A Guide
to
the works and remains
of
**Benjamin Wills Newton**

A Guide
to
the works and remains
of
**Benjamin Wills Newton**

Compiled by
C.W.H. Griffiths, M.A.

publications

pearlpublications.co.uk

Contact: info@pearlpublications.co.uk

*A Guide to the Works and Remains of Benjamin Wills Newton*

ISBN 978-1-901397-12-3 Paperback
ISBN 978-1-901397-13-0 Hardback
ISBN 978-1-901397-14-7 EBook

First published 2023.

The moral rights of the author are asserted.

Copyright © 2023 by C.W.H. Griffiths.

All rights reserved. No part of this publication may be reproduced or transmitted in any form or by any means without acknowledgement.

British Library CIP Data available.

BISAC: REF004000; REL108020; BIO018000

We acknowledge with thanks:

> Permission from The John Rylands University Library of the University of Manchester to quote from items held in the Fry Collection

> Permission to quote from various items of the original Fry Collection now held by Tom Chantry

If any rights have been inadvertently infringed, the publisher apologises, and asks that the omission be excused. Pearl Publications undertakes to correct any such unintentional oversight in subsequent printings.

---

*A Pictorial Memoir of Benjamin Wills Newton: Supplement to 'A Guide to the Works and Remains of Benjamin Wills Newton'* is published separately. Paperback 978-1-901397-15-4. Hardback 978-1-901397-16-1. See the information given at the end of this book.

> *From the present time onward it may be expected that there will be some*
>
> *(they will at first, perhaps, be a few scattered individuals)*
>
> *who will give themselves earnestly, humbly, and prayerfully to search the Word of God,*
>
> *expecting to find in the Truth there*
>
> *taught with such definiteness, clearness, and harmoniousness*
>
> *as to preclude uncertainty*
>
> *and to afford a solid basis for practical unity.*

B.W. Newton. *Europe and the East*, Second Edition 1878, p.123.

# CONTENTS

| | |
|---|---|
| Personal Preface | 1 |
| Introduction | 3 |
| **PART 1** | |
| Section 1. Full index to published titles | 5 |
| Section 2. Libraries and collections | 35 |
| Section 3. Bibliography of B.W. Newton's published works | 43 |
| Section 4. Contributions to other publications | 159 |
| Section 5 Assessment of attributed publications | 171 |
| Section 6. Contributions to periodicals | 187 |
| Section 7. Articles in *The Christian Witness* | 201 |
| Section 8. Published notes of addresses, and posthumous quotations | 229 |
| **PART 2** | |
| Section 9. B.W. Newton correspondence | 275 |
| Section 10. Duplicated and manuscript items | 407 |
| Section 11. Indexes of B.W. Newton's works | 439 |
| Section 12. Miscellaneous Biographical Items and Memorabilia | 443 |
| Appendix 1 - Comparison of editions of *Thoughts on The Apocalypse* | 463 |
| Appendix 2 - Thematic arrangement of B.W. Newton's Principal Works | 497 |
| Appendix 3 - A select publications list relevant to the controversy of J.N. Darby with B.W. Newton, and B.W. Newton's separation from the Brethren | 509 |
| Advertisement of the Supplement *A Pictorial Memoir of Benjamin Wills Newton* | 523 |

## PERSONAL PREFACE

I began this research for my own benefit. I found reading the works of B.W. Newton extremely helpful to me spiritually. They opened to me an understanding of doctrine, practical sanctification, and prophecy. I naturally desired to read more. I was dismayed that there was no definitive list. The more I probed, the more I found previously unrecorded works. The inter-relation between publications was confusing. It was impossible to get an overview.

Over four decades the scope of the work grew. Many times, I reached one summit only to see several more beyond that needed to be conquered. Looking back it seems that I have followed in the footsteps of others before me, such as A.C. Fry, F.W. Wyatt and John Cox, in my conviction that the writings catalogued are unique and uniquely needed for the last times before the Lord returns. However, I am conscious that this has not been my chosen task. Had providence ordered my life otherwise, it was my earnest desire that it should have been spent in a busy pastoral and teaching ministry. I am conscious of personal failure, and unfitness for that calling, but trust that what I have done may yet have lasting value and bear fruit in the purposes of a sovereign God.

B.W. Newton has been known mainly through negative secondary sources. The object of this work is to provide a comprehensive overview of his published works, his letters and other directly related materials that have survived. They shed a very different light upon the man. The message that God gave him, beaten out on the anvil of tribulation, persecution, and disappointment, needs to be heard.

It is difficult to know where to begin with acknowledgements. Before the age of the internet I corresponded with more than a hundred librarians. The helpful criticism of Nigel Pibworth and the ready access to the Sovereign Grace Advent Testimony resources given by Stephen Toms must certainly be noted. Dr David Brady of the Christian Brethren Archive at the John Ryland University Library, Manchester, gave valued early help and encouragement, as has the CBA throughout. Permission has been granted to quote from manuscript materials relating to the Fry Collection. We are also grateful for the permission given to make free use of Susan Noble's description of the items in 'The Fry Collection'.

In the later stages of the work Tom Chantry, who now holds the once 'lost' items of 'The Fry Collection' graciously gave me repeated access to compare, collate and summarise them, and permission to include the information in this Guide.

However, my greatest appreciation is for the collaboration of Timothy Stunt, who gave constant encouragement over more than thirty-five years. His detailed criticism and correction, particularly of the correspondence section, could have been provided by no-one else. His personal knowledge of many of the sources, and his professionalism, spurred me to more diligent effort, and extended the scope of the work.

Whilst acknowledging my debt to others, I take full responsibility for any inaccuracies, faults, or shortcomings. The design and execution of the work is solely my own. I trust that I may be forgiven for any neglect in acknowledging my debt to any individuals or institutions. In a work undertaken over such a long period, it is inevitable that some of the cataloguing, and indeed ownership, of a few of the items may have changed. In such rare circumstances I trust I have given sufficient information for them to be tracked down. Likewise, in this day when 'of making many books there is no end', I have no doubt failed to list some more recent reprints.

Having benefited from the largesse of others, without which this work would have been impossible, permission is given for the free quotation of this *Guide*, provided the source is acknowledged.

C.W.H. Griffiths, September 2023

# INTRODUCTION

There are two parts of this *Guide*.

**Part 1** catalogues published materials. It begins with a full index of all known titles of published works, or articles in periodicals. It lists and assesses any anonymous published material of which B.W. Newton has been suggested as the author. The first part of this *Guide* therefore consists of

1. Full index to the titles of published works by, or ascribed to, B.W. Newton.
2. Libraries and collections where B.W. Newton's published works are principally located.
3. Bibliography of B.W. Newton's published works.
4. Contributions made by B.W. Newton to other publications.
5. Assessment of anonymous publications ascribed to B.W. Newton.
6. B.W. Newton's contributions to periodicals.
7. Articles in *The Christian Witness* ascribed to B.W. Newton.
8. Publications derived from notes of addresses, and posthumously published letters and manuscripts.

**Part 2** of the *Guide* describes manuscript and typescript material, and ephemera that have survived. This second part therefore consists of

9. Known correspondence directly relating to B.W. Newton from various sources. This has been summarised and arranged in date order. Where correspondence is held by the Christian Brethren Archive we have given the catalogue numbers.
10. Manuscript and duplicated materials. These are principally, but not exclusively, those originally in 'The Fry Collection'. We have only listed the items in the Fry Collection that are of direct relevance to this *Guide*. We have given an outline of relevant material in the Archive to show what is available. We have given the remainder of the material not in the CBA in greater detail, insofar as we have access to it.
11. Indexes of B.W. Newton's Works. These are (with one exception) in typescript and MS. They represent early attempts to index his published works by Bible text and by subject.
12. Miscellaneous Biographical items and Memorabilia. This catalogues reference biographical material under six headings: A. Biographical Records and Personal Effects; B. Pictures; C. Conduct of Meetings; D. Consideration of B.W. Newton as a writer; E. Items Relating to his Death; F. Reminiscences.

**Appendices**

We have added three Appendices that we hope will be of use and interest to readers.

Appendix 1. Comparison of the Editions of *Thoughts on The Apocalypse*.
Appendix 2. A Thematic Arrangement of B.W. Newton's Principal Works.
Appendix 3. A Select Publications List Relevant to the Controversy of J.N. Darby with B.W. Newton, and his Separation from The Brethren.

It is regretted that we were unable to fulfil our original intention of including a pictorial and illustrated appendix in this volume. Incorporating it would have doubled its cost, because of the colour printing requiremens. It is therefore intended to publish this separately as a supplement to the *Guide*. An advertisement of its contents is given at the end of this volume.

With the growth of print on demand reprint publications, the need for this book is greater than when it was commenced. Randomly published editions old and new, under varying titles, some falsely attributed as publications of B.W. Newton, have made it more difficult than ever to gain an overview of B.W. Newton's teaching.

This work enables serious readers and researchers to take a strategic view of his works. For those intent on republishing what he wrote, it gives a bird's eye view of the maze of interlocking, extracted, combined, and re-written works. It uncovers important documents that have been all but lost through anonymous publication, or through their inclusion in long forgotten journals.

We have allowed some overlapping or repeat of reference notes and description so that the sections of the book can be used relatively independently.

# SECTION 1

## FULL INDEX OF TITLES
## OF WORKS BY, OR ASCRIBED TO,
## B.W. NEWTON

# FULL INDEX OF TITLES
# OF WORKS BY, OR ASCRIBED TO, B.W. NEWTON

**Notes**

1. This section is a comprehensive alphabetical index of the titles of B.W. Newton's published works. It aims to include all titles by which they have been referred to, or known (e.g. cover titles or titles in publishers' lists).[1] In this alphabetical listing the initial definite and indefinite articles (a, an, the) have been ignored.[2]
2. Titles of works published by B.W. Newton, or titles given to reprints of his published works, are in capital letters.
3. All other items are in lower case.
4. The second column indicates the Section of this *Guide* where the publication is described.
5. Some items appear in more than one section; for example, if an item appeared firstly in a periodical and was later published separately. Likewise, where an item was published anonymously but B.W. Newton's authorship can be proven, there will be a description in Section 3, B.W. Newton's Published Works, and an assessment in Section 5, Anonymous Publications Ascribed to B.W. Newton, which will show how his authorship is confirmed.
6. For the sake of completeness, this index includes some items that have been wrongly attributed to B.W. Newton. The evidence against his authorship of these is given in Section 5.
7. Non-English titles are listed in strict alphabetical sequence (regardless of whether they have the definite article in their original language).
8. The reference to editions of non-English titles (e.g. French Edition) relates to their language, not their place of publication.

| 1. | THE 1260 DAYS OF ANTICHRIST'S REIGN FUTURE | Section 3, Published Works |
|---|---|---|
| 2. | ACCEPTANCE WITH GOD | Section 3, Published Works |
| 3. | Acceptance, Worship, and Service. Thoughts on Hebrews 1-8. | Section 8, Derivative Publications *Watching and Waiting*. NM 6.4 |
| 4. | Access. Sustainment. Service | Section 8, Derivative Publications *Patmos Series*. NP 6 |
| 5. | ACCETTAZIONE CON DIO | Section 3, Published Works |
| 6. | THE ACKNOWLEDGEMENT OF GOD BY EARTHLY GOVERNMENTS, BEING FIVE PAPERS ISSUED AT VARIOUS TIMES BY THE LATE BENJAMIN WILLS NEWTON | Section 3, Published Works |
| 7. | ADDRESS RESPECTING THE METHODS OF THE SALVATION ARMY | Section 3, Published Works |

---

[1] Letter by letter sequence is used, e.g. *Christ and His Church...* precedes *Christendom...*, which in turn precedes *The Christian...*, which precedes *Christ, Our Suffering Surety*.
[2] e.g. *An Erroneous Mode...* immediately precedes *Erroneous Statements....*

# SECTION 1: INDEX OF TITLES

| 8. | AIDS TO PROPHETIC ENQUIRY | Section 3, Published Works |
|---|---|---|
| 9. | THE ALTERED TRANSLATION OF GENESIS 2:5, AS GIVEN IN THE REVISED VERSION, CONSIDERED | Section 3, Published Works |
| 10. | ANCIENT TRUTHS RESPECTING THE DEITY AND TRUE HUMANITY OF THE LORD JESUS | Section 3, Published Works |
| 11. | ANSWERS TO QUESTIONS ON THE PROPRIETY OF LEAVING THE CHURCH OF ENGLAND | Section 3, Published Works |
| 12. | ANSWERS TO THE QUESTIONS LATELY CONSIDERED AT A MEETING HELD IN PLYMOUTH ON SEPTEMBER 15TH 1834 AND THE FOLLOWING DAYS: CHIEFLY COMPILED FROM NOTES TAKEN AT THE MEETING [Henry Borlase and B.W. Newton co-authors] | Section 4, Contributions to Other Publications |
| 13. | An Anthology (No.1) 'Reminiscences' of Lectures in Stafford Rooms. | Section 8, Derivative Publications. Studies Series. NS 1 |
| 14. | Anthology (No.2) 'Reminiscences' of Bible Readings, etc. at Newport, I.W. | Section 8, Derivative Publications. Studies Series. NS 2 |
| 15. | Anthology (No.3) 'Reminiscences' of Bible Readings, etc. at Newport, I.W. | Section 8, Derivative Publications. Studies Series. NS 3 |
| 16. | Antichrist and Babylon with an exposition of Daniel 11 | Section 8, Derivative Publications. Studies Series. NS 4 |
| 17. | ANTICHRIST, EUROPE AND THE EAST | Section 3, Published Works |
| 18. | THE ANTICHRIST FUTURE | Section 3, Published Works |
| 19. | THE ANTICHRIST FUTURE, ALSO THE 1260 DAYS OF ANTICHRIST'S REIGN FUTURE | Section 3, Published Works |
| 20. | 'Apostolic Succession', a Review of 'Protestant Christendom. | Section 8, Derivative Publications. *Time of the End Series* NT 5 |
| 21. | APPOINTMENTS OF GOD IN JUSTICE AND MERCY CONSIDERED | Section 3, Published Works |
| 22. | Armageddon. (Reprinted from *Perilous Times*). | Section 8, Derivative Publications. *Time of the End Series* NT 23. [Not by B.W. Newton] |
| 23. | ATONEMENT AND ITS RESULTS | Section 3, Published Works |
| 24. | ATONEMENT SAVETH | Section 3, Published Works |
| 25. | BABYLON AND EGYPT | Section 3, Published Works |
| 26. | 'Babylonianism'. Its Manifestation and Doom. | Section 8, Derivative Publications. *Time of the End Series* NT 14 |
| 27. | BAPTISM (1) | Section 3, Published Works |
| 28. | BAPTISM (2) | Section 3, Published Works |

SECTION 1: INDEX OF TITLES

| 29. | The Baptism of the Holy Spirit | Section 8, Derivative Publications. Misc. NM 4.4 |
|---|---|---|
| 30. | 'Baptism' What it signifies  Who the Right Subjects | Section 8, Derivative Publications. *Patmos Series.* NP 18 |
| 31. | Believer's Life work, 'Gold, Silver, Precious Stones, Wood, Hay, Stubble' | Section 8, Derivative Publications. *Patmos Series.* NP 4 |
| 32. | Believers' Prospects or the Saints in Glory. A Millennial Picture. | Section 8, Derivative Publications. *Time of the End Series.* NT 4 |
| 33. | THE BLOOD THAT SAVETH | Section 3, Published Works |
| 34. | The Book of Daniel | Section 6, Contributions to Periodicals. *The Investigator* |
| 35. | A BRIEF SKETCH OF THE PROGRESS OF PROPHETIC ENQUIRY, ETC | Section 3, Published Works |
| 36. | BRIEF STATEMENTS IN THE FORM OF ANSWERS TO QUESTIONS | Section 3, Published Works |
| 37. | The Broad Church | Section 8, Derivative Publications. Misc. NM 1.1 |
| 38. | THE BURNT OFFERING | Section 3, Published Works |
| 39. | B.W. NEWTON ON MINISTRY AND ORDER IN THE CHURCH OF CHRIST | Section 3, Published Works |
| 40. | B.W. Newton's addresses on Hebrews | Section 10, Duplicated and Manuscript Items (SGAT) |
| 41. | The Calling of the Gentiles the 'New Meat Offering'. Romans 15 and 16 | Section 8, Derivative Publications. *Patmos Series.* NP 29 |
| 42. | A Catechism on the Four Great and Universal Empires, and the Kingdom by Which They will be Succeeded, as Mentioned in the Book of the Prophecies of Daniel | Section 5, Anonymous Publications Ascribed to B.W. Newton. [Inconclusive evidence on authorship] |
| 43. | CATHOLICITY IN A DISPENSATION OF FAILURE, A SURE TOKEN OF APOSTASY | Section 3, Published Works |
| 44. | Characteristics of the Gospel of Matthew | Section 8, Derivative Publications. *Studies Series.* NS 16 |
| 45. | Christ and his Church as related to the Nations | Section 8, Derivative Publications. *Teachers of the Faith and Future.* NM 8.7 |
| 46. | CHRISTENDOM: A RETROSPECTIVE AND PROSPECTIVE OUTLINE | Section 3, Published Works |
| 47. | Christendom: its Course and Doom | Section 8, Derivative Publications. *Studies Series.* NS 5 |

| | | |
|---|---|---|
| 48. | THE CHRISTIAN AND JEWISH REMNANTS AT THE TIME OF THE END | Section 3, Published Works |
| 49. | CHRIST, OUR SUFFERING SURETY: HEBREWS 2:10 AND 5:7 | Section 3, Published Works |
| 50. | 'Christian Progress' or 'Faith and Discipleship' | Section 8, Derivative Publications. *Patmos Series.* NP 33 |
| 51. | The Christian Remnant and the Jewish Remnant at 'The Time of the End' | Section 8, Derivative Publications. *Time of the End Series.* NT 18. |
| 52. | CHRIST'S RETURN – NOT SECRET BUT IN MANIFESTED GLORY | Section 3, Published Works |
| 53. | CHRIST'S SECOND COMING. IT WILL BE PRE-MILLENNIAL | Section 3, Published Works |
| 54. | Church Principles | Section 8, Derivative Publications. *Perilous Times.* NM 5.3 |
| 55. | The Claims of God Met! How? | Section 8, Derivative Publications. *Patmos Series.* NP 34 |
| 56. | Classified List and General Index of the Works of the late Benjamin Wills Newton | Section 11, Indexes of B.W. Newton's Works |
| 57. | CLEANSING THE LEPER. LEVITICUS 14 | Section 3, Published Works |
| | | Section 7, Articles in *The Christian Witness* |
| 58. | The Cleansing of the Leper, Leviticus 14 | Section 8, Derivative Publications. *Studies Series.* NS 6 |
| 59. | COME IL SANGUE CI SALVA? | Section 3, Published Works |
| 60. | THE COMING OF THE LORD | Section 3, Published Works |
| 61. | THE COMING OF THE LORD. EVENTS CONNECTED THEREWITH | Section 3, Published Works |
| 62. | THE CONSECRATION OF THE PRIESTS | Section 3, Published Works |
| 63. | Consecutive Events in connection with the 'Day of the Lord'. | Section 8, Derivative Publications. *Time of the End Series.* NT 16 |
| 64. | Conversation on Romans 5:13 and 14. | Section 8, Derivative Publications *Watching and Waiting.* NM 6.8 |
| 65. | CONVERSATION ON THE SEVENTEENTH CHAPTER OF REVELATION | Section 3, Published Works |
| 66. | Conversations and notes re – B.W. Newton, 'Rough notebook' | Section 10, Duplicated and Manuscript Items (SGAT) |
| 67. | Conversion. What is it? | Section 8, Derivative Publications. *Patmos Series.* NP 41 |

SECTION 1: INDEX OF TITLES

| 68. | Correspondence regarding R. Pearsall Smith | Section 6, Contributions to Periodicals. *The Record* |
|---|---|---|
| 69. | Correspondence respecting 'The London Review' | Section 6, Contributions to Periodicals. *The Record* |
| 70. | Correspondence, etc. [Compiled by Lord Congleton] | Section 4, Contributions to Other Publications |
| 71. | Counsels to Converts | Section 8, Derivative Publications. *Perilous Times* and *Watching and Waiting*. NM 5.1 |
| 72. | 'Creation's Groan' and 'the Glory that should Follow'. Romans 8:19 - 23 | Section 8, Derivative Publications. *Patmos Series*. NP 36 |
| 73. | Dark Sayings upon the Harp | Section 8, Derivative Publications. *Studies Series*. NS 32 |
| 74. | DAVID, KING OF ISRAEL | Section 3, Published Works |
| 75. | DAVID RESTORING THE ARK | Section 3, Published Works |
| 76. | THE DAY OF THE LORD, A LECTURE ON ZECHARIAH 14 | Section 3, Published Works |
| 77. | DEFENCE IN REPLY TO THE PERSONAL ACCUSATIONS OF MR DARBY | Section 3, Published Works |
| 78. | The Disciples' Prayer | Section 8, Derivative Publications. *Patmos Series*. NP 30 |
| 79. | The Dispensations | Section 7, Articles in *The Christian Witness*. [Beyond Reasonable Doubt by B.W. Newton] |
| 80. | THE DOCTRINE OF SCRIPTURE RESPECTING BAPTISM, BRIEFLY CONSIDERED | Section 3, Published Works |
| 81. | DOCTRINES OF POPERY | Section 3, Published Works |
| 82. | DOCTRINES OF POPERY AS ESTABLISHED BY THE COUNCIL OF TRENT, CONSIDERED. ON ORIGINAL SIN | Section 3, Published Works |
| 83. | DOCTRINES OF POPERY ON HOLY SCRIPTURE AND TRADITION, AS ESTABLISHED BY THE COUNCIL OF TRENT, CONSIDERED | Section 3, Published Works |
| 84. | Doctrines of the Church in Newman Street | Section 7, Articles in *The Christian Witness*. [by B.W. Newton] |
| 85. | DOCTRINES OF THE CHURCH IN NEWMAN STREET, CONSIDERED | Section 3, Published Works |

| | | |
|---|---|---|
| 86. | DR TREGELLES'S GREEK TESTAMENT; REMARKS ON SOME OBSERVATIONS OF THE BISHOP OF GLOUCESTER AND BRISTOL ON DR TREGELLES'S REVISED TEXT OF THE GREEK NEW TESTAMENT | Section 3, Published Works |
| | | Section 5, Anonymous Publications Ascribed to B.W. Newton. [Beyond Reasonable Doubt by B.W. Newton] |
| 87. | DUTY OF GIVING HEED TO THE PREDICTIONS OF SCRIPTURE RESPECTING EVENTS THAT ARE TO PRECEDE THE RETURN OF OUR LORD | Section 3, Published Works |
| 88. | AN EFFECT OF THE DOCTRINES ANIMADVERTED ON IN PRECEDING TRACTS | Section 3, Published Works |
| 89. | EGYPT, PALESTINE AND SYRIA, THEIR PROSPECTS IN PROPHECY | Section 3, Published Works |
| 90. | EINE GEGENWÄRTIGE SELIGKEIT IN CHRISTO | Section 3, Published Works |
| 91. | Elementary Studies in Leviticus 14 on the Leper Cleansed | Section 8, Derivative Publications. *Studies Series*. NS 6 |
| 92. | Elementary Studies in Leviticus 23 on the Seven 'Feasts of the Lord' | Section 8, Derivative Publications. *Studies Series*. NS 7 |
| 93. | Elementary Studies in the Book of Daniel | Section 8, Derivative Publications. *Studies Series*. NS 8 |
| 94. | Elementary Studies in 'the Canticles' on the Practical Walk of Faith | Section 8, Derivative Publications. *Studies Series*. NS 9 |
| 95. | Elementary Studies in the Facts of Prophetic Scripture, Part One | Section 8, Derivative Publications. *Studies Series*. NS 10 |
| 96. | Elementary Studies on Doctrinal Subjects in the Epistle to the Romans | Section 8, Derivative Publications. *Studies Series*. NS 11 |
| 97. | Elementary Studies on the Facts of Prophetic Scripture in the Book of Daniel and the Book of Revelation. Part Two, Revised. | Section 8, Derivative Publications. *Studies Series*. NS 12 |
| 98. | Elementary Studies on the Offerings in the Book of Leviticus | Section 8, Derivative Publications. *Studies Series*. NS 13 |
| 99. | England and the Ten Kingdoms | Section 8, Derivative Publications. *Perilous Times*. NM 5.4 |
| 100. | ENGLAND'S FUTURE COURSE IN THE EAST | Section 3, Published Works |
| 101. | 'Entrance into the Holiest'. By what means? On what Ground? In what title? | Section 8, Derivative Publications. *Patmos Series*. NP 14 |
| 102. | AN ERRONEOUS MODE OF STATING THE GOSPEL, CONSIDERED | Section 3, Published Works |
| 103. | ERRONEOUS STATEMENTS CONCERNING THE ATONEMENT AND ITS RESULTS (PART FIRST) | Section 3, Published Works |

| | | |
|---|---|---|
| 104. | ERRONEOUS STATEMENTS CONCERNING THE ATONEMENT AND ITS RESULTS (PART SECOND) | Section 3, Published Works |
| 105. | ERRONEOUS STATEMENTS CONCERNING THE ATONEMENT AND ITS RESULTS (PART THIRD) | Section 3, Published Works |
| 106. | ETERNAL RECONCILIATION, BEING THE SUBSTANCE OF A DISCOURSE RECENTLY DELIVERED IN LONDON | Section 3, Published Works |
| 107. | EUROPE AND THE EAST | Section 3, Published Works |
| 108. | EUROPEAN PROSPECTS (AD 1863) | Section 3, Published Works |
| 109. | EVENTS THAT ARE TO PRECEDE THE RETURN OF THE LORD. THE DUTY OF GIVING HEED TO THE PREDICTIONS OF SCRIPTURE | Section 3, Published Works |
| 110. | THE EXCELLENCY OF THE PERSON OF CHRIST UNALTERABLE. REMARKS ON THE DOCTRINE OF OLSHAUSEN | Section 3, Published Works |
| 111. | THE EXERCISE OF WORLDLY AUTHORITY | Section 3, Published Works |
| 112. | An Exposition of Isaiah 53 with Acts 8:26-40 | Section 8, Derivative Publications. *Patmos Series.* NP 1 |
| 113. | An Exposition of the Epistle to the Ephesians | Section 8, Derivative Publications. *Studies Series.* NS 14 |
| 114. | EXPOSITORY TEACHING ON THE MILLENNIUM AND ISRAEL'S FUTURE | Section 3, Published Works |
| 115. | Extracts from 'A Narrative of Facts' [by Robert Baxter] | Section 4, Contributions to Other Publications |
| 116. | Extracts from Bishop Pearson's Exposition of the Apostle's Creed [published by B.W. Newton] | Section 4, Contributions to Other Publications. |
| 117. | EXTRACTS FROM THE SECOND SERIES OF 'AIDS TO PROPHETIC ENQUIRY'... COMPARED WITH EXTRACTS FROM 'THE DAILY NEWS' AND 'STANDARD', ETC | Section 3, Published Works |
| 118. | EXTRACTS FROM THE WORKS OF B.W. NEWTON, FOR THE MOST PART REPRINTED FROM *WATCHING AND WAITING* | Section 3, Published Works |
| 119. | EXTRACTS FROM TWO TRACTS, ENTITLED 'REMARKS ON THE SUFFERINGS OF THE LORD JESUS' AND OBSERVATIONS ON A TRACT ENTITLED 'THE SUFFERINGS OF CHRIST AS SET FORTH IN A LECTURE ON PSALM 6, CONSIDERED' AND QUOTATIONS FROM OTHER PAPERS | Section 3, Published Works |
| 120. | Facts of Prophetic Scripture, Studies in Daniel and Revelation | Section 8, Derivative Publications. *Studies Series.* NS 12 |

# SECTION 1: INDEX OF TITLES

| | | |
|---|---|---|
| 121. | The Final Division of the Roman Empire into Ten Kingdoms, with Map of Suggested Sub-Divisions. | Section 8, Derivative Publications. *Time of the End Series.* NT 22 |
| 122. | THE FINAL PERSEVERANCE OF RUSSIA INCONSISTENT WITH THE DECLARATIONS OF SCRIPTURE | Section 3, Published Works |
| 123. | THE FIRST AND SECOND CHAPTERS OF THE EPISTLE TO THE ROMANS, CONSIDERED, WITH REMARKS ON CERTAIN DOCTRINES… | Section 3, Published Works |
| 124. | FIRST ANXIETY OF EVERY SOUL AWAKENED | Section 3, Published Works |
| 125. | THE FIRST RESURRECTION AND THE REIGN IN RIGHTEOUSNESS | Section 3, Published Works |
| 126. | The First Resurrection | Section 7, Articles in *The Christian Witness*. [Not by B.W. Newton] |
| 127. | FIRST SERIES OF AIDS TO PROPHETIC ENQUIRY | Section 3, Published Works |
| 128. | FIVE LETTERS ON EVENTS PREDICTED IN SCRIPTURE AS ANTECEDENT TO THE COMING OF THE LORD | Section 3, Published Works |
| 129. | The Forgiveness and Restoration of Israel. Psalms 18 and 118. | Section 8, Derivative Publications. *Time of the End Series.* NT 10 |
| 130. | FOUNDATION TRUTHS | Section 3, Published Works |
| 131. | Fry Collection (summary) | Section 10, Duplicated and Manuscript Items |
| 132. | Fry Manuscript (summary) | Section 10, Duplicated and Manuscript Items |
| 133. | The Future Siege of Jerusalem | Section 6, Contributions to Periodicals. *The Investigator* |
| 134. | GEDANKEN ÜBER THEILE DES DRITTEN BUCHES MOSE. AUS DEM ENGL. ÜBERS1: DAS BRANDOPFER (3 BUCH MOSE 1 KAP) ALS TYPUS AUF CHRISTUS BIBLISCH ERÖRTERT | Section 3, Published Works |
| 135. | GESÙ CHE LAVA I PIEDI AGLI APOSTOLI | Section 3, Published Works |
| 136. | Gleanings in 1 and 2 Peter (No 1) | Section 8, Derivative Publications. *Gleanings Series.* NM 2.1 |
| 137. | Gleanings in the 'Book of Exodus' (No 3) | Section 8, Derivative Publications. *Gleanings Series.* NM 2.3 |
| 138. | Gleanings in the 'Book of Numbers' (No 2) | Section 8, Derivative Publications. *Gleanings Series.* NM 2.2 |
| 139. | God and 'the Heathen'. Romans 1 | Section 8, Derivative Publications. *Patmos Series.* NP 35 |
| 140. | GOSPEL TRUTHS | Section 3, Published Works |

# SECTION 1: INDEX OF TITLES

| 141. | GREAT PROTESTANT TRUTHS, BEING TWO OF 'THE LEICESTERSHIRE LECTURES' | Section 3, Published Works |
|---|---|---|
| 142. | The Greek New Testament, edited from Ancient Authorities… [Quarto Edition] [S.P. Tregelles] | Section 4, Contributions to Other Publications |
| 143. | The Greek New Testament, edited from Ancient Authorities… [Manual Edition] [S.P. Tregelles] | Section 4, Contributions to Other Publications |
| 144. | GREEK OF ROMANS 1 | Section 3, Published Works |
| 145. | 'Hades' Ephesians 4:8 and 'Mosaic Cosmogony' - or Remarks on the fifth of the Essays and Reviews. | Section 8, Derivative Publications. *Patmos Series.* NP 43 |
| 146. | THE HARLOT OF BABYLON | Section 3, Published Works |
| 147. | The 'Holy Spirit'; His Office and Work | Section 8, Derivative Publications. *Patmos Series.* NP 37 |
| 148. | How B.W. Newton Learned Prophetic Truth | Section 8, Derivative Publications. *Watching and Waiting.* NM 7 |
| 149. | HOW DOES THE BLOOD SAVE? | Section 3, Published Works |
| 150. | 'How to Study Prophecy' illustrated from Zech. 12-14. | Section 8, Derivative Publications. *Time of the End Series.* NT 8 |
| 151. | 'Human Progress'. Its Course and Doom, or Withdrawal unto Perdition. | Section 8, Derivative Publications. *Patmos Series.* NP 22 |
| 152. | IL GIORNO DEL SIGNORE | Section 3, Published Works |
| 153. | Il Glorioso Avvenimento e Il Regno Personale del Nostro Signore Gesù Cristo | Section 5, Anonymous Publications Ascribed to B.W. Newton. [Not by B.W. Newton] |
| 154. | IL SANGUE CHE SALVA | Section 3, Published Works |
| 155. | Imputed Obedience | Section 8, Derivative Publications. Misc. NM 4.3 |
| 156. | IN A DISPENSATION OF FAILURE, CATHOLICITY A SURE TOKEN OF APOSTASY | Section 3, Published Works |
| 157. | IN QUAL MODO IL SANGUE SALVA? | Section 3, Published Works |
| 158. | In the Courts of God: 'Guilty' or 'Guiltless'. Romans 1-4 | Section 8, Derivative Publications. *Patmos Series.* NP 25 |
| 159. | Index of Scripture references in the works of B.W. Newton | Section 11, Indexes of B.W. Newton's Works |
| 160. | Index of texts explained or referred to in the works of Benjamin Wills Newton | Section 11, Indexes of B.W. Newton's Works |
| 161. | Individual Gifts | Section 8, Derivative Publications. *Studies Series.* NS 15 |

| | | |
|---|---|---|
| 162. | 'Instead of' or 'the Lord will Provide'. Reflections for Good Friday | Section 8, Derivative Publications. *Patmos Series.* NP 38 |
| 163. | An Introduction to the Book of Hebrews | Section 8, Derivative Publications. *Watching and Waiting.* NM 6.10 |
| 164. | Instruction for the Church concerning 'The Kingdom of God'. | Section 8, Derivative Publications. *Time of the End Series.* NT 6 |
| 165. | Isaiah 40-49 | Section 8, Derivative Publications. *Studies Series.* NS 43 |
| 166. | ISAIAH 53, CONSIDERED: BEING AN EXTRACT FROM A WORK ENTITLED 'THOUGHTS ON SCRIPTURAL SUBJECTS' | Section 3, Published Works |
| 167. | IS IT WRONG TO EXPECT CERTAIN PREDICTED EVENTS PREVIOUS TO THE RETURN OF THE LORD JESUS? A LETTER TO A FRIEND | Section 3, Published Works |
| 168. | ISRAEL AND JERUSALEM | Section 3, Published Works |
| 169. | ISRAEL IN THE DAYS OF HAGGAI AND ZECHARIAH; WITH A NOTE UPON THE PROPHECY OF HAGGAI, BOTH REPRINTED FROM 'OCCASIONAL PAPERS ON SCRIPTURAL SUBJECTS', ALSO A LECTURE UPON ZECHARIAH 3 | Section 3, Published Works |
| 170. | 'Israel's Future' in the Earth. Isa. 24-27. | Section 8, Derivative Publications. *Time of the End Series.* NT 3 |
| 171. | ISRAEL'S PROSPECTS IN THE MILLENNIUM, BEING THE SUBJECT OF A LECTURE DELIVERED JULY 1st 1856 AT DUKE STREET CHAPEL, ST JAMES PARK, LONDON | Section 3, Published Works |
| 172. | Israel's Rejection and the Gentiles' Acceptance of Jesus of Nazareth, Characteristics of the Gospel of Matthew. | Section 8, Derivative Publications. *Studies Series.* NS 16 |
| 173. | IS SALVATION BY THE OBEDIENCE OF A DIVINE SUBSTITUTE A FICTION? | Section 3, Published Works |
| 174. | Is the Exercise of Worldly Authority consistent with Discipleship? | Section 7, Articles in *The Christian Witness* [by B.W. Newton] |
| 175. | JERUSALEM | Section 3, Published Works |
| | | Section 7, Articles in *The Christian Witness* [by B.W. Newton] |
| 176. | JÉRUSALEM ET L'HOMME DE PÉCHÉ | Section 3, Published Works |
| 177. | JERUSALEM, ITS FUTURE HISTORY | Section 3, Published Works |
| 178. | JÉRUSALEM. SON HISTOIRE FUTURE | Section 3, Published Works |
| 179. | JERUSALEMS BEDEUTUNG IN DER VERGANGENHEIT, GEGENWART UND ZUKUNFT | Section 3, Published Works |

SECTION 1: INDEX OF TITLES

| | | |
|---|---|---|
| 180. | Jesus, the Light contrasted with Darkness in the First Five Chapters of the Gospel of John | Section 8, Derivative Publications. *Bethany Series.* NM 4.1 |
| 181. | JESUS WASHING HIS DISCIPLES' FEET | Section 3, Published Works |
| 182. | Jewish Disabilities. | Section 6, Contributions to Periodicals. *The Morning Herald* |
| 183. | John the Baptist, the Place and Character of his Ministry and Baptism | Section 8, Derivative Publications. *Studies Series.* NS 17 |
| 184. | THE JUDGMENT OF THE COURT OF ARCHES AND OF THE JUDICIAL COMMITTEE OF THE PRIVY COUNCIL IN THE CASE OF ROWLAND WILLIAMS, D.D., ONE OF THE WRITERS IN THE 'ESSAYS AND REVIEWS', CONSIDERED | Section 3, Published Works |
| 185. | JUDGMENTS ON THE 'ESSAYS AND REVIEWS' | Section 3, Published Works |
| 186. | JUSTIFICATION AND SANCTIFICATION | Section 3, Published Works |
| 187. | JUSTIFICATION, BEING THE SUBSTANCE OF A DISCOURSE RECENTLY DELIVERED IN LONDON | Section 3, Published Works |
| 188. | The Kenite | Section 7, Articles in *The Christian Witness.* [Not by B.W. Newton] |
| 189. | The Kingdom of Heaven | Section 8, Derivative Publications. *Studies Series.* NS 18 |
| 190. | LA GIUSTIFICAZIONE, SAGGIO DI B.W. NEWTON DA UNA SIGNORA INGLESE | Section 3, Published Works |
| 191. | LA JUSTIFICATION OU COMMENT DIEU NOUS JUSTIFIE | Section 3, Published Works |
| 192. | LA JUSTIFICATION, SERMON PRÉCHÉ À LONDRES PAR B.W. NEWTON | Section 3, Published Works |
| 193. | La Pâque | Section 5, Anonymous Publications Ascribed to B.W. Newton. [Insufficient evidence of authorship] |
| 194. | La Pasqua | Section 5, Anonymous Publications Ascribed to B.W. Newton. [Insufficient evidence of authorship] |
| 195. | 'The Last End of the Indignation' Psalm 110 and 127. | Section 8, Derivative Publications. *Time of the End Series.* NT 7. |
| 196. | Latitudinarianism, its Development, Course and Downfall | Section 8, Derivative Publications. *Studies Series.* NS 19 |
| 197. | LECTURE ON THE PROPHECY OF THE LORD JESUS, AS CONTAINED IN MATTHEW 24,25 | Section 3, Published Works |

| 198. | Lectures on Matthew | Section 10, Duplicated and Manuscript Items (SGAT) |
|---|---|---|
| 199. | LECTURES ON PROPHECY | Section 3, Published Works |
| 200. | Lectures on St Matthew by B.W. Newton | Section 10, Duplicated and Manuscript Items (C.W.H. Griffiths) |
| 201. | Lectures on the Epistle to the Hebrews | Section 10, Duplicated and Manuscript Items (SGAT) |
| 202. | Lectures on the Epistle to the Romans | Section 8, Derivative Publications. Misc. [F.W. Wyatt]. NM 3 |
| 203. | Le Glorieux Avènement et Le Règne Personnel de Notre Seigneur Jésus-Christ | Section 5, Anonymous Publications Ascribed to B.W. Newton. [Not by B.W. Newton] |
| 204. | LE MONDE À VENIR | Section 3, Published Works |
| 205. | LE PROFEZIE DEL SIGNOR GESÙ CRISTO, COME SI TROVANO NEI CAPITOLI 24 E 25 DELL' EVANGELO DI S. MATTEO | Section 3, Published Works |
| 206. | THE LEPROSY | Section 3, Published Works |
| 207. | LE SANG QUI SAUVE | Section 3, Published Works |
| 208. | LETTER FROM B.W. NEWTON TO J. CLULOW, 18 APRIL 1845. | Section 3, Published Works |
| 209. | Letter on Hyper-Calvinism | Section 8, Derivative Publications. *Perilous Times.* NM 5.2 |
| 210. | A LETTER ON SUBJECTS CONNECTED WITH THE LORD'S HUMANITY | Section 3, Published Works |
| 211. | Letter on the Beacon Controversy | Section 6, Contributions to Periodicals. *The Christian Observer* |
| 212. | Letter on the objects of a believer's life. | Section 8, Derivative Publications. *Watching and Waiting.* NM 6.5 A |
| 213. | Letter on the Person of the Lord | Section 8, Derivative Publications. NM 1.2 |
| 214. | A LETTER ON WORSHIP AND MINISTRY | Section 3, Published Works |
| 215. | Letter regarding Spiritualism | Section 8, Derivative Publications. From A.J.W. Dalzell. NM 11.2 |
| 216. | A LETTER TO A FRIEND CONCERNING A TRACT RECENTLY PUBLISHED IN CORK | Section 3, Published Works |
| 217. | LETTER TO A FRIEND ON A REPLY TO THE ENQUIRY 'IS IT WRONG TO EXPECT CERTAIN PREDICTED EVENTS PREVIOUS TO THE RETURN OF THE LORD JESUS?' | Section 3, Published Works |

SECTION 1: INDEX OF TITLES

| | | |
|---|---|---|
| 218. | A LETTER TO A FRIEND ON THE STUDY OF PROPHECY | Section 3, Published Works |
| | | Section 7, Articles in *The Christian Witness* |
| | | Section 5, Anonymous Publications Ascribed to B.W. Newton. [Beyond Reasonable Doubt by B.W. Newton] |
| 219. | LETTER TO CLULOW | Section 3, Published Works |
| 220. | Letter to Mr I. Arnold Lake | Section 8, Derivative Publications *Teachers of the Faith and Future*. NM 8.8 |
| 221. | Letter to Rev. John Cox regarding the funeral of his only child | Section 8, Derivative Publications. *Teachers of the Faith and Future*. NM 8.3 A |
| 222. | A LETTER TO RICHARD WALDO SIBTHORPE, B.D., LATE FELLOW OF MAGDALEN COLLEGE, OXFORD ON THE SUBJECT OF HIS RECENT PAMPHLET | Section 3, Published Works |
| 223. | A LETTER TO THE BRETHREN AND SISTERS IN CHRIST, WHO MEET FOR COMMUNION IN EBRINGTON STREET, PLYMOUTH; CONTAINING REMARKS ON A RECENT TRACT, CIRCULATED AMONGST THEM | Section 3, Published Works |
| 224. | A LETTER TO THE MINISTER OF SILVER STREET CHAPEL, TAUNTON IN REPLY TO HIS RECENT LECTURE AGAINST THE PRE-MILLENNIAL ADVENT OF THE LORD | Section 3, Published Works |
| 225. | The Light of the World | Section 7, Articles in *The Christian Witness*.[Not by B.W. Newton] |
| 226. | THE LITERAL TRANSLATION OF 2 THESSALONIANS 3:1-10 | Section 3, Published Works |
| 227. | 'The Little Remnant under 'Antichrist'. Psalms 10, 16 and 18. | Section 8, Derivative Publications. *Time of the End Series*. NT 9 |
| 228. | Luke 18 v15,16 (an address) | Section 10, Duplicated and Manuscript Items (SGAT) |
| 229. | Manna. What is it? | Section 8, Derivative Publications. *Patmos Series*. NP 42 |
| 230. | MAP OF THE TEN KINGDOMS OF THE ROMAN EMPIRE | Section 3, Published Works |
| 231. | MATTHEW 13 | Section 3, Published Works |
| 232. | THE MEAT OFFERING | Section 3, Published Works |

| | | |
|---|---|---|
| 233. | Memorial versus Idolatry or the 'Table of the Lord' and the 'Table of Devils' | Section 8, Derivative Publications. *Patmos Series.* NP 20 |
| 234. | The Message of Moses and the Apostles contrasted | Section 8, Derivative Publications. *Studies Series.* NS 19A |
| 235. | The Message to the Churches - Ephesus | Section 8, Derivative Publications. *Patmos Series.* NP 8 |
| 236. | The Message to the Churches - Laodicea | Section 8, Derivative Publications. *Patmos Series.* NP 19 |
| 237. | The Message to the Churches - Pergamos | Section 8, Derivative Publications. *Patmos Series.* NP 12 |
| 238. | The Message to the Churches - Philadelphia | Section 8, Derivative Publications. *Patmos Series.* NP 17 |
| 239. | The Message to the Churches - Sardis | Section 8, Derivative Publications. *Patmos Series.* NP 15 |
| 240. | The Message to the Churches - Smyrna | Section 8, Derivative Publications. *Patmos Series.* NP 11 |
| 241. | The Message to the Churches - Thyatira | Section 8, Derivative Publications. *Patmos Series.* NP 13 |
| 242. | The Metropolis of the World - Babylon. The Metropolis of Scripture - Jerusalem. | Section 8, Derivative Publications. *Time of the End Series.* NT 20 |
| 243. | THE MILLENNIUM AND ISRAEL'S FUTURE | Section 3, Published Works |
| 244. | THE MILLENNIUM AND THE EVERLASTING STATE | Section 3, Published Works. |
| 245. | THE MILLENNIUM AND THE EVERLASTING STATE | Section 6, Contributions to Periodicals. *The Journal of Prophecy* |
| 246. | The 'Millennium'. Creation's Groan Hushed! The Curse Removed. | Section 8, Derivative Publications. *Time of the End Series.* NT 13 |
| 247. | MODERN DOCTRINES RESPECTING SINLESSNESS CONSIDERED. EXTRACTED FROM 'THOUGHTS ON SCRIPTURAL SUBJECTS' | Section 3, Published Works |
| 248. | MOSAIC COSMOGONY | Section 3, Published Works |
| 249. | Moses and the Gentile Family | Section 7, Articles in *The Christian Witness* [by B.W. Newton] |
| 250. | Moses's Heavenly Glory | Section 7, Articles in *The Christian Witness* [Not by B.W. Newton] |
| 251. | Moses's Loss of Canaan | Section 7, Articles in *The Christian Witness* [Not by B.W. Newton] |
| 252. | MOSES, THE CHILD OF FAITH | Section 3, Published Works |
| 253. | NARRATIVES FROM THE OLD TESTAMENT | Section 3, Published Works |
| 254. | THE NATIONS IN RELATION TO CHRIST AS IN THE SECOND PSALM | Section 3, Published Works |

| | | |
|---|---|---|
| 255. | NATURAL RELATIONS OF MEN AND GOVERNMENTS TO GOD | Section 3, Published Works |
| 256. | The Nazarite | Section 7, Articles in *The Christian Witness* [Probably by B.W. Newton] |
| 257. | THE NEW WORLD ORDER, OR PREMILLENNIAL TRUTH DEMONSTRATED | Section 3, Published Works |
| 258. | 'NO CONDEMNATION TO THEM WHO [sic] ARE IN CHRIST JESUS' (ROMANS 8) | Section 3, Published Works |
| 259. | NOTE ON 1 PETER 2:24 | Section 3, Published Works |
| 260. | NOTE ON 1 PETER 2:24 | Section 6, Contributions to Periodicals. *The Journal of Prophecy* |
| 261. | Note on 2 Peter 3:2 and Revelation 2:2 | Section 6, Contributions to Periodicals. *The Journal of Prophecy* |
| 262. | Note on Faith | Section 8, Derivative Publications. From A.J.W. Dalzell. NM 11.1 |
| 263. | Note on Psalm 68:4 | Section 6, Contributions to Periodicals. *The Journal of Prophecy* |
| 264. | NOTE ON THE LORD'S SUPPER | Section 3, Published Works |
| 265. | NOTES EXPOSITORY OF THE GREEK OF THE FIRST CHAPTER OF ROMANS WITH REMARKS ON THE FORCE OF CERTAIN SYNONYMS, ETC | Section 3, Published Works |
| 266. | Notes of an address on Zechariah 11 | Section 8, Derivative Publications. *Watching and Waiting*. NM 6.2 |
| 267. | Notes on Ezekiel | Section 8, Derivative Publications *Watching and Waiting*. NM 6.3 |
| 268. | Notes on Joshua 5:6-12. Fact, Faith, and Experience | Section 5, Anonymous Publications Ascribed to B.W. Newton. [Probably by B.W. Newton] |
| 269. | Notes on Psalm 73 | Section 8, Derivative Publications. *Watching and Waiting*. NM 6.9 |
| 270. | NOTES ON SOME STATEMENTS OF R. PEARSALL SMITH (REPRINTED FROM 'THE RECORD' NOVEMBER 2 1874 | Section 3, Published Works |
| 271. | NOTES ON THE GREEK OF ROMANS ONE | Section 3, Published Works |
| 272. | Notice of Daniel Williams' Reasons | Section 7, Articles in *The Christian Witness*. [Insufficient evidence to determine authorship] |
| 273. | Notice of Mr Tucker's Sermon | Section 7, Articles in *The Christian Witness* [Not by B.W. Newton] |

| | | |
|---|---|---|
| 274. | OBSERVATIONS ON A TRACT ENTITLED 'THE SUFFERINGS OF CHRIST AS SET FORTH IN A LECTURE ON PSALM 6', CONSIDERED | Section 3, Published Works |
| 275. | OCCASIONAL PAPERS ON SCRIPTURAL SUBJECTS I - IV | Section 3, Published Works |
| 276. | THE OLD TESTAMENT SAINTS | Section 3, Published Works |
| | | Section 6, Contributions to Periodicals. *The Journal of Prophecy* |
| 277. | THE OLD TESTAMENT SAINTS NOT EXCLUDED FROM THE CHURCH IN GLORY, WITH SOME REMARKS ON THE HERESY OF MARCION | Section 3, Published Works |
| 278. | THE OLD TESTAMENT SAINTS NOT EXCLUDED FROM THE CHURCH OF GOD | Section 3, Published Works |
| 279. | The Olive Tree and its Branches. The Doom of Israel and Christendom | Section 8, Derivative Publications. *Patmos Series*. NP 7 |
| 280. | On Isaiah 52:13 - 53 | Section 7, Articles in *The Christian Witness* [Not by B.W. Newton] |
| 281. | ON JUSTIFICATION THROUGH THE BLOOD AND RIGHTEOUSNESS OF A SUBSTITUTE | Section 3, Published Works |
| 282. | ON LUKE 21 | Section 3, Published Works |
| 283. 284. | ON LUKE 21 ON SANCTIFICATION BY THE BLOOD OF JESUS | Section 4, Contributions to Other Publications [with notes by J.G. Deck] |
| | | Section 3, Published Works |
| 285. | ON THE CLEANSING OF THE LEPER | Section 3, Published Works |
| 286. | ON THE DUTY OF GIVING HEED TO THE PREDICTIONS OF SCRIPTURE RESPECTING EVENTS THAT ARE TO PRECEDE THE RETURN OF OUR LORD | Section 3, Published Works |
| 287. | ON THE EXERCISE OF WORLDLY AUTHORITY | Section 3, Published Works |
| 288. | ON THE NATURAL RELATIONS OF MEN AND GOVERNMENTS TO GOD, EXTRACTED FROM THE THIRD SERIES OF 'AIDS TO PROPHETIC ENQUIRY' | Section 3, Published Works |
| 289. | ON THE PROPHECIES RESPECTING THE JEWS AND JERUSALEM, IN THE FORM OF A CATECHISM | Section 3, Published Works |
| 290. | ON THE SECOND PSALM. A REPRINT FROM 'OCCASIONAL PAPERS' | Section 3, Published Works |
| 291. | ON THE SPREAD OF NEOLOGY IN ENGLAND, EXTRACTED FROM THE THIRD NUMBER OF 'OCCASIONAL PAPERS' | Section 3, Published Works |
| 292. | ON THE WORDS 'THIS GENERATION' | Section 3, Published Works |

SECTION 1: INDEX OF TITLES

| 293. | On Zechariah 11 | Section 7, Articles in *The Christian Witness* [Probably by B.W. Newton] |
|---|---|---|
| 294. | THE ONE ALL SUFFICIENT OFFERING | Section 3, Published Works |
| 295. | One Man's Sin contrasted with 'The One Righteousness'. Romans 5 | Section 8, Derivative Publications. *Patmos Series*. NP 26 |
| 296. | ORDER OF EVENTS CONNECTED WITH THE APPEARING OF CHRIST AND HIS MILLENNIAL REIGN. EXTRACTED FROM THE THIRD SERIES OF 'AIDS TO PROPHETIC ENQUIRY' | Section 3, Published Works |
| 297. | OUR ALTAR, HEBREWS 13 v10 | Section 3, Published Works |
| 298. | OUR GOVERNMENTAL ACKNOWLEDGEMENT OF GOD, FIVE PAPERS ON THE MORAL AND RELIGIOUS QUALIFICATIONS OF LEGISLATORS IN THE PARLIAMENT OF GREAT BRITAIN | Section 3, Published Works |
| 299. | PA FODD Y MAE Y GWAED YN CADW? | Section 3, Published Works |
| 300. | PARABLES OF MATTHEW 13 | Section 3, Published Works |
| 301. | The parting charge of Mr Newton to his friends. | Section 8, Derivative Publications. *Teachers of the Faith and Future*. NM 8.9 |
| 302. | The Passover. Exodus 12. | Section 5, Anonymous Publications Ascribed to B.W. Newton. [Insufficient internal evidence of authorship] |
| 303. | THE PEACE SACRIFICE | Section 3, Published Works |
| 304. | PENSÉES SUR L'APOCALYPSE | Section 3, Published Works |
| 305. | THE PERFECT SACRIFICE | Section 3, Published Works |
| 306. | Persecution of Protestants in Spain | Section 4, Contributions to Other Publications [one of the contributors] |
| 307. | THE PERSONAL RETURN OF THE LORD JESUS CHRIST NECESSARY TO THE INTRODUCTION OF MILLENNIAL BLESSING | Section 3, Published Works |
| 308. | PETIT CATÉCHISME OU DEMANDES ET RÉPONSES SUR LES PROPHÉTIES CONCERNANT LES JUIFS ET JÉRUSALEM | Section 3, Published Works |
| 309. | 'The Pilgrimage of Truth' | Section 8, Derivative Publications. *Studies Series*. NS 40 |
| 310. | 'PLAIN PAPERS' ON GOSPEL THEMES | Section 3, Published Works |

# SECTION 1: INDEX OF TITLES

| | | |
|---|---|---|
| 311. | A poem by Mr Newton | Section 8, Derivative Publications *Teachers of the Faith and Future*. NM 8.4 |
| 312. | A Prayer of Mr Newton | Section 8, Derivative Publications *Watching and Waiting*. NM 6.7 |
| 313. | Prayers of Mr Newton | Section 8, Derivative Publications *Teachers of the Faith and Future*. NM 8.5 |
| 314. | PREDICTED EVENTS – A LETTER TO A FRIEND IN REPLY TO THE QUESTION, 'IS IT WRONG TO EXPECT…?' | Section 3, Published Works |
| 315. | PREMILLENNIAL TRUTH DEMONSTRATED | Section 3, Published Works |
| 316. | PREMILLENNIALISM DEMONSTRATED TO BE TRUTH | Section 3, Published Works |
| 317. | 'Prepared unto Glory!' How? | Section 8, Derivative Publications. *Patmos Series*. NP 5 |
| 318. | PRIESTHOOD AND SACRIFICE ESSENTIAL TO WORSHIP | Section 3, Published Works |
| 319. | The Probable Course of Events up to the 'Time of the End'. | Section 8, Derivative Publications. *Time of the End Series*. NT 2 |
| 320. | PROPHECIES CONCERNING THE JEWS AND JERUSALEM | Section 3, Published Works |
| 321. | PROPHECIES RESPECTING THE JEWS AND JERUSALEM IN THE FORM OF A CATECHISM | Section 3, Published Works |
| 322. | Prophecy and Ritualism | Section 6, Contributions to Periodicals. *Old Truths* |
| 323. | PROPHECY. HOW TO READ IT, OR SCRIPTURE ITS OWN INTERPRETER, FROM 'THE FIRST SERIES OF AIDS TO PROPHETIC ENQUIRY' | Section 3, Published Works |
| 324. | 'The Prophecy of Habakkuk' | Section 8, Derivative Publications. *Patmos Series*. NP 21 |
| 325. | THE PROPHECY OF THE LORD JESUS AS CONTAINED IN MATTHEW 24 AND 25, CONSIDERED | Section 3, Published Works |
| 326. | PROPHECY OF THE LORD JESUS AS CONTAINED IN MATTHEW 24 BRIEFLY CONSIDERED | Section 3, Published Works |
| 327. | A Prophetic Forecast of Professing Christianity | Section 8, Derivative Publications. *Time of the End Series*. NT 19. |
| 328. | A PROPHETIC MAP OF THE WORLD; INTENDED TO EXHIBIT ITS GENERAL CONDITION AT THE END OF THE AGE: ALSO SOME EXTRACTS ON THE SAME SUBJECT FROM 'THOUGHTS ON THE APOCALYPSE' | Section 3, Published Works |

# SECTION 1: INDEX OF TITLES

| 329. | PROPHETIC PSALMS IN THEIR RELATION TO ISRAEL, BRIEFLY CONSIDERED | Section 3, Published Works |
|---|---|---|
| 330. | THE PROPHETIC SYSTEM OF MR ELLIOTT AND DR CUMMING CONSIDERED, EXTRACTED FROM THE FIRST SERIES OF 'AIDS TO PROPHETIC ENQUIRY' | Section 3, Published Works |
| 331. | The Propitiation of Christ | Section 7, Articles in *The Christian Witness* [Insufficient Evidence regarding authorship] |
| 332. | PROPOSITIONS FOR THE SOLEMN CONSIDERATION OF CHRISTIANS | Section 3, Published Works |
| 333. | The Prospects of Egypt, Edom, Nineveh, Moab, Tyre etc. | Section 8, Derivative Publications. *Studies Series.* NS 20 |
| 334. | PROSPECTS OF THE TEN KINGDOMS OF THE ROMAN EMPIRE, BEING THE THIRD SERIES OF 'AIDS TO PROPHETIC ENQUIRY' | Section 3, Published Works |
| 335. | THE PROSPECTS OF THE WORLD, IN CONNECTION WITH THE APPROACHING RETURN OF THE LORD JESUS CHRIST | Section 3, Published Works |
| 336. | THE PROSPECTS OF THE WORLD, IN CONNECTION WITH THE APPROACHING RETURN OF THE LORD JESUS CHRIST | Section 5, Anonymous Publications Ascribed to B.W. Newton. [by B.W. Newton] |
| 337. | 'Protection', 'Acceptance', 'Blessing'. The Blood of Christ | Section 8, Derivative Publications. *Patmos Series.* NP 31 |
| 338. | Psalms 1-8 | Section 8, Derivative Publications. *Patmos Series.* NP 23 |
| 339. | Psalm 119. Christ's Daily Life Work for us | Section 8, Derivative Publications. *Patmos Series.* NP 39 |
| 340. | The Purpose of God according to Election in Romans 9 - 11 | Section 8, Derivative Publications. *Patmos Series.* NP 28 |
| 341. | QU'EST-CE QUE L'ÉPHA DE ZACHARIE 5? OU L'EXPOSITION DE 1851 CONSIDÉRÉE EN RAPPORT AVEC LES PRINCIPES DE LÉGISLATION MODERNE | Section 3, Published Works |
| 342. | THE RECHABITES, JEREMIAH 35. A TRACT COMPILED FROM NOTES OF A LECTURE DELIVERED IN DUKE STREET CHAPEL, ST JAMES'S PARK JULY 8TH 1855. | Section 3, Published Works |
| 343. | 'The Recompense of the Reward'. Genesis 3 and Hebrews 11. | Section 8, Derivative Publications. *Time of the End Series.* NT 12 |
| 344. | Reflections for the New Year in the Parables of Matthew 25 | Section 8, Derivative Publications. *Patmos Series.* NP 10 |

# SECTION 1: INDEX OF TITLES

| 345. | Reflections for the Season, December 25th | Section 8, Derivative Publications. *Patmos Series.* NP 9 |
|---|---|---|
| 346. | REFLECTIONS ON THE CHARACTER AND SPREAD OF SPIRITUALISM | Section 3, Published Works |
| 347. | REFLECTIONS SUGGESTED BY THE PRESENT MOVEMENT IN ENGLAND AGAINST ROMANISM. A LETTER TO A FRIEND | Section 3, Published Works |
| 348. | REGENERATION IN ITS CONNEXION WITH THE CROSS: THE SUBSTANCE OF A LECTURE DELIVERED IN DUKE STREET CHAPEL, ST JAMES'S PARK | Section 3, Published Works |
| 349. | Reliance on Christ | Section 6, Contributions to Periodicals. *Old Truths* |
| 350. | The Religious Tendencies of the Times [by James Grant] | Section 4, Contributions to Other Publications |
| 351. | REMARKS ON A BOOK ENTITLED 'NATURAL LAW IN THE SPIRITUAL WORLD' BY HENRY DRUMMOND, FRSI, FGS, BEING THE SUBSTANCE OF FOUR LECTURES GIVEN IN LONDON | Section 3, Published Works |
| 352. | REMARKS ON A TRACT ENTITLED 'JUSTIFICATION IN THE RISEN CHRIST' | Section 3, Published Works |
| 353. | REMARKS ON 'MOSAIC COSMOGONY', BEING THE FIFTH OF THE 'ESSAYS AND REVIEWS', EXTRACTED FROM THE THIRD NUMBER OF THE 'OCCASIONAL PAPERS ON SCRIPTURAL SUBJECTS' | Section 3, Published Works |
| 354. | REMARKS ON MR TROTTER'S PAMPHLET | Section 3, Published Works |
| 355. | Remarks on Parts of the Epistle to the Galatians | Section 8, Derivative Publications. *Studies Series.* NS 21 |
| 356. | REMARKS ON R. PEARSALL SMITH'S EDITION OF HYMNS SELECTED FROM THOSE OF THE LATE F.W. FABER, D.D., PRIEST OF THE ORATORY OF ST. PHILIP NERI, BROMPTON | Section 3, Published Works |
| 357. | REMARKS ON THE PROPHETIC STATEMENTS OF MR FLEMING | Section 3, Published Works |
| 358. | REMARKS ON THE REVISED ENGLISH VERSION OF THE GREEK NEW TESTAMENT | Section 3, Published Works |
| 359. | REMARKS ON THE SUFFERINGS OF THE LORD JESUS: A LETTER ADDRESSED TO CERTAIN BRETHREN AND SISTERS IN CHRIST. | Section 3, Published Works |
| 360. | Remarks on the Ten Kingdoms of the Roman World | Section 5, Anonymous Publications Ascribed to B.W. Newton. [by B.W. Newton] |

SECTION 1: INDEX OF TITLES

| 361. | REMARKS ON THE TEN KINGDOMS OF THE ROMAN WORLD WITH A MAP | Section 3, Published Works |
|---|---|---|
| 362. | Reminiscence of an exhortation from Revelation 12 | Section 8, Derivative Publications. *Watching and Waiting*. NM 6.6 |
| 363. | Reminiscences of Mr B.W. Newton's Ministry on Prophecy, Part II | Section 8, Derivative Publications. *Studies Series*. NS 23 |
| 364. | Reminiscences of Mr B.W. Newton's Ministry, Part I | Section 8, Derivative Publications. *Studies Series*. NS 22 |
| 365. | A REMONSTRANCE TO THE SOCIETY OF FRIENDS | Section 3, Published Works |
| 366. | REPLY TO A TRACT OF MR TROTTER ENTITLED 'WHAT ARE MR NEWTON'S PRESENT DOCTRINES AS TO THE HUMAN NATURE AND RELATIONSHIPS OF THE LORD JESUS CHRIST?' | Section 3, Published Works |
| 367. | RETFÆRDIGGJÖRELSEN OG HELLIGGJÖRELSEN. UDVALG AF BWN'S VARKER. AUTORISEERET OVERSÆTTELSE EFTER ORIGINALENS 2 UDG. KRA. (1900) | Section 3, Published Works |
| 368. | Retranslations in the New Testament | Section 7, Articles in *The Christian Witness*. Beyond Reasonable Doubt by B.W. Newton |
| 369. | Retranslations of Some Passages in the Epistles | Section 7, Articles in *The Christian Witness*. Not by B.W. Newton |
| 370. | Retranslations of various portions of Holy Scripture extracted from the works of the late B.W. Newton. | Section 10, Duplicated and Manuscript Items (SGAT) |
| 371. | Review of Mr Peter's Letter | Section 7, Articles in *The Christian Witness* [by B.W. Newton] |
| 372. | 'Riches of Grace' as seen in the Tabernacle | Section 8, Derivative Publications. *Patmos Series*. NP 32 |
| 373. | ROMANS 7, CONSIDERED | Section 3, Published Works |
| 374. | SALVATION BY SUBSTITUTION | Section 3, Published Works |
| 375. | 'Salvation' What the Instrumentality? What the Link? | Section 8, Derivative Publications. *Patmos Series*. NP 16 |
| 376. | SCRIPTURAL PROOF OF THE DOCTRINE OF THE FIRST RESURRECTION | Section 3, Published Works |
| 377. | SCRIPTURAL PROSPECTS | Section 3, Published Works |
| 378. | SCRIPTURAL TRUTHS | Section 3, Published Works |

| | | |
|---|---|---|
| 379. | THE SECOND ADVENT NOT SECRET, BUT IN MANIFESTED GLORY | Section 3, Published Works |
| 380. | THE SECOND ADVENT OF OUR LORD NOT SECRET BUT IN MANIFESTED GLORY | Section 3, Published Works |
| 381. | The Second Appearing and Personal Reign of the Lord Jesus Christ | Section 5, Anonymous Publications Ascribed to B.W. Newton. [Not by B.W. Newton] |
| 382. | A SECOND LETTER TO A FRIEND ON THE STUDY OF PROPHECY | Section 3, Published Works |
| 383. 384. | A SECOND LETTER TO A FRIEND ON THE STUDY OF PROPHECY<br>A SECOND LETTER TO THE BRETHREN AND SISTERS IN CHRIST, MEETING FOR COMMUNION IN EBRINGTON STREET | Section 7, Articles in *The Christian Witness*<br>Section 5, Anonymous Publications Ascribed to B.W. Newton. [Beyond reasonable doubt by B.W. Newton]<br>Section 3, Published Works |
| 385. | SECOND SERIES OF 'AIDS TO PROPHETIC ENQUIRY' | Section 3, Published Works |
| 386. | SECOURS POUR L'ÉTUDE DE LA PROPHÉTIE, TRADUIT LIBREMENT DE L'ANGLAIS DE BWN. | Section 3, Published Works |
| 387. | Selections from Mr B.W. Newton's Teachings | Section 8, Derivative Publications. *Studies Series.* NS 22,23 |
| 388. | The Sermon on the Mount. An Outline | Section 8, Derivative Publications. *Studies Series.* NS 24 |
| 389. | THE SERVICE OF THE PRIESTS ON THE EIGHTH DAY (LEV. 9) | Section 3, Published Works |
| 390. | THE SEVEN PARABLES OF THE THIRTEENTH OF MATTHEW DISPENSATIONALLY CONSIDERED | Section 3, Published Works |
| 391. | THE SEVENTH CHAPTER OF THE EPISTLE TO THE ROMANS, CONSIDERED | Section 3, Published Works |
| 392. | The 'Signs of the Times'. Matthew 24 and 25. | Section 8, Derivative Publications. *Time of the End Series.* NT 17. |
| 393. | THE SIMILARITIES AND THE CONTRASTS BETWEEN THE PRESENT AND COMING DISPENSATIONS | Section 3, Published Works |
| 394. 395. | THE SIMILARITIES AND THE CONTRASTS BETWEEN THE PRESENT AND COMING DISPENSATIONS<br>THE SIN OFFERING (LEVITICUS 4 AND 5) | Section 4, Contributions to Other Publications<br>Section 3, Published Works |
| 396. | Some Characteristics of the Millennial Age. | Section 8, Derivative Publications. *Time of the End Series.* NT 21 |

# SECTION 1: INDEX OF TITLES

| 397. | 'Songs of Thanksgiving' | Section 8, Derivative Publications. *Time of the End Series.* NT 11 |
|---|---|---|
| 398. | SPIRITISM | Section 3, Published Works |
| 399. | A STATEMENT AND ACKNOWLEDGEMENT RESPECTING CERTAIN DOCTRINAL ERRORS | Section 3, Published Works |
| 400. | STATEMENT OF DOCTRINE | Section 3, Published Works |
| 401. | Statement of Doctrines held by a Body of Christians [compiled by Arthur Andrews] | Section 4, Contributions to Other Publications |
| 402. | Studies in 2 Chronicles | Section 8, Derivative Publications. *Studies Series.* NS 26 |
| 403. | Studies in Galatians | Section 8, Derivative Publications. *Studies Series.* NS 21 |
| 404. | Studies in Leviticus | Section 8, Derivative Publications. *Studies Series.* NS 25 |
| 405. | Studies in Parts of 2 Chronicles | Section 8, Derivative Publications. *Studies Series.* NS 26 |
| 406. | Studies in Parts of the Book of Genesis | Section 8, Derivative Publications. *Studies Series.* NS 27 |
| 407. | Studies in Parts of the First Epistle to the Corinthians | Section 8, Derivative Publications. *Studies Series.* NS 28 |
| 408. | Studies in Parts of the Gospel of John | Section 8, Derivative Publications. *Studies Series.* NS 29 |
| 409. | Studies in Parts of the Gospel of Matthew | Section 8, Derivative Publications. *Studies Series.* NS 30 |
| 410. | Studies in Parts of the Second Epistle to the Corinthians | Section 8, Derivative Publications. *Studies Series.* NS 31 |
| 411. | Studies in Some of the Psalms | Section 8, Derivative Publications. *Studies Series.* NS 32 |
| 412. | Studies in the Book of Daniel | Section 8, Derivative Publications. *Studies Series.* NS 8 |
| 413. | Studies in 'the Canticles' | Section 8, Derivative Publications. *Studies Series.* NS 40 |
| 414. | Studies in the Epistle of 1 John | Section 8, Derivative Publications. *Studies Series.* NS 33 |
| 415. | Studies in the Epistle of James | Section 8, Derivative Publications. *Studies Series.* NS 34 |
| 416. | Studies in the Epistle to the Ephesians | Section 8, Derivative Publications. *Studies Series.* NS 14 |

| | | |
|---|---|---|
| 417. | Studies in the Epistle to the Galatians condensed from the commentary by Martin Luther. | Section 8, Derivative Publications. *Studies Series.* [Not by B.W. Newton] |
| 418. | Studies in the Epistle to the Hebrews | Section 8, Derivative Publications. *Studies Series.* NS 35 |
| 419. | Studies in the Epistle to the Philippians | Section 8, Derivative Publications. *Studies Series.* NS 36 |
| 420. | Studies in the Epistle to the Romans | Section 8, Derivative Publications. *Studies Series.* NS 11 |
| 421. | Studies in the Epistles of 1 and 2 Timothy | Section 8, Derivative Publications. *Studies Series.* NS 37 |
| 422. | Studies in the Facts of Prophetic Scripture | Section 8, Derivative Publications. *Studies Series.* NS 10 |
| 423. | Studies in the First Epistle to the Corinthians | Section 8, Derivative Publications. *Studies Series.* NS 31 |
| 424. | Studies in the Gospel of John | Section 8, Derivative Publications. *Studies Series.* NS 29 |
| 425. | Studies in the Gospel of Matthew | Section 8, Derivative Publications. *Studies Series.* NS 30 |
| 426. | Studies in the Lives of Jonah, Job and Philemon | Section 8, Derivative Publications. *Studies Series.* NS 38 |
| 427. | Studies in the Prophecy of Isaiah | Section 8, Derivative Publications. *Studies Series.* NS 39 |
| 428. | Studies in the Psalms | Section 8, Derivative Publications. *Studies Series.* NS 32 |
| 429. | Studies in the Second Epistle to the Corinthians | Section 8, Derivative Publications. *Studies Series.* NS 31 |
| 430. | Studies in the 'Song of Solomon' | Section 8, Derivative Publications. *Studies Series.* NS 40 |
| 431. | Subject index and index of texts | Section 11, Indexes of B.W. Newton's Works |
| 432. | Subject index to the works of B.W. Newton | Section 11, Indexes of B.W. Newton's Works |
| 433. | SUBSTANCE OF A LECTURE ON LUKE 21 | Section 3, Published Works |
| 434. | The Sufferings of Christ on Three Separate Occasions | Section 8, Derivative Publications. *Studies Series.* NS 41 |
| 435. | A Synopsis of Isaiah 40-49 and 59-61 | Section 8, Derivative Publications. *Studies Series.* NS 42 |
| 436. | The Ten Kingdoms. Their Government and Probable Final Re-arrangement in accordance with Daniel 2, 7 and 8. | Section 8, Derivative Publications. *Time of the End Series.* NT 15 |

| 437. | THAT HE MIGHT GATHER INTO ONE ALL THINGS IN CHRIST; EVEN IN HIM | Section 3, Published Works |
|---|---|---|
| 438. | THEOLOGICAL OPINIONS OF REV. JOSEPH COOK OF BOSTON, BRIEFLY CONSIDERED (PART I) | Section 3, Published Works |
| 439. | THINGS CLEAN AND UNCLEAN (LEVITICUS 11) | Section 3, Published Works |
| 440. | Things pertaining to this life | Section 8, Derivative Publications. *Patmos Series*. NP 2 |
| 441. | 'Things that accompany Salvation' - or the practical walk of the 'saved'. Romans 12 - 14 | Section 8, Derivative Publications. *Patmos Series*. NP 24 |
| 442. | Things that must shortly come to pass. | Section 8, Derivative Publications. *Time of the End Series*. NT 1 |
| 443. | Things you always wanted to know about Bible Prophecy – 39 Key Questions answered. | Section 8, Derivative Publications. *Studies Series*. NS 10 |
| 444. | THE THIRD SERIES OF 'AIDS TO PROPHETIC ENQUIRY' | Section 3, Published Works |
| 445. | Thoughts on Ministry | Section 7, Articles in *The Christian Witness*. [Insufficient evidence to confirm authorship] |
| 446. | Thoughts on Nehemiah | Section 7, Articles in *The Christian Witness*. [Beyond reasonable doubt by B.W. Newton] |
| 447. | THOUGHTS ON PARTS OF LEVITICUS | Section 3, Published Works |
| 448. | THOUGHTS ON PARTS OF THE EPISTLE TO THE ROMANS | Section 3, Published Works |
| 449. | THOUGHTS ON PARTS OF THE PROPHECY OF ISAIAH | Section 3, Published Works |
| 450. | THOUGHTS ON PARTS OF THE SONG OF SOLOMON | Section 3, Published Works |
| 451. | THOUGHTS ON SCRIPTURAL SUBJECTS | Section 3, Published Works |
| 452. | THOUGHTS ON THE 24th MATTHEW | Section 3, Published Works |
| 453. | THOUGHTS ON THE APOCALYPSE | Section 3, Published Works |
| 454. | THOUGHTS ON THE APOSTASY OF THE PRESENT DISPENSATION | Section 3, Published Works |
| 455. | THOUGHTS ON THE APOSTASY OF THE PRESENT DISPENSATION | Section 5, Anonymous Publications Ascribed to B.W. Newton. [Beyond reasonable doubt by B.W. Newton] |

| 456. | Thoughts on the Apostasy of the Present Dispensation | Section 7, Articles in *The Christian Witness*. [Beyond reasonable doubt by B.W. Newton] |
|---|---|---|
| 457. | THOUGHTS ON THE CHRISTIAN AND JEWISH REMNANTS AT THE TIME OF THE END | Section 3, Published Works |
| 458. | THOUGHTS ON THE DEATH OF CAPTAIN BIRD ALLEN AND OTHER CHRISTIANS ENGAGED IN THE NIGER EXPEDITION | Section 3, Published Works |
| 459. | THOUGHTS ON THE END OF THE AGE, BEING IN PART COMPILED FROM SOME NOTES OF LECTURES DELIVERED AT SIDMOUTH AND ELSEWHERE | Section 3, Published Works |
| 460. | THOUGHTS ON THE HISTORY OF PROFESSING CHRISTIANITY AS GIVEN IN THE PARABLES OF MATTHEW 13 | Section 3, Published Works |
| 461. | Thoughts on the Lord's Prayer | Section 8, Derivative Publications. Misc. NM 1.3 |
| 462. | Thoughts on the Tabernacle | Section 7, Articles in *The Christian Witness*. [by B.W. Newton] |
| 463. | THOUGHTS ON THE WHOLE PROPHECY OF ISAIAH | Section 3, Published Works |
| 464. | THOUGHTS ON UNFULFILLED PROPHECY | Section 3, Published Works |
| 465. | The 'Time of the End'. A Résumé of Prophetic Truth translated from the French. | Section 8, Derivative Publications. *Patmos Series*. NP 40 |
| 466. | The Times of Restitution. Acts 3:19 - 21 | Section 6, Contributions to Periodicals. *The Investigator* |
| 467. | TRACTS ON DOCTRINAL SUBJECTS | Section 3, Published Works |
| 468. | THE TRESPASS OFFERING | Section 3, Published Works |
| 469. | THE TRUE UNITY OF THE CHURCH OF GOD IN TIME AND ETERNITY | Section 3, Published Works |
| 470. | Truths concerning Christ as the Redeemer | Section 6, Contributions to Periodicals. *Old Truths* |
| 471. | THE TWELVE HUNDRED AND SIXTY DAYS OF ANTICHRIST'S REIGN FUTURE, A SECOND TRACT, WRITTEN WITH RELATION TO CERTAIN LECTURES RECENTLY DELIVERED AT THE TOWN HALL, WORTHING | Section 3, Published Works |
| 472. | Twelve Prayers by B.W. Newton | Section 8, Derivative Publications *Watching and Waiting*. NM 6.1 |

SECTION 1: INDEX OF TITLES

| | | |
|---|---|---|
| 473. | UEBER DIE EWIGE VERSÖHNUNG, EIN TRAKTAT | Section 3, Published Works |
| 474. | UEBER DIE RECHTFERTIGUNG | Section 3, Published Works |
| 475. | 'Under Sin, Under Law, Under Grace'. Romans 6 - 8 | Section 8, Derivative Publications. *Patmos Series*. NP 27 |
| 476. | Valera's Spanish Bible of 1602. An appeal to Protestant Christians [by S.P. Tregelles. Prefatory notes by B.W. Newton] | Section 4, Contributions to Other Publications |
| 477. | A VINDICATION OF 'A REMONSTRANCE TO THE SOCIETY OF FRIENDS' | Section 3, Published Works |
| 478. | WHAT IS THE EPHAH OF ZECHARIAH 5? OR, THE EXHIBITION OF 1851 CONSIDERED IN RELATION TO THE PRINCIPLES OF MODERN LEGISLATION | Section 3, Published Works |
| 479. | What is the Pearl Testimony? (Compilation A.C. Fry) | Section 8, Derivative Publications. Misc. NM 10 |
| 480. | THE WHITE ROBE (REVELATION 7:9-17) | Section 3, Published Works |
| 481. | THE WHITE ROBE (REVELATION 7:9-17) | Section 5, Anonymous Publications Ascribed to B.W. Newton. [Beyond reasonable doubt by B.W. Newton] |
| | | Section 3, Published Works |
| 482. | 'THE WHOLE FAMILY' EPHESIANS 3:5. IS IT 'EVERY FAMILY' OR IS IT 'THE WHOLE FAMILY OF THE REDEEMED'? | Section 8, Derivative Publications. *Bethany Series* No.3. |
| 483. | Wilderness Wanderings and Heavenly Guidance | Section 8, Derivative Publications. Patmos Series. NP 3 |
| 484. | 'The Word of Jesus and the Voice of the Son of God' | Section 8, Derivative Publications. *The Bethany Series*. NM 4.2 |
| 485. | The World in Crisis | Section 8, Derivative Publications. *Watching and Waiting*. NM 6.1 |
| 486. | THE WORLD TO COME | Section 3, Published Works |
| | | Section 7, Articles in *The Christian Witness*. |
| 487. | THE WRECK AND THE ROCK | Section 3, Published Works |
| 488. | ZECHARIAH 5 RETRANSLATED WITH NOTES. BEING AN EXTRACT FROM THE SECOND EDITION OF 'THOUGHTS ON SCRIPTURAL SUBJECTS' | Section 3, Published Works |

| 489. | ZECHARIAH 5. THE VISION OF THE EPHAH CONSIDERED IN RELATION TO THE PRINCIPLES OF MODERN LEGISLATION | Section 3, Published Works |

# SECTION 2

## LIBRARIES AND COLLECTIONS WHERE B.W. NEWTON'S PUBLISHED WORKS ARE LOCATED

# LIBRARIES AND COLLECTIONS WHERE B.W. NEWTON'S PUBLISHED WORKS ARE LOCATED

The libraries with the most important collections of B.W. Newton's books are noted by abbreviation. We have only identified other libraries and collections if they hold unique or rare items.

This *Guide* is the result of extensive searches with hundreds of national, provincial, and theological libraries. It is therefore probable that in some cases library holdings may have changed. No liability is accepted for unsuccessful journeys to remote libraries!

The abbreviations used for the main libraries and collections are as follows:

| | |
|---|---|
| BIOLA | Bible Institute of Los Angeles |
| Bo | Bodleian Library, Oxford |
| BL | British Library |
| CBA | The Christian Brethren Archive, The John Ryland University Library of Manchester. Catalogue references are given where known, e.g. CBA 6998. |
| CG | Items held by C.W.H. Griffiths |
| CU | Cambridge University Library |
| EC | Items held by the late Edwin Cross in 1992. |
| EL | Evangelical Library, London |
| Fratelli | The Library of the Brethren Assembly in Vechia, Florence |
| I | Italian National Library, Florence (Fondo Guicciardini) |
| Sc | National Library of Scotland |
| SG | Collection of the Sovereign Grace Advent Testimony, Chelmsford (NB This collection has been examined in its entirety, but it is uncatalogued. Therefore, only older and unusual items in this collection are recorded). |
| SNL | Spanish National Library (Fondo Usoz) |
| T | Library of Trinity College, Dublin |
| TC | Items held in the private collection of Tom Chantry |
| U | Union Catalog, USA |

Wherever possible, sources with public access have been given. As explicit permission has not been given to publicise the source, the following references given in the text are not identified –ID, NP.

**Description of Important Collections Relevant to Section 3, Bibliography of B.W. Newton's Published Works.**

## 1. THE CHRISTIAN BRETHREN ARCHIVE

The Christian Brethren Archive of the John Rylands University Library of the University of Manchester is probably the largest collection of printed books, periodicals, manuscripts, and archival materials relating to 'the Brethren Movement'. Its webpage describes the objective of the archive as follows:

'The purpose of the Christian Brethren collection is to preserve materials that document the history of the Brethren movement and make these materials available to researchers and interested parties. The Archive holds these materials in trust for future generations, and therefore they can only be examined in the Special Collections Reading Room of the John Rylands University Library.'

The chief interest in the Archive in relation to B.W. Newton is that it houses the Fry Collection. More detailed information on the Fry Collection is given in Section 10, Duplicated and Manuscript Items. However, the Archive has acquired several important Brethren collections, and has received gifts of books, manuscripts and other material since its foundation in 1979. The Archive has 16,000 books, pamphlets and tracts. These inevitably include many of B.W. Newton's published works, and many anonymous early works that may have been written by him. It is therefore an important point of access for these, and we have consequently referenced their presence in the Christian Brethren Archive (CBA) in Section 3, B.W. Newton's Published Works, and Section 8, Publications Produced from Notes of Addresses, and Posthumously Published Letters and Manuscripts.

We have also consulted the attributions to anonymous articles in the *Christian Witness* given in the *Echoes of Service* Collection, which is now in the Christian Brethren Archive, in our assessment of B.W. Newton's possible authorship (in Section 7, Articles in *The Christian Witness*).

The former Archivist of the Collection, Dr David Brady, helpfully assisted in identifying anonymous articles that may have been written by Mr Newton, and we have had the full co-operation of the CBA throughout this research.

The author of this *Guide* has also contributed a number of important items to the Archive, either as copies, or as originals; either personally, or through encouragement to others to place them in the Archive, as he has also done in relation to the Sovereign Grace Advent Testimony Collection.

It is in many senses a strange anomaly that someone who was so bitterly attacked by the Brethren during his lifetime, and who spent 50 years disavowing any connection with the movement, should have most of his surviving publications, manuscripts and ephemera stored in the Christian Brethren Archive. We are nevertheless thankful that this material is thereby securely preserved.

## 2. THE SOVEREIGN GRACE ADVENT TESTIMONY

It is beyond the remit of this *Guide* to narrate the history of those who have sought to maintain B.W Newton's teaching on prophetic and other matters through the twentieth and twenty first centuries.[1]

However, some comments are needed to understand the origins and role of the SGAT:

1. To account for the provenance of relevant materials in the SGAT Collection.
2. To highlight the importance of the magazines *Perilous Times* and *Watching and Waiting* as a source for biographical information regarding B.W. Newton.

---

[1] It is hoped that an account of the two decades after B.W. Newton's death will be published shortly, charting the activities of such as Edward Crossley, Arthur Andrews, Lancelot Holland, John Cox (jun.), Lucas Collins, C.T. Walrond, F.W. Wyatt, A.C. Fry, and Arthur Dalzell. There is some information regarding this period in the soon to be published *Arthur J.W. Dalzell: B.W. Newton's Physician and the Kyneton Settlement*.

> 3. To understand how the SGAT became the primary publisher of B.W. Newton's works.

The Sovereign Grace Advent Testimony is difficult to describe. It is not an organisation, insofar as it has no formal membership. What became its magazine was started by a distinctly different group twenty years before it came into existence. It did not set out to be a publisher, but has become the main publisher and distributor of B.W. Newton's works. It did not set out to keep an archive, but it now holds important original items and duplicated books relevant to B.W. Newton's life and ministry. It has had two secretaries in the 102 years since it was formed in 1918/1919.[1] For most of its existence the role of SGAT secretary has been combined with that of the editor of a quarterly (once monthly) magazine, *Watching and Waiting*.

B.W. Newton's conviction throughout his ministry was that the true Church is in a condition of weakness and division. 'Individual agency' is the means God has chiefly used for the revival of truth during the last eighteen hundred years 'since the darkness first set in'.[2] He therefore did not found a church or sect. Still less did he found a branch of the Brethren. It is therefore unsurprising that at his death there were no organised and co-ordinated arrangements to promote his teachings, although there were centres of interest in his teachings and ministry on the Isle of Wight, in Worthing, and in London.

G.T. Hunt[3], a Director of Hunt, Barnard and Co [printers] of London and Aylesbury, began producing *Perilous Times*, a four paged monthly magazine, in 1899 in co-operation with others of B.W. Newton's circle who contributed to it. It was chiefly a response to the 'Downgrade' Movement of the Free Church Council. None of its objects related directly to the correct understanding of prophecy. The magazine continued until March 1919, when it was enlarged and relaunched as *Watching and Waiting: Light for 'Perilous Times'*. At that point it reaffirmed its original objectives, but the common bond of the readership was clearly adherence to the teaching – particularly to the prophetic teaching – of B.W. Newton. The content of the magazines closely followed his teaching, and recorded many recollections of his ministry, often in the obituaries of those who had known him.

Hunt, Barnard and Co. also produced a large body of material from notes of B.W. Newton's addresses, including one substantial book on The Epistle to the Romans – see Section 8, Publications Produced from Notes of Addresses, and Posthumously Published Letters and Manuscripts for a fuller account of Hunt, Barnard's publishing, and of the B.W. Newton-related content of the two magazines.

When B.W. Newton's wife died in 1906, her will provided for a Trust Fund to safeguard and propagate B.W. Newton's works. Money from this was used to continue issuing the works of Mr Newton. It operated separately from the magazines *Perilous Times* and *Watching and Waiting*, and used Lucas Collins as its publisher. He followed a strict principle of publishing only what B.W. Newton had himself

---

[1] George Hazelton Fromow from 1919 until his death in 1974, and Stephen A. Toms from 1974 to the present.
[2] Comments attributed to B.W. Newton in *Old Truths*, Prophecy and Ritualism - 1867 (Vol. 2), p.237.
[3] George Turnor Hunt, 1855-1936. Obituary *Watching and Waiting* February 1936, p.9. The *Watching and Waiting* obituary quotes *The Bucks Herald* and *The Bucks Advertiser* obituaries. Died Jan. 4th 1936. A photograph of him as an old man is reproduced in *A Pictorial Memoir of Benjamin Wills Newton* – the supplement to this Guide.. See the Advertisement at the end of this volume.

approved and published. See Section 12, Miscellaneous Biographical Items, D. B.W. Newton as a writer, 1.4 Publishing by B.W. Newton's trustees.

The Sovereign Grace Advent Testimony was formed when 'leading members of 'the Strict Baptist Community' announced their 'Manifesto' in December 1919. The original eleven convenors had organised regular meetings in 1918, intended to counter the teaching of The Advent Testimony and Preparation Movement.[1] Their object was twofold; to maintain a simple futurist position on prophecy (premillennial and post-tribulation); and to do so as Calvinists, separate from the declension of the mainstream Churches.

The SGAT's open letter and invitation to its London meetings was noticed with interest (and some reservations) by *Watching and Waiting*.[2] However, in time the magazine-readers and the meeting-attenders grew together, and came to embrace others of widely different ecclesiology in their 'Advent Testimony'.[3] The fusion was complete in 1931, when George Fromow, who had been the secretary of the SGAT since its formation and one of the original signatories of the 'Manifesto', became the editor of *Watching and Waiting*[4]. By 1931 most of those who had known B.W. Newton's London ministry were elderly. Books and manuscript notes of B.W. Newton's ministry were bequeathed to the SGAT and were stored by the secretary, G.H. Fromow, in his large house in Chiswick, for redistribution or safekeeping. As Hunt Barnard ceased publishing materials derived from notes of B.W. Newton's ministry, the SGAT took over the role of storing and distributing these materials as well. Unbound printed materials of B.W. Newton's published works were acquired in the period after the Second World War, and were bound and distributed.

The SGAT currently (2021) has an industrial unit for book storage in Essex, which includes a library of older books and tracts by various authors. All the early publications in the SGAT library are recorded in this *Guide* (Section 3, B.W. Newton's Published Works). MS and typescript materials are recorded in Section 10, Duplicated and Manuscript Items, with a further description of this part of the SGAT Collection.

## 3. BIOLA UNIVERSITY LIBRARY AND ARCHIVES

BIOLA University was founded as The Bible Institute of Los Angeles in 1908 on the model of the Moody Bible Institute. It has a large collection of Brethren works, and with them items by, and related to, B.W. Newton, This Brethren aspect of its library and archive developed from the personal interest of Arnold D. Ehlert, who was librarian at BIOLA between 1954 and 1974.[5]

---

[1] Now known as the Prophetic Witness Movement International. It was founded in 1917 to promote 'any moment rapture', premillennial pretribulation teaching.

[2] *Watching and Waiting*, December 1919, p.93 'While we cannot accept all that Strict Baptists teach, we can and do endorse all that is contained in this letter' (which gave the SGAT Manifesto).

[3] At a later time Percy Heward spoke at its meetings, and Edwin Kirk was for a time the SGAT chair. Bishop Thompson (a former Free Church of England bishop) was also a frequent speaker later. During G.H. Fromow's time as secretary, the SGAT also had an attachment with the International Council of Christian Churches.

[4] George Hazelton Fromow (1889-1974). His obituary is given in *Watching and Waiting* July-August 1974, p.49.

[5] Arnold Douglas Ehlert (1909-1998). He produced *Brethren Writers: A Checklist with an Introduction to Brethren Literature and Additional Lists* (1969), following on from his earlier dissertation, *A Bibliographic History of Dispensationalism* (1944).

## 4. GUICCIARDINI COLLECTION (FONDO GUICCIARDINI)

This collection is in the Italian National Library at Florence. Count Piero Guicciardini (1808-1886) was a converted Italian nobleman. He commenced an indigenous Brethren work in Tuscany. A period of persecution followed, which led to his exile, part of which he spent in England between 1851 and 1860, associating with West Country Brethren. S.P. Tregelles maintained an interest and involvement in the cause of the Gospel in Italy long after Newton's break from Darby, although we have no evidence of contact between S.P. Tregelles or B.W. Newton with the Count.[1] Count Guicciardini presented his library to the Biblioteca Nazionale in Florence in 1877, when a greater degree of religious liberty had been restored to Tuscany.

The collection is a large one that includes 15th to 19th century publications, with many rare items from the pre-Reformation and Reformation period. It also includes a large number of nineteenth century pamphlets, many of them written by Brethren. Some are the sole surviving copies. The collection was meticulously re-catalogued in 1983. Timothy Stunt assisted in the identification of many of the items.[2]

## 5. FRATELLI COLLECTION

The Fratelli Collection[3] of early Brethren material is in the library of the Brethren Assembly at Via Vigna Vechia, Florence, Italy. Manuscript attributions of early anonymous items are important, as they derive from Eliza Browne[4]. She corresponded with J.L. Harris in the early years of the Plymouth Assembly and received copies of tracts from him, evidently with indications of authorship. She was possibly the step-daughter of J.L. Harris, who was living in Plymouth in the 1830s and 40s. She moved to Florence in about 1850-51. Some items bearing her name in manuscript also found their way into the Guicciardini Collection, which was donated to the Italian National Library (at Florence) in 1887.

We have been able to verify some of Eliza Browne's attributions of B.W. Newton's authorship, e.g. *Remarks on the Ten Kingdoms of the Roman World* and the anonymous tract *Baptism* (see Section 5, Anonymous Publications Ascribed to B.W. Newton).

## 6. USOZ COLLECTION

We have not personally accessed the Usoz Collection of the Spanish National Library in Madrid. We do not know if it contains manuscript records that would be relevant to this *Guide*. We have recorded the publications by B.W. Newton listed in library catalogue in this bibliography, some of which are unique surviving copies.

---

[1] But see S.P. Tregelles on Daniel p.212n, and the letter from S.P. Tregelles to B.W. Newton (undated, but April 1854).
[2] More background to the Guicciardini Collection may be found in 'Understanding the Past in the City of Florence', by Timothy Stunt (In *The Harvester*, September 1983). A detailed account is given in *Un Riforatore Toscano dell'epoca del Risorgimento, il Conte Guicciardini (1808-1886)*, by S. Jacini, Florence 1940; and in *Piero Guicciardini, un riformatore religioso nell'Europa dell'ottocento* by L. Giorgi and M. Rubboli, Florence, 1988.
[3] More background to the Fratelli Collection may be found in 'Understanding the Past in the City of Florence', by Timothy Stunt (In *The Harvester*, September 1983). Daisy Ronco's *Risorgimento and the Free Italian Churches* (1996) gives a full account.
[4] Eliza Browne was probably the step-daughter of James Lampen Harris (for a time Mr Newton's co-elder at Plymouth), the daughter of his second wife (see T.C.F. Stunt *The Life and Times of Samuel Prideaux Tregelles*).

B.W. Newton and S.P. Tregelles had a strong interest in Manuel Matamoros (1834-1866)[1] in the early 1860s, and in the tribulations of the Spanish Protestants during the period 1855-1865. S.P. Tregelles's wife was a fluent Spanish speaker. See (1) the references to the appeal for the republishing of Valera's Protestant Spanish translation of the Bible, Section 4, B.W. Newton's Contributions to Other Publications (2) the references to Spain and Matamoros in Section 9, B.W. Newton's Correspondence, and (3) the flier requesting financial support for persecuted Protestants in Spain in Section 4, B.W. Newton's Contributions to Other Publications.

Luis de Usoz y Río (1806-1865)[2] was related to Manuel Matamoros by marriage. He amassed a large personal library of Protestant works. He was an acquaintance of George Borrow (author of *The Bible in Spain*), who received him in London in 1839. His widow donated most of his library, including 29 published items by B.W. Newton, to the Spanish National Library. In the listing of items in the Usoz Collection we have simply referred to the books as being in the Spanish National Library (SNL).

---

[1] *Manuel Matamoros: His Life and Death. A Narrative of the Late Persecution of Christians in Spain* by William Greene, 3rd Edition 1889 gives more information regarding Manuel Matamoros. There are strictures on this account in CBA 7181 (30). See too T.C.F. Stunt, *The Life and Times of Samuel Prideaux Tregelles*, 8.6, The Spanish Dimension.

[2] An account of Luis de Usoz, and further background, is given in *Historia de los Heterodoxos Españoles*, Marcelino Menéndez y Pelayo. (Ed. D. Enrique Sánchez Reyes), Madrid 1946, p.319 ff., where Usoz is referred to as a Quaker.

# SECTION 3

## BIBLIOGRAPHY OF B.W. NEWTON'S PUBLISHED WORKS

# BIBLIOGRAPHY OF B.W. NEWTON'S PUBLISHED WORKS

## Works Listed

This part of the *Guide* lists every item published separately by B.W. Newton, later reprints, and items derived from these published works. Works published anonymously are included in this part of the *Guide* if they are beyond reasonable doubt by B.W. Newton. This section does not include items published by others on the basis of notes of addresses. Those are listed in Section 8, Section 8, Publications Produced from Notes of Addresses, and Posthumously Published Letters and Manuscripts. This section does not generally include extracts of his works that have been published by others, unless this is important on account of the rareness of the item.

## Content of the entries

The entry for each item includes
1. A brief description of the contents.
2. Points of interest – e.g. its position in relation to a particular controversy.
3. Its relation to other works.
4. A list of any works published elsewhere that are included in it.
5. A list of any works that have been extracted from it.
6. Formal publication details, including the principal repositories where editions were located as this bibliography was being compiled.

## Titles

The bibliography records every title by which each work was known, whether the formal title, that appearing on the binding, in publishers' lists, or in later editions. Variations of titles are listed alphabetically and, where necessary, are referred to in the main entry. Bound compilations of published works were issued from time to time. The titles of these bindings are given, and the component publications in them listed.

The principal title where description of contents is given is generally the latest title used by Mr Newton himself.

## Date

ND indicates that the work is not dated and that it has not been possible to establish the date by other means.
[1846?] indicates the possible date.
[c.1846] indicates the probable date that the item was published.
[1846] indicates virtual certainty of the date, although it is not given in the publication.

## Editions

Distinguishing the editions of some of the items is difficult for various reasons. It appears that on some occasions the publication of an item as a part of another work has been regarded as 'the first edition', and no separate first edition exists. In the case of the *Five Letters on Events Predicted in Scripture as Antecedent to the Coming of the Lord*, MS circulation of the item seems to have been considered to be 'the First Edition'. In the Case of *The Prophecy of the Lord Jesus as Contained in Matthew 24 and 25, Considered*, it developed from another tract of a different name, and it is different from a tract of almost the same name. We have highlighted the difficulties and have at times adopted the designation 'proto-edition' of an earlier tract.

## Publishers and Printers

At the time of the earlier publications of B.W. Newton, the roles of printer, publisher and distributer were less defined. The printer is not generally noted in this Guide, unless there are no indications of the publisher.

Print on Demand re-issuing of B.W. Newton's works creates a difficulty for a Guide such as this. Except in a few instances (where a publication is likely to be otherwise unobtainable or inaccessible) we have not listed older items produced by Print on Demand publishers.

See the further comments made on printing and publishing in Section 12 – Miscellaneous Biographical Items and Memorabilia, D. B.W. Newton as a Writer, 1. His Publishers.

## Alphabetical sequence

In this main bibliography, the English definite and indefinite articles are ignored when these are the first words in a title. Otherwise, this part of the *Guide* is strictly letter by letter alphabetical. Non-English titles are listed in alphabetical sequence (even if they have the definite article in their original language).

## Scripture References

Where roman numerals have been used for chapters of the Bible, these have been altered to conform to modern usage.

## Size

As many of the items as possible have been viewed personally. This has not been possible in every case. As library conventions vary, it is difficult to give completely accurate measurements. The measurements are included as an indication of the size of the work. The measurements are those of the binding edge.

## THE 1260 DAYS OF ANTICHRIST'S REIGN FUTURE

See *The Twelve Hundred and Sixty Days of Antichrist's Reign Future.*

## ACCEPTANCE WITH GOD

A Gospel tract. There is some confusion in the numbering of the editions.

No copies of the First Edition have been located. The end of the text of the Second Edition has 'B.W. Newton, 1859', indicating that date.

Second Edition
    1860                  Geo Hunt (printer), London      16cm    4p.      BL,I

? Edition
    [1859-1869][1]       Houlston & Wright, London     10cm    4p.      CBA

Sixth Edition
    1900                  Houlston & Sons, London       10cm    11p.     BL

Seventh Edition
    [1900][2]             Houlston & Sons, London       10cm    11p.     CBA

Ninth Edition
    [c.1910?]           Lucas Collins, London          10cm    11p.     SG

? Edition       (noted in *Watching and Waiting* Jan. 1924)
    1924                  Hunt, Barnard, Aylesbury

? Edition       (noted in *Watching and Waiting* Sept. 1936)
                          SGAT or Hunt, Barnard                 4p.     CBA?

'Eighth' Edition
    [c.1950]            E.J. Burnett, Worthing         10cm    18p.     BL,CBA

'Ninth' Edition
    1965                  SGAT, London                 17cm    4p.      SG

Arabic Edition
    No copies have been located. *Watching and Waiting*, January and December 1939 refers to this as 'recently published'. It was translated and published in Jerusalem by a converted Arab, Shukri H. Khouri (obituary *Watching and Waiting* July/August 1941).

Italian Edition – *Accettazione con Dio*
    1874    V.J. Arduin (printer), Menton    10cm    8p.      French National Library

---

[1] From publisher's dates
[2] From publisher's dates

Norwegian Edition

This was probably produced, but no copies have been located. See letter to Miss Leake, 12th August 1895 (Section 9, B.W. Newton's Correspondence), CBA 7050, pp.245-247.[1]

## ACCETTAZIONE CON DIO

Italian Edition of *Acceptance with God*.

## THE ACKNOWLEDGEMENT OF GOD BY EARTHLY GOVERNMENTS, BEING FIVE PAPERS ISSUED AT VARIOUS TIMES BY THE LATE BENJAMIN WILLS NEWTON

The frontispiece title is *Our Governmental Acknowledgement of God, Five Papers on the Moral and Religious Qualifications of Legislators in the Parliament of Great Britain, by the late Benjamin Wills Newton*. The cover indicates that these were 'reprinted by permission'.

The five papers consist of
1. A letter from Mr Newton published in *The Morning Herald*, January 2nd 1852 regarding 'Jewish Disabilities', under the pseudonym 'Χριστιανος' [Christianos = A Christian]. See Section 6 – Letters and Articles by B.W. Newton Published in Periodicals, *Morning Herald*, for further comment.

And four pamphlets concerned with lobbying, being addressed variously to members of the legislature, constituencies, and Parliament, as follows:

2. Observations on the Parliamentary Oaths Bill.
    This takes the form of a series of propositions. It is dated 1882.
3. Shall Atheism force on us an Alteration of our Laws?
    This 'enquiry' is dated February 26th 1883.
4. Affirmation – What is it?
    This is dated April 1883.
5. The Affirmation of the Society of Friends.
    This is undated. It is not addressed to a particular audience, but is evidently contemporaneous with 4, above.

1900    'Privately printed [for F.W. Wyatt]        18cm    41p.    EL,CBA

## ADDRESS RESPECTING THE METHODS OF THE SALVATION ARMY

This is a critical examination of the methods of William Booth's movement, and in particular of its Arminianism. It is perhaps significant that Mr Newton published *Atonement and Its Results*, and *Atonement Saveth* in the same year.

It attracted a reply from a member of the Salvation Army, which attacked Mr Newton's statements on particular redemption. [*Atonement for Every One*, by Admiral Edmund Gardiner Fishbourne, 1882,

---

[1] See also the preface to *The Sabbath and Lord's Day* by John Cox, jun., in which he refers to the first edition of his booklet having been published in 1896 at the request of a friend in Norway, and afterwards translated into that language.

Elliott Stock, London, 10cm, 32p Bo, BL]. Admiral Fishbourne only referred to Mr Newton's *Address Respecting the Methods of the Salvation Army* in his reply.

    1882      Houlston & Sons, London      16cm    23p.    BL,Bo,CBA,CU,EL

## AIDS TO PROPHETIC ENQUIRY

There were three 'Series' of *Aids to Prophetic Enquiry* published. The other two came to be known by other titles *Babylon and Egypt* (Second Series), and *Prospects of the Ten Kingdoms* (Third Series). The First Series was always known by the title *Aids to Prophetic Enquiry*. In its original form, the book drew principally from two earlier works:
 1. *Thoughts on Unfulfilled Prophecy.*
 2. The first edition of *The Prophecy of the Lord Jesus as contained in Matthew 24.*

In a publisher's list (1862) it was subtitled *A Brief Sketch of the Progress of Prophetic Enquiry.*

As with *Thoughts on the Apocalypse* and with *Babylon and Egypt*, there is confusion regarding editions of the book, as three publishers produced 'Second Editions'. The Partridge and Oakey edition seems to have followed the other two. It gives two different renderings of the 'Advertisement to the Second Edition', and the publisher was therefore aware of the confusion created.

The sequence of the contents of the three editions follows on the next pages.

| 1st Edition 1848 | 2nd Edition 1850-3 | 3rd Edition 1881 | Comments |
|---|---|---|---|
| Remarks on the Prophetic Statements of Mr Fleming. 21p. | -- | -- | Moved to the end of the 2nd and 3rd Editions, but unchanged, |
| -- | Advertisement to the Second Edition. 2p. | -- | Describes the changes made from 1st Edition |
| -- | -- | Preface to the Third Edition. 6p. | Reflective on the times and developments |
| -- | Introductory Observations 15p. | Introductory Observations. 21p. | Minor editing with minor additions. Most notably in final footnote of 3rd Edition |
| -- | No Poetic Exaggeration in the Language of Scripture. 16p. | No Poetic Exaggeration in the Language of Scripture. 20p. | Virtually unchanged. Minor additions and explanations |
| -- | Some Objections to the Doctrine of the Millennial Reign considered. 11p. | Some Objections to the Doctrine of the Millennial Reign considered. 16p. | Virtually unchanged. Minor additions and explanations. |
| On Zechariah 12. 14. sub-headed 'Introductory Observations'. 4p. | -- | -- | Explains basic principles in understanding prophecy, and indicating why he has chosen Zech. 12-14 as an example. |
| On Zechariah 12 and 13. 9p. | On Zechariah 12 and 13. 11p. | On Zechariah 12 and 13. 13p. | Virtually unchanged 1st to 2nd Minor additions and explanations 2nd to 3rd. |
| On Zechariah 14. 12p. | On Zechariah 14. 13p. | On Zechariah 14. 17p. | Virtually identical in all three editions |
| Futurity of the Manifestation of Antichrist – his connection with Jerusalem. 16p. | Futurity of the Manifestation of Antichrist – his connexion with Jerusalem. 21p. | Futurity of the Manifestation of Antichrist – his connexion with Jerusalem. 27p. | Some significant changes 1st to 2nd, e.g. regarding Antichrist's area of origin 2nd and 3rd are virtually identical. |

| | | | |
|---|---|---|---|
| Characteristics of Antichrist in the words of Scripture. 5p. | Passages of Scripture respecting Antichrist compared. 11p. | Passages of Scripture respecting Antichrist compared. 12p. | The 1st Edition simply quoted a series of topical Scriptures. The 2nd and 3rd Editions give a fuller account with only minor additions in the 3rd Edition. |
| Extracts from Irenæus, Jerome, Cyril &c. respecting Antichrist. 6p. | -- | -- | Omitted because similar, fuller quotations are given in *Prospects of the Ten Kingdoms* (1st ed. 1849) |
| Thoughts on Matthew 24. 16p. | Thoughts on Matthew 24. 17p. | Thoughts on Matthew 24. 22p | Virtually identical in all three editions |
| On Luke 21. 9p. | On Luke 21. 10p. | On Luke 21. 21p. | Virtually identical 1st to 2nd Edition. Substantial addition in 3rd Edition (after p.123 2nd and p.158 3rd) – 5 classes of people at the Lord's return etc. |
| -- | Remarks on the Prophetic Statements of Mr Fleming.[1] 22p. | Remarks on the Prophetic Statements of Mr Fleming. 20p. | Moved from the beginning of the First Edition. The third adds a substantial footnote at p.187 regarding the year-day system. |
| -- | The Prophetic System of Mr Elliott[2] and Dr Cumming.[3] considered[4]. §1 22p. | The Prophetic System of Mr Elliott and Dr Cumming considered §1. 29p. | 3rd adds a substantial updating footnote at p.201. Otherwise virtually identical. |
| -- | §2. [the year-day theory]. 15p. | §2. [the year-day theory]. 20p. | Virtually identical 2nd to 3rd Editions |
| -- | §3 [Mr Elliott on Rev. 13 and 17]. 20p. | §3 [Mr Elliott on Rev. 13 and 17]. 12p. | Virtually identical 2nd to 3rd Editions |
| -- | §4 [Principles to be observed in interpreting the Book of Revelation]. 20p. | §4 [Principles to be observed in interpreting the Book of Revelation]. 13p. | Replacement of paragraph (2nd, p.204 and 3rd, p.270) |
| -- | -- | Scriptural Proof of the Doctrine of the First Resurrection. 36p. | -- |

| | | | |
|---|---|---|---|
| -- | -- | Remarks on Bishop Wordsworth's Lectures on the Apocalypse.[5] 77p. | -- |
| -- | -- | Remarks on Indefectibility. 27p. | [Christendom is not indefectible] |
| -- | -- | Present Tendencies. 42p. | -- |
| -- | Appendix. Antichrist to be King of Assyria and Babylon – present prospects of those countries… 14p. | Appendix. Antichrist to be King of Assyria and Babylon – present prospects of those countries… 19p. | Virtually identical 2nd to 3rd Editions |
| -- | -- | Extracts from the Works of Dr Lightfoot[6] [regarding Bishop Wordsworth's Lectures]. 5p. | -- |

The First Edition has no preface or introduction. The advertisement to the Second Edition states that quotations from Revelation have been modified to follow Dr Tregelles's work on the Greek 'lately published'.

The following works were extracted from *Aids to Prophetic Enquiry*, and were subsequently published separately:

---

[1] *The Rise and Fall of Papacy* (143 pages) by Rev. Robert Fleming (Junior) (1660? – 1701) appeared to have predicted the French Revolution, using the year-day system, and predicted a weakening of the Papacy in 1848. His book was republished in 1848, and caused a sensation. It contained a chapter on 'The Principles of Apocalyptical Interpretation'.

[2] Edward Bishop Elliott (1793-1875) published *Horæ Apocalypticæ, or, A Commentary on the Apocalypse, Critical and Historical* in four volumes in 1844, republishing in 1846, 1847, 1848, 1850, and 1862. He was the leading historicist writer of the day and, when his predictions of the End of the Age in 1865/1866 failed, he revised his date to 1941, thus relieving himself of further embarrassment.

[3] Rev. John Cumming (1807-1881) was a prolific writer on eschatology, and against the Papacy. A historicist, he published *Apocalyptic Sketches* in 1848, a second volume in 1850, and a third volume in 1858. He predicted the End of the Age as coming between 1848 and 1867.

[4] *Futurism Considered*, by Richard Gwatkin, 1860, p.iii refers to seven lectures given at Worthing Town Hall on historicist lines that were arranged by the Rector of Broadwater, Worthing in reply to B.W. Newton's lectures there. The speakers included E.B. Elliott. Gwatkin's book gives his two lectures in this series, which are explicitly directed against B.W. Newton, and reply to *The Prophetic System of Mr Elliott and Dr Cumming, Considered*. For further information see the entry for *The Antichrist Future*.

[5] Christopher Wordsworth (1807-1885), Bishop of Lincoln, was a nephew of the poet William Wordsworth. He was a High Churchman. He delivered his *Lectures on the Apocalypse, Critical, Expository, and Practical* at the University of Cambridge in 1848, and they were published in 1849 (535 pages). They made various predictions regarding the Papacy, and the growth of infidelity.

[6] Dr John Lightfoot (1602-1675)

## Section 3 - Bibliography of B.W. Newton's Published Works

1. *The Prophetic System of Mr Elliott and Dr Cumming.*
2. *Scriptural Proof of the Doctrine of the First Resurrection.*
3. *The First Resurrection and the Reign in Righteousness* (an edited version of 3.).
4. *Prophecy. How to Read it.*

First Edition     Cover title, *Aids to Prophetic Inquiry.*
    1848     James Nisbet & Co, London     18cm     100p.     BL,Bo,CU,I,Sc,T

Second Edition (1) 'considerably enlarged'
    1850     James Nisbet & co, London     18cm     ii+220p.     BIOLA,CBA,EL,I

Second Edition (2) 'considerably enlarged'
    1853     Houlston & Wright, London     18cm     ii+220p.     CBA,EL

Second Edition (3) 'considerably enlarged'
    1853     Partridge & Oakey, London     18cm     iv+220p.     CG

Third Edition 'considerably enlarged'. Preface is dated February 1881.
    1881     Houlston & Sons, London     18cm     x+469p.     BL,Bo,CBA,CU, EL,Sc,SG

Fourth Edition (photographic reprint of Third Edition)
    [2015]     SGAT, Chelmsford     18cm     x+469p.     SG

A new binding 'from stored sheets' was made by the SGAT, London in 1948 (*Watching and Waiting*, April/June 1948 p.151).

French Edition,
    *Secours pour l'Étude de la Prophétie. Traduit librement de l'anglais de BWN.*
    1866     Georges Bridel Lausanne     21+276p.     Swiss National Library

## THE ALTERED TRANSLATION OF GENESIS 2:5, AS GIVEN IN THE REVISED VERSION, CONSIDERED

This is a defence of six-day creation against the theory of evolution, geological assumptions, and the notion of 'pre-Adamic man', all countenanced by the Revised Version translation of this verse. The pamphlet contains valuable notes on Greek and Hebrew. Mr Newton also published *Remarks on the New Testament Translation of the Greek New Testament*, which gives his assessment of the New Testament translation of the Revised Version.

*Perilous Times* (April 1901 p.2) referred to this as having been published by Lucas Collins. There does not appear to have been a Second Edition. Houlston's stock was taken over by Lucas Collins, and overstickers were used on the previous publisher's name.

The SGAT rebound *Remarks on 'Mosaic Cosmogony…'* into paperback format in 1973, and included the remaining copies of this pamphlet with it.

    1888     Houlston & Sons, London     18cm     76p.     BIOLA,BL,Bo,CBA,CU,EL,Sc

## ANCIENT TRUTHS RESPECTING THE DEITY AND TRUE HUMANITY OF THE LORD JESUS

This is considered by some to have been B.W. Newton's final and definitive statement on the controversy that arose in Plymouth in 1847, insofar as it touches on the humanity of the Lord Jesus. Its publication was followed by *Christ, Our Suffering Surety...*, which deals with other issues raised in that controversy.

It drew a reply from Edward Dingle, a diffuse writer on religious and scientific matters – *An Examination of a Recently Published Pamphlet Entitled 'Ancient Truths Respecting the Deity and True Humanity of the Lord Jesus'*, (1858, published for the author by W. Brendon, 17cm, 37p, BL).

First Edition
    1857    Houlston & Wright, London    17cm    28p.    BL,Bo,CBA,CU,I,Sc,SG,T

Second Edition
    1869    Houlston & Wright, London    17cm    30+4p.    CBA

'Second Edition' [Third Edition] bound with *Christ, Our Suffering Surety*, and *Note on 1 Peter 2:24*. This had the collective title of the three booklets - *Ancient Truths.... Christ, Our Suffering Surety.... Note on 1 Peter 2:4*.
    1893    Houlston & Sons, London    18cm    (29p.)    BIOLA,BL,Bo,CBA,CU,EL,Sc

## ANSWERS TO QUESTIONS ON THE PROPRIETY OF LEAVING THE CHURCH OF ENGLAND

This is B.W. Newton's reply to five objections raised by a Churchman to another (evidently a friend of Mr Newton's), who had left the Church of England. This is an important little tract as it establishes Mr Newton's (and probably the Ebrington Street assembly's) position on the Church, separation from evil, the ministry, and worship, at an early point in Brethren history. It has not been possible to identify the persons and places referred to in the tract, as these are indicated only by their initial letters. Mr Newton's authorship is confirmed by his initials at the end of the tract.

    1841    1, Warwick Square, London    18cm    18p.    I, New College (Edinburgh)
             John Wertheimer & Co, Printer

## ANTICHRIST, EUROPE AND THE EAST

This is a collection of separately published pamphlets that were bound together, and published as books, on at least two occasions.

It was advertised in the publisher's list of the Second Edition of *Scriptural Proof of the Doctrine of the First Resurrection* (1868). Several similar compilations were produced c.1866.

The edition advertised in *Gospel Truths* (1872) *and the* 1902 publication under this title consists of:
1. The Antichrist Future
2. The Twelve Hundred and Sixty Days of Antichrist's Reign Future.
3. Conversation on the Seventeenth Chapter of Revelation.
4. What is the Ephah of Zechariah 5?
5. The Final Perseverance of Russia Inconsistent with the Declarations of Scripture.

6. England's Future Course in the East.

    1902    London        18cm    (pamphlet page-numbered)    EL

## THE ANTICHRIST FUTURE

The First Edition is headed 'London, 1859. To those in Worthing who favoured me with their presence at lectures recently given by me there'. The Rector of Broadwater, Worthing arranged a series of historicist lectures in reply, including two by his father, E.B. Elliott.[1]

The Second Edition was also re-published posthumously with another tract, and the resulting item is titled, *The Antichrist Future, also the 1260 days of Antichrist's reign future*. The tract was included in the compilation *Antichrist, Europe and the East*.

First Edition
    1859    Houlston & Wright, London    16cm    27p.    BL,Bo,CU

Second Edition
    1859(*sic*)    Houlston & Wright, London    17cm    27p.    Bo,Sc,SG

## THE ANTICHRIST FUTURE, ALSO THE 1260 DAYS OF ANTICHRIST'S REIGN FUTURE

This is a reprint of the Second Edition of *The Antichrist future*, with the tract *The Twelve Hundred and Sixty Days of Antichrist's Reign Future, a Second Tract written with relation to certain Lectures recently delivered at the Town Hall, Worthing*. See further details given in the separate entries for each of these tracts.

Libraries have listed this as the Second Edition, but it was only produced in this form once. This booklet is therefore evidently the 'Second Edition' of the two component tracts.

First Edition
    1900    Houlston & Sons, London    18cm  11+83p.  BIOLA,BL,Bo,CBA,CU,EL,Sc,SG
              and Lucas Collins, London

Second Edition (reprint of the First Edition)
    1999    SGAT, Chelmsford    18cm    11+83p    SG

---

[1] For further information on these events in Worthing and the subsequent results see *Mr Newton at Worthing* by C.W.H. Griffiths. *Futurism Considered*, by Richard Gwatkin, 1860, p.iii refers to four lectures having been given by 'Rev' B.W. Newton and four by Rev R[obert] Govett. If they were given at the same time, this is the only evidence we have of B.W. Newton working collaboratively with Robert Govett. Their positions would have diverged with Govett's publication of his commentary on the Book of Revelation in 1861-1864. The Rector of Broadwater, Worthing (E.B. Elliott's eldest son) arranged seven lectures at Worthing Town Hall on historicist lines in November and December 1859. The speakers included E.B. Elliott. Gwatkin's book gives his two lectures in this series that are explicitly directed against B.W. Newton and defending E.B. Elliott's views. For many years during the life, and after the death of B.W. Newton, there was in Worthing a strong body of Christians supportive of B.W. Newton and his teachings. This was particularly connected with Thomas Graham Graham, John Cox, jun., and E.J. Burnett. Obituary of T.G. Graham is in *Perilous Times*, January, February. March, April, and May 1906. Died 29th December 1905, aged 81 years. Obituary of John Cox jun., who spent the last 21 years of his life living and ministering in Worthing, *Perilous Times*, April 1915, p.113. Died aged 86. Obituary of Ernest John Burnett. Younger brother of W.E. Burnett, *Watching and Waiting*, July-August 1959, p.159. Died aged 82.

## APPOINTMENTS OF GOD IN JUSTICE AND MERCY CONSIDERED

This is concerned with substitutionary atonement and the federal headship of Christ. B.W. In regard to Christ's headship Newton emphasised the importance of distinguishing between the believer's legal oneness with Christ as Federal Head of the redeemed, and his living union with Christ by the Spirit. It quotes and responds to an article in *The Expositor* in December 1885, ten years earlier

    1895    Houlston & Sons, London    18cm    ii+55p.    BIOLA,BL,Bo,CBA,CU,EL,Sc
          and Arthur Andrews, Ryde, IW

Chinese Edition
    Referred to in *Watching and Waiting* (Nov/Dec. 1940) as being produced by 'a Chinese brother'. No copies have been located. It is probable that the missionary W.E. Burnett's ministry gave rise to this initiative.[1]

## ATONEMENT AND ITS RESULTS

This was compiled from five other works, which were revised by the author for inclusion in this book. The component works are:

1. *Atonement Saveth* (1882)

2. On Justification through the Blood and Righteousness of a Substitute (from *Occasional Papers on Scriptural Subjects No.1*, 1861).

3. On Sanctification by the Blood of Jesus (from *Occasional Papers on Scriptural Subjects, No.2*, 1862).

4. On Sanctification through the Spirit (from *Occasional Papers on Scriptural Subjects, No.2*, 1862).

5. Thoughts on Practical Sanctification (from *Occasional Papers on Scriptural Subjects, No.4*, 1866).

6. Jesus washing His Disciples' Feet (from *Occasional Papers on Scriptural Subjects No.3*, 1863).

3, 4, and 5 above, together with *Justification, being the Substance of a Discourse recently delivered in London*, were heavily edited to create the tract *Justification and Sanctification* (c.1910).

A Norwegian tract with the title, *Retfærdiggjörelsen og Helliggjörelsen*, (Justification and Sanctification) may include extracts from *Atonement and Its Results*.[2]

Compare the content of B.W. Newton's *Tracts on Doctrinal Subjects*.

---

[1] William Edward Burnett (1862-1950), an associate of B.W. Newton, who commenced the Evangelical Protestant Mission to the Chinese in 1893. He left for China in 1883, first serving with the China Inland Mission. He died in China. Obituary *Watching and Waiting*, September-October 1950, p.69, and January-February 1951, p.106-108

[2] See letter to Miss Leake, 18th January 1875, CBA 7050, pp.242-244 regarding Norwegian translations. See also the preface to *The Sabbath and Lord's Day* by John Cox, jun. in which he refers to the first edition of his booklet having been published in 1896 at the request of a friend in Norway, and afterwards translated into that language.

First Edition
    1882       Houlston & Sons, London          17cm    121p.    BL,Bo,CBA,CU,Sc

Second Edition
    1902       Houlston & Sons, London          18cm    120p.    BIOLA,CBA,EL
                 Lucas Collins, London   [printed F.W. Sargeant, Ryde, IW]

Third Edition
    1965       SGAT, London                     18cm    91p.     BIOLA,CBA,CU,EL,Sc

Arabic Edition
    Translated and published by Shukhri H Khouri (Jerusalem) between December 1939 and July 1941 (*Watching and Waiting*, January 1939, December 1939 and July/August 1941(obituary)).

Chinese Edition
    This is referred to in *Watching and Waiting* November/December 1940, as being produced by 'a Chinese brother'. No copies have been located. It is probable that the missionary W.E. Burnett's ministry gave rise to this initiative.[1]

## ATONEMENT SAVETH

This deals with the priestly work of the Lord Jesus towards God the Father in his one oblation. Through it, he has satisfied the demands of Divine Government and procured pardon, acceptance, and rewardability for his people. It was included in *Atonement and Its Results* in the same year as the First Edition.

First Edition
    1882              Houlston & Sons, London         18cm    16p.     BL,Bo,CU

Second Edition
    1912              Lucas Collins, London           17cm    16p.     CBA,EL

## BABYLON AND EGYPT

This was originally *Aids to Prophetic Enquiry. Second Series*. The title changed with each edition. Finally, considerably augmented, it became popularly known as *Babylon and Egypt*.

B.W. Newton had an item, 'The Times of Restitution. Acts 3:19-21', published in *The Investigator* in September 1832, when he evidently expected the final fulfilment of Babylon Prophecies in 'the mystic Babylon'. His view changed by 1836. See the notes on the article in Section 6, B.W. Newton's Letters and Articles Published in Periodicals in this *Guide*, and S.P. Tregelles, *Three Letters to the author of 'A Retrospect of Events That Have Taken Place Amongst the Brethren'*, Second Edition 1894 p.69.

---

[1] William Edward Burnett (1862-1950), an associate of B.W. Newton who commenced the Evangelical Protestant Mission to the Chinese in 1893, having left for China in 1883, first serving with the China Inland Mission. He died in China. Obituary *Watching and Waiting*, September-October 1950, p.69, and January-February 1951, p.106-108.

The First Edition of *Babylon and Egypt* sets out to prove that Biblical prophecies predict a restoration and destruction of the Babylon on the Euphrates. It also seeks to demonstrate that the Biblical prophecies regarding Babylon have not yet been fulfilled. B.W. Newton gathered topographical information regarding this from Sir Henry Rawlinson, who was in Baghdad.[1]

To this, in the Second Edition, was added 'Supplementary Remarks on Prospects of the East' (11 pages). The other variations between the First and Second Editions, apart from a few textual changes, are:
1. Pages 73-76 (Second Edition) new comment on events after 1848.
2. Pages 93, 94 (Second Edition) Additional quotations from authorities, and deletions (e.g. on the word 'mountain' as connected with Babylon).
3. After the end of Appendix D ('Rome: Its Desolation and Revival') of the First Edition, the Second Edition added a two page section on Rome as the seven hilled city.

The Third Edition 'substantially enlarged, and amended' the Second Edition by the following additions and changes:
1. A 10 page preface affirming the literal meaning of Scripture as the guide to prophecy.
2. Pages 191-378 (Third Edition) add 'The Future of Egypt and Other Nations as Described in Isaiah 19, and elsewhere'.
3. Pages 379-556 (Third Edition) add 'A Retrospective and Prospective Outline' [of Christendom].
4. Pages 557-602 (Third Edition) adds a 'Postscript' in three sections:
    a. Comments on an article on 'Socialism and the Papacy'.
    b. 'Extracts from Augustine, etc' ['which I have elsewhere published'], demonstrating the confusion of thought of ancient and modern writers regarding the present age and the Millennium.
    c. 'Notes on Dr Pusey's Statements' in his *Eirenicon* (see on 'The Judgment of the Court of Arches' in *Occasional Papers on Scriptural Subjects No.4* (1866) for further material relating to this).
5. It replaces Appendix E of the Second Edition (which considered Revelation 17:18, demonstrating that the phrase $\eta$ $\varepsilon\chi o\upsilon\sigma\alpha$ $\beta\alpha\sigma\iota\lambda\varepsilon\iota\alpha\nu$ (reigneth, A.V.) has an abstract sense rather than referring to the (then) present; and the last two pages that the Second Edition added to Appendix D) with a new Appendix E, 'Catechism on the Seventeenth Chapter of the Revelation' (pp.620-642). The comment on this verse was removed to *Thoughts on the Apocalypse*, Second Edition, under Notes on Revelation 17 and 18, See Appendix 1 of this Guide, Comparison of Editions of *Thoughts on The Apocalypse*, loc. cit.

Four other publications were derived from *Babylon and Egypt*:

---

[1] Reference is made to Sir Henry Rawlinson in the Fry Manuscript (CBA 7049), p.317. Dr J.P. Riach introduced him to Mr Newton. See the note too in *Babylon and Egypt* (3rd edition) p.56n. There is a letter from Sir Henry Rawlinson dated 12th April 1849 giving topographical and demographic information referenced in Section 9, B.W. Newton's Correspondence, in this Guide. See too the reference to another letter in Appendix 1, Comparison of Editions of Thoughts on The Apocalypse – under Thoughts on chapter 18.

## Section 3 - Bibliography of B.W. Newton's Published Works

1. *Extracts from the Second Series of 'Aids to Prophetic Enquiry', Compared with Extracts from the 'Daily News' and 'Standard', etc.*
2. *Conversation on the Seventeenth Chapter of Revelation*, also published as *The Harlot of Babylon*.
3. *Christendom: a Retrospective and Prospective History* (posthumous).
4. *Egypt, Palestine and Syria – Their Prospects in Prophecy* (posthumous).

The First Edition was critically reviewed in *The Quarterly Journal of Prophecy* (Horatius Bonar), Vol. 2, 1850, pp.480-484.

Quotations are included in the anthology *B.W. Newton on Ministry and Order in the Church of Christ*.

Publication details of the First Edition are confused because of the involvement of three publishers (cf. *Aids to Prophetic Enquiry* and *Thoughts on the Apocalypse*). Library cataloguing is also confused because of the reference to three series of the *Aids to Prophetic Enquiry*.

Interestingly, although the engraved map of Babylon and its environs is dated '1849' in the First Edition, it is dated '1854' in the Second Edition, perhaps indicating that it was reprinted and circulated separately prior to the Second Edition. In *Thoughts on the Apocalypse* (Second Edition, p.295, Third Edition, p.402), Mr Newton stated that he submitted this sketch of the plain of Babylon to the approval of Colonel Chesney[1] prior to its publication.

First Edition (1)
    1849    James Nisbet, London    18cm    144+2p.  BL,I

First Edition (2)
    1849    Houlston & Stoneman, London    17cm    ?    Bo,CU,Sc

First Edition (3)
    1853    Partridge, London    20cm    146p.    Emmaus Bible College

First Edition (4) *Aids to Prophetic Enquiry. Second Series. on Babylon and its Revival.*
    1857    Houlston & Stoneman, London    19cm    144+2p.  NP

Second Edition 'Revised' – *Babylon, Its Revival and Final Desolation, Being the Second Series of 'Aids to Prophetic Enquiry'*. Cover title simply *Babylon*.
    1859    Houlston & Wright, London    ?cm    164p.    EL,SG,U

Third Edition 'Revised and Enlarged' – *Babylon: Its Future History and Doom, with Remarks on the Future of Egypt and Other Eastern countries*. The Preface is dated 'July 1890. London'.
    1890    Houlston & Sons, London  18cm  xvi+642p.  BIOLA, BL,Bo,CBA,CU,EL,Sc,SG,T
    Preface 'July 1890'

Fourth Edition (Third Edition photographically reprinted).
    2015    SGAT, Chelmsford    18cm    xvi+642p.[2]    SG

---

[1] Francis Rawdon Chesney (1789–1872). Chesney carried out extensive exploration and mapping of the rivers Euphrates and Tigris in 1835, and subsequently.
[2] Bottom line of page 27 missing.

A new binding 'from stored sheets' was made by the SGAT in 1948 (*Watching and Waiting*, April-June 1948 p.151).

## BAPTISM (1)

Publisher's list title for *Doctrine of Scripture Respecting Baptism, Briefly Considered.*

## BAPTISM (2)

This is an anonymously published tract. It is identical to Appendix A in *A Remonstrance to the Society of Friends*. It may either have been published separately before inclusion as an appendix (in which case it would be one of B.W. Newton's earliest known tracts), or extracted from the larger item.

1835?  Cornwall Street, Plymouth and Central Tract Depot, 1 Warwick Square, London; Rowe, Plymouth (printer)

17cm  4p.  Fratelli Collection, Florence

## THE BLOOD THAT SAVETH

This is a Gospel Tract. A second tract, *How Does the Blood Save?* is the sequel. The first three editions have not been located or dated. There is some confusion in the numbering of the editions (cf. *Acceptance with God* – First Edition 1859). Some of the tracts are in small format, which accounts for the variation in the number of pages.

| Edition | Date | Publisher | Size | Pages | Location |
|---|---|---|---|---|---|
| ? Edition | [1853-1869][1] | Houlston & Wright, London | 18cm | 8p. | CG |
| Fourth Edition | [185?] | Geo Hunt, printer | 18cm | 4p. | BL |
| Fifth Edition | 1860 | Geo Hunt, printer | 12cm | 8p. | CBA,I |
| Seventh Edition | [1900-1904][2] | Lucas Collins/Houlston & Sons | 10cm | 20p. | EC |
| Eighth Edition | [1900-1904][3] | Houlston & Sons/Lucas Collins | 10cm | 20p. | CBA |
| Ninth Edition | [1900-1904][4] | Houlston & Sons, London | 10cm | 20p. | CBA |
| 'Eighth' Edition | c.1950 | E.J. Burnett, Worthing | 10cm | 12p. | BL |

---

[1] Publisher's dates
[2] Publisher's dates
[3] Publisher's dates
[4] Publisher's dates

? Edition – *The Blood that Saves*
    c.1966            SGAT, London                20cm    5p.     CBA,SG

Arabic Edition
    Translated and published by Shukri H. Khouri (Jerusalem) 'recently' – *Watching and Waiting*, January 1939 p.6.

French Edition – *Le Sang qui Sauve.*
    Listed in *Watching and Waiting* September 1939.

German Edition?
    See letter from S.P. Tregelles to B.W. Newton dated 17th July 1862.

Italian Editions – *Il Sangue che Salva.*
    1884            De Angelis, Naples         10cm    14p.    I
                  MS note 'translated by Lady Otway[1]
    1886            Gennaro De Angelis, Naples    10cm    14p.    I

Norwegian Edition
    No copies have been located, but this was probably published. See letter to Miss Leake, 12th August 1895 (CBA 7050 p.245) noted in Section 9, B.W. Newton's Correspondence.

## BRIEF SKETCH OF THE PROGRESS OF PROPHETIC ENQUIRY, ETC

Publisher's list title for *Aids to Prophetic Enquiry* (first series).

## BRIEF STATEMENTS IN THE FORM OF ANSWERS TO QUESTIONS

Strictly speaking this has no title, but is headed, 'The following Statements in the form of Answers to Questions will be found to give the general substance of the Doctrines which I hold and desire to teach, on the subjects to which they refer, with regard to our Lord's humanity'. W.B. Neatby listed it in his *A history of the Plymouth Brethren* under the title that we have adopted.

It was written more for his friends than against his opponents. In a letter to 'Mrs Browne' dated 3rd April 1848, he referred to a 'consecutive statement of his doctrines on the subject of the recent controversy', which he had left with Ebrington Street to publish if they wished. A copy of the *Brief Statements* was attached to the letter.

The item is dated 11th July 1848, presumably the date that it was printed. It was printed after 'the Bath Conference' (10th May 1848), where J.N. Darby, and some of B.W. Newton's former colleagues at Plymouth, condemned him for error. It is a plain statement in response to such attacks. It again affirms his orthodoxy.

It may be compared with *Statements I Desire to Oppose,* a manuscript in B.W. Newton's own hand currently held by Tom Chantry (see Section 10, Duplicated and Manuscript Items)

It is listed in CBA 6998 (1848(9), folio 9) as a 'Statement of Doctrine'.

---

[1] Lady Eliza Price Noble Otway [*née* Campbell], c.1831-1910. See letter of B.W. Newton dated 26th May 1871

The *Brief Statements* were reprinted in *Watching and Waiting* July/September 1994, pp.171, 174 (from a photocopy of Dr Ulrich Bister's copy).

    1848    Jenkin Thomas, printer, Plymouth    12cm    7p.    ID

## THE BURNT OFFERING

Part 1 of Vol. 1 of the First Edition of *Thoughts on parts of Leviticus*. The parts circulated separately before they were bound up into the First Edition.

## B.W. NEWTON ON MINISTRY AND ORDER IN THE CHURCH OF CHRIST

This is an anthology of B.W. Newton's writings and attributed works on this subject. The material is slightly edited – 'such changes as have been made are for the sake of clarity, and to delete material not directly relevant to the present purpose'. It was produced before the re-emergence of MS material that throws further light on how Mr Newton's own meetings were ordered (1) after he started his work at Duke Street, London, (2) at the closure of the Bayswater work, and (3) at the end of his life. See Section 10, Duplicated and Manuscript, Items – items held by Tom Chantry, and MS items recovered by the CBA in 2011. Also see
Section 12, Miscellaneous Biographical Items – Conduct of Meetings, etc.
It gives extracts from the following:

### From published writings

1. *Babylon and Egypt.*
2. *The Doctrine of Scripture Respecting Baptism.*
3. *Doctrines of Popery. On Holy Scripture and Tradition.*
4. *Europe and the East.*
5. *A Letter to Richard Waldo Sibthorpe [sic], B.D., Late Fellow of Magdalen College, Oxford on the Subject of his Recent Pamphlet,.*
6. 'Notes on 1 Corinthians 1', from *Occasional Papers on Scriptural Subjects No.2.*
7. 'Parables of Matthew 13' from *Prospects of the Ten Kingdoms.*
8. *Remarks on Mr R. Pearsall Smith's Edition of Hymns Selected from those of the Late F.W. Faber.*
9. *Remarks on the Revised English Version of the Greek New Testament.*
10. *A Second Letter to the Brethren and Sisters Meeting for Communion at Ebrington Street.*
11. *Thoughts on Parts of Leviticus.*
12. *Thoughts on the Apocalypse.*

### From publications based on notes of his lectures

1. *Anthology (No.3) 'Reminiscences' of Bible Readings, etc. at Newport, I.W.* (NS 3).
2. *Church Principles* (NM 5.3 – CBA 7060).
3. *An Exposition of the Epistle to the Ephesians* (NS 14).
4. *Individual Gifts* (NS 15).

5. 'Presidency of Holy Spirit', the appendix of Patmos Series 37 – *'The Holy Spirit'; His Office and Work* (NP 37).
6. *Studies in the Epistles of 1 and 2 Timothy* (NS 37).

**From unpublished sources**

A previously unpublished letter to Arthur Andrews (CBA 7187).

    1999    Pearl Publications, Ashford, Middlesex    20.5cm    127p.    CBA,SG

## CATHOLICITY IN A DISPENSATION OF FAILURE, A SURE TOKEN OF APOSTASY

This concerns the predicted apostasy of Christendom, and the need for true believers to take a position of separation from it.

It was included in a compilation, *Doctrines of Popery*.

First Edition – *In a Dispensation of Failure, Catholicity the Sure Token of Apostasy; Being the Substance of a Lecture Lately Delivered in London.*
    1851    James Nisbet & co, London    17cm    25p.    SG,SNL

Second Edition – Title as the First Edition
    [1853-1869][1]    Houlston & Wright, London    17cm    24p.    SG

Third Edition – *Catholicity in a Dispensation of Failure, a Sure Token of Apostasy.*
    1892    Houlston & Sons, London    17cm    iv+42p.    CBA,SG
           and Arthur Andrews, Ryde, IW

(Fourth Edition) – Title as the Third Edition. Edited and without 'Advertisement' or footnotes.
    1900    Lucas Collins, London    17cm    24p.    EL,SG
           Hunt, Barnard (printer)

## CHRISTENDOM: A RETROSPECTIVE AND PROSPECTIVE OUTLINE

This was the principal addition made to the Third Edition of *Babylon and Egypt*.. It records the history and failure of Christendom, and its predicted judgement.

This item is not to be confused with a pamphlet produced posthumously on the basis of notes of a lecture, and titled *Christendom: Its Course and Doom* (for which, see Section 8, Publications Produced from Notes of Addresses, and Posthumously Published Letters and Manuscripts - NS 5).

Very minor additional notes are provided in this re-publication, identified by square brackets. There is an explanatory account of 'the Lincoln Judgment given on p.184 (see *Babylon and Egypt*, Third Edition, p.531). Indexes are provided.

    1912    Hunt, Barnard and co, London & Aylesbury    17cm    iv+184p.    CBA,EL,SG

---

[1] Publisher's dates

## THE CHRISTIAN AND JEWISH REMNANTS AT THE TIME OF THE END

These were two of the *Five Letters on Events Predicted in Scripture as Antecedent to the Coming of the Lord*, published together under this title.

    1866    Houlston and Wright    18cm    24p.    ID

## CHRIST, OUR SUFFERING SURETY: HEBREWS 2:10 AND 5:7

This concerns the Person and work of the Lord Jesus. The opening page makes plain that this item was intended as a complement to *Ancient Truths Respecting the Deity and True Humanity of the Lord Jesus*. *Ancient Truths...* is principally concerned with the nature of the Lord's humanity. This tract is concerned with his suffering, and touches on many of the issues of J.N. Darby's controversy with B.W. Newton; Christ's suffering with, and for, his people; the nature of his suffering; whether his suffering was wholly substitutionary; and the use of the Psalms as a means to understanding the Lord's inner spiritual experiences. A bound compilation volume including this (as a Second Edition), *Ancient Truths*, and *Note on 1 Peter 2:24*, was produced, and offered for sale on a publisher's list in *Occasional Papers on Scriptural Subjects No.1*, (1861). No new title was used for the compilation, but simply the titles of the three works, commencing with *Ancient Truths*.

First Edition

    1858    Houlston & Wright, London    17cm    65p.    BL,Bo,CBA,CU,I, Sc,T

'Second Edition'. This is referred to as the 'Second Edition' when republished with *Note on I Peter 2:24* as *Ancient Truths...Christ, Our Suffering Surety...Note on 1 Peter 2:24*

    1893    Houlston & Sons, London,    17cm    118p.    SG
              and Arthur Andrews, Ryde

## CHRIST'S RETURN – NOT SECRET BUT IN MANIFESTED GLORY

This is the title of Irish Christian Mission (ICM) Edition of *The Second Advent of Our Lord Not Secret but in Manifested Glory*.

## CHRIST'S SECOND COMING. IT WILL BE PRE-MILLENNIAL

This was produced to provide an answer to post-millennialism.

It is a 'virtually unedited' reprint of *The Personal Return of the Lord Jesus Necessary to the Introduction of Millennial Blessing*, together with, *Examination of 'Christ's Second Coming: Will it be Premillennial?' by David Brown, DD*, which was published in three parts in *Occasional Papers on Scriptural Subjects*.[1]

    [1991]    SGAT, Chelmsford    18cm    100p.    CBA,SG

---

[1] David Brown, DD, Principal of the Free Church College Aberdeen. The book ran through seven editions in his lifetime (1803-1897). David Brown first issued his book in parts, but substantially enlarged it in the second edition (1849). The 6th edition had 468 pages. See the letter of David Brown to B.W. Newton dated 29th June 1861, noted in Section 9, B.W. Newton's Correspondence.

## CLEANSING THE LEPER. LEVITICUS 14

This is an exposition of the chapter, drawing spiritual lessons from it for the believer and for Israel. It was not included in *Thoughts on parts of Leviticus*, which concludes at Leviticus 13. Mrs Stirling made a hand-written copy, presumably late in B.W. Newton's life.

However, B.W. Newton later made clear to his close associates that he 'abjured' the tract 'altogether', as he erred in the way that he spoke of cleansing and the obedience in v.8 and following. Verse 8 onwards rather 'teaches by contrast. 'The Law made nothing perfect; but there is a cleansing in Christ that makes us perfect, that there is no more sacrifice for sins. You cannot put away what is put away. Sin is so entirely put away that 'there is no more offering for sin. Cleansed εις το διηνεκες.' [Heb. 7:3; 10:12, 14 –'continually', 'for ever']. The first part was a prelibation of the '8th day washing' (v8 onwards) that will be ours at Christ's coming, when we shall not only be cleansed in fact, but in experience from the sorrow of indwelling sin.[1]

It was originally published anonymously as an article in *The Christian Witness* (Vol. 4 October 1837), under the title 'Cleansing the Leper' (see Section 7, Articles in *The Christian Witness*). One of the editions of the tract (the one published jointly by The Tract Depot, Plymouth and The Tract Depot, London) is anonymous. The Tract Depot, London, edition has his name at the end of the text. It is not known which edition was earlier. The *Studies Series*, published posthumously on the basis of notes of lectures, included *Elementary Studies in Leviticus 14 on the Leper Cleansed* (NS 6) with no verbal similarity (see note on this in Section 8, Publications Produced from Notes of Addresses, and Posthumously Published Letters and Manuscripts).

[Edition A] *On the Cleansing of the Leper*.
    [1837-40?]    Tract Depot, Plymouth    16.5cm  12p.  SG
                       and Tract Depot, London
                       J.B. Rowe, Plymouth (printer)

[Edition B] *Cleansing the Leper*.
    [1837-40?]    Tract Depot, London    20cm  12p.  SNL
                       Printed by C[lulow] and S[oltau] (Plymouth)

Manuscript copy by Mary Stirling – *Cleansing the Leper*.
    [1890-1905?]    CBA

## COME IL SANGUE CI SALVA?

Italian Edition of *How does the blood save?*

---

[1] CBA 7064, pages 265-269, 281-287 –conversations with B.W. Newton 13th, 14th and 18th November 1898.

## THE COMING OF THE LORD or
## THE COMING OF THE LORD. EVENTS CONNECTED THEREWITH

This is the title of a compilation volume first made c.1866. It consisted of various works by Mr Newton. The title was listed at the end of the First Edition of *Thoughts on the Prophecy of Isaiah* (1868), along with other compilations - *Antichrist, Europe and the East*, and *Israel and Jerusalem*.

It consisted of:
1. *The Duty of Giving Heed...*
2. *The Second Advent of Our Lord Not Secret...*
3. *The Prophecy of the Lord Jesus (Matt. 24).*
4. *Order of Events Connected with the Appearing of Christ...*
5. *The Christian and Jewish Remnants....*
6. *Scriptural Proof of the Doctrine of the First Resurrection.*
7. *The Day of the Lord.*
8. *A Letter to the Minister of Silver Street Chapel...*

Eight other works were included in variant collections using the same title, and some of the above items were omitted. The copy belonging to A.C. Fry of Newport, Isle of Wight had *Prophetic Psalms in Relation to Israel* (1900 edition) in the compilation, from which it may be concluded that this was a generic name used for any such collections over a period of about 35 years.

Bibliographic listings have not been examined, cross-referenced or recorded here, as there were such significant changes in the composition. Copies are held by EL and SG.

## THE CONSECRATION OF THE PRIESTS

This is Part 1 of Vol. 2 of the First Edition of *Thoughts on Parts of Leviticus*.

## CONVERSATION ON THE SEVENTEENTH CHAPTER OF REVELATION

This was originally an appendix of the volume that became known as *Babylon and Egypt*. It was written in the form of a dialogue, and shows that the Babylon of Revelation 17 is not Rome, either papal or pagan.

It was later bound up in the compilation *Antichrist, Europe and the East*.

First Edition
    1855    Partridge, Oakey and co, London    18cm    22p.    Bo,BL,CU,Sc,T

Second Edition
    1878    Houlston & Sons, London    18cm    22p.    SG

Third Edition
    1925    E.J. Burnett, Worthing    18cm    22p.    CBA

(Fourth) Edition - *The Harlot of Babylon. The Revelation Chapter 17 in Conversation.*
    (1968)    SGAT, London    22.5x9cm    22p.    SG

(Fifth) Edition - *The Harlot of Babylon. The Revelation Chapter 17 in Conversation.*
    199[?]    Irish Christian Mission, Belfast    22.5x9cm    22p.    CG

## DAVID, KING OF ISRAEL

This is a spiritual commentary on the life of David.

There is some confusion regarding editions, apparently due to the involvement of two publishers (see *Aids to Prophetic Enquiry, Babylon and Egypt,* and *Thoughts on the Apocalypse* for similar instances). We have been unable to inspect the First Edition.

Chapter 4 of the Second Edition, *David Restoring the Ark*, was published separately.

First Edition (1)
    1851    James Nisbet, London    18cm    119p.    I

First Edition (2)
    1851    Partridge, Oakey, London    8cm    [119p.?]    SNL

Second Edition – with an additional chapter and notes
    'The present edition has been revised throughout, but has not been materially altered. The chief difference is the addition of a new chapter on "The Threshing-floor of Araunah the Jebusite", with appended "Notes on the Thirtieth Psalm"'.
    1874    Houlston & Sons, London    18cm    vi+168p    BL,Bo,CBA,CU,EL,Sc,SG,T

Third Edition (photographic reprint of the Second Edition)
    [2015]    Houlston & Sons, London    18cm    vi+168p    SG

A new binding of the Second Edition 'from loose sheets' was made by the SGAT in 1953 (*Watching and Waiting*, January/February 1953).

## DAVID RESTORING THE ARK

This was a chapter (21 pages) from the Second Edition of *David, King of Israel*, Second Edition, that was published separately.

    1851    J. Nisbet, London    17cm    21p.    SG, CBA

## THE DAY OF THE LORD, A LECTURE ON ZECHARIAH 14

This short work proved to be one of B.W. Newton's most popular. It focussed on a passage that had greatly influenced his early understanding of prophetic truth. It is a simple introduction to the study of prophecy.

It was originally delivered as a lecture 'very soon after' the operations of the British forces off the coast of Syria in the autumn of 1840 (see footnote to p.7 of the Ninth Edition).

See also Notes on Zechariah 14, first printed as a section of *Occasional Papers on Scriptural Subjects No.2*, and posthumously as a chapter of *Expository Teaching on the Millennium and Israel's Future*. See also the Note on Zechariah 14 in *Aids to Prophetic Enquiry*.

First Edition – *The Day of the Lord. Notes, Comprising the Substance of a lecture, by B.W. Newton, on Zechariah 14.*
  [c.1840/1]    The Tract and Stationery Depot, Exeter    17cm    20p.    SNL,SG
  and 1, Warwick Square, London

Second Edition – *The Day of the Lord, a Lecture on Zechariah 14.*
  1858    Houlston & Wright, London    16cm    24p.    BL,Bo,CU Sc,SG,T

Third Edition – *The Day of the Lord, a Lecture on Zechariah 14*
  1861    Houlston & Wright, London    17cm    23p.    SG

Fourth or Fifth Edition
  1869    Houlston & Wright, London    17cm    22p.    SG

Sixth Edition – *The Day of the Lord, a Lecture on Zechariah 14*
  1891    Houlston & Sons, London    17cm    23p.    CBA,SG

Seventh Edition
  Not located

Eighth Edition
  1931    E.J. Burnett, Worthing    17cm    24p.    CBA,EL

Ninth Edition – *The Day of the Lord, a Lecture on Zechariah 14.*
  1954    E.J. Burnett, Worthing    17cm    23p.    CG

(Tenth) Edition – *The Day of the Lord, a Lecture on Zechariah 14.*
  [1993]    Irish Christian Mission, Belfast    21cm    23p.    CG

Arabic Edition
  Translated and published by Shukri H Khouri (Jerusalem) 'recently' – *Watching and Waiting* January 1939 p.6.

Italian Edition – *Il Giorno del Signore: Discorso sopra il capitolo 14 di Zaccaria.*
  1886    Claudiana, Florence (printer)    18cm    23p.    Bollettino delle pubblicazioni italiane (1887)[1]

Norwegian Edition
  This was possibly produced – see letter to Mrs Leake (1895) in CBA 7050 pp.245-247.[2]

## DEFENCE IN REPLY TO THE PERSONAL ACCUSATIONS OF MR DARBY

B.W. Newton prepared this when Brethren from other parts visited Plymouth in 1846 to investigate the charges made against him by J.N. Darby. It was published and circulated separately.

---

[1] This title is listed in the *Bollettino delle pubblicazioni italiane* (1887), but it is not in the Fondo Guicciardini catalogue. However, an index card provided by the Biblioteca Nazionale Centrale, Florence in 1985 identifies it as Fondo Guicciardini.
[2] See also the preface to *The Sabbath and Lord's Day* by John Cox, jun. in which he refers to the first edition of his booklet having been published in 1896 at the request of a friend in Norway, and afterwards translated into that language.

It was sent, with a lengthy letter (dated 25th November 1846) from the leaders of the Ebrington Street, Plymouth, Meeting, to the Rawstorne Street Meeting on their summons to Mr Newton. The *Defence* was reprinted in Lord Congleton's *Correspondence etc. Relating to Mr Newton's Refusal to Appear Before the Saints at Rawstorne Street, London…According to the Two Citations Which Issued from them November 20th to 15th December 1846*[1], pp.21-30. A copy of this is in the CBA.

The *Defence* is also referred to in an undated letter [Jan. 1846] by Mr Newton (the original of this is with TC; CBA 7180(26) (Xerox copy); F.W. Wyatt's copy MS Book 2, p.81 (TC); A.C. Fry's secondary copy CBA 7049, pp.356-362.

No original, separately printed, copy of the *Defence* has been located.

## THE DOCTRINE OF SCRIPTURE RESPECTING BAPTISM, BRIEFLY CONSIDERED

In this work, B.W Newton argued the case for believer's baptism, leaning heavily upon I Peter 3:21. The Second [posthumous] Edition is 'word for word' with the first, but in one volume, with one set of numbered appendices.

Note also the tract 'Baptism' (2), included as an appendix in *A Remonstrance to the Society of Friends*, and the Patmos Series booklet on baptism (NP 18), noted in Section 8, Publications Produced from Notes of Addresses, and Posthumously Published Letters and Manuscripts.

Quotations are included in the anthology *B.W. Newton on Ministry and Order in the Church of Christ*.

First Edition (in two parts)
    1859    Houlston & Wright, London    17cm    56+81    BIOLA,BL,Bo,CBA,CU,Sc,T

Second Edition
    1907    Lucas Collins, London    18cm    iv+150p.    BL,CBA,EL,SG

## DOCTRINES OF POPERY

This is a compilation of four works:
1. *Doctrines of Popery as Established by the Council of Trent. No.1 On Holy Scripture and Tradition.*
2. *Doctrines of Popery as Established by the Council of Trent. No. 2 On Original Sin.*
3. *Reflections Suggested by the Present Movement in England against Romanism.*
4. *In a Dispensation of Failure, Catholicity, a Sure Token of Apostasy.*

The copy held by The Evangelical Library, London is bound up with *On the Spread of Neology in England*.

    1867    Houlston & Wright, London    Pages as pamphlets    SG,EL

---

[1] See notes on the Correspondence in Section 4, Contributions to Other Publications in this Guide.

## DOCTRINES OF POPERY AS ESTABLISHED BY THE COUNCIL OF TRENT, CONSIDERED. ON ORIGINAL SIN

B.W. Newton's thoughts on this were later developed in 'Falsification of the Meaning of the Word 'Justify' at the Council of Trent', published in *Occasional Papers on Scriptural Subjects No.1*, (1861).

This item was bound up in the compilation *Doctrines of Popery*.

    1851    James Nisbet and co, London    17cm    28p.    BIOLA,CBA,I,SG

## DOCTRINES OF POPERY ON HOLY SCRIPTURE AND TRADITION, AS ESTABLISHED BY THE COUNCIL OF TRENT, CONSIDERED

This was bound up in the compilation *Doctrines of Popery in 1867*.

In the introduction to the Second Edition (1883), Mr Newton stated of this book 'I wish it to be read in connexion with Remarks that I have just published on an article in 'The Quarterly Review' respecting texts of the Greek New Testament founded on ancient authorities'. These 'Remarks' were later reprinted in *Remarks on the Revised English Version of the Greek New Testament* (Chapter 18 and following). The article to which Mr Newton referred was by Dean Burgon[1] (See Evangelical Library Annual Lecture 1975 on S.P. Tregelles). It was probably the article in *The Quarterly Review*, dated October 1881 (No.304, Vol. 152), although articles on the Revised Version also appeared in January and April 1882.

An extract (2 pages) from this was published in the *Bible League Quarterly* October- December 1978, under the title 'A Brief Word on the Verbal Inspiration of Scripture'.

Quotations are included in the anthology *B.W. Newton on Ministry and Order in the Church of Christ*.

First Edition
    1851    James Nisbet and co, London    17cm    ii+79p.    BL,CBA,I,SG

Second Edition
    1883    Houlston & Sons, London    18cm    86+2p.    BL,Bo,CBA,CU,EL,Sc

## DOCTRINES OF THE CHURCH IN NEWMAN STREET, CONSIDERED

This pamphlet is against Irvingism.

It first circulated as a tract (see CBA 7049 p.373). It then appeared in *The Christian Witness*, Vol. 1, April 1835 as an article. It was 'some time afterwards' reprinted as a tract with additional material included in a preface (see B.W. Newton's *A Statement and Acknowledgement Respecting Certain Doctrinal Errors* p.5).

A Second Edition of Vol. 1 of *The Christian Witness* was published in 1838, which included the article in its modified form. The enlarged article was a focus of attack by J.N. Darby and his friends upon

---

[1] John William Burgon (1813 –1888), Dean of Chichester, who wrote in a manner B.W. Newton deplored, both because of the violence and levity of his language, and because 'the object of the writer is to invalidate the authority of the earliest documents by which God has been pleased to transmit to us the revelation of His will'.

B.W. Newton, regarding its alleged teaching on the humanity of the Lord Jesus. The tract is referred to in J.N. Darby's *Observations on a Tract Entitled, 'Remarks on the Sufferings of the Lord Jesus'*, pp.38-43, 95. In *A Statement and Acknowledgement Respecting Certain Doctrinal Errors* B.W. Newton drew attention to the fact that the tract had taught the same doctrine that J.N. Darby later objected to, and that it had circulated widely with the approval of the Brethren up until that time. John Cox, jun.'s *Earnest Expostulation...* reaffirms this; 'This pamphlet was widely circulated by the Brethren in this country and India for twelve years before they discovered anything wrong in the statements in question'. He added that it was 'productive of much good, and is known to have been useful to many who might otherwise have become entangled with Irvingism'. This pamphlet is also referred to in a letter from Mr Newton dated 24th January 1845 (copied in CBA 7049 p.373) as follows, 'The tract, having found its way to India, was thought serviceable against Irvingism, and was republished at Madras by the Church Mission Press; so they evidently considered it not heresy'.

S.P Tregelles's notes on the tract (8th November 1847) were added to B.W. Newton's *A Statement and Acknowledgement Respecting Certain Doctrinal Errors* as an appendix (see note there and in Section 9, B.W. Newton's Correspondence). S.P. Tregelles also referred to the circumstances of its withdrawal by B.W. Newton in his *Three Letters to the Author of 'A Retrospect of Events That Have Taken Place Amongst the Brethren'*.

This pamphlet, along with the two tracts - *Remarks on the Sufferings of the Lord Jesus*; and *Observations on a Tract Entitled 'The Sufferings of Christ as Set Forth in a Lecture on Psalm 6, Considered'* - were withdrawn by Mr Newton in 1847 in *A Statement and Acknowledgement*. The latter two were withdrawn 'for reconsideration'.[1]

There is perhaps a sign of early rivalry between J.N. Darby and B.W. Newton in that J.N. Darby published his own tract on Irvingism, also in 1835 – *A Letter to a Clergyman on the Claims and Doctrines of Newman Street*.

For further comments on Irvingism see, *Extracts from 'A Narrative of Facts, Characterizing the Supernatural Manifestations in Members of Mr Irving's Congregation and Other Individuals, and Formerly in the Writer Himself', by Robert Baxter*, published by B.W. Newton in 1836, and with an appendix by him. Further notes on this publication are in the Section 4, B.W. Newton's Contributions to Other Publications of this *Guide*.

The Madras edition is the only copy of the tract that has been located, but the text of the tract is extant in volumes of *The Christian Witness*.

B.W. Newton made further comment on Irvingism in his tract *Salvation by Substitution*, appendix iv, which was extracted and reprinted from *Occasional Papers on Scriptural Subjects No.4*. It has been suggested that B.W Newton participated in a correspondence regarding "Newmanism" in the *Record*, but we have been unable to trace it.

---

[1] See the discussion of the status of these tracts in *Judge Righteous Judgement*, 1867, and *An Earnest Expostulation*, 1869, both by John Cox, jun. See also the letter of B.W. Newton to an unknown person dated 24th January 1845, Noted in Section 9 of this Guide, B.W. Newton's Correspondence.

First Edition
    1835    - not located.

Church Mission edition
    1836    'Printed at the Church Mission Press', Madras
                        18cm    vi+18p.        Yale University Library.[1]

MS notes
    [1838]    Tract Depot, Plymouth    18cm    24p.           BL

## DR TREGELLES'S GREEK TESTAMENT; REMARKS ON SOME OBSERVATIONS OF THE BISHOP OF GLOUCESTER AND BRISTOL ON DR TREGELLES'S REVISED TEXT OF THE GREEK NEW TESTAMENT

We have concluded that this is beyond all reasonable doubt by B.W. Newton, although it does not bear his name. See the discussion of authorship in Section 5, Anonymous Publications Ascribed to B.W. Newton.

The Bishop of Gloucester and Bristol (Charles John Ellicott 1816-1905) was later one of the Committee responsible for producing the Revised Version. Whilst making the highest commendation of Tregelles's Greek New Testament as faithful labour, and a unique collection of assorted critical materials, the bishop had commented that it is mechanical in approach, and sometimes fails to show 'critical instinct' and 'scholarly sagacity'. The pamphlet replies to this demeaning comment, as 'his remarks have caused pain to the friends of Dr Tregelles'. B.W. Newton also replied to the Bishop of Gloucester's criticism and his approach in *Remarks on the Revised English Version of the Greek New Testament*.

The item was reprinted in *Teachers of the Faith and Future*, by G.H. Fromow.

    1870    Samuel Bagster & Sons, London           21.5cm  8p.    CG

## DUTY OF GIVING HEED TO THE PREDICTIONS OF SCRIPTURE RESPECTING EVENTS THAT ARE TO PRECEDE THE RETURN OF OUR LORD

This originated from one of the *Five Letters on Events Predicted in Scripture as Antecedent to the Coming of the Lord* (1847). The letter from which it was derived was entitled *Is it Wrong to Expect Certain Events Previous to the Return of the Lord Jesus?* The complicated development of this group of publications is given in the entry concerned with the *Five Letters*...

At the same time that this pamphlet was issued with this title, it was also included in *Occasional Papers on Scriptural Subjects No.1*, where the title is, 'On the Duty of Giving Heed to the Predictions of Scripture Respecting Events That Intervene Between the Departure and Return of the Lord'. It is there described as 'in part a reprint'. Although it has minor improvements and a different ending, it is plain that Mr Newton was following the original letter, rather than the amended version that appeared in the *Five Letters* in 1845.

---

[1] Beinecke Rare Books Library, in Volume 851 of the College Pamphlets Collection.

First Edition
    1861    Houlston & Wright, London    17cm    28p.    BL,Bo,CU,Sc,T

'Second Edition'
    1867    Houlston & Wright, London    17cm    28p.    SG

'Second Edition'
    1893    Houlston & Sons, London    17cm    28p.    EL,SG

'Third Edition' – as the First Edition apart from notes.
    1913    Lucas Collins, London    18cm    32p.    BL,Bo,EL,SG

'Fourth Edition' – *Events That Are to Precede the Return of Our Lord. The Duty of Giving Heed to the Predictions of Scripture.*
    1972    SGAT, London    18cm    23p.    CBA,SG

## AN EFFECT OF THE DOCTRINES ANIMADVERTED ON IN PRECEDING TRACTS

This is the unnumbered sequel to the five *Tracts on Doctrinal Subjects*. The others were produced in 1877, and circulated as a bound set. This followed seven years later.

It considers a pamphlet written by an unidentified (but professed evangelical) clergyman to his Diocesan against Romanist and ritualistic teaching. He had forwarded his letter to B.W. Newton. It had disappointed and intensely pained B.W. Newton. He considered that it showed the effect of the tendency considered in the earlier tracts, which centred upon the teaching of Dr Patrick Fairbairn. According to this doctrine the Atonement was not made by the shedding of Christ's blood (as if it were polluted by our sins), but by the blood subsequently offered and symbolically sprinkled. He likewise contended against the writer's idea that expiatory sacrifice was neither vicarious nor penal in its nature. B.W. Newton quoted a number of authorities in support of his position (including 8 pages from Bunyan's *Pilgrim's Progress*).
    1884    Houlston & Sons, London    18cm    38p.  BL,Bo,CU,EL,Sc,T

## EGYPT, PALESTINE AND SYRIA, THEIR PROSPECTS IN PROPHECY

This is composed of extracts from the Third Edition of *Babylon and Egypt*. It was first published in *Watching and Waiting*, September 1946, and reproduced from that as the pamphlet.

    1947    SGAT, London    16.5x10cm    20p.    BL,SG

## EINE GEGENWÄRTIGE SELIGKEIT IN CHRISTO

German Edition of *No Condemnation to Them Who Are in Christ Jesus*.

## ENGLAND'S FUTURE COURSE IN THE EAST

This was Part 2 of *Europe and the East*.

## AN ERRONEOUS MODE OF STATING THE GOSPEL, CONSIDERED

This is No.2 of the *Tracts on Doctrinal Subjects*. It examines the doctrines of general atonement (or 'at-one-ment'); Arminian appeals to 'come to Christ'; and for the sinner "to do his part" in the work of conversion. The tract was produced after the popular D.L. Moody rallies in London in 1875 and 1876, but makes no direct allusion to him. It refers to Thomas Erskine, R. Pearsall Smith, and the book *Frank: The Record of a Happy Life* (by Hannah Whitall Smith, R. Pearsall Smith's wife).

First Edition
    1877                Houlston & Sons, London         18cm   23p   .BL,Bo,CBA,EL,Sc

Second Edition
    1933                S.R. Cottey, London            18cm   26p.    CBA,EL
                      (printed by Hunt, Barnard, London and Aylesbury)

## ERRONEOUS STATEMENTS CONCERNING THE ATONEMENT AND ITS RESULTS (PART FIRST)

This is No.3 of the *Tracts on Doctrinal Subjects*.

Parts First, Second and Third of the consideration of *Erroneous Statements* are a continuous narrative. This tract is concerned with confusion regarding Christ's work of Atonement; controversy regarding 'indwelling sin' two years earlier [probably R. Pearsall Smith's campaigns]; and statements made at a large annual evangelical conference, which intended to reply to the controversial views, but adopted statements in Patrick Fairbairn's[1] *Typology of* Scripture. Those statements declare that Christ's blood became an 'unclean or accursed thing' in the work of atonement. B.W. Newton maintains from Scripture that the Cross is a place of wrath and judgement, but also of 'a sweet smelling savour'; therefore Christ, his life and his blood could not have become polluted or unclean.

      1877     Houlston & Sons, London        18cm   19p.    BL,Bo,CBA,EL,Sc

## ERRONEOUS STATEMENTS CONCERNING THE ATONEMENT AND ITS RESULTS (PART SECOND)

This is No.4 of the *Tracts on Doctrinal Subjects*.

Parts First, Second and Third of the consideration of *Erroneous Statements* are a continuous narrative. This tract is concerned with statements of Patrick Fairbairn that Christ 'sank under the stroke of death as an outcast from Heaven' and that he was 'laden with guilt and pollution'. He also opposes a similar statement by C.H. Mackintosh.[2] An appendix (14 pp.) deals in detail with statements in Fairbairn's *The Typology of Scripture*. The tract emphasises the need for Christ, as priest, to be perfect in his work on the Cross, without sin attaching to him. He only 'bore our sins' in the sense that 'He took on himself the *reatus* or legal ascription of our guilt, so as to subject Himself to the penalties voluntarily incurred by Him because of such ascription'. He quotes A.A. Hodge *The Atonement* in

---

[1] Patrick Fairbairn (1805-1874), Free Church of Scotland minister. He was Principal, and Professor of Church History and Exegesis, at the Free Church College, Glasgow from 1856 to 1874.
[2] 'Sin attaching to the life which the Lord Jesus laid down on the Cross', C.H. Mackintosh on Genesis, p.71.

support of his statements.[1]

    1877    Houlston & Sons, London    18cm    32p    BL,Bo,CBA,EL,Sc

## ERRONEOUS STATEMENTS CONCERNING THE ATONEMENT AND ITS RESULTS (PART THIRD)

This is No.5 of the *Tracts on Doctrinal Subjects*.

Parts First, Second and Third of the consideration of *Erroneous Statements* are a continuous narrative. This tract responds to statements made at a recent evangelical conference, which are faulty in their understanding of sanctification. Its statement, based on the writings of Patrick Fairbairn, was that the sprinkling of the blood of Christ is 'life being diffused all over and through the soul'. B.W. Newton contends rather that 'The great primary, fundamental change effected for all believers by the Atonement, and finished on the Cross, is a change in the governmental relation in which God stands to them, so that their relation becomes one of grace and abiding favour, and is no longer one of wrath. The believer thereby has "no more *conscience* of sins"'.

    1877    Houlston & Sons, London    18cm    21p.    BL,Bo,CBA,EL,Sc

## ETERNAL RECONCILIATION, BEING THE SUBSTANCE OF A DISCOURSE RECENTLY DELIVERED IN LONDON

This product of Mr Newton's early ministry in London is an exposition of Romans 5.

It was published with three other pamphlets to form *Gospel Truths*, where it was revised by the author in the Second Edition. It was also bound up with four other pamphlets to form the compilation *Thoughts on Parts of the Epistle to the Romans*.

First Edition
    1852    Partridge & Oakey, London    16cm    22p.    BL,Bo,CU

Second Edition
    1856    Houlston & Stoneman, London    16cm    23p.    I,SG

Third Edition
    1861    Houlston & Wright, London    16cm    22p.    SG

German Edition
    Ueber die Ewige Versöhnung, Ein Traktat
    1860    Fricke, Halle    16cm    31p.    BL,CBA,CU

## EUROPE AND THE EAST

This was originally published as a commentary on the Crimean War (1854-56) in the light of prophecy.

---

[1] Archibald A. Hodge, *The Atonement*. See also A.A. Hodge, *Systematic Theology*, and John Owen's consideration of Penal Substitution in Vol. 5 *Works, Chapter 8*.

The First Edition was published in two parts, though with continuous pagination. The two parts were:
1. The final perseverance of Russia inconsistent with the declarations of Scripture.
2. England's future course in the East.

The First Edition of *Europe and the East* had only 73 pages. No copies of the first part, as separately published, have been located.

The changes from the First to the Second Edition are as follows:
1. The Second Edition has a preface of 4 pages, dated June 1878, giving the context of the original tract, and comment on its fulfilled and unfulfilled aspects.
2. Very minor changes were made to the First Edition text. The changes are in brackets.
3. A lengthy additional section (pp.67-128) was added to the second part, with the note 'This section was not in the First Edition. With the exception of the few last sentences, it was written in August 1878'.
4. After the original appendix (pp.129-140), which is dated February 1855, the Second Edition has a continuation of the appendix, dated April 1879 – 'the subjoined remarks were not in the Appendix of the First Edition.' The new section (pp.140-155) reflects on the outcome of the Crimean War, and the topic generally.
5. There is a further new section of the appendix (pp.156-176), which commences, 'Whilst engaged in writing the last of the preceding pages, some papers were sent to me from Scotland bearing on the controversy which is now agitating "The Free Church"' [of Scotland].[1] It notes that the Free Church and the Congregational Union 'have been penetrated by the principles of the day'.

*Europe and the East* was bound up with four other works in the compilation *Antichrist, Europe and the East*.

Quotations from it are included in the anthology '*B.W. Newton on Ministry and Order in the Church of Christ*'.

First Edition - *Europe and the East. Part 2. England's Future Course in the East.*
    1855    Partridge, Oakey and Co, London  16cm    29p. [pp.45-73]    BL

First Edition (incl. Parts 1 and 2)
    1855    Partridge, Oakey & co, London    16cm    73p.    BL,Bo,CU,Sc,T

Second Edition – enlarged. Preface 'June 1878'.

---

[1] Presumably the turmoil surrounding the heresy trial of William Robertson Smith. The pamphlet quoted was possibly *Infidelity in Aberdeen Free College...*, published anonymously. This was also a time of controversy concerning the Declaratory Act, relating to Confessional Subscription.

| | | | | |
|---|---|---|---|---|
| 1878 | Houlston & Sons, London | 18cm | 176p. | BL,Bo,CBA,CU,EL,Sc,T |

A new binding of 'stored sheets' of the Second Edition was made in 1948 (*Watching and Waiting* June 1948 p.151)

## EUROPEAN PROSPECTS (AD 1863)

This was extracted from *Occasional Papers on Scriptural Subjects No.3* (1863) and reprinted posthumously, together with a coloured Map of the 'Ten Kingdoms of the Roman Empire'.

Hunt, Barnard and Co published edited extracts from this published work as *The Time of the End* Series No.22 (NT 22), titled, *The Final Division of the Roman Empire into Ten Kingdoms, with a Map of Suggested Sub-Divisions,* in 1910 [noted in Section 8, Publications Produced from Notes of Addresses, and Posthumously Published Letters and Manuscripts]. It would be interesting to speculate on the interaction between Hunt, Barnard, who published many attributed and edited works, and Lucas Collins whose item here (produced in the same year) was determinedly 'without any alteration'.

First Edition – 'without any alteration'.
| | | | | |
|---|---|---|---|---|
| 1910 | Lucas Collins, London | 17cm | 54p. | BIOLA,BL |

Second Edition – 'without any alteration'.
| | | | | |
|---|---|---|---|---|
| 1924 | E.J. Burnett, London | 17cm | 53p. | CBA |

## EVENTS THAT ARE TO PRECEDE THE RETURN OF THE LORD. THE DUTY OF GIVING HEED TO THE PREDICTIONS OF SCRIPTURE

Title of the 'Fourth' Edition of *On the Duty of Giving Heed to the Predictions of Scripture Respecting Events That Are to Precede the Return of the Lord.*

## THE EXCELLENCY OF THE PERSON OF CHRIST UNALTERABLE. REMARKS ON THE DOCTRINE OF OLSHAUSEN

Hermann Olshausen (1796–1839) was a German theologian who rejected the Reformation doctrine of substitutionary righteousness. His works were published in English throughout the nineteenth century.

In their booklet *J.N. Darby and B.W. Newton. A Timely Testimony Concerning the Two Original Leaders of the Plymouth Brethren*, Lewis Longfield and A.E. Clarke refer to this as a tract by Mr Newton. It is a section of *Thoughts on Scriptural Subjects*, and was evidently at one stage circulated separately, although no copies of it have been located.

## THE EXERCISE OF WORLDLY AUTHORITY

See *On the Exercise of Worldly Authority.*

## EXPOSITORY TEACHING ON THE MILLENNIUM AND ISRAEL'S FUTURE

This is a posthumous collection of items from *Occasional Papers on Scriptural Subjects*, Nos. I, 2 and 4, together with two separately published tracts.

| | |
|---|---|
| On Isaiah 18 | from No.1 |
| Notes on Isaiah 18 | from No.1 |
| Notes on Zechariah 14 | from No.2 |
| On the First Psalm | from No.2 |
| Notes on Psalm 1 | from No.2 |
| On the Second Psalm | from No.2 |
| Notes on Psalm 2 | from No.2 |
| Notes on Psalm 68 | from No.4 |
| Notes on Psalm 84 | from No.4 |

The articles were published with the pamphlets *Israel's Prospects in the Millennium*, and *The Millennium and the Everlasting State*.

The component items were all as revised by the author with a view to republication. The book has an index, and an index of texts. With reference to Psalm 68, see also the Note on Psalm 68:4 in the *Quarterly Journal of Prophecy*, January 1867 (Vol. 19), pp.80-81 – noted in Section 6, B.W. Newton's Letters and Articles Published in Periodicals.

First Edition. It includes 2 indexes – of Scriptures quoted, and subjects
    1913    Lucas Collins, London    18cm    v+192p.    BL,CBA,EL

Second Edition (photographic reprint of the First Edition]
    [2015]    SGAT, Chelmsford    18cm    v+192p.    SG

## EXTRACTS FROM THE SECOND SERIES OF 'AIDS TO PROPHETIC ENQUIRY'… COMPARED WITH EXTRACTS FROM 'THE DAILY NEWS' AND 'STANDARD' ETC

This is a brief tract highlighting the accuracy of B.W. Newton's statements on the likely fulfilment of prophecy. It was perhaps instigated by, or published by, Ker Baillie Hamilton[1], in view of the nature of the publication, the publisher (not Houlston), and the location.

The Second Series of *Aids to Prophetic Enquiry* later came to be known as *Babylon and Egypt*.

    1868    William Brackett, printer, Tunbridge Wells    17cm    11p.    BL

## EXTRACTS FROM THE WORKS OF B.W. NEWTON, FOR THE MOST PART REPRINTED FROM 'WATCHING AND WAITING'

This is the index title given by the British Library to three separate works filed under the same shelf mark:

1. *Egypt, Palestine, and Syria, Their Prospects in Prophecy.*
2. *The New World Order, or Pre-Millennial Truth Demonstrated.*
3. *Scriptural Prospects.*

---

[1] Ker Baillie Hamilton, 1804-1889. Former colonial governor of Grenada, Newfoundland, and Antigua and the Leeward Islands. Buried in Tunbridge Wells. See notes on Section 9, B.W. Newton's Correspondence, November 1871 onwards and on *Prospects of the Ten Kingdoms* in Section 3. See *Dictionary of Canadian Biography*, Vol. 11. See *A Pictorial Memoir of Benjamin Wills Newton* – the supplement to this Guide - for a picture of him with further notes..

## EXTRACTS FROM TWO TRACTS, ENTITLED 'REMARKS ON THE SUFFERINGS OF THE LORD JESUS' AND 'OBSERVATIONS ON A TRACT ENTITLED "THE SUFFERINGS OF CHRIST AS SET FORTH IN A LECTURE ON PSALM 6, CONSIDERED"' AND QUOTATIONS FROM OTHER PAPERS

This is a defence of Mr Newton's orthodoxy, and the orthodoxy of the tracts in question, by quotation, analysis, and commentary, produced by John Cox, jun. The title page is headed 'Private and Confidential'. It was evidently intended as a vindication to Mr Newton's friends, rather than an entry into the controversy with his traducers.

  1867 (no publisher)     18cm 34p. SG

## THE FINAL PERSEVERANCE OF RUSSIA INCONSISTENT WITH THE DECLARATIONS OF SCRIPTURE

This is the first of the two parts that made up the First Edition of *Europe and the East*.

## THE FIRST AND SECOND CHAPTERS OF THE EPISTLE TO THE ROMANS, CONSIDERED, WITH REMARKS ON CERTAIN DOCTRINES RECENTLY PROMULGATED BY THE SAVILIAN PROFESSOR OF GEOMETRY [REV. BADEN POWELL, 1796-1860] AND THE REGIUS PROFESSOR OF GREEK [BENJAMIN JOWETT 1817-1893], IN THE UNIVERSITY OF OXFORD

The exposition of the two chapters of Romans is supplemented with a fifty page 'appendix' illustrating the text 'professing themselves to be wise, they became fools' (Rom. 1:22).

The doctrines of the Rev. Baden Powell consisted chiefly in the denial of the Mosaic account of creation. He commended 'Mr Darwin's masterly volume'. Benjamin Jowett was a denier of regeneration; of Christ's freedom from error; of atonement by blood shedding; of original sin; and of the effect of Adam's sin as Federal Head of mankind.

The publication is commended, and Mr Newton's exposition of Habakkuk 2:4 in it is examined, in *The Christian Annotator*, 16th February 1856 p.61, and March 1st 1856 pp.75,76. Further comment on Rev. Baden Powell's teaching is given in *Reflections Suggested by the Present Movement in England against Romanism* p.11.

This item was included in the compilation *Thoughts on Parts of the Epistle to the Romans*.

First Edition
  1856 Houlston & Stoneman, London 16cm iv+120p. BL,Bo,CBA,CU,Sc,SG,T

Second Edition
  1897 Houlston & Sons, London  18cm iv+125p. BL,Bo,CBA,CU,EL,Sc

## FIRST ANXIETY OF EVERY SOUL AWAKENED

This was a gilt edged Gospel card, which quotes the opening of the first chapter of *Thoughts on Parts of Leviticus*. The card was printed following the publication of the extract under the title 'Concern for Salvation' in *Perilous Times*, July 1901.

  [c 1902] Hunt, Barnard, Aylesbury  ?cm 1 or 2p. Not known.

## THE FIRST RESURRECTION AND THE REIGN IN RIGHTEOUSNESS

A modified edition of *Scriptural Proof of the Doctrine of the First Resurrection*.

## FIRST SERIES OF AIDS TO PROPHETIC ENQUIRY

See *Aids to Prophetic Enquiry*.

## FIVE LETTERS ON EVENTS PREDICTED IN SCRIPTURE AS ANTECEDENT TO THE COMING OF THE LORD

The complex web of publications relating to this item is set out in the diagram that follows the description and publication details.

These 'letters' were the focus of the earliest controversy of J.N. Darby with B.W. Newton.

Around 1840, or slightly earlier, Mr Newton wrote letters to several individuals. We do not know the addressees, apart from the statement that the first was to 'a friend who resides in Norfolk'. These letters were copied by hand, and circulated (together with some notes on 2 Thessalonians 2, which were subsequently printed in the First Edition of *Thoughts on the Apocalypse*).

Mr Newton stated 'Some years ago, I wrote five letters on subjects connected with the study of prophecy. They were not printed, but circulated in manuscript. Copies were made by various persons, and widely disseminated, not only in this country, but in Canada, India and elsewhere'.[1]

J.N. Darby described an interview with B.W. Newton regarding the letters in about 1840[2]. He subsequently wrote his objections to Mr Newton. The correspondence was on the letters generally, but chiefly on the Parable of the Wheat and Tares (in the first letter). Mr Newton wrote a letter to him in reply.[3] The correspondence was seen by many. Miss Jeremie asked for permission to take extracts from the doctrinal parts of Mr Newton's reply. Mr Newton later explained how Miss Jeremie's notebooks, and the copies made from them, led J.N. Darby to make false allegations of deceit, and suppression of materials by Mr Newton.[4]

Until 1845, although many had asked Mr Newton to publish the letters, he declined to, as he did not wish to give offence to J.N. Darby or to seem to have a desire for controversy on the subject. However, he resolved to publish the first letter in the summer of 1845, but removed one 'severe' passage 'for love's sake'.[5] There was a prefaced note to the item, 'It is now published, with some omissions and alterations – but in substance, it remains the same'. Alterations were made to the first

---

[1] In his *Defence in Reply to the Personal Accusations of Mr Darby*.
[2] J.N. Darby, *Narrative of Facts*, pp.16-18, included in Collected Writings, vol. 20.
[3] The two original undated letters from J.N. Darby together with a copy of Mr Newton's reply (also undated, in Miss Toulmin's hand) were listed in CBA 6998 as in 'Folio 1' of the Fry Collection, but were lost. They have now been recovered and are in Tom Chantry's collection. See Section 9, B.W. Newton's Correspondence at c.1840/41.
[4] See Letter of Miss Jeremie to B.W. Newton dated 19th January [1846] in Section 9, Correspondence, and in the Fry MS, CBA 7049 pp.363,365, Noted in Section 10, Duplicated and Manuscript Items
[5] *Defence in Reply to the Personal Accusations of Mr Darby*.

## Section 3 – Bibliography of B.W. Newton's Published Works

letter to counter allegations (in a just published tract) that Mr Newton believed the Holy Spirit resided in the teachers only, and that the Ebrington Street Assembly held 'other popish principles'.

S.P. Tregelles wrote, 'Amongst other alterations there were some paragraphs added: and besides the omissions (that of one paragraph in particular) there were various abridgements in order to bring the whole into a more condensed form'[1].

Despite Mr Newton's openness regarding the changes, J.N. Darby accused him of bad faith, and alleged that he had deliberately and deceitfully inserted material to defend himself in the then current controversy between the two men. S.P. Tregelles set out the charges that J.N. Darby made at a meeting, in his published *Letter to H. Gough of 16th December 1846*[2]. As Mr Newton commented, 'Surely, if there had been any intention on my part to deceive, it would have been a strangely foolish thing to print the letter at variance with the MS, when the MS. was in everybody's hands'.[3]

Perhaps the most significant addition was a 'Supplementary Letter' that gave 'Answers to particular questions in relation to the Wheat and Tares' at the end of the publication. It answered J.N. Darby's objections, and was copied from a letter to him. J.N. Darby referred to it as 'the famous appendix of which so much has been said'.[4] It appears that Miss Jeremie circulated this 'appendix' in manuscript form.

S.P. Tregelles published all the *Five Letters* in 1847, together with the Appendix of the first letter. In doing so he wrote, 'The following letters were written about seven years ago, and have been copied and circulated in MS. form by many Christians who felt the solemn importance of the truths which they were written to evince from Scripture. A desire has often been expressed that they should be printed. It is not necessary now to give any detail of the reasons which have hitherto prevented this being done; they have now been placed by the writer in the hands of the Editor, with full permission for him to give them whatever publicity he may see fit'.

Rev. John Cox, sen. stated that the letters were printed [individually?] before they were published in their original form by S. P. Tregelles in 1847.[5] However, in the absence of any surviving printed copies of the other letters before 1847, or indeed, of a First Edition of the *Five Letters*, it is probable that:

1. Only the first letter was printed before 1847.
2. The 1847 edition was a 'Second Edition' only insofar as either (a) the first letter had already been printed (although it had had two printings), or (b) in recognition of the manuscript 'edition' that had been in circulation.

---

[1] Preface to the Second Edition' of the *Five Letters*
[2] See the note on this in see the note in Section 9, B.W. Newton's Correspondence, and in Appendix 3, A Select Publications List
[3] Quoted by W.B. Neatby, in *A History of the Plymouth Brethren*, p.114
[4] See Manuscript Items recovered by the Christian Brethren Archive. Manuscript copy in B.W. Newton's own hand, CBA FRY/1/6/6, noted in Section 10, Duplicated and Manuscript Items. A copy of 'The Answers to Particular Questions' in Mr Newton's hand is also now in the CBA in a (copy) letter to J.N. Darby, which we have placed at c.1843 in the listing of Correspondence in Section 9 of this *Guide*. J.N. Darby's comments on it are in his *Collected Writings 20* p.19 – *Narrative of Facts*.
[5] When he republished two of the letters as *Thoughts on the Christian and Jewish Remnants at the Time of the End* in 1866

The *Five Letters* are individually titled:
1. 'Is it wrong to expect certain predicted events previous to the Return of the Lord Jesus?'
2. 'On the Christian Remnant'.
3. 'On the Jewish Remnant'.
4. 'Are the Christian Remnant part of the Church of the Firstborn?'
5. 'Is the Church directed in Scripture to expect a secret Coming of the Lord Jesus?'

See the separate entry for the publication details of the first letter. *The Christian and Jewish Remnants at the Time of the End*, (letters two and three) was a separate publication in 1866, and was included in the compilation, *The Coming of the Lord*.

Hunt, Barnard published a pamphlet posthumously on the same subject as letters 2 and 3, apparently from notes of addresses by Mr Newton, under the title *The Christian Remnant and the Jewish Remnant at 'The Time of the End'* (NT 18) – see Section 8, Publications Produced from Notes of Addresses, and Posthumously Published Letters and Manuscripts.

First Edition – see discussion above. Not located.

Second Edition – with preface by S.P. Tregelles.
    1847    James Nisbet, London    17cm    viii+76p.    SG,SNL

Third Edition – a reprint of the Second Edition, with S.P. Tregelles's preface.
    1877    Houlston & Sons, London  17cm  viii+76p.  BIOLA,BL,Bo,CBA,CU,EL,Sc,SG

Section 3 – Bibliography of B.W. Newton's Published Works

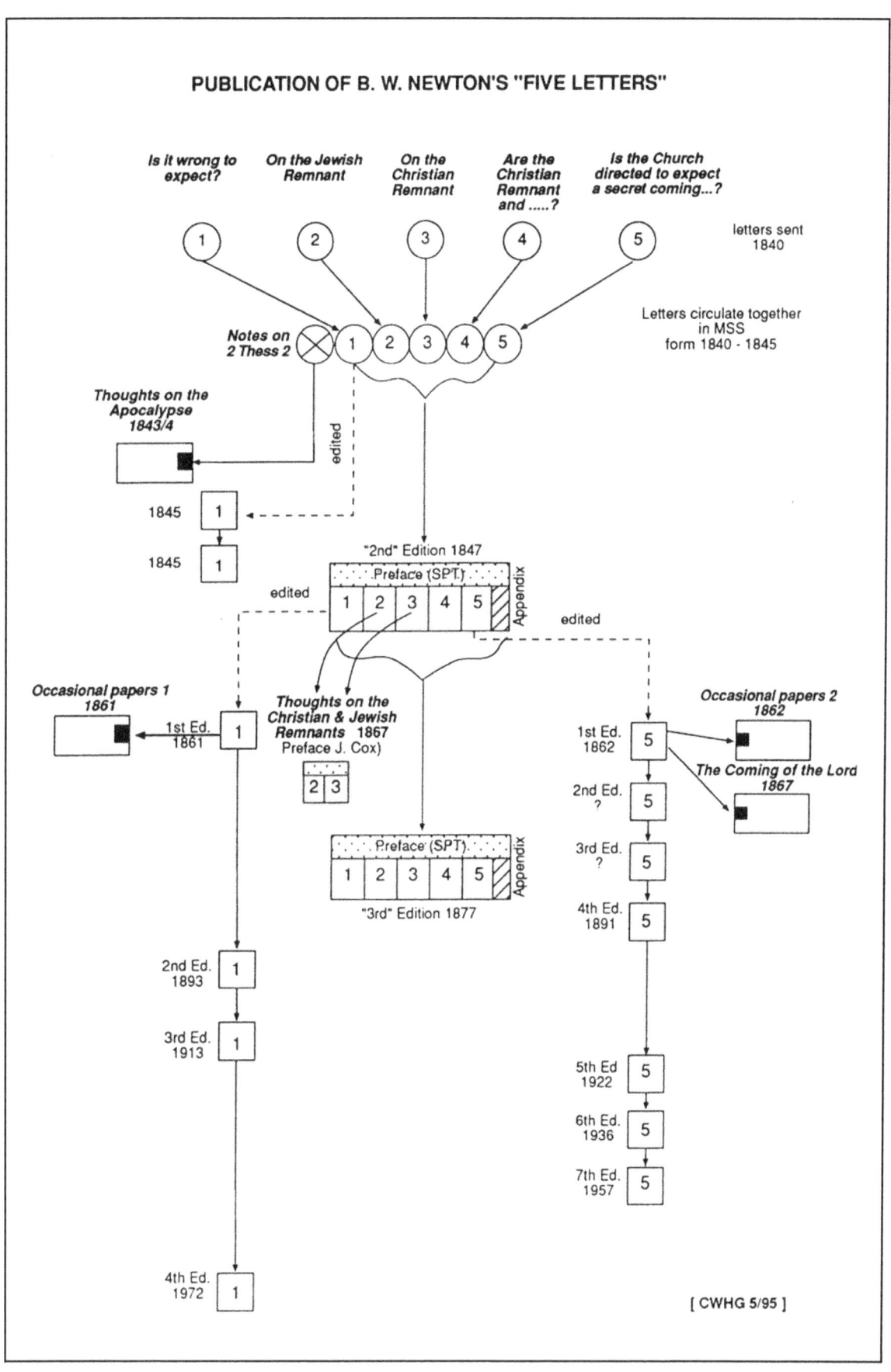

## FOUNDATION TRUTHS

This title was given to at least two overlapping compilations of Mr Newton's works. One of these was made in 1867 and is referred to in Napoleon Noel's *History of the Brethren*. The contents page of the 1867 compilation has, 'the above papers have been published from time to time, and are now bound together'.

The items that were included in compilations with this title are as follows. The contents of the 1867 edition held by the Evangelical Library are indicated by an asterisk.

1. *Acceptance with God.*
2. **Ancient Truths Respecting the Deity and True Humanity of the Lord Jesus.*
3. *Appointments of God in Judgment and Mercy Considered.*
4. *Atonement and Its Results.*
5. *The Blood that Saveth.*
6. **Christ, Our Suffering Surety. Hebrews 2:10 and 5:7.*
7. *Is Salvation by the Obedience of a Divine Substitute a Fiction?*
8. **Jesus Washing His Disciples' Feet.*
9. **Note on I Peter 2:24.*
10. **On Justification through the Blood and Righteousness of a Substitute*
11. **On Sanctification by the Blood of Jesus.*
12. **Propositions for the Solemn Consideration of Christians.*
13. *Regeneration in its Connexion with the Cross.*
14. **Salvation by Substitution.*
15. *Tracts on Doctrinal Subjects.*

Copies of the 1867 edition are held by CBA, EL, and New College, Edinburgh.

A Houlston & Wright edition is held by SG that differs from the 1867 collection.

CG has another (later?) edition.

## GEDANKEN ÜBER THEILE DES DRITTEN BUCHES MOSE. AUS DEM ENGL. ÜBERS. 1: DAS BRANDOPFER (3 BUCH MOSE 1 KAP) ALS TYPUS AUF CHRISTUS BIBLISCH ERÖRTERT

German Edition of *Thoughts on Parts of Leviticus Vol.1 No.1 – The Burnt Offering*.

## GESÙ CHE LAVA I PIEDI AGLI APOSTOLI

Italian Edition of *Jesus Washing His Disciples' Feet*.

## GOSPEL TRUTHS

This brings together four separately published works:
1. *Justification, Being the Substance of a Discourse.*
2. *Eternal Reconciliation.*
3. *No Condemnation to Them Who Are in Christ Jesus.*
4. *Regeneration in Its Connexion with the Cross.*

First Edition
    1869    Houlston & Wright, London    18cm    101p.    BL,Bo,EL,Sc,T

Second Edition 'New Edition Revised' (Preface 'February 1872')
    1872    Houlston & Sons, London    18cm    v+102p.    CBA,EL

Third Edition
    1885    Houlston & Sons, London    18cm    v+102p.    SG?

Fourth Edition – with preface of Second Edition
    1901    Houlston & Sons, London    18cm    viii+102p.    BIOLA,CBA,EL,SG

Chinese Edition

    Referred to in *Watching and Waiting* November / December 1940 p.189, as 'by a Chinese brother'. No copies have been located. It is probable that the missionary W.E. Burnett's ministry gave rise to this initiative.[1]

Norwegian Edition

    This was probably produced. See letter to Miss Leake, 12th August 1895 (CBA 7050 pp.245-247). No copies have been located.

## GREAT PROTESTANT TRUTHS, BEING TWO OF 'THE LEICESTERSHIRE LECTURES'

See under the separate titles:
1. *Priesthood and Sacrifice Essential to Worship.*
2. *The True Unity of the Church of God in Time and Eternity.*

These were bound together, and given this title in B.W. Newton's publisher's list in *Occasional Papers on Scriptural Subjects No.1*.

## GREEK OF ROMANS 1

See *Notes Expository of the Greek of Romans 1.*

## THE HARLOT OF BABYLON

A posthumous reprint of Appendix E of the Third Edition of *Babylon and Egypt*. This was originally published under the title *Conversation on the Seventeenth Chapter of Revelation*, which see.

## HOW DOES THE BLOOD SAVE?

This is a Gospel tract written as the sequel to *The Blood That Saveth*. It has not been possible to construct a list of the dates of all the editions of this tract. the First Edition no doubt followed the First Edition of *The Blood that Saveth*, sometime prior to 1860.

---

[1] William Edward Burnett (1862-1950), an associate of B.W. Newton who commenced the Evangelical Protestant Mission to the Chinese in 1893, having left for China in 1883, first serving with the China Inland Mission. He died in China. Obituary: *Watching and Waiting*, September-October 1950, p.69, and January-February 1951, p.106-108.

## Section 3 - Bibliography of B.W. Newton's Published Works

Fourth (?) Edition
    [1882]        Houlston & Sons, London      10cm    14p.    BL,Bo,CU

Fifth Edition
    In Houlston & Sons publisher's list 1898.

Sixth Edition
    [1900-1904][1]    Houlston & Sons/      10cm    15p.    CBA
                        Lucas Collins, London

Seventh Edition
    [1900-1904][2]    Houlston & Sons/      10cm    15p.    SG
                        Lucas Collins, London

Eighth? Edition
    [1904-1914][3]    Hunt, Barnard & Co, Aylesbury    10cm    16p.    BL

Ninth? Edition
    c.1924.  Probably another edition, referred to in *Watching and Waiting*, February 1924, p.320.

Tenth? Edition
    c.1966        SGAT, London             18cm    6p. (2 folds)    CBA

Arabic Edition
    *Watching and Waiting*, December 1939 refers to a recently published Arabic Edition by Shukri H. Khouri (Jerusalem). See *Watching and Waiting*, January and December 1939. No copies have been located.

Italian Edition (A) - *Come il Sangue ci Salva?* –Translated by 'Lady Otway'.
    1884    De Angelis, Naples        18cm    10p.    I

Italian Edition (B) -*In Qual Modo il Sangue Salva?*
    1887        Claudiana, Florence (printer)    15cm    8p.    Bollettino delle
                                                                 pubblicazioni italiane (1887)[4]

Norwegian Edition
    Probably produced. See letter to Miss Leake, 12th August 1895 (CBA 7050 p.245).

Welsh Edition – *Pa Fodd y mae y Gwaed yn Cadw?*[5]
    c.1895    A.E. Dimmer, Ryde, IW    10x7.5cm    15p.    SG, National Library of Wales

---

[1] Publisher's dates.
[2] Publisher's dates.
[3] Publisher's dates.
[4] This title is listed in the *Bollettino delle pubblicazioni italiane* (1887), but it is not in the Fondo Guicciardini catalogue. However, an index card provided by the Biblioteca Nazionale Centrale, Florence in 1985 identifies it as Fondo Guicciardini.
[5] See T.C.F Stunt, *Life and Times of Samuel Prideaux Tregelles* p47ff and G.H. Fromow *Teachers of the Faith and Future* for Tregelles's knowledge of Welsh and his evangelistic work in Wales. He had his tract *The Blood of the Lamb and the Union of Saints* printed in Welsh.

## IL GIORNO DEL SIGNORE

Italian Edition of *The Day of the Lord*.

## IL SANGUE CHE SALVA

Italian Edition of *The Blood that Saveth*.

## IN A DISPENSATION OF FAILURE, CATHOLICITY A SURE TOKEN OF APOSTASY

Title of the First Edition of *Catholicity in a Dispensation of Failure, a Sure Token of Apostasy*.

## IN QUAL MODO IL SANGUE SALVA?

Italian Edition of *How Does the Blood Save?*

## ISAIAH 53, CONSIDERED: BEING AN EXTRACT FROM A WORK ENTITLED 'THOUGHTS ON SCRIPTURAL SUBJECTS'

The comments on the chapter follow the pattern used in *Thoughts on the Apocalypse*, and *Thoughts on Parts of Leviticus*, of an overview of the chapter, followed by a verse by verse exposition, which here makes comment upon the Hebrew. In *Thoughts on Scriptural Subjects*, the two parts are two separate chapters – 'On Isaiah 53', and 'Notes on Isaiah 52:13 to end, and on Isaiah 53'. B.W. Newton expounded the opening verses as applying specifically of the future cry of Israel in the day of its repentance.

No record has been found of a First Edition. It seems likely that the initial issuing of the exposition in *Thoughts on Scriptural Subjects* has been regarded as the First Edition. This appears to be confirmed by the 1898 Houlston publisher's list, which specifies the editions of other items, but not of this.

It was extracted from the Second Edition of *Thoughts on Scriptural Subjects* in the year of its publication, and therefore incorporates the author's amendments to its First Edition.

'Second Edition'
    1896    Houlston & Sons, London    19cm    92p.    BIOLA,BL,Bo,CBA,CU,Sc

## IS IT WRONG TO EXPECT CERTAIN PREDICTED EVENTS PREVIOUS TO THE RETURN OF THE LORD JESUS? A LETTER TO A FRIEND

This was the first of the *Five Letters on Events Predicted as Antecedent to the Coming of the Lord*, which was published separately in this modified form in 1845. For a fuller account of the publishing of these letters, see the separate item for the *Five Letters*.

Although the typography was the same, this tract appeared under two variant titles, and differing publisher's details. It has not been possible to determine which was the earlier, but both must have been produced in or near 1845.

This tract was modified and printed as an article in *Occasional Papers on Scriptural Subjects* No.1 titled, 'On the Duty of Giving Heed to the Predictions of Scripture Respecting Events That Intervene

Between the Departure and Return of the Lord', and from that it was published as a new tract under the title *Duty of Giving Heed to the Predictions of Scripture Respecting Events That Are to Precede the Return of Our Lord*.

Edition (A) – *Predicted Events. A Letter to a Friend in Reply to the Enquiry, 'Is It Wrong to Expect Certain Predicted Events Previous to the Return of the Lord Jesus?'*
    [1845]    I.K. Campbell, 1 Warwick Square, London    17cm    23p.    EC (incomplete)
              and 5, Cornwall Street, Plymouth.

Edition (B) – *Is It Wrong to Expect Certain Predicted Events Previous to the Return of the Lord Jesus? A Letter to a Friend*
    [1845]    Tract Depot, Cornwall Street, Plymouth    17cm    23p.    CBA

## ISRAEL AND JERUSALEM

This was a compilation of Mr Newton's works made c.1866. It is listed in the end papers of the Second Edition of *Thoughts on the Prophecy of Isaiah* 1968, along with *Antichrist, Europe and the East*, and *The Coming of the Lord*. A copy is held at BIOLA.

It consisted of:
1. *Israel's Prospects in the Millennium.*
2. *Jerusalem. Its Future History.*
3. *The Millennium and the Everlasting State.*
4. *Old Testament Saints Not Excluded from the Church of God.*
5. *On the Prophecies Respecting the Jews and Jerusalem in the Form of a Catechism.*
6. *Prophetic Psalms in Their Relation to Israel, Briefly Considered.*
7. *The World to Come.*

## ISRAEL IN THE DAYS OF HAGGAI AND ZECHARIAH; WITH A NOTE UPON THE PROPHECY OF HAGGAI, BOTH REPRINTED FROM 'OCCASIONAL PAPERS ON SCRIPTURAL SUBJECTS', ALSO A LECTURE UPON ZECHARIAH 3

The first two component parts of this booklet were extracted from *Occasional Papers on Scriptural Subjects No.2*. The lecture upon Zechariah 3 was given at Duke Street Chapel, Westminster on 27th June 1858. Mr Newton approved these notes of the lecture (with certain additions) shortly before his death, with a view to publication. A Chinese Edition may have been produced. It was translated by 'a Chinese brother', who resolved to 'wait in faith for the time of the Lord to come to print' (*Watching and Waiting*, November/December 1940). It is probable that the missionary W.E. Burnett's ministry gave rise to that initiative.[1]

    1911    Lucas Collins, London    18cm    62p.    CBA,EL

---

[1] William Edward Burnett (1862-1950), an associate of B.W. Newton who commenced the Evangelical Protestant Mission to the Chinese in 1893, having left for China in 1883, first serving with the China Inland Mission. He died in China. Obituary *Watching and Waiting*, September-October 1950, p.69, and January-February 1951, p.106-108.

## ISRAEL'S PROSPECTS IN THE MILLENNIUM, BEING THE SUBJECT OF A LECTURE DELIVERED JULY 1ST 1856 AT DUKE STREET CHAPEL, ST JAMES PARK, LONDON

Mr Newton published this as a tract. It concludes with three appendices (1) A Note on the Distinction Between the Millennial and Post-Millennial Earth, (2) A Note on 2 Peter 3, and (3) A Note on converted Israel's enjoyment of all the personal and everlasting blessings of the Gospel in the Millennium and beyond.

This tract was posthumously brought together with other works in *Expository Teaching on the Millennium and Israel's Future*, with revisions the author had made before his death.

    1856    Houlston & Stoneman, London    16cm    38p.    BL,Bo,CBA,CU,Sc,SG,T

## IS SALVATION BY THE OBEDIENCE OF A DIVINE SUBSTITUTE A FICTION?

This is a spirited defence of the Reformation doctrine of the substitutionary imputation of Christ's merit to the believer on account of Christ's obedience and suffering. It was occasioned by denials of the doctrine and, in particular, a 'recent' lecture. This was one of the points of contention with J.N. Darby.

First Edition
    1893    Houlston & Sons, London    18cm    16p.    BL,Bo,CU, EL,Sc,SG
            Arthur Andrews, Ryde, IW
Second Edition
    1898    Houlston & Sons, London    18cm    16p.    CBA

## JERUSALEM

See *Jerusalem, Its Future History*.

## JÉRUSALEM ET L'HOMME DE PÉCHÉ

French Edition of *Jerusalem, Its Future History*.

## JERUSALEM, ITS FUTURE HISTORY

This originated as an anonymous article in *The Christian Witness* of January 1835 under the simple title *Jerusalem*. See discussion of authorship Section 7, Articles in The *Christian Witness*. The Plymouth Tract Depot reprinted it with the same title. Although it was expanded in later editions, the earliest edition had additional footnotes that were later omitted. The pamphlet was included in the compilation *Israel and Jerusalem*.

The title of the German Edition is more informative of the content.

[Proto edition] *Jerusalem*.
    [1835?]    Plymouth Tract Depot    16cm    20p.    SG
             and Central Tract Depot, London
First Edition
    1852    Partridge and Oakey, London    16cm    48p.    BL,Bo,CU,Sc,SG,T

Second Edition
  ND [Pre-1861]¹    Houlston & Wright, London    18cm    48p.    CBA,BIOLA

Third Edition
  1908    Lucas Collins, London    18cm    58p.    BL,CBA,EL,Sc

Arabic Edition
  Translated and published by Shukri H. Khouri (Jerusalem) between December 1939 and July 1941. See *Watching and Waiting*, January 1939, December 1939, and July/August 1941 (obituary). No copies have been located. See also the reference to Ibrahim Bastoli who translated 'some works' of Mr Newton into Arabic (*Watching and Waiting*, March 1956 p.221).

French Editions
  Edition A. *Jérusalem et l'Homme de Péché*. Reprint of 'Proto edition'.
    [1835-1947?]    Dépôt de Traités,    17.5cm    19p.    I
                    39 Bath Street Jersey, C.I.

  Edition B. *Jérusalem et l'Homme de Péché, 2 Chr. 7:6* [sic]. Reprint of 'Proto edition'.
    [1835-1947?]    Dépôt de Traités,    17cm    19p.    I
                    39 Bath Street Jersey, C.I.

  Edition C. *Jérusalem. Son Histoire Future.*
    1854    Geneva    18cm    ?    Swiss National Library

  Edition D. *Jérusalem. Son Histoire Future.*
    1884    E. Béroud, Geneva    18cm    66p.    French National Library

German Edition. *Jerusalems Bedeutung in der Vergangenheit, Gegenwart und Zukunft* [Jerusalem's significance in the past, present, and future].
  1857    Beck, Berlin    18cm    32p.    BL

## JÉRUSALEM. SON HISTOIRE FUTURE

French Edition of *Jerusalem, Its Future History*.

## JERUSALEMS BEDEUTUNG IN DER VERGANGENHEIT, GEGENWART UND ZUKUNFT

German Edition of *Jerusalem, Its Future History*.

## JESUS WASHING HIS DISCIPLES' FEET

This is an exposition of John 13:10. It was occasioned by denials that the cleansing of Christ for sin on the basis of His one offering is continuously effectual throughout the believer's earthly life.

It originally appeared in *Occasional Papers on Scriptural Subjects No.3*, 1863, and was later included in *Atonement and Its Results* (1882), as revised by the author. It was posthumously reprinted in its revised form from *Atonement and Its Results*.

---

¹ Publisher's list, *Occasional Papers on Scriptural Subjects No.1*.

First Edition
    1866     Houlston & Wright, London     16cm    22p.    BIOLA,BL,Bo,CU,Sc

Second Edition
    1874     Houlston & Sons, London     16cm    22p.    CG

Third Edition – 'reprinted from *Atonement and Its Results*'.
    1902     Houlston & Sons, London     18cm    20p.    BIOLA,CBA

Italian Edition. *Gesù che Lava i Piedi agli Apostoli.*
    1886     Claudiana, Florence     16cm    19p.    Bollettino delle pubblicazioni italiane (1887)[1]

## THE JUDGEMENT OF THE COURT OF ARCHES AND OF THE JUDICIAL COMMITTEE OF THE PRIVY COUNCIL IN THE CASE OF ROWLAND WILLIAMS, D.D., ONE OF THE WRITERS IN THE 'ESSAYS AND REVIEWS', CONSIDERED

The publication of the *Essays and Reviews* marked the onset of liberalism in the Church of England in the same way that J.H. Newman's *Tracts for the Times* heralded Anglo-Catholicism. Dr Rowland Williams (1817-1880) contributed an essay on 'Bunsen's Biblical Researches'. Baron Bunsen (1791-1860) was one of the most advanced modernists of his day. The Bishop of Salisbury took action against Dr Williams in the ecclesiastical courts, but he was exonerated by the decision of the Privy Council. Mr Newton examines the implications for the Established Church, and for the nation. The issues involved are the inspiration of Scripture, and eternal punishment, but Mr Newton also gives comment on the errors of the Anglo-Catholics regarding baptismal regeneration, and their rejection of Israel's future.

An account of the circumstances of the Privy Council judgement is given in *The 'Archbishop' of Canterbury and 'Modern' Christianity* by W. Lancelot Holland, pp.23-31 (1898, 225p – EL). The then Archbishop of Canterbury (Archbishop Temple) was a contributor to the first of the *Essays and Reviews*.

Mr Newton also wrote against Dr William's contribution to the *Essays and Reviews* in *Remarks on 'Mosaic Cosmogony'*…

*Judgment of the Court of Arches…* was extracted from *Occasional Papers on Scriptural Subjects No.4*, which also included a Postscript relating to it. It also gave an extract from a message by Lord Shaftesbury expressing his concern regarding the spread of modernism in England. See further notes there.

    1866     Houlston & Wright, London  20cm  iii+126p.  BIOLA,BL,Bo,CBA,CU,EL,Sc,T

## JUDGMENTS ON THE 'ESSAYS AND REVIEWS'

Publisher's list title for *Judgment of the Court of Arches…*

---

[1] This title is listed in the *Bollettino delle pubblicazioni italiane* (1887), but it is not in the Fondo Guicciardini catalogue. However, an index card provided by the Biblioteca Nazionale Centrale, Florence in 1985 identifies it as Fondo Guicciardini.

## JUSTIFICATION AND SANCTIFICATION

This is a combination of *Justification, Being the Substance of a Discourse Recently Delivered in London*, and three papers on sanctification from *Atonement and Its Results*, brought together in a heavily edited form. It is somehow related to the Norwegian pamphlet (Second Edition 1910), *Retfærdiggjörelsen og Helliggjörelsen* [Justification and Sanctification], 'selected from Benjamin Wills Newton's works. Authorised translation after the original. Second Edition'. The Norwegian pamphlet almost certainly has an earlier date than the Hunt Barnard one. It may have different content, or the English content that was translated into Norwegian may be the basis of this tract.

First Edition
    c.1910    Hunt, Barnard and Co, London and Aylesbury    16cm    16p.    CBA,EL

Second Edition – 'recently issued' – *Watching and Waiting*, November/December 1959.
    1959    SGAT London    ?    ?    ?

Third Edition
    c.1967    SGAT, London    15cm    16p.    SG

## JUSTIFICATION, BEING THE SUBSTANCE OF A DISCOURSE RECENTLY DELIVERED IN LONDON

The basis of this tract was a lecture on Romans 5:1-11. In it Mr Newton argued for the forensic and declaratory sense of 'justification' – the believer having Christ's righteousness imputed to him. He argued against both the papist and modernistic definition of 'making righteous'.

The tract was combined with four other works to form the compilation *Thoughts on Parts of the Epistle to the Romans*, and, with three other works, to form *Gospel Truths*. It was also included in an edited form in *Justification and Sanctification*. It is not to be confused with, *On Justification through the Blood and Righteousness of a Substitute*.

First? Edition
    1852    Partridge and Oakey, London    16cm    22p.    BL,Bo,CU,I,Sc,T

Second Edition
    Not located.

Third Edition
    1856    Houlston & Stoneman, London    18cm    22p.    I,SG

French Editions
    [Edition A] - *La Justification, Sermon Prêché à Londres par B.W. Newton.*
        1854    E Béroud, Geneva    16?cm    31p.    French National Library

    [Edition B] - *La Justification Ou Comment Dieu Nous Justifie.*
        According to *Perilous Times* (September 1902) this was circulated in France, Belgium and Switzerland.
            Bridel & Co, Lausanne,    18cm    32p.    CBA, Swiss National Library
            Paris and Lyons

German Edition. *Ueber die Rechtfertigung*. This tract did not identify the author.
    1860      Wupperthaler Traktat-Geseltshaft, Barmen      16cm    25p    CBA
               T.F. Steinhans, printer

Italian Edition. *La Giustificazione, Saggio di B.W. Newton tradotto in italiano da Una Signora Inglese*.
    1875      J.V. Arduin, Menton                16?cm    26p.    French National Library

## LA GIUSTIFICAZIONE, SAGGIO DI B.W. NEWTON TRADOTTO IN ITALIANO DA UNA SIGNORA INGLESE

Italian Edition of *Justification, Being the Substance of a Discourse*.

## LA JUSTIFICATION OU COMMENT DIEU NOUS JUSTIFIE

French Edition of *Justification, Being the Substance of a Discourse*..

## LA JUSTIFICATION, SERMON PRÊCHÉ À LONDRES PAR B.W. NEWTON

French Edition of *Justification, Being the Substance of a Discourse*.

## LECTURE ON THE PROPHECY OF THE LORD JESUS, AS CONTAINED IN MATTHEW 24,25

This was the title of the Second Edition of *Prophecy of the Lord Jesus as Contained in Matthew 24 and 25, Considered*.

## LECTURES ON PROPHECY

This is an early compilation of five tracts. Three of them are ascribed to Mr Newton (one shared with J.L. Harris, and another accompanied by notes of J.G. Deck). Two are anonymous.

The component works are:

1) *The Personal Return of the Lord Jesus Necessary to the Introduction of Millennial Blessing* (1842), by B.W. Newton.
*The Prospects of the World in Connection with the Approaching Return of the Lord Jesus Christ* (1842), anonymous, but clearly by Mr Newton. See Section 5, Anonymous Publications Ascribed to B.W. Newton

2) *The Similarities and the Contrasts between the Present and Coming Dispensations* (1842), severally by J.L. Harris and B.W. Newton.

3) *Christ Not Yet Seated on the Throne of David* [1840], anonymous, but attributed to S.P. Tregelles in EC's copy of the tract and acknowledged by S.P. Tregelles in his letter to B.W. Newton of 31st August 1862. See Section 9, B.W. Newton's Correspondence.

4) *On Luke 21* (1843), by B.W. Newton, with notes added by J.G. Deck.

    ND [1843?]      J.K. Campbell, London    16cm    pages as tracts    SG

## LE MONDE À VENIR

French Edition of *The World to Come*.

## LE PROFEZIE DEL SIGNOR GESÙ CRISTO, COME SI TROVANO NEI CAPITOLI 24 E 25 DELL' EVANGELO DI S. MATTEO

Italian Edition of *The Prophecy of the Lord Jesus as Contained in Matthew 24 and 25, Considered*.

## THE LEPROSY

Vol. 2, No.4 of the First Edition of *Thoughts on Parts of Leviticus* (issued in as a series).

## LE SANG QUI SAUVE

French Edition of *The Blood that Saveth*.

## LETTER FROM B.W. NEWTON TO J. CLULOW, 18 APRIL 1845.

This was sent to Joseph Clulow, one of the four leading Brethren at Plymouth who supported Mr Newton in the initial controversy with J.N. Darby. In this letter, Mr Newton gave his account of the meeting of thirteen leading Brethren that took place in mid-April 1845. It was called to discuss the charges that J.N. Darby was making against him (B.W. Newton). In his *Narrative of Facts* (*Collected Writings*, vol. 20 p.34, etc), J.N. Darby alleged that this was a false account (see H.H. Rowdon, *Origins of the Brethren* p.241). In an appendix to this published letter, Mr Newton gave 16 doctrinal positions that he sought to maintain.

This publication was originally in the Fry Collection. It was listed by T.C.F. Stunt in the first cataloguing of the early Brethren papers held by Mr C.E. Fry (CBA 6998). However, it was one of the items that were not transferred to the Christian Brethren Archive. No other copies of the letter as a separate published tract have been located. It was printed 'for private circulation only', and dated 18th April 1845.

According to F.W. Wyatt's 'calendars' (CBA/1/2/2 – CBA/1/2/15) the MS copy had an appendix in Newton's own hand. The letter was reprinted, without the appendix, in Lord Congleton's *Correspondence, etc. Relating to Mr Newton's Refusal to Appear Before the Saints at Rawstorne Street, London*.[1] The appendix of 16 doctrinal statements was reprinted in S.P. Tregelles's *Three Letters to the author of 'A Retrospect of Events That Have Taken Place Amongst the Brethren'* on pages 64-66. See further notes on this publication in Appendix 3, Select Publications.

Tom Chantry has the manuscript in the handwriting of B.W. Newton that was probably referred to by F.W. Wyatt. It commences 'It is my desire to maintain…'. It gives the first thirteen of the sixteen statements printed by S.P. Tregelles (it is possible there is a missing sheet); nine statements that he desires to oppose; and a solemn protest against the Church being made a deliberative assembly.

See Section 9, B.W. Newton's Correspondence.

---

[1] See notes in the Section 9, B.W. Newton's Correspondence, in this Guide.

## A LETTER ON SUBJECTS CONNECTED WITH THE LORD'S HUMANITY

This was issued by B.W. Newton early in 1848. It followed the doctrinal controversy with J.N. Darby. Mr Newton had, in the preceding months, left the Brethren. The letter is addressed to 'my dear brethren and sisters' – evidently to those who remained loyal to him.

In the tract, Mr Newton distinguished between the personal, and relative, positions of the Lord Jesus whilst he was here on earth. Whilst he admitted that he had wrongly stated Christ to have been under certain specific results of Adam's sin, used wrong theological terms, and had made a wrong application of Romans 4, he strongly defended the orthodoxy of *Observations on a Tract...* , and *Remarks on the Sufferings of the Lord Jesus...*, taken as a whole. He sought to demonstrate this by reproducing part of *Observations on a tract...*, in an appendix, dealing with the doctrine of vicariousness. He denied that he had ever held the error of the imputation of Adam's sin that others attributed to him (p.32).

J.N. Darby rejected the tract out of hand in his *Remarks on 'A Letter on Subjects Connected with the Lord's Humanity'* (October 1848, *Collected Writings* vol.15), although initially J.G. Bellett wrote a letter approving of it (W.B. Neatby *History of the Plymouth Brethren*, p.150). J.N. Darby's pamphlet itself came in for criticism from one of Mr Newton's circle. A reply was published entitled, *The point at issue; or Observations by R.C. Johnson on 'Remarks by J.N. Darby on "A letter on Subjects Connected with Our Lord's Humanity'"*.[1] Horatius Bonar also severely criticised J.N. Darby's tract in *The Quarterly Journal of Prophecy*, 1849 p.209.

In the appendix to a letter to George F [sc. James]. Walker of Teignmouth dated 10th April 1848, Mr Newton modified his quotation from this pamphlet, according to F.W. Wyatt, who makes the following comments. The quotation he made began at p.23 'as I have found that many....' and ends at p.29 'had drawn as thick clouds round him' but omits the long paragraph on pp.26,27 'Neither in life...had so appointed'. It also makes alterations in the second paragraph 'which are improvements' as follows: 'In the 1st para quoted 'respecting these doctrines' for 'respecting these Tracts'.[2] 'The personal position of the Lord Jesus is that which pertained to Himself – alone and individually regarded. The relative position is that which pertained to Him in consequence of His connexion with others – i.e. man and Israel. If He had said when He had taken flesh, "I am come to claim that which is personally due to myself in my present individual relation to God" He would have assumed a personal position. If on the contrary, He did not say this, but said, "I have come to receive things which are not due to myself personally, but I will willingly remain under them because they are the portion of those with whom I have associated myself by taking their flesh" – then He assumed a relative position. To his personal position (I speak of Him after He had assumed flesh) nothing but blessing was due. Even as an Israelite under Law ...'.

Establishing the month that Mr Newton's 'Letter' was published is problematic. It has been variously dated in bibliographies as July or October 1848, but J.N. Darby was not in the habit of waiting for 2-5 months before responding to B.W. Newton's publications, and his reply was

---
[1] Dated December 15th 1848 (published by Jenkin Thomas (printer), Plymouth, 20p, SGAT.
[2] This appears to be an error by Wyatt as the paragraph in the original reads 'respecting my doctrines'.

published in December 1848. However, unless the appendix of the letter to G.J. Walker preceded the publication (and was therefore not 'an improvement' as F.W. Wyatt suggests, but an earlier version), a date earlier than 10th April 1848 is to be presumed, which posits a yet longer delay in J.N. Darby's reply. See Section 9, B.W. Newton's Correspondence regarding the letter to G.J. Walker and also the comments on *Brief Statements in the Form of Answers to Questions*, published 11th July 1848.

[1848]   Jenkin Thomas, 9, Cornwall St, Plymouth (printer)   16cm   55p.   EC, ID

## A LETTER ON WORSHIP AND MINISTRY

The letter was sent from Plymouth, dated 14th May 1846, to A.A. Rees. It appears to have been published about that time (by A.A. Rees?), but no copies have been located. G.V. Wigram included the letter in *Plain Evidence Concerning Ebrington Street; as to the Nature of the System Now Pursued Thereby* - a polemical attack on B.W. Newton's principles.[1]

Rev. A.A. Rees[2] reprinted the original letter in September 1875 [without G.V. Wigram's strictures]. He wrote in that republication, 'After losing sight of the following letter for nearly thirty years, a printed copy of it fell into my hands the other day, in the South of England, & I reprint it for private circulation, to show that, almost from the beginning, there was a variety of views among leading "Brethren", even at Plymouth, as to the principle and degree of open Ministry & Worship'.

It appears that Rev. A.A. Rees then wrote to B.W. Newton in 1882 asking him if he still held the principles set forth in his original letter to him. That letter was answered by a reply on B.W. Newton's behalf, dated 15th November 1882, from C.Y. Biss, together with a covering note explaining why Dr Biss was replying on his behalf.

We have been unable to locate a copy of the 'Letter' as printed by A.A. Rees. F.W. Wyatt heads his copy/transcript as 'A Letter from B.W. Newton to A.A. Rees, on the Subject of Worship and Ministry among 'the Brethren'.

Reprinted for private circulation 'Sunderland, Sept. 1875'. Manuscript copy in F.W. Wyatt's hand (7 pages) CBA FRY/1/6/4. See Section 9, B.W. Newton's Correspondence

## A LETTER TO A FRIEND CONCERNING A TRACT RECENTLY PUBLISHED IN CORK

This 'Letter' was a reply to a polemic tract by the Brethren leader, John Marsden Code (1805-1873), which, condemning B.W. Newton, spoke of 'this fearful doctrine', 'heretical opinion', etc. J.M. Code's tract is *Remarks on Mr Newton's Doctrine on the Sufferings of Christ*.[3]

In his tract, Mr Newton clearly re-stated his position on the humanity and sufferings of Christ, and suggested a tendency to Docetism and Eutychianism in his opponents. He quoted a hymn by J.G.

---

[1] *Plain Evidence concerning Ebrington Street; as to the Nature of the System Now Pursued Thereby* by George V. Wigram, published by J.B. Rowe, Plymouth, and 1, Warwick Square London (Xerox copy CBA 14182), 24 pages. The letter by B.W. Newton takes up 6 pages of the publication.

[2] For further information on A. A. Rees, and his views on worship and ministry, see: The Early Development of Arthur Augustus Rees and his Relations with the Brethren, by Timothy C.F. Stunt, *Brethren Archivists and Historians Network Review* (BAHNR) 4:22-35.

[3] 1850. Published by George Purcell & Co, Cork, 16cm, 12p, EC.

Deck, freely used by the Brethren since 1837. The Brethren hymn writer had used the expression 'our mortal flesh and blood partake' of Christ - the very doctrine of which Mr Newton had been accused. This led J.G. Deck to publish *Confession of a Verbal Error in a Hymn* (14th November 1850). The circumstances of this are recounted with wry humour in W.B. Neatby's *History of the Plymouth Brethren* (pp.144-146). See too F.F. Bruce *The Humanity of Christ*, p.7. J.G. Deck had been associated with Mr Newton a few years earlier in the tract *On Luke 21*. See also the letter to him dated 1st November 1847 in Section 9, B.W. Newton's Correspondence.

In 1848 Mr Newton had published and circulated *Extracts from Bishop Pearson's Exposition of the Apostles' Creed* (which also included quotations on the human nature of Christ from Calvin's *Institutes*). This was now circulated as an appendix to this tract.

    1850    Houlston & Stoneman, London    17cm    34p.    BL,CBA,I,SG

## LETTER TO A FRIEND ON A REPLY TO THE ENQUIRY 'IS IT WRONG TO EXPECT CERTAIN PREDICTED EVENTS PREVIOUS TO THE RETURN OF THE LORD JESUS?'

Alternative title for *Is It Wrong to Expect...*, which see.

## A LETTER TO A FRIEND ON THE STUDY OF PROPHECY

This was first published as an article in *The Christian Witness* of October 1835. It was subsequently published as a tract. It is unanimously attributed to B.W. Newton, and, from our assessment, we have concluded that it is beyond reasonable doubt by him. See Section 7, Articles in *The Christian Witness* for the basis of this conclusion, which also comments on F. Roy Coad's allegation of partial rapture teaching in this tract. It was followed by *A Second Letter to a Friend on the Study of Prophecy*. The letters are 'signed' XZ.

The letter sets out general principles to be followed regarding the interpretation of unfulfilled prophecy; the means of bringing in Millennial blessing at the Coming of the Lord; the nature of the judgements of the Day of the Lord; and believers dwelling in the Heavenly Jerusalem.

*The Christian Witness* Vol. 2.
    October 1835,    Pages 341-355    -    15p.    CBA

Separately published.
    [ND]    Central Tract Depot, London    18cm    12p.    CBA,SG

## LETTER TO CLULOW

Frequent reference is made in histories of the Brethren to 'Letter to Clulow'. See *Letter from B.W. Newton to J. Clulow, 18 April 1845*.

## A LETTER TO RICHARD WALDO SIBTHORPE [sic], B.D., LATE FELLOW OF MAGDALEN COLLEGE, OXFORD ON THE SUBJECT OF HIS RECENT PAMPHLET

R.W. Sibthorp (1792-1879)[1] was a friend of Mr Newton's in his early years at Oxford, and after his conversion (see *Teachers of the Faith and Future* by G.H. Fromow, p.4, and CBA 7049, pp.176-184). Sibthorp had earlier written *The Character and Tokens of the True Catholic Church* (1827, Dr Williams Library London), defending the Protestant position, but throughout his later life he 'halted between two opinions'. He seceded to Rome in 1841, but rejoined the Church of England again within two years (one wonders whether his old friend's 'letter' to him had some effect). He seceded to Rome for a second time in 1865, but left instructions just before his death for an Anglican burial.

The occasion of this tract by Mr Newton was Sibthorp's first secession, and his publication of *Some Answer to the Inquiry 'Why Are [sic] You Become a Catholic?'* (London, 1842). It drew eight other responses apart from Mr Newton's, including those of W. Dodsworth, W. Palmer, and R.H. Herschell. Sibthorp published a reply to some of his critics under the title *A Further Answer to the inquiry 'Why Have [sic] You Become a Catholic'* (London, 1842). He makes no specific reference to Mr Newton in it.

In his tract Mr Newton argued against the claims of the Church of Rome, and also indicated some of his own views on Church government. Quotations are included in the anthology *B.W. Newton on Ministry and Order in the Church of Christ*.

[Edition A] by 'W.B. Newton' [sic].
    1842    D. Walther, London    21cm    32p.    CG

[Edition B]
    1842    D. Walther, London    21cm    32p.    New College, Edinburgh

## A LETTER TO THE BRETHREN AND SISTERS IN CHRIST, WHO MEET FOR COMMUNION IN EBRINGTON STREET, PLYMOUTH; CONTAINING REMARKS ON A RECENT TRACT, CIRCULATED AMONGST THEM

This is the first part of Mr Newton's reply to J.N. Darby's criticism of his *Thoughts on the Apocalypse*. J.N. Darby's first criticisms were issued in parts during the summer of 1845(?), and were later published as *An Examination of Statements Made in the 'Thoughts on the Apocalypse' by B.W. Newton; and an Enquiry How Far They Accord with Scripture* (*Collected Writings*, Vol. 8 pp.1-320). Following Mr Newton's *Letter to the Brethren and Sisters...*, J.N. Darby produced *An Answer to 'A Letter to the Brethren and Sisters in Christ...'*. Mr Newton then wrote *A Second letter to the Brethren and Sisters in Christ...*, making brief reference to J.N. Darby's *An Answer...* . J.N. Darby thereupon concluded the paper

---

[1] See letter of B.W. Newton to his mother dated 28th April 1829. For further information regarding his visit to the Continent (with B.W. Newton) see *Report of the Religious Tract Society*, (London 1830), pp.82-97. Further biographical information regarding Sibthorp in *Richard Waldo Sibthorp: A Biography Told Chiefly in His Own Correspondence*, by J. Fowler (London 1890), and T.C.F. Stunt *From Awakening to Secession*, index and *passim*. See also Michael Trott, *The Life of Richard Waldo Sibthorp* (Brighton 2005). He was the first to secede to Rome of those associated with the Tractarian Movement. The sensation that ensued, and its consequent impact on the leaders of the movement, is well described in *W.G. Ward and the Oxford Movement*, by Wilfrid Ward [his son] 1889, p193ff. CBA 7064 records a statement of B.W. Newton that R.W. Sibthorp sent a message to him on his death bed that he had 'died a protestant'.

duel with *Answer to 'A Second Letter to the Brethren and Sisters in Christ'...* (*Collected Writings*, Vol. 8, pp.344-377). This all took place in 1845. An account of the exchange is given in *The Origins of the Brethren* by H.H. Rowdon, p.240.

This 'Letter' contains an appendix in which S.P. Tregelles gave his response to J.N. Darby's criticism of B.W. Newton's (and the Greek New Testament's) translation of Psalm 110:1 – Appendix C, 7 pages, dated September 1st 1845.

    1845    Warwick Square, London    18cm    63p.    Bo,SG
           and 5, Cornwall Street, Plymouth

## A LETTER TO THE MINISTER OF SILVER STREET CHAPEL, TAUNTON, IN REPLY TO HIS RECENT LECTURE AGAINST THE PRE-MILLENNIAL ADVENT OF THE LORD

John Jackson, the minister of the Silver Street Baptist Chapel in Taunton, had published a lecture he had given under the title, *The Pre-Millennial Advent and Earthly Reign of Jesus Christ, Irreconcilable with the Character of the Christian Dispensation and Common Sense, and with the Priestly Office and Perpetual Intercession of our Lord in Heaven. A Lecture Delivered at Silver Street Chapel, Taunton on the Evening of Wednesday November 13th 1844* (published by James Barnicott, Taunton, 43p – Taunton Public Library Archive).

Mr Newton had given a series of three lectures on prophetic subjects in the weeks preceding, and John Jackson had attended. There are some interesting comments in Jackson's tract as to how Mr Newton dealt with his questions to him at the meeting.

In his tract, John Jackson refers to those associated with Mr Newton in the town, and it may be significant that 'both he and the Church became discouraged by a dwindling membership, and in June, 1845 Mr Jackson resigned' (*Centenary History of Silver Street Baptist Church*, 1914).

In his tract Mr Newton defended himself against misquotations and misrepresentations, and gave a strong defence of the premillennial Advent of the Lord. In an appendix, he included an extract from 'the Baptists' Confession of Faith' 1660, showing early prevalence of premillennial views. He also quoted one of his earlier tracts, *Thoughts on Unfulfilled Prophecy*.[1]

First Edition
    (1845)    May, London, bookseller, Taunton    18cm    36p.    SG,SNL

Second Edition
    1851    No copies located

Third Edition, Revised
    1863    Houlston & Wright, London    18cm    36p.    BL,Bo,CBA,CU,EL,Sc,SG,T

(Fourth) Edition
    Edited and issued under the title *The New World Order, or Premillennial Truth Demonstrated, An Answer to the Post-millennial, A-millennial, Anti-millennial Theories.*
    (1943)    SGAT, London    16cm    20p.    BIOLA,BL,CBA

---

[1] See notes on *Thoughts on Unfulfilled Prophecy*, which was published anonymously.

(Fifth) Edition
> Reprint of the edited (Fourth) Edition, under the revised title – *Premillennialism Demonstrated to be Truth*.
> (199?)  Irish Christian Mission, Belfast          15cm    19p.    CG

## THE LITERAL TRANSLATION OF 2 THESSALONIANS 3:1-10

This is a short item extracted from Mr Newton's translation of the passage in *Prospects of the Ten Kingdoms*.

> ND [c.1915] Tuckers Publishing Office, London    10cm    1p.    SG

## MAP OF THE TEN KINGDOMS OF THE ROMAN EMPIRE

This map appeared in two almost identical forms. It was bound in a folder 24x15cm. In the version of the map with this title, the boundary of the Roman Empire in Britain was drawn at the wall of Antoninus. This map was reissued in *European Prospects (AD 1863)*. It was also reproduced from Mr Newton's 'plate' in W.L. Holland's *The 'Archbishop' of Canterbury and 'Modern' Christianity* (1898, 225p – EL). In an otherwise identical issue of the map (also dated 1863), bound in some copies of *Occasional Papers on Scriptural Subjects* (1861-1866) the Roman Empire extends to cover the whole of mainland Scotland. See also *A Prophetic Map of the World* (1846), and *Map of the Countries Contained in the Roman Empire in the Time of Trajan*, bound in *Remarks on the Ten Kingdoms of the Roman World with a Map* (1841 – map dated 1840).

> [1900-1914]    Lucas Collins, London          48 x 56.5cm    EL,BIOLA

## MATTHEW 13

Cover title of *Thoughts on the History of Professing Christianity as Given in the Parables of Matthew 13*.

## THE MEAT OFFERING

Part 2 of Vol. I of the First Edition of *Thoughts on Parts of Leviticus*, which was originally published separately in a series.

## THE MILLENNIUM AND ISRAEL'S FUTURE

Cover title of *Expository Teaching on the Millennium and Israel's Future*.

## THE MILLENNIUM AND THE EVERLASTING STATE

This was first published anonymously as an article in *The Quarterly Journal of Prophecy* (Vol. 9, July 1857, pp.263-269). It was a reply to a letter from 'an enquirer' (Vol. 9, p.89) who had asked for a response on the subject of 'the duration of the restored kingdom of Israel and under them of the universal kingdom of Christ on earth'. B.W. Newton's tract considers the use of the word 'everlasting' in Scripture; the nature of the reign of the saints; the circumstances of Israel and Jerusalem in the Millennium; and what follows the Millennium. It does not respond to the letter in a detailed way, but describes the distinctions between the Millennium and the Everlasting State, clearing away some of the difficulties. The article led to a further article by another correspondent; another letter resulting from that; and led to a second article from the second correspondent. See the further comment in Section 4, B.W. Newton's Contributions to Other Publications.

The article that appeared in *The Quarterly Journal of Prophecy* was reprinted (also anonymously), as this tract. The tract was later incorporated into *Expository Teaching on the Millennium and Israel's Future*, published posthumously, but with 'the author's revisions' (CG has the copy with the author's handwritten revisions).

(First Edition)
    1858    Geo Hunt, London    18cm    12p.    BIOLA, CBA

(Second Edition) '…extracted from *The Quarterly Journal of Prophecy*, edited by Horatius Bonar, DD'.
    ND (199?)    Irish Christian Mission, Belfast    15cm    11p.    CG

## MODERN DOCTRINES RESPECTING SINLESSNESS CONSIDERED. EXTRACTED FROM 'THOUGHTS ON SCRIPTURAL SUBJECTS'

This extract has particular reference to two pamphlets by R. Pearsall Smith[1], entitled, *Through Death to Life*, and *Holiness through Faith*… R. Pearsall Smith promoted 'holiness teaching', and was effectively the founder of the Keswick Movement. Later in life he was a leading member of the Psychical Research Society.[2] Mr Newton wrote other works to counter R. Pearsall Smith's influence and teaching - *Remarks on R. Pearsall Smith's Edition of Faber's Hymns…*, *Notes on Some Statements of R. Pearsall Smith*, and *The Seventh Chapter of the Epistle to the Romans, Considered*. See also the item published on the basis of notes of an address, *The Baptism of the Holy Spirit* (NM 4.4) (noted in Section 8, Publications Produced from Notes of Addresses, and Posthumously Published Letters and Manuscripts); CBA 7004, copies in B.W. Newton's hand of letters referring to the works of R. Pearsall Smith (Section 10, Duplicated and Manuscript Items); and the correspondence in 'The Record' noted in this *Guide* (Section 4, B.W. Newton's Contributions to Other Publications).

First Edition
    1873    Houlston & Sons, London    17cm    80p.    BL,Bo,CBA,CU, Sc,T

Second Edition
    1896    Houlston & Sons, London    17cm    89p.    SG

## MOSAIC COSMOGONY

Cover title of *Remarks on 'Mosaic Cosmogony'*…

## MOSES, THE CHILD OF FAITH

This consists of devotional reflections on the life of Moses, applied to the believer's position and walk.

---

[1] Robert Pearsall Smith (1827 - 1899) was a leader in the Holiness Movement in the United States, and the 'Higher Life' movement in Great Britain.
[2] See *Watching and Waiting* March-April, and May-June 1942.

There are close similarities between this book and an anonymous article that appeared in the April 1839 edition of *The Christian Witness* – 'Moses and the Gentile Family'. At times there is close verbal agreement. We have concluded that that article was also by B.W. Newton. See discussion of authorship of in Section 7, Articles in *The Christian Witness*.

The enlarged Third Edition incorporated the First Edition unchanged, as its first chapter.

First Edition
    1851    James Nisbet & Co, London    18cm    16p.    I,SG,SNL

Second Edition
    [Not located]

Third Edition ('reprinted in a somewhat enlarged form' – May 1892).
    1892    Houlston & Sons, London    18cm    64p.    BL,Bo,CBA,CU,Sc,SG

Fourth Edition ('reprint of the Third Edition').
    There were minor changes to this edition – Greek words transliterated and additional references given.
    1928    E.J. Burnett, Worthing    18cm    64p.    SG

A 'new binding from loose sheets' (of the 1892 edition?) was made in 1954 (*Watching and Waiting*, Jan./Feb. 1954, p.14).

## NARRATIVES FROM THE OLD TESTAMENT

This consists of an earlier tract, *The Rechabites*, and five items reprinted from *Occasional Papers on Scriptural Subjects*, Nos. 1, 2 and 4. The introduction, The Old Testament Saints Not Excluded from the Church in Glory (itself a reprint of an earlier tract in modified form) was subsequently published separately.

The items from *Occasional Papers on Scriptural Subjects* were:
1. Abraham's History in Genesis 12.
2. Abraham and Lot. Genesis 13.
3. Jacob's History in Genesis 28.
4. Jacob's History in Genesis 29, etc.
5. On Leviticus 10, the Sin of Nadab and Abihu.

First Edition
    1886    Houlston & Sons, London    18cm    xxxix+128p    BIOLA,BL,Bo,
                                                                                                                CBA,CU,EL,SG,Sc,U

Second Edition (photographic reprint of the First Edition)
    [2015]    SGAT, Chelmsford    18cm    xxxix+128p    SG

## THE NATIONS IN RELATION TO CHRIST AS IN THE SECOND PSALM

This is the title of an SGAT edition of On the Second Psalm. A Reprint from 'Occasional Papers' [No.2].

## NATURAL RELATIONS OF MEN AND GOVERNMENTS TO GOD

Publisher's list title of *On the Natural Relations of Men and Governments to God*.

## THE NEW WORLD ORDER, OR PREMILLENNIAL TRUTH DEMONSTRATED

Edited version of *A Letter to the Minister of Silver Street Chapel, Taunton…*

## 'NO CONDEMNATION TO THEM WHO [sic] ARE IN CHRIST JESUS' (ROMANS 8), A TRACT COMPILED FROM NOTES OF A LECTURE DELIVERED IN DUKE STREET CHAPEL, ST JAMES' PARK, APRIL 6TH 1856

The date of the lecture should be 1855, as appears from a footnote in the text that is added to its reprinting in *Gospel Truths*, where it is said to have been given on Good Friday 1855. The publisher's advertisement of it in the Second Edition of *The Day of the Lord* also corrects the date to 1855, as does Anna Newton's [his mother's] copy in the SGAT Collection.

The exposition was later incorporated into the compilation *Thoughts on Parts of the Epistle to the Romans*, and, in a revised form, into *Gospel Truths*.

First Edition
    1856    Houlston & Stoneman, London    16cm    21p.    BL,Bo,CU,EL,I,SC,SG,T

Second Edition
    1862    Houlston & Wright, London    16cm    21p.    SG

German Edition - *Eine Gegenwärtige Seligkeit in Christo*.
    It has not been possible to check this against the First Edition, which has not been viewed. There are minor variations between this, and the tract as it appeared in *Gospel Truths*.
    1857    Hamburg    16cm    12p.    Landesbibliotek, Oldenburg

## NOTE ON 1 PETER 2:24

This was extracted from *The Quarterly Journal of Prophecy* (October 1859) in an identical form, apart from the omission of an introductory paragraph in the journal. It was later incorporated into *Ancient Truths Respecting the Deity and True Humanity of the Lord Jesus*, together with *Christ, Our Suffering Surety…*

It is a scholarly dissertation on the verse. It quotes Hebrew, Greek, and Latin, and questions the 1611 (Authorised Version) translation. It draws out the theological significance of the verse as correctly translated in relation to the Atonement.

First Edition
    1859    Houlston & Wright. London    17cm    14p.    BL, Bo, Sc, SG

'Second Edition' – When republished with *Ancient Truths...*, and *Christ, Our Suffering Surety...* it is there also referred to as the 'Second Edition'.

    1893    Houlston & Sons, London    17cm    118p.    SG
            and Arthur Andrews, Ryde

## NOTE ON THE LORD'S SUPPER

This is an extract from *Thoughts on Scriptural Subjects*, published separately.

    1907    Lucas Collins, London    ?    5p.    Kings College, London

## NOTES EXPOSITORY OF THE GREEK OF THE FIRST CHAPTER OF ROMANS WITH REMARKS ON THE FORCE OF CERTAIN SYNONYMS, ETC

This was at first intended to be an appendix to *The First and Second Chapters of the Epistle to the Romans, Considered...*, but was excluded as unsuitable for a work intended for general circulation. It was presumably also excluded from *Thoughts on Parts of the Epistle to the Romans* for the same reason. It consists of scholarly, suggestive, comments on the Greek of the chapter.

    1856    Houlston & Stoneman, London    19cm    11+156p.    BL,Bo,CBA,CU,EL,Sc,T,U
            Preface 'May 20 1856, 70 Finchley New Road, London'

The SGAT bound 'Loose papers' of this with paperback covers in 1974 (*Watching and Waiting*, January 1974, p.15). It was then given the cover title *Greek of Romans One*.

## NOTES ON THE GREEK OF ROMANS ONE

Cover title of the original edition of *Notes Expository of the Greek of the First Chapter of Romans with Remarks on the Force of Certain Synonyms, etc.*

## NOTES ON SOME STATEMENTS OF R. PEARSALL SMITH (REPRINTED FROM 'THE RECORD' NOVEMBER 2 1874

This was circulated as a separate item, and was later reprinted in *Lectures on the Epistle to the Romans* (see comment on that work, which was produced from notes of Mr Newton's addresses in Section 8, Publications Produced from Notes of Addresses, and Posthumously Published Letters and Manuscripts). The Evangelical Library, London, has the full correspondence in bound volumes of *The Record*. For other works relating to R. Pearsall Smith see the entry for *Modern Doctrines respecting Sinlessness, Considered*.

See the comments on this and other articles that appeared in *The Record* in Section 6, B.W. Newton's Letters and Articles Published in Periodicals

    ND [1874?]    27.5cm    1p.    CBA

## OBSERVATIONS ON A TRACT ENTITLED 'THE SUFFERINGS OF CHRIST AS SET FORTH IN A LECTURE ON PSALM 6, CONSIDERED'

This tract, dated September 1st 1847, was Mr Newton's second response to J.L Harris and C. McAdam's pamphlet. His first response had been *Remarks on the Sufferings of the Lord Jesus: a Letter addressed to certain Brethren and Sisters in Christ*. He had, in his earlier tract, simply stated his doctrine, but in this one he directly answers J.L. Harris's allegations. In this tract Mr Newton defended the doctrine that he actually held (rather than that attributed to him) and challenged the doctrinal statements of his opponents. He nevertheless wrote graciously and humbly. He wrote in his introduction that he never saw one line of the notes on Psalm 6 before J.L. Harris printed them. He denied the accuracy of many items in the notes, and certainly the construction that his opponents placed upon them. He added, 'That on this, and many other occasions, I may have spoken unguardedly and without sufficient precision of thought and expression, and so have given just reason for the present chastisement, I willingly admit; and I desire to mark the rod, and who has appointed it. At the same time I increasingly feel, after writing the present tract, that the doctrine intended to be conveyed will bear, as a whole, most rigid [i.e. rigorous] examination by the Word of God'.

The pamphlet drew a polemic attack from J.N. Darby in *A Plain Statement of the Doctrine on the Sufferings of Our Blessed Lord* (1847) [J.N. Darby, *Collected Writings,* Doctrinal No.4, Vol. 15), and in a note in the Second Edition of his *Observations on a Tract Entitled, 'Remarks on the Sufferings of the Lord Jesus'*.

CBA 6998 1847, folio 3, listed the 'Copy by Miss Toulmin of notes taken by Miss Kate Gidley at N's address on Psalm 6', which were those used by J.L Harris and C. McAdam to make their attack upon B.W. Newton. This item disappeared from the Fry Collection before it was catalogued at the Christian Brethren Archive. It has still not been located following Ian Deighan's purchase of the library of the late Ulrich Bister. There is likewise an item listed in CBA 6998 as 'original fragment from N's mother re-Lecture on Psalm 6' (1847, folio 10), but this is also missing from the Fry Collection and, so far as can be ascertained, has not been recovered. See the note of a letter from George Treffry to Amy J.T. Toulmin, dated 11th June 1847 in Section 9 of this *Guide*, B.W. Newton's Correspondence.

Mr Newton later withdrew his two tracts 'for reconsideration', in *A Statement and Acknowledgement Respecting Certain Doctrinal Errors* (1847). He nevertheless held that it was the doctrine that could be inferred from the tracts that was the danger, not what he had himself intended to convey. The reasons for his withdrawal of the tracts are given in *Christ, Our Suffering Surety...*, pp.64, 65.

After leaving Plymouth, he included quotations from this tract in his *A Letter on Subjects Connected with the Lord's Humanity* (1848). Neither the *Observations...* nor the *Remarks...* were reissued by Mr Newton, but John Cox, jun. published *Extracts from Two Tracts, Entitled 'Remarks On The Sufferings Of The Lord Jesus' and 'Observations On A Tract Entitled "The Sufferings Of Christ As Set Forth In A Lecture On Psalm 6, Considered"', and Quotations from Other Papers* in 1867 as a 'private and confidential' pamphlet, in which he demonstrated that what Mr Newton taught was not in error.

| | | | | |
|---|---|---|---|---|
| 1847 | J.K. Campbell, 1 Warwick Square London and Tract Depot, Plymouth | 18cm | 89p. | SG |

## OCCASIONAL PAPERS ON SCRIPTURAL SUBJECTS

These four volumes contain a variety of material. Most of this was incorporated in later publications or appeared separately, although there are several notable exceptions.

There was a hiatus between the third and fourth numbers. A bound issue of *Occasional Papers, Nos. 1, 2, and 3* was published in 1863 as 'Volume 1'. Probably a continuation of annual publication was intended, but not fulfilled. The correspondence record indicates that 1863 and 1864 was a time of personal ill health for B.W. Newton. *Occasional Papers on Scriptural Subjects No.4* is advertised as 'Volume 2' on a publisher's list.

Prior to his death, Mr Newton began preparing the *Occasional Papers on Scriptural Subjects* for republication, but only completed the first volume (see the 'Advertisement' in *Thoughts on Parts of the Song of Solomon*, and the prefatory note in *Expository Teaching on the Millennium and Israel's Future*), and part of the second. C.W.H. Griffiths has the volume containing Mr Newton's manuscript corrections. In the summary of contents of each item, we have noted where changes are indicated, and if they were published in a revised form.

Papers from *Occasional Papers on Scriptural Subjects* appear in or as the following works:
1. *Atonement and Its Results.*
2. *Christ's Second Coming. It Will Be Pre-millennial.*
3. *Duty of Giving Heed to the Predictions of Scripture Respecting Events That Are to Precede the Return of the Lord.*
4. *European Prospects (AD 1863).*
5. *Expository Teaching on the Millennium and Israel's Future*
6. *Israel in the Days of Haggai and Zechariah; with a Note upon the Prophecy of Haggai.*
7. *Jesus Washing His Disciples' Feet.*
8. *The Judgment of the Court of Arches*
9. *Narratives from the Old Testament.*
10. *The Old Testament Saints Not Excluded from the Church in Glory.*
11. *On Justification through the Blood and Righteousness of a Substitute.*
12. *On Sanctification by the Blood of Jesus.*
13. *On the Second Psalm.*
14. *On the Spread of Neology in England.*
15. *The Prophecy of the Lord Jesus in Matthew 24 and 25, Considered.*
16. *Remarks on 'Mosaic Cosmogony'…*
17. *Remarks on the Revised English Version of the Greek New Testament.*
18. *Salvation by Substitution.*
19. *The Second Advent of Our Lord Not Secret, but in Manifested Glory.*
20. *Thoughts on Parts of the Song of Solomon.*

## OCCASIONAL PAPERS ON SCRIPTURAL SUBJECTS No.1 (117 pages)

1. On Justification Through the Blood and Righteousness of a Substitute (12 pages).
   Reprinted separately, and also published in a revised form in A*tonement and Its Results*.

2. On the Song of Solomon, Chapter 1 from Verses 5 to 11 Inclusive (11 pages).
   Included in a revised form in *Thoughts on Parts of the Song of Solomon*. CG has Mr Newton's amended copy used for the reprint.

3. On Ephesians 3:15 (3 pages).
   Included in *Remarks on the Revised English Version of the Greek New Testament*, and in *The Whole Family*. Mr Newton revised this, but it has not been published in its revised form. CG has Mr Newton's amended copy.

4. On the Omission of the Greek Article before Definite Words with Especial Reference to Ephesians 3:15 (11 pages).
   Included in revised form in the first chapter of *Remarks on the Revised English Version of the Greek New Testament*. Mr Newton made later revisions to this, but it has not been published in that revised form. CG has Mr Newton's amended copy.

5. On the Duty of Giving Heed to the Predictions of Scripture Respecting Events That Are to Intervene between the Departure and Return of the Lord (17 pages).
   A footnote to the contents of *Occasional Papers on Scriptural Subjects No.1* says 'this paper is in part a reprint and may be obtained separately'. This was one of the *Five Letters on Events Predicted as Antecedent to the Coming of the Lord*. This item was later reprinted under the title *On the Duty of Giving Heed to the Predictions of Scripture Respecting Events That Are to Precede the Return of Our Lord*.

6. On Isaiah 18 (3 pages).
   This was reprinted posthumously in *Expository Teaching on the Millennium and Israel's Future* with the author's revisions.

7. Notes on Isaiah 18 (11 pages).
   This was reprinted posthumously in *Expository Thoughts on the Millennium and Israel's Future* with the author's revisions.

8. Examination of a Work Entitled 'Christ's Second Coming, Will It Be Premillennial?' by Rev. David Brown, DD (11 pages). Part 1.
   This was reprinted with other parts of the series on David Brown's book in *Christ's Second Coming, It will be Pre-Millennial.*[1]

9. Note on the Words Λογιζομαι, to Impute, Rom. 4:6: Ελλογεω, to Enter in Account, Rom. 5:13, Λογιζομαι ΕΙΣ, to Impute FOR, Rom. 4:5 (5 pages).

---

[1] David Brown, DD, Principal of the Free Church College Aberdeen. His book ran through seven editions in his lifetime (1803-1897). David Brown first issued his book in parts. He substantially enlarged the second edition (1849). The 6th edition had 468 pages. See the letter from David Brown to B.W. Newton dated 29th June 1861.

Chapter 10 of *Remarks on the Revised English Version of the Greek New Testament* recasts these comments. Mr Newton made later revisions to this article, but it has not been published in revised form. CG has B.W. Newton's amended copy. See also the letter of Mr Newton 20th April 1858.

10. *Falsification of the Meaning of 'Justify' at the Council of Trent* (9 pages).
    Mr Newton amended one sentence of this, but it has not been published in revised form. CG has Mr Newton's amended copy. A similar theme, although not in identical words, is followed in *Doctrines of Popery as Established by the Council of Trent. No.2; on Original Sin*.

11. Notes on 2 Peter 1 (17 pages).
    This is a verse by verse exposition from the Greek. Not republished.

## OCCASIONAL PAPERS ON SCRIPTURAL SUBJECTS No.2 (173 pages)

1. On Sanctification by the Blood of Jesus (11 pages).
   Reprinted separately, and also included, in a revised form, in *Atonement and Its Results*.

2. On Sanctification through the Spirit (9 pages).
   Included, in a revised form, in *Atonement and Its Results*.

3. On the Song of Solomon from Chapter 2, Verse 8 to Verse 17 Inclusive (11 pages).
   Reprinted posthumously in *Thoughts on Parts of the Song of Solomon* with the author's revisions. CG has Mr Newton's amended copy.

4. Abraham and Lot, Genesis 13 (13 pages).
   Included in *Narratives from the Old Testament*.

5. The Second Advent of Our Lord Not Secret but in Manifested Glory (14 pages).
   This was one of the *Five Letters on Events Predicted as Antecedent to the Coming of the Lord*, and was also published separately.

6. Examination of a Work Entitled 'Christ's Second Coming, Will It Be Premillennial?' by Rev. David Brown, D.D. (17 pages). Part 2.
   Reprinted in *Christ's Second Coming: It will be Pre-Millennial*[1] with the other parts of this series from *Occasional Papers on Scriptural Subjects Nos.1-3*.

7. Israel in the Days of Haggai and Zechariah (13 pages).
   Reprinted with Mr Newton's amendments with the following article (*Note on the Prophecy of Haggai*), and a lecture upon Zechariah 3, under the omnibus title, *Israel in the Days of Haggai And Zechariah; with A Note Upon The Prophecy Of Haggai, Both Reprinted From 'Occasional Papers On Scriptural Subjects', Also A Lecture upon Zechariah 3*. Minor corrections were made. CG does not have Mr Newton's amended copy.

---

[1] See comment on this in *Occasional Papers on Scriptural Subjects, No.1* in Section 3, B.W. Newton's Published Works.

8. Note on the Prophecy of Haggai (7 pages).
Reprinted with Mr Newton's amendments, together with the preceding article (*Israel in the Days of Haggai and Zechariah*), and a lecture upon Zechariah 3, under the omnibus title, *Israel in the Days of Haggai And Zechariah; with A Note Upon The Prophecy Of Haggai, Both Reprinted From 'Occasional Papers On Scriptural Subjects', Also A Lecture upon Zechariah 3*. CG has Mr Newton's amended copy. Minor corrections were made.

9. On the Force of the Present Tense in Greek and Hebrew (7 pages).
Expanded in *Remarks on the Revised English Version of the Greek New Testament*, chapter 7. Mr Newton made minor changes to this, but it has not been published in revised form. CG has Mr Newton's amended copy.

10. On 1 Corinthians, Chapter 1 (22 pages).
A verse by verse exposition. Not repeated elsewhere. S.P. Tregelles refers to this in a letter to Mr Newton dated 16th January 1864, which is in the Christian Brethren Archive (CBA 7181(60). Mr Newton made minor corrections to this, but it has not been published in revised form. CG has Mr Newton's amended copy.
Quotations are included in the anthology *B.W. Newton on Ministry and Order in the Church of Christ*.

11. Notes on Zechariah 14 (19 pages).
Reprinted posthumously in *Expository Thoughts on the Millennium and Israel's Future* with the author's revisions.

12. On the First Psalm (5 pages).
Reprinted posthumously in *Expository Thoughts on the Millennium and Israel's Future* with the author's revisions.

13. Notes on Psalm 1 (4 pages).
Reprinted posthumously in *Expository Thoughts on the Millennium and Israel's Future* with the author's revisions.

14. On the Second Psalm (7 pages).
Reprinted posthumously in *Expository Thoughts on the Millennium and Israel's Future* with the author's revisions. It was also reprinted separately

15. Notes on Psalm 2 (14 pages).
Reprinted posthumously in *Expository Thoughts on the Millennium and Israel's Future* with the author's revisions. CG has Mr Newton's amended copy. It was not included in the separate publication of the preceding item (On the Second Psalm).

## OCCASIONAL PAPERS ON SCRIPTURAL SUBJECTS No.3 (200 pages)

1. Jesus Washing His Disciples' Feet (12 pages).
Reprinted in *Atonement and Its Results,* subject to the author's revisions, and republished from that separately.

2. Jacob's History in Genesis 28 (11 pages).
   Reprinted in *Narratives from the Old Testament*.

3. On the Song of Solomon from Verse 7 to 16 of Chapter 4 (15 pages).
   Reprinted in *Thoughts on Parts of the Song of Solomon* with the author's revisions.

4. Examination of a Work Entitled 'Christ's Second Coming, Will It Be Premillennial?' by Rev. David Brown, D.D. (19 pages). Part 3.
   Reprinted in *Christ's Second Coming: It Will Be Pre-Millennial*[1], together with the other parts of this series in *Occasional Papers on Scriptural Subjects*, Nos. 1-3.

5. Note on Dr Brown's Interpretation of 2 Thessalonians 2:8 (6 pages).
   Reprinted in *Christ's Second Coming: It will be Pre-Millennial.*[2]

6. Note on Matthew 24:34 (7 pages).
   This was reproduced from an earlier work - *Lecture on the Prophecy of the Lord Jesus, as Contained in Matthew 24, 25* where it was a section entitled, On the Words 'This Generation'. It was also included in the subsequent (but significantly different) publication, *The Prophecy of the Lord Jesus as Contained in Matthew 24 and 25, Considered*. It was also published separately as *On the Words 'This Generation'*.

7. Remarks on 'Mosaic Cosmogony', being the fifth of the *Essays and Reviews* (38 pages).
   Reprinted separately with revisions, with the same title, but including the following item (Note on the Locality of Hades), and 'supplementary remarks'.

8. Note on the Locality of Hades (9 pages).
   Reprinted separately with revisions with the preceding item (Remarks on 'Mosaic Cosmogony'...), and 'supplementary remarks'.

9. European Prospects (29 pages).
   Reprinted posthumously, separately and without amendment, as *European Prospects. (AD 1863)*.

10. Note on the Spread of Neology in England (13 pages).
    This was published 'to be read in connexion with the preceding paper' (European Prospects). It was published separately, and included in the compilation *Doctrines of Popery*.

11. Uses of $Ευλογεω$ in the New Testament, Especially with Reference to 1 Corinthians 10:16 (7 pages).
    Not reprinted.

12. Notes on the Greek of Ephesians 1 from Verses 1 to 11 Inclusive (34 pages).
    These notes were not reprinted, apart from the comments on $υιοθεσια$ (Eph. 1:5), which were included in in *The Old Testament Saints Not Excluded from the Church in Glory*, with

---

[1] See comment on this in the item in *Occasional Papers on Scriptural Subjects, No.1*.
[2] See item 5 of *Occasional Papers on Scriptural Subjects, No.3*, and the note on the item in *Occasional Papers on Scriptural Subjects, No.1*.

slight amendments at the beginning and end. S.P. Tregelles commented on the Greek text of Ephesians 1:6 in a letter to Mr Newton dated 9th December 1863, which is in the Christian Brethren Archive (CBA 7181(59)) (see Section 9, B.W. Newton's Correspondence). Mr Newton completed his notes on Ephesians 1 in *Occasional Papers on Scriptural Subjects, No.4* .

## OCCASIONAL PAPERS ON SCRIPTURAL SUBJECTS No.4 (262 pages)

1. Thoughts on Practical Sanctification (17 pages).
   Reprinted with revisions in *Atonement and Its Results*.

2. Jacob's History in Genesis 29, etc. (12 pages).
   Reprinted in *Narratives from the Old Testament*.

3. On the Song of Solomon from Chapter 5:2 to Chapter 6:3 (9 pages).
   Reprinted posthumously with other items from this series in *Occasional Papers on Scriptural Subjects* and with the author's revisions, as *Thoughts on Parts of the Song of Solomon*.

4. On the Song of Solomon from Chapter 6:20, to end (11 pages).
   Reprinted posthumously with other items from this series in *Occasional Papers on Scriptural Subjects* and with the author's revisions, as *Thoughts on Parts of the Song of Solomon*.

5. On Leviticus 10 – The Sin of Nadab and Abihu (15 pages).
   Reprinted in *Narratives from the Old Testament*.

6. The Judgment of the Court of Arches and of the Judicial Committee of the Privy Council, in the Case of the Rev. Rowland Williams, D.D., One of the Writers in the *Essays and Reviews*, Considered [84 pages].
   
   Introduction (6 pages).
   Section I. Remarks on Dr Lushington's Judgement (20 pages).
   Section II. On the Judgement Pronounced by the Judicial Committee of the Privy Council (20 pages).
   Appendix A. Note on Mr Wilson's Rejection of the Doctrine of Eternal Punishment (6 pages).
   Appendix B. Doctrine of the English Reformers on Baptism (7 pages).
   Appendix C. Dr Pusey and his *Eirenicon* (22 pages) – See *Babylon and Egypt*, Third Edition 'Postscript', p.577 in connection with this.
   Appendix D. The Future of Israel Denied by Modern Maintainers of Catholicity (3 pages).
   
   This item was also printed as a separate tract. See separate listing for further information.

7. Salvation by Substitution [46 pages].
   It included the following appendices:

Appendix I. Dr Steane on Imputed Righteousness[1] (7 pages).
Appendix II. Clarkson on Imputation (5 pages).
Appendix III. Extracts from the Bishop of Ossory on Justification (4 pages).
Appendix IV. Note on the Doctrines of Mr Irving[2] (8 pages).
This item was also printed separately.

8. Notes on the Greek of Ephesians 1 verse 12 to end (21 pages).
This continued from the notes on the earlier part of the chapter, which were published in *Occasional Papers on Scriptural Subjects, No.3* (see note). They were not reprinted.

9. Notes on Psalm 68 (19 pages).
This was reprinted posthumously in *Expository Teaching on the Millennium and Israel's Future*, with the author's amendments.

10. Notes on Psalm 84 (17 pages)
This was reprinted posthumously in *Expository Teaching on the Millennium and Israel's Future*, with the author's amendments.

11. Postscript – Note on 'Ecce Homo' (10 pages).
This is a 'postscript' to Mr Newton's comments on the *Judgments of the Court of Arches...* published in *Occasional Papers on Scriptural Subjects, No.4*. It relates to *Ecce Homo: A Survey of the Life and Work of Jesus Christ* by Sir John Robert Seeley (1834-1895). This was a neologian production on the humanity of Christ, originally published anonymously, but later acknowledged. Mr Newton saw it as undermining many of the fundamental doctrines of Christianity. This postscript was not republished, but John Cox, jun. quoted from it at length with other material on Sir John R Seeley's publication in *Old Truths*, 1868, pp.36-41.

12. 'The following extract is from an excellent speech of Lord Shaftesbury at the Annual General Meeting of the Church Pastoral Aid Society in 1866 (2 pages).
This is included at the end of *Occasional Papers on Scriptural Subjects, No.4* (in some copies?) on unnumbered pages, following on from the 'Postscript' on *Ecce Homo*. Shaftesbury refers to *Ecce Homo* as 'that most pestilential book ever vomited, I think, from the jaws of hell'.

13. Map (55x47cm).
The map appears at the end of bound volumes of *Occasional Papers on Scriptural Subjects*. It is not clear if it relates directly to *Occasional Papers on Scriptural Subjects, No.4* or is an addition to the entire set.
'The coloured part of this map is intended to suggest the probable territorial arrangements that will be found in the Roman Empire when finally divided into Ten Federal Kingdoms'.

---

[1] Commending Dr Edward Steane's book, *Imputed Righteousness*. But note the 'interruption of his friendship' with Dr Steane as a result of Steane associating with Dr Stanley. See correspondence 8th March 1873 onwards and item 76 in CBA 7049.
[2] See further comments on B.W. Newton's response to Irvingism in the notes on *Doctrines of the Church in Newman Street*.

This map was reprinted in almost identical form as *Map of the Ten Kingdoms of the Roman Empire*. The map bound with *Occasional Papers on Scriptural Subjects* included the whole of mainland Scotland within the Roman boundary, which subsequent maps did not.

*Occasional Papers on Scriptural Subjects, No.1.*
    1861    Houlston & Wright, London    24cm    117p.    BL,Bo,BIOLA,CBA,CU, EL,Sc,SG,U

*Occasional Papers on Scriptural Subjects, No.2.*
    1862    Houlston & Wright, London    24cm    173 p.    BL,Bo,BIOLA,CBA,CU,EL,U?

*Occasional Papers on Scriptural Subjects, No.3.*
    1863    Houlston & Wright, London    24cm    200p.    BL,Bo,BIOLA,CBA,CU,EL,U?

*Occasional Papers on Scriptural Subjects, No.4.*
    1866    Houlston & Wright, London    24cm    264p.    BL,Bo,BIOLA,CBA,CU,EL,U?

## THE OLD TESTAMENT SAINTS

This was reprinted, without amendment, from *The Quarterly Journal of Prophecy* (Vol. 9, April 1857) where it appeared anonymously with interesting footnotes by the editor (Horatius Bonar). Two letters from William Trotter[1] followed its publication (July 1857 and October 1857), accompanied by many strictures on those by the editor of the Journal.

Two sections of *Thoughts on Parts of the Prophecy of Isaiah* – 'The True Unity of the Church of God in Time and Eternity' and, 'Note on the Unity of the Redeemed' - deal with the same theme in different ways.[2]

The article was later incorporated in a modified form in The Old Testament Saints Not to Be Excluded from the Church in Glory – the opening chapter of *Narratives from the Old Testament*. It was reprinted from this as *The Old Testament Saints Not to Be Excluded from the Church in Glory: with Some Remarks on the Heresy of Marcion*.

Printed separately, it has the editor's (H. Bonar's) footnotes.

[First? Edition] ('Reprinted from the *Quarterly Journal of Prophecy*').
    ND [1857?]   Burns and Co, Printers, Paddington    17cm    12p.    SG

[Second? Edition] ('Reprinted from the *Quarterly Journal of Prophecy*').
    ND [1858-61?]   Varty, printer, Bishopsgate (London)    17cm    14p.    CG

---

[1] William Trotter (1818-1865). An associate of J.N. Darby, and author of *The Origin of so-called Open-Brethrenism, The Whole Case of Plymouth and Bethesda*. See note on B.W. Newton's *Reply to a tract of Mr Trotter entitled 'What are Mr Newton's present doctrines as to the human nature, and relationships, of the Lord Jesus Christ?'* in this section of the Guide.

[2] T.C.F. Stunt, *The Life and Times of Samuel Prideaux Tregelles*, p43n, notes this subject as a key issue in the controversy between B.W. Newton and the Darbyites, and that S.P. Tregelles was of one mind with B.W. Newton, publishing a pamphlet *Eternal Life and those who receive it* in September 1845.

## THE OLD TESTAMENT SAINTS NOT EXCLUDED FROM THE CHURCH OF GOD

Title of the Second Edition of *The Old Testament Saints*.

## THE OLD TESTAMENT SAINTS NOT EXCLUDED FROM THE CHURCH IN GLORY, WITH SOME REMARKS ON THE HERESY OF MARCION

This consists of Prefatory Remarks; the first chapter of *Narratives from the Old Testament* (itself a modified version of an earlier tract, *The Old Testament Saints*, which see); a chapter from *Thoughts on Parts of the Prophecy of Isaiah* (Note on Marcionism); and *The Condition of Sons, Remarks on the Right Translation of υιοθεσια, in Ephesians 1:5*, taken from *Occasional Papers on Scriptural Subjects No.3*, with minor amendments at the beginning and end. A short 'Note on Hebrews 11:40' is added before the appendix.

First Edition
    1887    Houlston & Sons, London    18cm    68p.    BL,Bo,CBA,CU, EL,Sc,U

Second Edition (reprint of the First Edition)
    1999    SGAT, Chelmsford    18cm    68p.    SG

Canadian Editions

    First Edition - *The Old Testament Saints Not Excluded from the Church of God* (as No.25 of 'Ministry for Heart and Conscience). A publisher's preface (12 pages) is added, together with pages 24-47 of *Expository teaching on the Millennium and Israel's Future*, reprographically reproduced from the original items.
    ND [1995]    Ministry for the Difficult Last Days, Vancouver    19cm    73p.    CG

    Second Edition - Titled *That He Might Gather Together into One All Things in Christ; Even in Him.*
    [1998?]    Ministry for the Difficult Last Days, Vancouver    19cm    73p.    ?

## THE ONE ALL SUFFICIENT OFFERING

This is a compilation of extracts from *Thoughts on Parts of Leviticus* (e.g. on Leviticus 2:11). It was reprinted from *Watching and Waiting*, Sept. /Oct. 1953 pp.352 ff.

    [1953]    SGAT, London    16.5cm    7p.    CG

## ON JUSTIFICATION THROUGH THE BLOOD AND RIGHTEOUSNESS OF A SUBSTITUTE

This was extracted from *Occasional Papers on Scriptural Subjects No.1* (1861). It was later revised, and included in *Atonement and Its Results* (1882).

First Edition
    1862    Houlston & Wright, London    17cm    ?    Bo,CU,Sc,T

Second Edition
>    1866    Houlston & Wright, London         17cm    22p.    CBA

## ON LUKE 21

This is introduced as follows: 'The following pages contain the substance of a lecture by B.W. Newton at Crediton, on part of the 21st of Luke; the notes have been added by James G. Deck. Luke 21 from verse 8 to the end of the chapter'.

This tract drew a reply, probably from J.N. Darby, entitled *Examination of a Tract 'On Luke 21, the Substance of a Lecture by B.W. Newton, the Notes by J.G. Deck'* 1843, 1 Warwick Square ([ND] Groombridge and Sons, London 17cm, 12p, CBA (5618(37)).

This exposition is of particular interest as it shows J.G. Deck, the Brethren hymn writer, standing with B.W. Newton on prophetic matters immediately before the start of the open controversy with J.N. Darby. In the controversy, J.G. Deck threw in his lot with J.N. Darby, and was evidently embarrassed that Mr Newton later quoted his hymn in his defence (see *A Letter to a Friend Concerning a Tract Recently Published at Cork*).

*On Luke 21* was included in the compilation *Lectures on Prophecy*.
One of the chapters of *Aids to Prophetic Enquiry* (First Series) is an exposition of Luke 21, but the two are not verbally similar.

See the letter from B.W. Newton to J.N. Darby [ND, but c.1843] regarding the End of the Age and 'the Tares', which may refer to this tract and *Prophecy of the Lord Jesus as contained in Matthew 24, Briefly Considered*.

>    1843    C & S [Clulow and Soltau]         16cm    11p.    I, SG
>            and Campbell, 1, Warwick Square

## ON SANCTIFICATION BY THE BLOOD OF JESUS

This was printed separately in the same year that it appeared in *Occasional Thoughts on Scriptural Subjects* No.2. It was later incorporated, in a revised form, into *Atonement and Its Results* (1882).

>    1862    Houlston & Wright, London         16cm    21p.    BL,Bo,CU,Sc

## ON THE CLEANSING OF THE LEPER

Title of an edition of *Cleansing the Leper*.

## ON THE DUTY OF GIVING HEED TO THE PREDICTIONS OF SCRIPTURE RESPECTING EVENTS THAT ARE TO PRECEDE THE RETURN OF OUR LORD

See *Duty of Giving Heed to the Predictions of Scripture…*

## ON THE EXERCISE OF WORLDLY AUTHORITY

This first appeared in *The Christian Witness*, Vol. 4, July 1837. The subsequent tract is identical to the article. The title in *The Christian Witness* describes the content more clearly – Is the Exercise of Worldly Authority Consistent with Discipleship? See discussion of authorship in Section 7, Articles in *The Christian Witness*. Editions were not numbered.

See *On the Natural Relations of men and Governments to God* on a related theme.

First [??] Edition
    [ND]    John Wertheimer, London    16cm    16p.    SG

Second [??] Edition
    c.1850 – When republication was announced in *Perilous Times*, March 1901, it was said to have been 'out of print for about 50 years'. No copies located.

Third [??] Edition
    1901    Lucas Collins, London    16cm    16p.    BIOLA?,Bo,CBA,EL

Fourth [??] Edition
    [ND 1925??]    Robert Stockwell, printer, Borough, SE [London]    16cm    16p.    CBA, EL

## ON THE NATURAL RELATIONS OF MEN AND GOVERNMENTS TO GOD, EXTRACTED FROM THE THIRD SERIES OF 'AIDS TO PROPHETIC ENQUIRY'

In this tract, Mr Newton warned believers against taking a position of worldly authority in which they cannot act solely in obedience to the Bible. See the similar theme in *On the Exercise of Worldly Authority*. The Third Series of 'Aids to Prophetic Enquiry' was later known as *Prospects of the Ten Kingdoms*.

First Edition
    1850    James Nisbet & Co    17cm    16p.    Bo, BL,CU,Sc,SG

Second Edition
    1873    Houlston & Sons, London    17.5cm    20p.    CBA,SG

## ON THE PROPHECIES RESPECTING THE JEWS AND JERUSALEM, IN THE FORM OF A CATECHISM

This tract, in question and answer format, is chiefly concerned with the future of Jerusalem before and during the Millennium.

[First Edition]
    [ND]    Plymouth Tract Depot    17.5cm    12p.    CBA

Second Edition
    1855    Partridge, Oakey & Co, Oxford    17.5cm    22p.    SG,SNL

Third Edition
    1866    Houlston & Wright, London    16cm    28p.    BIOLA, CBA

Fourth Edition – *Prophecies Respecting the Jews and Jerusalem Considered. In the Form of a Catechism.*
    'Identical with the Third Edition'.
        1888    Houlston & Sons, London        17.5cm  31p.     BIOLA,CBA,EL,SG

[Fifth?] Edition 'A new edition', *Watching and Waiting*, October/December 1949, p.294
        1949    No copies located

[Sixth?] Edition
    *Prophecies concerning the Jews and Jerusalem in the form of Questions. and Answers*
        [1993]    Irish Christian Mission, Belfast        21cm  31p.     CG

[Seventh?] Edition *Prophecies respecting the Jews and Jerusalem Considered. In the Form of a Catechism.*
        [2002]    SGAT, Chelmsford        21cm  14p.     SG

French Edition. *Petit Catéchisme, ou Demandes et Réponses sur les Prophéties Concernant les Juifs et Jérusalem.*
        1856    A Petit-Pierre, Paris    16cm    36p.    French National Library, Paris

## ON THE SECOND PSALM. A REPRINT FROM 'OCCASIONAL PAPERS'

This was extracted from *Occasional Papers on Scriptural Subjects No.2*. The exposition also appeared in *Expository Teaching on the Millennium and Israel's Future*. On the Second Psalm did not include the article 'Notes on Psalm 2', which followed in *Occasional Papers*.

First [?] Edition
        1900    Lucas Collins, London        12.5cm  16p.     BL, CBA

Second [?] Edition
    *The Nations in Relation to Christ as in the Second Psalm.*
    This edition was unedited, apart from the introduction of sub-headings, and the removal of Hebrew words. It was a reprint of the article as it appeared in *Watching and Waiting* May/June 1952.
        [1952]    SGAT, London        16.5cm  12p.     BIOLA,CBA,U

Second [?] Edition
    *The Nations in relation to Christ as in the Second Psalm.*
    This was a reprint of the Second [?] Edition
        [1999]    SGAT, London        21cm  6p.     SG

## ON THE SPREAD OF NEOLOGY IN ENGLAND, EXTRACTED FROM THE THIRD NUMBER OF 'OCCASIONAL PAPERS'

In this tract, Mr Newton made observations on the modernism of his day, with particular reference to Dr Stanley[1]; Bishop Colenso[2]; and developments at Oxford. He made some characteristic

---
[1] Arthur Penrhyn Stanley (1815-1881), Dean of Westminster.
[2] John William Colenso (1818-1843), Bishop of Natal, whose heterodoxy was a catalyst for the first Lambeth Conference (1867). T.C.F. Stunt, *Life and Times of Samuel Prideaux Tregelles* notes that Colenso had been a pupil of S.P. Tregelles's friend Henry Addington Graves, vicar of Charles Church, Plymouth.

comments on the responsibilities of Governments. It was extracted from *Occasional Papers on Scriptural Subjects No.3* (1863). It was also included in an 1865 binding of the compilation *Doctrines of Popery*.

    1865    Houlston & Wright, London    17.5cm  24p.    BL,Bo,CU,Sc,T

### ON THE WORDS 'THIS GENERATION'

This was extracted from the Second Edition of *The Prophecy of the Lord Jesus as Contained in Matthew 24, 25, Considered* (the Second Edition was titled *Lecture on the Prophecy of the Lord Jesus as contained in Matthew 24,25*). This item also appeared in *Occasional Papers on Scriptural Subjects No.3* under the heading 'Note on Matthew 24:34'.

    [ND]    Hunt and Elliott. London    18cm  12p.    SG

### THE ONE ALL SUFFICIENT OFFERING

This consists of edited extracts from *Thoughts on Parts of Leviticus*. It was reprinted from *Watching and Waiting* September/October 1953 p.352.

    [1953]    SGAT, London    16cm  8p.    CG

### ORDER OF EVENTS CONNECTED WITH THE APPEARING OF CHRIST AND HIS MILLENNIAL REIGN. EXTRACTED FROM THE THIRD SERIES OF 'AIDS TO PROPHETIC ENQUIRY'

*The Third Series of 'Aids to Prophetic Enquiry'* came to be known as *Prospects of the Ten Kingdoms*, and hence the title of the Third Edition of this item was changed to *...Extracted from 'Prospects of the Ten Kingdoms'*. The work is an epitome of the sequence of future events. It is concerned with the return of the Lord; conditions in the Millennium; and the New Heavens and New Earth.

First Edition
    1850    J. Nisbet, London    17.5cm  38p.    CBA

Second Edition, Revised
    1874    Houlston & Sons, London    17.5cm  55p.    CBA

Third Edition
    1911    Lucas Collins, London    17?cm  56p.    BIOLA,EL,SG

### OUR ALTAR, HEBREWS 13:10

This is No.1 of *Tracts on Doctrinal Subjects*. It deals with the objective sacrifice, and work of satisfaction, on the cross. He states emphatically that the Cross is our altar, and that the work of atonement was completed on the Cross, in opposition to contrary statements. It also develops from this to consider the position of believers gathering 'outside the gate' of ecclesiasticism.

This item is not to be confused with A Note on Hebrews 13:10, which is a section of *Thoughts on Scriptural Subjects*.

    1877    Houlston & Sons, London    17cm  20p.    BL,Bo,CBA,CU,EL,SC

## OUR GOVERNMENTAL ACKNOWLEDGEMENT OF GOD, FIVE PAPERS ON THE MORAL AND RELIGIOUS QUALIFICATIONS OF LEGISLATORS IN THE PARLIAMENT OF GREAT BRITAIN

This is the title page title of *The Acknowledgement of God by Earthly Governments*.

## PA FODD Y MAE Y GWAED YN CADW?

Welsh Edition of *How does the Blood Save?*

## PARABLES OF MATTHEW 13

Publisher's list title of *Thoughts on the History of Professing Christianity in the Parables of Matthew 13*.

## THE PEACE SACRIFICE

Part 3 of Vol. 1 of the serialised First Edition of *Thoughts on Parts of Leviticus*. As with the other parts, it was circulated separately.

## PENSÉES SUR L'APOCALYPSE

French Edition of *Thoughts on the Apocalypse*.

## THE PERFECT SACRIFICE

American Edition of *Thoughts on Parts of Leviticus*.

## THE PERSONAL RETURN OF THE LORD JESUS CHRIST NECESSARY TO THE INTRODUCTION OF MILLENNIAL BLESSING

This tract was produced from notes taken at the Mechanics Institute, Plymouth on November 4th 1841. It provides an answer to post-millennialists who argue that the preaching of the Gospel is the instrumentality that will be used to introduce millennial blessing.

It was included in the compilation, *Lectures on Prophecy*. It was also reprinted in *Christ's Second Coming; it will be Premillennial*, with minor alterations.

First (?) Edition
    1841    Rowe, London                        12.5cm  18p.    ? (seen)

Second (?) Edition
    1841    Hamilton Adams & Co, London    12.5cm  18p.    CBA, SG

Third (?)Edition as part of *Lectures on Prophecy* with *First Lecture…* added to the title.
    1842    John Wertheimer, London        17.5cm  18p.    CBA

## PETIT CATÉCHISME, OU DEMANDES ET RÉPONSES SUR LES PROPHÉTIES CONCERNANT LES JUIFS ET JÉRUSALEM

French Edition of *On the Prophecies Respecting the Jews and Jerusalem in the Form of a Catechism*.

## 'PLAIN PAPERS' ON GOSPEL THEMES

Henry Varley's obituary of Mr Newton in *The Christian*, 20th July 1899 lists this as one of Mr Newton's works. No work is known by this title, and, as there are (other) errors in the obituary, it may be assumed that another work is meant, possibly *Occasional Papers on Scriptural Subjects*. *Plain Papers on Prophetic and other Subjects* (1855) was an anonymous Brethren publication advocating an any-moment, pre-tribulation rapture, and is therefore plainly not by Mr Newton. That item was condemned in a footnote by Horatius Bonar to the *Quarterly Journal of Prophecy* publication of *The Old Testament Saints not excluded from the Church in Glory*.

## PREDICTED EVENTS. A LETTER TO A FRIEND IN REPLY TO THE ENQUIRY, 'IS IT WRONG TO EXPECT CERTAIN PREDICTED EVENTS PREVIOUS TO THE RETURN OF THE LORD JESUS?'

This is one of the *Five Letters on Events Predicted as Antecedent to the Coming of the Lord*. See details under the *Five Letters*, and the alternative title, *Is It Wrong to Expect Certain Predicted Events Previous to the Return of the Lord Jesus? A Letter to a Friend*.

## PREMILLENNIAL TRUTH DEMONSTRATED

Publisher's list title of *The New World Order, or Premillennial Truth Demonstrated*, which was an edited version of *A Letter to the Minister of Silver Street Chapel, Taunton*.

## PREMILLENNIALISM DEMONSTRATED TO BE TRUTH

The title of the Irish Christian Mission (ICM) edition of *The New World Order, or Premillennial Truth Demonstrated*, which is an edited version of *A Letter to the Minister of Silver Street Chapel, Taunton*.

## PRIESTHOOD AND SACRIFICE ESSENTIAL TO WORSHIP

This is No.2,087-88 of 'The Penny Pulpit'. Its full title is *Leicester Lectures on Great Protestant Truths, the Second Lecture, 'Priesthood and Sacrifice Essential to Worship', Delivered on Wednesday Evening, March 30th 1853 in the New Hall, Leicester by Benjamin Wills Newton (Formerly Fellow of Exeter College, Oxford), Rev. G.W. Straton, Rector of Aylestone in the Chair*.

The address was based on Hebrews 9 and 10. It sets out the Protestant position, against the teachings of the Church of Rome.

It was reprinted in *Watching and Waiting*, January/February 1959.

The other Leicester Lecture known to have been by Mr Newton was *The True Unity of the Church of God in Time and Eternity*. The two were apparently bound together as *Great Protestant Truths, Being Two of the Leicestershire [sic] Lectures* – as indicated in a publisher's list in *Occasional Papers on Scriptural Subjects No.1*.

    1853    T.J. Paul, London    22cm    15p.    CBA

## PROPHECIES CONCERNING THE JEWS AND JERUSALEM

Title of the Irish Christian Mission (ICM) edition of *On the Prophecies Respecting the Jews and Jerusalem in the Form of a Catechism*.

## PROPHECIES RESPECTING THE JEWS AND JERUSALEM IN THE FORM OF A CATECHISM

Publisher's list title of *On the Prophecies Respecting the Jews and Jerusalem in the Form of a Catechism*.

## PROPHECY. HOW TO READ IT, OR SCRIPTURE ITS OWN INTERPRETER, FROM 'THE FIRST SERIES OF AIDS TO PROPHETIC ENQUIRY'

This is catalogued in a publisher's list in *Regeneration in its Connexion with the Cross* (1860). The item is undated, but the earliest other publication of Mr Newton's works in the publisher's list is 1858.

    ND [1859?]   Geo Hunt, London                12.5cm  4p.     CBA,SG

## THE PROPHECY OF THE LORD JESUS AS CONTAINED IN MATTHEW 24 AND 25, CONSIDERED

This has been one of the most widely circulated of Mr Newton's works. *How B.W. Newton Learned Prophetic Truth* (NM 7 in the listing of posthumous works based on MSS and lecture notes in Section 8, Publications Produced from Notes of Addresses, and Posthumously Published Letters and Manuscripts) highlights Matthew 24 as one of the passages that most strongly influenced him in his early search for prophetic truth. The first of the *Five Letters… (Is It Wrong to Expect…)* also deals with Matthew 24, as does the distinct tract *Prophecy of the Lord Jesus as Contained in Matthew 24 <u>Briefly</u> Considered* (c. 1843). Furthermore, *Aids to Prophetic Enquiry* (First Series) has a chapter titled, Thoughts on Matthew 24, which has similar content.

The verbal agreement, and arrangement of the commentary and notes; have led us to consider *Thoughts on the End of the Age* to be the First Edition of this work. This tract was criticised briefly in J.N. Darby's *An Examination of the Statements made in the 'Thoughts on the Apocalypse'* (*Prophetic Writings*: Vol. 8 p.209n)[1].

After the Second Edition, the work remained virtually unchanged.

One of the appendices added to the Second Edition is the expanded parable, *The Wreck and the Rock*, which had circulated separately earlier, and had also drawn a response from J.N. Darby. See the further comment under that publication title.

A further item is added to the Second Edition - *On the Words 'This Generation'*. It was later circulated separately, and was also incorporated into *Occasional Thoughts on Scriptural Subjects No.3*, as 'Note on Matthew 24:34'.

First Edition - *Thoughts on the End of the Age, Being in Part Compiled from Some Notes of Lectures Delivered at Sidmouth, and Elsewhere*.

    1845    J Harvey, Sidmouth                11cm   37p.    Bo,CBA,I,U

---

[1] It was also criticised in *Analysis, by a Student of Prophecy, of 'Thoughts on the Apocalypse' by B.W. Newton of Plymouth* [by R.M. Beverley] pp.49-51.

Second Edition - *Lecture on the Prophecy of the Lord Jesus as Contained in Matthew 24,25 with Notes and Appendix.*
    1857    Houlston & Stoneman, London    18cm    102p.    SG,Toronto University

Third Edition - also *'with notes and appendix'*.
    1879    Houlston & Sons, London    18cm    103p.    BL,Bo,CBA,CU,EL,Sc,T

Fourth Edition
    1902    Houlston & Sons and Lucas Collins, London    18cm    112p.    BIOLA,CBA,U

Fifth Edition
    1930    E.J. Burnett, Worthing    18cm    108p.    BIOLA,U

A new binding 'of stored sheets' was made in 1948 (*Watching and Waiting*, April/June 1948, p.151), probably of the Fourth Edition.

Sixth Edition
    1969    SGAT, London    18cm    108p.    BL,CBA,EL,SG

Seventh Edition
    1982    SGAT, Chelmsford    18cm    108p.    SG

Italian Edition - *Le Profezie del Signor Gesù Cristo Come si Trovano nei Capitoli 24 e 25 dell Evangelo di S. Matteo: Osservazioni con Note ed Appendici. Traduzione dall' Inglese.*
    1887    Claudiana [printer], Florence    16cm    116p.    Bollettino delle pubblicazioni italiane (1887)[1]

Chinese Edition?

*Watching and Waiting* (November/December 1940) stated that a translation had been made, and 'a Chinese brother' was 'wait[ing] in faith for the time of the Lord to come to print'. Because of increased costs, publication had been delayed. It is probable that the missionary W.E. Burnett's ministry gave rise to this initiative.[2]

## PROPHECY OF THE LORD JESUS AS CONTAINED IN MATTHEW 24 BRIEFLY CONSIDERED

This short tract, apart from its title, has no verbal similarity with any of the editions of the widely circulated *Prophecy of the Lord Jesus as Contained in Matthew 24 and 25, Considered*. It may be regarded as the seedbed of ideas later developed. It is consistent with the later publication in its divisions of Matthew 24, and its exposition of 'this generation'. It has an appendix (pp.18-20), written in response to an anonymous tract 'containing remarks on one of my recent lectures in this place' which he received 'whilst engaged in writing the preceding pages'.

---

[1] This title is listed in the *Bollettino delle pubblicazioni italiane* (1887), but it is not in the Fondo Guicciardini catalogue. However, an index card provided by the Biblioteca Nazionale Centrale, Florence in 1985 identifies it as Fondo Guicciardini.
[2] William Edward Burnett (1862-1950), an associate of B.W. Newton who commenced the Evangelical Protestant Mission to the Chinese in 1893, having left for China in 1883, first serving with the China Inland Mission. He died in China. Obituary *Watching and Waiting*, September-October 1950, p.69, and January-February 1951, p.106-108

The First Edition of *Thoughts on the Apocalypse* (1844 p.95) refers to 'A tract entitled *Thoughts on the 24th of Matthew* (1, Warwick Square, London)', which may be this tract. It evidently predates *Thoughts on the End of the Age* (1845) - the title of the precursor of *Prophecy of the Lord Jesus as Contained in Matthew 24 and 25, Considered…*

*Prospects of the World in Connection with the Approaching Return of the Lord Jesus Christ* [which we have concluded to be by B.W. Newton] refers to a tract *Prophecy in the 24th Matthew Considered* – 'sold at 1 Warwick Square, London' (on page 9n), which we again conclude to be this tract.

See the letter from B.W. Newton to J.N. Darby ND [c.1843] regarding the End of the Age and 'the Tares', which may also refer to this tract, and the tract *On Luke 21…*

    ND [1843?]   Plymouth, *The Christian Witness*       12.5cm  20p.     CBA
                    and Tract Depot

### A PROPHETIC MAP OF THE WORLD; INTENDED TO EXHIBIT ITS GENERAL CONDITION AT THE END OF THE AGE: ALSO SOME EXTRACTS ON THE SAME SUBJECT FROM 'THOUGHTS ON THE APOCALYPSE'.

This is a world map. Other maps produced by B.W. Newton are of 'the prophetic earth', e.g. the *Map of the Ten Kingdoms of the Prophetic Earth*.

The twenty pages of introduction to the map expand on the theme of 'the classes of persons [who] will then exist on the earth', which is then illustrated cartographically. A similar account to this introduction is found again in *Aids to Prophetic Enquiry* (Third Edition, pp.162 ff.), which perhaps removed the need for further editions of it, as Mr Newton considered *Aids to Prophetic Enquiry* to be foundational to *Thoughts on the Apocalypse* (see *Aids to Prophetic Enquiry* Second Edition page vi – footnote).

The 'extracts' from *Thoughts on the Apocalypse* are the exposition of chapters 13 and 17-18.

Not only does the map incorporate an extract from *Thoughts on the Apocalypse*, contrariwise some bindings of the First Edition of *Thoughts on the Apocalypse* include the introduction to the map numbered in roman numerals. The French Edition (1847) incorporated the map, and the introduction to it, with consecutive numbering.

We may assume that it was produced after the completion of *Thoughts on the Apocalypse*, with a view to inclusion in the published book.

    1846     Hamilton, Adams, London and Plymouth       BL,Bo,CU,Sc, SG,U
              Map: 29x41cm. Text: 17cm   xx+138p.

### PROPHETIC PSALMS IN THEIR RELATION TO ISRAEL, BRIEFLY CONSIDERED

In this pamphlet Mr Newton maintained that the Psalms as a whole have a specific reference to the land and people of Israel. It considers various Psalms that have been erroneously interpreted exclusively of the Church. He expounds them as relating to Israel's future. Particular comments are made on Psalms 2,8,10,12,14,18,53,72,74,76, 79,80,83,98,100,110,124,134.

First Edition

|  |  |  |  |  |
|---|---|---|---|---|
| [1858] Houlston & Sons, London | 16cm | 42p. | BIOLA,BL,Bo,CBA,CU,EL,Sc,U(?) |

Second Edition
    1900    Houlston & Sons, London    17cm    42p.    BIOLA,BL,Bo,CBA,CU,EL,Sc

(Third Edition)
    ND [199?]    Irish Christian Mission, Belfast    15cm    42p.    CG

## THE PROPHETIC SYSTEM OF MR ELLIOTT AND DR CUMMING CONSIDERED, EXTRACTED FROM THE FIRST SERIES OF 'AIDS TO PROPHETIC ENQUIRY'

In this Mr Newton examined the writings of these two men, notable for their historicist interpretation of the Book of Revelation – *Horae Apocalypticae* by Edward Bishop Elliott (1793-1875), and *Apocalyptic Sketches* by Dr John Cumming (1807-1881). See further notes with the *Aids to Prophetic Enquiry* listing.

    1850    James Nisbet & Co, London    17cm    59p.    BL,Bo,CU,I,Sc,SG,T

## PROPOSITIONS FOR THE SOLEMN CONSIDERATION OF CHRISTIANS

This is a manifesto of Mr Newton's position on the Deity and Humanity of the Lord Jesus, the Atonement, and prophetic truth. The seventeen propositions are, in part at least, corrective of the views of J.N. Darby and his followers.

This publication very quickly ran through three editions, and was advertised by the publication of *Three Reviews* [from *Old Truths*, *The Morning Advertiser*[1], and *The Record*] of a Tract by Mr B.W. Newton entitled 'Propositions for the Solemn Consideration of Christians' (1866 – no publisher – 16cm, 12p, CBA). This promotional publication was reprinted in *Watching and Waiting*, October/ December 1948 pp.205 ff.

The *Propositions* were also reviewed in the *Quarterly Journal of Prophecy* (Vol. 17, 1865 pages 77-79).

The whole pamphlet was reprinted in *Teachers of the Faith and Future* by G.H. Fromow.

First Edition (dated June 1864)
    1864    Houlston & Wright, London    18cm    22p.    BL,Bo,CU,Sc,T

Second Edition
    1865    Houlston & Wright, London    18cm    22p.    CBA

Third Edition
    1867    Houlston & Wright, London    12.5cm    24p.    CBA,Sc

Fourth Edition
    1892    Houlston & Sons, London    18cm    36p.    BL,Bo,CU,EL,Sc,SG

Fifth Edition (The text is identical to the Fourth Edition)
    ND [1955?]  G.L. Silverwood-Browne, Wembley    18cm    36p.    CG

---

[1] *The Morning Advertiser*, editor James Grant. See the note on his *The Religious Tendencies of the Times: or How to Deal with the Deadly Errors of the Day*, in the section on Contributions to other Publications.

## PROSPECTS OF THE TEN KINGDOMS OF THE ROMAN EMPIRE, BEING THE THIRD SERIES OF 'AIDS TO PROPHETIC ENQUIRY'

*Aids to Prophetic Enquiry* was the original name given to three books, published as three 'Series'. The First Series became known by the primary title (*Aids to Prophetic Enquiry*). The Second Series became known as *Babylon and Egypt*, and the Third Series became known as *Prospects of the Ten Kingdoms*.

As well as a consideration of the ten future kingdoms of prophecy, a considerable part of the book is taken up with exposition of the Book of Daniel, and 2 Thessalonians 2. *Watching and Waiting* (September/October 1955 p.175) referred to it as 'the most notable of all B.W. Newton's prophetic works'.

The First Edition has an 'Appendix D' (2 pages), On the Septuagint Version of Daniel. This was left out of the Second Edition.

A Conclusion (79 pages) was added after the appendices in the Second Edition, headed 'Remarks on the Franco-Prussian War and Its Results'.

Chapter 12 of the Second Edition, On 2 Thessalonians 2, expands a translation and comments that had circulated with Mr Newton's *Five Letters…*, and which were earlier published in the First Edition of *Thoughts on the Apocalypse*.

As with *Aids to Prophetic Enquiry, First Series*, and *Aids to Prophetic Enquiry Second Series*, [*Babylon and Egypt*], there is confusion of publishers and the dates of the First Edition of this work. The 1863 date given in the Union Catalog is not easily explicable.

*A Letter to a Friend, Requesting Attention to a Work Entitled, 'Prospects of the Ten Kingdoms of the Roman World [sic]'* by Ker Baillie Hamilton, CB[1], was produced to advertise the Second Edition (1881 Houlston & Sons, London, 17cm, 16p, BL,Bo,CBA,T). See notes in Section 9, B.W. Newton's Correspondence, November 1871 onwards.

Five items were extracted from *Prospects of the Ten Kingdoms*, and issued separately under the following titles:
1. *What is the Ephah of Zechariah 5? or, The Exhibition of 1851 Considered in Relation to the Principles of Modern Legislation.*
2. *Thoughts on the History of Professing Christianity as Given in the Parables of Matthew 13.*
3. *On the Natural Relations of Men and Governments to God.*
4. *Order of Events Connected with the Appearing of Christ and the Millennial Reign.*
5. *A Literal Translation of 2 Thessalonians 2:1-10.*

*Scriptural Prospects* incorporated two brief extracts from it.

---

[1] Ker Baillie Hamilton, 1804-1889. Former colonial governor of Grenada, Newfoundland, and Antigua and the Leeward Islands. Buried in Tunbridge Wells. See notes in Section 9, B.W. Newton's Correspondence, November 1871 onwards. See *Dictionary of Canadian Biography, Vol. 1*. See also the notes on *Extracts from the Second Series of 'Aids to Prophetic Enquiry'… Compared with Extracts From 'The Daily News' and 'Standard' etc*. A picture of him is included in *A Pictorial Memoir of Benjamin Wills Newton* – the supplement to this Guide. See the Advertisement at the end of this volume.

First Edition
    1849    James Nisbet & Co, London    18cm    274p.    BIOLA,BL,Bo, CBA,CU,EL,Sc,SG,U,T

    1853    Partridge, Oakey & Co, London    18cm    274+iip.    EL

    1863    Houlston & Wright, London    20cm    274p.    U

Second Edition, 'Revised'
    1873    Houlston & Sons, London    18cm    viii+491p.    BIOLA,BL, Bo, CBA,CU,Sc,SG,T,U

Third Edition. Revised and Abridged (the editing and reduction was done by E.J. Burnett – *Watching and Waiting* September/October 1955 p.174).
    1955    G.L. Silverwood-Browne, Wembley    17cm    vi+271p.    CBA,EL

Fourth Edition. Revised and Abridged (A reprint of the Third Edition subject to a few minor amendments, and with the addition of a forward by Pastor James Payne. Dated from the review in *Watching and Waiting*, January/February 1964).
    ND [1963/4] SGAT, London    17cm    viii+271p.    CBA

Fifth Edition (A reprint of the Fourth Edition).
    ND [1976]    SGAT, Chelmsford    17cm    viii+271p.    SG

Sixth Edition (A photographic reprint of the Second Edition).
    [2015]    SGAT, Chelmsford    17cm    viii+271p.    SG

## THE PROSPECTS OF THE WORLD, IN CONNECTION WITH THE APPROACHING RETURN OF THE LORD JESUS CHRIST

We conclude that this anonymous tract was certainly by B.W. Newton. See the discussion of authorship in Section 5, Anonymous Publications Ascribed to B.W. Newton.

In it he examined the means by which millennial blessing will be introduced. He wrote of the revival of the countries of the Eastern Mediterranean. The scope of the coming apostasy will be the 'Roman world', not just the western half of it. Christ's Millennial Reign is described.

Edition 1
    [ND]    [Plymouth] C[lulow] & S(oltau)    16cm    24p.    SG
              J. Wertheimer, printer, London

Edition 2. Title add: *Second Lecture.*
    1842    London, 1, Warwick Square    16cm    24p.    I
              J. Wertheimer, printer, London

Edition 3 (perhaps identical to Edition 2). *Second Lecture.*
    1842    London [Central Tract Depot]    17cm    24p.    CBA

## QU'EST-CE QUE L'ÉPHA DE ZACHARIE 5? OU L'EXPOSITION DE 1851 CONSIDÉRÉE EN RAPPORT AVEC LES PRINCIPES DE LÉGISLATION MODERNE

French Edition of *What is the Ephah of Zechariah 5?...*

## THE RECHABITES, JEREMIAH 35. A TRACT COMPILED FROM NOTES OF A LECTURE DELIVERED IN DUKE STREET CHAPEL, ST JAMES'S PARK JULY 8ᵀᴴ 1855.

In this tract, the Rechabites are used to demonstrate the duty and blessings of separation for the believer. This item was later included in *Narratives from the Old Testament*.

    1856    Houlston & Stoneman, London    17cm    22p.    SG

## REFLECTIONS ON THE CHARACTER AND SPREAD OF SPIRITUALISM

In this work, Mr Newton presented a careful examination of the teachings of Scripture on spiritualism, with notes on Old Testament words and expressions. He also made comment on contemporary writings.

Part of the 'Note on Deuteronomy 8:9-14' in this book was reprinted as *Note on Spiritualism*, in the Second Edition of *Thoughts on Parts of the Prophecy of Isaiah*.

First Edition
    1876    Houlston & Sons, London    18cm    88 (? )p.    Bo,BL,CU,Sc,T

Second Edition   Appendix (20 pages) added. Preface 'January 1882'.
    1882    Houlston & Sons, London    18cm    88p.    Bo,BL,CBA,CU,EL,Sc

American Edition - 'reprinted from the London Edition. 2d Edition'
    1882-    Willard Tract Repository, Boston    ?cm    123p.    U

## REFLECTIONS SUGGESTED BY THE PRESENT MOVEMENT IN ENGLAND AGAINST ROMANISM. A LETTER TO A FRIEND

This is No.3 of the *Doctrines of Popery* series.

In the tract, Mr Newton questioned whether Romanism was the chief enemy of the Church, and warned of the secular 'latitudinarian' principles that were being used to resist its advance. He called for opposition on separated and strictly Biblical lines.

The 'letter' is dated December 30th 1850.

Notes from it on 2 Peter 3:2 and Rev. 2:2 were reprinted in *The Quarterly Journal of Prophecy* Vol. 19, 1867, p.390 – see Section 4, B.W. Newton's Contributions to Other Publications.

    1851    James Nisbet & Co, London    18cm    21p.    CBA,SG

## REGENERATION IN ITS CONNEXION WITH THE CROSS: THE SUBSTANCE OF A LECTURE DELIVERED IN DUKE STREET CHAPEL, ST JAMES'S PARK

The tract gives Mr Newton's thoughts on John 3:1-15, and, in particular 'the serpent of brass', and 'born of water'.

This, together with three other works, were later brought together to form *Gospel Truths*.

First Edition
    1860    Houlston & Wright, London and    17cm    34p.    SG
              Geo Hunt, Bible and Tract Depot, London

Second Edition
    1864    Houlston & Wright, London    17cm    34p.    CBA

### REMARKS ON A BOOK ENTITLED 'NATURAL LAW IN THE SPIRITUAL WORLD' BY HENRY DRUMMOND, FRSI[1], FGS, BEING THE SUBSTANCE OF FOUR LECTURES GIVEN IN LONDON

In his book, Henry Drummond[2] had sought a harmony between evolutionary 'science', and religion, on the basis of common laws prevailing in both. His book had a wide circulation and influence, and ran through at least eight editions in the nineteenth century. Mr Newton opposed his liberal view of Scripture.

    1884    Houlston & Sons, London    18cm    192p.    CBA,EL

### REMARKS ON A TRACT ENTITLED 'JUSTIFICATION IN THE RISEN CHRIST'

The tract to which B.W. Newton referred was by the Brethren writer, Charles Stanley (1821-1888). The error of Charles Stanley's tract is a rejection of justification as a result of Christ's finished work on the cross. A very similar issue was at the root of the Stuart, or Reading, division of the Exclusive Brethren (1885). In his pamphlet, Mr Newton also opposed the similar teaching of another Brethren writer, C.H. Mackintosh (1820-1896), a close colleague of Charles Stanley. He pointed out the parallels of this doctrine with Roman Catholic teaching.

This item was later included in *Thoughts on Scriptural Subjects*, which see.

First Edition
    1870    Houlston & Sons, London    18cm    29p.    BL,Bo,CU,Sc

Second Edition. – 'Reprinted from *Thoughts on Scriptural Subjects*'.
    1896    Houlston & Sons, London    17cm    30p.    CBA

### REMARKS ON 'MOSAIC COSMOGONY', BEING THE FIFTH OF THE 'ESSAYS AND REVIEWS', EXTRACTED FROM THE THIRD NUMBER OF THE 'OCCASIONAL PAPERS ON SCRIPTURAL SUBJECTS'

The *Essays and Reviews* were written by Anglican clergymen, and were of a very theologically liberal character. Mr Newton referred to them in at least five of his works. They led to a legal contest in the Church courts. The Judicial Committee of the Privy Council finally sanctioned some of the views expressed. This 'Judgment of the Court of Arches' was itself the subject of detailed examination by Mr Newton in *Occasional Papers on Scriptural Subjects No.4*.

---

[1] FRSI [sic]. FRSE?
[2] Henry Drummond (1851-1897). Not to be confused with Henry Drummond (1786-1860), the Irvingite apostle.

In these *Remarks* Mr Newton argued against the essay by Charles Wycliffe Goodwin (1818-1891) and others, who rejected the literality of the Genesis creation narrative.

The Third Edition revised *Remarks on 'Mosaic Cosmogony'...*, and added another chapter from *Occasional Papers on Scriptural Subjects No.3*, entitled, Note on the Locality of Hades, with very minor amendments (mainly deletions). To these were added Supplementary Remarks (13 pages), and a Proposed Article of Faith (2 pages).

*Mosaic Cosmogony*, as Mr Newton's work came to be known (assuming the title of the essay that it opposed!), was later bound up with *The Altered Translation of Genesis 2:5 as given in the Revised English Version, Considered*.

[First Edition]
    1864    Houlston & Wright, London    25cm    59p.    BL,Bo,CU,EL,Sc,T

Second Edition?

    It is probable that the 1864 edition was regarded as the Second Edition, in view of its earlier publication in *Occasional Papers on Scriptural Subjects No.3*. No copies of a Second Edition have been located.

Third Edition, 'Revised' 'with slight additions'.
    1882    Houlston & Sons, London    18cm    103p.    BIOLA,BL,Bo,CBA,CU,Sc,U

A paperback binding was made from loose papers, and issued by SGAT in 1973, when it was bound up with *The Altered Translation of Genesis 2:5 as given in the Revised English Version, considered* (*Watching and Waiting*, November/December 1973 p.383).

## REMARKS ON MR TROTTER'S PAMPHLET

See: *Reply to a Tract by Mr Trotter Entitled 'What are Mr Newton's Present Doctrines as to the Human Nature and Relationships of the Lord Jesus Christ?'*.

## REMARKS ON R. PEARSALL SMITH'S EDITION OF HYMNS SELECTED FROM THOSE OF THE LATE F.W. FABER, D.D., PRIEST OF THE ORATORY OF ST. PHILIP NERI, BROMPTON

F.W. Faber was the principal hymn writer of the nineteenth century Tractarian (or Anglo-Catholic) movement. In this publication Mr Newton severely censured both Faber's hymns, and the publication of a selection of them by a professed evangelical, R. Pearsall Smith.

The cover has 'printed for the author', and does not name a publisher. A statement is made at the end of the preface – 'As it is not my wish that this pamphlet should have a wide or unrestricted circulation, I have not placed it with my usual publishers, but have retained it in my own hands'. For further comments on Mr Newton's engagement with R. Pearsall Smith, see *Modern Doctrines Respecting Sinlessness Considered*. A correspondence that he (B.W. Newton) had published in *The Record* at this time may have induced him to issue the book to the public at large.

Quotations are included in the anthology *B.W. Newton on Ministry and Order in the Church of Christ*.

    1874    Houlston & Sons, London    17cm    vi+128p.    BL,CBA,EL

## REMARKS ON THE PROPHETIC STATEMENTS OF MR FLEMING

This is a chapter of *Aids to Prophetic Enquiry*. It formed the first chapter of the First Edition. It has not been located as a separate tract, but the Second Edition of *Aids to Prophetic Enquiry* has a footnote, 'This paper was first published in 1848', this could, however simply indicate that it was published within the First Edition of *Aids to Prophetic Enquiry* in 1848, rather than as a separate tract. On Robert Fleming's book see the comment under *Aids to Prophetic Enquiry*.

## REMARKS ON THE REVISED ENGLISH VERSION OF THE GREEK NEW TESTAMENT

Mr Newton was devoted to the study of the Greek text of the New Testament. He supported the great work of his first wife's cousin[1], S.P. Tregelles, in his work on a critical revision of the Greek New Testament. There is much reference to S.P. Tregelles's work in this book.

In these *Remarks* Mr Newton was very critical of the Revised Version New Testament translation. He regarded its publication as 'a matter of intense regret'. On the other hand, he forcefully rejected the theory of textual preservation proposed by Dean Burgon. In this publication he devoted considerable attention to the *Quarterly Review* in which Dean Burgon's response to the Revised Version was published. He opposed both the principles that he expressed there, and 'the violence of his attack'. Although not referred to by name in this book, it is made clear, in Mr Newton's *Doctrines of Popery on Holy Scripture and Tradition, as Established by the Council of Trent, Considered*, Second Edition that his comments refer to Dean Burgon.

See also the comments relating to F.J.A. Hort in the Correspondence section, and the comments in Section 4, B.W. Newton's Contributions to Other Publications in connection with S.P. Tregelles's Greek New Testament.

These *Remarks* include some items that had been published earlier:
1. On the Omission of the Greek Article Before Definite Words
    (from *Occasional Papers on Scriptural Subjects No.1*).
2. Note on the Words λογιζομαι, etc
    (in a modified form from *Occasional Papers on Scriptural Subjects No.1*).
3. On the Force of the Present Tense in Greek and Hebrew
    (in a revised form from *Occasional Papers on Scriptural Subjects No.3*).

Another work, *The Altered Translation of Genesis 2:5 as given in the Revised English Version*, also comments on the Revised Version.

*The Whole Family. Ephesians 3:5...* republished extracts from these *Remarks*.

Quotations from these *Remarks* are included in the anthology *B.W. Newton on Ministry and Order in the Church of Christ*.

---

[1] The mother of B.W. Newton's first wife, Hannah (née Abbott 1799-1846) was Sarah Abbott (née Tregelles 1772-1802). She was a younger sister of S.P. Tregelles's grandfather.

The book was originally published in three parts – Part 1 (1881), Part II (1882), and Part III (1883), although the publication date of the complete volume is given as 1881.

    1881    Houlston & Sons, London    18cm    iv+355p.    BIOLA,BL,Bo,CBA, CU (Part 3),EL,Sc,U

## REMARKS ON THE SUFFERINGS OF THE LORD JESUS: A LETTER ADDRESSED TO CERTAIN BRETHREN AND SISTERS IN CHRIST.

This was written in response to J.L. Harris's *The Sufferings of Christ as set forth in a lecture on Psalm 6* (1847 – J.K. Campbell, Tract Depot, 1 Warwick Square, London: W. Balle, Exeter: J.B. Rowe, Plymouth - 17cm – 76p – BL). The editor's preface to J.L. Harris's tract is signed: 'Christopher McAdam, Countess Wear, Exeter, July 1847'. The text of the tract ends 'Yours affectionately in the Lord, J.L. Harris. To Mr C McAdam, Brampford, Speke, June 1847'.

The hostile tract of J.L. Harris, Mr Newton's former companion in the ministry at Plymouth, criticised a MS account of one of his (Mr Newton's) lectures. The notes had been made and circulated by Amy J.T. Toulmin, Mr Newton's cousin (see CBA 7180(36), from notes taken by Kate Gidley. It appears that the original notes were in the Fry Collection (see CBA 6998 1847, folio 3), but they are now lost. It is plain from Mr Newton's second response to the pamphlet (*Observations on a Tract, entitled, 'The Sufferings of Christ as set forth in a lecture on Psalm 6, considered'*) that he neither saw, nor sanctioned, the notes that had been circulated, and that they did not fairly represent his teaching. For a (critical) account of how such MS notes were circulated see J.N. Darby *Observations on a Tract entitled 'Remarks…'*, pp.87,88.

In this tract Mr Newton defined his understanding of the nature and purpose of the life-sufferings of the Lord Jesus, without directly referring to J.L. Harris's tract. B.W. Newton's tract is written in a gracious spirit, and concludes (p.41) 'I would only say how deeply sensible I feel of the imperfections of these remarks. It is a subject solemn, so full, so varied in its connexions, that I should have greatly hesitated to write on it, unless circumstances had appeared to constrain. Many things are omitted that might have been said; and there may be errors as well as imperfections. But my comfort is that we have to do with One who does not upbraid nor make an offender for a word. Liberality, generousness, kindness of soul, as well as mercy, characterize God. If He should be extreme to mark what is done amiss, who could stand? But there is forgiveness with Him that He may be feared. It is only when I think of His grace that I have any hope of blessing either to myself or others, from writing or speaking these things. But that encourages me and I trust in Him to commend what may be true to your consciences in His fear, and to enable you to discern between things that differ'.

It subsequently became necessary for him to answer his accusers more directly, as J.N. Darby quickly published his *Observations on a Tract Entitled, 'Remarks on the Sufferings of the Lord Jesus: A Letter Addressed to Certain Brethren and Sisters in Christ'* (1847 – Campbell, London – 17cm - 67p – BL. *Collected Writings* Vol. 15). This was a vitriolic attack on Mr Newton's character and integrity. He accused him of being an agent of Satan, and the bearer of the vilest heresy. J.N. Darby also accused Mr Newton of plagiarism in connection with [Rev.] Andrew A. Bonar's commentary on Leviticus (published 1846) – 'such as it is, Newton's tract is much borrowed from it'. He urged all to oppose and reject Mr Newton, and his teaching. This led to Mr Newton's response to his critics in *Observations on a Tract, entitled, 'The Sufferings of Christ as Set Forth in a Lecture on Psalm 6, Considered'*".

Mr Newton later withdrew this tract [*Remarks...*] for reconsideration, together with his *Observations* on J.L. Harris's remarks, when he published *A Statement and Acknowledgement respecting Certain Doctrinal Errors*. However, certain passages were subsequently published by him in *A Letter on Subjects Connected with the Lord's Humanity*, and in 1867 his close associate, John Cox, jun. published *Extracts from the Two Tracts Entitled, 'Remarks on the Sufferings of the Lord Jesus...' and 'Observations on a Tract...' and Quotations from Other Papers*, as a 'private and confidential' pamphlet. It would be fair to say that the status of the two pamphlets was as described at the end of his life by his close associate, W.L. Holland (In *The 'Archbishop' of Canterbury and 'Modern' Christianity*, 1898), 'withdrawn owing to certain deductions that were capable, apart from the context, of being made from it'. There are further comments on Mr Newton's reasons for withdrawal of the tracts in *Christ, Our Suffering Surety* (Second Edition, pp.63-70).

The tract is dated July 26th 1847.

First Edition
    1847    Campbell, Warwick Square, London    17cm    50p.    SG,EC
             and Plymouth

Second Edition. Advertised in *Observations on a Tract entitled...* (dated September 1st 1847) as 'recently published'.
    1847    Campbell and Tract Depot,    ?    ?    ?
             Cornwall St, Plymouth

## REMARKS ON THE TEN KINGDOMS OF THE ROMAN WORLD WITH A MAP

Although this was published anonymously and never formally under B.W. Newton's name, it is certain it was by him. See the discussion in Section 5, Anonymous Publications Ascribed to B.W. Newton.

The tract reviews the divisions of prophetic history in relation to God's dealings with Jerusalem. With the aid of the map, it delineates the area of the last Gentile empire, within the boundary of the Roman Empire at its fullest extent. As in later publications, B.W. Newton took the boundaries of the Roman Empire in the time of Trajan as being the likely limits of the rule of the Ten Kingdoms. A concluding note, added to the 1841 edition, comments, 'It should have been mentioned that Persia is not included in the Roman Empire ... Bavaria should have been mentioned together with Switzerland, as included in the Roman Earth'. The Map is dated 1840.

First (?) Edition
    1841    G.S. Lee, Plymouth    15cm    12p.    I

Second (?) Edition
    1844    Tract Depot, London    17.5cm    12p.    I

French Edition
> *Remarques sur Les Dix Royaumes du Monde Romain.*
> 1843     J. Wertheimer, London                                17.5cm    12p.    I

## A REMONSTRANCE TO THE SOCIETY OF FRIENDS

This is Mr Newton's earliest substantial work, and his first contribution to the Beaconite controversy among the Quakers. That controversy led to the virtual demise of the Evangelical party among the Society of Friends.[1]

Mr Newton's work consists for the most part of quotations of leading Friends on doctrinal matters, and an examination of the quotations given in the light of Scripture.

It drew a reply, *Strictures on a Late Publication Entitled, 'A Remonstrance to the Society of Friends'* (1836 – J&A Arch, London – 21cm – 43p – BL, Library of the Society of Friends, London), which is attributed to Joseph Treffry (1771-1851), Mr Newton's uncle.

The pamphlet also provoked an article, and a published correspondence between B.W. Newton and J.J. Gurney[2] in *The Christian Observer* (see October 1835 pp.629-642, and Appendix 1836 pp.791,792, and (Newton's reply) April 1836 pp.221-225).

Robert Govett used the *Remonstrance* as a reference source, showing the heterodoxy of the Quakers, in his book *The Trinity* (1874).

The appendix of Newton's *Remonstrance* was published anonymously with the simple title *Baptism*, although it is not clear whether this was circulating before or after the publication of the *Remonstrance…* Publication details of this are given in this Section under *Baptism (2)*.

> 1835    Nisbet & Co, London    (Plymouth – printed)    18cm    vi+104+2[3] p.
> 
>                                                                                 BL,CBA,U

## REPLY TO A TRACT OF MR TROTTER ENTITLED 'WHAT ARE MR NEWTON'S PRESENT DOCTRINES AS TO THE HUMAN NATURE AND RELATIONSHIPS OF THE LORD JESUS CHRIST?'

In this brief tract Mr Newton defended himself against the allegations of William Trotter (1818-1865), a staunch ally of J.N. Darby.

A private letter by Mr Newton commenting upon William Trotter's allegations against him had come into the hands of William Trotter. He published it with commentary upon each paragraph, in his

---

[1] See *Early Brethren and the Society of Friends* by T.C.F. Stunt, Christian Brethren Research Fellowship 1970 (This research item has been republished with some amendments as Chapter 2 of *The Elusive Quest of the Spiritual Malcontent: Some Early Nineteenth-Century Ecclesiastical Mavericks*, by T.C.F. Stunt., 2015); and *The Beacon Controversy in the Society of Friends 1835-1840. A Bibliography* by Jolyon Hall 1968.

[2] J.J. Gurney was a leading evangelical Quaker, who had upheld verbal inspiration at the Quaker Yearly Meeting in 1836. See T.C.F. Stunt, *Early Brethren and the Society of Friends*: Christian Brethren Research Fellowship Occasional Paper No.3, 1970, p.7 (This research item has been republished with some amendments as Chapters 1 and 2 of *The Elusive Quest of the Spiritual Malcontent: Some Early Nineteenth-Century Ecclesiastical Mavericks*, by T.C.F. Stunt., 2015).

[3] The pagination repeats pp.25,26.

tract entitled *What are Mr Newton's Present Doctrines as to the Human Nature and Relationships of the Lord Jesus Christ?* [1850 – James Nisbet, London, and J.B. Rowe, Plymouth – 17.5cm – 58p – BL,CBA].

Only a handwritten copy of B.W. Newton's reply is known to have survived, in the hand of Amy J.T. Toulmin, Mr Newton's cousin. It has been corrected in another hand, evidently with access to the original, in which the title page is also copied.

The handwritten copy does not name the author, but it is written in the first person to a tract directed against B.W. Newton.

William Trotter also reproduced his version of the controversial events of 1845-1849 in a lengthy letter of 15th July 1849, which was published as a pamphlet – *'Origin of Open Brethren'* or *'The Whole Case of Plymouth and Bethesda'*. See also the reference to his correspondence to *The Quarterly Journal of Prophecy* upon B.W. Newton's article, Old Testament Saints, which appeared in it (Section 6 - Letters and Articles by B.W. Newton Published in Periodicals).

    1850    James Nisbet & Co, London    ?    approx. 12pp.    EC

## RETFÆRDIGGJÖRELSEN OG HELLIGGJÖRELSEN. UDVALG AF BWN'S VARKER. AUTORISEERET OVERSÆTTELSE EFTER ORIGINALENS 2 UDG. KRA. (1900)

[Justification and Sanctification. Selected from BWN's works. Authorised translation after the original. Second Edition (1900)]. We have not been able to examine the pamphlet or to obtain a translation. An English pamphlet, *Justification and Sanctification*, was produced by Hunt, Barnard, possibly ten years later, and may have been the text that was translated.

The Norwegian connection is most likely explained by Mr Newton's letter to Miss Leake 18th January 1895 (CBA 7050 pp.242-244). See also the preface to John Cox, jun., *The Sabbath and Lord's Day* in which he refers to the First Edition of his booklet having been published in 1896 at the request of a friend in Norway, and afterwards translated into that language.

The First Edition has not been traced.

Second Edition
    ND (c.1900)   Johannes Björnstads [printer]  ?  ?  Norwegian National Library, Oslo

## ROMANS 7, CONSIDERED

Publisher's list title of *The Seventh Chapter of the Epistle to the Romans, Considered*, and the cover title of SGAT's 'binding of loose papers' of the pamphlet.

## SALVATION BY SUBSTITUTION

This was compiled from notes of a lecture given on Christmas Day, 25th December 1865. It was first published in *Occasional Papers on Scriptural Subjects No.4* (1866).

In it Mr Newton declared unequivocally the substitutionary nature of the Lord's sufferings. He also advocated the free offer of the Gospel to sinners. Appended to the main treatise are several lengthy corroborating quotations from other writers, and a refutation of Edward Irving's doctrine.

First Edition
    [1866]    Houlston & Wright, London    17cm    68p.    BL,Bo,CU,Sc,T

Second Edition
    [1878]    Houlston & Sons, London    18cm    80p.    BL,Bo,CBA,CU, Sc,SG

Third Edition
    1909    Lucas Collins, London    16cm    80p.    BL,CBA,EL

There was a paperback binding of loose papers of the Second Edition with a cover giving as the publishers 'SGAT, London', and 'G.H. Fromow, Chiswick'. This was most probably the reviewed edition available 'from ourselves', *Watching and Waiting*, May/June 1965, p.335.

## SCRIPTURAL PROOF OF THE DOCTRINE OF THE FIRST RESURRECTION

This tract was later incorporated in the Third Edition of *Aids to Prophetic Enquiry* (First Series), 1881. Additional footnotes were then added.

When it was included in *Aids to Prophetic Enquiry*, a note regarding the Bampton Lectures of Samuel Waldegrave was deleted (pp.26-30 Second Edition, *Scriptural Proof…*). *Babylon and Egypt* (Third Edition, p.574) refers to this note on Mr Waldegrave's opinions, which is evidently unique to this separately published tract.

A note on Rev. 20:5, 'The rest of the dead lived not' (pp.34-36 Second Edition *Scriptural Proof…*) was also deleted when it was incorporated into *Aids to Prophetic Enquiry*.

First Edition
    1858    Houlston & Wright, London    16cm    36p.    BL,Bo,CU,I,Sc,SG,T

Second Edition
    1868    Houlston & Wright, London    16cm    36p.    CBA,EL,SG

[Third Edition]. This is an edited version with the title *The First Resurrection and the Reign in Righteousness*. It was reprinted from *Watching and Waiting*, March/April 1951. It was reviewed as a tract in *Watching and Waiting*, July/August 1951.
    ND [1951]    SGAT, London    16cm    26p.    BIOLA,EL

[Fourth Edition]
    This is a reprint of the Third Edition under the same title (*The First Resurrection…*).
    ND [1987]    SGAT, Chelmsford    16cm    26p.    SG

[Fifth Edition]. This is a reprint of the Third Edition under the same title (*The First Resurrection…*).
    ND [199?]    Irish Christian Mission, Belfast    15cm    26p.    CG

## SCRIPTURAL PROSPECTS

This consists of two short extracts from *Prospects of the Ten Kingdoms*, and one from *Thoughts on the Apocalypse*. The extracts were reprinted from *Perilous Times* (September 1908 p.159; January 1910 p.231; April 1912 p.353). In the bound volume No.9 of *Watching and Waiting* this tract was inserted at p.116 with the April/May/June 1944 magazine.

    ND [1943/44]   SGAT, London                 18cm    4p.    BL,SG

## SCRIPTURAL TRUTHS

These are 24 × 4 page tracts, which were also bound up in book form. They are extracts from the writings of Mr Newton – for example, No.1 is extracted from *Prospects of the Ten Kingdoms*, Second Edition pp.296 ff.

*Perilous Times* (p.192) reported in April 1902 that they would be 'ready shortly'. Mrs Stirling's bound volume (at CBA) is dated 1907, and was published by John F Shaw, London. However, this probably simply refers to the binding of the volume.

The SGAT report for 1963 (in *Watching and Waiting* March/April 1963) states we 'have bound up several hundred of the little volume, *Scriptural Truths*'.

    c.1901   John Shaw & Co, London        16cm   98p.    SG

    c.1902   Hunt, Barnard, Aylesbury     11cm   100p.   CBA,SG

## THE SECOND ADVENT NOT SECRET, BUT IN MANIFESTED GLORY

This is the title given to the Seventh Edition of *The Second Advent of our Lord not Secret but in Manifested Glory*.

## THE SECOND ADVENT OF OUR LORD NOT SECRET BUT IN MANIFESTED GLORY

This is an item in *Occasional Papers on Scriptural Subjects No.2* (1862), from which it was reprinted. It covers the same theme as the fifth of the *Five Letters on Events Predicted in Scripture as Antecedent to the Coming of the Lord*, which was titled, *Is the Church Directed in Scripture to Expect a Secret Coming of the Lord Jesus?*. Although the two items commence with a consideration of 1 Thess. 4, there is little further similarity (see, however, the account of the development of the letters under the entry for *Five Letters on Events Predicted...*).

The tract reviews the Scriptural evidence against a secret coming of the Lord Jesus, and gives a succession of predicted events for which the believer should watch as appointed signs of the Lord's near return.

As with other publications in this *Guide*, it may be that the publication of the item in *Occasional Papers on Scriptural Subjects*, and even the earlier similar item in the *Five Letters...*, account for the inability to locate copies of the Second and Third Editions, as the publisher accepted these as the earlier editions.

[First Edition]
    1862   Houlston & Wright, London          18cm   26p.    SG

Second Edition          not located.

Third Edition           not located.

Fourth Edition
    1891    Houlston & Sons, London                    16cm    27p.    CBA,EL,SG

Fifth Edition
    1922    C.M. Tucker                                16cm    28p.    EL

Sixth Edition. Greek words transliterated.
    1936    E.J. Burnett, Worthing                     16cm    28p.    BIOLA,CBA

Seventh Edition - *The Second Advent not Secret, but in Manifested Glory*, slightly edited.
    1957    G.L. Silverwood-Browne, Wembley            15cm    19p.    BIOLA,CBA

[Eighth Edition] - *Christ's Return not Secret, but in Manifested Glory*.
    1993    Irish Christian Mission, Belfast           15cm    19p.    CG

[Ninth Edition] - *The Second Advent not Secret, but in Manifested Glory* slightly edited. A reprint of the Seventh Edition.
    [2003]          SGAT, Chelmsford                   21cm    12p.    SG

## A SECOND LETTER TO A FRIEND ON THE STUDY OF PROPHECY

This was first published as an article in *The Christian Witness* of January 1836. It was subsequently published as a tract. It is unanimously attributed to B.W. Newton, and from our assessment we have concluded that it is beyond reasonable doubt by him. See consideration of authorship in Section 7, Articles in *The Christian Witness* for the basis of this conclusion. It was preceded by *A Letter to a Friend on the Study of Prophecy*. The letters are both 'signed' XZ.

The second letter was produced to supplement the first, to set out the Scriptural evidence for the millennial glory of the saints, and to comment on the significance of the progressive nature of millennial blessing.

*The Christian Witness* Vol. 3     January 1836    Pages 39 - 57     19 pages

    [ND]    Central Tract Depot, London                ?       ?       CBA, SG

Two editions not located.

Fourth Edition
    1840    J. Clulow & H. Soltau, Plymouth            18cm    23p.    CBA, SG

## A SECOND LETTER TO THE BRETHREN AND SISTERS IN CHRIST, MEETING FOR COMMUNION IN EBRINGTON STREET

This is one of the pamphlets that that followed Mr Newton's publication of *Thoughts on the Apocalypse*. After his commentary was issued, J.N. Darby produced his censure, *An Examination of the Statements made in 'Thoughts on the Apocalypse' by B.W. Newton, and an Enquiry How Far They Accord with Scripture*. Mr Newton made reply with his *A Letter to the Brethren and Sisters in Christ Meeting for Communion in Ebrington Street, Plymouth, Containing Remarks on a Recent Tract Circulated among Them*. A further censure then came from J.N. Darby, under the title, *Answer to a 'Letter to the Brethren and Sisters Who Meet for Communion in Ebrington Street'*. This *Second Letter...* from B.W. Newton is mainly concerned with J.N. Darby's first response. Only the final ten pages were a formal reply to J.N. Darby's *Answer...* This pamphlet responds to J.N. Darby on regeneration, the incarnation, circumcision, union with Christ, and other issues. It does not deal with differences of interpretation of the Book of Revelation.

B.W. Newton discontinued the literary duel when J.N. Darby persisted, and published his *Answer to a 'A Second Letter to the Brethren and Sisters Who Meet for Communion in Ebrington Street'*. The three challenges by J.N. Darby are all in his *Collected Writings*, Vol. 8. The whole sequence of the publications took place in 1845. This *Second Letter...* was also criticised in *Remarks on 'The Wreck and the Rock'*, pp.17,18,31,32. (published anonymously, but owned by J.N. Darby in his *A Plain Statement of the Sufferings of our Blessed Lord*, p.113).

Quotations from this tract are included in the anthology *B.W. Newton on Ministry and Order in the Church of Christ*, as giving evidence of Mr Newton's views on Church order.

    1845    I.K. Campbell, 1 Warwick Square    16cm    68p.    CBA, SG
                London and Plymouth
                [Tract Depot] 5, Cornwall Street.

## SECOND SERIES OF 'AIDS TO PROPHETIC ENQUIRY'

The original title of *Babylon and Egypt*.

## SECOURS POUR L'ÉTUDE DE LA PROPHÉTIE, TRADUIT LIBREMENT DE L'ANGLAIS DE B.W.N.

French Edition of *Aids to Prophetic Enquiry*.

## THE SERVICE OF THE PRIESTS ON THE EIGHTH DAY (LEV. 9)

This is Part 2 of Vol. II, of the serialised *Thoughts on Parts of Leviticus*.

## THE SEVEN PARABLES OF THE THIRTEENTH OF MATTHEW, DISPENSATIONALLY CONSIDERED

Title of the First Edition of *Thoughts on the History of Professing Christianity as Given in Matthew 13*.

## THE SEVENTH CHAPTER OF THE EPISTLE TO THE ROMANS, CONSIDERED

In this work Mr Newton expounded and applied the chapter in both its general statement, and verse by verse. He opposed perfectionist views, and the views of those who deny the application of verses 13 to 24 to the believer. The last 27 pages of the booklet are concerned with Romans 2 rather than Romans 7.

The publication of the Second Edition in 1872 coincided with Mr Newton's opposition to R. Pearsall Smith's teaching, and in this context it was reviewed in *The Record* (9th December 1872). See also notes on *Modern Doctrines Respecting Sinlessness Considered*.

This item was included in the compilation, *Thoughts on Parts of the Epistle to the Romans*.

First Edition
    1860    Houlston & Wright, London    18cm    90p.    BL,Bo,I,Sc,SG,T,U[edition?]
           Geo Hunt, London.

Second Edition - apparently identical to the First Edition.
    1873    Houlston & Sons, London    16cm    84p.    BIOLA,CBA,EL

Third Edition (photographic reprint of the Second Edition)
    [2016]    SGAT, Chelmsford    16cm    84p.    SG

A new binding of the Second Edition in paperback from loose papers was made in 1955 (*Watching and Waiting*, March/April 1955).

## THE SIMILARITIES AND THE CONTRASTS BETWEEN THE PRESENT AND COMING DISPENSATIONS

The frontispiece of the tract reads as follows: 'This tract, being the substance of two lectures at the Mechanics Institute, Plymouth, December 2nd 1841 by J.L. Harris and B.W. Newton is printed from notes taken at the time and subsequently printed'. This wording may suggest two editions.

The pamphlet is in two halves, the second headed 'BWN', which consists of 12 pages.

Both halves deal with dispensational similarities and differences. Mr Newton in his part argued the importance of looking for the soon coming of the Lord Jesus.

The item was included in the set of tracts known as *Lectures on Prophecy*.

(First Edition?)
    ND [1842]    John Wertheimer & Co,    16cm    24p.    SG
                   Finsbury Circus, London

(Second Edition?)
    1842    Central Tract Depot, London    16cm    24p.    CBA, EC

## THE SIN OFFERING (LEVITICUS 4 AND 5)

This was Part 4 of Vol. I, of the serialised *Thoughts on Parts of Leviticus*.

## [SPIRITISM]

The correct title of this series of extracts from Mr Newton's works is not known. They were reprinted as a tract from articles in *Watching and Waiting* between June and October 1919. The tract is referred to in the October 1919 issue, p.70. No copies have been located.

## A STATEMENT AND ACKNOWLEDGEMENT RESPECTING CERTAIN DOCTRINAL ERRORS

This was Mr Newton's final statement before he left the Brethren. A 'Memorandum' on page 207 of MS Book 1 (TC) has the following note in F.W. Wyatt's hand 'On 26th of this year 1847. B.W. Newton published *A Statement and Acknowledgement Respecting Certain Doctrinal Errors*. Tregelles begged him not to do so, and N hesitated for hours under Tregelles pleading that N's adversaries would make an evil use of it. At last he signed it, and sent it to press'. The origin of the comment is not given, but is probably from Miss Amy J.T. Toulmin.

In this 'Statement' Mr Newton confessed his error in placing Christ in any association with the federal headship of Adam as a means of accounting for the sufferings that he bore. He withdrew any such statement that he had made, and rejected any such statements that had been attributed to him. In it he also withdrew 'for reconsideration' the two tracts, *Remarks on the Sufferings of the Lord Jesus…*, and *Observations on a tract entitled, 'The Sufferings of Christ…'*. He explained how his position had been arrived at in the controversy against the teachings of Edward Irving, and how he had guarded the doctrine with limitations in his own mind, and in his teaching. He stated that he had never personally made the deductions that some had drawn regarding Christ's fitness for the work of the atonement.

In this tract he was essentially acknowledging the sin of carelessness, and the lack of clarity in his statements – see his comments in *A Letter on Subjects connected with the Lord's Humanity* (pp.32,33).

He concluded, 'I desire that this may be considered as an expression of my deep and unfeigned grief and sorrow, especially by those who may have been grieved or injured by false statement, or by any consequences thence resulting'.

The last two pages are an appendix by S.P. Tregelles – 'A Brief Account of Mr Newton's Paper on the Doctrines of the Church in Newman Street'. The original of S.P. Tregelles's 'Brief Account…' was dated 8th November 1847, and 'was written in reply to a private inquiry and not for publication'. According to the 'Rough Notes'[1], the original of S.P. Tregelles's notes were in Folio 8 and/or 9, but are now missing from the Fry Collection.

Mr Newton moved from Plymouth after the publication of the tract. See Section 9, B.W. Newton's Correspondence for this date for background.

In the weeks that followed the publication of this pamphlet, B.W. Newton's erstwhile colleagues in the Ebrington Street meeting (J.E. Batten, H. Soltau, J. Clulow, W.B. Dyer) withdrew, publishing their personal confessions of error as a means of distancing themselves from B.W. Newton. J.N. Darby disallowed Mr Newton's sincerity, and published his *Notice of the Statement and Acknowledgement of Error Circulated by Mr Newton*[2] (J.N. Darby, Collected Writings Vol. 15).

The *Statement* was reprinted as Appendix B of *A History of the Brethren Movement* by F. Roy Coad [Paternoster Press – 1968 – 327p – BL]. It was also reprinted in Chapter 28 of *Teachers of the Faith and Future*, by George H. Fromow (2nd Edn. pp.158-161). It is followed by the statement by G.H. Lang,

---

[1] 'The Rough Notes' (In the Christian Brethren Archive as FRY/1/2/1 - see 'Manuscript Items added to the Fry Collection in 2011' item 7, in this Guide).

[2] Notice J.N. Darby's nuanced change in his reference to the pamphlet. There is a subtle difference between 'the statement and acknowledgement of error, circulated by B.W. Newton', and 'A statement and acknowledgement respecting an error'. B.W. Newton always held that it was the statements in his final two tracts in the controversy that were at fault, together with some in his statements in *Doctrines of the Church in Newman Street*, - from which others could draw erroneous conclusions that he himself neither intended not held.

'If it be asked why so thorough a confession and withdrawal did not end the controversy, the answer must be that Mr Newton's opponents had ceased to walk in love, and therefore carnal influences, such as bitterness, ambition, a party spirit, overcame them'.

First Edition (dated November 26th 1847).
    ND [1847]   [No Publisher] Plymouth      18cm    10p.    ID

Second Edition
    1907    No printer – 'privately reprinted'    16cm    10p.    CBA

## STATEMENT OF DOCTRINE

CBA 6998 (1948 Folio 9) refers to this as dated 11th July 1848. It is therefore to be identified with *Brief Statements in the Form of Answers to Questions*, which has the same date.

## SUBSTANCE OF A LECTURE ON LUKE 21

See *On Luke 21…*

## THAT HE MIGHT GATHER INTO ONE ALL THINGS IN CHRIST; EVEN IN HIM

Title given to *The Old Testament Saints not Excluded from the Church in Glory, with Some Remarks on the Heresy of Marcion*, Canadian Edition, published by 'Ministry for the Last Difficult Days'.

## THEOLOGICAL OPINIONS OF REV. JOSEPH COOK OF BOSTON, BRIEFLY CONSIDERED (PART I)

Joseph Cook of Boston, Lincolnshire had some acceptance in Evangelical circles. Mr Newton considered his teachings pantheistic. He opposed him, and in doing so defended the doctrines of total depravity, the sole authority of Scripture, propitiation and atonement, the resurrection of the body, and creation.

In a notice at the end of the book, Mr Newton declares his intention to publish 'a short second number with appendix' – hence the book was titled 'Part I'. No record of any such further volume has been found.

    1881    Houlston & Sons, London    18cm    xii+125p.    BL,Bo,CBA,CU,EL,Sc,SG

## THINGS CLEAN AND UNCLEAN (LEVITICUS 11)

This was Part 3 of Vol. 2 of the serialised *Thoughts on Parts of Leviticus*.

## THE THIRD SERIES OF 'AIDS TO PROPHETIC ENQUIRY'

The original title of *Prospects of the Ten Kingdoms*.

## THOUGHTS ON PARTS OF LEVITICUS

B.W. Newton commented on ten chapters of the Book of Leviticus in this work. In the first part he related the ceremonial law of the offerings to the saving work of Christ. C.H. Spurgeon in his *Commenting on Commentaries* seemed to be only aware of Volume 1 of this work, but wrote, 'It treats of the offerings in a manner deeply spiritual and helpful'.

Details of the publishing are confused. The 'First Edition' was issued between 1852 and 1857 in a series of tracts in 'two volumes' with successive numbering. A Second Edition, by another publisher, appeared in 1857. In 1861 'a new edition' of volume 1 was advertised in the Second Edition of *The Day of the Lord* as 'just published'. It was also advertised in *Gospel Truths* 1872.. No separate copies of the second edition of 'Volume 1' have been located.

The edition that appeared in 1898 was not called the Third Edition, but 'A New Edition, revised'. It does not refer to any Second Edition.

The parts issued separately in the serialised publication were:

Volume 1
1. The Burnt Offering (Chapter 1) – 1852.
2. The Meat Offering (Chapter 2) – 1852.
3. The Peace Sacrifice (Chapter 3) – 1852.
4. The Sin Offering (Chapters 4 and 5) – 1852.
5. The Trespass Offering (Chapter 6) – 1853.

Volume 2
1. On Leviticus 8. The Consecration of the Priests – 1854.
2. On Leviticus 9. The Service of the Priests on the Eighth Day – 1857.
3. Things Clean and Unclean (Chapter 11) – 1857.
4. The Leprosy (Chapter 13) -1857.

There are other expositions on parts of Leviticus by Mr Newton. It is therefore perhaps surprising that these were not included in any of the editions. These further items include:

1. On Leviticus 10. The Sin of Nadab and Abihu, in *Occasional Papers on Scriptural Subjects No.4*, and later included in *Narratives from the Old Testament*.
2. *Cleansing the Leper* (Chapter 14); and
3. The Feasts of Israel as appointed in Leviticus 23, in *Thoughts on Scriptural Subjects*.

Two items extracted from *Thoughts on Parts of Leviticus* and published separately are:

1. *The One All-Sufficient Offering*.
2. *The First Anxiety of Every Soul Awakened* (also reprinted in G.H. Fromow's *Teachers of the Faith and Future*).

Quotations are included in the anthology *B.W. Newton on Ministry and Order in the Church of Christ*.

First Edition
   Volume 1st
      1852-1857      Partridge, Oakey and Co         17cm    ?       ?
   Volume 2nd
      1852-1857      Partridge, Oakey and Co         17cm    136p.   BL,Bo,CBA CU,Sc,SG,T
         [NB some of the library listings of the series are incomplete and may include volume 1]

Second Edition
  Volume 1
    1857     Houlston & Wright, London            17cm    240p.    CBA,U
  Volume 2
    ND [1857?] Houlston & Wright, London          17cm    136p.    EL,SG
(Third Edition) - New Edition, Revised
    1898     Houlston & Sons, London              18cm    397+7p.  CBA,EL,U
(Fourth Edition)
    2011     SGAT, Chelmsford                     18cm    397+7p.  SG
             and Tentmaker Publications, Stoke-on -Trent

American Editions – *The Perfect Sacrifice.*
*The Perfect Sacrifice* is an edited edition of Volume 1. Mr Newton's original is described as having consisted of an 'essay' on each of the offerings, together with notes. The preface proceeds to describe *The Perfect Sacrifice* as follows: 'The present edition consists only of the essays, into which have been inserted such portions of the notes as seemed desirable for the more full presentation of the author's views. Some footnotes have been added by the editor from the writings of the author, and from other sources. There has been no change of the author's language except in a few instances where a mere verbal correction has been made'.
  (Edition 1)
  1870       American Baptist Publication Society
                              17cm    178p.    University of Michigan Library, Philadelphia
  (Edition 2)        (A short run print republication).
    2006     University of Michigan    ?    180p.    University of Michigan Library

German Edition of Vol. 1, Part 1 (The Burnt Offering). *Gedanken über Theile des dritten Buches Mose. Aus dem Engl. übers 1: Das Brandopfer (3 buch Mose 1 kap) als Typus auf Christus biblisch erörtert.*
  1861 Fricke, Halle  16cm  78p.    CBA,Nordelbischen Kirchenbibliothek Hamburg

Chinese Edition
  Referred to in *Watching and Waiting,* November/December 1940 p.189 as having been produced by 'a Chinese brother'. No copies have been located. It is probable that the missionary W.E. Burnett's ministry gave rise to this initiative.[1]
    [1940?]  ?                                    ?       ?        ?

---
[1] William Edward Burnett (1862-1950), an associate of B.W. Newton who commenced the Evangelical Protestant Mission to the Chinese in 1893, having left for China in 1883, first serving with the China Inland Mission. He died in China. Obituary *Watching and Waiting,* September-October 1950, p.69, and January-February 1951, p.106-108

## THOUGHTS ON PARTS OF THE EPISTLE TO THE ROMANS

This was a compilation of the various works. The volume at the Evangelical Library, London, consists of the following:
1. *The First and Second Chapters of the Epistle to the Romans, Considered.*
2. *Justification* [Romans 5:1-11].
3. *Eternal Reconciliation* [Romans 5].
4. *Romans 7 Considered.*
5. *No Condemnation to Them Who Are in Christ Jesus* [Romans 8].

The volume belonging to A.C. Fry, now in the possession of the SGAT is evidently later. It consists of:
1. *Notes Expository of the Greek of Romans 1.*
2. *The First and Second Chapters of the Epistle to the Romans Considered.*
3. *Romans 7 Considered.*
4. *Gospel Truths* (itself a compilation of *Justification*; *Eternal Reconciliation*; *No Condemnation...*; and *Regeneration in its Connexion with the Cross*.

*Thoughts on Parts of the Epistle to the Romans* is not to be confused with *Lectures on the Epistle to the Romans*. That is a posthumous production based on notes of lectures given by Mr Newton, for which see Section 8, Publications Produced from Notes of Addresses, and Posthumously Published Letters and Manuscripts.

| 1867 | Houlston & Wright, London | 17.5cm | individual numbering | EL,U |
| ND [1900?] | No publisher | 17.5cm | individual numbering | SG |

## THOUGHTS ON PARTS OF THE PROPHECY OF ISAIAH

This work follows the same pattern as Mr Newton's 'Thoughts' on Leviticus, and on the Book of Revelation. There is an essay on each chapter (Thoughts), followed by textual 'Notes', including B.W. Newton's translation of each verse upon which it comments does not always follow the Masoretic reading[1].

There are several excursuses. These additional notes are concerned with:
1. Spiritualism [in the Second Edition].
2. Marcionism [in the First and Second Editions].
3. The Unity of the Redeemed [in the First and Second Editions]. This follows the Note on Isaiah 6:1 in the First Edition. [cf. *The True Unity of the Church of God in Time and Eternity*; and *Old Testament Saints Not Excluded from the Church in Glory*, each of which deal with the same theme, but in different ways].

---

[1] On page 45 of the Second Edition, he commends J.A. Alexander's commentary, 'This I value most of any critical work on Isaiah that I have seen. Whilst altogether repudiating conjectural emendations of the Hebrew text, I do not defer always to the accentuation nor to the pointing of the printed editions – neither the accentuation nor the pointing being of Divine authority'.

4. Note on Three Quotations From the Old Testament in Hebrews 2:12,13 [in the First and Second Editions].[1]

The First Edition was published as 'Volume 1', the Second Edition proceeds no further than the First (i.e. to Isaiah 9:7), and the reference to it as 'Volume 1' disappeared. As with several other works, the First Edition was issued in parts. Three 'parts' were issued during 1868. The Bodleian Library has parts 1 and 3.

There are minor additions to the text and footnotes (e.g. p.81n) in the Second Edition.

The contents of the Second Edition are as follows:

1. Thoughts and Notes on Isaiah 1 (45 pages)
2. Thoughts and Notes on Isaiah 2 (28 pages)
3. Note on Spiritualism (14 pages)
4. Thoughts and Notes on Isaiah 3 and 4 (21 pages)
5. Thoughts and Notes on Isaiah 5 (34 pages)
6. Thoughts and Notes on Isaiah 6 (31 pages)
7. Note on Marcionism (22 pages)
8. Note on the Unity of the Redeemed (23 pages)
9. Thoughts and Notes on Isaiah 7 (37 pages)
10. Thoughts and Notes on Isaiah 8 – 9:1-7 (48 pages)
11. Note on Three Quotations from the Old Testament in Hebrews 2:12,13 (12 pages)

Part of the Note on Spiritualism was later included in *Reflections on the Character and Spread of Spiritualism*. The Note on Marcionism was incorporated into *Old Testament Saints Not to be Excluded from the Church in Glory; with Some Remarks on the Heresy of Marcion*.

The SGAT added further material from notes of Mr Newton's lectures to the First Edition to form *Thoughts on the Whole Prophecy of Isaiah*, which see. This therefore lacked the additional notes and additional comments in the Second Edition (e.g. the comments on Isa. 1:3,19). In the SGAT production the Note on the Unity of the Redeemed was taken out of square brackets, and followed on as if it were a note on Isaiah 6:1, as the First Edition.

First Edition
    1868    Houlston & Wright, London    18cm    302p.    BIOLA,BL,Bo,CU,SG,Sc

Second Edition
    1894    Houlston & Sons, London    18cm    316p.    BIOLA,CBA,EL,U

There was a binding of loose papers of the Second Edition by SGAT in 1950 (*Watching and Waiting*, January/February 1951 p.102).

---

[1] B.W. Newton contends that the verses in Hebrews do not quote Isaiah 8:18, as is commonly asserted, but rather 2 Sam. 22:3

## Section 3 - Bibliography of B.W. Newton's Published Works

### THOUGHTS ON PARTS OF THE SONG OF SOLOMON

This was posthumously published as a separate item. It brings together Mr Newton's comments on the Song of Solomon that had appeared in *Occasional Papers on Scriptural Subjects*, Nos. 1,2,3, and 4. Mr Newton had begun revising these before his death, but only completed the item that appeared in *Occasional Papers on Scriptural Subjects, No.1*, to which he made minor changes (CG holds the volume, which has his emendations). These minor changes were incorporated in the publication. It is devotional and spiritual, rather than providing verse by verse notes upon the text.

    1906    Lucas Collins, London    18cm    100p.    BIOLA,BL,CBA, EL,SG,U

Chinese Edition

    Referred to in *Watching and Waiting* November / December 1940 p.189, by 'a Chinese brother'. No further details are known or copies located. It is probable that the missionary W.E. Burnett's ministry gave rise to this initiative.[1]

### THOUGHTS ON SCRIPTURAL SUBJECTS

This is a work on similar lines to *Occasional Papers on Scriptural Subjects*, being a collection of articles, but, unlike *Occasional Papers on Scriptural Subjects*, it centres upon one theme – justification and atonement. It replies to attempts to undermine these key Reformation doctrines. The preface quotes an otherwise unpublished letter by S.P. Tregelles in which he also sounds a warning against such theological trends[2].

The contents of the Second Edition are as follows:

1. The Lord's Day our Sabbatic Day
2. The Feasts of Israel as Appointed in Leviticus 23.
3. Note on Hebrews 13:10.[3]
4. Note on the Lord's Supper.
5. Notes on Certain Statements of Dean Goode on the Eucharist.[4]
6. Remarks on a Tract Entitled 'Justification in the Risen Christ'.[5]
7. Romans 4:25 Considered in Connection with the Preceding Paper.
8. On Isaiah 53.
9. Notes on Isaiah 52:13 to End, and on Isaiah 53.

---

[1] William Edward Burnett (1862-1950), an associate of B.W. Newton who commenced the Evangelical Protestant Mission to the Chinese in 1893, having left for China in 1883, first serving with the China Inland Mission. He died in China. Obituary *Watching and Waiting*, September-October 1950, p.69, and January-February 1951, p.106-108

[2] See the note on this letter, listed at 17th December [1869] in Section 9 of this Guide, B.W. Newton's Correspondence

[3] This is not to be confused with the tract *Our Altar, Hebrews 13:10*.

[4] *The Nature of Christ's Presence in the Eucharist, or the True Doctrine of the Real Presence Vindicated in Opposition to the Fictitious Real Presence Asserted by Archdeacon Denison, Mr (late Archdeacon) Wilberforce, and Dr Pusey* by William Goode (1801-1868), Dean of Ripon.

[5] *Justification in the Risen Christ; or 'The Faith which was Once Delivered to the Saints'*, by Brethren writer C. Stanley (1821-1890). He was the editor of the periodical *Things Old and New* after C.H. Mackintosh.

10. On the Imputation of Adam's Sin, and Christ's Righteousness.
11. Representative and Personal Condition of Believers Contrasted.
12. The Excellency of the Person of Christ Unalterable. Remarks on the Doctrines of Olshausen.[1]
13. Modern Doctrines Respecting Sinlessness Considered.[2]
14. On the Use of the Preposition ANTI [αντι] in the New Testament.
15. Appendix [This is a commendation of *The Atonement* by A.A. Hodge, and *The Doctrine of the Atonement as taught by the Apostles* by G. Smeaton, with a lengthy quotation from Dr Smeaton's book, and of John Calvin on Osiander (in Latin)].
16. Zechariah 5 Re-translated.
17. Notes on Zechariah 5.

At least one previously published work was included in it – *Remarks on a Tract Entitled, 'Justification in the Risen Christ'*. The Second Edition added two chapters, 'Zechariah 5 Re-translated', and 'Notes on Zechariah 5'. It also added 2 pages of corrigenda!

*Note on the Lord's Supper*; *Modern Doctrines respecting Sinlessness, Considered*; *Isaiah 53, Considered* (chapters 8 and 9); and *Zechariah 5 Re-translated* were subsequently extracted, and published separately. If *The Excellency of the Person of Christ Unalterable* was published separately, this was also extracted from it.

*Perilous Times* (June 1915 pp.126,127) gives a translation of Isaiah 53 compiled from *Isaiah 53, Considered*, which was extracted from this work.

First Edition
    1871    Houlston & Sons, London    18cm    xii+389p.    BL,Bo,CBA,CU,EL,Sc,T,U

Second Edition. – 'Revised, and republished without any material alteration, and with very slight addition'. Two chapters were added, and the section on Isaiah 53 was slightly extended. The 'Advertisement' to the edition is dated 'September 1896'.
    1896    Houlston & Sons, London    18cm    vii+426+6p.    CBA,U

Third Edition (photographic reprint of the Second Edition)
    [2015]    SGAT, Chelmsford    18cm    xii+389p.    SG

## THOUGHTS ON THE 24TH MATTHEW

Referred to in the First Edition of *Thoughts on the Apocalypse* (p.95). Believed to be the same as *Prophecy of the Lord Jesus as contained in Matthew 24, Briefly Considered*.

---

[1] Hermann Olshausen (1796–1839) was a German theologian who rejected the Reformation doctrine of substitutionary righteousness. His works were published in English throughout the nineteenth century.

[2] This is chiefly concerned with the writings of Robert Pearsall Smith (1827-1899), who was a leader in the Holiness movement in the United States, and the 'Higher Life' movement in Great Britain.

## THOUGHTS ON THE APOCALYPSE

### The publication date

It was originally issued in twelve parts. In his *Advertisement* to the Second Edition, Mr Newton gave the date of its first publication as 1843. The Brethren writer William Kelly also stated that it was produced in 1843 in *The Coming and Day of the Lord*. However, the First Edition indicates a publication date of 1844, and S.P. Tregelles in his *An Account of the Printed Text of the Greek New Testament*, 1854 (p.270 note) stated that Mr Newton followed the revised Greek text that he published in 1844, and that the First Edition of *Thoughts on the Apocalypse* was (accordingly) published in 1844. This disparity can be resolved if the parts publication commenced in 1843 and Mr Newton had access to S.P. Tregelles's unpublished text, as he prepared the *Thoughts on the Apocalypse* for publication.[1]

There is further confusion regarding date, as *The Observations on 2 Thess. 2* (pp.182-186 of the First Edition) has an additional note, which commences, 'Since the above was written'. It goes on to refer to 'the events of the present year (1846)' - despite the frontispiece giving the date as 1844, and of the book giving some evidence of being made up from the part-work.

The publisher's note in the First Edition of the *Second Series of the 'Aids to Prophetic Enquiry'* [otherwise titled *Babylon*] 1849, p.94, refers to the separate sections of *Thoughts on the Apocalypse* chapters 13 and 17 as still being available separately.

### The book's development and structure

In view of the importance of the book, a detailed account and comparison of the editions is given Appendix 1 of this *Guide*.

In his *Commenting on Commentaries* C.H. Spurgeon simply described the book as "Of the Futurist School. Condensed and instructive". In B.W. Newton's own words, 'The Revelation, in its prophetic parts, belongs to the closing hour of human history'. The characteristics of the period which the Revelation treats are 'Christ hidden with God – Israel blinded – the Gentiles supreme and glorious – the Church suffering'.

*Thoughts on the Apocalypse* gives 'thoughts' on the teaching of a chapter or chapters, followed by notes, mainly on the text, on the text of the same chapter(s). The book therefore established the pattern for Mr Newton's other commentaries – i.e. a discourse on a passage of Scripture, followed by more detailed notes on the text.

The Second Edition enlarged the first (by approximately one third), but the central themes of the book are unaltered. Despite the violent attacks upon the First Edition by J.N. Darby and his followers, the Second Edition does not refer to him or controversy, and makes few discernible changes in response to his criticisms. An example of B.W. Newton's editing is given in *A Pictorial*

---

[1] See also the comment on the Advertisement of the Second Edition in Appendix 1, Comparison of Editions of *Thoughts on The Apocalypse*, of this *Guide*, and the note on B.W. Newton's personal Greek New Testament (dated 1842 by him) in Section 12, Miscellaneous Biographical Items and Memorabilia. It shows heavy use on the pages of the Book of Revelation, and MS corrections in Mr Newton's hand, probably to Griesbach's edition. It is likely that he made the amendments to that personal Greek Testament before Tregelles's work on the text of the Revelation was published.

*Memoir of Benjamin Wills Newton* – the supplement to this Guide. See the Advertisement at the end of this volume. The third, posthumous, edition is a word for word reprint of the second, with additional notes and indexes. However, Mr Newton hoped to revise it before his death, particularly in relation to Revelation 7. See F.W. Wyatt's letter, included in our comparison of the editions, given in Appendix 1.

### *Thoughts on the Apocalypse* and J.N. Darby

The differences with J.N. Darby on prophecy became more apparent after the publication of his (J.N. Darby's) *Notes on the Book of Revelations* [sic]; *to Assist Inquirers in Searching into that Book* (1839) and the circulation of B.W. Newton's *Five Letters…* (1840). The second of those *Five Letters* was designed to demonstrate that believers will serve and suffer throughout the closing period of the present dispensation. In it Mr Newton outlined the book of Revelation, and expressed the view that 'a more minute interpretation of the Revelation would, as I believe, greatly confirm the statement I have made'.

Following the publication of *Thoughts on the Apocalypse* J.N. Darby came to Plymouth in 1845 and published there a lengthy[1] diatribe against it (also in parts) under the title, *An Examination of the Statements made in 'Thoughts on the Apocalypse' by B.W. Newton, and an Enquiry How Far They Accord with Scripture* [1845 – ii+372p – BL,CBA. *Collected Writings*, Vol. 8]. The spirit in which J.N. Darby's 'examination' was written was later severely criticised in *The Quarterly Journal of Prophecy* (Vol. 1 1849 pp.71,72). Mr Newton replied with *A Letter to the Brethren and Sisters in Christ Meeting for Communion in Ebrington Street, Plymouth, Containing Remarks on a Recent Tract Circulated among Them* (1845). J.N. Darby then wrote *Answer to 'A Letter to the Brethren and Sisters in Christ Who Meet for Communion in Ebrington Street, Plymouth'* (1845) [*Collected Writings* Vol. 8]. Mr Newton followed with *A Second Letter to the Brethren and Sisters in Christ Meeting for Communion in Ebrington Street* (1845). Determined, as ever, to have the last word, J.N. Darby followed with *Answer to 'A Second Letter to the Brethren and Sisters in Christ Who Meet for Communion in Ebrington Street, Plymouth'* (*Collected Writings* Vol. 8). There the literary correspondence ceased, although Mr Newton's *Thoughts on the Apocalypse* was also criticised in *Remarks on 'The Wreck and the Rock'* (1846 - published anonymously, but owned by J.N. Darby in his *A Plain Statement of the Sufferings of our Blessed Lord*, p.113).

Robert Mackenzie Beverley, another Brethren writer, published his own critical reply under the title, *Analysis, by a Student of Prophecy, of 'Thoughts on the Apocalypse' by B.W. Newton of Plymouth* [1845 – Longman, Brown, Green and Longmans, London – 17cm - 51p - BL,Bo,CU,Sc,T].

### Related publication issues

In 1846 Mr Newton issued *A Prophetic Map of the World; Intended to Exhibit its General Condition at the End of the Age; also Some Extracts on the Same Subject from 'Thoughts on the Apocalypse'*. This reprinted pages 155-293 of the First Edition (Rev. 13-18). The 20 pages of explanation of the map, numbered in roman numerals, with the map itself, were included in some of the bindings of the First Edition, and in the French Edition, where consecutive numbering was used with the rest of *Pensées sur*

---

[1] Peter Embley, in his thesis *The Origins and Early Development of the Plymouth Brethren*, reckoned that it ran to 200,000 words. It was longer than the book it censured.

*l'Apocalypse*. A similar account to this 'explanation' is found in *Aids to Prophetic Enquiry* (Third Edition, pp.162 ff.), which perhaps removed the need for it to appear in the Second Edition of *Thoughts on the Apocalypse*.

The publisher of the First Edition is given in *Aids to Prophetic Enquiry, Second Series* [Babylon] p.94, as 'Nisbet and Co and Hamilton and Adams, London'. There is also some confusion regarding the publisher of the Second Edition (cf. the First Edition of *Aids to Prophetic Enquiry*).

Quotations are included in the anthology *B.W. Newton on Ministry and Order in the Church of Christ*. A pamphlet, *Scriptural Prospects* (1943/4) reprinted one short extract from the Third Edition.

First Edition (in parts)
    1843    J.B. Rowe, Plymouth    18cm    337p.    BL,CBA

First Edition (one volume)
    1844    Hamilton, Adams & Co, London    18cm    337p.    BL,Bo,CBA,Sc SG,T

First Edition (with map, and its introduction).
    1844 [6?]    Hamilton, Adams & Co, London    18cm    xx+337p.    SG

Second Edition, revised.
    (The 'Advertisement' of the Second Edition (pp.5-7) gives the publication details as London, October 18th 1853).
    1853    Partridge & Oakey, London    22cm    vii+377p.    Bo,BL,CBA,Cu,Sc,T,U
    1853    Houlston & Wright, London    22cm    vii+377p.    Bo,BL,CBA,Cu,Sc,T,U
    1853    Houlston & Sons, London    22cm    vii+377p.    Bo,BL,CBA,Cu,Sc,T,U

Third Edition - a 'word for word' reprint, but adds a prefatory note, footnotes, modernises some spellings, and adds appendices.
    1904    Houlston & Sons London    22cm    ix+515+8p.    BIOLA,BL,CBA,EL,SG,U
              and Lucas Collins, London

Fourth Edition (photographic reprint of the Third Edition)
    [2015]    SGAT, Chelmsford    22cm    ix+515+8p.    SG

French Edition - *Pensées sur l'Apocalypse. Ouvrage Traduit de l'Anglais.*
        (with the map and its introduction).
    1847    Libraire Protestante, Paris, Imprimerie de Marc Ducloux et comp$^e$
        16cm    xviii+363p.+map    French National Library    I,CG

## THOUGHTS ON THE APOSTASY OF THE PRESENT DISPENSATION

This first appeared in the January 1838 edition of *The Christian Witness*. In Section 7, Articles in *The Christian Witness* we conclude that it is beyond reasonable doubt the work of B.W. Newton. See there for a full assessment of authorship. The tract is virtually identical to the article. The only changes are such as the addition of an exclamation mark!

As a tract, it was bound up in a set entitled *Truth for the Times*. The second tract in the set (*The Character of Office in the Present Dispensation*) was by J.N. Darby.

First Edition (In *Truth for the Times*).
    [1838?]    Tract Depot, Plymouth    17cm    20p.    SG

Second Edition (*Truth for the Times No.1*).
    [ND]    Tract Depot, Plymouth and    17cm    20p    I
           Central Tract Depot, London

## THOUGHTS ON THE CHRISTIAN AND JEWISH REMNANTS AT THE TIME OF THE END

This consists of two of the *Five Letters on Events Predicted in Scripture as Antecedent to the Coming of the Lord - On the Christian Remnant*, and *On the Jewish Remnant*. It has a preface by Rev. John Cox.

This item is not to be confused with *The Christian Remnant and the Jewish Remnant at 'The Time of the End'*.[1]

    1866    Houlston & Wright, London    18cm    24p.    BL,Bo,CBA, CU,Sc,T

## THOUGHTS ON THE DEATH OF CAPTAIN BIRD ALLEN AND OTHER CHRISTIANS ENGAGED IN THE NIGER EXPEDITION

This tract relates to the failure of the Niger missionary and anti-slavery expedition (1841), which had been patronised by Prince Albert. The main thrust of the tract is the danger of pursuing right objects through wrong means.[2]

The Christian Brethren Archive, Manchester has two handwritten copies, one from the Fry Collection (CBA 7046), and the other by Mary Stirling. Mary Stirling's copy supplies the wording and format of the title page, which is missing from the other, and from the printed copy in the Fratelli Collection.

    1842    J.B. Rowe, Plymouth    16cm    12p.    Fratelli (Vechia, Florence)

## THOUGHTS ON THE END OF THE AGE, BEING IN PART COMPILED FROM SOME NOTES OF LECTURES DELIVERED AT SIDMOUTH AND ELSEWHERE

We consider this the First Edition of *Prophecy of the Lord Jesus as Contained in Matthew 24 and 25, Considered*, which see.

## THOUGHTS ON THE HISTORY OF PROFESSING CHRISTIANITY AS GIVEN IN THE PARABLES OF MATTHEW 13

This pamphlet was extracted from *Prospects of the Ten Kingdoms*, First Edition (1849).

---

[1] This was based on an address by Mr Newton. It was No.18 in the *Time of the End Series*, published posthumously. For the note on that tract see Section 8, Derivative Publications.

[2] For further comment on slavery, see B.W. Newton's note on Rev. 18:13 in the Third Edition of *Thoughts on the Apocalypse*, and his letter to his mother dated 22nd April 1830.

It sets out Mr Newton's distinctive interpretation, that the sequence of seven parables in Matthew 13 represents a prophetic history of the Church. He demonstrated the difficulty that the parables present to the post-millennial view, and to the expectation of a secret rapture of the Church. The Parable of the Pearl was a key element in his exposition, and strengthened his expectation of a powerful end-time testimony to the Gospel, centring on Jews and Jerusalem, immediately before the return of the Lord. A.C. Fry produced a duplicated booklet, largely based on Mr Newton's writings, setting out this hope [A.C. Fry, *What is meant by the Pearl Testimony?* 12 pages – CBA[1]].

It is uncertain whether there was a separate 'Second Edition' of this tract. The date given for the Second Edition in the 1897 edition (the 'Third' Edition) corresponds with the date of the Second Edition of *Prospects of the Ten Kingdoms*, and the publishers may have considered publication in the *Prospects...* to be the Second Edition of the tract.

Quotations are included in the anthology *B.W. Newton on Ministry and Order in the Church of Christ*

The Hunt, Barnard *Time of the End Series* tract, *A Prophetic Forecast of Professing Christianity*. (NT 19) also gives an exposition of the parables of Matthew 13.[2]

First Edition - *The Seven Parables of the Thirteenth of Matthew Dispensationally Considered.*
    1850 [1849?]    James Nisbet & Co, London    17cm    30p.    SNL

Second Edition – not located.
    1873 – date given in the Third Edition (see comments above)

Third Edition – the Second Edition 'reprinted'.
    1897    Houlston & Sons, London    18cm    42p.    CBA,SG

[Fourth] Edition - *Parables of Matthew 13. History of Professing Christianity.*
    [ND -1950?] SGAT, Chiswick    18cm    42p.    CG

## THOUGHTS ON THE WHOLE PROPHECY OF ISAIAH

This was a compilation of

1. *Thoughts on Parts of the Prophecy of Isaiah*, <u>First</u> Edition.
2. *Isaiah 53, Considered: Being an Extract from a Work Entitled 'Thoughts on Scriptural Subjects'*. This consisted of two chapters of *Thoughts on Scriptural Subjects*.
3. Notes of addresses published by Hunt, Barnard.[3]
    NS 39 *Studies in the Prophecy of Isaiah.*
    NS 42 *A Synopsis of Isaiah 40-49 and 59-61.*

---

[1] See note under NM 10 in Section 8, Publications Produced from Notes of Addresses, and Posthumously Published Letters and Manuscripts.

[2] See note under NT 19 in Section 8, Publications Produced from Notes of Addresses, and Posthumously Published Letters and Manuscripts.

[3] See Section 8, Publications Produced from Notes of Addresses, and Posthumously Published Letters and Manuscripts.

It was an attempt to produce a commentary on the whole prophecy. Some of the chapters of Isaiah (those based on the notes of addresses) have extremely brief comments on them. See the component items) for further detail of the contents.

    1975    SGAT, London    18cm    viii+308p.    CBA,EL,SG

## THOUGHTS ON UNFULFILLED PROPHECY

In this tract Mr Newton answered 'some of the difficulties that are supposed to impede enquiry into unfulfilled prophecy'.

Parts of this tract closely resemble the second chapter of *Aids to Prophetic Enquiry*. The appendix of *A Letter to the Minister of Silver Street Chapel, Taunton* (First Edition 1845) refers to it as 'a tract still in circulation written by me some years ago'.

    c.1840    Tract Depot, Plymouth    16cm    20p.    CBA, SG

## TRACTS ON DOCTRINAL SUBJECTS

These tracts were issued separately and successively. They are:
1. *Our Altar (Hebrews 13:10)*.
2. *An Erroneous Mode of Stating the Gospel, Considered.*
3. *Erroneous Statements Concerning Atonement and Its Results (Part 1st).*
4. *Erroneous Statements Concerning Atonement and Its Results (Part 2nd).*
5. *Erroneous Statements Concerning Atonement and Its Results (Part 3rd).*

The tracts are chiefly concerned with the work of Christ on the Cross for his people; cf. *Atonement and Its Results*. For detail of the content of the tracts, and their publication details, see the individual entries in this Section.

The five tracts were bound together, with this title. A sixth unnumbered tract followed seven years later (1884) - *An Effect of the Doctrines Animadverted on in Preceding Tracts*. From its allusion to 'the preceding tracts', it may have been bound up, or circulated with, them, but we have not found evidence of this.

    1877    Houlston & Sons, London    17cm    118p.[1]    BL,Bo,Sc.

## THE TRESPASS OFFERING

This is Part 5 of Vol. 1 of the First Edition of *Thoughts on Parts of Leviticus*. It was initially published separately as a series issue.

## THE TRUE UNITY OF THE CHURCH OF GOD IN TIME AND ETERNITY

This is one of the Leicester lectures on 'Great Protestant Truths', along with *Priesthood and Sacrifice Essential to Worship*. Its full title was *Leicester Lecture on Great Protestant Truths (Second Series). The Fourth Lecture 'The True Unity of the Church of God in Time and Eternity'*. Delivered on Tuesday Evening,

---

[1] Total pages. The Tracts are numbered separately. 156 pages, if *An Effect of the Doctrines Animadverted on in Preceding Tracts* is counted.

*April 18th 1854, in the New Hall, Leicester, by Benjamin Wills Newton (Formerly Fellow of Exeter College, Oxford). Rev. Samuel Adams of Thornton in the Chair.* It was published in *The Penny Pulpit* (it was number 2,231-32), which consisted of 'sermons by ministers of various denominations', and was published in monthly parts, numbered consecutively.

The theme of this lecture was taken up in two other items by B.W. Newton, 'Old Testament Saints', and 'The Unity of the Redeemed', in the Second Edition of *Thoughts on Parts of the Prophecy of Isaiah*.

The two tracts by B.W. Newton from this series were bound together as *Great Protestant Truths, being two of the Leicestershire Lectures* – as indicated in a publisher's list in *Occasional Papers on Scriptural Subjects No.1*.

It was reprinted in *Watching and Waiting*, July/August 1959, but was there dated incorrectly. An extract (pp.314-315) appeared in *Old Truths*, Vol. 2 (1867) p.237.

    1854    The Penny Pulpit    21cm    17p.    CBA

## THE TWELVE HUNDRED AND SIXTY DAYS OF ANTICHRIST'S REIGN FUTURE, A SECOND TRACT, WRITTEN WITH RELATION TO CERTAIN LECTURES RECENTLY DELIVERED AT THE TOWN HALL, WORTHING

This tract replies to the objections of historicists who identify the Antichrist with the Papacy, and deny that 1260 days of his ascendancy are literal days. The 'certain lectures' were not B.W. Newton's own lectures (referred to in *The Antichrist Future*), but a series of seven on historicist lines arranged at Worthing Town Hall in November/December 1859 by the Rector of Broadwater, Worthing (the son of E.B. Elliott) in an attempt to refute the Futurist position. The lecturers include E.B. Elliott himself[1]. See the notes given in the separate entry for *Antichrist Future*.

This tract was also published in *The Antichrist Future, also the 1260 days of Antichrist's Reign Future*, which brought together both tracts that resulted from the Worthing lectures.[2] The tracts were also bound up in the compilation *Antichrist, Europe and the East*.

    ND [1860]    Houlston and Wright, London    16cm    41p.    BL,Bo,CU,Sc,T

## UEBER DIE EWIGE VERSÖHNUNG, EIN TRAKTAT

German Edition of *Eternal Reconciliation, Being the Substance of a Discourse Recently Delivered in London*.

## UEBER DIE RECHTFERTIGUNG

German Edition of *Justification, Being the Substance of a Discourse Recently Delivered in London*.

---

[1] See *The Prophetic System of Mr Elliott and Dr Cumming considered*, included in *Aids to Prophetic Enquiry*.

[2] See the soon to be published *Mr Newton at Worthing* by C.W.H. Griffiths. For many years during the life and after the death of B.W. Newton there was a strong body of Christians supportive of B.W. Newton and his teachings in Worthing. This was particularly connected with John Adams, Thomas Graham Graham, and E.J. Burnett. Obituary of T.G. Graham, *Perilous Times*, January, February. March, April, and May 1906. Died 29th December 1905, aged 81 years. Obituary of Edward John Burnett, younger brother of W.E. Burnett, *Watching and Waiting*, July-August 1959, p.159.

## A VINDICATION OF 'A REMONSTRANCE TO THE SOCIETY OF FRIENDS'

Mr Newton published *A Remonstrance to the Society of Friends* in 1835, at the time of the Beacon controversy. It drew a reply, *Strictures on a Late Publication Entitled 'A Remonstrance to the Society of Friends'* that is attributed to Joseph Treffry (1771-1851), his uncle. The *Strictures...* accused Mr Newton of misrepresenting the Society of Friends by incorrect and imperfect quotations of William Penn, and of other leading Quaker writers. Mr Newton, in his reply to this, strengthened his complaint against the Christology and the soteriology of the Quakers[1].

    1836    Nisbet & Co, London    18cm    72p.    CBA

## WHAT IS THE EPHAH OF ZECHARIAH 5? OR, THE EXHIBITION OF 1851 CONSIDERED IN RELATION TO THE PRINCIPLES OF MODERN LEGISLATION

This tract highlights the detrimental influence of commercial expediency upon Government policy. Mr Newton saw this as tending towards the situation symbolically represented in the vision of the ephah in Zechariah 5.

T.C.F. Stunt, *Life and Times of Samuel Prideaux Tregelles* notes that Tregelles attendance at the Exhibition apparently led to a period of estrangement between them (a reminiscence of Mr Newton in CBA 7064 p142), perhaps corroborated by the publication of Tregelles *Remarks on Daniel* (1852), which took a different line from Mr Newton on the interpretation of Daniel 11 and 12.

The item was included in the Second Edition of *Prospects of the Ten Kingdoms* (1873), and in the compilation *Antichrist, Europe and the East*.

First Edition
    1851    James Nisbet & Co, London    17cm    37p.    BL,I,SG

Second Edition
    1855    Partridge & Oakey, London    17cm    37p.    SG

Third Edition
    1862    Houlston & Wright, London    17cm    38p.    Bo,SG

Fourth Edition. Combined with *Zechariah 5 Re-translated with Notes*. Retitled, *Zechariah 5: the Vision of the Ephah considered in relation to the Principles of Modern Legislation*.
    1912    Lucas Collins, London    17cm    40p.    BL,CBA,EL

French Edition - *Qu'est-ce que l'Épha de Zacharie 5? ou l'Exposition de 1851 Considérée en Rapport avec les Principes de Législation Moderne*.
    1856    Lausanne    18cm    ?    Swiss National Library

---

[1] For information on B.W. Newton and the Beacon Controversy, see T.C.F. Stunt, *Early Brethren and the Society of Friends: Christian Brethren Research Fellowship Occasional Paper No.3* (This research item has been republished with some amendments as Chapter 2 of *The Elusive Quest of the Spiritual Malcontent: Some Early Nineteenth-Century Ecclesiastical Mavericks*, by T.C.F. Stunt., 2015), and *The Beacon Controversy in the Society of Friends 1835-1840. A Bibliography*, by Jolyon Hall, 1968 (Library of the Society of Friends, London).

## THE WHITE ROBE (REVELATION 7:9-17)

This is a children's Gospel tract. It answers the question of fitness for heavenly glory. The frontispiece appears to be a missionary scene.

This was published anonymously. However, we consider that B.W. Newton's authorship of it is beyond reasonable doubt. See the discussion in Section 5, Anonymous Publications Ascribed to B.W. Newton. It is undated, but the association with Mrs Stirling suggests a date towards the end of the nineteenth century.

    [ND 1890??]   Dublin Steam Printing Company     13cm   16p.   CBA

Reprinted in *Watching and Waiting*, October – December 1989, pp.187-189.

## 'THE WHOLE FAMILY' EPHESIANS 3:5. IS IT 'EVERY FAMILY' OR IS IT 'THE WHOLE FAMILY OF THE REDEEMED'?

This tract combined an extract from *Occasional Papers on Scriptural Subjects No.1*, and an extract from *Remarks on the Revised English Version of the Greek New Testament*. It was issued by LB [Louisa A Balch? 1876-1959] as a critique of the Revised Version rendering of the verse, which had been quoted by King George V, in his 1934 Christmas Day message. This appears on some publishers' lists as *Bethany Series No.3*, and is therefore noted in Section 8, Publications Produced from Notes of Addresses, and Posthumously Published Letters and Manuscripts.

    1935    G.H. Fromow, London     10cm   13p.   BL

## THE WORLD TO COME

The tract describes the characteristics of the millennial period. It first appeared in *The Christian Witness*, Vol. 1, April 1834. Very few changes were made to it through the various editions. As with other publications, there is some confusion regarding the early editions. The printing in *The Christian Witness* may be counted as the First Edition in subsequent numbering.

In CBA 7049 (from CBA 7062) the record of his 'reminiscences' reads 'I once wrote an article in *The Christian Witness* on the World to Come, which was praised by Powerscourt, and by Darby, and others'.

(First Edition)
    ND [c.1835]   J Clulow & H Soltau, Plymouth    17cm   16p.   EC

(Second Edition)
    ND [c.1842]   Wertheimer, Lea & Co, London    17cm   16p.   CBA,EL

Third Edition – not located
    ? [before 1868 – publisher's list in *Thoughts on Parts of the Prophecy of Isaiah*, First Edition 1868, and *The Seventh Chapter of the Epistle to the Romans, Considered*, Second Edition 1873].

Fourth Edition – not located.

Fifth Edition
    1887    Houlston & Sons, London         17cm    16p.    BIOLA,CBA

Sixth Edition
    1897    Houlston & Sons, London         17cm    16p.    BIOLA,CBA,EL

Seventh? Edition
*Watching and Waiting* (October/December 1948, p.220) refers to the tract having been 're-issued'. No copies have been located, and, as no mention was made of this as a new publication in the SGAT Annual Reports of 1948 or 1949, this is suspect as a further edition. Perhaps further copies became available at this time, as several other publications were then bound up 'from loose sheets'.

French Edition (1) - *Le Monde à Venir*
    1837    Tract Depot, 1 Warwick Square         17cm    16p.    I
            London (printed by J Wertheimer, London)

French Edition (1) - *Le Monde à Venir*
    ND      Dépôt de Traités, Jersey and          17cm    21p.    I
            1, Warwick Square, London (printed by R Gosset, Jersey)

Norwegian Edition – Possibly produced c.1900.
See Mr Newton's correspondence with Mrs Leake in 1895 (CBA 7050), and the biographical note in connection with *Retfærdiggjörelsen og Helliggjörelsen*.

## THE WRECK AND THE ROCK

In this short item Mr Newton used an analogy to demonstrate the dispensational standing of disciples whilst the Lord Jesus was with them, and thereby opposed the distinctions that J.N. Darby made between Jewish and Church blessings.

It was probably originally reprinted from *A Letter to the Brethren and Sisters who meet for Communion in Ebrington Street, Plymouth…*, in which it appeared as Appendix A, although it is there described as 'a familiar illustration which has been found useful in assisting the thoughts of many'. It figured largely in the dispute with J.N. Darby. J.N. Darby wrote a reply, *Remarks on 'The Wreck and the Rock'* (published anonymously, but owned by J.N. Darby in his *A Plain Statement of the Sufferings of our Blessed Lord*, p.113). Mr Newton referred to his pamphlet in his *Observations on a Tract*, p.83 (1847) as having been published 'recently', and also responded to J.N. Darby's reply. The tract (with one or two minor amendments and slight additions to the footnotes) was later included in the Second Edition of *The Prophecy of the Lord Jesus as Contained in Matthew 24,25, Considered.* (1857).

    ND [1846?]   C(lulow) & S[oltau], Plymouth       18cm    4p.    ID

## ZECHARIAH 5 RETRANSLATED WITH NOTES. BEING AN EXTRACT FROM THE SECOND EDITION OF 'THOUGHTS ON SCRIPTURAL SUBJECTS'

This extract was also issued with *What is the Ephah of Zechariah 5…?* under the title, *Zechariah 5. The Vision of the Ephah considered in Relation to the Principles of Modern Legislation*. Those close to B.W. Newton valued his translations of Scripture. Note the MS volume held by SGAT - Retranslations of various portions of Holy Scripture extracted from the works of the late B.W. Newton, described in Section 10, Duplicated and Manuscript Items.

    1896    Houlston & Sons, London    18cm    8p.    BL,Bo,CU,Sc,SG

## ZECHARIAH 5. THE VISION OF THE EPHAH CONSIDERED IN RELATION TO THE PRINCIPLES OF MODERN LEGISLATION

This is the title given to the Fourth Edition of *What is the Ephah of Zechariah 5…?*, combined with *Zechariah 5 retranslated with notes*.

# SECTION 4

## CONTRIBUTIONS TO OTHER PUBLICATIONS

## CONTRIBUTIONS TO OTHER PUBLICATIONS

**B.W. Newton contributed to, or his name is linked with, the following publications:**

1. *Answers to the Questions Lately Considered at a Meeting Held in Plymouth on September 15th 1834 and the Following Days: Chiefly Compiled from Notes Taken at the Meeting by Henry Borlase and B.W. Newton* (1834).

2. *Correspondence, etc.,* published by Lord Congleton (1846).

3. *Extracts from 'A Narrative of Facts'* by Robert Baxter (1836).

4. *Extracts from Bishop Pearson's Exposition of the Apostles' Creed* (1848).

5. *The Greek New Testament, Edited from Ancient Authorities...* by S.P. Tregelles [Quarto Edition] (published 1857-79).

6. *The Greek New Testament, as Edited from Ancient Authorities,* by S. P. Tregelles [Manual Edition] (1881).

7. *On Luke 21,* by B.W. Newton, notes by J.G. Deck (1843).

8. *Persecution of Protestants in Spain* (1862).

9. *The Religious Tendencies of the Times,* by James Grant (1869).

10. *The Similarities and the Contrasts between the Present and Coming Dispensations,* J.L Harris and B.W. Newton (1842).

11. *Statement of Doctrines held by a Body of Christians ...* compiled by Arthur Andrews (1897)

12. *Valera's Spanish Bible of 1602. An Appeal to Protestant Christians* (1856).

## 1. ANSWERS TO THE QUESTIONS LATELY CONSIDERED AT A MEETING HELD IN PLYMOUTH ON SEPTEMBER 15TH 1834 AND THE FOLLOWING DAYS: CHIEFLY COMPILED FROM NOTES TAKEN AT THE MEETING BY HENRY BORLASE AND B.W. NEWTON

Lady Powerscourt arranged annual prophetic conferences, which most of the early Brethren leaders attended, including Mr Newton (with his first wife) in 1833. He wrote later that he had little agreement on prophetic matters with the other attendees, apart from William de Burgh, an Irish clergyman[1]. In 1834 some who were prevented from attending the Powerscourt Prophetic Conference in Ireland met in Plymouth, and considered the same questions as were considered at Powerscourt. The meetings were held at the Mechanics Institute, Plymouth.[2] Henry Borlase[3], B.W. Newton, J.L. Harris, and T. Dowglass[4] arranged the meetings. In his preface to the Second Edition Tregelles says, 'many Christian Ministers were invited as well as others, and many attended'. It undoubtedly took a different view of prophecy from that of the conferences in Ireland. In CBA 7064, p40 describes the meeting as the 'best time' and 'very unanimous and delightful'.

This publication is a valuable aid to understanding this early period, in that its statements have a bearing on Church order. Tregelles's republication of the pamphlet in 1847 is significant in view of developments at Plymouth at the time. A copy of the First Edition has not been located, but it is understood to have been bound up with some copies of the First Edition of the 1835 series of *The Christian Witness*. According to the Burdet Morris bibliographical index of Devon, the First Edition was published in 1834.

First Edition [1834] Although no copy of this has been located, an account of it is given under 'Borlase' in *Bibliotheca Cornubiensis* by G.C. Boase and W.P. Courtney.

Second Edition, omitting the word 'lately' from the title. Edited by S.P. T[regelles] who added further comment, but made only minor, marked corrections to the text. His preface is identified 'Plymouth, February 6th 1847'.
    1847    Plymouth                                     17cm              BL
    1847    James Nisbet & Co. London           17cm    84p.    I, SG

---

[1] William Burgh, later William de Burgh (1801-1866).

[2] See CBA 7064 p. 40.

[3] Henry Borlase (1806-1835) seceded from the ministry of the Church of England in 1832. *Papers by the late Henry Borlase, connected with the Present State of the Church* was published after his death. His influence upon B.W. Newton's ecclesiology was very significant. Two of B.W. Newton's close associates on the Isle of Wight at the end of his life, in 1892, Edward Crossley and Arthur Andrews, published *Extracts from the Writings of the Late Henry Borlase on Subjects Connected with the Present State of the Church*.

[4] Thomas Dowglass was an acquaintance of B.W. Newton at Oxford. After moving to Salcombe, and a period of co-operation with the work at Plymouth, he defected to Irvingism and became an Angel Evangelist with the Irvingites. B.W. Newton thereupon found himself lecturing against Dowglass's teaching in Salcombe. See T.C.F. Stunt, *From Awakening to Secession*, pp.298, 299. In CBA 7049, p.141,142, A.C. Fry (presumably following F.W. Wyatt) calls him 'Douglas'.

## 2. CORRESPONDENCE ETC. RELATING TO MR NEWTON'S REFUSAL TO APPEAR BEFORE THE SAINTS AT RAWSTORNE STREET, LONDON, ACCORDING TO THE TWO CITATIONS WHICH ISSUED FROM THEM, NOVEMBER 20TH, TO DECEMBER 6TH 1846.

This was a collection of the letters and other items, concerning the attempt of the leaders of the London Brethren Meeting at Rawstorne Street to arraign Mr Newton before them. It gives both the summons, and the response of the leaders of the Plymouth Meeting, including B.W. Newton. Lord Congleton (John Vesey Parnell 1805-1883) published it. He was one of the early leaders of the Brethren, and was himself involved in trying to mediate between B.W. Newton and J.N. Darby and his friends, who attacked him. Evidently Lord Congleton felt it was better for the wider community to have copies of the actual documents and letters relevant to the controversy than to rely upon partisan accounts that were being issued on J.N. Darby's side. The documents are without comment. Among these important documents, the following items are included:

**Letter from B.W. Newton to J. Clulow, 18 April 1845.** (Part 1, Appendix A, pp.33-34)

> This letter is dated April 18th 1845. It was printed separately for private circulation, and a handwritten appendix by Mr Newton was in the original Fry Collection. See Section 3, B.W. Newton's Published Works, and Section 9, B.W. Newton's Correspondence.

**Letter dated 25th November 1846 from H.W. Soltau, Joseph Clulow, J.E. Batten and W.B. Dyer to W.H. Dorman** (pp.9–21)

> This letter was also previously 'printed but not published' with the note 'A copy of this letter may be obtained, on application, either personally or by letter, to Mr Campbell, 1 Warwick Square, London or 5 Cornwall Street Plymouth' [17cm, ID]. It was issued in this way 'for the information of many who desire to be furnished with our reasons for counselling our brother, Newton, to decline a certain meeting, proposed to be held at Rawstorne-street, London'.

**Letter dated 9th December 1846 to W.H. Dorman and H. Gough. from B.W. Newton, H.W. Soltau, W.B. Dyer, J. Clulow and J.E. Batten.**

> This was a brief and firm reply to the threat of excommunication proposed by the London, Rawstorne Street, Brethren Meeting. It declared, 'The Meeting you propose is entirely opposed to the directions of the Word of God'.

**A Defence in Reply to the Personal Accusations of Mr Darby** (pp.21 - 30)

> This is the only printed version of this tract that has been located. It was probably published a short time after January 1846. However, if it was published before the summons from Rawstorne Street, it is unclear why it was necessary for that meeting to be sent a copy. It deals largely with Mr Darby's allegations regarding Mr Newton's *Five Letters*... See Section 3, B.W. Newton's Published Works (under *Defence*). See the notes on related letters during this period in Section 9, B.W. Newton's Correspondence.

> 1846     Tract Depot, Plymouth     17cm    50p.    CBA

## 3. EXTRACTS FROM 'A NARRATIVE OF FACTS, CHARACTERIZING THE SUPERNATURAL MANIFESTATIONS IN MEMBERS OF MR IRVING'S CONGREGATION AND OTHER INDIVIDUALS, AND FORMERLY IN THE WRITER HIMSELF', BY ROBERT BAXTER

This pamphlet consists of extracts from Robert Baxter's longer book – *A Narrative of Facts, Characterizing the Supernatural Manifestations in Members of Mr Irving's Congregation and Other Individuals in England and Scotland, and Formerly in the Writer Himself* (Second Edition) *with Preface* [April 1833] *on the Spiritual Influence Permitted to Satan, and Remarks on Mr Irving's and the Morning Watch's Reviews of the Narrative* - 1833 - James Nisbet, London - 18cm - xlvii+155 pages – BL.

B.W. Newton evidently produced and published this. The appendix, which summarises the main arguments against the supernatural manifestations, is followed by the subscription, 'B.W. Newton'. However, the first paragraph of the 'Preliminary Remarks' ['February 1833'] at the beginning of the 'Extracts' gives the impression that the pamphlet is issued by Robert Baxter[1]. It was produced after Mr Newton's *Doctrines of the Church in Newman Street* had appeared in *The Christian Witness*, and at the time when Mr Newton's larger, Second Edition, tract of that title began to circulate.

B.W. Newton refers to Baxter's book in *Occasional Papers on Scriptural Subjects* No.4, p.195.

    1836    'Printed and sold by' Thomas P. Dixon, Falmouth    20cm    20+2p.    BL

## 4. EXTRACTS FROM BISHOP PEARSON'S EXPOSITION OF THE APOSTLES' CREED

This consists of quotations from Bishop Pearson's classic exposition[2], together with an extract from John Calvin's *Institutes*. It was issued by B. W. Newton in 1848 from Plymouth, together with the introductory statement, 'The following extracts will, I believe, be found useful in illustrating to some minds the Scripture Doctrines of the real Humanity and Sufferings of our blessed Lord and Saviour Jesus Christ'.

Its issuing by Mr Newton was a clear statement of his own orthodoxy after the disruption at Plymouth, and following his own departure from Brethrenism in December 1847. It was published before July 1848. In *A Letter on Subjects connected with the Lord's Humanity*, Mr Newton says of it, 'which I have just published'.

The *Extracts*... were later printed as an appendix to *A Letter to a Friend Concerning a Tract Recently Published at Cork* (1850).

    1848    [printed and sold by] Jenkin Thomas, Plymouth    17cm    12p.    CG

    [ND]    [printed by] B.R. Peake, London    17cm    12p.    CBA

---

[1] Robert Baxter (1802-1889) was one of the Irvingite 'prophets' who left the movement. He also produced *Irvingism, Its Rise, Progress and Present State*, 1836 (at EL bound with his *Narrative of Facts*).

[2] *Exposition of the Creed*, first published in 1659 by John Pearson (1613 – 1686), later Bishop of Chester.

## 5. THE GREEK NEW TESTAMENT, EDITED FROM ANCIENT AUTHORITIES WITH THEIR VARIOUS READINGS IN FULL. AND THE LATIN VERSION OF JEROME BY S.P. TREGELLES [Quarto Edition]

Mr Newton gave practical support to S.P. Tregelles in the preparation of his monumental work. It was first issued in parts to subscribers.

Because of his failing health, the final part, Part 6 - the Book of Revelation - was prepared for publication 'under the general superintendence of B.W. Newton', and two of the sections of the 'Introductory Notice' to this part in 1872 are by Mr Newton. They are both simple factual statements relating to the circumstances of his (Mr Newton's) involvement. The first (14 lines) is dated 'March 1872', and concluded with 'B.W. Newton'. The second is a 'P.S.' to this (9 lines and concluded with the initials 'B.W.N.'). The postscript indicates that 'the present introduction, like the introductions to the preceding parts is intended to be temporary only. The substance of these introductions will be comprised in the Prolegomena, which is being prepared…'. The Prolegomena appeared when the book was finally published, after a lengthy delay, and made no mention of B.W. Newton. See letter F.J.A. Hort to Mrs S.A. Tregelles, 24th January 1876, after S.P. Tregelles's death, and the subsequent correspondence in Section 9 of this *Guide*. This gives the explanation why Mr Newton is not mentioned in the Prolegomena. As F.J.A. Hort refused to include a preface prepared by Mr Newton. He [Mr Newton] therefore requested all mention of his name to be removed from the Greek Testament. Mr Newton wanted S.P. Tregelles's principles to be set out in the Prolegomena, with stated assurances that no posthumous changes were made to his text.

    1857 -1879 Samuel Bagster, London    23cm    1070+56p.    BL,EL

C.W.H. Griffiths has a volume of this full quarto edition, which he had bound from printer's signatures for bookbinding stored by the SGAT. These include the above brief statements by B.W. Newton.

## 6. THE GREEK NEW TESTAMENT, AS EDITED FROM ANCIENT AUTHORITIES, BY SAMUEL PRIDEAUX TREGELLES [Manual Edition]

Mrs S.A. Tregelles, S.P. Tregelles's widow had committed his Greek New Testament to F.J.A. Hort for publication after the death of her husband. This resulted in the publication of the quarto edition.

Westcott and Hort's Greek New Testament was published in 1881, and the Revised Version New Testament also in 1881 under the significant influence of F.J.A. Hort.[1] We know from B.W. Newton's *Remarks on the Revised English Version…*, his strong objection to Westcott and Hort's Greek New Testament. He evidently felt the need to promote the different approach adopted by S.P. Tregelles by keeping his Greek New Testament in print in an accessible format. The full quarto version had sold out, and there was no prospect of it being reprinted[2]. In a letter dated, 23rd November 1882, from A. Prideaux (brother of Mrs S.A. Tregelles, S.P. Tregelles's widow) to B.W. Newton. He (Mr Prideaux) reported that he had seen his sister. He and she were very glad that Mr Newton was

---

[1] See B.W. Newton, *Remarks on the Revised English Version of the Greek New Testament'*.
[2] The SGAT store has printer's bookbinding signatures of the quarto edition of S.P. Tregelles' Greek New Testament, presumably purchased from the publisher by B.W. Newton or his adherents.

willing to take on all that concerned Dr Tregelles's works. He expressed the hope that it would be possible to bring out a manual version of S.P. Tregelles's Greek New Testament.[1]

Before his death S.P. Tregelles had been greatly pained by the use made of his text by Joseph Bryant Rotherham. He had used the text as the basis of his revision of *The New Testament Critically Emphasised*. See Section 9, B.W. Newton's Correspondence, letter by B.W. Newton dated 2nd January 1894.

We do not know who B.W. Newton worked with to achieve the publication of the manual version of S.P. Tregelles's Greek New Testament, although S. Bloxsidge may have been included.[2] It is hard to believe, however, now that he was again involved with its publication, that B.W. Newton was not one of the 'editors' who wrote the preface to the manual version, which was published in 1887. The preface is 7 pages.

CG has B.W. Newton's personal copy of this edition. It has 'B.W.N.' embossed on the spine. There are six manuscript additions to the Corrigenda, believed to be in B.W. Newton's hand.

    1881    Samuel Bagster and Sons, London  18cm    xi+602p. BL, [CG]

## 7. ON LUKE 21. THE FOLLOWING PAGES CONTAIN THE SUBSTANCE OF A LECTURE BY B.W. NEWTON AT CREDITON, ON PART OF THE 21ST OF LUKE. THE NOTES HAVE BEEN ADDED BY JAMES G. DECK (1843)

This was evidently published with Mr Newton's approval. J.G. Deck's contribution is clearly defined. Comment on Mr Newton's contribution is therefore included in Section 3, B.W. Newton's Published Works.

## 8. PERSECUTION OF PROTESTANTS IN SPAIN

This two page 'circular for private distribution' is an appeal for financial support for Christians persecuted and imprisoned in Spain. Manuel Matamoros[3], the leader of a group of Spanish Protestants had, with others, been condemned to 4 years penal servitude in the galleys, and they had to bear the cost of their own prosecution.

Contributions were invited to be made to:
    Messrs Bagsters and sons; Messrs Seeley; Office of Protestant Institute; Rev. Charles J. Goodhart; William Long; Samuel Worralt; B.W. Newton; S. P Tregelles. 'Dr Tregelles will undertake the transmission to Spain of the sums collected'.

---

[1] Mrs Tregelles died soon after the publication of the manual edition, on 15th September 1882.
[2] See letters to Mr Bloxsidge, dated 5th April 1871, and 30th October 1872. Hunt, Barnard later circulated his booklet, *Inspired Words Realised*. Died June 15th 1928 aged 86 years. Graduate of Exeter College. Brief obituary *Watching and Waiting*, August 1928
[3] Manuel Matamoros-Garcia (1834-1868). For a favourable view of Matamoras, see *Manuel Matamoros and his Fellow Prisoners in Spain*, by William Greene, 3rd Edition 1889. See the note on the Usoz Collection in Section 2 of this Guide.

## Section 4 – Contributions to Other Publications

See the letters from S.P. Tregelles to B.W. Newton, dated 5th February 1862, and 12th October 1862 in Section 9, B.W. Newton's Correspondence. By 19th December 1864 S.P. Tregelles had lost all confidence in Matamoros. See his letter to B.W. Newton of that date.

    February 3rd 1862                                   20cm    2p.     BL

## 9. 'THE RELIGIOUS TENDENCIES OF THE TIMES: OR HOW TO DEAL WITH THE DEADLY ERRORS OF THE DAY' BY JAMES GRANT

James Grant produced this book in 1869. In it he attacked errors of Brethrenism, and Mr Newton's alleged views. Mr Newton wrote letters to him and convinced him of his orthodoxy. James Grant had these made into a circular, which he inserted in the book to correct the views he had expressed regarding him. *Perilous Times* reprinted the circular (September 1909, pp.211, 212). Grant later wrote *The Plymouth Brethren, their History and Heresies*, in which he presented Mr Newton as very much the innocent party in the Plymouth controversy. He was the editor of *The Morning Advertiser*, which favourably reviewed Mr Newton's *Propositions*... See also the correspondence of B.W. Newton with John Cox, jun. regarding this in MS Book 1 (TC) pp.403 ff. Noted in Section 9, B.W. Newton's Correspondence at 19th May 1869, and 26th May 1869.

    1869    London                             17cm    ?     BL

## 10. THE SIMILARITIES AND THE CONTRASTS BETWEEN THE PRESENT AND COMING DISPENSATIONS

This was produced on the basis of notes taken from lectures delivered by J.L. Harris and B.W Newton. Authorship of the two parts is clearly distinguished, and it is therefore included in Section 3, B.W. Newton's Published Works.

## 11. A STATEMENT OF DOCTRINES HELD BY A BODY OF CHRISTIANS MEETING IN THE EVANGELICAL PROTESTANT CHAPEL, NEWPORT STREET, RYDE, ISLE OF WIGHT. COMPILED BY ARTHUR ANDREWS

This was bound up in a volume titled 'Newton's Works' owned by A.C. Fry. The connection of Mr Newton with these 34 articles is further described in a reprint of the *Statement*... by S.R. Cottey, titled simply, *A Statement of Doctrinal Belief*. It declared, 'This Statement of Doctrinal Belief is based on [it was almost identical in form] that prepared for a Protestant Evangelical Assembly at Ryde, Isle of Wight, and approved by the late B.W. Newton in 1897'. This was reprinted in *Watching and Waiting* January, February, April, May and August 1931 with the description 'Approved by Mr B.W. Newton, for an Assembly in Ryde in 1897'.

It must be regarded as doubtful whether B.W. Newton had a hand in its preparation or whether he merely assented to its contents. The approval of B.W. Newton of the statement may be questioned. CBA 7064 p1 (note dated 8th September 1897) quotes Mr Newton as highlighting a deficiency in 'A.A.'s confession or creed'. B.W. Newton in CBA 7064, p70 (dated 18th September 1897) is again critical 'Only think of A.A. bringing out a long 'Confession of Faith' and so little in it about the work of the Holy Ghost! Hardly touched on! Persons are as dark as possible about it'. B.W. Newton was estranged from Edward Crossley (see correspondence) who had built the Chapel, and perhaps Arthur Andrews too, before his death.

Arthur Andrews seems to have been the compiler. He had produced *The Doctrine of the Sacraments compiled by A.A.* [published by the 'Evangelical Protestant Chapel, Ryde'. SG] in 1895. Articles 21, 22, and 23 of this were identical with those of the larger 'Statement'. The only significant difference is a change of nomenclature from 'sacrament' to 'ordinance'.

W. Lancelot Holland incorporated 8 of the articles into his *Old Paths for a New Century; or, Foundation Truths for the Church of God (In Twenty Nine Articles of Faith)*, 12th September 1899.

The Chapel was built by Edward Crossley[1] in 1893. B.W. Newton withdrew from that fellowship in July 1896 (see the Correspondence section at this date). A.A. Andrews also withdrew. The date of the *Statement* is therefore curious. According to C.E. Fry, Arthur Andrews closed the chapel - see item C.4, Reminiscence from C.E. Fry (from his father A.C. Fry) to C.W.H. Griffiths, in Section 12, Miscellaneous Biographical Items.

Although Edward Crossley seemed to have given a final rebuff to B.W. Newton in his letter of 4th August 1896, perhaps there was a reconciliation. When he died 21st January 1905 he left the Evangelical Protestant Chapel in Newport Street, Ryde (and a substantial proportion of his estate) to Arthur Andrews to continue the work there.

[First Edition] - *A Statement of Doctrines held by a Body of Christians...*
    1897    F.W. Sargent, Ryde    17cm    24p.    SG

[Second Edition] *A Statement of Doctrinal Belief*
    1931    S.R. Cottey, London    17cm    27p.    SG,CBA

## 12. VALERA'S SPANISH BIBLE OF 1602. APPEAL TO PROTESTANT CHRISTIANS, RESPECTING THE REPRINTING OF THIS VERSION

This pamphlet has a short prefatory note, subscribed 'B.W.N.'. Its date and place is given in the pamphlet as 'London, May 17th 1856'. It says 'It may be desirable to state, that this tract does not emanate from the Committee of the Trinitarian Bible Society, nor are they in any way connected with it. It is written by an individual who earnestly desires the circulation of correct Protestant versions of the Holy Scriptures in Spain, and elsewhere'.[2] The tract is otherwise anonymous.

---

[1] Edward Crossley (1841 – 21 January 1905), prominent businessman, Liberal MP. (1885-1892) and mayor of Halifax. See CBA 7048, Fellow of the Royal Astronomical Society. He became attached to B.W. Newton after hearing a lecture of his in London (CBA 7064, p58.) He had a summer home on the Isle of Wight to which he retired. A sermon of his was printed in Watching and Waiting, Jan.-Feb. 1950, pp.10-13. *The Isle of Wight Observer*, 18th November 1893 indicates that Edward Crossley's chapel was then being built and Arthur Andrews would assist him in his ministerial work. See *Fissures in Late-Nineteenth-Century English Nonconformity: A Case Study in One Congregation* by Dale A. Johnson in *Church History: Studies in Christianity and Culture*, Vol. 66, Issue 04, December 1997, pp.735-749, Cambridge University Press.

[2] The Trinitarian Bible Society reprinted the Valera Spanish Gospel of Matthew in 1845, the New Testament in 1858, and the whole Bible in 1868. B.W. Newton rightly states that he was not connected with the T.B.S. Committee, but he was a subscribing member of the T.B.S. from 1852 onwards, and he collected gifts from various people for the Spanish Scripture fund. Information obtained from the T.B.S. records (letter from the secretary dated 15th August 1985 to C.W.H. Griffiths). *The Word of God among All*

It is possible that B. W. Newton was the author of the whole pamphlet, and that he was simply writing in the third person to remain anonymous. He, as others, was linked with Manuel Matamoros, a Spanish Christian worker, and the campaign for the release of the 'Spanish Prisoners' (see in this section the leaflet *Persecution of Protestants in Spain*). He was also a subscribing member of the Trinitarian Bible Society from 1852 onwards. However, it is likely that the author of the Appeal, apart from the Preface, was S.P. Tregelles. The reasons for this conclusion are:

1. A volume of tracts by S.P. Tregelles passed down from A.C. Fry includes the tract.
2. It would be the only example of B.W. Newton introducing his own tract in this way. He would not thereby have remained anonymous to 'Protestant Christians' as his initials were widely known.
3. S.P. Tregelles's wife Sarah was fluent in Spanish, and in 1855-6 Dr Tregelles produced 'The Versions of Scripture for Roman Catholic Countries: an Appeal to the British and Foreign Bible Society'.
4. S.P Tregelles was very committed to the republication of Valera's Spanish version[1]. For further background see Chapter 4, 'Early Operations', in *The Word of God among all Nations. A Brief History of the Trinitarian Bible Society 1831-1981*, by Andrew J Brown. Cf. T.C.F. Stunt, *The Life and Times of Samuel Prideaux Tregelles*,(2020) 99-100.

If it was by S.P. Tregelles, it was synchronous with his (S.P Tregelles's) appeal to the British and Foreign Bible Society, mentioned above, in the same year, and by the same publishers.

1856    Houlston & Stoneman, London    18cm    72p.    BL, CBA, Trinitarian Bible Society.

---

*Nations. A Brief History of the Trinitarian Bible Society 1831-1981* makes various references to the Spanish Bible and to S.P. Tregelles.
[1] Cypriano de Valera (1531-1602), Spanish protestant Bible translator.

# SECTION 5

## ASSESSMENT OF ANONYMOUS PUBLICATIONS ASCRIBED TO B.W. NEWTON

# ASSESSMENT OF
# ANONYMOUS PUBLICATIONS ASCRIBED TO B.W. NEWTON

## Items published when B.W. Newton was associated with the Brethren

As a general observation, it should be noted that many, perhaps most, of the multitude of early Brethren tracts were anonymous. There was no need or incentive to determine authorship at the time. Mr Newton was a prolific writer. Some of his early works were published anonymously. There is a high probability that he wrote some of the anonymous tracts produced by Clulow and Soltau's Plymouth Tract Depot.

Some sets of *The Christian Witness* (the first periodical of the developing "Brethren" movement) have the authors (or who the owner of the volumes thought were the authors) indicated by manuscript notes or initials. We have carried out an assessment of these ascriptions in Section 7, Articles in *The Christian Witness*. However, whilst one can understand the desire of a later possessor of a set of *The Christian Witness* to have initials against the anonymous articles, in the case of independently circulating anonymous tracts the imperative was generally not there. In relation to these, there are generally not the conflicting claims to authorship that exist with *The Christian Witness* ascriptions.

## Items included in Section 3 - B.W. Newton's Published Works

Some anonymously published tracts by Mr Newton are included within Section 3, B.W. Newton's Published Works. We have done this where:

1. The tract was developed into a later item, and published under his name (e.g. *Jerusalem*).
2. The tract was later incorporated into a publication by B.W. Newton (e.g. *The Wreck and the Rock*).
3. The tract was extracted from a publication published by him (e.g. *Baptism*, from *A Remonstrance to the Society of Friends*).
4. The tract is a translation of an acknowledged tract (e.g. *Jérusalem et l'Homme de Péché*).

## Assessment of the Anonymous Items

The tracts and other items considered in this section do not fall into the above categories, but they have been ascribed to B.W. Newton by different sources. We have assessed each of them on the basis of internal and external evidence. We have also entered the publications in Section 3, B.W. Newton's Published Works where we have concluded that the item was certainly, or beyond reasonable doubt, by B.W. Newton.

# Section 5 – Assessment of Anonymous Publications Ascribed to B.W. Newton

## Summary

1. *A Catechism on the Four Great and Universal Empires, and the Kingdom by Which They will be Succeeded, as Mentioned in the Book of the Prophecies of Daniel* — The internal evidence is inconclusive, and there is no external evidence. It cannot be assumed that B.W. Newton was the author

2. *Dr Tregelles's Greek Testament; Remarks on Some Observations of the Bishop of Gloucester and Bristol on Dr Tregelles's Revised Text of the Greek New Testament* — Beyond Reasonable Doubt by B.W. Newton.

3. *Notes on Joshua 5:6-12. Fact, Faith, and Experience* — Probably by B.W. Newton.

4. *A Letter to a Friend on the Study of Prophecy* — Beyond reasonable doubt by B.W. Newton.

5. *The Passover. Exodus 12* — There is insufficient internal evidence to determine the authorship, and the external evidence is uncertain.

6. *The Prospects of the World* — Certainly by B.W. Newton

7. *Remarks on the Ten Kingdoms of the Roman World* — Certainly by B.W. Newton.

8. *The Second Appearing and Personal Reign of the Lord Jesus Christ* — Not by B.W. Newton.

9. *A Second Letter to a Friend on the Study of Prophecy* — Beyond reasonable doubt by B.W. Newton.

10. *Thoughts on the Apostasy of the Present Dispensation* — Beyond reasonable doubt by B.W. Newton.

11. *Valera's Spanish Bible of 1602 Appeal to Protestant Christians, respecting the Reprinting of this Version* — The Preface by B.W. Newton certainly; the Tract by S.P. Tregelles beyond reasonable doubt

12. *The White Robe* — Beyond reasonable doubt by B.W. Newton.

# 1. A CATECHISM ON THE FOUR GREAT AND UNIVERSAL EMPIRES, AND THE KINGDOM BY WHICH THEY WILL BE SUCCEEDED, AS MENTIONED IN THE BOOK OF THE PROPHECIES OF DANIEL

This interesting publication was produced at Plymouth in 1840. It was evidently a widely circulating tract as the copy with which we are familiar indicates that the printing was the 'second thousand'. B.W. Newton produced two publications titled 'Catechism' – one regarding the 'Harlot of Revelation 17' and the other regarding 'The Jews and Jerusalem'. Its teaching appears to be broadly in harmony with that of B.W. Newton. Nigel Pibworth therefore suggested that it might be by B.W. Newton.

**External Evidence**

None known

**Internal Evidence**

All the Scripture references were noted. A comparison of comments on texts was made, mainly through C.W.H. Griffiths's Scripture indexing of older works by Mr Newton, but also by Wyatt's index of texts of some later works.

1. The use of distinctive expression 'The Book of the Prophecies of Daniel' in the title of the book. We could find no evidence that B.W. Newton used this name for the book elsewhere.

2. The observation made regarding the imagery used to describe the empires in Daniel 2, and the imagery used in Daniel 7; namely, that Daniel 2 describes the character of their power, and Daniel 7 describes the exercise of their power (p. 3). We could find no comparable statements.

3. The listing of countries within the last empire (p. 6, 7). We could find no close equivalent to the list.

4. The distinctive interpretation of the expression 'the desire of women' as referring to the Messiah in Daniel 11:37, p.9. I could find no comparable interpretation.

5. The assumption of the title 'Lucifer' by Antichrist, Isa. 14:12, 13, p.7. 'He appears also to have assumed the name of Lucifer, son of the morning or day-star, one of the names of the Lord himself'.
   *Answers to the Questions… at Plymouth* (1834) p.62 has the following statement, - '"Lucifer" as blasphemously assuming Christ's character of the morning star'. However, Answers… was edited by Mr Newton and Henry Borlase, and records the outcome of a Conference.

6. The writer of the Catechism's translation in 1 John 4:3 (p.9). 'Jesus Christ come (εληλυθυτα [*sic.* for εληλυθοτα]) in the flesh' p.9. *A Remonstrance to the Society of Friends* (1835) (p. 27) has the 'Jesus Christ come (εληλυθοτα) in the flesh'.

7. The observation made on the description of the fourth beast (Antichrist) in Rev. 13:2. 'The same power is symbolized by a beast compounded of the three beasts, which in Daniel 7 symbolize the first three universal empires', p.7. The first edition of Thoughts on the Apocalypse (1844/5), p. 160, has 'The lion of Babylon, the bear of Persia, the leopard of Greece, [but N.B.] and the fourth or Roman beast (see Dan. 7) unite their forms to symbolize him.

CONCLUSION: **The internal evidence is inconclusive, and there is no external evidence. It cannot be assumed that B.W. Newton was the author.**

> There could be other contenders for the authorship of *The Catechism…*, for example S.P. Tregelles, and J.L. Harris, who was lecturing on Prophecy with B.W. Newton in 1841 – see *The Similarities and the Contrasts between the Present and Coming Dispensations*.

1840    J.B. Rowe (printer). Tract Depot, Plymouth   16cm   12p.   CBA

## 2. DR TREGELLES'S GREEK TESTAMENT; REMARKS ON SOME OBSERVATIONS OF THE BISHOP OF GLOUCESTER AND BRISTOL ON DR TREGELLES'S REVISED TEXT OF THE GREEK NEW TESTAMENT

This is dated August 1870, and has a preface, 'The continued prostration of the strength of Dr Tregelles under severe illness renders it quite impossible for him, at present, to undertake anything that requires mental exertion. The following Remarks, therefore, have been written by a friend, to whom Dr Tregelles has committed the general oversight of the publication of his work'.

The Bishop of Gloucester and Bristol (Charles John Ellicott 1816-1905) was later one of the Committee responsible for producing the Revised Version. The bishop made the highest commendation of Tregelles's Greek New Testament as faithful labour, and as a unique collection of assorted critical materials. However, he commented that it was mechanical in approach and sometimes fails to show 'critical instinct' and 'scholarly sagacity'. It is to such remarks that this pamphlet replies, as 'his remarks have caused pain to the friends of Dr Tregelles'. The author defends the principles upon which Dr Tregelles worked.

**External evidence**

1. It has been bound into a volume with the cover title *Textual Criticism of the Greek New Testament. S.P. Tregelles*, received by C.W.H. Griffiths from C.E. Fry. The binding of the book is identical with the manual edition of S.P. Tregelles's Greek New Testament, which has the initials B.W.N. (i.e. his personal copy) embossed on the spine. Both have a gold crown embossed on the front cover. The volume on textual criticism has had a repair to the spine. It is therefore not possible to determine whether it also has B.W.N. embossed on it. Extracts in F.W. Wyatt's hand, and an item with B.W. Newton's signature have been bound into it. The pamphlet is professedly not by S.P. Tregelles. The items in the book most likely derive from the personal possession of B.W. Newton.

2. A further copy is bound into a matching volume of the same provenance with the cover title, *The Printed Text of the Greek N.T. S.P. Tregelles*. In this volume it has the initials 'BWN' at the end in F.W. Wyatt's hand.

3. A letter written by Mrs Tregelles on her husband's behalf to Mr Newton dated 4th June 1870 [CBA 7181(111)] refers to her husband's inability to collate the readings of the Codex Sinaiticus. Bishop Ellicott devalued S.P. Tregelles's work by commenting that he had not had access to the Codex Sinaiticus. In this pamphlet the author affirms Dr Tregelles's esteem for the Codex Sinaiticus, and states that he had intended to make a collation of its readings in the

Gospels, where he had not had access to it. His ill-health had prevented him. The preface to the Manual Edition of S.P. Tregelles' Greek New Testament includes similar statements.

4. A letter written by Mrs Tregelles on her husband's behalf to Mr Newton dated 1st June 1870 [CBA 7181(110)] refers to C.J. Ellicott, although not regarding the comments which are the subject of this pamphlet.

5. Dr Tregelles had suggested that Mr Newton should write to C.J. Ellicott on another matter some years earlier, in a letter dated 5th October 1864 [(CBA 7181(77)].

**Internal evidence**

In the 'Introductory Notice' to the last part of Dr Tregelles's Greek New Testament (Quarto edition), dated March 1872, Mr Newton describes his role – 'having undertaken the general superintendence of the issue of this concluding Part…'. This is surely the same person who had been given 'the general oversight of the publication of his work'.

CONCLUSION: **Beyond Reasonable Doubt by B.W. Newton.**

    1870    Samuel Bagster & Sons, London    21.5cm  8p.    CG

## 3. A LETTER TO A FRIEND ON THE STUDY OF PROPHECY

This first appeared as an article in *The Christian Witness*. It was afterwards circulated as a separate tract. We have concluded that it is beyond reasonable doubt by B.W. Newton.

For the assessment leading to this conclusion see Section 7, Articles in *The Christian Witness*, and the entry in Section 3, B.W. Newton's Published Works.

CONCLUSION: **Beyond reasonable doubt by B.W. Newton.**

Publication and location details given in Section 3, B.W. Newton's Published Works

## 4. NOTES ON JOSHUA 5:6-12. FACT, FAITH, AND EXPERIENCE

The tract applies the analogy of Israel's journey to Canaan to the believer's progress through the Christian life.

**External evidence**

1. This is in a bound volume in the Fratelli Collection.[1] It is bound next to *Baptism*, which, although anonymously published, has been shown to be by B.W. Newton (it was extracted from *A Remonstrance to the Society of Friends*).
2. This tract bears the hand-written ascription 'B. Newton', believed to be in the hand of Eliza Browne[2]. *Baptism* bears the same ascription in the same hand.

---

[1] See the note on the Fratelli Collection for its association with the Plymouth meeting and J.L. Harris.
[2] See the note on Eliza Browne in Section 2, Libraries and Collections, the Fratelli Collection.

**Internal Evidence**

1. We have been unable to find evidence that this is elsewhere quoted, or used as a framework of thought, in any of B.W. Newton's writings.
2. The only parallel that we have been able to identify is with the analogy that believers stand 'with staves in their hands ready to depart' (Exodus 12:11 - see p.1 and compare with *On Luke 21*, p.10, and *The Personal Return of the Lord Jesus*, p.18).
3. Two statements imply 'higher life' teaching, which is uncharacteristic of B.W. Newton – 'The majority of us only know the wilderness' – 'Till they reach Gilgal they are uncircumcised' (page 3).

CONCLUSION: **Probably by B.W. Newton.**

> [ND] Plymouth, Tract Depot, Cornwall Street   17cm 4p.   Fratelli
> ('and sold at the following depots...Exeter...Hereford...London')
> Printer: J.B. Rowe, Plymouth

## 5. THE PASSOVER. EXODUS 12

This is a brief four page tract. It considers the typical correspondence between the Israelites leaving Egypt and the gathering of believers out of the world to everlasting glory.

**External evidence**

The Fondo Guicciardini has seven copies of the tract. There is a manuscript note on one of the French Editions - 'by Mr Newton, I believe'. The author of the note is unknown.

S.P. Tregelles wrote a letter to B.W. Newton dated 12th August 1858, advising regarding the circulation of tracts in Italian. That would have been after this tract had been produced, but it would indicate an interest in publishing in Italian at that time.

**Internal evidence**

There is no parallelism between the treatment of the Feast of the Passover in *Thoughts on Scriptural Subjects* and this tract. However, the exposition of *Thoughts on Scriptural Subjects* is based on Leviticus 23, not on Exodus 12. There are significant differences in the ordinances of Exodus 12 and their description in Leviticus 23.

The author concurs with B.W. Newton's representation of the evil character of leaven (cf. p.3 and *Prospects of the Ten Kingdoms*, p.165), but this was probably the general view among the early Brethren.

Likewise, the author expected the destruction of the world, not its betterment (cf. p.1 and *The Prospects of the World*, p.4). This was again, however, the predominant view among early Brethren.

CONCLUSION: **There is insufficient internal evidence to determine the authorship, and the external evidence is uncertain.**

## Section 5 - Assessment of Anonymous Publications Ascribed to B.W. Newton

First (?) Edition
    [ND]    London, James Manchee (Late Campbell)    17cm    4p.    I
                Plymouth, Brendon, printer

French Edition - La Pâque.

  [Edition 1]
    [ND]    Plymouth, J. Clulow and H. Soltau    17.5cm    4p.    I [4 copies]
             London, 1, Warwick Square
                printed by J. Wertheimer and Co.

  [Edition 2]
    1838    London, Tract Depot, 1, Warwick Square    17cm    11 [1] p. I
                printed by J. Wertheimer and Co.

Italian Edition - La Pasqua.

    1857    Genoa, printer G. Parodini    17cm    4p.    I

## 6. THE PROSPECTS OF THE WORLD IN CONNECTION WITH THE APPROACHING RETURN OF THE LORD JESUS CHRIST

This was produced from an address or lecture. It refers to 'you who are assembled'. It takes an overview of prophecy, rejecting post-millennialism and hopes of present earthly glory. The writer considers the future changes and prospects of the Gentile world, and of Jerusalem. It briefly recounts the whole period of Scripture prophecy.

**External evidence**

The external evidence is very strong.

1. It is in a volume owned by Anna Newton, his mother, held by the Sovereign Grace Advent Testimony. Articles not by B.W. Newton are all marked.

2. It appears as one of a published set of *Lectures on Prophecy* in the SGAT collection.[1] It is followed by *The Similarities and the Contrasts between the present and the Coming Dispensations* in the compilation. The half of that tract written by B.W. Newton (the other half was by J.L. Harris) states on p.22, 'I told you in a former lecture of the great ruling nations of the earth, and of their present prospects'. That is precisely the subject of *The Prospects of the World*.

3. It quotes *Remarks on the Ten Kingdoms of the Roman Empire*, which is likewise independently attributed to B.W. Newton (footnote on p.14).

---

[1] London, J.K. Campbell. This also included *The Personal Return of the Lord Jesus Christ necessary to the introduction of Millennial Blessing; Christ Not Yet Seated on the Throne of David;* and *The Substance of a Lecture on Luke 21*. Interestingly, *London Publishers and Printers c.1800-1870* by P.A.H. Brown dates the publishing of John Keylock Campbell of 1, Warwick Square, London as 1848-1850 - after B.W. Newton had left the Brethren, despite the fact that Warwick Square was the principal clearing house for Brethren tracts. However, the British Library has a J K Campbell catalogue dated as early as January 1847..

### Internal evidence

The internal evidence is likewise conclusive.

1. The material is thoroughly consistent with other writings by B.W. Newton - for example on the extent of the Roman Empire.

2. The author refers to *Prophecy in the 24th of Matthew, Considered* [p.9n], which we believe to be *Prophecy of the Lord Jesus as Contained in Matthew 24 Briefly Considered*.

3. The author also recommends material by, or attributed to, S.P. Tregelles - papers on 'Babylon' and 'Egypt' in *The Christian Witness*, p.7; and 'The Man of Sin', p.11. [For further reference to S.P. Tregelles's article on Babylon, see comments on B.W. Newton's article in *The Investigator*, September 1832, pp.53–55, 'The Times of Restitution. Acts 3:19 – 21', in Section 6, B.W. Newton's Letters and Articles Published in Periodicals].

4. The writer refers to his meeting with Michael Solomon Alexander, a rabbi who was converted and baptised in Plymouth in 1825, and who set sail to become the first Anglican bishop of Jerusalem on 7th December 1841. This meeting is corroborated by report of a lecture given in 1887 in '*Apostolic Succession*', a Review of' '*Protestant Christendom*', No.5 of the *Time of the End* Series, a derivative publication produced posthumously.[1]

**CONCLUSION: Certainly by B.W. Newton.**

Edition 1
    [ND]    [Plymouth] C[lulow] & S(oltau)    16cm    24p.    SG
              J. Wertheimer, printer, London

Edition 2 Add 'Second Lecture' to the title.
    1842    London, 1, Warwick Square    16cm    24p.    I
              J. Wertheimer, printer, London

Edition 3 (perhaps identical with Edition 2) Add 'Second Lecture' to the title.
    1842    London [Central Tract Depot]    17cm    24p.    CBA

## 7. REMARKS ON THE TEN KINGDOMS OF THE ROMAN WORLD

The tract is an outline of future prophetic history. It identifies the pivotal importance of the status of Jerusalem. It considers the Times of the Gentiles, and the Scriptural basis for a, yet future, tenfold division of the Roman Empire. Bound with it is a coloured map titled 'Map of the Countries contained in the Roman Empire in the Time of Trajan'.[2] The map was 'published by Lee and Catford, Plymouth and Truro', and is dated 1840. In view of its separate dating it probably circulated separately.

---

[1] See the 1904 Supplementary Note added to the Note on Rev. 11:8 in the Third Edition of *Thoughts on the Apocalypse* (pp. 213, 214), commented on in Appendix 1. A Comparison of the Editions of *Thoughts on the Apocalypse* for further information and other references to him in B.W. Newton's works.

[2] Page 9 refers to 'the Map which this Tract is intended to accompany', which suggests this.

### External Evidence

1. The extent of the revived Roman Empire is taken from this tract, and quoted in a footnote in *The Prospects of the World* (*Remarks…*, p.8 and *Prospects of the World…* p.14n).

2. Parts of the tract *Jerusalem* are very close to this tract - both in subject matter, and verbally. There is a paragraph of virtual verbal agreement on page 6 (cf. p.6 of *Jerusalem*, the early edition).

3. There is a manuscript attribution (by Eliza Browne?[1]), 'by Mr Newton' on the French Edition.

### Internal Evidence

1. The author's map gives the boundary of the future Ten Kingdoms as the fullest extent of the Roman Empire in the time of Trajan. This concurs with all Mr Newton's other comments upon the subject. See, for example *Prospects of the Ten Kingdoms* pp.27,28, where the period of Trajan's imperial rule is taken to be definitive. There are no significant differences between the limits of this map, and others produced for B.W. Newton - indeed a note on the map draws attention to Ireland, Persia, and Arabia as being outside the Roman Empire[2] a distinctive view held by B.W. Newton.

2. The author expects a future revival of the literal Euphratean city of Babylon (p.11).

3. In writing of Antichrist, the author links Isaiah 14:13 and Daniel 11:45. Compare p.12 with *Aids to Prophetic Enquiry* (Third Edition) p.91.

**CONCLUSION: Certainly by B.W. Newton.**

First (?) Edition
    1841    G.S. Lee, Plymouth                      15cm    12p.    I

Second (?) Edition
    1844    Tract Depot, London                 17.5cm  12p.    I

French Edition - *Remarques sur Les Dix Royaumes du Monde Romain.*
    1843    J. Wertheimer, London              17.5cm  12p.    I

NB The Map is dated 1840

## 8. THE SECOND APPEARING AND PERSONAL REIGN OF THE LORD JESUS CHRIST; A DISCOURSE ON 'THY KINGDOM COME' - MATT 6:10

### External Evidence

The sole indication that this work may be by B.W. Newton is the cataloguing of the Fondo Guicciardini[3]. It indicates it was by him by placing his name in brackets, and with a question mark, after the French and Italian Editions of the tract. No authority is given by the Collection for

---

[1] Eliza Browne. See the note on the Fratelli Collection in Section 2, Libraries and Collections
[2] 'It should have been mentioned that Persia is not included in the Roman Empire. According to the prophecy in Ezekiel 38:5, it is to be connected not with the western, but with the Russian or Muscovite nations. Bavaria should have been mentioned, together with Switzerland, as included in the Roman earth'.
[3] Fondo Guicciardini. See Section 2, Libraries and Collections.

attributing the tract to Mr Newton. The Guicciardini catalogue makes no mention of the English title and *Le Glorieux Avènement* is not a precise translation of *The Second Appearing*.

**Internal Evidence**

The tract has been examined in detail, but it has not been possible to draw out any conclusive evidence. One line of enquiry that seemed promising, but proved problematical is the reference that the author of the tract makes to 'the sequel', which would make plain certain points from Matthew 24. Unfortunately, it has proved impossible to categorically identify the sequel. For example, the French Edition of *The World to Come* follows it in the Fondo Guicciardini catalogue. *A Catechism of the Four Great Universal Empires*[1] follows it in the CBA Collection (CBA 5700(3)), and (interestingly) *Prophecy of the Lord Jesus as Contained in Matthew 24, Briefly Considered* follows it in the copy in the SGAT Collection. There is therefore no unequivocal external evidence from collections of tracts.

The internal arguments for and against B.W. Newton's authorship may be summarised as follows:

<u>For B.W. Newton's authorship</u>

1. On p.10 the author adopted 'all the tribes of the land' as the translation of Matthew 24:30, and links this with Revelation 1:7. This is also done in *Thoughts on the End of the Age*, p.21; and *Thoughts on the Apocalypse*, p.61.
2. The author clearly regarded the Old Testament saints as a part of the Church (p.13).
3. The author translated and expounded Revelation 5:10 as reigning 'over the earth', (p.15). This is also done in the *A Letter to a Friend on the Study of Prophecy* (p.12), *A Second Letter to a Friend on the Study of Prophecy* (p.7), and *Thoughts on Leviticus*, p.317 ('on and over the earth').
4. The position of believers is described as standing 'with their staff in their hand' (p.18). Compare this with the comments made in Notes on *Joshua 5:6-12. Fact, Faith, and Experience*, which was probably by B.W. Newton.
5. Two of the French Editions were published from Geneva. B.W. Newton did publish works from Geneva.

<u>Against B.W. Newton's authorship</u>

1. Even the Second Edition of the tract (1839) was distributed from the London Central Tract Depot. There is no mention of Plymouth on any of the publication details.
2. This was a very widely circulating tract. If it were by Mr Newton, it is surprising that it is not alluded to, or quoted, by him, so far as we can ascertain.
3. There appears to be little, if any, statement from which B.W. Newton might later wish to distance himself. It was being republished as late as 1852 (French Edition). It would have surely been withdrawn before that point if he had any difficulty with it. If it was truly by him, why did he not own or make use of a very successful tract elsewhere?
4. Mr Newton gave no extended exposition of Matthew 6:10 elsewhere.

---

[1] *A Catechism of the Four Great Universal Empires* is a tract of unknown authorship, which has some similarities with B.W. Newton's writings, but has no external sources attributing it to him. It does not comment on Matthew 24.

5. The printer who B.W. Newton used for his Geneva publications, 'E Béroud', is different from theprinters of the two French Editions of this tract in the Fondo Guicciardini.

6. Georges Kaufmann (1809-1884), who published the French Editions, was a hymn writer among J.N. Darby's followers in Switzerland.[1] It is extremely unlikely that one of J.N. Darby's supporters would be publishing anything by B.W. Newton as late as 1852 when he (Kauffman) was also publishing works by J.N. Darby (e.g. *Pensées sur Philippiens 3*).[2]

7. The printer of this tract at Vevey (E. Buvelot) published J.N. Darby's *Lettre à M. le Ministre Guers au Sujet de sa Note Sure les Erreurs de M. J.* [sic] *B. Newton…* in 1853. It is unlikely that the same firm would have knowingly carried a title by B.W. Newton at this stage in the controversy only a year earlier.

**CONCLUSION: Not by B.W. Newton.**

First (?) Edition
    [ND]    Tract Depot, London    17cm    20p.    CBA

Second Edition
    1839    Central Tract Depot, London    17cm    24p.    SG

Third Edition
    ?    ?    ?    ?    ?

Fourth Edition
    [1842?]    Tract Depot, London    ?    22p.    BL,CBA (5700(3))

French Editions

    [Edition 1] *Le Glorieux Avènement et Le Règne Personnel de Notre Seigneur Jésus-Christ. Traduit de l'anglais, et Réimprimé sur la Seconde Edition de Genève.*
        [ND]    Jersey Tract Depot and    17.5cm  22p.    I
        1, Warwick Square

    [Edition 2] *Le Glorieux Avènement et le Règne Personnel de Notre Seigneur Jésus-Christ. Discours sur Matth 6:10: Que ton Règne Vienne. Traduit de l'Anglais sur la Seconde Edition de Genève.*
        1840    Georges Kaufmann (?S.I.? France?)17cm    24p.    I

    [Edition 3] *Le Glorieux Avènement et Le Règne Personnel de Notre Seigneur Jésus-Christ. Discours sur Matthieu 6:10: Que ton Règne Vienne. Quatrième édition.*
        1852    Georges Kaufmann [publisher], Geneva.    17cm    23p.    I
            E. Buvelot [printer], Vevey

    Italian [Maltese] Edition. *Il Glorioso Avvenimento e il Regno Personale del Nostro Signore Gesù Cristo.*
        1848    Gabriele Vassalli, printer, Valletta    14cm    35p.    I

---

[1] See F.C[uendet], *Souvenez-vous de vos Conducteurs*, Vevey, 1966, p.68. Information from T.C.F. Stunt.
[2] We are very grateful for the observations of T.C.F. Stunt on Geneva publishers in relation to this item.

## 9. A SECOND LETTER TO A FRIEND ON THE STUDY OF PROPHECY

This first appeared as an article in *The Christian Witness*. It was afterwards circulated as a separate tract. We have concluded that it is beyond reasonable doubt by B.W. Newton, and have therefore included it in Section 3, B.W. Newton's Published Works.

For the assessment leading to this conclusion, see Section 7, Articles in *The Christian Witness*.

**CONCLUSION: Beyond reasonable doubt by B.W. Newton.**

Publication and location details given in Section 3, B.W. Newton's Published Works.

## 10. THOUGHTS ON THE APOSTASY OF THE PRESENT DISPENSATION

This first appeared in the January 1838 edition of *The Christian Witness*. In our assessment of attributed *Christian Witness* articles (Section 7), we conclude that it is beyond reasonable doubt the work of B.W. Newton. See there for a full assessment of the tract. The tract is virtually identical to the article. The only changes are such as the addition of an exclamation mark.

As a tract, it was bound up in a set entitled *Truth for the Times*. The second tract in the set (*The Character of Office in the Present Dispensation*) was by J.N. Darby.

**CONCLUSION: Beyond reasonable doubt by B.W. Newton.**

First Edition (In *Truth for the Times*).
    [1838?] Tract Depot, Plymouth      17cm    20p.    SG

Second Edition (*Truth for the Times No.1*).
    [ND] Tract Depot, Plymouth and      17cm    20p.    I
    Central Tract Depot, London

## 11. VALERA'S SPANISH BIBLE OF 1602. APPEAL TO PROTESTANT CHRISTIANS, RESPECTING THE REPRINTING OF THIS VERSION

Our assessment of this item is given in Section 4, B.W. Newton's Contributions to Other Publications. We believe that the British Library cataloguing of the whole tract as by 'B.W.N.' is incorrect, although the preface certainly is by him.

**CONCLUSION: The Preface by B.W. Newton certainly; the Tract by S.P. Tregelles beyond reasonable doubt.**

Publication and location details given in Section 4, B.W. Newton's Contributions to Other Publications.

## 12. THE WHITE ROBE (REVELATION 7:9-17)

This is a children's' Gospel tract. It deals with the question of fitness for heavenly glory. The frontispiece is what appears to be a missionary scene.

## External Evidence

1. It is bound up in Vol. 16 of B.W. Newton's works, dated 1901 - The Stirling Collection[1].
2. As well as being in a volume of B.W. Newton's works, the tract has a MS entry at the end of the text (but before a hymn which concludes it) 'By B.W. Newton. M.A.'. This ascription is in the handwriting of Mary E.J. Stirling.
3. The date of the collection (2 years after B.W. Newton's death), and the printer, make it unlikely that it was issued by his friends on the basis of notes of an address. Such known items were from the Isle of Wight circle, or from Hunt, Barnard (see Section 8, Publications Produced from Notes of Addresses, and Posthumously Published Letters and Manuscripts).

## Internal Evidence

1. It is difficult to make any conclusive assessment of the internal evidence for Mr Newton's authorship as the tract is necessarily simple, and does not deal with any distinctive or controversial issues.
2. Horatius Bonar produced *The White Robes: A tract for Sabbath School Children* –'*the substance of a sermon preached to Sabbath school children, Sept. 13, 1840*', Kelso Tracts No.12, but, apart from the Scripture text upon which it was based, there are no significant similarities.

There is no reason for doubting the ascription of this tract to B.W. Newton. We have therefore included it in Section 3, B.W. Newton's Published Works.

CONCLUSION: **Beyond reasonable doubt by B.W. Newton.**

    ND    Dublin Steam Printing Company    12.5 x 9 cm    16p.    CBA

Reprinted in *Watching and Waiting*, October/December 1989, pp.187-189.

---

[1] The Stirling Collection. See Section 10, Duplicated and Manuscript Items.

# SECTION 6

## LETTERS AND ARTICLES BY B.W. NEWTON PUBLISHED IN PERIODICALS

# LETTERS AND ARTICLES BY B.W. NEWTON
# PUBLISHED IN PERIODICALS

B.W. Newton is known to have written anonymously to several newspapers, but as he did not use a consistent pseudonym, it is a matter of conjecture how far he used these media to express his views. He likewise contributed to several theological or prophetic periodicals. Again, it is not known how far he did so anonymously. Meticulous following of leads has its place in identifying a contribution, but sometimes it is pure serendipity. The helpful comments of Timothy Stunt on several matters in this section are gratefully acknowledged.

Attributed items published posthumously in *Perilous Times*, *Watching and Waiting*, and elsewhere, are not listed here, but are found in Section 8, Publications Produced from Notes of Addresses, and Posthumously Published Letters and Manuscripts.

A separate section of this *Guide* assesses the authorship of the articles in *The Christian Witness* that have been attributed to him.

The periodicals to which he is known to have contributed that we consider here were as follows:
1. *The Christian Observer.*
2. *The Investigator.*
3. *The Morning Herald.*
4. *The (Quarterly) Journal of Prophecy.*
5. *Old Truths.*
6. *The Record.*

## THE CHRISTIAN OBSERVER

**Letter on the Beacon Controversy** - April 1836 (pp.221-225).

The full title of this publication was *The Christian Observer, conducted by members of the Established Church*. It was published by members of the so-called 'Clapham Sect', which included William Wilberforce.

This letter was written in the context of the Beacon Controversy.[1] *The Christian Observer* had noted the controversy in its May 1835 issue. It gave a literature review of it, and comment, in its October 1835 issue (pp.629-642). This mainly considered the quotations given by B.W. Newton in his *Remonstrance to the Society of Friends*. Joseph John Gurney[2] then wrote to the paper on 'the Orthodoxy of Friends' (published Appendix 1835 pages 791.792), replying to Mr Newton's *Remonstrance*.

Mr Newton's letter was a reply to that letter. Mr Newton's shows that he was supported in his *Remonstrance* by Church of England clergymen, and 'a well-known dissenting minister'. B.W. Newton's *A Vindication of 'A Remonstrance to the Society of Friends'* quotes J.J. Gurney's *Essays* (pp.18-20), and his letter to *The Christian Observer (p.62)*.

Although 'The Christian Observer' gives J.J. Gurney the title 'Mr', B.W. Newton is titled 'Rev.' in this Church of England paper.

---

[1] For more information on the Beacon Controversy see the notes on B.W. Newton's *Remonstrance to the Society of Friends* in Section 3, B.W. Newton's Published Works of this Guide.
[2] Joseph John Gurney (1788 – 1847) was a leader in the Evangelical wing of the Quakers in Britain, and the brother of Elizabeth Fry, the prison reformer. He, as she, was a social reformer with considerable influence. He asserted the primacy of Scripture, but was a moderate who did not separate from the Quakers at the time of the Beacon Controversy. Between 1837 and 1840, his preaching in America was, ironically, the cause of major division amongst the Quakers there. The Orthodox Friends (already separate from the more extreme 'Hicksites') split between 'Gurneyite' and 'Wilburite' factions

## THE INVESTIGATOR

This journal's full title was *The Investigator, or Monthly Expositor and Register, on Prophecy*. It was issued between 1831 and 1836. Joshua W. Brooks[1] (a historicist) edited it.

The articles by B.W. Newton that appeared in *The Investigator* were as follows:

1. The Times of Restitution. Acts 3:19 – 21.
2. The Future Siege of Jerusalem.
3. The Book of Daniel.

These articles are important, as they give an indication of B.W. Newton's prophetic position at a very early date. The authorship of the articles is identified by the initials 'BWN' only. The first is from Plymouth. S.P. Tregelles confirmed B.W. Newton's authorship (see below). J.N. Darby also contributed to this paper in 1832 (p.334).

**Article 1 'The Times of Restitution. Acts 3:19 – 21'** - September 1832, pp.53-55.

The article has the subscript 'B.W.N. Plymouth June 15th 1832'.

B.W. Newton frequently used these Scripture verses in discussion of the Millennium in his later ministry. In the article there is some discussion of the Greek, and of the futurity of Matthew 24. *Modern Fanaticism Unveiled* by Mrs Thalia S. Henderson, first published in 1831 and written against Irvingism, seems to have been the stimulus for the contribution. Her book has a chapter on Prophecy.

In the article Mr Newton viewed the prophesied destruction of Babylon – 'the Euphratean city' as a past event. He expected that Isaiah 13, which predicted it, will find its exhaustive fulfilment only in 'the mystic Babylon'. In his *Three Letters…*[2], S.P. Tregelles commented on the change in Mr Newton's expectation regarding the re-establishment of 'the Euphratean city', and identified himself as the author of an article on Babylon that appeared in *The Christian Witness*. He wrote, 'That Mr Newton should, in 1832 have written differently on the subject can occasion no surprise; three years after this, the evidence was placed before him, which showed that the ancient prophecies against Babylon have not met with their literal accomplishment…When the paper in *The Investigator* was mentioned a few years ago to Mr Newton, it had entirely passed from his memory…I gave a brief outline of what I then knew of the present state of the site and plain of Babylon, and of the non-fulfilment of the predictions of Isaiah and Jeremiah in *The Christian Witness* for July 1836'.

---

[1] Rev. Joshua William Brooks (1790-1882), Church of England minister, and later Prebendary of Lincoln Cathedral. He was the author of A *Dictionary of Writers on the Prophecies: With the Titles and Occasional Description of Their Works*, 1835 (listing upwards of 2,100 titles), and of *Elements of Prophetical Interpretation*, 1836. He was a historicist, whose own 'hypothesis' allegedly included the completion of 'the 6,000 years' and the return of Christ in 1836! For more information regarding him, see *The Prophetic Faith of our Fathers* by Leroy Edwin Froom.

[2] S.P. Tregelles, *Three Letters to the Author of 'A Retrospect of Events That Have Taken Place Amongst the Brethren*, Second Edition 1894, p.69.

At the conclusion of the article, Mr Newton commends William Burgh's *Lectures on the Second Advent*.

### Article 2 'The Future Siege of Jerusalem' - 1833, pp.45-49.

This followed on from an allusion in Article 1 to 'a future siege of Jerusalem, previous to the Millennium'. Matthew 24 is the basis for expecting the future siege.

The exposition articulates the key points of his later expositions of Matthew 24, notably: that it refers to a time of 'unexampled tribulation', which is followed 'immediately after' by the return of the Lord Jesus; that 'immediately' is the emphatic word of the chapter; that 'this generation' refers to the ungodly 'race'. The article links Matthew 24 with Daniel 11 and 12, and with Zechariah 12 and 14. It offers a reply to those who suppose that the destruction of Jerusalem by Titus in AD 70 fulfilled Matthew 24.

The subscript of the article is simply 'Your's faithfully, B.W.N.'

The article was reprinted in *Watching and Waiting*, October-December 2011, pp.310-316.

### Article 3 'The Book of Daniel' – 1834, pp.286-292.

This was intended to be 'a few brief and general remarks on the book of Daniel'. It contains Mr Newton's characteristic explanation of the prophetic visions of the book. 'I believe it will be found that Daniel supplies a brief, but continuous history of those Gentile nations by which Jerusalem was trodden down, until the time of her destruction by the Romans; that during the present Jewish dispersion, *all continuous history ceases*, and is not resumed until Jerusalem again assumes a national existence, and is again the object of Gentile violence'. It considers the prophetic parts of the book.

The subscript is, 'I am, &c. B.W.N.'

There is a remarkable editorial footnote to the article (it takes up nearly a page), which explains why by B.W. Newton did not have any further articles published in the journal. The footnote rejects comments by Mr Newton as 'not interpretation at all, but mere hypothesis', and that 'B.W.N. is apparently deluding himself', etc.

The article was reprinted in *Watching and Waiting*, January-March 2012, pp.7-13.

## THE [QUARTERLY] JOURNAL OF PROPHECY

Horatius Bonar began, and edited, *The Journal of Prophecy* (sometimes known as *The Quarterly Journal of Prophecy*). In considering J.N. Darby's attacks on B.W. Newton, it was detached in its comments (although it was less favourable to Darby). Mr Newton's *Aids to Prophetic Enquiry* did not receive a particularly favourable review. It did however harden its tone towards J.N. Darby, who was in its later issues associated with Socinianism. It reviewed Mr Newton's main works, and he became an occasional contributor. The periodical also viewed the works of Rev. John Cox, sen., favourably. He was probably also a contributor. The SGAT possesses Vols. 3, 4, and 5, apparently owned by Rev. John Cox sen., in which there are marginal corrections to the text of some articles. A further SGAT volume has a manuscript ascription of an exposition to S.P. Tregelles.[1]

Unfortunately, most of the published articles were anonymous, and the personal records of Horatius Bonar are lost.[2]

The articles known to be by B.W. Newton that appeared in *The Quarterly Journal of Prophecy* are as follows:

1. The Old Testament Saints.
2. The Millennium and the Everlasting State.
3. Note on 1 Peter 2:24.
4. Note on Psalm 68:4.
5. Notes on 2 Peter 3:2; Rev. 2:2.

**Article 1. The Old Testament Saints** - April 1857 (Vol. 9).

This was published anonymously. It provoked two letters in response from William Trotter (July and October 1857). It was published as a separate tract by Mr Newton, and was later incorporated into *Narratives from the Old Testament* in a modified form. See the description of the tract given in Section 3, B.W. Newton's Published Works.

**Article 2. The Millennium and the Everlasting State** - July 1857 (Vol. 9), pp.263-269.

This is an anonymous article, which later appeared as an (anonymous) tract under the same title. It was slightly edited by Mr. Newton, and his changes were incorporated into it in the posthumous *Expository Teaching on the Millennium and Israel's Future*. He therefore acknowledged his authorship by the correction for republication.

The context of the article was as follows:

The article was a response to a detailed letter from 'An Enquirer', Brighton, December 4th 1856, published in Vol. 9, 1857, pp.89-92, which sought clarification on 'the duration of the restored

---

[1] See note in SGAT copy Vol. 10, p.237. The exposition ascribed to S.P. Tregelles consists of several articles on Matthew 24.
[2] Most of the manuscripts and letters of Horatius Bonar were destroyed at the death of his sister (1941) [see PhD dissertation by Benjamin Ray Oliphint, 1951].

kingdom of Israel and under them of the universal kingdom of Christ on earth'. The "Enquirer" highlighted the apparent problems of sequencing Revelation 21:1-5 after the preceding chapter, and again with the remainder of chapter 21.

The Article by B.W. Newton appeared on pages 263-269 of the same volume (July 1857 (Vol. 9)). See *Expository Teaching on the Millennium and Israel's Future* in Section 3, B.W. Newton's Published Works for comment on the content.

A lengthy reply to B.W. Newton's article appeared in the January 1860 issue (Vol. 12, pp.26-35) of *The Quarterly Journal of Prophecy* under the heading 'The New Heavens and Earth'. The unnamed author took issue, in particular, with the statement, 'all that bears the likeness of the first Adam disappears for ever. None will be admitted into the New Earth, except those in whom both mortality and sin have ceased to be', i.e. that the New Heavens and Earth are not created until the close of the Millennium. The writer contends that 'the New Earth and the Millennial Earth are identical'. He claims that B.W. Newton's view rests on the 'suitability' of the present earth and heavens for believers made like Christ as the Last Adam. The reply questions the distinction made between Rev. 21:1-8, and 21:9 – 22:21. 'If 22:3 must be limited, why should not also 21:4 be limited?' '21:1-8 is the rough sketch, 21:9 – 22:21 is the finished picture'. It discussed the difficulty of making distinctions in Isa. 65:17-25. It argues that the predicted conflagration in 2 Peter 3 is at 'the beginning of the day of the Lord'. It adds Psa. 1:3, 97:3, Isa. 14:1, Mic. 1:3,4, Isa. 33:12,14, and Isa. 24:6 to this argument.

T.B. Lane (Vol. 12, April 1860, pp.199-202) and Arthur Hall (Vol. 12, April 1860, pp.202-203) responded to the new article. Mr Lane also rejected the argument from 'suitability', but questioned the writer of the second article's interpretation of the quoted Scripture passages. In particular, he stated that the object of 2 Peter 3 was to emphasise the certainty, not the timing of the fiery judgement. Arthur Hall also considered the passages quoted, and concluded with a comparison of the two states, endeavouring to show where they differ.

The reply that followed from the author of 'The New Heavens and Earth' (Vol. 12, July 1860, pp.205-219) asserted, (1) The Millennial Earth and the New Earth are identical. The difference lies between the millennial and eternal states. (2) It argued that the object of 2 Peter 3 is not just to demonstrate the certainty, but also the imminence of the Day of the Lord. The conflagration must therefore take place at its start. He replied to the objections of both respondents (T.B. Lane and Arthur Hall) in detail.

**Article 3. 'Note on 1 Peter 2:24'** - October 1859 (Vol. 11) pp.387-389.

This was separately published (without the introductory paragraph) in the same year. It was later published with *Ancient Truths Respecting the Deity and True Humanity of the Lord Jesus*, and *Christ, Our Suffering Surety...*. This is probably the item referred to in Horatius Bonar's letter to B.W. Newton, dated 31st December 1877 (see Section 9, B.W. Newton's Correspondence), which refers to the necessity of having the article republished. For more information see the note on *Ancient Truths...* in Section 3, B.W. Newton's Published Works.

**Article 4. Note on Psalm 68:4** - January 1867 (Vol. 19), pp.80-81.

'Notes on Scripture' were a regular feature in the Journal. The author is not normally indicated. It was presumably usually the editor. The notes in this issue are short sections on the following Scriptures (commencing at, p.78): 1 Cor. 15:29, Eph. 3:4, Psalm 68:4.

The (last) note, on Psalm 68:4, has at the end 'B.W. Newton' in capital letters. The others are anonymous. It is unclear whether B.W. Newton was the author of all three items. It is safest to assume that he was only the author of the last – see the note on Article 5, below.

This note on Psalm 68 appears to be an original item. We have been unable to locate it reproduced elsewhere [although compare the item on Psalm 68 in *Expository Thoughts on the Millennium and Israel's Future*]. It concerns the second return of Israel to their land, which will be accompanied by chastisement, and then blessing.

**Article 5. Note on 2 Peter 3:2 and Rev. 2:2** - October 1867 (Vol. 19), p.390.

'Notes on Scripture' were a regular feature of the Journal. The author is not usually indicated. It was presumably normally the editor. The notes in this volume are short sections on the following Scriptures, from pages 385-390:

Rom. 8:19-22, Psalm 94:12, Lev. 16, 1 Cor. 1:17, Gal. 1:1, 2 Tim. 2:2, 2 Peter 3:2, and Rev. 2:2.

Although the set of notes has at the end of the last 'B.W. Newton' in capitals, they are evidently not all written by him, as the first has a subscript indicating it is a quotation from Thomas Brooks, the third indicates that it is a quotation from *Old Truths*. The others are not attributed. Either B.W. Newton was only the author of the last, or he submitted the collection of notes to the Journal, and therefore was the author of the notes on Psalm 94:12, 1 Cor. 1:17, Gal. 1:1, 2 Tim. 2:2, 2 Peter 3:2, and Rev.2:2. The notes are short, and would be difficult to trace in his published works.

The note on 2 Peter 3:2 and Rev. 2:2 are an extract from B.W. Newton's *Reflections Suggested by the Present Movement in England against Romanism*, pp.13,14.

## OLD TRUTHS

This was edited by John Cox jun., the son of Rev. John Cox, Mr. Newton's close friend.

Works by Mr Newton were reviewed, and many extracts were published in this short-lived periodical. We have not attempted to catalogue all of these items. The source of the articles is not generally indicated.

A pamphlet was compiled from some of the articles [*The Testimony of Mr B.W. Newton concerning the Divinity and Humanity of the Lord Jesus. Extracted from 'Old Truths'* – 1867 – 8 pages – CBA].

We have assessed all the articles that appeared in *Old Truths*. The following articles cannot be identified as coming from any other work, but are attributed to B.W. Newton in the periodical.

**Article 1, Prophecy and Ritualism** - 1867 (Vol. 2), p.237.

> The source of this is unknown. It may be an original article.
>
> This short article highlights Romanist pretentions, which lay claim to such Scriptures as Isa. 49:23, Isa. 2:2, and Zech. 6:13. The article emphasises that all of these and similar verses relate to a future dispensation. "The Catechism of Pope Pius IV derives almost all its plausibility from the misapplication of millennial texts". He concludes that unless Romanists and ritualists can wrest the promises from Israel, they cannot claim them for themselves.
>
> The true Church is in a condition of weakness and division. 'Individual agency' is the means God has chiefly used for the revival of truth during the last eighteen hundred years 'since the darkness first set in'.

**Article 2, Truths concerning Christ as the Redeemer** - 1867 (Vol. 2), pp.244, 245.

> The source for this is unknown. It may be an original article.
>
> This sets forth, and develops, six statements.
>
> 1. The Lord Jesus was, as declared in the Athanasian Creed, 'perfect God and perfect Man'.
> 2. The Lord Jesus was never, either on the cross or in life in 'moral distance from God'.
> 3. The obedience and sufferings of the Lord Jesus in life, and in death, were exclusively on account of his believing people.
> 4. The whole course of the obedience and suffering of the Lord the Redeemer was fore-ordained and appointed in the counsels of eternity.
> 5. All the sufferings, and all the obedience, of the Lord Jesus were, from the first to the last, voluntary; none were constrained.
> 6. The work required for the redemption and justification of God's believing people was completed on the cross.

**Article 3, Reliance on Christ** - 1868 (Vol. 3), pp.230, 231.

The source of this is unknown. It may be an original article. Similar statements are made in *David, King of Israel* (p.1).

It defines the ground of our justification as 'reliance on the Divine mercy remitting sin for Christ's sake', 'a reliance of the heart on God'. It sets this against the teaching of the Church of Rome, and describes what 'reliance' means.

## THE RECORD

The Record was a newspaper that commenced publication on 1st January 1828. It took a strong evangelical, and Calvinist, position.[1]

In relation to item 1 below, B.W Newton was acquainted with the editor of the short-lived *London Review* (Blanco White), and several of the contributors. He used a nom de plume because 'I do not wish to come into open collision yet with the Editor and Contributors whom I am in the habit of meeting occasionally' as he said in a letter to his mother postmarked 28th April 1829.[2] It was for that reason he used a pseudonym in the first two letters below.

There may have been further items, including a correspondence on Irvingism, which has not been located.[3]

### 1. Correspondence respecting 'The London Review' - 27th and 30th April 1829.

These two letters were signed 'W', but are identified as being by Mr Newton in the letter to his mother cited above. These two letters comment on *The London Review* and describe it as having an unscriptural tone, and being weak on essential doctrines. They complain about certain statements in the second issue of the *London Review*, concerning the doctrines of the Fall, and Eternal Punishment.

### 2. Three further letters by 'W' followed

Published correspondence was limited to an average of 2 or 3 letters per paper and certain noms de plume appear as regular correspondents. We cannot confirm that the following items were by B.W. Newton, although they appeared under the letter 'W' over the following sixteen months.

**15th June 1829** - Regarding the compromising of Protestant soldiers made 'to minister to the debasing idolatries of Popery'.

**1st July 1830** - Responding to a correspondence on Churchmen attending dissenting places of worship 'where the Gospel is not faithfully preached in the parish Church'.

**6th September 1830** - On punctuality of those attending religious and charitable societies.[4]

---

[1] There is further background to *The Record* and its supporters in *Evangelicalism and Public Life*, a thesis by Ian Rennie, Toronto 1962 (copy at Cambridge University Library).
[2] Quoted in *From Awakening to Secession* by T.C.F. Stunt, T&T Clark, 2000, p.214. Original letter CBA 7179(6), F.W. Wyatt's copy MS Book 2 (TC), pp.36-37. A.C. Fry's secondary copy CBA 7049, pp.169-170.
[3] Checked April 1829 – end 1832, and 1870-1899 (A few lacks in British Library Newspaper Library between these dates), although the paper did oppose Irvingism. See the issue of 21st November 1831 quoted in *Edward Irving and his Circle* by A.L. Drummond, p.208.
[4] Exeter College Archives lists B.W. Newton as attending most Governing Body meetings [as a Fellow] from November 1827 – June 1830, and then one in December 1830.

### 3. Correspondence regarding R. Pearsall Smith - 2nd November 1874

This is introduced by the editor's statement, 'we have been induced to comply with the urgent request of friends to insert the following criticisms on some of his [Pearsall Smith's] statements, from the pen of an eminent scholar'.

Although Mr Newton had recently written against the views of Pearsall Smith[1], this appears to have been written by him specifically on the then current debate. It relates to Mr Christopher's letter to *The Record*, dated October 19th 1874.

The article is identified as by 'B.W. Newton' when it was republished posthumously, titled *Notes on Some Statements of R. Pearsall Smith (Reprinted from 'The Record', November 2 1874)* - see the listing in Section 3, B.W. Newton's Published Works. It was included as an appendix in *Lectures on the Epistle to the Romans*[2]. Other items which relate to this controversy and Mr Newton appeared in the 9th December 1872, 30th April 1873, and 23rd September 1874 editions of the paper.

There is a copy of the printed letter in Manuscript Book 1 (held by Tom Chantry), p.59.

---

[1] *Modern Doctrines respecting Sinlessness, Considered* (1873), and *Remarks on R. Pearsall Smith's edition of Hymns Selected from those of the late F.W. Faber...* (1874)

[2] See the note on this in Section 8, Publications Produced from Notes of Addresses, and Posthumously Published Letters and Manuscripts.

## THE MORNING HERALD

'**Jewish Disabilities**'. A letter published January 2nd 1852.

The letter bore the pseudonym 'ΧΡΙΣΤΙΑΝΟΣ' (Christianos = A Christian) when published.

There was political agitation from the 1820s onwards to remove 'Jewish Disabilities'. Finally, in 1858, the Jews Relief Act (which started its progress through Parliament as the Jewish Disabilities Bill), removed all barriers to Jews being elected to, and sworn in as, members of Parliament.

Evangelicals were divided on the legislation. B.W. Newton took the position that 'avowed rejection of the Scriptures, or any part thereof, is a moral disqualification for legislative authority'.

The letter was republished posthumously by F.W. Wyatt in 1900, as one of the items in 'The Acknowledgement of God by Earthly Governments'. We have F.W. Wyatt's authority for identifying it as by B.W. Newton. The booklet was printed 'by permission'. It therefore had Mr Newton's approval.

We have not checked *The Morning Herald* for other contributions by ΧΡΙΣΤΙΑΝΟΣ

# SECTION 7

## ARTICLES IN 'THE CHRISTIAN WITNESS' ASCRIBED TO B.W. NEWTON

# ARTICLES IN 'THE CHRISTIAN WITNESS' ASCRIBED TO B.W. NEWTON

*The Christian Witness* was the first periodical of the nascent Brethren Movement. It was produced at Plymouth between 1834 and 1841. Most of the articles published in *The Christian Witness* were anonymous. Some of the annual bound volumes of *The Christian Witness* have manuscript notes identifying the authors of articles. Unfortunately, these ascriptions are not consistent, and it is necessary to test their validity. The ascriptions of one owner have unfortunately been accepted at face value by several writers on the history of the controversy as it affected B.W. Newton.[1]

These ascriptions present particular problems. A volume of mostly anonymous articles presents a challenge to its owner. There is an obvious danger of speculation to get a name against every article. On the other hand, many of the writers may have later wished to leave the early anonymous tracts and articles unclaimed in view of the bitter controversies, hostile scrutiny, and reassessment of personal views and allegiances that took place in the years that followed.

Our assessment is only concerned with establishing or discounting B.W. Newton's authorship of articles. However, what we have undertaken does have a wider value in establishing or discounting the reliability of different sets of handwritten ascriptions.

We have not summarised or commented upon the content of the articles, beyond what is necessary to consider authorship. Nor have we carried out a search to see if any of the items considered were republished as tracts and acknowledged by other authors. We have, of course, compared each article with known tracts and publications by B.W. Newton.

We have examined the external and internal evidence for Mr Newton's authorship of all articles that are ascribed to him in the sets of volumes to which we have had access. Caution needs to be used with these, as even the ascriptions attributed to J.L. Harris (the one time editor) can be shown on occasion to be incorrect (e.g. in relation to J.N. Darby by reference to his *Collected Writings*). The only conclusive external evidence is where the author himself owns (or in the case of controversy does not disown) an article as his. Five of the articles considered were published as tracts under Mr Newton's name.

The internal evidence used is the comparison of thought, exposition, characteristic translation, and verbal parallelism with his published works. This has been facilitated by:
1. F.W. Wyatt's index of texts used in B.W. Newton's 48 principal works.
2. Lucas Collins' subject index of B.W. Newton's principal works.
3. A supplementary index of texts and subjects in B.W. Newton's other published works compiled by the writer of this *Guide* for his own use.
4. The index of texts and subjects in posthumously published articles and notes of addresses, which we have prepared and included as an appendix to Section 8, Publications Produced from Notes of Addresses, and Posthumously Published Letters and Manuscripts.

---

[1] Jonathan Burnham in his PhD research appears to have unadvisedly accepted all the ascriptions to Mr Newton in one set of *The Christian Witness*, thus giving credence to the opinion of its one time owner. This gives the impression that the authorship of *The Christian Witness* articles is established, and burdens Mr Newton with certain items that he did not write (for example, 'The Kenite' and the doubtful article 'The Propitiation of Christ').

**The limitations of this part of the assessment** are perceived to be as follows:
1. There has not been detailed examination of the writings of possible alternative authors of the articles.
2. The views that appear from this distance to be distinctively B.W. Newton's may at the time have been commonly held amongst Brethren.
3. It is likely that partners in the ministry at Plymouth, including, for example, J.L. Harris, and Percy F. Hall, would have come to some common understanding of Scripture and, perhaps, have adopted characteristic translations of particular verses. An instance of the danger is *Signs of the Coming of the Lord* by W.B. Dyer, which for some time was known only by J.N. Darby's critical comments in *Remarks on 'The Wreck and the Rock'* - a tract by B.W. Newton - it was therefore assumed by one authoritative library to have been by Mr Newton.
4. A powerful article might justifiably be taken up and used in the writings of another person. Quotation of another work is no guarantee of common authorship. For example, the article *Jerusalem* by B.W. Newton has reference to another article, which all sources attribute to Percy F. Hall.
5. A person's views may change over a long lifetime. Although Mr Newton held many distinctive positions with remarkable consistency, we cannot be sure, for example, that the way in which he subdivided the book of Romans in 1841 would be the same as in 1870.
6. There are a limited number of contemporary (1834-1841) works by B.W. Newton that can be used for close comparison.

Speculation has no part in this research.[1] Even with 100% consistency of manuscript attribution, B.W. Newton authorship of any article cannot be held as certain unless:
1. It was later republished under his own name.
2. He acknowledges it as his in other writings.
3. It is closely quoted in his other works.

There are some articles where authorship is virtually confirmed, but it does not meet these three criteria. Where the attributions to an article are unanimous, the article is found to be consistent with his teaching in other publications, and articles mutually corroborate each other, we may conclude that such were 'beyond reasonable doubt' by Mr Newton. Thus the two *Letters on the Study of Prophecy* could hardly be more strongly corroborated internally or externally, but we have been unable to show that Mr Newton either owned them, or that they were directly quoted in other works. Although produced at a time when anonymity did not appear to matter, we believe that in such cases we must heed Mr Newton's own maxim regarding his works. Published or unpublished material not clearly owned by him should not form the basis of controversial conjectures or allegations.

---

[1] The need for caution is apparent as at least one contributor who used his own name for some articles, but at other times used pseudonymous initials. The article in *The Christian Witness*, July 1836 on 'Babylon' ends with the initials 'F.G.', but it is claimed by S.P. Tregelles in his *Three Letters to the author of 'A Retrospect...'*, p.69.

## Identification of the articles to be considered

This study has not examined every article that appeared in The Christian Witness. Only those which appear in any of the manuscript attributions to him have been considered. It is therefore theoretically possible that something by him has escaped the net, although this must be unlikely. We drew upon as many sets as we could locate that have MS ascriptions of the authors.

None of these sets gives any ascriptions to the 1841 Christian Witness, However, Jonathan Burnham[1] identifies 'Thoughts on Ministry', The Christian Witness (1841) as being by him, though anonymous. We are unsure of the authority for this attribution, but we have nevertheless carried out an assessment of it.

In addition, it has also been suggested by Nigel Pibworth that the following articles may be by B.W. Newton.

- The Harmony and Diversity of the 4 Gospels.
- A Letter on the Dispensational Study of Scripture.

We therefore included an assessment of these articles

## Note on referencing

In the case of six of the articles that appeared in tract form, the page references refer to the tract's page numbering rather than that of *The Christian Witness*. This is perhaps unfortunate, but they had been indexed and assessed prior to this present study.

These articles are:

1. Jerusalem.
2. A Letter to a Friend on the Study of Prophecy.
3. A Second Letter to a Friend on the Study of Prophecy.
4. Is the Exercise of Worldly Authority consistent with Discipleship?
5. The Cleansing of the Leper.
6. On the Apostasy of the Present Dispensation.

---

[1] In Jonathan D. Burnham, *A Story of Conflict. The Controversial Relationship between Benjamin Wills Newton and John Nelson Darby* Printed Sources.

## Summary of Conclusions

**Certainly by B.W. Newton**
    The World to Come
    Jerusalem
    Doctrines of the Church in Newman Street
    Is the Exercise of Worldly Authority consistent with Discipleship?
    The Cleansing of the Leper
    Thoughts on the Tabernacle
    Moses and the Gentile Family
    Review of Mr Peter's Letter

**Beyond Reasonable Doubt by B.W. Newton**
    Retranslations in the New Testament
    A Letter to a Friend on the Study of Prophecy
    A Second letter to a Friend on the Study of Prophecy
    Thoughts on the Apostasy of the Present Dispensation
    Thoughts on Nehemiah
    The Dispensations

**Probably by B.W. Newton**
    On Zechariah 11
    The Nazarite

**Insufficient Evidence to Determine Authorship**
    The Propitiation of Christ
    Notice of Daniel Williams' Reasons
    A Letter on the Dispensational Study of Scripture
    Thoughts on Ministry (probably by Mr Newton or S.P. Tregelles)

**Not by B.W. Newton**
    On Isaiah 52:13 - 53
    The Light of the World
    The First Resurrection
    Notice of Mr Tucker's Sermon
    The Kenite
    Retranslations of Some Passages in the Epistles
    Moses's Loss of Canaan
    Moses's Heavenly Glory

## Section 7 – Articles in *The Christian Witness* ascribed to B.W. Newton

### All ascriptions that include reference to Mr Newton

| Conclusion | Volume | Article | #1 | #2 | #3 | #4 | #5 | #6 | #7 | #8 |
|---|---|---|---|---|---|---|---|---|---|---|
| Insufficient evidence | *Vol. 1,* 1/34 | On the Propitiation of Christ | BWN | BWN | - | Newton | Newton | BWN | BWN | - |
| Yes | Apr-34 | The World to Come | BWN | BWN | - | Newton | Newton | BWN | BWN | - |
| No | Apr-34 | On Isaiah 52:13 – 53 | JGB | JGB | - | JGB | JGB | JGB | BWN | - |
| Yes | Jul-34 | Review of Mr Peter's letter | BWN | BWN | - | Newton | Newton | BWN | BWN | - |
| Beyond reasonable doubt | Jul-34 | Retranslations in the New Testament | BWN | BWN | - | Newton | Newton | BWN | - | - |
| Probably | Oct-34 | On Zechariah 11 | JND | JND | - | Newton | Newton | BWN/JLH | BWN | - |
| Yes | *Vol. 2,* 1/35 | Jerusalem | BWN | - | Newton | Newton | Newton | BWN | BWN | BWN |
| Yes | Apr-35 | Doctrines of the Church in Newman St. | BWN | - | BWN | Newton | Newton | BWN | BWN | BWN |
| No | Apr-35 | The Light of the World | Hall | - | Hall | Hall | Hall | PFH | BWN(?) | BWN |
| No | Jul-35 | The First Resurrection | JLH | - | Harris | JLH | Harris | JLH | BWN | BWN |
| Beyond reasonable doubt | Oct-35 | A Letter.........On Prophecy | BWN | - | Newton | Newton | Newton | BWN | BWN | BWN |
| Beyond reasonable doubt | *Vol. 3,* 1/36 | 2nd Letter.....On Prophecy | BWN | - | Newton | Newton | Newton | BWN | BWN | BW Newton |
| Yes | *Vol. 4,* 7/37 | Is … Worldly Authority…Discipleship? | BWN | - | Newton | Newton? | N | JLH/BWN | BWN | - |
| Insufficient evidence | Jul-37 | Notice of Williams Reasons | WHD | - | - | Darby or Dorman | Newton** | BWN | BWN | - |
| Yes | Oct-37 | The Cleansing of the Leper | BWN | - | Newton ? | Newton | N | BWN | BWN | - |
| Beyond reasonable doubt | *Vol. 5,* 1/38 | On the Apostasy | BWN | - | BWN | - | N | BWN | BWN | - |
| No | Jan-38 | Notice of Mr Tucker's Sermon | Hall | - | BWN | - | Harris | BWN/JLH | | - |
| Beyond reasonable doubt | Jan-38 | Thoughts on Nehemiah | BWN | - | BWN | - | N | BWN | BWN | - |
| Yes | Apr-38 | Thoughts on the Tabernacle | BWN | - | BWN | - | N | BWN | BWN | - |
| Beyond reasonable doubt | Jul-38 | The Dispensations | BWN | - | BWN | - | N | BWN | BWN | - |
| Yes | *Vol. 6,* 4/39 | Moses and the Gentile Family | BWN | - | Newton | - | Newton | BWN | - | - |
| No | Oct-39 | The Kenite | PFH | - | Bellett | - | N? Hall | PFH | - | - |
| No | Oct-39 | Retranslations of Some Passages in the Epistles | BWN? | - | Fitzgerald | F | Newton** | BWN?/JF | - | - |
| Probably | Oct-39 | The Nazarite | BWN | - | Newton | - | Newton | BWN | - | - |
| No | *Vol. 7,* 4/40 | Moses's Loss of Canaan | - | - | Bellett | JG Bellett | N † | JGB | JGB | - |
| No | Apr-40 | Moses's Heavenly Glory | - | - | Bellett | JG Bellett | N † | JGB | JGB | - |
| Insufficient evidence | *Vol. 8,* 1/41 | A Letter on the Dispensational Study of Scripture | - | - | - | - | - | - | - | - |
| Insufficient evidence | Jan-41 | Thoughts on Ministry | - | - | - | - | - | - | - | - |

See notes on the following page on the ownership, etc. of the sets used for this table

## Notes on the sets used

Unfortunately, several of the sets referred to have changed hands since this assessment was prepared. It is hoped that they will be easily traceable from the information given.

#1 Copy belonging to the late W.R. Lewis, *Echoes of Service*, Bath. Ascriptions were supplied by Charles E. Franck, whose wife's mother (née Soltau) was 'a great personal friend of J.L. Harris, and he gave these names to her' – now at CBA.

#2 The library of Bible Institute of Los Angeles has copy of 1834 inscribed 'The names opposite the articles are taken from Mr Harris' Edition. He was the editor'.

#3 Copy belonging to William Kelly. In the Kelly Archive.

#4 Copy belonging to Edwin Cross and consulted in 1992. Its whereabouts is unknown.

#5 Copy owned by David Angell.
    \** Later? handwriting.
    † Crossed out in pencil.

#6 Copy owned by Roy Huebner.

#7 Copy owned by F. Roy Coad. See *History of the Brethren Movement* by F. Roy Coad (1968) p.131.

#8 Copy held at the Evangelical Library, London. Inscribed 'Wilkies'.

Our conclusion is that #1 is the most reliable set of ascriptions. This must have implications for ascriptions to other authors.

## ON THE PROPITIATION OF CHRIST

<u>Volume 1</u>　　　January 1834　　　pp.32 - 35　　　4 pages

All the ascriptions that we have located indicate this is by Mr Newton, but there are nevertheless difficulties, and it has not been possible to verify this by any internal or other external evidence. Indeed, the internal evidence points away from his authorship.

The article distinguishes between 'two important branches of truth'.
1. A 'universal propitiation' 'by means of which, all men are, in an important sense, objects of the direct favour of God' (I Tim 4:10). Propitiation is seen as the means of procuring common grace.
2. The election of the Church. 'An act of special grace, whereby He removes the barrier from some, though not all, and plucks the Church "like a brand from the burning"'.

We can find no reference to this twofold division of the work of propitiation anywhere else in Mr Newton's writings, either before or after this article. Indeed, it is definitely contradicted again and again. Writing in the Beaconite controversy in 1835 and 1836, he very definitely argues against any notion of partial reconciliation on the grounds of the sacrifice of Christ (see *Remonstrance…* p.11 and *Vindication…* pp.65-71). Later publications are equally forthright. *Tracts on Doctrinal Subjects No.2*, pp.6,7 states 'Under the imputation of the value of this work believers (but they only) stand … On all others "wrath abideth". <u>Their</u> sins, instead of being taken away, remain for judgement. The Governmental relation of God to <u>them</u> is marked by Sinai - not Zion. They stand in the presence of unpropitiated holiness'. *A Letter to Richard Waldo Sibthorpe [sic], B.D., Late Fellow of Magdalen College, Oxford on the Subject of his Recent Pamphlet*, (1841), pp.26-34, although it has a lengthy discussion of propitiation, makes no reference to it as the grounds of common grace. See too *Occasional Papers on Scriptural Subjects No.4*, p.97, and CBA 7057 pp.26-34.

Quite apart from the theological issue, we have been unable to find any close parallels with other works showing verbal agreement, in his use of Scripture, or in the other subject matter of the article. It simply does not resemble any other work by him in content.

CONCLUSION – **Insufficient Evidence to prove or disprove B.W. Newton's authorship**.

B.W. Newton's authorship of this article is doubtful and, at very least, unproven.

## THE WORLD TO COME

<u>Volume 1</u>　　　April 1834　　　pp.174 - 187　　　14 pages

This was published by B.W. Newton himself in virtually identical form. It ran to eight or nine editions, including two in French. See Section 3, Published Works for details.

He also owned it in the reminiscences recorded in the Fry MS CBA 7049 (where it has been extracted by A.C. Fry from CBA 7062).

CONCLUSION – **Certainly by B.W. Newton.**

## ON ISAIAH 52 v13 - 53

<u>Volume 1</u>　　　April 1834　　　　　pp.187 - 195　　　　　9 pages

Apart from F. Roy Coad's copy, all of the ascriptions attribute this article to J.G. Bellett.

We have compared it closely with Mr Newton's writings, and can find no similarity of thought or interpretation.

The article considers that the Church is addressing herself in the passage. However, Mr Newton interpreted the words strictly as the words of repentant Israel in the future. See 'Notes on Isaiah 52:13 to end, and on Isaiah 53' in *Thoughts on Scriptural Subjects* (included in *Isaiah 53, Considered: Being an Extract from a Work Entitled 'Thoughts on Scriptural Subjects'*).

The article attributes the words of verses 7-9, and verses 11,12, to the Father. Mr Newton did not do so in his 'Notes on Isaiah 52:13 to end, and on Isaiah 53'.

B.W. Newton wrote that in some of the verses Jehovah himself speaks, but indicates this at verse 8, not at those verses stated in the article (see 'Notes on Isaiah 52:13 to end, and on Isaiah 53').

Page 182 accredits the Church as still being 'the pillar and ground of truth'. All B.W. Newton's extant writings contend that the Church is in ruins, and forfeited its I Tim 3:15 standing shortly after the Apostles died. On this verse see, *A Letter to Richard Waldo Sibthorpe [sic], B.D., Late Fellow of Magdalen College, Oxford on the Subject of his Recent Pamphlet* p.22, and *A Letter on Subjects connected with the Lord's Humanity* p.17. The fall of the Church is maintained as an incontrovertible fact in *Doctrines of the Church in Newman Street* (Christian Witness 1835 p.128), and *A Second Letter to … Ebrington Street* (1845) pp.3-28. See too the quotations from other works in *B.W. Newton on Ministry and Order in the Church of Christ*. If the 'Review of Mr Peters Letter' in the same volume is by B.W. Newton, the fallen nature of the Church is again maintained on p.303.

**CONCLUSION – Not by B.W. Newton.**

There is no significant evidence in favour of B.W. Newton's authorship, but there is significant evidence against.

## REVIEW OF MR PETER'S LETTER

<u>Volume 1</u>　　　July 1834　　　　　pp.300 - 310　　　　　11 pages

The review refers to the publication, *A Letter by John William Peter, late Incumbent of Langford, Berks, on his resignation of his living, and secession from the Established Church.*

All the sets with attributions that have this volume ascribe it to Mr Newton.

The article speaks much of the state of the Church, and the basis of believers gathering. It argues against the democratic principle in the government of the Church. It is completely consistent with his principles as highlighted in *B.W. Newton on Ministry and Order in the Church of Christ*.

The writer opposes majority decisions 'the least spiritual will surely be the most numerous' (p.309). He denies any hope of an 'ordered Church' in this day of apostasy (p.309).

B.W. Newton wrote in a similar vein in his *Answers to Questions on the Propriety of leaving the Church of England* in 1841, in which he refers to 'a correspondence undertaken some years ago', although it cannot be identified with these comments.

There is an interesting reference on page 308 to 'unity - the pearl which apostasy has lost, but it should be the anxious effort of our lives to recover'. Mr Newton later held a very distinctive interpretation of this parable of Matthew 13, which saw in the singularity of the pearl the unity of God's faithful remnant at the last time. Nearly all commentators interpret the pearl in the parable as Christ, for whom the believer searches and finds with rejoicing. For a summary of B.W. Newton's teaching on the parable see *What is the Pearl Testimony?* by A.C. Fry.[1]

A brief note on John Peters [sic] is given in H.H. Rowdon's article *Secession from the Established Church in the Early Nineteenth Century* (Vox Evangelica 1964, p.84).

The article is quoted in *A Story of Conflict, the Controversial Relationship between Benjamin Wills Newton and John Nelson Darby*, by Jonathan D. Burnham p.82, and p.85 in relation to office and order in the Church.

There is confirmation of Mr Newton's authorship in CBA 7049 (from CBA 7062), where the record of his 'reminiscences' reads 'I once wrote an article in *The Christian Witness* on the *World to Come*, which was praised by Powerscourt, and by Darby, and others. In the next number I wrote a review of a book by a clergyman named Peters [sic] who left the Church of England, and by so doing reduced himself to poverty. I praised the work very much. They blamed my article extremely; didn't like it'.

CONCLUSION – **Certainly by B.W. Newton.**

## RETRANSLATIONS IN THE NEW TESTAMENT

<u>Volume I</u>     July 1834     pp.356 - 360     4 pages

Four of the five authorities for authorship attribute this article to B.W. Newton. The fourth is silent on authorship. The external evidence that it is by Mr Newton is strengthened, as the article is referred to in his *Remonstrance…* (1835 p.105), and in *A Second Letter to a Friend on the Study of Prophecy* (Fourth Edition p.15).

The internal evidence is equally strong. The retranslations are as follows:

<u>1) 2 Peter 3:9 'not desiring'</u>
The same translation is used in B.W. Newton's *Letter to the Minister of Silver Street Chapel* (1845), and in *A Letter to a Friend on the Study of Prophecy* (1835).
The translation is not used in *The World to Come* either in the original, or in later editions, although this could be accounted for as being because the tract was written before this article, and it was kept in its original form. See too the discussion of $\theta\epsilon\lambda\omega$ and $\beta ou\lambda o\mu\alpha\iota$ in *Occasional Papers on Scriptural Subjects No.3*, pp.298 - 300.

---

[1] See on NM 10 in Section 8, Publications Produced from Notes of Addresses, and Posthumously Published Letters and Manuscripts.

2) John 17:24

Translated as here in *Occasional Papers on Scriptural Subjects No.3*, p.199.

3) 2 Corinthians 5:9

The same translation with the same argument is found in the *Remonstrance...* (1835), p.103.

4) Philippians 1:21,22

No use of these verses by B.W. Newton has been found.

5) Hebrews 4:3

The translation is found in *Occasional Papers on Scriptural Subjects No.2*, p.97, and in *Remarks on the Revised Version*, p.81.

6) 2 Corinthians 5:15

B.W. Newton quotes this in the *Remonstrance...* (page 35), but does not own it. It is simply quoted as from *The Christian Witness*. He also similarly applies the laver to baptism on p.88 of *A Remonstrance....* The verse is quoted very similarly in *Doctrine of Scripture respecting Baptism* (1859, p.10 of Second Edition), and *Appointments of God...* (1895, p.54).

7) Romans 8:19 - 23

The translation of 'expectancy' for 'hope' in this verse is not clearly found elsewhere. However the distinctive phrasing of the verse, which is the same as Tregelles's Greek Testament, is found again in *Occasional Papers on Scriptural Subjects No.2*, p.114.

8) Acts 3:19 - 21

B.W. Newton comments on the same verses in *The Investigator* Vol. 2 (1832-33) in an article entitled 'The Times of Restitution'. There, as here, it is affirmed that the Greek word οταν is never used in the New Testament to signify 'when', but should be translated 'but so'. So too in *Jerusalem, its Future history* (*The Christian Witness*, January 1835; and Third Edition, pp.14 and 58); *The World to Come*; and *Occasional Papers on Scriptural Subjects No.4*, pp.207, 208. *A Second Letter to a Friend on the Study of Prophecy* quotes this as giving the literal translation (Fourth Edition, p.15n).
There is the strongest internal and external evidence for believing that this article was by B.W. Newton, although it does not appear to have been directly quoted and owned by him in his writings.

CONCLUSION – **Beyond reasonable doubt by B.W. Newton**

## ON ZECHARIAH 11

Volume 1     October 1834     pp.404 - 409     6 pages

This is an intriguing item, as it is introduced as follows – 'In connection with a paper which appeared in the last number, we would make a few further remarks on this important chapter'. The earlier article (pp.283 - 287, July 1834) is reliably attributed to J.N. Darby. If Mr Newton's authorship were proven, it would, perhaps, be the earliest record of their disagreement.

The authorities that we have used are equally split between authorship by B.W. Newton, and authorship by J.N. Darby. Roy Huebner's set introduces the idea that it may have been by J.L. Harris or B.W Newton. It must be said that the presumption of anyone reading the articles and knowing that the first was by Darby would surely have been that the second was by him also. This must strengthen the case for B.W. Newton's authorship when attributions run against this presumption.

If this is by B.W. Newton, it is conceivable that the discussion at the 'Meeting at Plymouth on September 15th 1834, and following days' - notably the Wednesday considerations - gave rise to this article (see *Answers to the Questions ... Plymouth* published October 1834 p.37 with footnote). Both this second article, and *Answers to the Questions…* take the 'bands and beauty' metaphor further than the first article, and apply it to the Church. This article applies it to the principles of gathering to be followed by believers.

B.W. Newton makes this application of 'bands and beauty' to the Church, in *Thoughts on the Apocalypse* (p.27). The 'Notes of an address on Zechariah 11', which was published in *Watching and Waiting* April and June 1924 does likewise.[1]

CONCLUSION – **Probably by B.W Newton**

## JERUSALEM

<u>Volume 2</u>    January 1835        pp.19 - 36              18 pages

This was published in identical form by the Plymouth Tract Depot, with the same title. It was the precursor of an enlarged and modified tract *Jerusalem, its Future History*, which first appeared in 1852. Although both *The Christian Witness* article and the Plymouth Tract were anonymous, *Jerusalem, its Future History* was not. It appeared under B.W. Newton's name.

CONCLUSION – **Certainly by B.W. Newton**

## DOCTRINES OF THE CHURCH IN NEWMAN STREET

<u>Volume 2</u>    April 1835          pp.113 - 128            16 pages

<u>Volume 2</u>    Second Edition  1837?   pp.113 - 128 + 121* - 128*   22 pages

CBA 7049 p.375 indicates that this circulated (anonymously?) as a tract before it was included as an article in *The Christian Witness*. *The Christian Witness* article was anonymous. It was then reprinted as a tract in slightly enlarged form. No copies of this (Plymouth) tract have been located, but the Madras edition (1836) bears B.W. Newton's name. B.W. Newton also owns the article, and the tract, in *A Statement and Acknowledgement Respecting Certain Doctrinal Errors*. The additions to the original article were incorporated in the Second Edition of *The Christian Witness*. Asterisked pages were added to preserve the page numbering of the remainder of the volume.

See Section 3, B.W. Newton's Published Works for further comment on the tract.

CONCLUSION – **Certainly by B.W. Newton.**

## THE LIGHT OF THE WORLD

<u>Volume 2</u>    April 1835          pp.187 -202             16 pages

---

[1] We have noted this item under the reference NM 6.2 in Section 8, Publications Produced from Notes of Addresses, and Posthumously Published Letters and Manuscripts.

Four of the six attributions identify this as by Percy F. Hall[1]. One of the two that attribute it to Mr Newton has a question mark, indicating doubt.

We have been unable to find in Mr Newton's works:

1. The application of 'The New Jerusalem' to the Church (p.199), rather than to a heavenly location.

2. The application of 'the Tree of Life' to Christ (p.199). cf. *A Letter to a Friend on the Study of Prophecy* where the writer speaks of the Tree 'whether symbol or reality', but does not apply it to the Lord.

Where Mr Newton does quote this passage, he refers it to the New Testament Church, and to the nation of Israel in the Millennium ('a city set on a hill'), rather than seeing 'the light of the world' as an abiding characteristic of the Church (see *Babylon and Egypt*, p.373).

We can find no clear similarities with Mr Newton's writings.

CONCLUSION –**Not by B. W. Newton.**

There is no significant evidence in favour of B.W. Newton's authorship.

## THE FIRST RESURRECTION

<u>Volume 2</u>   July 1835   pp.203 - 224   22 pages

We have found nothing in this article that is inconsistent with B.W. Newton's teaching, but it is not clearly and distinctly corroborated in his writings. The doctrine of the First Resurrection was strongly held amongst millenarians in the early nineteenth century. It was one of the marks of recovery of prophetic truth.

The internal evidence is as follows:

### In favour of Mr Newton's authorship

<u>Romans 4:25</u>. (pp.204, 206). The author follows the translation for which B.W. Newton strongly contends (See *Remonstrance...* (1835) pp.11 and 76, and *Propositions...* (1864) p.19). This was not universally held amongst Brethren and, for example, Darby's Bible translation does not adopt it.

<u>Daniel 7:18</u>. The author follows, and applies, the Authorised Version marginal reading, as does B.W. Newton in *Aids to Prophetic Enquiry* (page 301).

<u>Revelation 5:10</u>. (p.214). The same translation is found in *A Letter to a Friend on the Study of Prophecy*, p.5, but not in (other) writings by B.W. Newton. Note, however, that it is not a unique translation, and is found in Darby's Bible translation.

<u>Isaiah 25:8.</u> A similar argument on this verse is found in *Aids to Prophetic Enquiry*, p.301.

---

[1] Captain Percy Francis Hall (1804-1884). One of the early Brethren at Plymouth, who separated from J.N. Darby in 1866 with others, because of his teaching on the sufferings of Christ, which he and others equated with the error that J.N. Darby and J.L. Harris had attributed to B.W. Newton.

## Against Mr Newton's authorship

Hebrews 10:10 and Romans 7:4 (p.204). We have been unable to find any similar emphasis on the body of Christ in relation to resurrection.

Revelation 20:5 (p.213)   B.W Newton does not use this amended translation elsewhere.

Galatians 3:17:5 (p.213)   B.W Newton does not use this amended translation elsewhere.

John 5:19 (p.215)   B.W Newton does not use this amended translation elsewhere.

John 5:29 (p.215)   B.W Newton does not use this amended translation elsewhere.

B.W. Newton wrote *Scriptural Proof of the Doctrine of the First Resurrection*, but there is no similarity in the structure of the two items.   In Mr Newton's 'Scriptural Proof' he uses other proof texts.

Further evidence against Mr Newton's authorship is that Eliza Browne's copy of this, as an independent tract in the Fratelli Collection (Third Edition, Plymouth Tract Depot and London, 1838. printed in Kendal), is endorsed 'J. Harris'.

The balance of external evidence is against B.W. Newton's authorship.   The testimony of Eliza Browne's copy (#1) is particularly important as it purports to give J.L. Harris's identification of authors, and affirms that he wrote this article![1]   The similarities in use of Scripture and doctrine could easily be accounted for by the closeness of B.W. Newton and J.L. Harris in the ministry at Plymouth.

CONCLUSION - **Probably not by B.W. Newton.**

## A LETTER TO A FRIEND ON THE STUDY OF PROPHECY

Volume 2   October 1835   pp.341 - 355   15 pages

## A SECOND LETTER TO A FRIEND ON THE STUDY OF PROPHECY

Volume 3   January 1836   pp.39 - 57   19 pages

Page numbering of quotations is taken from the tract of *A Letter to a Friend…*, and from the Fourth Edition of the *A Second Letter to a Friend…*

Both of the articles were published as tracts.   The *Second Letter…* ran to at least four editions, the fourth being produced in 1840.   The letters are 'signed' XZ.

Both are clearly by the same author.   Any conclusions on authorship must apply equally.

### External evidence

1. The two articles are attributed to Mr Newton by all the sources identified.
2. In addition, the letters are found in a book of B.W. Newton's tracts owned by A.J.T. Toulmin and Anna Newton (his mother), which are all by B.W. Newton, except where otherwise indicated by the owners.

---

[1] For further information regarding Eliza Browne see The Fratelli Collection in Section 2, Libraries and Collections

3. A number of Mr Newton's tracts are 'Letters'.

**Internal evidence**

In favour of Mr Newton's authorship

The evidence in favour of B.W. Newton's authorship is substantial. Both articles very closely reflect B.W. Newton's thought on a number of issues. What follow are examples. A number of other parallels could have been added.

1. *A Second Letter...* (p.15) refers to the article on 'Retranslations in the New Testament' on Acts 3:21 (*The Christian Witness*, Vol. 1, p.360), which is also strongly attested as being by B.W. Newton.

2. Close similarity in comments on 2 Peter 1:21. The prophecy of Scripture is not <u>set forth</u> upon the authority of <u>individuals</u> (*A Letter...*, p.1, and *A Remonstrance...*, p.101).

3. Comparison of Matthew 16:28 and 2 Peter 1:16, in connection with the Transfiguration (*A Letter...*, p.1, and *World to Come*, p.6).

4. The author adopted the relationship of the Courts of the Temple as a type of millennial arrangements. This is found in *A Second Letter...*, p.9 and p.11, in *Prospects of the Ten Kingdoms*, pp.344, 345, and in *Thoughts on the Apocalypse* p.303. In 'Thoughts on the Tabernacle' (*The Christian Witness* April 1838), B.W. Newton says that this relationship 'has often been noticed in this work' (p.175n). Taken together, this is a very strong evidence of the identity of the authors.

5. The author used Isaiah 26:1 and Zechariah 11 together to demonstrate events that will precede Millennial blessing (*A Letter...*, p.3, and *Aids to Prophetic Enquiry*, p.5).

6. The author followed the same dispensational divisions as B.W. Newton (*A Letter...* pp.3,4, and *Aids to Prophetic Enquiry* pp.50,51).

7. Revelation 5:10 'The saints are not reigning over (επι) the earth (*A Letter...*, p.5, and *Thoughts on Leviticus*, p.317. Similar statements are made).

8. The author contrasted the riches of Babylon (Revelation 13) with the consecration of earth's riches to the Lord in the Millennium. (*A Second Letter...*, p.18, and *Thoughts on the Apocalypse*, pp.253, 254 and pp.405, 406).

9. The author considered Israel gathered around Sinai as typical of gathering around Jerusalem (Mount Zion) in the Millennium. (*A Second Letter...*, p.9, and *Thoughts on the Apocalypse*, p.300).

10. The author stated that Israel will have a dual role in the Millennium, as administrator of blessing, and as minister of chastisement. (*A Second Letter...*, p.18, and *Babylon and Egypt*, pp.295, 296).

11. The author linked Zechariah 12:10 and Genesis 45:5, depicting Christ as the True Joseph sent beforehand to preserve life. (*A Second Letter...* p.22, and *Prospects of the Ten Kingdoms*, p.331).

<u>Against Mr Newton's authorship</u>

1. There is no evidence that B.W. Newton used 'XZ' as a pseudonym elsewhere.

2. It is surprising that these seminal articles, which evidently had a wide circulation, were not incorporated into, or quoted, in B.W. Newton's later works.

3. The lack of later quotations could be accounted for if these articles presented teaching that Mr Newton later moved from, but, so far as we can see, they do not. We cannot agree with F. Roy Coad that the (first) 'Letter' teaches a partial rapture[1], as a reconciliation with J.N. Darby's view. Mr Newton always taught the preservation of the Church from the judgements at the Day of the Lord (See, for example, *Babylon and Egypt* pp.285, 286 and, indeed, the 'Second Letter'), but not from the reign of Antichrist. Mr Newton, although he speaks of 'some who will be preserved *from* not *through* this period of judgement', does not speak of any partial number of believers who will not be so preserved, or who will be caught up to be with the Lord when he comes. The author does not speak of two second comings. The 'period of judgement' to which he refers is the final judgement on Antichrist and his hosts, and upon the Tares.[2]

4. Some very distinctive ideas are not reflected in concurrent works or developed in later works by B.W. Newton, e.g. The use of 1 Kgs. 10:5 (*A Second Letter...*, p.10) - 'the ascent' of Solomon likened to the Lord's ascent into the Heavenly Jerusalem.

5. We do not know of any reference to these 'letters' by J.N. Darby, who took great exception to B.W. Newton's *Five Letters...*, and wrote against them. This is surprising, as they circulated widely as tracts.

**CONCLUSION - Beyond reasonable doubt by B.W. Newton**

These 'Letters' were undoubtedly by B.W. Newton, but it is difficult to explain why they have not been directly owned or quoted by B.W. Newton elsewhere.

## IS THE EXERCISE OF WORLDLY AUTHORITY CONSISTENT WITH DISCIPLESHIP?

<u>Volume 4</u>     July 1837          pp.251 - 265          15 pages

This was published by B.W. Newton as a tract with identical content, under the title *On the Exercise of Worldly Authority*.

**CONCLUSION Certainly by B.W. Newton**

---

[1] F. Roy Coad, *History of the Brethren Movement* (1968), p.131.
[2] On Govett's teaching, see S.P. Tregelles's letter to B.W. Newton, dated 26th July 1864, in which he says he may answer some of Govett's views in his projected publication, *The First Resurrection*. In that publication S.P. Tregelles states emphatically, 'this is the *first* resurrection, so no resurrection of believers can possibly precede it'.

## REVIEW OF DANIEL WILLIAMS 'REASONS FOR LEAVING THE COMMUNION OF THE BAPTISTS...'

<u>Volume 4</u>　　　July 1837　　　　　　pp.295 - 296　　　　　　2 pages

This is a brief article with only two paragraphs of introduction. The remainder is a quotation of Daniel Williams's tract. There is too little material to determine whether it bears the hallmarks of Mr Newton's writing.

It may have been attributed to Mr Newton as it was thought to be in a similar vein to the consideration of Mr Peter's letter in Volume 1. #1 attributes it to W.H.D. - W.H. Dorman[1] (or W.H. Darby[2]?). Daniel Williams's 'Reasons' was (later?) published as a tract by the Central Tract Depot, London (catalogue in a tract dated 1840 held by SG).

CONCLUSION - **Insufficient evidence to determine authorship.**

## THE CLEANSING OF THE LEPER.　LEVITICUS 14

<u>Volume 4</u>　　　October 1837　　　　pp.363 - 372　　　　　　10 pages

B.W. Newton published this as a tract. See Section 3, B.W. Newton's Published Works. It is referred to in CBA 7064, pages 265-269, 281-287 –conversations with B.W. Newton 13th, 14th and 18th November 1898, in which he makes plain that he then altogether 'abjured' the tract. See the further information given in Section 3.

CONCLUSION - **by B.W. Newton.**

## THOUGHTS ON THE APOSTASY OF THE PRESENT DISPENSATION

<u>Volume 5</u>　　　January 1838　　　　pp.83 - 99　　　　　　　7 pages

The page numbering of these comments is taken from the tract of the same title which was published from this article. It appeared as the first part of a series, *Truth for the Times*. Interestingly, the second was by J.N. Darby.

**External Evidence**

1. All of the copies of *The Christian Witness* with attributions agree that this is by B.W. Newton.

2. It is also attributed to Mr Newton in the Fratelli Collection, Florence (by E. Browne, a correspondent of J.L. Harris, who sent her many Plymouth tracts, She was quite possibly related to J.L. Harris).

3. *The Bible Treasury* (Ed. William Kelly) (Vol. 14, p.269) discusses B.W. Newton's view of the ministry by quoting this tract.

4. It is included in a volume of tracts by B.W. Newton held by the Sovereign Grace Advent Testimony in Chelmsford.

---

[1] W.H. Dorman (1838-1878). He left congregationalism for the Brethren in c.1838, but later separated from J.N. Darby in 1866 with Percy Hall, Thomas Newberry and others.

[2] W.H. Darby (1790-1880), J.N. Darby's older brother, who joined W.H. Dorman's protest against J.N. Darby's teaching on the sufferings of Christ in 1866, and later left the Brethren.

5. *Thoughts on…* was frequently used in B.W. Newton's writings (as noted in G.H. Fromow *Teachers of the Faith and Future*).

**Internal Evidence**

<u>For Mr Newton's Authorship</u>

Internal evidence is substantial, and its statements closely mirror those of Mr Newton elsewhere. What follows are examples of many instances that could have been cited. Its teaching is very much in harmony with what is given in the collection *B.W. Newton on Ministry and Order in the Church of Christ*.

1. It agrees with Mr Newton's writings regarding the commencement and end of the present dispensation - from the Flood to the revelation of the Son of Man in glory. It also agrees on the divisions within the dispensations (cf. pages 7 and 8, and *Aids to Prophetic Enquiry*, p.53).

2. It argues against election of Church officers by the people, with the exception of deacons (pp.10,11, cf. *B.W. Newton on Ministry and Order in the Church of Christ*, p.58).

3. It is quite close verbally when speaking of the 'awful warnings' of Peter and Jude to those who speak evil of dignitaries, and dissenters who join themselves with them (p.10, and *Prospects of the Ten Kingdoms*, p.310).

4. It opposes Dr Pye Smith, as elsewhere in Mr Newton's writings (p.12, and *Remarks on the Revised English Version…*, p.24 - where he comments on his translation of I Timothy 3:16 and of his opposition to the authority of the Song of Solomon; *Occasional Papers on Scriptural Subjects No.1*, p.116; *Occasional Papers on Scriptural Subjects No.3*, p.82; *Remarks on 'Mosaic Cosmogony'…*, p.26).

5. The Church decayed 'within 100 years' of the death of the Apostles, p.15 (cf. 60 years - *B.W. Newton on Ministry and Order in the Church of Christ*, p.89, and *Remarks on the Revised English Version…*, pp.270, 271).

6. It makes an analogy between Israel's rapid apostasy regarding the golden calf, and the apostasy of the Church (p.17, and *B.W. Newton on Ministry and Order in the Church of Christ*, pp.89, 90; *Doctrines of Popery*, p.71,72).

7. Links the gathered Church now with those who went outside the camp to Moses (p.17, and *Catholicity in a Dispensation of Failure…*, pp.18,19).

8. Teaches 'double separation' on the analogy of separation from Egypt and separation from Israel's idolatry (p.17, and *Thoughts on Parts of the Prophecy of Isaiah*, p.10; *Prospects of the 10 Kingdoms*, p.471; and *A Letter to Richard Waldo Sibthorpe [sic], B.D., Late Fellow of Magdalen College, Oxford on the Subject of his Recent Pamphlet*, p.25).

9. Views Christ as exercising all the power of his Father's throne, but not yet seated on his own throne (p.17n, and *Thoughts on Parts of the Prophecy of Isaiah*, p.61,62 et al).

10. Rests upon Ephesians 4:11,12 as a consolation in the present broken state of the Church (p.18, and *B.W. Newton on Ministry and Order in the Church of Christ*, p.107).

Against Mr Newton's authorship

1. The use of the term 'spiritual Jews' of the Church (p.6) is uncharacteristic and unusual of Mr Newton.

2. The application of Romans 2:24 to the Church has not been found elsewhere (p.9).

3. The quotation from the Shepherd of Hermas is not used elsewhere as proof of the apostasy of the Apostolic Fathers (p.19).

CONCLUSION – **Beyond reasonable doubt by B.W. Newton.**

## NOTICE OF MR TUCKER'S SERMON

<u>Volume 5</u>      January 1838      pp.99 - 110      12 pages

There is confused external evidence on the authorship of this article. The sets indicate Hall, or Harris, or Newton, or Newton/Harris.

The writer had 'seceded from the establishment' (p.109). The article deals with issues of ministering, and priestly authority. It seems reasonable to conclude that the article may have been written by a former ordained clergyman. Harris resigned as a perpetual curate at Plymstock in 1832.

There is a link with the previous article in *The Christian Witness*, 'Thoughts on the Apostasy of the Present Dispensation', which refers to Mr Tucker's sermon. If the two articles had been by the same author, it would have been more likely that the two would have been combined.

We have not been able to identify any internal evidence that this was by B.W. Newton, despite the fact that B.W. Newton wrote extensively regarding the Church of England.

It has few Scriptural quotations that could be compared with his writings.

Mr Newton had contacts with the Church Missionary Society, and with Madras (*Doctrines of the Church in Newman Street* was published by the Church Mission Press in Madras in 1836). This could have led to Mr Tucker's Sermon coming into his hands.

Mr Newton made some use of the Sermon in his earlier article, but may have passed it to J.L. Harris as the more appropriate person to review it.

CONCLUSION – **Not by B.W. Newton**

There is little evidence in favour of B.W. Newton's authorship, and there are reasons against it.

## THOUGHTS ON NEHEMIAH: OR, BLESSING IN AN APOSTATE DISPENSATION

<u>Volume 5</u>      January 1838      pp.111 - 115      5 pages

The example of Nehemiah was, for B.W. Newton, the clearest guide as to how the believer should act in the present ruin of the Church. He repeatedly refers to the work and times of Nehemiah in his writings.

**External Evidence**

1. All of *The Christian Witness* sets that make an attribution refer this to B.W. Newton.

2. The example of Nehemiah was mentioned in both *Thoughts on the Apostasy of the Present Dispensation*, and in this article, linking with its title. It follows on in sequence from it with only the notice of Mr Tucker's sermon (itself perhaps a follow on from *Thoughts on the Apostasy of the Present Dispensation*) in between.

3. The expression 'Thoughts on' is characteristic of B.W. Newton's writings.

**Internal evidence**

1. Page 112 relates 'It has already been remarked in a former paper' how each human dispensation ends in failure. *Thoughts on the Apostasy…*, makes such remarks.

2. The author contends for the unity of the Church as including both Israel and Gentile believers – 'indissolubly united in one body, even the Church'.

3. It is very similar in thought to 'The Example of Nehemiah' (*B.W. Newton on Ministry and Order in the Church of Christ*, pp.109 - 114), see especially 'His labour was not in vain, etc.' (p.115), and 'his labour was not unaccepted' (*B.W. Newton on Ministry and Order in the Church of Christ*, p.114 - footnote 39).

4. The analogy between the walls broken down, and the walls of truth around the Church likewise broken, is made on p.113 and in *Europe and the East*, p.119, and *Remarks on R. Pearsall Smith's Edition of Faber's Hymns*, p.110.

**CONCLUSION - Beyond reasonable doubt by B.W. Newton.**

The article was reprinted in *Watching and Waiting*, January – March 1998, pp.75-77.

## THOUGHTS ON THE TABERNACLE

<u>Volume 5</u>     April 1838          pp.174 - 180          7 pages

This article is unanimously ascribed to B.W. Newton by the sets with attributions that we have located.

B.W. Newton owns this article by a loose quotation from it in a footnote introduced in the Second Edition of *Thoughts on the Apocalypse* regarding the looking-glasses used to make the Laver (p.178 on *Thoughts on the Apocalypse*, p.60. The note is absent from the First Edition.

There are a number of parallels with B.W. Newton's writings, including, for example:

1. The article refers to gold as representing the Divine nature of Christ, in its full excellency as appreciated in Heaven, and therefore found only in the inner courts of the Tabernacle (compare p.177n, and *Thoughts on the Apocalypse*, p.492 and p.23n).

2. The article states that Adam was ψυχικος and earthy. He was therefore unfit for Heaven, even before he fell (p.177, and *Remarks on 'Mosaic Cosmogony'…* pages 70 and 71).

CONCLUSION – **Certainly by B.W. Newton.**

## THE DISPENSATIONS

<u>Volume 5</u>    July 1838    pp.285 -308    24 pages

This is a substantial and important article.   All the sets attest it to be by B.W. Newton. It is not known to have circulated as an independent tract.   There are some differences with his published writings.  This article was not incorporated in whole or in part in other works.

**Internal Evidence**

<u>For Mr Newton's Authorship</u>

The strongest internal evidence for Mr Newton's authorship of the article derives from the footnote on page 294.  There the author effectively claims ownership of the comments made in 'Thoughts on the Tabernacle', and compares the Temple with the millennial arrangements.   This also links the article with A *Second Letter to a Friend on the Study of Prophecy* (See 'Thoughts on the Tabernacle', p.175n, and comments on *A Second Letter to a Friend on the Study of Prophecy* in this section of the *Guide*), which is also strongly attested to Mr Newton.

There are other parallels, for example the following:

1. The article parallels the comments on the Greek word οικονομια, and discusses 'economy' and 'Dispenser'.  Page 285, and *Occasional Papers No.2*, p.192.

2. The article translates Hebrews 11:4 as a more 'abundant' sacrifice (not 'excellent').   Page 287, and *Thoughts on Leviticus*, p.231.

3. The limits of the present dispensation concur with B.W. Newton's writings.  Page 288, and *Aids to Prophetic Enquiry*, p.14.

4. The article speaks of Christ voluntarily identifying Himself with Israel's circumstances, p.291.  Compare *Observations on a Tract…on Psalm 6*, p.24.

5. There is similar treatment of Jer. 31:22 on p.293 to that in *Doctrines of the Church in Newman Street* (1835), p.121; *A Second Letter…Ebrington Street*, (1845), p.23; and in *A Letter on Subjects connected with the Lord's Humanity* (1848), p.9.  Compare Bishop Pearson's use of the verse in his commentary on the Apostles' Creed, Art. 3, (born of the Virgin Mary), p.250.  B.W. Newton viewed Bishop Pearson as an exemplar of orthodoxy, and published a corroborating quotation from him at the time of the controversy.  He refers to his position on this in a letter to John Cox, jun. dated 19th May 1869.

6. The comparison of Ephesians 1:22 and Hebrews 2:8 (pp.303, 304) is closely paralleled in both *Thoughts on the Apocalypse* pp.511, 512, and *A Letter to…Ebrington Street*, pp.18,19.

7. The writer not only understands 'the Regeneration' of Matthew 19:28 to be the Millennium, but elaborates the analogy from personal regeneration to show the imperfection of the Millennium, (pp.306, 307, and *Babylon and Egypt*) pp.344, 345.

### Against B.W. Newton's authorship

The writer proposes a different chapter division in Revelation 21 to that given in *Thoughts on the Apocalypse*. The article would make the first 6 verses of chapter 21 a chapter in itself (page 307). *Thoughts on the Apocalypse* makes a simple chapter division at Rev. 21 verse 8.

**CONCLUSION – Beyond reasonable doubt by B.W. Newton.**

There is very strong evidence for believing this to be by B.W. Newton - principally the use that he makes of the Temple and Millennium analogy, by which the author links himself both with 'Thoughts on the Tabernacle' and also (indirectly) with the *A Second Letter...on Prophecy*, both of which we confirm to be by B.W. Newton.

## MOSES AND THE GENTILE FAMILY

<u>Volume 6</u>     April 1839          pp.183 -190          8 pages

No other author of this article is suggested by the sources of attributions.

The most obvious comparison to make is with B.W. Newton's booklet *Moses, the Child of Faith* (1851). There are close similarities between the two, and at times close verbal agreement. This evidence may be summarised as follows:

1. The author uses the unusual expression 'the child of faith' of Moses (pp.184, 185, and 187).

2. There are a number of loose parallels in expression and content - compare, for example,
   pages 5 and 6 and   *Moses, the Child of Faith*, pages 184, 185.
   pages 9 and 10   and   *Moses, the Child of Faith*, page 186.
   page 11   and   *Moses, the Child of Faith*, page 187.

3. Probably the closest verbal correspondence is at *The Christian Witness* p.13, and *Moses, the Child of Faith* p.187, viz.:

   *The Christian Witness* That little word 'there' shows he had, in faith, put himself beyond the wilderness and its circumstances, and he was looking back upon it as a thing that was passed.

   M.C.F *The word 'there' was one that went beyond and out of the circumstances then present around him, and spoke of them all as past.*

4. The writer adopts the same derivation for 'Gershom' (*The Christian Witness*, p.11 and *Moses, the Child of Faith*, p.187) i.e. 'a stranger there' (as the Gesenius/Tregelles Lexicon) rather than A.V. margin 'a stranger here'. The article and the book make the same argument upon this etymology.

**CONCLUSION – Certainly by B.W. Newton.**

## THE KENITE

<u>Volume 6</u>     October 1839          pp.302 -320          19 pages

Only one of the attributions indicates that this article may be by B.W. Newton, and then adds a question mark and suggests that it may be by Percy F. Hall.

The internal evidence is equally dismissive of B.W. Newton's authorship. There is a clear comparison of subject matter between this article and B.W. Newton's pamphlet *The Rechabites* (1856), which was later incorporated in *Narratives from the Old Testament*. There is no evidence of parallelism or verbal agreement.

1. *The Rechabites* traces their history from Abraham. This article traces their history from Reuel.
2. 'Be to us instead of eyes' (Numbers 10:31) is differently interpreted (*The Christian Witness* pp.307, 308 and *Narratives from the Old Testament*, pp.84, 85).
3. The article seems to be uncharacteristically speculative, e.g. Caleb and Joshua were the spies who carried the grapes. Heber had not committed Israel's sin, etc.

**CONCLUSION - Not by B.W. Newton.**

There is no significant evidence in favour of B.W. Newton's authorship.

## RETRANSLATIONS OF SOME PASSAGES IN THE EPISTLES

<u>Volume 6</u>     October 1839          pp.361 - 371          9 pages

The attribution of this article to B.W. Newton is puzzling, as it is made (albeit with a question mark) in what we have concluded to be the most authentic attribution of articles.

The reason for perplexity is that the article is sub-headed 'continued from page 362, vol. 4' and continues (as the first article) in the first person. There is no doubt regarding the author of the first article. A letter from J.F(itzgerald) precedes the article in volume 4. It ends 'should you judge the following renderings worthy of insertion, I may, upon some future occasion, with the Lord's help and permission, add a few to their number'. Although the previous article is identically titled '... Epistles' it only dealt with passages in 1 and 2 Corinthians.

The verse considered here is not identified (it was Colossians 1:24). Either this was simply an editorial or printing mistake, or the editor assumed continuity of the comments (by the same author as in volume 4) on 2 Cor. 5:5-11.

It would appear that this is conclusive evidence in favour of J.F(itzgerald)'s authorship and against B.W. Newton's authorship. There may have been some confusion with the 'Retranslations in the New Testament', Vol. 1, which are undoubtedly by B.W. Newton.

**CONCLUSION - Not by B.W. Newton.**

## THE NAZARITE - NUMBERS 6

<u>Volume 6</u>     October 1839          pp.371 - 378          8 pages

There is strong external evidence for the authorship of this article by B.W. Newton. Four sources ascribe it to him.

**Evidence in favour of B.W. Newton's authorship:**

There is some internal evidence for the authorship of the article by B.W. Newton:

1. Wine is used as an emblem of earthly joy (*The Christian Witness*, p.372n, and *Narratives from the Old Testament*, p.94).

2. Lamentations 1:12 ('any sorrow like unto my sorrow', etc.) is applied to the Lord Jesus (page 376, so too *Observations on a Tract…on Psalm 6*, p.372).

3. Referring to the cleansing of the leper, the author used the same expression as in the article on 'The Cleansing of the Leper' – 'Hair is the sign of natural grace and comeliness' (*The Christian Witness*, p.373, and *Cleansing the Leper*, p.5).

4. The Nazarite is referred to throughout as a type of Christ (So too in *Observations…on Psalm 6*, p.41).

5. The author applies Jeremiah 31:22 ('the new thing in the earth') to the Lord Jesus (page 373), a favourite application by B.W. Newton[1], perhaps derived by him from Bishop Pearson.

**Evidence against B.W. Newton's authorship:**

*Answers to the Questions …. Plymouth* (page 38) by B.W. Newton and Henry Borlase applies the Nazarite vow differently to the Lord Jesus. Rather than being a lifelong symbolic Nazarite, *Answers to the Questions…Plymouth* pictures him as assuming Nazarite separation on the night of his betrayal, by refusing to drink the fruit of the vine any more. However, this publication was based on notes of the meetings, and may not exclusively reflect the ideas of those who produced it.

CONCLUSION - **Probably by B.W. Newton.**

## MOSES' LOSS OF CANAAN

<u>Volume 7</u>     April 1840     pp.153 - 156     4 pages

## MOSES' HEAVENLY GLORY

<u>Volume 7</u>     April 1840     pp.156 - 160     5 pages

These two articles are taken together, as the same writer claims authorship of both (see start of 'Moses' Heavenly Glory').

All of the ascriptions that we have, except #5, refer these articles to J.G. Bellett. Even the one ascription to B.W. Newton is crossed out in pencil. If there were not strong reasons for believing otherwise, those who made these ascriptions would have surely assumed the same authorship as the article in the previous volume, 'Moses and the Gentile Family'.

We have been unable to find any internal evidence in favour of Mr Newton's authorship. The following points weigh against it:

---

[1] See the letter dated 19th May 1869, referring to this verse, and a tract, noted in Section 9 of this Guide.

1. The article very distinctively makes the rod that budded a symbol of Christ's resurrection (p.154). Although B.W. Newton also applies the things of the Sanctuary, including the rod that budded, to Christ's work, he does not adopt this analogy (*Thoughts on Leviticus*, pp.323, 324, and cf. *Gleanings in the Book of Exodus*, pp.50, 51).

2. The second article says Moses was raised 'quite above the Jewish or earthly level'. It would be uncharacteristic of B.W. Newton to equate 'Jewish' with 'earthly' in this way.

CONCLUSION - **Not by B.W. Newton.**

There is no significant evidence in favour of B.W. Newton's authorship.

## A LETTER ON THE DISPENSATIONAL STUDY OF SCRIPTURE

<u>Volume 8</u>     January 1841          pp.29-47          19 pages

Whilst no known ascriptions have been located in relation to volume 8, it has been suggested that this 'Letter' may be by B.W. Newton.

**Evidence of possible authorship by B.W. Newton:**

1. The writer refers to three great spheres of Divine action, for which there are similarities in the article 'The Dispensations' and *Aids to Prophetic Enquiry* (which, however, makes a five-fold division). It must be noted that B.W. Newton did not maintain a rigid dispensational system, and in 'The Dispensations' a diversity in unity is proposed. The divisions made on page 32 of this article do not tally with those on page 298 of 'The Dispensations' (but those in this article are avowedly not comprehensive – 'I do not enumerate these as all the dispensational divisions of our vast period').

2. The emphasis on the successive failure of each dispensation is not strongly present. cf. *Thoughts on the Apostasy of the Present Dispensation*, etc.

3. The author argues for one of the Dispensations as being from *the Incarnation* to the end of the world. Surely, B.W. Newton would have begun not from the Incarnation, but from the great cry 'It is finished' (cf. the controversy with J.N. Darby on Christ's Federal Headship).

4. The author argues for the oneness of the redeemed family in which there are only temporary differences (p.41) - very much on B.W. Newton's side of the controversy with J.N. Darby.

5. The author's statement 'are not all claiming national or worldly aid' is in line with Mr Newton's comments on the disastrous Niger Expedition in his *Thoughts on the Death of Captain Bird Allen* (1842), but also reflects a wider sentiment amongst the early Brethren.

6. We have been unable to find any parallels with the references to 'the Prayer of the Spirit' (Eph. 1), and 'The Prayer of the Son' (John 17).

7. In dealing with the dispensations, the writer does not refer to the 'dispensation' of Gentile supremacy.

8. The view of 'the mercies of God' (Rom. 12:1) as providing the motivation to service (pp.40, 41) has not been found elsewhere. The commentary from notes of B.W. Newton's addresses, *Lectures on the Epistle to the Romans*, takes a different view, and says that it is by means of the mercies of God (i.e. the Blood, etc.) that we offer reasonable service. In the one, the emphasis is on engaging our minds, in the other on minds renewed by grace.

9. We have found no evidence elsewhere that B.W. Newton viewed Romans 3:20 as the end of a major division in the Epistle (p.42).

CONCLUSION – **insufficient evidence to prove or disprove B.W. Newton's authorship.**

There are no overwhelming difficulties with this having been by B.W. Newton. However, there is not a balance of evidence in favour at present. Without one ascription or clear parallel with his other works, his authorship is unproven.

## THOUGHTS ON MINISTRY

<u>Volume 8</u>     April 1841          pp.75-88          14 pages

Whilst no known ascriptions have been located in relation to volume 8, it has been suggested by Jonathan D. Burnham[1] that this may be by B.W. Newton.

The article rejoices in the 'great' 'long-neglected' truths that had been recovered – notably, 'meeting simply in the name of Jesus'. However, it makes a distinction between ministry in a general sense (washing the disciples' feet), and ministry in a particular sense, linked to the building up of the Church. It distinguishes between access through our heavenly calling as a priest, which is free to all, and 'gifts developed to some'. It observes misunderstandings regarding this in the developing movement of which the writer was a part.

The article appears to us to be thoroughly in line with B.W. Newton's position, as evidenced, for example, in the anthology, *B.W. Newton on Ministry and Order in the Church of Christ*. However, this was no doubt also the position of all the Plymouth leadership, and of S.P. Tregelles, who later defended and wrote in more detail on this type of order and 'pastoral relations' that were applied at Plymouth.

**Internal evidence in favour of B.W. Newton's authorship:**

1. The article speaks of 'the need, nay the necessity, of pastorship' (p.78). This is much in line with 'Church Principles' (NM 5.3 – in Section 8, Publications Produced from Notes of Addresses, and Posthumously Published Letters and Manuscripts).

2. The article refers to the Apostles and their delegates by whom a standard for qualification of elders could be determined (page 86). See *B.W. Newton on Ministry and Order in the Church of Christ*, p.71, where this role is described.

---

[1] Jonathan D. Burnham, *A Story of Conflict, the Controversial Relationship between Benjamin Wills Newton and John Nelson Darby* bibliography – B.W. Newton.

3. It takes a developmental view of specific gifts for the body of Christ (such as teaching or rule, p.78). This is again much in line with 'Church Principles', and *Thoughts on the Apostasy of the Present Dispensation* (p.10, which also emphasises the need for rule).

4. The article lays special importance on being 'addicted' to the ministry of the saints, and on submission to the ministry of those who *are* addicted to this ministry (1 Cor. 16:15, pp.85,86). This is again emphasised in 'Church Principles' (see *B.W. Newton on Ministry and Order in the Church of Christ*, pp.107,108). This is the closest parallel we have found with Mr Newton's works.

5. 'Thoughts on …' is a trademark title of Mr Newton's works.

**Internal evidence against on B.W. Newton's authorship:**

1. On page 76, Heb. 8:5 and 9:23 are linked together. They also appear on the same page in *A Second Letter to a Friend … on the Study of Prophecy* (p.10). Both give the things of the Tabernacle as a pattern – but this article refers it to the relation of the heavenly standing of the Church, and *A Second Letter…* as patterns of the future connection of earth and Heaven in the Millennium.

2. The writer several times quotes the Greek of Scripture references (p.83 κυριευουσιν, and οι εξουσιαζοντες; p.85 εταξαν). Mr Newton does not appear to quote or explain the Greek of these verses elsewhere.

3. As far as we are aware, this article was not cited by J.N. Darby or his friends in their attacks on B.W. Newton, which alleged changes in the government of the Plymouth Assembly.

**Internal evidence in favour of S.P. Tregelles's authorship:**

1. It is quite possible that the article was by S.P. Tregelles. He withdrew his earlier tract *The Blood of the Lamb and the Union of Saints* (see CBA 7049, p.307), and later wrote *Pastoral Relations*, in which he closely parallels several approaches presented in this article.

2. S.P. Tregelles repeatedly uses the somewhat unusual word 'pastorship' in Pastoral Relations [although B.W. Newton also uses it, e.g. in his letter dated 20th November 1879].

3. S.P. Tregelles distinguishes pastor and teacher in a similar manner (in *Pastoral Relations*, pp.21,90).

4. There is a further close parallel in discussion of those who 'addicted' themselves to the ministry, and of submission to them (*Pastoral Relations*, pp.85-87, 108ff).

**CONCLUSION – insufficient evidence to prove or disprove B.W. Newton's authorship.**

There is a lack of conclusive evidence that this was written by B.W. Newton. It is equally possible that S.P. Tregelles wrote it.

# SECTION 8

## PUBLICATIONS DERIVED FROM NOTES OF ADDRESSES
### AND
## POSTHUMOUSLY PUBLISHED LETTERS AND MANUSCRIPTS

# Section 8 - Published notes of addresses, and posthumous quotations

# PUBLICATIONS DERIVED FROM NOTES OF ADDRESSES
## AND
## POSTHUMOUSLY PUBLISHED LETTERS AND MANUSCRIPTS

**Contents of this section**

Introduction

*Studies Series*

*Patmos Series*

*Time of the End Series*

Miscellaneous Items
- NM 1  Items published by W. Lancelot Holland
- NM 2  *Gleanings Series*
- NM 3  *Lectures on the Epistle to the Romans*
- NM 4  Items compiled by Frank Kennedy
- NM 5  Items published in *Perilous Times*
- NM 6  Items published in *Watching and Waiting*
- NM 7  *How B.W. Newton Learned Prophetic Truth*
- NM 8  Items published in *Teachers of the Faith and Future*
- NM 9  Items published in *Early Brethren and the Society of Friends*
- NM 10 *What is the Pearl Testimony?* by A.C. Fry
- NM 11 Quotations by A.J.W. Dalzell in *Atonement is not Reconciliation* (1900)

Subject and Scripture Index of the items in this section

### INTRODUCTION TO THIS SECTION

This part of the *Guide* records derivative publications - notes of addresses, letters, and other spoken and written records of Mr Newton that were not intended for publication, and were therefore not authorised, scrutinised or corrected by him.

### Caution regarding this material

This has been kept as a separate part of the bibliography. Such a distinction is necessary, as the error that J.N. Darby and his followers attributed to Mr Newton was based upon their construction on alleged statements by him. These were printed with a bitter critique by J.L. Harris in 1847. Mr Newton's comments on that particular pamphlet are a sufficient warning of the dangers inherent in such material purporting to be by him. In his reply, *Observations on a Tract Entitled 'The Sufferings of Christ as Set Forth in a Lecture on Psalm 6, Considered'*, he stated the following: 'About eighteen months ago I was giving lectures on some of the Psalms. Notes of one of these being taken, not in short hand, by one of those present, were afterwards copied and lent by the possessor to some of her friends. I never saw one line of those notes, nor indeed knew of their existence (though aware that such notes were often taken) until I heard that they were read and severely censured in a meeting convened in Exeter for the purpose. Shortly afterwards they were published, accompanied by the strictures upon which I now comment. This was done without any communication having been made to me, and therefore no opportunity was afforded me of avowing or disavowing any of the sentiments, or of rendering any explanation or even giving my judgement as to the accuracy of the notes....The fact that I am accustomed in such lectures to occupy an hour, and not unfrequently more, whereas the notes can easily be read in twenty minutes, sufficiently proves that much must have been omitted. Indeed it is the necessary habit of any who take notes, not in short hand, to note the new or most prominent sentiments, and to pass by those which are more familiar. Yet the latter may be very important in the way of explanation - definition of terms and connexion.....I would further take the opportunity of stating, that I am not responsible for any notes of my lectures that may be now or at any future time circulated, unless they are accompanied by my signature'.

Mr Newton derived many of his publications from his own notes of sermons and lectures as is apparent from Section 3, B.W. Newton's Published Works, but he was always very meticulous in his preparation of works for publication, as a correspondent to *Watching and Waiting* testified, evidently from first-hand knowledge, 'Mr Newton ... wrote with the utmost care, often destroyed what he wrote, and rewrote it, sometimes several times' (*Watching and Waiting*, Oct. 1935 p.83). The author's manuscript notes for the Second Edition of *Thoughts on the Apocalypse* (in the possession of C.W.H. Griffiths) also show great attention to detail.

One of his close associates later in life, W.L. Holland, expresses similar caution regarding publication of notes purporting to be by Mr Newton. He wrote 'Study any work that has been written during the past sixty years by B.W. Newton (not any unrevised sermon notes, nor any tract that was withdrawn owing to certain deductions that were capable, apart from the context, of being made from it, nor the distorted sayings attributed to him by his enemies), and you will find that what you read will, with God's blessing, be for your edification in the Truth of God'.[1]

The same caution was felt by those of Mr Newton's circle who published the posthumous notes. *Reminiscences of Mr B.W. Newton's Ministry* (NS 22 & 23) has on the title page the statement, 'The compiler is alone responsible should any error be found in these pages'. Frank Kennedy in the *Bethany Series* (NM 4.1, and NM 4.2) declares 'As these notes were not revised by the late B.W. Newton, the compiler accepts all responsibility'. It may also be noted that most of the items listed here appear at first sight to be anonymous. It is only in the publisher's lists and on later bindings that they are described as being by Mr Newton.

This reticence was evidently not accidental, but reflects unwillingness to have a revered teacher again unjustly charged with error. It is a matter of regret that later republication, bookseller's lists, and library and archive catalogues fail to make this distinction. Consequently, some superficial Edwardian publications are now passed off as 'by B.W. Newton'.

These publications are nevertheless valuable in confirming some issues of Mr Newton's theological and prophetic teachings, and in giving comments on particular persons and events.

---

[1] Walter Lancelot Holland, *The Archbishop of Canterbury and Modern Christianity* p.202 (1898).

## Note regarding Hunt, Barnard and Co.

Most of this section catalogues notes of his addresses that were published posthumously in the decade after his death. From 1895 onwards, notes of Mr Newton's addresses began to be published, initially by Yelf Brothers on the Isle of Wight[1]. The printing (and reprinting of several of the Yelf Brothers items) was then taken up in earnest by Hunt, Barnard and Co of Aylesbury in 1899. At the same time Hunt Barnard also commenced printing the magazine *Perilous Times*. The perceived value of such notes to Mr Newton's circle is attested by the number of the tracts and publications involved, and by the enthusiasm with which they were circulated. The following quotation from *Perilous Times* (June 1908, p.143) is a testimony to this. 'Since we first began to supply "recommended publications" [1901] 48,684 of these have been supplied, of which 1,650 were works by the late Mr B.W. Newton.[2] These books or tracts have all been sent out ... at cost or less, so that it has been purely a labour of love'.

The extent to which notes were kept and later published is remarkable. It is evident that some form of shorthand was used in most cases (see *Origins of the Brethren*, by H.H. Rowdon pp.58, 59). In the case of *Lectures on the Epistle to the Romans*, the notes concerned were taken over a 33 year period, and some, when published, were already 64 years old. By then, the actual addresses must have been long forgotten, and the note taker was probably already dead. They nevertheless were sufficient to produce a 529 page book. The extent to which records may differ in such circumstances can be illustrated by comparison. *Reflections for the Season, December 25th* (Patmos Series 9; NP 9) and *'Gleanings' in the 'Book of Exodus'* (Gleanings Series No 3 - NM 2.3) are evidently different records of the same message.

One person was primarily responsible for most of the Hunt, Barnard publications. Jane Thornton Daniels (died 15/9/1914 aged 76 years[3]) compiled and prepared the *Studies*, *Patmos*, *Time of the End*, and *Gleanings* Series for publication (*Perilous Times*, Sept. 1914 p.77). With her passing, the flow of 'new' items all but ceases. Frank Kennedy (1858-1933) evidently attempted to continue this task, and *Watching and Waiting* March 1933 (p.22) states, 'He edited numerous MSS of Mr B.W. Newton's, several of which he had printed...' (see NM.4).

Some of the materials recorded in this section have been extracted from the manuscripts now in the Fry Collection of the Christian Brethren Archive in the John Ryland Library of Manchester University. It has not been thought necessary to precisely identify the source in these instances. Our

---

[1] Yelf Brothers sesquicentennial anniversary was celebrated by the publication of *Printers' Pride. The House of Yelf at Newport Isle of Wight 1816-1966. The Study of a Family Printing Business*, by A.N. Daish, Yelf Brothers 1967. Unfortunately, their order books are lost for the period when items related to B.W. Newton were published.

[2] The 1,650 were works that he himself had published. Virtually all the 'recommended publications' were published notes of Mr Newton's addresses, and they are here again distinguished from 'works by the late Mr B.W. Newton'. The publishing of these items is largely a testimony to G.T. Hunt, the senior partner of the firm. George Turnor Hunt, 1855-1936. As with many of B.W. Newton's associates, he retired to Worthing and attended Chatsworth Hall. Obituary *Watching and Waiting*, February 1936, p.9. The *Watching and Waiting* obituary quotes *The Bucks Herald* and *The Bucks Advertiser* obituaries. Died Jan. 4th 1936. A photograph of him as an old man is reproduced in *A Pictorial Memoir of Benjamin Wills Newton* – the supplement to this Guide. See the Advertisement at the end of this volume.. See Section 2, Libraries and Collections, Sovereign Grace Advent Testimony for further notes on the work of C.T. Hunt and his company.

[3] Obituary *Perilous Times* September 1914.

view is that most were drawn from other sources than those manuscripts held by A.C. Fry.  See Section 10, Duplicated and Manuscript Items for further information on 'the Fry Collection'.

Reported statements by B.W. Newton in the Fry Collection (often those made late in life in private conversations) have been published in connection with the controversy with J.N. Darby[1]. These are often brief quotations used to support an interpretation of events. In our view it is as precarious and unfair to use these as it was to use his reported statements on Psalm 6 as the *casus belli* of the controversy with J.N. Darby. It would perhaps be apt to quote his letter of 1st June 1885, 'it is beyond the power of any living individual to write an accurate or truthful account of the complications of Brethrenism during the last forty years'. This part of the *Guide* does not attempt to catalogue these quotations. We have, however, included a number of miscellaneous items at the end of this section where some reported statements and MS notes from the Fry Collection and elsewhere have been published. We have suggested some reading on the other side of the controversy with J.N. Darby in Appendix 3.

This section did not fall within the original plan for a bibliography. A full library index would be difficult, as most were anonymous and were not attributed to B.W. Newton when originally published. This section does not therefore identify the holdings of these items by other than the following libraries:

| | |
|---|---|
| Bible Institute of Los Angeles | BIOLA |
| Christian Brethren Archive, Manchester | CBA |
| Evangelical Library, London | EL |
| Sovereign Grace Advent Testimony | SG |
| Items held by C.W.H. Griffiths are indicated by CG | |

## Arrangement of this part of the Guide

This section of the Guide is divided into four sub-sections. It is followed by an index of the principal Scripture passages and subjects dealt with in these publications. We have given our own numbering to each of these items - NP, NS etc. - for ease of reference. However, we have listed series (such as *Patmos Series*) in their numbered order. Readers seeking a reference to a particular item are therefore advised to use the full alphabetical list of publications in Section 3 of this *Guide* to find the reference number of a particular pamphlet or article.

The first part has been termed the *Studies Series* (Items given the prefix NS). There is very considerable variation in cover, first page, list, and different edition titles to these items. They are listed unnumbered by Hunt, Barnard as the *Studies Series*. They, in fact, predate the involvement of Hunt, Barnard in such publication. W.R. Yelf or Yelf Brothers or W.R. Yelf of Newport, Isle of Wight published at least nine of these items in the last few years of the nineteenth century. They are, however, so closely intertwined by reprints and revisions that they have been grouped together.

---

[1] For example in *The Origins of the Brethren* by Harold H Rowdon (Pickering and Inglis, 1967), *A History of the Brethren Movement* by F. Roy Coad (Paternoster Press, 1968), *From Awakening to Secession* by T.C.F. Stunt, T&T Clark, 2000, and *A Story of Conflict: The Controversial Relationship between Benjamin Wills Newton and John Nelson Darby* by Jonathan D Burnham (Paternoster Press, 2004).

## Section 8 - Published notes of addresses, and posthumous quotations

Apart from the initial definite or indefinite article, they have been listed in strict alphabetical order, with cross-referencing of the various alternative titles.

Separate sections have been allotted to the *Patmos Series* (NP) and *The Time of the End Series* (NT). Both were numbered and produced in a uniform format. These have been kept in the order given them by the publisher (which is also the publication date order). Apart from the first two of the Patmos Series, they all bear the publisher's numbering.

The last section is a miscellany of books, pamphlets, and items published by others in books and periodicals (listed here as NM). They have been grouped together by periodical, publisher, or originator.

All the titles in this section, with their reference number, are given in Section 1, Index to Titles.

The dates given to otherwise undated items have been achieved after much meticulous and painstaking comparison of references to their publication in periodicals, the publisher's lists and to price changes etc. The date format is as follows:
    (1901) = virtual certainty.
    (c.1901) = a high degree of probability.
    (1901?) = there are good grounds for assuming this date.

## STUDIES SERIES

This consists of a number of pamphlets, some of which were first published by W.R. Yelf (later Yelf Brothers) of Newport, Isle of Wight. So far as can be ascertained, all were reprinted, some in a revised form, by Hunt, Barnard of Aylesbury.[1]

## Bound Volumes

The pamphlets were bound together on a number of known occasions, although the content of the volumes varied, depending upon which *Studies* were then in print. The following dates and titles of bound up volumes have been identified:

*Elementary Studies in Doctrinal and Prophetic Subjects*
   As only 'a few copies, cloth bound' were available in 1902, it may be that these items had been bound up by Yelf Brothers. If so, Yelf would also have had to have produced an edition of NS 12, 35, and 39, as these were included with other Yelf publications - NS 6,7,9,10,11,22 and 23.

*Elementary Studies* – vols. 1, 2, and 3.
   These were bound in cloth in 1909.

Studies Series in three volumes (titles not known).
   Bound in hardback c.1925.

*Old Testament Studies,* and *New Testament Studies*
   Bindings under these titles were reported in 1937, 1955 and 1962.

## Individual Items

These are unnumbered, and are therefore listed here alphabetically. The numbering and referencing is ours.

### NS 1. An Anthology (No.1) 'Reminiscences' of Lectures in Stafford Rooms.

Different from *Reminiscences...* (NS 22 23).
References in the text indicate that the notes were taken around 1888. CBA 7188(1) is a note of lectures to be given at the Stafford Rooms in May 1887. Stafford Rooms Y.M.C.A. was near Edgware Road, London. See also NT 5, which was probably also given as a lecture at the Stafford Rooms.
These are not personal or circumstantial reminiscences relating to B.W. Newton, but a series of short comments he made on Scripture texts and subjects. The notes cover the following texts and subjects:
   Atonement; baptism; Psa. 94; Isa. 30:9-14; Psa. 11; Luke 17:21; river of Eden; cherubim and seraphim.

   (1912)          Hunt, Barnard          32 pages          EL,SG

---

[1] The possible exception is NS 19A. *The Message of Moses and the Apostles Contrasted.*

### NS 2. Anthology (No.2) 'Reminiscences' of Bible Readings, etc. at Newport, I.W.

Different from *Reminiscences...* (NS 22, NS 23).

References in the text indicate that the notes were taken around 1889 or later.

These are not personal or circumstantial reminiscences relating to B.W. Newton, but a series of short comments he made on Scripture texts and subjects. The notes cover the following texts and subjects:

> 1 Tim. 2:14; Zech. 13:1-5; Dan. 12:2; Hades; Matt. 24; 2 Cor. 8:5; Isa. 9-12; Hos. 2:15; Parliamentary Oaths Bill; 1888 (Bradlaugh); 'The Army of God' 1888; Matt. 10:34; 1 Cor. 3.

> (1912)      Hunt, Barnard      24 pages      EL,SG

### NS 3. Anthology (No.3) 'Reminiscences' of Bible Readings, etc. at Newport, I.W.

Different from *Reminiscences...* (NS 22, NS 23)

These are not personal or circumstantial reminiscences relating to B.W. Newton, but a series of short comments he made on Scripture texts and subjects. The notes cover the following texts and subjects:

Lev. 16; laying on of hands; Gen. 1-4; Lev. 19:27; Rev. 1:1; Isa. 22; Heb. 10:8; 2 Cor. 1:20; 2 Cor. 5:14; 1 Tim. 3:16; Gal. 1:13; Matt. 13:45 (the Pearl); Jude; Ezek. 30:15; Matt. 16:26; Psa. 4:1.

A section from it was reprinted in the anthology, *B.W. Newton on Ministry and Order in the Church of Christ* – see Section 3, B.W. Newton's Published Works.

> (1913)      Hunt, Barnard      18 pages      EL,SG

### NS 4. Antichrist and Babylon with an Exposition of Daniel 11

'Condensed from a course of lectures given at Mildmay' (1876? See NS 5).

The notes show Isa. 13 and 14 to be unfulfilled, and comment on Daniel 11.

> (1908)      Hunt, Barnard      16 pages      EL,SG

### ~ Characteristics of the Gospel of Matthew

See Israel's Rejection and the Gentiles' Acceptance of Jesus of Nazareth (NS 16).

### NS 5. Christendom: its Course and Doom

The study is based on Matthew 24.

'The following pages are condensed from a course of lectures given at Mildmay in 1876'.[1]

> (1908)      Hunt, Barnard      20 pages      CBA,SG

---

[1] Other lectures at Mildmay were NS 4, and NS 19. See CBA 7064 p.29, where he notes his preaching at Mildmay ended his 'seclusion' at Winchester, but that he was then excluded from Mildmay because he 'protested against the Archbishop of Canterbury in reference to Universal Atonement'.

(Second? Edition) 'by Benjamin Wills Newton'.
199?   Irish Christian Mission   21 pages   CG

## ~ The Cleansing of the Leper, Leviticus 14

See NS 6

## ~Dark Sayings upon the Harp

See Studies in Some of the Psalms (NS 32).

## NS 6. Elementary Studies in Leviticus 14 on the Leper Cleansed

Included in *Studies in Leviticus* (NS 25). *The Cleansing of the Leper* in Leviticus 14 was also the subject of an article in *The Christian Witness*, and a separate early publication.

(ND)   W.R. Yelf   29 pages   SG

## NS 7. Elementary Studies in Leviticus 23 on the Seven 'Feasts of the Lord'

Included in *Studies in Leviticus* (NS 25).

(ND)   W.R. Yelf   31 pages   SG

## NS 8. Elementary Studies in the Book of Daniel

Reprinted as *Studies in the Book of Daniel*, and as part of *Elementary Studies in the Facts of Prophetic Scripture in the Book of Daniel and the Book of Revelation* (NS 12).

(First Edition)
1895   W.R. Yelf   43? pages   SG
(Second Edition) - *Studies in the Book of Daniel*
(1912)   11.5cm   Hunt, Barnard   16 pages   SG

## NS 9. Elementary Studies in 'the Canticles' on the Practical Walk of Faith

This was the 'First Series'. The 'Second Series' was titled *Studies in the Song of Solomon* (NS 40). Selected passages are used to describe the believer in different conditions.

1895   Yelf bros.   26 pages   SG

## NS 10. Elementary Studies in the Facts of Prophetic Scripture, Part One

The pamphlet consists of short statements and proof texts. There is no evidence of B.W. Newton producing such a summary himself. It is clearly not from an address by him. Perhaps it was drawn up by his friends with his approval, as *A Statement of Doctrines Held by a body of Christians Meeting in the Evangelical Protestant Chapel, Newport Street, Ryde, Isle of Wight*, compiled by Arthur

Andrews (1897).[1] Although the early editions do not claim any direct link with B.W. Newton, they would not have been so circulated if he disapproved of them.

Part Two is *Elementary Studies on* [sic] *the Facts...* (NS 12).

First Edition
    1892            W.R. Yelf            ?            ?

Second Edition - Part One, Revised
    1895            W.R. Yelf            23 pages        SG

(Third? Edition   Another edition about 1911?) '7th thousand' 'Hunt, Barnard and Co' on the front page.
    (1915)          Hunt, Barnard       18 pages        SG

(Fourth? Edition)
    (1940)          S.R. Cottey, Chiswick    18 pages        CG

(Fifth? Edition)
    (c.1943)  SGAT, Chiswick       18 pages        CG

(Sixth? Edition) - *Things You Always Wanted to Know about Bible Prophecy – 39 Key Questions answered,*' 'by Benjamin Wills Newton'.
    1993            Irish Christian Mission   23 pages        CG

German Edition (per publisher's list)
    (1911)          Hunt Barnard?             ?

### NS 11. Elementary Studies on Doctrinal Subjects in the Epistle to the Romans

This consists of a brief summary of each chapter, followed by short text by text comments on each chapter.

First Edition
    1896            W.R. Yelf            24 pages       BIOLA

Second Edition   Reprinted from First Edition
    (1914)          Hunt Barnard         24 pagesBIOLA,CBA,SG

### NS 12. Elementary Studies on the Facts of Prophetic Scripture in the Book of Daniel and the Book of Revelation. Part Two, Revised.

As with NS 10, it is impossible to determine how far, if at all, this derived directly from B.W. Newton. Note the great emphasis which the posthumous Third Edition of *Thoughts on the Apocalypse* lays on its being a 'word for word' reprint, using square brackets to identify anything added. Note too the letter of F.W. Wyatt to Miss Martin, reproduced in Appendix 1 of this *Guide*, in which he emphasises that when that edition was issued the publishers avoided even including a change of view he had had after the 1853 Second Edition. That change is not incorporated in this publication, and in many aspects it gives a more elaborate and detailed prophetic outline than B.W. Newton's book does (e.g. on Revelation 11 and 12).

---
[1] See notes in Section 6 of this Guide, Contributions to Other Publications.

Part One is *Elementary Studies in* [sic] *the Facts....* See the notes there regarding these two publications on prophecy.

Also see *Elementary Studies in the Book of Daniel* (NS 10).

(First Edition)
   (c.1911)     Hunt Barnard               40 pages           BIOLA
(Second Edition)
   (1922)           Hunt Barnar               32 pages           EL,SG
(Third Edition) 'by B.W. Newton'. Lithographic reprint from serialisation in *Watching and Waiting* from Jan./Feb. to Sept./Oct. 1968.
   (1969)           SGAT, London            55 pages           SG

## NS 13. Elementary Studies on the Offerings in the Book of Leviticus

Included in *Studies in Leviticus* (NS 25)

   1896              Yelf Bros                 18 pages           SG

## NS 14. An Exposition of the Epistle to the Ephesians

Half of the tract is concerned with chapter 1, but there are comments on the whole of the Epistle. A section from it was reprinted in the anthology *B.W. Newton on Ministry and Order in the Church of Christ*.

Sometimes listed as *Studies in the Epistle to the Ephesians*.
   (1908)           Hunt, Barnard             48 pages           CBA,SG

## ~ Facts of Prophetic Scripture, Studies in Daniel and Revelation

See *Elementary Studies in the Facts of Prophetic Scripture in the Book of Daniel and the Book of Revelation, Part Two* (NS 12).

## NS 15. Individual Gifts

The appendix of *Studies in the Song of Solomon, Second Series* (NS 40), published separately. It shows the analogy between Nehemiah's work, and the believer's work in this present age. It was reprinted in the anthology *B.W. Newton on Ministry and Order in the Church of Christ*. It was also reprinted in *Watching and Waiting*, October–December 2003, pp.122, 123.

From a publisher's list c.1925

## ~~Isaiah 40-49

List title of *A Synopsis of Isaiah 40-49 and 59-61* (NS 43).

## NS 16. Israel's Rejection and the Gentiles' Acceptance of Jesus of Nazareth: Characteristics of the Gospel of Matthew.

This comments chiefly on Matthew chapters 1 and 2.
It gives as a supplying address (Lucas Collins) 43, Blandford Street, Baker Street, London, W.

| (1909) | Hunt Barnard | 14 page s | CBA,SG |

## NS 17. John the Baptist, the Place and Character of his Ministry and Baptism

This is based on Matthew 3.

| (1909) | Hunt Barnard | 16 pages | CBA,SG |

## NS 18. The Kingdom of Heaven

A brief note on the present mystery and future manifestation of the Kingdom of Heaven.

| (1909) | Hunt Barnard | 4 pages | EL,SG |

## NS 19. Latitudinarianism, its Development, Course and Downfall

From lectures at Mildmay (1876? See NS 5)
This pamphlet comments on the godless permissiveness of modern systems of government.
Also supplied from (Lucas Collins), 43, Blandford Street, Baker Street, London, W.

| 1907 | Hunt, Barnard | 15 pages | EL,SG |
| (Second? Edition) | Titled, *'Latitudinarianism' End Time Apostasy* 'by Benjamin Wills Newton'. | | |
| 199? | Irish Christian Mission, Belfast | ? | ? |

## NS 19A. The Message of Moses and the Apostles Contrasted

Reference is made to this in *Studies on Parts of the Second Epistle to the Corinthians* (NS 31), p.12. It is therefore pre-1902, and possibly published by Yelf brothers. No copies have been located, despite correspondence with the printer. It is presumed that this may have been from notes of Mr Newton.

## ~ 'The Pilgrimage of Truth'

Sub-title of *Studies in the 'Song of Solomon', Second Series* (NS 40).

## NS 20. The Prospects of Egypt, Edom, Nineveh, Moab, Tyre etc.

Ammon, Tyre, and Philistia are the 'et cetera'.

| (1906) | Hunt, Barnard | 20 pages | BIOLA,EL,SG |

## NS 21. Remarks on Parts of the Epistle to the Galatians

This gives comments on Galatians 2-4.

    (1908)          Hunt, Barnard          22 pages          CBA,SG

## NS 22. Reminiscences of Mr B.W. Newton's Ministry, Part I

This was published in two parts. It has a disclaimer – 'The compiler is alone responsible should any error be found in these pages'.

Different from the three *Anthology...* publications with the title *Reminiscences...* (NS 1, NS 2, NS 3). The first page title of this, and of NS 23, is *Selections from Mr B.W. Newton's Teachings*.

These are not personal or circumstantial reminiscences relating to B.W. Newton, but a series of comments he made on Scripture texts and subjects. It gives various counsels for Christian living. It has particular comments on Psa. 84; 2 Cor. 6; Eccles. 1; Jere. 20.

    (Before 6/1902)    Yelf Bros          32 pages          CG

## NS 23. Reminiscences of Mr B.W. Newton's Ministry on Prophecy, Part II

This was published in two parts. It has a disclaimer – 'The compiler is alone responsible should any error be found in these pages'.

Different from the three *Anthology...* publications with the title *Reminiscences...* (NS 1, NS 2, NS 3). The first page title of this, and of NS 22, is *Selections from Mr B.W. Newton's Teachings*.

These are not personal or circumstantial reminiscences relating to B.W. Newton, but a series of comments he made on Scripture texts and subjects. The text indicates two dates for these notes, 1870 and 1886.

Comment is made upon the following portions of Scripture:

Isa. 29:11 & 12; Isa. 8; Isa. 25:7; Dan. 9:27; Isa. 10. Reference is made to the contrast between Christ and Antichrist, 'The Assyrian', Nebuchadnezzar, Jerusalem; various European developments; various people, including: Francis Newman, Prime Minister William E. Gladstone, Charles Bradlaugh;

    (Before 6/1902)    Yelf Bros          36 pages          EL

## ~ Selections from Mr B.W. Newton's Teachings

First page title of each part of *Reminiscences of B.W. Newton's Ministry* (NS 22, NS 23).

## NS 24. The Sermon on the Mount. An Outline

Comments on Matthew 5.

    (1909)          Hunt, Barnard          16 pages          CBA,SG

## ~~Studies in 2 Chronicles

See *Studies in Parts of 2 Chronicles* (NS 26).

## ~~Studies in Galatians

See *Remarks on Parts of the Epistle to the Galatians* (NS 21).

## NS 25. Studies in Leviticus

This brought together three earlier works, *Elementary Studies on Leviticus 14* (NS 6), *Elementary Studies on Leviticus 23* (NS 7), and *Elementary Studies on the Offerings in the Book of Leviticus* (NS 13). It was an 'enlarged edition', which included comments on other chapters of Leviticus. An article in *The Christian Witness*, and a publication by Mr Newton had the title *Cleansing the Leper: Leviticus 14* [or, *On the Cleansing of the Leper: Leviticus 14*], but these are distinct from this publication with no verbal similarity.

(1908)  Hunt, Barnard  48 pages  SG

## NS 26. Studies in Parts of 2 Chronicles

This has notes on 2 Chronicles 16-20,30,34, and Isa. 38-40.

(c.1905)  Hunt, Barnard  36 pages  SG

## NS 27. Studies in Parts of the Book of Genesis

This has notes on Genesis 1-32.

(1904)  Hunt, Barnard  48 pages  BIOLA,EL,SG

## NS 28. Studies in Parts of the First Epistle to the Corinthians

Comments on the whole book, apart from chapters 6-9.

(1902)  Hunt, Barnard  32 pages  BIOLA,CBA,SG

## NS 29. Studies in Parts of the Gospel of John

This has comments on chapters 3,5,6,9,10,13-17,19-21. The comments on John chapter 3 were published in the Patmos Series No.41 *Conversion. What Is It?* (NP 41) at about the same time. The printing in Patmos is in identical typography and content apart from a very brief appendix. Likewise, the comments on John chapter 6 were also published in the Patmos Series No.42 *Manna. What is it?* (NP 42) in identical typography.

(1911)  Hunt, Barnard  47 pages  CBA,SG

### NS 30. Studies in Parts of the Gospel of Matthew

There are comments on nearly the entire Gospel.
Time of the End Series No.19 (NT 19), which concerns the parables of Matthew 13, was extracted from this. Those parables are also treated in *Prospects of the Ten Kingdoms*, and - extracted from it - *Thoughts on the History of Professing Christianity as Given in the Parables of Matthew 13*. (Section 3, Published Works).

    (1904)        Hunt, Barnard        60 pages        BIOLA,CBA,SG

### NS 31. Studies in Parts of the Second Epistle to the Corinthians

Chapter 10 is the only chapter of the epistle upon which there is no comment.

    (1903)        Hunt, Barnard        36 pages        BIOLA,CBA,SG

### NS 32. Studies in Some of the Psalms

References in the text indicate three dates for the notes, 1870, 1886, and 1889.
Comment is made on most of the Psalms, giving their future prophetic significance.
Sub-titled *Dark Sayings upon the Harp'*.

    (1905)        Hunt, Barnard        68 pages        EL,SG

### ~ Studies in the Book of Daniel

See *Elementary Studies in the Book of Daniel* (NS 8).

### ~~Studies in 'the Canticles'

See *Studies in the Song of Solomon* (NS 40).

### NS 33. Studies in the Epistle of 1 John

This includes a closing note on 2 and 3 John.

    (1906)        Hunt, Barnard        38 pages        BIOLA,CBA,SG

### NS 34. Studies in the Epistle of James

This has notes on the whole of the epistle, and two different sets of notes on James 4 and 5.

    (c.1905)        Hunt, Barnard        36 pages        BIOLA,CBA,SG

### ~~Studies in the Epistle to the Ephesians

See *An Exposition of the Epistle to the Ephesians* (NS 14).

### ~~Studies in the Epistle to the Galatians Condensed from the Commentary by Martin Luther

(Published 1908). It is plain from *Perilous Times* May 1909, p.196 that this was not derived from Mr B.W. Newton, but it is found in Hunt, Barnard's lists of the *Studies Series*. It is not to be confused with *Remarks on Parts of the Epistle to the Galatians* (NS 21), sometimes called *Studies in Galatians*.

### NS 35. Studies in the Epistle to the Hebrews

The notes comment on every chapter in varying length.

    (1902)        Hunt, Barnard        32 pages        BIOLA,CBA,SG

### NS 36. Studies in the Epistle to the Philippians

The notes comment on all four chapters.

    (1907)        Hunt, Barnard        20 pages        CBA,SG

### ~~Studies in the Epistle to the Romans

See *Elementary Studies on Doctrinal Subjects in the Epistle to the Romans* (NS 11).

### NS 37. Studies in the Epistles of 1 and 2 Timothy

The notes comment on all chapters in varying length.
A section from it was reprinted in the anthology *B.W. Newton on Ministry and Order in the Church of Christ*.

    (c.1906)       Hunt, Barnard        74 pages        BIOLA,CBA,SG

### ~ Studies in the Facts of Prophetic Scripture

See *Elementary Studies in the Facts of Prophetic Scripture* (NS 10).

### ~ Studies in the First Epistle to the Corinthians

See *Studies in Parts of the First Epistle to the Corinthians* (NS 28).

### ~ Studies in the Gospel of John

See *Studies in Parts of the Gospel of John* (NS 29).

### ~ Studies in the Gospel of Matthew

See *Studies in Parts of the Gospel of Matthew* (NS 30).

### NS 38. Studies in the Lives of Jonah, Job, and Philemon

    (1907)        Hunt, Barnard        20 pages        SG

### NS 39. Studies in the Prophecy of Isaiah

This has comments (some brief) on every chapter. It was used in the compilation, *Thoughts on the Whole Prophecy of Isaiah* (See Section 3, B.W. Newton's Published Works), where it was added in with one other series of notes - *A Synopsis of Isaiah 40-49 and 59-61* (NS 42), and two other publications by Mr Newton, in an attempt to produce a commentary on the whole prophecy.

    (1901)        Hunt, Barnard        48 pages        EL,SG

### ~ Studies in the Psalms

See *Studies in Some of the Psalms* NS 32

### ~ Studies in the Second Epistle to the Corinthians

See *Studies in Parts of the Second Epistle to the Corinthians* NS 31.

### NS 40. Studies in the 'Song of Solomon'

Sub-titled *The Pilgrimage of Truth*. This was also referred to as the *Second Series*, evidently a different set of lectures from those recorded in the *First Series*, which was *Elementary Studies in 'The Canticles'* (NS 9).

*Individual Gifts*, the appendix, which was based on the work of Nehemiah, was also published separately (NS 15). It was included in the anthology *B.W. Newton on Ministry and Order in the Church of Christ*.

    (c.1906)        Hunt, Barnard        40 pages        BIOLA,EL,SG

(Second Edition) - *Ministry for Heart and Conscience. No.26.*
    ND (1996?)    Ministry for the Last Difficult Days, Vancouver.    19cm  40 pages    CG

### NS 41. The Sufferings of Christ on Three Separate Occasions

The three separate occasions were, in the Wilderness, in Gethsemane and on the Cross.

    (c.1911)        Hunt, Barnard        12 pages        SG

### NS 42. A Synopsis of Isaiah 40-49 and 59-61

These notes were used in the compilation of *Thoughts on the Whole Prophecy of Isaiah* (see Section 3, B.W. Newton's Published Works of this *Guide*) in which it was edited with *Studies in the Prophecy of Isaiah* (NS 39), and two other publications by Mr Newton, in an attempt to produce a commentary on the whole prophecy.

    (1906)        Hunt, Barnard        12 pages        SG

**~~Things you always wanted to know about Bible Prophecy – 39 Key Questions answered.**

See *Elementary Studies in the Facts of Prophetic Scripture, Part One* (NS 10).

## PATMOS SERIES

The Patmos Series was produced by Hunt, Barnard in 11.5 x 9cm format. As noted in the introduction to this Section of the *Guide*, the content of the Series was the work of Jane Thornton Daniels. The various numbers of the Series were printed on paper of different colours.

The numbering that follows is the numbering given to the tracts by Hunt, Barnard. It is evident from differences in typography and price that there were different printings. It has not been possible to distinguish where different printings or revised editions are held by CBA, SG. Some assumptions have been made on this. There were several bindings of the Series, not necessarily including all the numbers. Bindings of the Series are known to have been made in 1902 and 1962.

There were also separate bindings of *The Message to the Seven Churches* (NP 8,11,12,13,15,17,18) (1903), and of notes on the epistle to the Romans (title not known) (NP 24-29) (1903).

### NP 1. An Exposition of Isaiah 53 with Acts 8:26-40

The title page indicates neither that it is the *Patmos Series* nor that it is the first in the series. *Perilous Times* (March 1901 p.1) states 'Miss Daniels, who has published several little books containing notes of addresses by Mr B.W. Newton, has another in the press on Isaiah 53 and Acts 8:26-40'. Compare the Chapters on Isaiah 53 in *Thoughts on Scriptural Subjects*, noted in Section 3, B.W. Newton's Published Works.

    (1901)                           16 pages             G
    (1915?) (price change)     16 pages             CBA,SG

### NP 2. Things Pertaining to This Life

This is an exposition of 1 Cor. 6:1-11.
It is labelled *Patmos Series*, but is unnumbered.
    (1901)                           16 pages             CBA,SG

### NP 3. Wilderness Wanderings and Heavenly Guidance

This is not about the Exodus, but is concerned with the believer's pathway through this life, illustrated mainly from the life of Jacob (esp. Gen. 27 & 28).
    (1901)                           15 pages             CBA,SG
    (1902?) (typography)     15 pages             CG

### NP 4. Believer's Life work, 'Gold, Silver, Precious Stones, Wood, Hay, Stubble'

These are notes on 1 Corinthians 3.
    (1901)                           16 pages             CBA,SG

### NP 5. 'Prepared unto Glory!' How?

This comments on 1 Corinthians 15. The answer to the question is therefore that we must be changed before we enter into glory.
    (1901)                           16 pages             CBA,SG

### NP 6. Access. Sustainment. Service

This is subtitled, *The Lessons of the Brazen and Golden Altars*. It concerns the Tabernacle.
    (1901)                    16 pages        CBA,SG

### NP 7. The Olive Tree and its Branches. The Doom of Israel and Christendom
This consists of comments on Romans 11.
    (1901)                    16 pages        CBA,SG
    (1940?) (price change)    16 pages        CG

### NP 8. The Message to the Churches - Ephesus
As well as dealing with this particular letter in Revelation 2:1-7, the tract also gives an introduction to all the 'Letters to the Churches' in Revelation 2 and 3.
Bound together with 11,12,13,15,17,19 as *The Message to the Seven Churches* (1903)
    (1901)                    16 pages        CBA,SG

### NP 9. Reflections for the Season, December 25th
This draws lessons from Exodus 32 – 33:11. It gives a warning concerning the apostasy of Christendom. It makes a parallel between Israel's actions in making a golden calf for a 'feast unto the Lord', and what is often made of Christmas. (Compare NP 23, and NM 2, NM 3).
    (1901)                    15 pages        CBA,SG
    (1903) (includes different list)   15 pages    CG

### NP 10. Reflections for the New Year in the Parables of Matthew 25
These give a warning to all those who professedly own the name of the Lord Jesus.
    (1901)                    15 pages        CBA,SG

### NP 11. The Message to the Churches - Smyrna
The (Brethren) view that these letters represent a prophetic sequence of Church history is refuted in this item.
Bound together with 8,12,13,15,17,19 as *The Message to the Seven Churches* (1903)
    (1902)                    14 pages        CBA,SG

### NP 12. The Message to the Churches - Pergamos
Bound together with 8,11,13,15,17,19 as *The Message to the Seven Churches* (1903).
    (1902)                    9 pages        CBA,SG

### NP 13. The Message to the Churches - Thyatira
Bound together with 8,11,12,15,17,19 as *The Message to the Seven Churches* (1903).
    (1902)                    19 pages        CBA,SG

### NP 14. 'Entrance into the Holiest'. By What Means? On What Ground? In What Title?
This consists of comments on Hebrews 10.
    (1902)             15 pages        CBA,SG

### NP 15. The Message to the Churches - Sardis
Bound together with 8,11,12,13,17,19 as *The Message to the Seven Churches* (1903).
    (1902)             15 pages        CBA,SG

### NP 16. 'Salvation' What the Instrumentality? What the Link?
This gives notes on 1 Corinthians 1:17-21.
    (1902)             17 pages        CBA,SG
    (c.1915) (price change)   17 pages        CG

### NP 17. The Message to the Churches - Philadelphia
Bound together with NP 8,11,12,13,15,19 as *The Message to the Seven Churches* (1903).
    (1902)             13 pages        CBA,SG

### NP 18. 'Baptism'. What it Signifies. Who the Right Subjects
    (1902)             16 pages        CBA,SG
Second Edition
    (1905?)           16 pages        CG

### NP 19. The Message to the Churches - Laodicea
Bound together with NP 8,11,12,13,15,17 as *The Message to the Seven Churches* (1903).
    (1902)             14 pages        CBA,SG

### NP 20. Memorial versus Idolatry or the 'Table of the Lord', and the 'Table of Devils
This gives comments on 1 Corinthians 10:16-21.
    (1902)             16 pages        CBA,SG

### NP 21. 'The Prophecy of Habakkuk'
See NS 22.
    (1902)             18 pages        CBA,SG

### NP 22. 'Human Progress'. Its Course and Doom, or Withdrawal unto Perdition.
This was the substance of a message given on 25th December 1861 (cf. NP 9, and NP 10). It was also given a week after 'human progress' had been praised at the funeral service of Prince Albert. The address was based principally upon the Prophecy of Habakkuk (See NS 21).
    (1902)             16 pages        CBA,SG

### NP 23. Psalms 1-8
This also contains some remarks about the Pentateuch.
   (1903)               18 pages         CBA,SG

### NP 24. 'Things that Accompany Salvation' - or the Practical Walk of the 'Saved'. Romans 12 - 14
This includes notes on 'the Christian Sabbath'.
NP 24 - 29 were bound together in 1903 as notes on the Epistle to the Romans (title not known).
   (1903)               16 pages         CBA,SG

### NP 25. In the Courts of God: 'Guilty' or 'Guiltless'. Romans 1 - 4
This has an appendix on the nature of Christ's Atonement.
NP 24 - 29 were bound together in 1903 as notes on the Epistle to the Romans (title not known).
   (1903)               16 pages         CBA,SG

### NP 26. One Man's Sin Contrasted with 'The One Righteousness'. Romans 5
NP 24 - 29 were bound together in 1903 as notes on the Epistle to the Romans (title not known).
   (1903)               16 pages         CBA,SG

### NP 27. 'Under Sin, Under Law, Under Grace'. Romans 6 - 8
NP 24 - 29 were bound together in 1903 as notes on the Epistle to the Romans (title not known).
   (1903)               16 pages         CBA,SG

### NP 28. The Purpose of God According to Election in Romans 9 - 11
NP 24 - 29 were bound together in 1903 as notes on the Epistle to the Romans (title not known).
   (1903)               16 pages         CBA,SG

### NP 29. The Calling of the Gentiles the 'New Meat Offering'. Romans 15 and 16
This tract expounds Romans 15 and 16 in the light of a Type given in Leviticus 23. It has an appendix on the Philippian Jailor (Acts 16).
NP 24 - 29 were bound together in 1903 as notes on the Epistle to the Romans (title not known).
   (1903)               16 pages         CBA,SG

### NP 30. The Disciples' Prayer
This expounds what is commonly known as The Lord's Prayer (Matthew 6:9-13).
   (1903)               12 pages         CBA,SG

### NP 31. 'Protection', 'Acceptance', 'Blessing'. The Blood of Christ
This gives notes on: Exod. 12; Lev. 16; Num. 19, and has an appendix on John 13.
   (1903)               12 pages         CBA,SG

## NP 32. 'Riches of Grace' as seen in the Tabernacle
This has notes on: The Atonement Money; The Laver; The Anointing Oil; The Incense.
(1903)　　　　　　16 pages　　　　CBA,SG

## NP 33. 'Christian Progress' or 'Faith and Discipleship'
This consists of notes on Matthew 8.
(1904)　　　　　　12 pages　　　　CBA,SG

## NP 34. The Claims of God Met! How?
The answer to the question is given in the subtitle *Substitution*. The pamphlet has comments on the book of Leviticus in general, and chapters 1-7 in particular.
(1904)　　　　　　14 pages　　　　CBA,SG

## NP 35. God and 'the Heathen'. Romans 1
(1904　　　　　　　12 pages　　　　CBA,SG

## NP 36. 'Creation's Groan' and 'the Glory That Should Follow'. Romans 8:19 - 23
(1904)　　　　　　12 pages　　　　CBA,SG

## NP 37. The 'Holy Spirit'; His Office and Work
This is more particularly an exposition of 2 Cor. 1:21,22, and of Rom. 8:16,17. It has an appendix on The Presidency of Holy Spirit in the assembly of believers, giving a reply to Brethren teaching. The appendix is extracted from a letter addressed to 'one who had once been with the Brethren' (It is in A.C. Fry's MS - CBA 7049, pp.310-314, which indicates that it is from 'Vol. 4, p.183'). The appendix was reprinted in the anthology *B.W. Newton on Ministry and Order in the Church of Christ*.
(1904)　　　　　　19 pages　　　　CBA,SG

## NP 38. 'Instead of' or 'the Lord Will Provide'. Reflections for Good Friday
This gives notes on Genesis 22 with an appendix on substitution based on 2 Cor. 5:14.
(1905)　　　　　　16 pages　　　　CBA,SG

## NP 39. Psalm 119. Christ's Daily Life Work for Us
The Psalm is viewed as a manifestation of the character of Christ. The pamphlet is mainly concerned with verses 113-120 of the Psalm, and imputation of righteousness.
(1905)　　　　　　12 pages　　　　CBA,SG

## NP 40. The 'Time of the End'. A Résumé of Prophetic Truth Translated from the French.
The French pamphlet has not been traced. Although it may represent a tract published by B.W. Newton in French, rather than notes of an address, as most of the Patmos Series, it is plain that the translation was not authorised by him. The tract consists of a summary of prophetic teaching under headings.
(1907)　　　　　　15 pages　　　　CBA,SG

| | | |
|---|---|---|
| (1911) (5th 1,000) | 15 pages | CG |

French Edition (presumably a reprinting of the original).

| | | |
|---|---|---|
| (1924) | ? | ? |

Spanish Edition

| | | |
|---|---|---|
| (1940) | ? | ? |

**NP 41. Conversion. What is it?**

This is a study in John 3. Apart from the addition of a very brief appendix (2 pages), this is identical in typography and content to the comment on the chapter that appears in NS 29 - *Studies in Parts of the Gospel of John*, which was published at about the same time. The item focusses on evangelistic method, and what follows from conversion. See also NP 42. *Manna. What is it?*

| | | |
|---|---|---|
| (1911) | 12 pages | CBA,SG |

**NP 42. Manna. What is it?**

This expounds John 6; Lk. 22; and 1 Cor. 10, in reference to communion with Christ.

This is identical in typography and content to the comment on the chapter that appears in NS 29, *Studies in Parts of the Gospel of John*, which was published at about the same time. See also NP 41. *Conversion. What is it?*

| | | |
|---|---|---|
| (1911) | 12 pages | CBA,SG |

**NP 43. 'Hades', Ephesians 4:8 and 'Mosaic Cosmogony' - or Remarks on the Fifth of the Essays and Reviews.**

The two halves of this provide a brief summary of Mr Newton's teaching, which is more fully developed in his publication *Remarks on 'Mosaic Cosmogony'....* This pamphlet deals with issues raised by geologists, and the theory of evolution.

| | | |
|---|---|---|
| (1913) | 16 pages | CBA,SG |

## TIME OF THE END SERIES

This Series was also produced in 11.5 x 9cm format by Hunt, Barnard. It commenced in 1902. It was also the work of Jane Thornton Daniels (see the introduction to this Section of the *Guide*). It seems unlikely that she prepared the last or the last two numbers, as these are not notes of Mr Newton's addresses. These last two were published at the end of her life, and after her death. The initial intention for the Series is given in a postscript to No.1, 'This rudimentary "Series" is intended to aid beginners on the study of prophecy. It comprises the "matter" of an introductory course on prophetic subjects'. The text indicates that NT 2 and NT 4 were from addresses given in 1877, and NT 5 in 1887. Therefore, the 'introductory course', if given as such by Mr Newton, would seem to consist of NT 1-4. There is a significant amount of circumstantial material in the first ten numbers. The T*ime of the End* Series deals exclusively with future prophecy, whereas the *Patmos Series* was generally concerned with doctrinal matters. However, the *Patmos Series* did have some numbers that were equally concerned with prophecy, for example NP 40, produced in 1907, which even had the title *Time of the End*.

Bound volumes of the Series, or part of it, were made in c.1905 and 1962.

**NT 1. Things that must shortly come to pass.**
The first page is headed, Things to Come. It is principally concerned with Antichrist's assault on Jerusalem.
(1902)  12 pages  CBA,SG
Second Edition
(1912?)  ?  SG

**NT 2. The Probable Course of Events up to the 'Time of the End'.**
The first page is headed, Passage of Events. It is especially concerned with the rise of Antichrist. The lecture is dated in the text as having been given in 1877.
(1902)  16 pages  CG
Second Edition  (has some corrections)
(1912)  16 pages  CBA,SG

**NT 3. 'Israel's Future' in the Earth. Isa. 24-27.**
This is an exposition of the chapters concerned, together with an Introduction on the apostasy of Israel and Christendom.
(1902)  16 pages  CBA,SG

**NT 4. Believers' Prospects or the Saints in Glory. A Millennial Picture.**
This is based on Revelation 4 and 5. There are comments on textual criticism, and on J.N. Darby's attack on *Thoughts on the Apocalypse*.
The lecture is dated in the text as having been given in 1877.
(1902)  16 pages  CBA,SG

**NT 5. 'Apostolic Succession', a Review of 'Protestant Christendom'.**

This deals with the Apostasy of Christendom. It refers to the establishment of the Anglican Archbishopric in Jerusalem, with Bishop Michael Solomon Alexander as its first incumbent.[1] From the text, we learn that the lecture was given in May 1887, presumably at the Stafford Rooms. See NS 1.

    (1903)               18 pages        CBA,SG

### NT 6. Instruction for the Church concerning 'The Kingdom of God'.

The starting point for this address is Rev. 4 & 5. It distinguishes the Kingdom introduced, and the Kingdom manifest.

    (1903)               18 pages        CBA,SG

### NT 7. 'The Last End of the Indignation' Psalm 110 and 127.

This is a straightforward exposition of the Psalms concerned. It also has a note on Daniel 11:41. The address is dated in the item as given in June 1886. It is dated in one of G.L. Silverwood-Browne's MS books as 20th Feb. 1886. See Section 10, Duplicated and Manuscript Items – C.W.H. Griffiths.

    (1903)               16 pages        CBA,SG

### NT 8. 'How to Study Prophecy' illustrated from Zech. 12 - 14.

In this Mr Newton outlines how he came to value prophetic truth. There are interesting parallels with *How B.W. Newton Learned Prophetic Truth* (NM 7). This lecture is also in a typescript book of C.T. Walrond held by SGAT (see Section 10, Duplicated and Manuscript Items), which dates the address as 22nd September 1887 at Newport IoW, from notes of Mr Bath.

    (1903)               16 pages        CBA,SG

### NT 9. 'The Little Remnant' under 'Antichrist'. Psalms 10, 16, and 18.

There is an appendix on Psalm 125:3.

    (1903)               16 pages        CBA,SG

### NT 10. The Forgiveness and Restoration of Israel. Psalms 18 and 118.

This additionally discusses the relation between the earthly and the heavenly Jerusalem. It has a note on Song of Solomon 6:10-13. In the text this is described as the culmination of a series of lectures on the restoration of Israel (NT 7-10?).

    (1903)               15 pages        CBA,SG

---

[1] See the 1904 Supplementary Note added to the Note on Rev. 11:8 in the Third Edition of *Thoughts on the Apocalypse* (pp. 213, 214), commented on in Appendix 1 of this Guide - A Comparison of the Editions of *Thoughts on the Apocalypse* for further information, and other references to him in B.W. Newton's works.

### NT 11. 'Songs of Thanksgiving'
This consists of a series of notes on the following chapters:
Exod. 15; Num. 21; Judg. 5; 2 Chr. 5; Psa. 73; Rev. 15.
    (1903/1904)        12 pages        CBA,SG

### NT 12. 'The Recompense of the Reward'. Genesis 3 and Hebrews 11
This is principally concerned with Abel.
    (1904)        12 pages        CBA,SG

### NT 13. The 'Millennium'. Creation's Groan Hushed! The Curse Removed
The first page title is Psalm 8. The Millennial Day.
    (1904)        12 pages        SG

### NT 14. 'Babylonianism'. Its Manifestation and Doom
This is an exposition of Daniel 4.
    (1906?)        11 pages        CBA,SG

### NT 15. The Ten Kingdoms. Their Government and Probable Final Re-arrangement in Accordance with Daniel 2,7, and 8
This also considers forms of Government in the light of Scripture.
    (1906?)        16 pages        CBA,SG
Revised Edition (8th Thousand).
    (c.1912)        16 pages        CG

### NT 16. Consecutive Events in connection with the 'Day of the Lord'
The first page title is The Day of the Lord. It is a summary outline of events which will immediately precede the return of the Lord.
    (1906)        16 pages        CBA,SG
'Revised Reprint' 8th 1000
    (1912)        16 pages        CG

Spanish Edition. Noted in *Watching and Waiting*, Nov. 1933, p.86
    No copies have been located

### NT 17. The 'Signs of the Times'. Matthew 24 and 25
This very briefly covers similar ground to *The Prophecy of the Lord Jesus as contained in Matthew 24 and 25, considered* (Section 3, Published Works).
    (1906?)        12 pages        CBA, SG

### NT 18. The Christian Remnant and the Jewish Remnant at 'The Time of the End'

This considers the moral and spiritual condition of faithful Christians, and elect (but unregenerate) Jews, immediately prior to the Lord's return.

This subject is also treated in *Five Letters on Events predicted as Antecedent to the Coming of the Lord* (Section 3, Published Works).

    (c.1909)        12 pages        CBA,SG

This item was reprinted in *Watching and Waiting* Oct-Dec 2013 and Jan–March 2014.

### NT 19. A Prophetic Forecast of Professing Christianity

This is an exposition of the parables of Matthew 13.

It was extracted from *Studies in Parts of the Gospel of Matthew* (NS 30).

This subject is also treated in *Prospects of the Ten Kingdoms*, and (extracted from it) in *Thoughts on the History of Professing Christianity as Given in the Parables of Matthew 13*. (Section 3, Published Works).

    (1910)        12 pages        CBA,SG

### NT 20. The Metropolis of the World - Babylon. The Metropolis of Scripture - Jerusalem

This compares and contrasts the two great cities of Scripture. It has an appendix on Daniel 8:19, "The last end of the indignation'.

    (1910)        19 pages        CBA,SG

### NT 21. Some Characteristics of the Millennial Age

This gives leading facts regarding the Millennium.

    (1910)        16 pages        CBA,SG

### (NT 22). The Final Division of the Roman Empire into Ten Kingdoms, with Map of Suggested Sub-Divisions

This is not based on Mr Newton's addresses. It was 'compiled from *European Prospects (AD 1863)*, which was published posthumously in 1910, excerpted from *Occasional Papers on Scriptural Subjects No.3* (see Section 3, B.W. Newton's Published Works).

    (1913)        16 pages        CG

Second Edition

    (1917?)       16 pages        CBA,SG

### (NT 23). Armageddon. (Reprinted from *Perilous Times*)

This is not by Mr Newton, but is the reprint of a series of articles that were first published in *Perilous Times* (November 1914 - February 1915). It reviews First World War circumstances, refers to the Kaiser, etc.

    (1917?)       19 pages        CBA,SG

## MISCELLANEOUS ITEMS NOT INTENDED FOR PUBLICATION BY MR NEWTON, BUT PUBLISHED BY OTHERS

# NM 1  Items published by W. Lancelot Holland

Walter Lancelot Holland (1852-1936) was a close associate of Mr Newton in his closing years. He published *The Monitor*, a periodical, prior to B.W. Newton's death. He later replaced it with *The Voice of Truth*, both apparently published monthly. No copies have been located. It is possible there was some Newton-related material of interest in these magazines.

He withdrew from Mr Newton shortly before his death.[1] He was, nevertheless an early contributor to *Perilous Times*. He became separated from most of Mr Newton's circle of friends in the first few years of the twentieth century, principally because of his adoption of the seventh day Sabbath. He features in a number of the manuscripts in Susan Noble's catalogue of the Fry Collection. A correspondence of 12 letters, involving A.C Fry and F.W. Wyatt, and with other papers regarding the Sabbath, was recovered by the Christian Brethren Archive in 2011. G.H. Fromow wrote a kindly obituary of him in *Watching and Waiting* when he died in 1936 aged 84 years. A copy of an engraving of him is reproduced in *A Pictorial Memoir of Benjamin Wills Newton* – the supplement to this Guide. See the Advertisement at the end of this volume.

### NM 1.1  The Broad Church
Comment that Mr Newton made whilst preaching on Hebrews 2:15, from a sermon taken down in shorthand in 1856.
The extract amounts to one paragraph.
It is recorded in *The 'Archbishop of Canterbury' and 'Modern' Christianity* (1898), pp.110, 111.

### NM 1.2  Letter on the Person of the Lord
W.L. Holland published extracts from a letter that he had received from B.W. Newton 'some two years ago'. It replies to Brethren attacks on Mr Newton's doctrine regarding the Suretyship of Christ and distinguishes Christ's circumstantial and personal position before God. It runs to three pages, and is probably Mr Newton's last recorded statement on the subject.
Published in *The Archbishop of Canterbury and Modern Christianity* (1898), in a section on 'The Holy Person of Our Lord Jesus Christ', between pages 195 and 202.

### NM 1.3  Thoughts on the Lord's Prayer
Published in *The Voice of Truth* (Ed. W.L. Holland), No.3. 1900 (Information from *Perilous Times* Sept. 1900 p.2). The author of this *Guide* would be pleased to hear of any surviving copies.
This item may possibly have been reproduced in NP 30 – *The Disciples' Prayer*.

---

[1] Two letters regarding W.L. Holland's withdrawal from B.W. Newton and his joining Frank White, dated 27th February 1899, and March 1899. The second letter gives B.W. Newton's reaction and comment on W.L. Holland's statements (CBA 7187(7), and 7187(10); Further biographical material regarding W.L. Holland is given in *The Gospel Magazine*, May 1896, p.305 ff. An engraving of him from the *Gospel Magazine* is reproduced in *A Pictorial Memoir of Benjamin Wills Newton* – the supplement to this Guide. See the Advertisement at the end of this volume.

# NM 2 <u>Gleanings Series</u>

These three booklets were produced Hunt, Barnard in the same 11.5 x 9cm format as the Patmos, and the Time of the End Series. They were prepared for publication by Jane Thornton Daniels (see the introduction to this Section of the *Guide*).

### NM 2.1 'Gleanings' in 1 and 2 Peter (No 1)

This consists of comments on 1 Peter 4 prefaced by brief notes on 1 Peter 3. There are also notes on 2 Peter 1:1-11 in the publication.
 (1903)   Hunt, Barnard   34 pages SG

### NM 2.2 'Gleanings' in the 'Book of Numbers' (No 2)

The comments in this are on chapters 1-4,6,7,19, and 21.
An appendix has thoughts on the blood of Christ.
 (1903)   Hunt, Barnard   30 pages SG

### NM 2.3 'Gleanings' in the 'Book of Exodus' (No 3)

This has notes on chapters 2-4,12,17,18, and on chapters 32 and 33. The notes on chapters 32 and 33 are similar to NP 9, which was preached from this passage on a Christmas day. It must surely have been an account of the same address by a different note taker.
 (1903)   Hunt, Barnard   52 pages SG

# NM 3 <u>Lectures on the Epistle to the Romans</u>

This book was prepared on the basis of 'very full notes' of lectures delivered by Mr Newton between 1854 and 1887. The notes were therefore up to 64 years old at the date of publication, and spanned 33 years of Mr Newton's teaching ministry. The book is a remarkable attempt to produce a substantial commentary from notes made by Mr Newton's hearers, but the exposition is sometimes uneven in its treatment of passages, and sometimes gives a two-fold exposition of a single passage.

CBA 7187(36) indicates that F.W. Wyatt was responsible for preparing the notes for publication. This is confirmed by a letter from A.C. Fry to F.W. Wyatt dated 4th April 1918, 'Mr Walrond tells me it is progressing. What a lot of work it has made for you!!'.[1]

A letter of Mr Newton, reprinted from *The Record* of 2nd November 1874, regarding statements of Pearsall Smith, is included at the end of the volume. See Section 6, B.W. Newton's Letters and Articles Published in Periodicals; and *Modern Doctrines Respecting Sinlessness, Considered* (1873), and *Remarks on R. Pearsall Smith's Edition of Hymns Selected from Those of the Late F.W. Faber...* (1874) in Section 3, B.W. Newton's Published Works.

 First Edition
   October 1918  C.M. Tucker, London  v + 529 pages  EL,SG

---

[1] One of the F.W. Wyatt letters held by C.W.H. Griffiths

Second Edition (photographic reprint of First Edition)
  [2015]           SGAT, Chelmsford          v + 529 pages        SG

'A new binding up' was carried out in July 1939 (*Watching and Waiting*, July 1939)

# NM 4 <u>Items compiled by Frank Kennedy</u>

Frank Kennedy (1858-1933) was a former society entertainer who was converted in the Torrey and Alexander Mission of 1905. He was afterwards led to a position of Biblical separation, greatly valuing Mr Newton's works. The story of his conversion is told in *The Mighty God and a Sinner*, first published in *Perilous Times* and later as a book by Hunt, Barnard.

### NM 4.1 The 'Bethany' Series No.1. 'Jesus, the Light Contrasted with Darkness in the First Five Chapters of the Gospel of John'
This was 'compiled from an address by B.W. Newton'.
  (1922/3)       Hunt, Barnard          11.5 x 9cm        24 pages        SG

### NM 4.2 The 'Bethany' Series No.2 'The Word of Jesus and the Voice of the Son of God'
This was 'compiled from an address by B.W. Newton'. The subject of the address was John 5:24-29.
  (1925)         Hunt, Barnard          11.5 x 9cm        31 pages        SG

### ~~[Bethany Series No.3] 'The Whole Family' Ephesians 3:15
This appears on some publisher's lists as *Bethany Series No.3*, although this is not indicated in the publication. It was not compiled by Frank Kennedy, but by 'LB' [Louisa A Balch? (1876-1959)]. This does not consist of notes of an address by Mr Newton, but is rather a compilation from his published works (see Section 3, B.W. Newton's Published Works).

### NM 4.3 Imputed Obedience
This was a tract published and circulated 'free of charge' by Frank Kennedy. It was compiled 'from a report of an address by B.W. Newton'. It was originally produced in 1930. No copies have been located, but it was reprinted in *Watching and Waiting* Jan/March 1947 (pp.58,59).

### NM 4.4 The Baptism of the Holy Spirit
This was compiled from notes of an address given by Mr Newton in 1887. It was circulated by Frank Kennedy to counter teaching current in his day on the Baptism of the Spirit.
It appears to have run to three editions, the third was enlarged with extracts from *Doctrine of Scripture Respecting Baptism, Briefly Considered*, and 'another of his works which he published privately' [*Remarks on R. Pearsall Smith's Edition of Hymns Selected from Those of the Late F.W. Faber*, p.104].
  (1930)            ?                    ?                 ?               ?

Section 8 - Published notes of addresses, and posthumous quotations

Second Edition
  ?                        ?                              ?                ?              ?
Third Edition, 'enlarged'
  (1934)                J. Tamblyn (printer)        10 x 12.5cm      4 pages      CBA,SG

# NM 5 Items published in *Perilous Times*

The 4 page monthly periodical *'Perilous Times', or Wayside Notes for 'Strangers and Pilgrims'* (*2 Timothy 3:1; Hebrews 11:13; 1 Peter 2:11*) began publication in 1899, the year of Mr Newton's death. It was promoted by Mr Newton's circle of friends to continue his testimony to various aspects of truth. For the first 16 years it was co-edited by John Cox, jun., and G.T. Hunt (of the printers Hunt, Barnard, Aylesbury). Following the death of John Cox, jun. in 1915[1] the editorial control passed solely to G.T. Hunt. In 1919 the paper was superseded by *Watching and Waiting - Light for Perilous Times* and was then enlarged to 8 pages. Mr Newton is frequently quoted in its pages. Only those portions that are clearly not from his published works are noted below.

### NM 5.1 Counsels to Converts

A letter sent by Mr Newton on 24th June 1883.
Published in *Perilous Times*, Vol. 1 (1899-1906) July 1905, p.1
It was subsequently published by Hunt, Barnard as a tract, *Counsels to Converts*.
    c.1905;   2 pages; CG.

### NM 5.2 Letter on Hyper-Calvinism

The letter is believed to be CBA 7031a, dated 1888 in the Fry Collection of the Christian Brethren Archive at Manchester. The letter is to a friend troubled by hyper-Calvinism. In it Mr Newton refers to perplexity about hyper-Calvinism as the first trial of his Christian life. See the note on the letter in Section 9, B.W. Newton's Correspondence, and in reference to his letter to his mother dated 30th December 1827.
    Published in *Perilous Times*, June and July 1906 Vol. 2 (1906-13), p.14 and p.22 under the title, Divine Sovereignty and Human Responsibility.

### NM 5.3 Church Principles

*Perilous Times* introduces this as follows: 'This valuable paper of Church principles was written by the late Mr B.W. Newton more than fifty years ago, but has not been previously printed'. It was written in 1846.
It is recorded MS Book 1, pp.38 ff. (held by Tom Chantry), F.W. Wyatt makes the following comments, dated 1905. 'The above MS BWN wished me to copy for myself, some where in 1885, as he did not intend to print it, but to let it remain in MS. He said that its publication as things now are (or then were) would do harm. Some years afterwards he told me how troubled he was

---

[1] Died March 26th 1915, aged 86. Obituary *Perilous Times*, April 1915, p.112. 'For many years he laboured earnestly at Bayswater with Mr Newton'. The funeral service was led by his nephew, the children's evangelist R. Hudson Pope.

losing the MS, having lent it to a Mr Anstey who unwarrantably took it to Canada. I offered to copy the above: I never saw or heard of the original being returned'.

It is also copied in CBA 7060 –'On Ministry.

The paper sets out Mr Newton's position on ministry, order, and gift in the Church. It is quoted extensively in *B.W. Newton on Ministry and Order in the Church of Christ*, an anthology of Mr Newton's works.

Published in *Perilous Times*, Vol. 2 (1906-13), pp.18-20;39,40;61,62;69-71;91,92;93,94;107.

### NM 5.4 England and the Ten Kingdoms

Brief quotation. 'Mr Newton used to say that...'

Quoted in *Perilous Times*, Vol. 2 (1906-1913), p.119.

## NM 6 Items published in *Watching and Waiting*

As noted in NM 5 above, *Watching and Waiting: Light for 'Perilous Times'* was initially an enlargement of *Perilous Times*. Over time it became the magazine of the Sovereign Grace Advent Testimony, most obviously when the secretary of the SGAT, George H. Fromow, became editor of *Watching and Waiting* in 1931. By this time the SGAT had widened its base to include on its platform those from a variety of backgrounds (other than just 'the Strict Baptist community'), united in their 'like precious faith', and, in particular, their simple futurist view of Biblical prophecy and appreciation of the works of Mr Newton[1]. George H. Fromow continued as editor of *Watching and Waiting* until his death in 1974. As with *Perilous Times*, Mr Newton is frequently quoted. It would be an enormous task of little obvious value to try to identify all the citations made in it from his published works. This Section of the *Guide* records here those quotations of material attributed to Mr Newton not published elsewhere. Section 3, B.W. Newton's Published Works notes reprints in *Watching and Waiting* of items that have become scarce.

### NM 6.1 The World in Crisis

A short quotation of one paragraph, introduced by the statement 'Mr Newton, speaking many years ago, uttered the following words...'

Published in *Watching and Waiting* December 1921, p.98.

### NM 6.2 Notes of an address on Zechariah 11

Published in *Watching and Waiting* April and June 1924 (p.9, and pp.23-26).

### NM 6.3 Notes on Ezekiel

These were 'from typescript notes, believed to be of addresses by B.W. Newton'. The notes were evidently published in outline only, as the issue which announces their proposed publication (December 1936) says 'these are extensive and may run through a whole year', and yet they appeared in only four issues: January, February, March, and May 1937 (pp.109-110; 116,117; 126,127;142,143).

---

[1] For further notes on the SGAT see Section 2, Libraries and Collections, The Sovereign Grace Advent Testimony.

### NM 6.4 Acceptance, Worship and Service. Thoughts on Hebrews 1-8
'Believed to be an address by B.W. Newton reported by F.W. Wyatt, hitherto unpublished'.
   Published in *Watching and Waiting* January 1940 (p.110).

### NM 6.5 A letter on the objects of a believer's life
This is a brief letter dated 2nd October 1890 from the Isle of Wight.
   Published in *Watching and Waiting* January/February 1942 (pp.15,16). G.L. Silverwood-Browne transcribed the letter, presumably from material lent to him by A.C. Fry on 25th December 1948 (MS book held by CG. Noted in Section 10, Duplicated and Manuscript Items).

### NM 6.6 Reminiscence of an exhortation from Revelation 12
Related by Mr W.H. Stirling, this is a brief reference to Mr Newton's perception of the testimony needed in the last days, as of the 'Glorious Woman' of Revelation 12.
   Published in *Watching and Waiting* October-December 1944 (pp.138-139).

### NM 6.7 A Prayer of Mr Newton
Published in Watching and Waiting July-September 1945 (p.162).
   Later published in Teachers of the Faith and Future by G.H. Fromow (NM 8).

### NM 6.8 Conversation on Romans 5:13 and 14
A conversation in Tunbridge Wells recounted by W.H. Stirling.
   Published in *Watching and Waiting* October-December 1947 (pp.128,129).

### NM 6.9 Notes on Psalm 73
'Notes of an exposition given in [sic] the Isle of Wight, March 31st 1872'.
   Published in *Watching and Waiting* April-June 1948 (pp.159-162).

### NM 6.10 An Introduction to the Book of Hebrews
'Not before published', 'slightly abbreviated and amended'.
The notes are dated 24th September 1851.
   Published in *Watching and Waiting* May-June 1972, and July-August 1972 (pp.231-233; 241-244).

### NM 6.11 Two Prayers by B.W. Newton
SGAT Annual Report 1945, back page. Bound up in volumes of *Watching and Waiting* magazines for that year.

## NM 7 How B.W. Newton Learned Prophetic Truth

This was first published in *Watching and Waiting* of March-April 1953. It was then produced as a separate tract. Later still, it was reprinted in G.H. Fromow's *Teachers of the Faith and Future*. It was published a second time in *Watching and Waiting* April-June 1991, pp.146-151. The narrative was taken from a manuscript entitled 'Draft or Protocol of a Tract for Publication'. The manuscript is in the Fry Collection of the Christian Brethren Archive at the John Ryland Library of Manchester University. It is in F.W. Wyatt's large manuscript book No 3, p.1 (CBA 7050). It is also reproduced in A.C. Fry's MS pp.84-94 (CBA 7049).

This item highlights Romans 11, Matthew 24, Zechariah 12 and 14, and the Book of Daniel as having a major influence upon him. Note the prominence of these in his earliest published works, and Compare NT 8.

 (c.1953)  SGAT, London  16 pages  BIOLA,CBA,SG

## NM 8 Items Published by G.H. Fromow in *Teachers of the Faith and Future*

See Appendix 3, A Select Publications List for a brief comment on the book. The items noted here are those reprinted in the book that do not appear to be from his published works.

First Edition
 1959  SGAT, London  160 pages  SG

Second Edition
 1969  SGAT, London  198 pages  CBA,EL,SG

### NM 8.1 A letter to Mr Newton's mother

This was sent from Exeter College, Oxford, and is dated 30th December 1827.

It gives an account of his conversion. It is also contained in the Fry Manuscript (CBA 7049). It is on pages 1-3 of the Second Edition of *Teachers of the Faith and Future*. See further notes in the Correspondence section of this *Guide*.

### NM 8.2 An extract from a letter to Mr Newton's mother

This is dated 8th of February 1851, and recounts the opening to ministerial labours that he had been given in London.

It is on pages 8 and 9 of the Second Edition. See the note in Section 9, B.W. Newton's Correspondence.

### NM 8.3 A letter to Rev. John Cox, sen. regarding the funeral of his only child

See Section 9, B.W. Newton's Correspondence. The letter is from Bayswater, and is dated simply '1855'. The burial took place on 22nd September 1855.

It is on pages 13 and 14 of the Second Edition. The letter copied by F.W. Wyatt was lost from the Fry Collection, but has now been recovered.

### NM 8.4 A poem by Mr Newton

This consists of two verses on the Lord's return. These are 'the only verses attributed to B.W. Newton'.[1] They were taken from the record of his life in Plymouth Library, which was destroyed during the Second World War.

It is on p.14 of the Second Edition.

### ~ 'How B.W. Newton Learned Prophetic Truth'

See NM 7.

This forms chapter three of the Second Edition (pp.15-22).

### NM 8.5 Prayers of Mr Newton

There are three prayers of Mr Newton recorded on pages 156-157 of the Second Edition. The first and third are reprinted from the 'Report of the 26th year of Witness' of the SGAT which is dated 17th February 1945 (p.6). The second is reprinted from *Watching and Waiting* July-September 1945 (p.162).

### NM 8.6 The Postscript of a letter to Mr Newton's mother

This is dated 23rd December 1827, and gives a brief exposition of Romans 1-3. The letter does not appear to be in the Fry Collection of the Christian Brethren Archive at Manchester. This postscript forms chapter 17 of the Second Edition. It is recorded on pp.106,107. See note in Section 9, B.W. Newton's Correspondence.

### NM 8.7 Christ and his Church as related to the Nations

This is from notes of an address given on March 21st 1855 on Revelation 6. The occasion was the day of humiliation for the Crimean War. This forms chapter 20 of the book, and is found on pages 114-122 of the Second Edition.

### NM 8.8 Letter to Mr I. Arnold Lake

This is dated June 1st 1885, and is from Orpington, Kent.

It gives a valuable overview of Mr Newton's relationship to the Brethren Movement.

It is on pages 162-164 of the Second Edition. For more detail, see the note in Section 9, B.W. Newton's Correspondence.

### NM 8.9 The parting charge of Mr Newton to his friends

This was a last message from him to his circle of friends. It is dated 21st May 1899. This was circulated in printed form after his death. A copy of this is now in the Christian Brethren Archive at Manchester University.

It is on p.164 of the Second Edition. It quotes from an 'In Memoriam' card printed at the time of his death. See Section 9, B.W. Newton's Correspondence for that date. A copy of this is included

---

[1] Some verses of non-religious verses of poetry by him are recorded in MS Book 2, p.157 – See reference in Section 10 Duplicated and MS items, G Items held by Tom Chantry, MS Book 2.

in *A Pictorial Memoir of Benjamin Wills Newton* – the supplement to this Guide. See the Advertisement at the end of this volume..

## NM 9 Letters relating to the Society of Friends [Quakers], quoted by Timothy C.F. Stunt in 'Early Brethren and the Society of Friends' (Christian Brethren Research Fellowship 1970).[1]

These letters are drawn from the Fry Collection held in the Christian Brethren Archive of the John Ryland Library at the University of Manchester. Extracts of the letters are quoted to meet the author's object. The following are noted:

| | | |
|---|---|---|
| 23rd April 1827 | To his mother | page 8 |
| 7th October 1827 | To his mother | page 8 |
| 30th December 1827 | To his mother | page 8 |
| 13th January 1828 | To his mother | page 8 |
| 22nd April 1830 | To his mother | page 10 |
| April 1837 | To his mother | pages 14-18 |

## NM 10 What is the Pearl Testimony? by A.C. Fry

Alfred C. Fry produced this duplicated booklet. This pamphlet was reprinted in *Watching and Waiting* July-September 1949, pp.266-267.

It consists mainly of extracts from the writings of B.W. Newton. It set out his distinctive view of the Parables of Matthew 13 - that they represent a prophetic history of the Church. B.W. Newton expected the sixth and final parable (of the Pearl) to be 'fulfilled' shortly before the return of the Lord. He perceived the 'pearl' as a believing, Jewish testimony to arise in Jerusalem before the end, which will have an evangelistic and aggressively Christian character. He often referred to this in his writings. Reference is also made to it in surviving manuscript notes of his addresses. See, in particular, the reference in the letter of F.W. Wyatt to Miss Martin, transcribed in Appendix 1, Comparison of Editions of Thoughts on The Apocalypse. In that F.W. Wyatt refers to A.C. Fry, and to B.W. Newton's changed view of 'the Manchild' in Rev. 7, which has a bearing upon this Pearl Testimony teaching.

                                                        12 pages        CBA

## NM 11 Quotations by A.J.W. Dalzell in *Atonement is not Reconciliation* (1900).

### NM 11.1 Note on Faith

This is a two page item (pages 11-13) according to the 'Addenda and Corrigenda' this was 'adapted from an unpublished MS. dictated by B.W. Newton'.

---

[1] This research item has been republished with some amendments as Chapters 1 and 2 of *The Elusive Quest of the Spiritual Malcontent: Some Early Nineteenth-Century Ecclesiastical Mavericks*, by T.C.F. Stunt., 2015.

**NM 11.2 Letter regarding Spiritualism**

A five line quotation of a letter from B.W. Newton to Dr Dalzell (page 147). Mr Newton evidently urged Christians to refrain from the use of the phonograph. The comment was made in the context of the growth of spiritualism.[1]

---

[1] Similar comments are made in CBA 7064, p132, 1st March 1898.

## SUBJECT INDEX OF SECTION 8 ITEMS

**Biblical Subjects**

| | |
|---|---|
| Cherubim & seraphim | NS 1 |
| Eden, River of | NS 1 |
| Hades | NS 2,43 |
| Kingdom of God | NS 18; NT 6 |
| Tabernacle | NP 22 |

**Biographical of Mr Newton**

| | |
|---|---|
| 'The Brethren' | NM 8.8,9,10 |
| J.N. Darby | NT 4 |
| Conversion of | NM 8.1 |
| Death of his child | NM 8.3 |
| Generally | NM 9,10 |
| London ministry | NM 8.2 |
| Poem by | NM 8.4 |
| Parting charge | NM 8.9 |
| Prayers of | NM 6.7,8.5 |
| Prophecy, how learned | NT 8; NM 7; NS 23(p.20) |
| 'Thoughts on the Apocalypse' | NT 4 |

**Christian living**

| | |
|---|---|
| | NS 9,22; NP2,4,6,33; NM 5.1,6.5 |
| Guidance | NP 3 |
| Practical gifts | NS 15 |

**Church Order**

| | |
|---|---|
| Baptism | NS 1; NP 18 |
| 'Broad Church' | NM 1.1 |
| 'Christian Sabbath' | NP 24 |
| Church principles | NM 5.3 |
| Laying on of hands | NS 3 |
| 'Presidency of the Spirit' | NP 37 |
| Table of the Lord | NP 20,42 |

**Dated Messages, letters etc.**

| | |
|---|---|
| 1827 | NM 8.1,8.6,10 |
| 1828 | NM 10 |
| 1830 | NM 10 |
| 1837 | NM 10 |
| 1851 | NM 6.9; 8.2 |
| 1854-1887 | NM 3 |
| 1855 | NM 8.3; 8.7 |
| 1856 | NM 1.1; 5.3? |
| 1861 | NP 22 |
| c.1869 | NM 9 |
| 1870 | NS 23,32 |
| 1872 | NM 6.9 |
| 1876 | NS 4,5,19 |
| 1877 | NT 2,4 |
| 1883 | NM 5.1 |
| 1885 | NM 8.8 |
| 1886 | NS 23 32; NS 32,48,62; NT 7,8 |
| 1887 | NS 1, NT 5; NM 4.4 |
| 1888 | NS 1; NM 5.2 |
| 1889 | NS 2,32 |
| 1890 | NM 6.5 |
| 1898 | NM 1.2 |
| 1899 | NM 8.9 |

**Doctrine**

| | |
|---|---|
| Atonement | NS 1; NP 14,16, |
| Baptism of the Spirit | NM 4.4 |
| Blood of Christ | NP 31; NM 2.2 |
| Conversion | NP 41 |
| Creation | NP 43 |
| Election | NP 28 |
| Faith | NM 11.1 |
| Federal Headship | NP 26 |
| Holy Spirit | NP 37 |
| Hyper-Calvinism | NM 5.2 |
| Imputed obedience | NM 4.3 |
| Person of the Lord | NM 1.2,8 |
| Substitution | NP 34,38 |
| Sufferings of Christ | NS 41 |
| Textual criticism | NT 4 |

**Government & politics**

| | |
|---|---|
| Bradlaugh | NS 2,23 |
| Crimean War | NM 8.7 |
| Europe | NS 23 |
| Forms of Government | NT 15 |
| Gladstone | NS 23 |
| Parliamentary Oaths | NS 2 |
| Permissive Society | NS 19 |

**People and Places**

| | |
|---|---|
| Bradlaugh | NS 2,23 |
| Darby, J.N. | NT 4 |
| Gladstone | NS 23 |
| Isle of Wight | NM 6.5; 6.9 |
| Mildmay | NS 4,5,19 |
| Newman, Francis | NS 23 |
| Newport, I of W | NS 2,3 |
| Stafford Rooms | NS 1 |

**Prophecy**

| | |
|---|---|
| Antichrist | NS 4,23; NT 1,9 |
| Babylon | NS 4; NT 20 |
| Babylonianism | NT 14 |
| Christendom | NS 5; NP 7,9; NT 3,5,19 |
| Christian remnant | NT 18 |
| Day of the Lord | NT 16 |
| Egypt etc. | NS 20 |
| Future events | NT 2,16 |
| How to study prophecy | NT 8; NM 7 |
| Human progress | NP 22 |
| Israel | NS 20; NT 3,9,10,18 |
| Jerusalem | NS 23; NT 1,10,20 |
| Millennium | NT 4,13,21 |
| Outline of prophecy | NS 10; NP 40; NT 1 |
| 'Pearl Testimony' | NS 3; NM 11 |
| Ten Kingdoms | NT 15; NM 5.4 |
| Time of the End | NP 40; NT 7, NM 6.6 |

# SCRIPTURE INDEX OF SECTION 8 ITEMS

## Genesis
| | |
|---|---|
| 1-4 | NS 3 |
| 1-32 | NS 27 |
| 3 | NT 12 |
| 22 | NP 38 |

## Exodus
| | |
|---|---|
| generally | NP 6 |
| 2-4 | NM 2.3 |
| 12 | NP 31; NM 2.3 |
| 15 | NT 11 |
| 17,18 | NM 2.3 |
| 32; 33:11 | NP 9; NM 2.3 |

## Leviticus
| | |
|---|---|
| 1-7 | NP 34 |
| 1-16 | NS 25 |
| 16 | NS 3; NP 31 |
| 19:27 | NS 3 |
| 23 | NS 25 |
| 27,28 | NP 3 |

## Numbers
| | |
|---|---|
| 1-4 | NM 2.2 |
| 6,7 | NM 2.2 |
| 19 | NP 31; NM 2.2 |
| 21 | NT 11; NM 2.2 |

## Judges
| | |
|---|---|
| 5 | NT 11 |

## 2 Chronicles
| | |
|---|---|
| 5 | NT 11 |
| 16-20 | NS 26 |
| 30 | NS 26 |
| 34 | NS 26 |

## Nehemiah
| | |
|---|---|
| generally | NS 15 (NS 40) |

## Job
| | |
|---|---|
| generally | NS 38 |

## Psalms
| | |
|---|---|
| most | NS 32 |
| 1-8 | NP 23 |
| 4:1 | NS 3 |
| 8 | NT 13 |
| 10 | NT 9 |
| 11 | NS 1 |
| 16 | NT 9 |
| 18 | NT 9,10 |
| 73 | NT 11; NM 6.9 |
| 84 | NS 22 |
| 94 | NS 1 |
| 110 | NT 7 |
| 118 | NT 10 |
| 119 | NP 39 |
| 125:3 | NT 9 |
| 127 | NT 7 |

## Ecclesiastes
| | |
|---|---|
| 1 | NS 22 |

## Song of Solomon
| | |
|---|---|
| most | NS 9,40 |
| 6:10-13 | NT 10 |

## Isaiah
| | |
|---|---|
| some | NS 39 |
| 8 | NS 23 |
| 9-12 | NS 2 |
| 10 | NS 23 |
| 13,14 | NS 4 |
| 22 | NS 3 |
| 24-27 | NT 3 |
| 25:7 | NS 23 |
| 29:11,12 | NS 23 |
| 30:9-14 | NS 1 |

## Isaiah (continued)
| | |
|---|---|
| 38-40 | NS 26 |
| 40-49 | NS 42 |
| 53 | NP 1 |
| 59-61 | NS 42 |

## Jeremiah
| | |
|---|---|
| 20 | NS 22 |

## Ezekiel
| | |
|---|---|
| all | NM 6.3 |
| 30:15 | NS 1 |

## Daniel
| | |
|---|---|
| generally | NS 12; NM 7 |
| 2 | NT 15 |
| 4 | NT 14 |
| 7 | NT 15 |
| 8 | NT 15 |
| 8:19 | NT 20 |
| 9:27 | NS 23 |
| 11 | NS 4 |
| 11:41 | NT 7 |
| 12:2 | NS 2 |

## Hosea
| | |
|---|---|
| 2:15 | NS 2 |

## Jonah
| | |
|---|---|
| generally | NS 38 |

## Habakkuk
| | |
|---|---|
| all | NP 21 |
| generally | NP 22 |

## Zechariah
| | |
|---|---|
| 11 | NM 6.2 |
| 12-14 | NT 8; NM 7 |
| 13:1-5 | NS 2 |

## Matthew
| | |
|---|---|
| most | NS 30 |
| 1,2 | NS 16 |
| 3 | NS 17 |
| 5 | NS 24 |
| 6:9-13 | NP 30; NM 1.3 |
| 8 | NP 33 |
| 10:34 | NS 2 |
| 13 | NT 19; NM 11 |
| 13:45 | NS 3 |
| 16:26 | NS 3 |
| 24 | NS 2,5; NM 7 |
| 24,25 | NT 17 |
| 25 | NP 10 |

## Luke
| | |
|---|---|
| 17:21 | NS 1 |
| 22 | NP 42 |

## John
| | |
|---|---|
| 1-5 | NM 4.1 |
| 3 | NS 29; NP 41 |
| 5:24-29 | NM 4.2 |
| 5,6 | NS 29 |
| 6 | NP 42 |
| 9,10 | NS 29 |
| 13 | NP 31 |
| 13-17 | NS 29 |
| 19-21 | NS 29 |

## Acts
| | |
|---|---|
| 8:26-40 | NP 1 |

## Romans
| | |
|---|---|
| all | NS 11; NM 3 |
| 1 | NP 35 |
| 1-3 | NM 8.6 |
| 1-4 | NP 25 |
| 4:4 | NM 11.1 |
| 5 | NP 26 |
| 5:13,14 | NM 6.8 |
| 6 8 | NP 27 |

## Romans (continued)

| | |
|---|---|
| 8:16,17 | NP 37 |
| 8:19-23 | NP 36 |
| 9-11 | NP 28 |
| 11 | NP 7; NM 7 |
| 11:6 | NM 11.1 |
| 12-14 | NP 24 |
| 15-16 | NP 29 |

## 1 Corinthians

| | |
|---|---|
| all exc. 6-9 | NS 28 |
| 1:17-21 | NP 16 |
| 3 | NS 2; NP 4 |
| 6:1-11 | NP 2 |
| 10 | NP 42 |
| 10:16-21 | NP 20 |
| 15 | NP 5 |

## 2 Corinthians

| | |
|---|---|
| all exc. 10 | NS 31 |
| 1:20 | NS 3 |
| 1:21,22 | NP 37 |
| 5:14 | NS 3; NP 38 |
| 6 | NS 22 |
| 8:5 | NS 2 |

## Galatians

| | |
|---|---|
| 1:13 | NS 3 |
| 2-4 | NS 21 |

## Ephesians

| | |
|---|---|
| all | NS 14 |
| 2:8 | NM 11.1 |
| 4:8 | NP 43 |

## Philippians

| | |
|---|---|
| generally | NS 36 |
| 1:29, 29 | NM 11.1 |

## 1 Timothy

| | |
|---|---|
| all | NS 37 |

## 1 Timothy (continued)

| | |
|---|---|
| 2:14 | NS 2 |
| 3:16 | NS 3 |

## 2 Timothy

| | |
|---|---|
| all | NS 37 |

## Philemon

| | |
|---|---|
| generally | NS 38 |

## Hebrews

| | |
|---|---|
| all | NS 35 |
| generally | NM 6.10 |
| 1-8 | NM 6.4 |
| 2:15 | NM 1.1 |
| 10 | NP 14 |
| 10:8 | NS 3 |
| 11 | NT 12 |

## James

| | |
|---|---|
| all | NS 34 |

## 1 Peter

| | |
|---|---|
| 3,4 | NM 2.1 |

## 2 Peter

| | |
|---|---|
| 1:1-11 | NM 2.2 |

## 1 John

| | |
|---|---|
| all | NS 33 |

## 2 John

| | |
|---|---|
| all | NS 33 |

## 3 John

| | |
|---|---|
| all | NS 33 |

## Jude

| | |
|---|---|
| generally | NS 3 |

## Revelation

| | |
|---|---|
| generally | NS 12 |
| 1:1 | NS 3 |
| 2,3 | NP 8,11,12,13,15,17,19 |
| 4,5 | NT 4,6 |
| 6 | NM 8.7 |
| 12 | NM 6.6; NM 11 |
| 15 | NT 11 |

# SECTION 9

## B.W. NEWTON CORRESPONDENCE

# B.W. NEWTON CORRESPONDENCE

1. This section is a chronological listing, mainly of correspondence to and from B.W. Newton.

2. Some letters between third parties have been recorded where these are of particular interest or relevance. Where this has been done, the summary of their contents draws attention to matters concerning him, rather than other extraneous content.

3. There are more than 500 letters directly relevant to B.W. Newton still extant, most of them held at the Christian Brethren Archive.[1]

4. Almost all of the letters recorded here are unpublished, and were not intended for publication.

5. Undated published letters that are not known in manuscript form (for example Newton's *Five Letters...*) are not recorded here, but are recorded in Section 3, B.W. Newton's Published Works.

6. Some letters recorded here have not been located. These have been identified from three main sources.

    a) T.C.F. Stunt made a list of letters, copies of letters, and some other items in 1962 (CBA 6998), prior to their loss from the Collection.[2] He made Xerox copies of a few of these items.

    b) A notebook held at the Christian Brethren Archive has an index of letters (CBA 7002).

    c) The 'Rough Notes' (a random collection of lists and calendars used by F.W. Wyatt and others to sort the correspondence) also provide some unique information. These are now held at the Christian Brethren Archive. See Section 10, Duplicated and Manuscript Items. These notes are catalogued in the CBA as FRY/1/2/1 – FRY/1/2/15, with a résumé prepared by C.W.H. Griffiths.

7. Some of the items in the Fry Collection are not in B.W. Newton's handwriting, but are copies by others or even (in the case of 'The Fry Manuscript', CBA 7049) copies of copies. However, there can be little doubt of the precision and faithfulness with which F.W. Wyatt, A.C. Fry, and others, recorded the words of their mentor, even when they may have reflected unfavourably upon him.

8. Mr Newton made handwritten copies of letters that he sent. There is therefore, at times, some uncertainty whether a letter was actually sent - see, for example, the letter to C. McAdam, written sometime after April 1845.

9. CBA 7181 consists of 123 letters and miscellaneous envelopes. It takes up 33 pages in Susan Noble's summary of the Collection. It is composed of letters sent by S.P. Tregelles and Mrs S.A. Tregelles[3]. The letters mainly concern Tregelles's circumstances, and his work of translation. We have restricted comment on these to matters relevant to B.W. Newton's circumstances or doctrine. Some of the originals have been lost. A manuscript book of 106 of the copied letters by F.W. Wyatt was recovered by the CBA in July 2011 (FRY/1/1/4). A photocopy of this is also held by the SGAT.

---

[1] Perhaps some of the credit for this remarkable legacy is attributable to the fact that the 1871 Census records that Mr Newton had a 'letter sorter' living at his address – presumably employed by him!

[2] See Section 10, Duplicated and Manuscript Items for an explanation of this loss. Most of the original copies have now been recovered, as noted at each letter

[3] S.P. Tregelles's wife, née Sarah Anna Prideaux (1807-1884, who was also his cousin).

10. We have added notes of certain key events and records relating to the personal life of Mr Newton (births deaths, etc), and have included Census data, to give context. Perhaps a yet more insightful biographical timeline could be achieved by integrating the dates of his published works and other contextual information, but that is beyond the scope of this *Guide*.

11. We have varied the font size and arrangement of text to highlight the items from, to, and concerning, B.W. Newton.

## Section 9 – B.W. Newton Correspondence

> **B.W. Newton was born 12th December 1807**[1]

> 25th March 1815      **From Mrs Amy Toulmin** [Amy J.T. Toulmin's mother]
>                                                                                                         Birmingham
>
> **To Mrs Anna Newton** [Mr Newton's mother]
> Regarding Mr and Mrs Toulmin's wish that she should stay with them in Birmingham for a year before 'Bene' is settled in school. Amy [J. Toulmin] (one year old), the Corn Laws, and Napoleon.
> F.W. Wyatt's copy MS Book 2 (TC) p.122. Copied in A.C. Fry's MS (CBA 7049), pp.18-21.

July 1823                   **From B.W. Newton's mother**      Location not given
         To B.W. Newton [at school]    c/o Rev. T[homas] Byrth, Diptford Parsonage,
                                                                                                    near South Brent, Devon
On the death of Amy Toulmin's mother[2]. Postscript regarding various domestic matters.
Copy CBA 7049, pp.50-55.

16th October 1825         From B.W. Newton           Exeter College
     **To his mother**
Regarding his journey to Oxford, College Rooms, and financial matters.
Original letter - TC. Listed in CBA 6998: F.W. Wyatt's copy MS Book 2 (TC), pp.10-12: A.C. Fry's secondary copy CBA 7049, pp.69-72.

> 11th December 1825   **From William Dalby**          Exeter College
>      **To Mrs [Anna] Newton**
> Assuring her of B.W. Newton's good performance and progress. 'His attention to the branch of Scriptural knowledge … has been exemplary'. 'His health seems comparatively re-established'.
> 1/2 page.
> F.W. Wyatt's copy MS Book 2 (TC) p.10. A.C. Fry's secondary copy CBA 7049, p.73.

30th June (postmark) [1826]     From B.W. Newton         Exeter College
     **To his mother**                 Plymouth
Responding to her letter that arrived on the day of the announcement of his election as a Fellow. The letter starts before the announcement. He speaks of his weariness and anxiety, 'O that I had a friend to keep up my spirits'. He then tells her of the announcement of his success with a further note, added at 10 am, when the result of his proposed election was known. Regards to Mr Byrth. 2 pages.

---

[1] His Birth Certificate was in the Fry Collection, and is currently held by Tom Chantry from items sold to him by Ian Deighan. See the note in Section 7, Miscellaneous Biographical Items and Memorabilia. His parents had married on 23rd March 1807. His father (also named Benjamin Wills Newton) died on the 1st December 1807. A picture of him given in *A Pictorial Memoir of Benjamin Wills Newton* – the supplement to this Guide. See the Advertisement at the end of this volume.

[2] Née Amy Jane Honeychurch. Born 18th May 1789. Died in U.S.A. 3rd June 1823. Her cousin, B.W. Newton's mother, and B.W. Newton himself, were beneficiaries of her will.

## Section 9 – B.W. Newton Correspondence

The letter is postmarked June 30 1828. F.W. Wyatt adds a note that this must be 1826; he affirms this from the list of dates in Mr Newton's own handwriting in his (Mr Newton's) copy of 'University Statutes'. The handwritten notes are given on page 118 of MS Book 2 as follows:

*Matriculated: Friday Dec. 10 1824*

*Elected Fellow: Friday June 30th 1826*

*Passed: Saturday May 17th 1828 – [took his examination and given a 1st class per page 96]*

*AB: Thursday July 2nd 1829.*

Original TC. Listed in CBA 6998 'original letters from B.W. Newton'. F.W. Wyatt's copy MS Book 2 (TC), p.30. A.C. Fry's secondary copy CBA 7049, pages 75-76.

| | | |
|---|---|---|
| 23rd April 1827 | From B.W. Newton | Oxford |
| **To his mother** | Plymouth | |

His academic career. Dr [Robert] Hawker, F.W. Newman, and various family members mentioned. 'What a revolution there has been in my views…I am more than apprehensive' [re-the Quakers]. 4 pages.

Quoted in *The Early Brethren and the Society of Friends* by T.C.F. Stunt, C.B.R.F., 1970[1], p.8: Quoted in *From Awakening to Secession* by T.C.F. Stunt, T&T Clark, 2000, p.200.

Original letter CBA 7179(1). F.W. Wyatt's copy MS Book 2 (TC), pp.13-14: Not in CBA 7049.

| | | |
|---|---|---|
| 26th August 1827 | From B.W. Newton | Oxford |
| **To his mother** | Plymouth | |

Regarding the difficulty of obtaining a First. Comments on [H. B.] Bulteel[2], and Henry Martyn's example of faith. 4 pages.

Original letter CBA 7179(2). F.W. Wyatt's copy MS Book 2 (TC), pp.14-15; A.C. Fry's secondary copy CBA 7049, pp.106-108.

| | | |
|---|---|---|
| 3rd September 1827 | From B.W. Newton | Oxford |
| **To his mother** | Plymouth | |

Sorrow at causing his mother concern. Comments regarding Henry Martyn. Assures his mother that he will not join a 'party'. References to [John] Newton, Scott, Adams, and Leighton, John Hawker, Mr Triggs, Bulteel, Dr Blackmore, C. Fox and Dr Hingston and [Abdiel] Harris. 4 pages.

Quoted in *From Awakening to Secession* by T.C.F. Stunt, T&T Clark, 2000, p.213.

Original letter CBA 7179(3), F.W. Wyatt's copy MS Book 2 (TC), pp.15-17: A.C. Fry's secondary copy CBA 7049, pp.108-112.

| | | |
|---|---|---|
| 22nd September 1827 | From B.W. Newton | Exeter College, Oxford |
| **To his mother** | Plymouth | |

---

[1] This research item has been republished with some amendments as Chapters 1 and 2 of *The Elusive Quest of the Spiritual Malcontent: Some Early Nineteenth-Century Ecclesiastical Mavericks*, by T.C.F. Stunt., 2015.

[2] For further information regarding Henry Bellenden Bulteel (1800-1866), see the other references to him in this correspondence listing, and the manuscript resources noted in Section 10 of this Guide. T.C.F. Stunt makes frequent reference to him in *From Awakening to Secession*. The index of his book gives a helpful summary of his life, and an appendix gives an account of his conversion.

On the trials of solitude and College life. Records his pleasure in Hebrew, and Bible reading. Comments on the Church of England's Articles, and its declension from the truth. References to Bulteel, Bisse of Worcester College, Dr Blackmore, and family members. 4 pages.
Original letter CBA 7179(4). F.W. Wyatt's copy MS Book 2 (TC), pp.17,18: A.C. Fry's secondary copy CBA 7049, pp.112-115.

[7] October 1827 (postmark)     From B.W. Newton          Exeter College, Oxford
    **To his mother**              Plymouth

On the possibility of mother moving nearer Oxford, spiritual thoughts, re-F.W. Newman. Includes comment on the deadness, and lack of evangelical faith among the Society of Friends. The letter is simply dated 'October 1827', but F.W. Wyatt notes that the postmark is the 7th. The original is not extant.
Quoted in *The Early Brethren and the Society of Friends* by T.C.F. Stunt, C.B.R.F, 1970, p.8. Quoted in *From Awakening to Secession* by T.C.F. Stunt, T&T Clark, 2000, p.209.
F.W. Wyatt's copy MS Book 2 (TC), pp.20-22: A.C. Fry's secondary copy CBA 7049, pp.116-119; Referred to in T.C.F. Stunt, *From Awakening to Secession*, pp.208,209.

23rd December 1827          From B.W. Newton          Exeter College, Oxford
    **To his mother**              Plymouth

Regarding his prospects at the University. Includes notes on Romans 1-3 as a postscript.
Quoted in *Teachers of the Faith and Future* by G.H. Fromow, Second Edition, 1969, pp.106,107.
Original TC. Listed as an original letter in CBA 6998. F.W. Wyatt's copy MS Book 2 (TC), pp.22-25. A.C. Fry's secondary copy CBA 7049, pp.116-119.

30th December 1827          From B.W. Newton          Exeter College, Oxford
    **To his mother**              Plymouth

References to the Quakers. His happiness that his mother has left the Quaker meeting, and that she and Amy [J.T. Toulmin] have attended 'the Church on the hill'. Comments that the Friends do not have the knowledge of God. Recounts his separation from the Friends [Quakers] and his own conversion. Reference to a book lent to him (B.W. Newton) by Hannah Abbott[1] on the Friends. Reference to Bulteel and [Rev. T.] Byrth.
T,C.F. Stunt links the account in this letter with H.B. Bulteel's invitation, a year earlier, to Mr Newton to attend Dr Hawker's Chapel at Plymouth with him [CBA 7059 p.110 – cf. the Fry MS (CBA 7049), p.137].[2] This would identify the unnamed minister in the letter as Dr Hawker, and would shed light on his reference to early difficulties with 'hyper-Calvinism' – see Section 8 of this *Guide*, Derived Publications, NM 5.2 Letter on Hyper Calvinism, and the note on the letter in this Correspondence listing in 1888.
4 pages.
Quoted in *The Early Brethren and the Society of Friends* by T.C.F. Stunt, C.B.R.F, 1970, p.8[3]. Quoted more fully, but somewhat inaccurately, in *Teachers of the Faith and Future*, by G.H. Fromow, 1969.

---
[1] His future wife.
[2] T.C.F. Stunt, *From Awakening to Secession*, p. 196
[3] This research item has been republished with some amendments as Chapters 1 and 2 of *The Elusive Quest of the Spiritual Malcontent: Some Early Nineteenth-Century Ecclesiastical Mavericks*, by T.C.F. Stunt., 2015.

Quoted in *From Awakening to Secession* by T.C.F. Stunt, T&T Clark, 2000, pp.195-197, 315.
Original letter CBA 7179(5). F.W. Wyatt's copy MS Book 2 (TC) 25-28: A.C. Fry's secondary copy CBA 7049, pp.125-128.

13th January 1828      From B.W. Newton      Exeter College
    **To his mother**      Plymouth

Regarding the apostasy of the Church. Approving reference to César Malan[1]. Disapproval of Quakerism, Arminianism, Methodism ('dreadful foe to Gospel truth'), Toiling in study, Clarke, and Bulteel.
Quoted in *The Early Brethren and the Society of Friends* by T.C.F. Stunt, C.B.R.F, 1970, pp.8,9.
Quoted in *From Awakening to Secession* by T.C.F. Stunt, T&T Clark, 2000, p.200.
Original letter - TC. Listed in CBA 6998: F.W. Wyatt's copy MS Book 2 (TC), pp.29-30: A.C. Fry's secondary copy CBA 7049, pp.143-145.

17th April 1828      **From F.W. Newman**      Temple Carig, Delgany
To B.W. Newton      Exeter College, Oxford

On various subjects, including Israel, and the Millennium.
Quoted in *From Awakening to Secession*, by T.C.F. Stunt, T&T Clark, 2000, pp.210-211.
Also quoted by T.C.F. Stunt in *Prisoners of Hope*, Paternoster, 2004, p.59n.
F.W. Wyatt's copy MS Book 2 (TC), pp.120-121: A.C. Fry's secondary copy CBA 7049, pp.62-65.

10th June 1828      **From Rev. Thomas Byrth**[2]      Latchford Parsonage,
                                                                                         [Warrington, Cheshire]
    To B.W. Newton

Congratulation upon B.W. Newton achieving his 'first class'.
F.W. Wyatt's copy MS Book 2 (TC), p.60: A.C. Fry's secondary copy CBA 7049, pp.55,56.

30th June 1828 [postmark]      From B.W. Newton
    **To his mother**

Wrongly recorded in CBA 6998 as 1828. This is the letter regarding his election to Fellowship at the University. See the entry at 30th June 182<u>6</u>.

15th August 1828      From B.W. Newton      Stercoke, near Wick, Caithness
    **To his uncle [Joseph Treffry]**      Plymouth

Defends his Calvinism. Desires to return to 'the congenial South'.
The copy from which FWW made his copy - TC. Listed in CBA 6998: F.W. Wyatt's copy MS Book 2 (TC), p.32: A.C. Fry's secondary copy CBA 7049, pp.148-151.

---

[1] For extensive discussion of the Swiss *Réveil* and Dr Henri Abraham César Malan (1787–1864) in the context of the development of B.W. Newton and his associates, see T.C.F. Stunt, *From Awakening to Secession*, passim and index.

[2] See other references to Thomas Byrth, B.W. Newton's schoolmaster, in this listing of correspondence. More information is given regarding him in T.C.F. Stunt, *From Awakening to Secession*, index, and pages 190-197.

## Section 9 – B.W. Newton Correspondence

5th April 1829 (postmark)    From B.W. Newton    Oxford
    **To his aunt [Miss E. Treffry]**    **Plymouth**
Regarding 'a minister's duty', and a visit to her. 4 pages.
Original letter - CBA 7179(13). F.W. Wyatt's copy MS Book 2 (TC), p.33: A.C. Fry's secondary copy CBA 7049, pp.164-165.

9th April 1829    From B.W. Newton    Exeter College
    **To his mother**    Plymouth
Regarding the offer to him of a professorship at Bishop's College, Calcutta, with a stipend of £800 per annum.
With a copy of an undated letter (enclosed, and copied by Wyatt and Fry) concerning this from T[homas] Woodroffe to the Principal of Magdalen Hall. [Newton spells 'Woodruffe', but Woodroffe in the *History of the Church Missionary Society*].
Original TC. CBA 6998 lists as original letter. F.W. Wyatt's copy MS Book 2 (TC), p.34. A.C. Fry's secondary copy CBA 7049, pp.165-167.

16th April 1829    From B.W. Newton    Exeter College
    **To his mother**    Plymouth
Regarding his rejection of the offer of the professorship at Bishop's College, Calcutta, in the face of his mother's resistance. Favourable impression of [the newly consecrated] Bishop of Calcutta [John Matthias Turner (died 1831), predecessor of Daniel Wilson]. Other family matters. Visits to Bushey, and to London.
Original letter - TC. Listed in CBA 6998: F.W. Wyatt's copy MS Book 2 (TC), pp.35,36. A.C. Fry's secondary copy CBA 7049, pp.167-169.

28th April 1829 (postmarked)    From B.W. Newton    Oxford
    **To his mother**    Plymouth
Reference to the earlier Calcutta proposal. Refers to letters he has written to *The Record* newspaper regarding *The London Review* under the nom de plume 'W'.[1] Refers to [R.W.] Sibthorpe [*sic*, for Sibthorp][2], [John] Newton's works, Boyes Bible, Mr Rosdew, and Mr Lampen. Speaks of his confidence and hope in Christ. 4 pages.
Quoted in *From Awakening to Secession* by T.C.F. Stunt, T&T Clark, 2000, p.214.
Original letter CBA 7179(6), F.W. Wyatt's copy MS Book 2 (TC), pp.36-37. A.C. Fry's secondary copy CBA 7049, pp.169-170.

23rd May 1829    From B.W. Newton    Oxford
    **To his mother**    Plymouth
Referring to his busyness, and plans for the long vacation. Stipulations for ministry to the servants. Thoughts on Amy J.T. Toulmin's growing faith in Christ. References to Bulteel, and Mary Coplestone. 4 pages.
Original letter - CBA 7179(7). F.W. Wyatt's copy MS Book 2 (TC), p.37. A.C. Fry's secondary

---

[1] See notes on these letters in Section 6, B.W. Newton's Letters and Articles Published in Periodicals
[2] See *A Letter to Richard Waldo Sibthorpe*, in Section 3, Published works for further information regarding Sibthorp.

copy CBA 7049, pp.175,176.

| 8th June 1829 | From B.W. Newton | Exeter College |

**To his mother** — Plymouth

Regarding the offer to him (B.W. Newton) of the Presidency of the College in Bombay where he would have the sole control of all the Church missions – 'but I suppose it is of no use to ask you for your consent'. Various plans for the long vacation. A 'kind friend' had given him a pony capable of pulling a 'gig' at 10 miles per hour. Otherwise inclined to accompany 'one of my most near and intimate friends' [i.e. R.W. Sibthorp] on a three week tour of the continent.
Original letter - TC. Listed in CBA 6998. F.W. Wyatt's copy MS Book 2 (TC), pp.39-40. A.C. Fry's secondary copy CBA 7049, pp.173-175.

19th June 1829      From B.W. Newton      Oxford

**To his mother** — Plymouth

Plans for the long vacation, and a journey to North Devon. Plans to leave Oxford on Monday 6th July 1829. 4 pages.
Original CBA 7179(8). F.W. Wyatt's copy MS Book 2 (TC), p.40. A.C. Fry's secondary copy CBA 7049, pp.175-176.

26th August 1829      From B.W. Newton      Berlin

**To his mother** — Plymouth

Describes tract distribution work with [R.W.] Sibthorpe [*sic*, for Sibthorp] in Prussia, Hanover, Denmark, and Saxony, with Switzerland the final intended destination.[1]
Quoted in *From Awakening to Secession* by T.C.F. Stunt, T&T Clark, 2000, p.215.
Original letter - TC. Listed in CBA 6998. F.W. Wyatt's copy MS Book 2 (TC), pp.41-44: A.C. Fry's secondary copy CBA 7049, pp.176-181.

13th November 1829 (postmark)      From B.W. Newton      Exeter College

**To his mother** — Plymouth

Regarding counsel to those on their deathbeds, various family, and personal, circumstances.
Original letter - TC. Listed in CBA 6998. F.W. Wyatt's copy MS Book 2 (TC), pp.44-45: A.C. Fry's secondary copy CBA 7049, pp.188-190.

22nd April 1830      From B.W. Newton      Exeter College, Oxford

**To his mother** — Plymouth

Visit to Mary [née Honeychurch[2]] and Samuel Ll[oyd][3] at Wood Green. Commends Mary's motherly labours. Regarding a petition against West Indian slavery that he had written to both

---

[1] For further information on this expedition to the Continent see CBA 7064 p36ff, and CBA 7049.
[2] A cousin of B.W. Newton's mother.
[3] Samuel Lloyd, son of founder of Lloyd's Bank. *A Pictorial Memoir of Benjamin Wills Newton* – the supplement to this Guide.- reproduces F.W. Wyatt's note regarding his relatedness to B.W. Newton. B.W. Newton's mother was first cousin to Samuel Lloyd's wife.

Houses of Parliament, and hoped to have signed by many members of the University.[1] Concludes 'West Indian slavery must be abomination in the sight of God'.[2] Plans of [H.B.] Bulteel to visit Plymouth. Pleasure at hearing of plans for regular tract distribution in Plymouth. Hopes to send remittance to clear his debts at Plymouth. Reference to Plymouth evangelical clergy[3] - Mr Hatchard, and Mr Carne. Concerning various family matters. 4 pages. Quoted in *The Early Brethren and the Society of Friends* by T.C.F. Stunt, C.B.R.F, 1970, p.10[4].

Original letter CBA 7179(9). F.W. Wyatt's copy MS Book 2 (TC) pp.46-47: A.C. Fry's secondary copy CBA 7049, pp.190-192.

24th June 1830           From B.W. Newton           Exeter College, Oxford
**To his mother**           Plymouth

Expresses sorrow at the unexpected death of his grandmother [Treffry]. Concern over her spiritual state before death, but thankful that Bulteel was present on the last day. References to family members. Refers to his arrangements for returning to Plymouth.
3 pages.
Original letter CBA 7179(10). F.W. Wyatt's copy MS Book 2 (TC), p.47B (extra page): A.C. Fry's secondary copy CBA 7049, p.193.

31st July 1830           From B.W. Newton           10 Gascoigne St, Plymouth
**To G.V. Wigram**           Glasgow

Regarding Wigram's investigation of tongues manifestations in Scotland. The nature of miracles in the book of Acts. The P.S. mentions J.N. Darby.

B.W. Newton's strictures on the manifestations quoted at length in *From Awakening to Secession* by T.C.F. Stunt, T&T Clark, 2000, p.253. Cf. T.C.F. Stunt, 'J.N. Darby and Tongues at Row: A Recent MS Discovery, *Brethren Historical Review* 12 (2016) p.7, 9.

F.W. Wyatt's copy MS Book 2 (TC), p.47A. A.C. Fry's secondary copy CBA 7049, pp.264-266. Not listed in CBA 6998.

---

[1] This has not been traced either at The Bodleian Library, or at the Parliamentary Archives, the Library of the House of Lords, or the House of Commons Library. If it was produced and sent, it is assumed to have been lost in the Great Fire at the Houses of Parliament in 1834. We have not checked the journals of either of the Houses of Parliament, where it should have been registered, even if it did not survive. This was a period in which there was considerable concern regarding slavery. There was a slave rebellion in Jamaica in December 1831.

[2] For further comment on nineteenth century slavery, see the note on Rev. 18:13 in the third edition of *Thoughts on the Apocalypse*, and note B.W. Newton's *Thoughts on the Death of Captain Bird Allen*, regarding the Niger Expedition.

[3] For further information regarding the Plymouth evangelical clergy at this time, see T.C.F. Stunt, *From Awakening to Secession*, pp.288, 289. John Hatchard (1794[?] – 1869), vicar of St Andrews, Plymouth. James Carne (1794[?] -1832), successor to Robert Hawker (1753–1827), the vicar of Charles Church, Plymouth. Attendance at Charles Church under Robert Hawker's preaching was one of the means of B.W. Newton's conversion. See the record of his conversations with F.W. Wyatt in CBA 7059, p.110, and the Fry Manuscript (CBA 7049), p.137.

[4] This research item has been republished with some amendments as Chapters 1 and 2 of *The Elusive Quest of the Spiritual Malcontent: Some Early Nineteenth-Century Ecclesiastical Mavericks*, by T.C.F. Stunt., 2015.

> **15th March 1832. Married his first wife, Hannah Abbott**[1] (a cousin of S.P. Tregelles)
>
> **Left Oxford 'entirely', because of Irvingism**[2] (CBA 7057, p.331)

15th March 1832          From B.W. Newton
    **To J.C. Jones**[3]
Letter resigning his Fellowship on account of his marriage.
Quoted in *From Awakening to Secession* by T.C.F. Stunt, T&T Clark, 2000, p.279.
Exeter College Archives MS A.I.8.

> 7th August 1833     **From C. Brenton**[4]
>     **To C.P. Golightly**
> 'Newton I have not seen since I was at Plymouth in October. He is conducting a school in conjunction with Mr Borlase who has seceded within the last year from the ministry of the Church of England'.[5]
> MS 1804, Lambeth Palace Archives, pages 79, 80. Quoted by T.C.F. Stunt in *From Awakening to Secession*, p.293, footnote 51, and p.298, footnote 75.

> 11th August 1832[6]     **From S[arah] W. Crewdson**
>     **To D. Crewdson**
> Comment on Benjamin and Hannah Newton's 'party' at Providence Chapel, Plymouth increasing. Quoted by T.C.F. Stunt, *From Awakening to Secession*, p.294. See too p.291.
> *Crewdson Papers*, Kendal/CRO: Cumbria County Record Office, WD/Cr/6/62

ND [23 September 1833]     From B.W. Newton     Glenmore, Wicklow, Ireland
    **To his mother**         Plymouth
Regarding his attendance at the Powerscourt Conference.
Although undated, a precise date can be identified by the reference to 'Monday morning' and other details of this Powerscourt Conference [as noted by Timothy Stunt].

---

[1] According to *Collectanea Cornubiensia*, by George Clement Boase, 1890.

[2] *Barclay Fox's Journal*, published 1979, p.82, refers to Mr Newton's coming to Falmouth to preach against Irvingism in December 1835. Robert Barclay Fox of Falmouth (1814-1875). Note also the incident recorded in CBA 7057 noted by T.C.F. Stunt in *The Elusive Quest of the Spiritual Malcontent*, p72n in connection with Irvingism.

[3] John Collier Jones (1770-1838); Rector of Exeter College, 1819-1838; Vice Chancellor 1828-1832.

[4] Charles Lancelot Lee Brenton (1807-1862).

[5] L.C.L. Brenton (1807-1862), was a contemporary of B.W. Newton at Oxford. He was at one time substitute curate of St Ebbe's, Oxford, and had himself seceded in December 1831. C.P. Golightly (1807-1885), another contemporary of B.W. Newton at Oxford, who, after some association with J.H. Newman, became a lifelong opponent of Romanism. There is background on both of these correspondents in T.C.F. Stunt, *From Awakening to Secession*.

[6] We have not viewed this letter, and we are unaware of its wider content. It is noted in T.C.F. Stunt, *From Awakening to Secession*, page 294, note 55. S.W. Crewdson, née Fox, was the cousin of B.W. Newton's first wife, (née Hannah Abbott). See the other letters, S.W. Crewdson to D. Crewdson, and further comment on the Crewdsons in T.C.F. Stunt, *Early Brethren and the Society of Friends*, passim. *Christian Brethren Research Fellowship Occasional Paper No.3*, 1970. This research item has been republished with some amendments as Chapter 2 of *The Elusive Quest of the Spiritual Malcontent: Some Early Nineteenth-Century Ecclesiastical Mavericks*, by T.C.F. Stunt, 2015.

Quoted in *From Awakening to Secession* by T.C.F. Stunt, T&T Clark, 2000, p.295 n60
Original letter - TC. Listed in CBA 6998: F.W. Wyatt's copy MS Book 2 (TC), p.50. A.C. Fry's secondary copy CBA 7049, pp.293-294

> 17th September [1833][1]      **From S[arah] W. Crewdson**
> **To D. Crewdson**
> Comment on Benjamin and Hannah Newton's 'party' at Providence Chapel, Plymouth, including reference to "the first interment that has taken place among them", which she had attended.
> Quoted by T.C.F. Stunt, *From Awakening to Secession*, p.294, 295 n61.
> *Crewdson Papers*, Kendal/CRO: Cumbria County Record Office, WD/Cr/6/65

26 January 1834      **From Aunt Lloyd**
     To B.W. Newton
'Mem[orandum] by Miss Toulmin'
Listed by F.W. Wyatt in CBA 7002, Index of Correspondence as on p.124 of MSS 2. Apparently no longer extant.

ND [1834?]      From B.W. Newton      (no location)
     **To his mother**      (no location)
Regarding the privilege of arousing the minds of those who slumber. The necessity of searching the Scriptures. The resurrection. The spiritual state of Uncle John in Canada. Urges his mother to 'Seek first the Kingdom of God'. Has a message for Uncle John [who is presumably with B.W. Newton's mother prior to embarkation for Canada – noted by Timothy Stunt].
Both this, and the following item, are undated. The sequence used by F.W. Wyatt's notebook is adopted here (rather than the CBA numbering) as it seems a better fit to the circumstances. 4 pages.
Original CBA 7179(12). F.W. Wyatt's copy MS Book 2 (TC), pp.51-52. A.C. Fry's secondary copy CBA 7049, pp.294-295.

ND [1834?]      From B.W. Newton      (no details)
     **To his mother**      (no location)
Gives warning concerning the present evil in the world. Requests that his mother sell some copies of *The Christian Witness*, and circulate some of his tracts. Reference to Amy J.T. Toulmin, family matters, and Uncle John's current journey from Falmouth to Quebec.
See note on preceding letter in reference to the sequence of these two undated letters. 4 pages.
Original CBA 7179(11) 4 pages. F.W. Wyatt's copy MS Book 2 (TC), p.52. A.C. Fry's secondary copy CBA 7049, pp.291-292.

---

[1] We have not viewed this letter, and are unaware of its wider content. It is noted in T.C.F. Stunt, *From Awakening to Secession*, page 293, note 51 in connection with B.W. Newton. S.W. Crewdson, née Fox, was the cousin of B.W. Newton's first wife, (née Hannah Abbott). The day is the old Quaker convention for Saturday. There is no record of the day of the month or year.

> '7th day night' [c.1834][1]  **From S[arah] W. Crewdson**   High Wycombe
> **To D. Crewdson**
> Comment on B.W. Newton giving up the "worldly glory" of the Oxford Colleges (on account of his resigning his Fellowship and leaving Oxford).
> *Crewdson Papers*, Kendal/CRO: Cumbria County Record Office, WD/Cr/6/85

10th April 183[7?] (postmark)   From B.W. Newton & wife   Sizergh [Hall, Kendal]
    **To his mother**   Plymouth

Regarding his preaching and encouraging in Kendal, principally with Quakers or former Quakers. References to J.N. Darby, J.L. Harris, and W. Crewdson. Itinerary possibly proceeding to Manchester and Liverpool.

The year is uncertain. In the index of F.W. Wyatt's MS Book 2 (TC) it appears to be 1838. At the item in MS Book 2, F.W. Wyatt states the final number is not legible due to want of ink, but suggests there may be evidence of pressure suggesting a '3'.

Quoted and discussed in *The Early Brethren and the Society of Friends*[2] by T.C.F. Stunt, C.B.R.F 1970, pp.14-18, where the date is clarified as 1837.

F.W. Wyatt's copy MS Book 2 (TC), pp.48-49. A.C. Fry's secondary copy CBA 7049, pp.296-299. Not listed as an original letter in CBA 6998.

4th January [1840?]   From B.W. Newton
    **To his mother**

Short note (6 lines). Agreeing with her sentiments. Reporting his good health.

Placed by Wyatt before the first exchange with J.N. Darby, but the letter implies he (B.W. Newton) is away from Plymouth, or alternatively that his mother was not there at the time.

F.W. Wyatt's copy MS Book 2 (TC), p.54.

ND [post-1840]   From B.W. Newton
    **To an unknown person** (but see CBA 7051/7052)

Refers to Mr Townsend's book on mesmerism.[3]

Copy of Original Transcript of letter CBA 7050, pp.19-29.

---

### Census 7th July 1841

Address: Little Saltram [?], Plymouth.
    B.W. Newton 34; Hannah Newton 42; servant 'born foreign parts'.

---

[1] See note 202. 'c.1834' is suggested by T.C.F. Stunt.
[2] This research item has been republished with some amendments as Chapter 2 of *The Elusive Quest of the Spiritual Malcontent: Some Early Nineteenth-Century Ecclesiastical Mavericks*, by T.C.F. Stunt., 2015.
[3] Rev. C.H. Townsend, *Facts in Mesmerism, with Reasons for a Dispassionate Inquiry into it*, First Edition 1840. See also the correspondence with Dr C.Y. Biss commencing 13th June 1887 regarding mesmerism.

## Section 9 – B.W. Newton Correspondence

c.1840,1841 **From J.N. Darby**
To B.W. Newton

Refers to his [J.N. Darby's] note, which has been the cause of B.W. Newton renouncing confidence in him. Refers to the [Five?] letters[1], and his (J.N. Darby's) assessment that B.W. Newton has taken up a 'false position'. Denies speaking harshly of him, or his writings, to others. Refers to [J.L.] Harris, and [H.W.] Soltau. 3 pages

Xerox copy of original CBA 7180(3); MS Book 2 (TC), pp.55-56: A.C. Fry's secondary copy CBA 7049, pp.320-321.

ND [c.1840,1841] **From J.N. Darby**
To B.W. Newton

Criticises B.W. Newton's [Five] Letters, and his papers in *The Christian Witness*. Urging that 'the letters' should not be circulated. Alleges B.W. Newton's 'love of influence'. States that he has no conviction as to a secret coming of the Lord, and that the 'proofs' of such are 'very feeble and vague'. [Replied to by CBA 7180(2)]. 4 pages.

Listed in CBA 6998 as an undated original letter. CBA 7180(1) Xerox copy of original. F.W. Wyatt's copy MS Book 2 (TC), p.56-57. A.C. Fry's secondary copy CBA 7049, pp.322, 323.

ND [c.1840-1] From B.W. Newton
**To J.N. Darby**

[Reply to CBA 7180(1)]. Assures Mr Darby of his affection, but expresses grief at his criticism of his papers, and his accusations against his integrity. States that he believes that J.N. Darby has departed from the truth on prophetic matters. States his intention to go on stating simply what he believes, and not speaking of others or against others. Requests J.N. Darby to clarify his objections to his tracts. Refers to [J.L.] Harris, and [J.G.] Bellett. 7 pages.

Original, a copy by Miss Amy J.T. Toulmin - TC. CBA 7180(2) Xerox of Miss Toulmin's copy (some missing). F.W. Wyatt's copy MS Book 2 (TC), pp.57-59. A.C. Fry's secondary copy CBA 7049, pp.324-328.

ND [1843?] From B.W. Newton
**To 'My beloved brother' [J.N. Darby]**

Concerning the Tares of Matthew 13, and in reality a reply to J.N. Darby's objections to the *Five Letters...* This became what J.N. Darby referred to as 'the famous appendix' to the *Five Letters...* It was circulated by Miss Jeremie, and was later published with the five letters in the 1847 edition to which S.P. Tregelles wrote a preface. It appears as a 'Supplementary Letter' (after the five) in the printed editions.

Manuscript copy of the letter in Mr Newton's hand, but without the reply to each of J.N. Darby's specific points is now in the CBA catalogued as FRY/1/6/6.

---

[1] The *Five Letters* referred to in this, and subsequent letters, relates to the letters eventually published as *Five Letters on Events Predicted in Scripture as Antecedent to the Coming of the Lord*. See Section 3, B.W. Newton's Published Works.

ND [1843?]　　　　　　　　　From B.W. Newton
**To 'My beloved brother' [J.N. Darby]**　　　　Plymouth

He referred to J.N. Darby's letter and to J.L. Harris's translation of 'the End of the Age'. He denied that he has said that the End of the Age is 'one definite moment marked by one event'. He contended strongly against J.N. Darby's view of judgement upon Israel. He replied that God has made a solemn promise – 'Blindness is happened to them not forever, but until the fulness of the Gentiles has come in'. He opposed the view (held by J.N. Darby) that in 2 Thess. 2 the Christians supposed that the Day of the Lord had come because they were suffering persecution – they 'knew perfectly' that their enemies would be judged first.

He stated 'I have for years concluded that the great turning point of the dispensation shall be when the Lord Jesus shall quit the throne of the Father and be brought before the Ancient of Days [Dan. 7:13,14]'. This will be unseen and unknown on earth 'until subsequent events manifest it'.

Requests the return of [pamphlets on] Luke 21 and Matt. 24.[1] Three pages of notes are attached, which respond to points in J.N. Darby's letter, which were published in *The Five Letters...* as 'Answers to Particular Questions'. See too 'the famous appendix' CBA FRY/1/6/6, noted in Section 10, Duplicated and Manuscript Items.

7 pages in B.W. Newton's handwriting, with the envelope, indicating J.N. Darby was in Plymouth. CBA.

[1844?]　　　　　　　　　From B.W. Newton
**To Dr [J.C.] Cookworthy** [envelope]

Answers the note of Dr Cookworthy regarding the predictions of the Lord Jesus in Matt. 16:28, Mark 9:1 and Luke 16:28 ('there be some standing here who shall not taste of death...'). States that it was fulfilled eight days afterwards by the Transfiguration. 2 Peter 1:16 also refers to the Transfiguration. The Transfiguration is a Scripture proof of manner and certainty of the Lord's advent in glory. Matt. 10:23 is one proof that neither Israel nor the world will be converted by the Gospel in this dispensation. Refers to 'the statements of the Tract'.

[Pencil note on the letter (Mrs L.S. Riach's handwriting) 'This was written about the year 1844 or before I think. This was given to me by Dr C's widow after his death...'. If *Thoughts on the End of the Age* is the tract referred to, the letter is after 1845].

3+1 pages.
Christian Brethren Archive, Box 23(10) (Ex-The Stirling Collection).

March 1844　　　　　　　　　From B.W. Newton
　　To unknown

The letter is concerning 2 Peter 3.

'The subject of 2 Peter 3 is evidently the destruction of the natural world, not of the <u>appearing</u> of the Day of the Lord, but IN the day of the Lord'. On verse 12, translates διɑ + accusative as 'in consequence of which' rather than A.V. 'wherein'

---

[1] *On Luke 21*? See Section 3, B.W. Newton's Published Works. That tract and J.N. Darby's reply are dated 1843. Matthew 24 may refer to *Prophecy of the Lord Jesus as contained in Matthew 24, briefly considered*. If so, this indicates J.L. Harris, J.G. Deck and S.P. Tregelles taking a common stand on prophetic matters at this stage. See, further, the compilation publication *Lectures on Prophecy*.

In his own hand, and headed 'Copy'. 6 pages.
Original - TC. No other reference to this letter has been found.

21st November 1844           From B.W. Newton           Plymouth
    **To Andrew Jukes**
The letter is about baptism.
'Clulow asks me to write one or two lines on your paper on baptism'. Mr Newton emphasises the 'great importance of keeping baptism as the sign of past regeneration'. Detailed consideration. Regarding his paper, does not wish to 'reject what is excellent and valuable in it.
It is listed in the 'Rough Notes'.[1] F.W. Wyatt's copy MS Book 1 (TC), p.60.

---

2nd January 1845 [*sic* for 1846]   **From R[obert] H. Rickards,** Plymouth
    **To T[homas] Lakeman, H.P.E[meric] de St Dalmas, R.W. Wolston** [of Brixham]   See entry at 2nd January 1846.

---

24th January 1845           From B.W. Newton           Plymouth
    **To 'My Beloved Brother'**
Refers to Christ's Federal Headship, and to his (B.W. Newton's) tract *Doctrines of the Church in Newman Street*. 'The tract, having found its way to India, was thought serviceable against Irvingism, and was republished at Madras by the Church Mission Press; so they evidently considered it not heresy'.
A.C. Fry's secondary copy CBA 7049, pp.373,374. Neither the original, nor an original copy, have been located.

30th March 1845           From B.W. Newton           Plymouth
    **To [J.L.] Harris, [H.W.] Soltau, and [J.E.] Batten**
Requests that they make 'a kind but decided protest', and express 'unequivocal disapproval' of J.N. Darby's actions in assuming the role of a universal censor. 'A most strange system of dispensational doctrines has become apparent among the brethren', which he describes. 'If he persists I can only regard him as one who creates divisions contrary to the doctrines we have received, and avoid him'. 4 pages
Draft in B.W. Newton's hand – TC, CBA 7180(4) Xerox copy of original draft. F.W. Wyatt's copy MS Book 2 (TC) pp.60-62. A.C. Fry's secondary copy CBA 7049, pp.328-331.

1st April 1845           From B.W. Newton
    **To J.N. Darby**
Accepts the explanation J.N. Darby had given to [J.L.] Harris and [J.E.] Batten, and accepts in good faith his (J.N. Darby's) statements that he had not come to Plymouth to be antagonistic. Abhors the strife, and desires to unite 'in all we can in love'. 3 pages.
Original copy in B.W. Newton's own hand. - TC. CBA 7180(6) Xerox copy of original. F.W. Wyatt's copy MS Book 2 (TC), p.62B: A.C. Fry's secondary copy CBA 7049, pp.332-333.

---

[1] 'The Rough Notes' –see 'Manuscript Items added to the Fry Collection in 2011' in this Guide, item 7. The 'notes' are catalogued in the Christian Brethren Archive as FRY/1/2/1).

## Section 9 – B.W. Newton Correspondence

Undated [April 1845]     **From J.N. Darby**
    To B.W. Newton                Gascoigne Street [Plymouth]

[Replies to CBA 7180(6)]. Professes not to know whom B.W. Newton means when he refers to 'us' (implies a party spirit). Denies he has adopted an antagonistic position. Charges B.W. Newton with acting badly towards many brethren. Refers to disagreement as 'a difference of interpretation on points of Scripture', which may be 'comparatively immaterial'. Refers to [J.E.] Batten, and [J.L.] Harris. 3 pages.

Original letter listed in CBA 6998 in folio 3, 1845. CBA 7180(7) Xerox copy of original. F.W. Wyatt's copy MS Book 2 (TC), pp.62 ff. : A.C. Fry's secondary copy CBA 7049, pp.333-334.

4th April 1845     From B.W. Newton
   **To J.N. Darby**

[Reply to CBA 7179(7)]. Explaining whom he (B.W. Newton) referred to as 'us' in his earlier letter. Comments adversely on the manner in which Darby came to Plymouth. Requests that J.N. Darby urgently provide names and circumstances to substantiate his (J.N. Darby's) allegations that he (B.W. Newton) had acted badly towards brethren. Deplores J.N. Darby's inadequate estimate of the differences between them. Regrets the conciliatory tone of his earlier letter. 'I should not have so written if I had been aware that you had so grave a charge against me'. 3 pages.

Original copy in B.W. Newton's own hand - TC. CBA 7180(8) xerox copy of original copy. F.W. Wyatt's copy MS Book 2 (TC), p.63. A.C. Fry's secondary copy CBA 7049, pp.334-335.

[April 1845 undated]     **From J.N. Darby**
    To B.W. Newton                Gascoigne Street [Plymouth]

[Reply to CBA 7180(8)]. Does not wish a 'paper controversy'. Relates the circumstances of his first coming to Plymouth. Proposes that he present his case to brethren who have expressed interest.

Quoted in *From Awakening to Secession* by T.C.F. Stunt, T&T Clark, 2000, p.291. 4 pages. Original letter listed in CBA 6998 in folio 4, 1845. Xerox copy of original CBA 7180(9). F.W. Wyatt's copy MS Book 2 (TC), p.64. A.C. Fry's secondary copy CBA 7049, pp.335-336.

[April 1845 undated]     From B.W. Newton
   **To J.N. Darby**

[Reply to 7180(9)]. Objects to J.N. Darby's denial of his (B.W. Newton's) Scriptural right to know what he has against him in his accusations of acting badly. Refuses to agree to J.N. Darby's effective proposal of a jury of 'the brethren' to judge his (J.N. Darby's) accusations. 2 pages.

Listed in CBA 6998 as in folio 4, 1845 (a copy in Mr Newton's hand). CBA 7180(10) Xerox copy of original (a copy in Mr Newton's hand). F.W. Wyatt's copy MS Book 2 (TC), p.64. A.C. Fry's secondary copy CBA 7049, pp.334-335.

[April 1845 undated]     **From J.N. Darby**
    To B.W. Newton                Gascoigne Street [Plymouth]

[Reply to 7180(10)]. Short note, refusing to enter into further correspondence. Accuses B.W. Newton of 'a systematic effort to form a sect'. 2 pages.
Original letter listed in CBA 6998 in folio 4, 1845. CBA 7180(11) Xerox copy of original. F.W. Wyatt's copy MS Book 2 –TC, p.64. A.C. Fry's secondary copy CBA 7049, p.337.

[April 1845 undated]         From B.W. Newton
   **To J.N. Darby**
[Reply to CBA 7180(11)]. States that J.N. Darby's last letter contained a new charge - forming a sect -, and requests that J.N. Darby provide particulars or withdraw the charge. 2 pages.
Original copy in Mr Newton's own hand - TC. Listed in CBA 6998 as in folio 4, 1845. CBA 7180(12) Xerox copy of original. F.W. Wyatt's copy MS Book 2 (TC), p.65. A.C. Fry's secondary copy CBA 7049, p.338.

18th April 1845         From B.W. Newton
   **To J[oseph] Clulow**
This gives an account of a recent meeting [of 13 brethren with J.N. Darby and B.W. Newton] at which B.W. Newton defended himself against the charges of trying to form a sect, and of denouncing the opinions of others. He specified the doctrines which he regarded as unscriptural, and which 'derange and subvert old truths which the Church of God has ever held sacred' in the letter, and in 16 doctrinal statements appended to it. His opposition is directed against a system, rather than against individuals.
Xerox copy of original CBA 7180(13), 4 pages.
This item was printed for private circulation, but no copies of that printing are known to have survived apart from that missing from the Fry Collection. It was reprinted without the appended doctrinal statements in Lord Congleton's *Correspondence etc. Related to Mr Newton's Refusal to Appear Before the Saints at Rawstorne Street, London...*, 1846 (Appendix A, pp.32-34). The appended doctrinal statements were reprinted in S.P. Tregelles's *Three Letters to the Author of 'A Retrospect of Events...'*, First Edition 1847, Second Edition 1894 (pp.64-66). See Rowdon *The Origins of the Brethren*, p.241 for a further account of the letter.
See Section 3, B.W. Newton's Published Works of this *Guide* as *Letter from B.W. Newton to J Clulow, 18 April 1845*.
Listed in CBA 6998 (1845, Folio 6) as 'Two copies of a letter from N. to J. Clulow. (One copy in print for private circulation, one with an appendix in N's hand)'.

[After April 1845 undated]     From B.W. Newton
   **To Mr [C.] McAdam**
Speaks of himself as tired. 'I trust I may be able to remain [at Plymouth] if it is right'. Describes the manner of J.N. Darby's coming to Plymouth. Regrets the intemperate tone of J.N. Darby's remarks. Suggests that, having found nothing that he (J.N. Darby) can attack Plymouth for, he has settled on a personal attack on him (B.W. Newton), and on his book *Thoughts on the Apocalypse*. States that J.N. Darby has held his position for the last 6 years. Desiring that others will tell J.N. Darby clearly and openly that his views are unsound and dangerous. Rejecting that this is a matter of interpretation only, but that it concerns important truths. References to J.L. Harris, and H.W. Soltau. 4 pages.

Draft or unsent original on B.W. Newton's handwriting - TC. CBA 7180(5) Xerox copy of original. Listed in CBA 6998 in folio 5, 1845. F.W. Wyatt's copy MS Book 2 (TC), p.66. A.C. Fry's secondary copy CBA 7049, pp.338-340.

[July 1845]          From B.W. Newton
     **To Mr [J.L.] H[arris]**

Refers to the unity of judgement amongst the leaders at Plymouth prior to J.N. Darby's arrival, and that, having failed to dent that unity, he (J.N. Darby) had focussed his attack upon his (B.W. Newton's) ministry. Referring to his 14 years of ministry at Plymouth. Rejecting the idea of a special prayer meeting with J.N. Darby for 'humiliation', in view of past experience of such meetings, and the animus displayed by J.N. Darby. The judgement of the appropriate subjects for such a meeting were not shared. Referring to the threat of Wigram to withdraw from him because of the meetings in London, at which B.W. Newton had explained his prophetic position (see letter from Wiggins dated 31st December 1845). Assuring him (J.L. Harris) that he values his co-operation 'beyond price', but advocates the 'sorrowful necessity' of allowing the cords of unity to hang very loosely at present.

Listed in CBA 6998 in folio 6 1845, but not in the CBA. F.W. Wyatt's copy MS Book 2 (TC), p.67. A.C. Fry's secondary copy CBA 7049, pp.341-343.

8th October 1845      **From J.L. Harris**      Linton
     To B.W. Newton

J.L. Harris addressed B.W. Newton as 'beloved brother', and went on to state 'The nine weeks which I passed in Plymouth previous to my leaving it on the occasion of my [second] marriage [9th September 1845 to Frances Farrish, daughter of Leigh Richmond] were to me the most painfully distressing of any that I have known since I left the Establishment in 1832'. [i.e. for J.L. Harris the pain began at the beginning of July, though in B.W. Newton's reply (the next letter) he (Newton) referred to 'since March … a gradual and increasing distance growing up between us']

J.L. Harris declared two convictions: that there is need for humiliation in the meeting at Plymouth, and his difference with the Brethren there regarding [the closing of] the Friday meeting. Stating that he does not intend to return to Plymouth to resume his ministry there. Regards this as the most painful step in his Christian life since leaving the Establishment. His difference of opinion regarding changes made 'in the diaconal department'. Referring to his marriage, [Captain, aka Admiral] William Haydon, Mary Smith, and H.W. Soltau; and to the health of B.W. Newton's wife. [CBA 7180(15) replies to this]. 8 pages.

Original letter- TC. CBA 7180(14) Xerox copy of the original. Listed in CBA 6998 as in folio 6, 1845. F.W. Wyatt's copy MS Book 2 (TC), p.72. A.C. Fry's secondary copy CBA 7049, pp.343-346.

[After 8th] October 1845      From B.W. Newton
     **To J.L. Harris**      Linton

[Reply to CBA 7180(14)]. Addressed Harris 'Beloved brother'. Expressed sorrow at the rift between himself and Harris, which had been growing since March. Judged [J.N.] Darby's visit

to Plymouth to have been 'of Satan'. Stated that he believed J.N. Darby's system affected 'the whole system' of Divine truth, and the whole Church of God. Were it not so, he would leave Plymouth. Refers to his wife, who is 'somewhat better', and to Mrs Harris. 3 pages.
Original or copy in Mr Newton's hand - TC. CBA 7180(15) Xerox copy of original copy. F.W. Wyatt's copy MS Book 2 (TC), p.73. A.C. Fry's secondary copy CBA 7049, pp.346-347.

November 1845          **From Miss H---n (of Cork)**
    To B.W. Newton
Of her corroborating B.W. Newton's statements regarding *The Five Letters...* in the face of J.N. Darby's accusations to Mr and Mrs McA[dam] of devious suppression of parts of them by B.W. Newton at a 'reading meeting' in their presence. That testimony was corroborated by a conversation with Mrs B—h.
Reference in B.W. Newton's *Defence*, and therefore also in Lord Congleton's *Correspondence, etc.*, pp.24,25.

> 26th November 1845   From **Lord Congleton, G[eorge] J. Walker, J[ohn] Moseley,**
>                                                           and **J.C. Cookworthy** Plymouth
>     **To J.N. Darby**
> Writing on behalf of B.W. Newton. Requesting that J.N. Darby should nominate 4 brethren to meet 4 nominated by B.W. Newton to enquire into, and report on, the charges made against B.W. Newton by J.N. Darby at a meeting in the Ebrington Street Chapel on 17th November 1845. Listing the charges, which related to B.W. Newton's *Five Letters...*, and his *Letter to Clulow*. See CBA 7180(16)(2) for the reply.
> Original copy listed in CBA 6998 as in folio 7, 1845. CBA 7180(16)(1) Xerox copy of original copy. F.W. Wyatt's copy MS Book 2 (TC), p.76. A.C. Fry's secondary copy CBA 7049, pp.347,348.

> 27th November 1845 [received]   **From J.N. Darby**
>     **To Lord Congleton, G[eorge] J. Walker, J[ohn] Moseley, and J.C. Cookworthy**
>                                   Addressed 'to J. Moseley at Mr Clulow's, 1 Boon's Place'.
> Replying to CBA 7180(16)(1).
> Refusing to nominate 4 as to a 'worldly tribunal', stating the issue is a matter of his conscience, and should be settled before 'the Church of God'. Alleging 'a long train of facts and circumstances' to be involved. Offering to give a personal account to the addressees, and suggesting that they inform themselves from others who were present at the meeting. Suggesting that B.W. Newton takes the matter up himself as a personal wrong. See CBA 7180(16)(3) for reply.
> Original copy listed in CBA 6998 as in folio 7, 1845. CBA 7180(16)(2) Xerox copy of original copy. F.W. Wyatt's copy MS Book 2 (TC) p.76. A.C. Fry's secondary copy CBA 7049, pp.348-351.

> 28th November 1845   From **Lord Congleton, G[eorge] J. Walker, J[ohn] Moseley,**
>                                                           and **J.C. Cookworthy** Plymouth
>     **To J.N. Darby**
> Replying to CBA 7180(16)(2).
> Expressing sadness that J.N. Darby admitted to having made the alleged statements, and had expressed no withdrawal or regret. Contesting that B.W. Newton should take this up as a private wrong, but stating that as J.N. Darby had made his charges against B.W. Newton's personal character to a large gathering, without first having given B.W. Newton the opportunity of

clearing himself of the charges, a different manner of proceeding is necessary. Denying that the issues were a matter of conscience, but simply matters of fact, which competent persons could evaluate. Reluctantly concluding that J.N. Darby's reply was an 'evasion'.
See CBA 7180(16)(4) for reply.
Original copy listed in CBA 6998 as in folio 7, 1845. CBA 7180(16)(3) Xerox copy of original copy. F.W. Wyatt's copy MS Book 2 (TC), p.76. A.C. Fry's secondary copy CBA 7049, pp.351,352.

---

Undated [end November 1845] **From J.N. Darby**
    **To Lord Congleton, G[eorge] J. Walker, J[ohn] Moseley and J.C. Cookworthy**
Replying to CBA 7180(16)(3)
Objecting that none of the correspondents had personal knowledge of the circumstances of his (J.N. Darby's) charges. Requesting to be able to take a copy of his first letter. Stating that the 'subject' can be evaded no longer. Referring to J.L. Harris and C. McAdam as confidants in the content of the first letter.
Original copy listed in CBA 6998 in folio 7, 1845. CBA 7180(16)(4) Xerox copy of original copy. F.W. Wyatt's copy MS Book 2 (TC), p.77. A.C. Fry's secondary copy CBA 7049, pp.352-353.

---

10th December 1845    **From Capt. R[ichard]. Courtenay Johnson**    Nice[1]
    To B.W. Newton

Letter of sympathy. The notes on the letter make its posting unclear.
Original letter - TC. F.W. Wyatt's copy MS Book 1 (TC), pp.150-153. Listed in F.W. Wyatt's list of S.P. Tregelles's letters in the 'Rough Notes' (In the Christian Brethren Archive as FRY/1/2/1).

12th December 1845    **From W[illiam] G[raeme] Rhind**    Plymouth
    To B.W. Newton

Declaring his support for B.W. Newton amidst accusations. Acquitting B.W. Newton of the charges brought against him.
Original letter - TC. CBA 7180(17) Xerox copy of original (incomplete). F.W. Wyatt's copy MS Book 1 p.154 (TC) (complete).

14th December 1845    **From Lord Congleton**
    To B.W. Newton    Plymouth

A brief note declaring that, having heard J.N. Darby's accusations [in Ebrington Street, Plymouth 17th November 1845] and B.W. Newton's explanations, 'I find no cause to suppose you had any intention of dishonesty or untruthfulness'. He held him 'fully acquitted' of the charges made against him [B.W. Newton]. 3 pages.
Original letter - TC. CBA 7180(18) Xerox copy of original. The letter was quoted in the answer to the Rawstorne Street Meeting's summons to B.W. Newton made by Soltau, Clulow, Batten, and Dyer, and dated 25th November 1846, separately printed – ID. Therefore also in Lord Congleton's *Correspondence, etc.*, p.17 – CBA.

---

[1] Postmark 'Nizza' in the Kingdom of Sardinia - now France.

> 17th December 1845  **From H.W. Soltau**  Plymouth
> To 'the Brethren and Sisters Breaking Bread in the Ebrington Street Room'
> A note from H.W. Soltau to the congregation. J.E. Batten, W.B. Dyer[1], and J. Clulow added a note concurring with his judgement that the charges against B.W. Newton were unjustified. The letter was quoted in the answer made by Soltau, Clulow, Batten, and Dyer to the Rawstorne Street Meeting's summons to B.W. Newton, and dated 25th November 1846.
> The letter of 25th November 1846 as separately printed – ID. Also included in Lord Congleton's *Correspondence, etc.*, pp.13,14 – CBA. Not listed in CBA 6998.

Undated [After 28th December 1845]  From B.W. Newton
    **To unknown**
Signed, but undated. Refers to the attempt to interfere with the work at Plymouth in which 'all regard to truth and uprightness has been set at naught'. Comments on the role [J.N.] Darby has played. In respect of ministry, he regards the new teaching as a denial of the mode the Holy Spirit has revealed Himself to be working in the Church. Refers to the secession meeting started by J.N. Darby and his friends at Raleigh Street.
[An attached note indicates the letter has been copied for Amy J.T. Toulmin]. 5 pages.
Copied extract listed in CBA 6998 in folio 8, 1845. CBA 7180(19) Xerox copy of original, A.C. Fry's secondary copy CBA 7049, pp.354,355.

30th December 1845  **From W.G. Rhind**  Plymouth
To B.W. Newton
    Declaring the view of himself, [R.H.] Rickards, [J.] Mosel[e]y and [W.] Morris that he (B.W. Newton) was 'entirely free from the charge of moral dishonesty'. Stating that Lord Congleton concurs with their judgement. Requesting that B.W. Newton put his explanation in writing. 2 pages.
The letter was quoted in the answer made by Soltau, Clulow, Batten, and Dyer to the Rawstorne Street Meeting's summons to B.W. Newton, and dated 25th November 1846. Original letter - TC. CBA 7180(20) Xerox copy of original. Incorrectly listed in CBA 6998 in folio 8, 1845 as '31st December 1845'. The letter of 25th November 1846 was separately printed – ID. Therefore it is also in Lord Congleton's *Correspondence, etc.*, pp.16 ff. CBA.

> 31st December 1845  **From George J. Walker**  Teignmouth
> To 'brethren
> Stating his judgement that J.N. Darby's charges against B.W. Newton are unfounded.
> 2 pages.
> Listed in CBA 6998 as an original letter in folio 8, 1845. CBA 7180(21) Xerox copy of original. Listed in 7002, F.W. Wyatt's index of correspondence as in MS Bk 1 p.154, but noted by CG when viewed.

31st December 1845  **From G[ilbert].L[ester]. Wiggins**  Tottenham
    To B.W. Newton

---
[1] William B. Dyer was the older brother of Henry Dyer. Both were later leaders in the Brethren Movement.

Letter of sympathy. Writes of his thankfulness that he brought Newton to Tottenham 'last Spring' [See letter B.W. Newton to J.L. Harris (July 1845)].
Original letter - TC. Listed in CBA 6998, F.W. Wyatt's copy MS Book 1 (TC), p.155.

31st December 1845     **From W.G Rhind**
   To B.W. Newton
Incorrectly listed in CBA 6998. See 30th December 1845.

[End of 1845]          From B.W. Newton
   **To a person unknown**
A portion of a letter. The letter was sent after the secession of J.N. Darby and those who followed him to Raleigh Street.
Mr Newton considers God has regarded with favour the work thus far carried out by those 'co-operating with me in ministry' on the principles of taking the Scriptures, and them alone, as their guide. Accordingly, he regards any attempt to interfere with the work as offensive to God, especially because a 'false and deceiving system' is being introduced. 'What then must be my judgement of the effect of the influence of the individual who is the chief pillar of these things, who boasts in his attempted work of destruction, and in the doctrines he has sought to propagate? How must I feel it my duty in all legitimate ways to discourage his ways for his own sake, and for the sake of the whole Church of God… The rule I prescribe for myself I could not but desire to prescribe to you'.
It is signed by Mr Newton, but undated. F.W. Wyatt comments 'I do not recognise the writer's handwriting'. endorsed 'Copied for Amy Jane [Toulmin] at her request'.
MS Book 2 (TC), p.78.

---

1st January 1846         **From W. Morris**              Exmouth
   To 'brethren'
Replying to 'yours of 29th ult.'. Relating the charges made by J.N. Darby against B.W. Newton (regarding *The Five Letters...*) at a meeting of 300 persons. The allegation was that he (B.W. Newton) had supressed two of five MS letters, and had substituted an appendix for those letters. J.N. Darby had also made allegations regarding the *Letter to Clulow* [*Letter from B.W. Newton to J Clulow, 18 April 1845*] at the meeting. Giving a reply to the accusations, and declaring B.W. Newton innocent of the charges. Referring to Miss Jeremie.
Original letter CBA 7180(22) 6 pages. F.W. Wyatt's copy in MS Book 2 (TC), p.85. A.C. Fry's secondary copy CBA 7049, pp.366-368.

---

2nd January 1845 [*sic* for 1846]  **From R[obert] .H. Rickards**      Plymouth
   To T[homas] Lakeman, H.P.E[meric] de St Dalmas[1], R[ichard].W[alter]. Wolston [of Brixham]
Referring to the charges made against B.W. Newton, which he, and many others, had investigated, and found to be groundless.
The origin of the letter was Plymouth [given as Exmouth in A.C. Fry's secondary copy CBA 7049. Rickards was *from* Exmouth]. The location is important as it explains their being addressed together. 2 pages.

---

[1] Henri Pierre Emeric de St Dalmas (1815-1904).

## Section 9 – B.W. Newton Correspondence

> Original letter listed in CBA 6998 in folio 8. 1845. CBA 7180(23) Xerox copy of original. F.W. Wyatt's copy in MS Book 2 (TC), p.85. A.C. Fry's secondary copy CBA 7049, pp.365,366.

> 5th January 1846     **From Lord Congleton**    1, Osnaburgh St, Regents Park, London
>    **To T[homas] Lakeman, H.P.E[meric] de St Dalmas, R.W. Wolston** [of Brixham]
> Exonerates Mr Newton of the charges of dishonesty, 'having heard both sides'. It is very similar to the note to B.W. Newton of 14th December 1845. It concludes 'Sad, sad work!'. 3 pages.
> Original letter listed in CBA 6998 in folio 8, 1845. CBA 7180(24) Xerox copy of original. F.W. Wyatt's copy in MS Book 2 (TC) p.85. A.C. Fry's secondary copy CBA 7049, p.365 (shortened).

[1846?]                   From B.W. Newton
     **To a person unknown**
The recipient seems to have published a tract, giving an untrue account of events in 1846. The letter refers to J.N. Darby. Mr Newton requests that the tract be withdrawn. The letter (draft or unsent original) was evidently written in that year.
Original copy - TC. Listed in CBA 6998 in folio 7, 1845.

January 1846              From B.W. Newton
     **To a person unknown**
Describing events at Plymouth. See previous items.
Listed in CBA 6998, folio 8, 1845, but now missing from the Fry Collection. Possibly the same as the item below, from B.W. Newton to 'a brother' (1846) re-Darby's recent pamphlets.

> 5th January 1846          **From J.N. Darby**
>    To 'Dearest brother'
> In the letter he rails against B.W. Newton (Mr N), and at the manner of ordering meetings at Ebrington Street. He concluded with a postscript. 'Poor dear Mrs N is very ill – I suppose dying off. But there is nothing to distress her now. She is quite peaceful, I hear'.
> Noted by F.R. Coad, *History of the Brethren Movement*, p.146.
> In *Letters of J.N. Darby*. Vol. 1, p.91.

[Jan] 1846                From B.W. Newton
     **To 'a brother'**
Replying to the correspondent's note of the previous month. Comments on [J.N.] Darby's recent pamphlets. The letter refers to a Defence that he (B.W. Newton) had written, but not yet published [see *Correspondence, etc.*, 1846, pp.21-30]. 'It seemed inappropriate to publish a reply to the extravagant claims of Mr Darby'. B.W. Newton considered 'the accusations will refute themselves'. 'One shrinks from personalities in print'. The letter comments on [J.N.] Darby's charges against him (B.W. Newton), relating to *Thoughts on the Apocalypse*. Comments on the ceasing of the Friday meeting, and the failure of the brethren to discipline [J.N.] Darby for his intemperate behaviour and accusations. Investigation of the allegations. [J.N. Darby's] assumption of a 'sub-apostolic' role. Proposals for resolving the dispute. Refers to the suggestion of a Church meeting to judge his [B.W. Newton's] case by voting as 'the very principle of Dissent 'against which we had been protesting for 14 years'. Refers to his ministry in London. Refers to [J.G.] Deck, [H.W.] Soltau, [J.E.] Batten, [J.] Clulow, [W.B.] Dyer, Sir A

Campbell, [W.G.] Rhind, [R.C.] Chapman, [J] Mozeley [*sic* for Moseley], [G.J.] Walker, Lord Congleton, [W.] Morris, [R.W.] Rickards, [G.V.] Wigram, Potter, [J.M.] Code, [C] Hargrove, and Steward.

No date given by F.W. Wyatt. The letter gives no indication of the day, month, or year.

10 pages.

Letter or draft copied in Mr Newton's hand – TC. CBA 7180(26) Xerox copy. F.W. Wyatt's copy MS Book 2 (TC), p.81. A.C. Fry's secondary copy CBA 7049, pp.356-362. It is probably the item listed in CBA 6998 in folio 8, 1845 as 'describing events at Plymouth', and dated 'Jan. 1846'.

ND [Spring 1846?]　　　　From B.W. Newton
　　**To J.G. Deck**

Replies to J.G. Deck's letter. Recounts the events of the previous twelve months, and particularly of J.N. Darby's first attack of 1845. Refers to [J.N.] Darby's charges against himself (B.W. Newton), and the attempt of Sir A. Campbell to resolve the matter through a general meeting. F.W. Wyatt dates it as spring 1846.

It may be an unfinished letter (i.e. it does not have concluding 'Yours sincerely', etc).

Original copy in Mr Newton's hand - TC. CBA 7180(25) Xerox copy. Listed in CBA 6998 as 2 copies in folio 6, 1845 - one copy of the letter in Miss Amy J.T. Toulmin's hand is sent by her to 'a brother at a distance'. 7 pages. F.W. Wyatt's copy MS Book 2 (TC), pp.69-72.

17th January 1846　　　　**From Frederick Prideaux**[1]
　　To B.W. Newton

From S.P. Tregelles's brother-in-law. Expressing sympathy.

MS Bk 1 p.158 (TC). Listed in CBA 6998.

> 18th January 1846　　　　**From S.P. Tregelles**　　　　Rome
> 　　**To Lord Congleton**
>
> Thanks Lord Congleton for his gift. Glad to hear news of Plymouth, although everything there is trying. Refers to individual blessing received.
>
> Listed in CBA 6998. F.W. Wyatt has a copy in his manuscript book of S.P. Tregelles's related correspondence recovered by CBA in July 2011 (FRY/1/1/4). The original is now held by Tom Chantry. Full transcription and TC reference in the Appendix to *Life and Times of Samuel Prideaux Tregelles*, T.C.F. Stunt.

19th January 1846　　　　**From Miss G[eorgina]. Jeremie**
　　To B.W. Newton

Remarking on J.N. Darby's (published) *Letter to the Saints Meeting in Ebrington Street...*, in relation to the appendix that Miss Jeremie had attached to B.W. Newton's *The Five Letters...*. It refers to J.N. Darby's statements and actions, and a conversation between Miss Jeremie and J.N. Darby. It is intended to clear B.W. Newton of the charges of dishonesty that J.N. Darby laid against him on account of the circulation of *The Five Letters...*. The circumstances are described in A.C. Fry's secondary copy, CBA 7049, S.P.

---

[1] Frederick Prideaux (1817-1891). Brother of S.P. Tregelles's wife (née Sarah Anna Prideaux). See *In Memoriam FP: a Letter to his Nephews and Nieces from FAP* in Section 12, Miscellaneous Biographical Items, of this Guide

## Section 9 – B.W. Newton Correspondence

Tregelles's preface to the published *The Five Letters...*, and B.W. Newton's *Defence*. 4 pages.
Original letter - TC. CBA 7180(27) Xerox copy. F.W. Wyatt's copy MS Book 2 (TC), p.86. A.C. Fry's secondary copy CBA 7049, pp.363-365.

7th February 1846          **From Lord Congleton**
    To B.W. Newton
Expresses fears about his own sectarian tendency, and consequent resolution to stay away from Plymouth.
Original letter - TC. Listed in CBA 6998. F.W. Wyatt's copy MS Book 1 (TC), p.158.

5th March 1846          From B.W. Newton          Plymouth
    **To William Berger**
Re the Investigation of J.N. Darby's charges. Explaining his (B.W. Newton's) principles.
cf. J.N. Darby *Account of the Proceedings at Rawstorne Street*: *Collected Writings* 20, Ecclesiastical 4.
Original (letter copied by Amy J.T. Toulmin) - TC. Listed in CBA 6998. F.W. Wyatt's copy MS Book 2 (TC), p.80.

10th March 1846  **From Edward Cronin (Brixton),**
    **Robert Howard (Tottenham), John E. Howard (Tottenham),**
    **Wm. Berger (Upper Clapton)**
    To B.W. Newton
A request for a meeting in view of 'the present distress'. CBA 7002 (F.W. Wyatt's listing of correspondence) suggests 'no person addressed, but like a circular'. One of 'the London Letters'.
cf. J.N. Darby *Account of the Proceedings at Rawstorne Street*: *Collected Writings* 20, Ecclesiastical 4, and Lord Congleton's *Correspondence, etc.*
Listed in CBA 6998 in folio 2, 1846 as in a circular 'containing the following letters'.
F.W. Wyatt's copy in MS Book 1 p.143 (TC).

20th March 1846          From B.W. Newton
    **To a 'brother' [Wm. Berger]**
The letter complains that the investigation into the dispute with Darby has not been planned with thought of Scriptural guidance. Offers to answer questions on paper. One of 'the London Letters'. 'Reply to the summons to Rawstorne Street...' is appended in another handwriting.
cf. J.N. Darby *Account of the Proceedings at Rawstorne Street*: *Collected Writings* 20, Ecclesiastical 4, and Lord Congleton's *Correspondence, etc.* 4 pages.
CBA 7180(28) Xerox copy. Listed in CBA 6998 in folio 2, 1846 as in a circular, where the recipient is identified as Wm. Berger.
F.W. Wyatt's copy in MS Book 1 p.143 (TC).

28th March 1846          **From Edward Cronin, etc.**
    To B.W. Newton
    One of 'the London Letters'. See letters at 10th March 1846 and following.

cf. J.N. Darby *Account of the Proceedings at Rawstorne Street*: *Collected Writings* 20, Ecclesiastical 4, and Lord Congleton's *Correspondence, etc...*
Listed in CBA 6998 in folio 2, 1846 as in a circular. F.W. Wyatt's copy in MS Book 1 p.145 (TC).

> 3rd April 1846        **From Messrs Soltau, B.W. Newton, Dyer, Clulow, and Batten**
>    **To Brethren in London**
> One of 'the London Letters'
> cf. J.N. Darby *Account of the Proceedings at Rawstorne Street*: *Collected Writings* 20, Ecclesiastical 4, and Lord Congleton's *Correspondence, etc.*
> Listed in CBA 6998 in folio 2, 1846 as in a circular also listed as a separately printed item ('various other tracts' No.32).
> It appears to have been originally in MS Book 1 (TC), but to have been removed.

> 4th April 1846        **From Lord Congleton**        Regent's Park, London
>    **To William Berger (Clapton)**
> Declining invitation to meet J.N. Darby and G.V. Wigram, because of J.N. Darby's defamation of B.W. Newton. 'I consider Mr Darby has made a division in the gathering of saints at Plymouth'. There is with the letter an attachment: Headed 'Rawstorne Street, Nov. 14 1846' referring to 'the meeting at E. Cronin's (10 Nov. 1846)' at which it was urged upon Mr Newton the need for investigation, which was challenged by some present.
> Original copy of a letter - TC. CBA 7180(29) Xerox copy. Listed in CBA 6998 in folio 2, 1846 as two copies, but only one copy located.

> 4th April 1846        **From S.P. Tregelles**        Rome
>    **To Lord Congleton**        Osnaburgh St, Regents Park, London
> Concerning Lord Congleton's gift. Regarding information given by Lord Congleton concerning Plymouth. 'It may be that several have practically forgotten in some measure their oneness with the whole body of Christ'. Speaks of 'grievous wolves' entering in, and of 'those within who speak perverse things'. Regarding fellowship and opportunities in Rome. Access to the Vatican MS to collate it. Requesting the letter be forwarded to Plymouth, and for B.W. Newton and John Howard to be advised of his progress with the Vatican.
> F.W. Wyatt has a copy in his manuscript book of S.P. Tregelles related correspondence recovered by CBA in July 2011 (FRY/1/1/4). Original letter - TC. Annotated transcription of the whole letter in T.C.F. Stunt, *Life and Times of Samuel Prideaux Tregelles* (2020) pp.209-14

6th April 1846        **From Edward Cronin**
   To B.W. Newton
One of 'the London Letters'
cf. J.N. Darby *Account of the Proceedings at Rawstorne Street*: *Collected* Writings 20, Ecclesiastical 4, and Lord Congleton's *Correspondence, etc...*
Listed in CBA 6998 in folio 2, 1846 as in a circular. F.W. Wyatt's copy in MS Book 1 p.149 (TC).

## Section 9 – B.W. Newton Correspondence

[April 1846]  **From H.W. Soltau, B.W. Newton, W.B. Dyer, Joseph Clulow, J.E. Batten**
  **To Edward Cronin etc.**

One of 'the London Letters'

cf. J.N. Darby *Account of the Proceedings at Rawstorne Street*: *Collected Writings* 20, Ecclesiastical 4, and Lord Congleton's *Correspondence, etc…*

Listed in CBA 6998, as a printed copy of the letter in folio 2, 1846. F.W. Wyatt's copy in MS Book 1 (TC).

8th April 1846     From B.W. Newton
  **To Brethren (Brixton)**

One of 'the London Letters'

cf. J.N. Darby *Account of the Proceedings at Rawstorne Street*: *Collected Writings* 20, Ecclesiastical 4, and Lord Congleton's *Correspondence, etc.*

Listed in CBA 6998 in folio 2, 1846 as in a circular. F.W. Wyatt's copy in MS Book 1 (TC).

13th April 1846     **From S.P. Tregelles**     Florence
  To B.W. Newton

Lengthy letter. Thankful for the improved account of 'cousin Hannah' [Newton's wife]. He is not well informed regarding events in Plymouth. He wants Clulow to write. Miss Pigeon has informed him. Grateful for the way the sisters in Clapham have been kept simple and true. Comments on the defects of 'Brethrenism'. Recounts his fortunes in Rome. The principal object of his visit has failed (to see the Codex Vaticanus). Refers to the Codex Amiatinus (Vulgate). Meetings with the Pope and Cardinals. 'It troubles me that I am only like one learning how to do such a work as that I have before me'. Reference to Lord Congleton and financial support. Reference to Emily Weston. 9 pages in F.W. Wyatt's copy.

Original letter - TC. Listed in CBA 6998. F.W. Wyatt has a copy in his manuscript book of S.P. Tregelles related correspondence recovered by CBA in July 2011 (FRY/1/1/4). The full text of the letter with notes is given in T.C.F. Stunt, *The Life and Times of Samuel Prideaux Tregelles*, Appendix of unpublished letters.

16th April 1846     **From Lord Congleton**
  To B.W. Newton

Describing the meeting in London, to which he had gone, although he was only there on the second day.

cf. J.N. Darby *Account of the Proceedings at Rawstorne Street*: *Collected Writings* 20, Ecclesiastical 4.

Original letter - TC. Listed in CBA 6998 as in folio 3, 1846. F.W. Wyatt's copy MS Book 1 (TC), p.158.

8th May 1846     **From Lord Congleton**
  To B. W. Newton

He states "there is scarcely anybody of those outside of Plymouth that approves of John Darby's conduct. There is scarcely anybody that does not feel that <u>as a fact</u> things at

Ebrington Street are in your hands'. However, suggests Newton should leave Plymouth for a season as soon as Mr Darby leaves. [As F.W. Wyatt comments, he could not, because his wife was dying].

Many corrections, amendments, and obliterations in the letter.

cf. J.N. Darby *Account of the Proceedings at Rawstorne Street*: Collected Writings 20, Ecclesiastical 4.

Original letter - TC. Listed in CBA 6998 in folio 3, 1846. F.W. Wyatt's copy MS Book 1 (TC), p.161.

14th May 1846          From B.W. Newton          Plymouth
**To 'My Dear Brother' [A.A. Rees]**[1]

A printed letter on worship and ministry. It was later reprinted for private circulation in September 1875 by A.A. Rees of Sunderland 'to show that, almost from the beginning, there was a variety of views among the leading 'Brethren", even at Plymouth, as to "The principle and degree of open Ministry and Worship"'. G.V. Wigram included it in his critical tract *Plain Evidence concerning Ebrington Street as to the Nature of the System now pursued thereby* (CBA 14182). Rev. A. A. Rees later wrote to B.W. Newton asking him if he was still in agreement with the letter - see the letter 15th November 1882 from C.Y. Biss to Rev. A.A. Rees.

See also Section 3, B.W. Newton's Published Works *Letter on Worship and Ministry*.

Transcript of the letter CBA 7065, pp.119-125. Transcript of the (published) letter in F.W. Wyatt's hand (7 pages) recovered by the CBA in July 2011, FRY/1/6/4. No printed copy has been located.

---

**18th May 1846 – Death of B.W. Newton's first wife (née Hannah Abbott).**

---

17th August 1846          From B.W. Newton          Plymouth
**To a person unknown**          Plymouth

On prophetic truth. The Archangel Michael, Melchizedek etc. Answers questions.

Copied by Wyatt in MS Book 1 (TC), p.163. Listed in the 'Rough Notes'.

---

29th September 1846    **From W.G. Rhind**        Ross
     **To H.W. Soltau**

Regarding B.W. Newton. Criticising J.N. Darby's reprehensible behaviour in connection with B.W. Newton, and his needing 'stern rebuke'. Referring to J.L. Harris in March 1845, and Rhind's statements at the Ebrington Street Chapel in December 1845. 4 pages.

Copy of the Letter in Amy J.T. Toulmin's hand – TC. Xerox copy of original CBA 7180(30), A.C. Fry's secondary copy CBA 7049, pp.368-369.

---

[1] For further information on A. A. Rees and his views on worship and ministry, see The Early Development of Arthur Augustus Rees and his relations with the Brethren, by Timothy C.F. Stunt, *Brethren Archivists and Historians Network Review* (BAHNR) 4:22-35.

## Section 9 – B.W. Newton Correspondence

5th November 1846      **From Lord Congleton**      Brighton
To 'My Dear Brother' [B.W. Newton]
Declining to accompany him to Oxford[1] or to identify himself with the Ebrington Street meeting. Condemns J.N. Darby's *Narrative of Facts…* as a 'shameful misrepresentation'.
Original letter - TC. Listed in CBA 6998. F.W. Wyatt's copy MS Book 2 (TC), p.89. A.C. Fry's secondary copy, CBA 7049, p.374.

11th November 1846
Listed in CBA 7002, F.W. Wyatt's index of correspondence, as 'summons to B.W. N. to appear to undergo investigation', as at p.165 of MS Book 1 (TC), followed by B.W. Newton's reply p.166. Is this confused with the next item?

12th November 1846      **From John (?) King – or S. Tomkins**
To B.W. Newton
Giving a set of questions for B.W. Newton to answer. The name is unclear from the handwriting. F.W. Wyatt in the 'Rough Notes' describes him as 'an unknown individual', 'an irresponsible private individual' who presented a set of 'horribly put' questions for Mr Newton to answer regarding 'your conduct', etc.
Listed in CBA 6998 in Folio 4, 1846, but the original has not been located.
[A note in MS Book 2 (TC) follows Lord Congleton's letter of 5th November 1846, and asks Mr Newton the following questions, which may relate to this item.
Re- 1. His willingness to undergo an investigation. 2. Whether his views on ministry are different from those of the majority. 3. Whether agreement on prophecy is essential to meeting at the Lord's Table. 4. Whether there is place for 'responsibility' in the Church, and whether it devolves upon one individual or appointment.]. See the note on the item of 11th November 1846.

Undated ['Saturday' 1846/7]      From B.W. Newton      Plymouth
**To unknown**      London
Referring to Mr Newton's visit to London and Oxford [see letter from Lord Congleton, dated 5 November 1846]. States that 'Wigram is, as you know, here'. G.V. Wigram had criticised Mr Newton for holding meetings in London, and threatened not to eat bread with him, 'nor meet with me, save at the Lord's Table'. Requests a note to confirm that he did nothing to deserve such treatment.
Original draft of a letter in Mr Newton's own hand - TC. Listed in CBA 6998, and the 'Rough Notes' in the end of 1846 Folio 7. F.W. Wyatt's copy MS Book 2 (TC), p.92.

---

[1] See undated letter [1846/7] also referring to a visit to Oxford. NB F.W. Wyatt states that that letter is to 'unknown', 'perhaps BWN'.

1846                        From B.W. Newton

**To Rawstorne Street**

Draft in B.W. Newton's hand of his reply to a summons from Rawstorne Street. This was probably the undated letter from B.W. Newton that F.W. Wyatt suggests may have been an unsent reply, which was replaced by the letter sent on the 9th December 1846.

cf. J.N. Darby *Account of the Proceedings at Rawstorne Street*: Collected Writings 20, Ecclesiastical 4.

Original draft - TC. Listed in CBA 6998 as in folio 4, 1846. F.W. Wyatt's copy MS Book 2 (TC), p.166.

20th November 1846     **From W.H. Dorman**            London
     To B.W. Newton           Plymouth

Requesting that B.W. Newton reconsider his refusal to meet the Brethren at Rawstorne Street to face the charges of J.N. Darby.

In Lord Congleton's *Correspondence, etc.*, pp.5,6.

---

23rd November 1846 **From H.W. Soltau**     7, Woodside, Plymouth
    **To R[obert] Howard**              Ashmore (Dorset)

Writes in defence of Mr Newton, and concerning J.N. Darby's hostility since his arrival in Plymouth in March 1845. Outlines the charges made against Mr Newton, and replies to them. Rejects a proposal that Mr Newton should remain silent in the face of the accusations. 10 pages. Original copy of the letter - TC. F.W. Wyatt's copy MS Book 2 (TC), pp.89-91 –A.C. Fry's secondary copy CBA 7049, pp.369-373. CBA 6998 notes two copies in different handwriting. Listed in CBA 6998 in folio 4 and 5 1846.

25th November 1846 **From H.W. Soltau**     7 Woodside [Plymouth]
    **To W.H. Dorman**            Southampton Street, Reading

On behalf of B.W. Newton. He and others had asked B.W. Newton to be able to answer W.H. Dorman's letter on 20th November 1846 in his stead, and had counselled him not to accept the invitation to the proposed meeting.

Original copy of the letter - TC. In Lord Congleton's *Correspondence, etc.*, p.6. Two copies in different handwriting listed in CBA 6998 folio 4,5, 1846.

---

25th November 1846 **From H.W. Soltau, Joseph Clulow, J.E. Batten, W.B. Dyer**
                                                                        7, Woodside, Plymouth

    **[To W.H. Dorman**           Reading]

Replying to W.H. Dorman's letter of 20th November 1846.

Outlines J.N. Darby's actions towards the fellowship at Plymouth from when he arrived in March 1845. His charges had passed from concern with prophetic issues, to Church order, to accusations against B.W. Newton's veracity. The investigation of the charges by the Ebrington Street fellowship is recounted. A copy of B.W. Newton's *Defence* was enclosed in the parcel, and the letter of the leaders at Ebrington Street to the congregation regarding the accusations against B.W. Newton (17th December 1845) was also copied, as were favourable letters from Lord Congleton (14th December 1845), and W.G. Rhind (30th December 1845). In the letter the correspondents object to the manner in which J.N. Darby has behaved at such meetings, and to G.V. Wigram's influence in London, and his bias. They also state 'we have always denied that the congregated Church is a deliberative assembly', protesting against the principles of Dissenters.

## Section 9 – B.W. Newton Correspondence

This letter was 'Printed, but not published' - for the information of many on why the correspondents counselled Mr Newton to decline the request for him to attend the proposed meeting at Rawstorne Street. 'A copy of the letter may be obtained, gratuitously, by brethren in the Lord, on application, either personally or by letter, to Mr Campbell, 1 Warwick-square, London, or 5, Cornwall Street, Plymouth' – ID.
The letter was also included in Lord Congleton's *Correspondence, etc.*, pp.9-21. CBA.

---

26th November 1846 **From J. Clulow** Plymouth
    **To W. H. Dorman** Southampton Street, Reading
A holding letter promising a full reply to his letter of 20th November 1846 by the following day.
In Lord Congleton's *Correspondence, etc...*, p.7

---

27th November 1846 **From W.H. Dorman** Southampton Street, Reading
    **To J. Clulow** Plymouth
Regretting the letters J. Clulow and H.W. Soltau had sent on B.W. Newton's behalf. He had acted upon Soltau's letter as a definitive refusal, and he would decline to read to the fellowship at Rawstorne Street any reasons that would be given for the refusal of B.W. Newton to answer their charges. Noting that J. Clulow's parcel of 25th November 1846 had just arrived.
In Lord Congleton's *Correspondence, etc*, pages 7,8.

---

24th November 1846        From B.W. Newton        Plymouth
    **To 'My Dear Brother' [Lord Congleton?]**
Replying to his letter. Apologising for the delay of his response, as he needed to consult the Brethren 'in this place'. He agreed with a way of proceeding, suggested by the correspondent, to enable each person gathering to satisfy themselves regarding the truth of 'the allegations printed and circulated against us'. This would involve three or four impartial individuals considering the charges made in the many tracts, and their answer from those gathered at Plymouth. 'We do not think there is any mode[?] in which the saints can rightly enter on the investigation of these things except they do it as individuals or as representing the gathering with which they are individually connected'.
Copy in B.W. Newton's hand. 2 pages. CBA.

---

4th December 1846 **From Joseph Clulow** Plymouth
    **To W.H. Dorman** 40, Southampton Street, Reading
Requesting the return of B.W. Newton's *Defence*, enclosed in Soltau's letter of 25th November 1846.
In Lord Congleton's *Correspondence, etc*, p.31 – CBA.

---

5th December 1846 **From W.H. Dorman** Reading
    **To J. Clulow** Plymouth
Returning B.W. Newton's pamphlet, *Defence*, and stating that he considered the letter of Soltau of 25th November unsatisfactory.
In Lord Congleton's *Correspondence, etc...*, p.31 - CBA

## Section 9 – B.W. Newton Correspondence

7th December 1846      **From W.H. Dorman and Henry Gough**     London
    To B.W. Newton

Final request ('the second citation') to B.W. Newton to appear before the Rawstorne Street meeting, with a deadline of 11th December for his reply, and threatening excommunication.
In Lord Congleton's *Correspondence, etc.*, pp.36,37 – CBA.
Original letter - TC. Listed in CBA 6998 as in folio 5, 1846.

9th December 1846      **From B.W. Newton, H.W. Soltau, W.B. Dyer, J. Clulow,**
                                 **J.E. Batten**      Plymouth
    To Messrs W.H. Dorman and H Gough

A reply with 'the most firm and decided negative' to the request made in Dorman and Gough's letter of 7th December 1846, as against principles that they had already declared. Warning against the course of action that they (the Rawstorne Street meeting) were proposing.
There is also an undated letter from B.W. Newton in MS Book 1 (TC), which Wyatt suggests may have been an unsent reply that was replaced by the one here. (See the entry before 20th November 1846).
Printed in Congleton's *Correspondence, etc.*, p.36 – CBA.
Original - TC. Original listed in CBA 6998 in folio 5, 1846.

---

10th December 1846    **From S.P. Tregelles**
    **To Henry Gough [for the Rawstorne Street Assembly]**

Declaring that the 'character, objects, and competency for discipline' of the meeting proposed the following evening is 'wholly contrary to the Word of God, and the authority of our Lord Jesus Christ'. It was read at the meeting by Henry Gough.
Included in the 'printed, not published' pamphlet in January 1847 - *A Letter from Mr Tregelles to Mr Gough relative to the exclusion of Mr Newton from the Lord's Table in Rawstorne Street, London*.
[Note on 1th December 1846 continued]. See the record of S.P. Tregelles's letter of 10th December, the letter of William Blake et al. to the Rawstorne Street Assembly dated 22nd January 1847, and the note in Appendix 3, Select Publications list regarding *A Letter from Mr Tregelles to Mr Gough*. It is quoted in full in W. Blair Neatby, *A History of the Plymouth Brethren*.
Included in CBA 13813, (Xerox copy) 24 pages. Original (ID).

---

ND [12th December 1846]      **From J. Scoble**      London
    **To Miss J[eremie]? [or T(oulmin)].**

The letter gives an account of the meeting in London. Mentioned in J.N. Darby's *Account of the Proceedings at Rawstorne Street* (there incorrectly spelled 'Scobell'). The date is derived from the reference to it in Frederick Prideaux's letter to S.P. Tregelles of 12th December 1846, which refers to the meeting having been 'the previous evening' – i.e. 11th December 1846. F.W. Wyatt copies the letter as to 'My Dear Miss J'. It is undated, but the original could possibly read 'My Dear Miss T'.
Original - TC. Listed in CBA 6998, F.W. Wyatt's copy in MS Book 1 (TC), p.140.

## Section 9 – B.W. Newton Correspondence

> 12th December 1846   **From Frederick Prideaux**[1],   5 Middleton Square
>   **To S.P. Tregelles**
> Gives an account of the previous evening's meeting at Rawstorne Street Meeting regarding B.W. Newton. Refers to Scoble at the meeting.
> Original copy of the letter - TC. Two copies listed in CBA 6998 in folios 1 and 5, 1846. One, according to the 'Rough Notes' was a duplicate in Miss Amy J.T. Toulmin's hand.
> F.W. Wyatt's copy MS Book 1 (TC) 136-139. CBA 7002, F.W. Wyatt's listing of correspondence, gives the date as 11th December 1846.

13th December 1846      **From W.H. Dorman and H. Gough**  London
    To B.W. Newton                Plymouth
Announcing B.W. Newton's excommunication from the fellowship of those gathering at Rawstorne Street, until he submits to an investigation by them of the charges made against him.
Original letter - TC. Reproduced in Lord Congleton's *Correspondence, etc,* p.50 – CBA.

> 15th December 1846  From **J. Clulow, H.W. Soltau, J.E. Batten, W.B. Dyer.**
>                                                         Plymouth
>   **To W.H. Dorman, and H. Gough, etc**. London
> Lengthy and careful reply protesting at the injustice, and oppressiveness of the actions of those associated with the Rawstorne Street meeting, and at their personal attack upon B.W. Newton. Repeats a number of their concerns and principles; for example questioning the apparent aspiration towards a 'Titus and Timothy' ministry by those who were acting with the Rawstorne Street meeting.
> The letter replies to 'your "communication" (Dated 7th December 1846)', but a postscript gives comment on 'your communication of 13th inst. excommunicating our brother Mr Newton which arrived whilst it was being drafted'.
> In Lord Congleton's *Correspondence, etc,* pp.37-50 – CBA.

> 16th December 1846  **From S.P. Tregelles**              Plymouth
>   **To H. Gough**            London
> This was a letter published 'by request' [of William Blake, John Scoble, and Frederick Prideaux].[2] It was a remonstrance to Henry Gough as a representative of the Rawstorne Street meeting. It objected to their novel procedure (excommunication is for unrepentant sinners); their novel offence (non-obedience to their summons); their adoption of an unscriptural procedure (the congregation as a deliberative assembly); their misuse of Matt. 18, and their ignoring of verse 15; their failure to state definite charges; their disregard of the investigation and exoneration that had already taken place at Plymouth; their disregard of Mr Newton's attempt to answer the charges by 'any fair, legitimate or Scriptural means' whilst he had been in London; their distortion of the need for a face to face meeting, claiming it to be 'a commandment of the Lord', and 'direction of the Holy Ghost'; their unreasonable demand for an immediate response; Mr Dorman's suppression of the reply from Plymouth; suppression of evidence and letters at the meetings (a sister was rebuked for questioning selective quotation from a letter); their false claim

---

[1] Frederick Prideaux (1817-1853). Brother of S.P. Tregelles's wife (née Sarah Anna Prideaux). See In Memoriam FP: a Letter to his Nephews and Nieces from FAP in Section 12, Miscellaneous Biographical Items, of this Guide

[2] Published as, *A Letter from Mr Tregelles to Mr Gough, relative to the exclusion of Mr Newton from the Lord's Table in Rawstorne Street, London.* 24 pages, 1847.

that all present concurred with the judgement (they should at least have stated it was a majority verdict. 'If you set up a democracy, you must do it properly'); that a reply was demanded under threat; that the manner of proceeding towards Plymouth implied metropolitan jurisdiction (as the Church of Rome claimed such a status); the weakness of the demand to 'satisfy their conscience' with no regard to the consciences of others; the contrast with the way that grave charges of dishonesty against Mr Wigram had been dealt with in 1844; the leading role taken by Mr Wigram despite his public maligning of B.W. Newton, and his unbridled animus against him. Mr Tregelles is thankful Mr Gough did read his letter of 10th December 1846 at the previous meeting. He disavows fellowship with Rawstorne Street on the grounds of their new position. There are three appendices giving detail of the events and circumstances.

See the record of S.P. Tregelles's letter of 10th December, the letter of William Blake et al. to the Rawstorne Street Assembly dated 22nd January 1847, and the note in Appendix 3, Select Publications list of this *Guide*. Quoted by Blair Neatby *A History of the Plymouth Brethren* p.128n. Printed in the pamphlet, *A Letter from Mr Tregelles to Mr Gough relative to the Exclusion of Mr Newton from the Lord's Table in Rawstorne Street, London*. I.K. Campbell, 1, Warwick Square, and at the Tract Depot, Plymouth,

24 pages. CBA 13813 (the only known copy).

---

25th December 1846  **From H.W. Soltau, J.E. Batten, W.B. Dyer, J. Clulow,** Plymouth

'**To the Saints at Rawstorne-street,** London, on whose behalf W.H. Dorman, and H. Gough have acted'

This letter reminds those at Rawstorne Street of the solemnity of placing a person outside of the Church and of handing over to Satan through excommunication. It therefore also highlights the grounds for such excommunication– (1) The nature of excommunicable sin, (2) Incontrovertible proof, (3) The hardened and impenitent condition of the subject, (4) That it should be 'the universal act of the whole Church', not simply of a 'majority concurring'.

It shows that the guidance of the Scriptures was not followed, and that some present did not concur with the judgement of 'this tribunal'. It points out the sectarian nature of the judgement as it is based on differences of principles.

[Note on letter 25th December 1846 contnued]. It concludes, 'We solemnly and unitedly avow our entire denial of its validity – We declare that obedience to it would be disobedience to the Lord; and obedience to the Lord demands disobedience to it, and thus record our solemn and earnest protest against it'.

Printed as a pamphlet entitled, *Remonstrance and Protest addressed to the Saints at Rawstorne Street, London, respecting their late act of Excluding Mr Newton, from the Lord's Table*, published at the Tract Depot, 5 Cornwall Street, Plymouth and sold by I.K. Campbell, 1, Warwick Square, London, 12 pages.  CBA 6374(2).

---

2nd January 1847  **From [J]ames [P]ringle Riach**[1]  Plymouth

To B.W. Newton

Confirming that J.N. Darby did accuse B.W. Newton with untruthfulness at the Ebrington Street meeting of 17th November 1845. The charges related to B.W. Newton's appendix to his *The Five Letters...* 4 pages.

MS Book 1 p.171 (TC); Xerox copy CBA 7180(31).

---

[1] James Pringle Riach (c1798-1865). Both he and his wife (Louisa Sophia) were intensely loyal supporters of Mr Newton and S.P. Tregelles throughout their lives.

## Section 9 – B.W. Newton Correspondence

> 8th January 1847     **From C. McAdam**     Countess Wear [Exeter]
>     **To George Treffry**[1]
> A note accompanying the return of the unopened parcel of booklets (Congleton's *Correspondence, etc...*) intended for the believers at Exeter. He states he disapproves of this means of disseminating information to the saints.
> Original - TC. F.W. Wyatt's copy in MS Book 1 (TC), p.172. In CBA 6998 it appears to be wrongly recorded as 10th January 1847, which was the date that it was sent to Miss Toulmin.

> 10th January 1847     **From [George] Treffry**
>     **To C. McAdam**
> Expresses surprise at C. McAdam's disapproval of the means used to convey information to the saints, as C. McAdam had circulated J.N. Darby's *Narrative of Facts*.
> This letter was enclosed in the letter of 19th January 1847 from Geo Treffry to Amy J.T. Toulmin.
> Original copy of letter - TC. Listed in CBA 6998 as in folio 1, 1847.

> 10th January 1847     **From C. McAdam**
>     **To [Geo.?] Treffry**
> Listed in CBA 6998. Appears to be an incorrect listing of the letter of 8th January 1847 that was enclosed in George Treffry's letter of 10th January 1847 to Amy J.T. Toulmin.

> 18th January 1847     **From George Treffry**     Exeter
>     **To Amy J.T. Toulmin**     Plymouth
> Describes the agitation in Exeter[2], and encloses correspondence with Mr McAdam (see letter listed at 8th January 1847). Regarding the circulation of the *Correspondence, etc...*, and the *Remonstrance....* 'I am getting into a regular hornet's nest'. Referring to S.P. Tregelles's Letter, T[reffry]'s note to C. McAdam, Mrs Roger and Mrs Turner, H.W. Soltau, Mr Woodman, J.L. Harris, and B.W. Newton. 4 pages.
> [Note on letter of 18th January 1847 continued]
> Original - TC. CBA 7180(32) Xerox copy of original. Listed in CBA 6998 in folio 1, 1847. F.W. Wyatt's copy in MS Book 1 (TC), p.171. CBA 7002, F.W. Wyatt's index of correspondence, gives the date as 10th January 1847.

22nd January 1847   **From G.V. Wigram** Treeby's, Grocer, Tavistock Place,
                                                                                                Plymouth
    To B.W. Newton,             Gasking Street [Plymouth]
An invitation to B.W. Newton to come to a proposed public investigation in London. Assuring Mr Newton of 'courtesy and fair-play', if he will come and be examined.
Original TC. Original letter listed in CBA 6998 1847, folio 1. F.W. Wyatt's copy in MS Book 1 (TC), p.173.

---

[1] B.W. Newton's cousin
[2] CBA FRY1/1/1 p.117 states 'I had a large work in Exeter. That was before Darby's affair'. ' had large congregations – perhaps 2,000'.

> **22nd January 1847**   **From William Blake, John Scoble, Frederick Prideaux**
> To the Brethren and Sisters in the Lord meeting for Christian fellowship
> in Rawstorne Street, London
> A letter that prefaced the published letter of S.P. Tregelles to Mr Gough. It states that they have been misrepresented as concurring in the act of excommunication of B.W. Newton by Rawstorne Street, though they strenuously objected to its unscriptural character. It explains that they requested permission to print Mr Tregelles's letter as it gives reasons why they cannot concur. The letter of S.P. Tregelles is dated 16th December 1846. See the record of that, and the note of it, under the date, and in Appendix 3, Select Publications list of this *Guide*.
> CBA 13813, 24 pages.

25th January 1847            From B.W. Newton            Plymouth
  **To 'a friend and sister'**
Replying to her note. Declaring the falseness of the charges in [J.N. Darby's] *Narrative of Facts*... Refers to a conversation between his (B.W. Newton's) mother and Sir A Campbell on [J.N.] Darby's accusations. An unfinished draft/copy? 4 pages.
Original - TC. CBA 7180(33) Xerox copy of original. Listed CBA 6998, 1847, folio 1. F.W. Wyatt's copy in MS Book 1 (TC), p.178.

> **30th January 1847**   **From H.W. Soltau**   7, Woodside, Plymouth
>   **To G.V. Wigram et al**
> Replying on behalf of W.B. Dyer, J.E. Batten, J. Clulow, and himself to a letter from G.V. Wigram et al, dated 22nd January Declining the invitation made to attend a meeting at Rawstorne Street Chapel; Regarding B.W. Newton's 'Reasons' being circulated to brethren. 4 pages.
> Original copy made by Soltau - TC.  CBA 7180(34) Xerox copy of original.
> F.W. Wyatt's copy in MS Book 1 (TC), p.174.

> **6th February 1847**   **From Chas Billett, Frederick Jackson, Edw. [W?]are,**
>   **William Whiting, Geo. Morrish, and G.W. Medes,** of Walworth
>   **To J. Hammond, W.T. Starling, and E. Leffler**
> This is the refusal of some at Walworth to attend the meeting regarding B.W. Newton at Rawstorne Street.
> [Note on letter of 6th February 1847 continued]. A printed copy of the letter, listed in CBA 6998 as in folio 2, 1847 is now missing. F.W. Wyatt's copy in MS Book 1 (TC), p.176, where it is noted as a 'Printed Circular'.

> **7th February 1847**   **From Lord Congleton**
>   **To J. Hammond, W.T. Starling, and E. Leffler**
> Refusal to attend the proposed meeting on February 9th. Enclosed a copy of S.P. Tregelles's *Letter to Gough* of last December [See note under letters of 10th and 16th December 1846].
> On February 27th Congleton published *Reasons for Leaving the Rawstorne Street Meeting*. Wigram replied to it in a tract dated 2nd April 1847.
> Original in Lord Congleton's own hand - TC. Listed in CBA 6998 as in folio 2, 1847. F.W. Wyatt's copy in MS Book 1 (TC), p.176.

10th February 1847 **From Lord Congleton**
    To B.W. Newton

Expressing disgust with Darby.
Original in his own hand - TC. CBA 7002, F.W. Wyatt's index of correspondence, lists it as at MS Book 1 p. 177 (TC) – not verified. Listed in CBA 6998 as in folio 2, 1847.

10th Feb. 1847 From B.W. Newton
    **To 'My Dear Sister in the Lord'**

Written with regard to the accusations made against him. 'I reject with abhorrence all notion of clergy and laity'. Called by F.W. Wyatt 'explanatory and expository'.
Original Copied in Miss Amy J.T. Toulmin's hand - TC. Listed in 6998 as in Folio 2. F.W. Wyatt's copy in MS Book 1 (TC), p.179.

> 30th April 1847 **From H.W. Soltau**
>     To R.C. Chapman
>
> Regarding the Friday night meeting.
> The letter states that he (R.C. Chapman) considers the extracts from Harris's letters respecting the Friday meeting to be a suppression of the truth.
> F.W. Wyatt's copy in MS Book 1 (TC), pp.182,183.

7th May 1847 From B.W. Newton     Plymouth
    **To Miss Egerton**     Darlington Street, Bath

Replying to her note. Answering charge [by Sir C. Brenton] that he (B.W. Newton) holds false doctrine in relation to Heb. 11:4 (Abel's sacrifice). 4 pages.
Original copy in Miss Amy J.T. Toulmin's hand - TC. CBA 7180(35) Xerox copy of original. F.W. Wyatt's copy in MS Book 1 (TC), pp.187 ff.

[May 1847] Undated **From Robert C. Chapman**,     Barnstaple
    To B.W. Newton

Invitation to visit and stay with him, in very jocular language. 'With much love'.
Original (copy) - TC. Listed in CBA 6998 as in folio 4, 1847. F.W. Wyatt's copy in MS Book 1 (TC), p.184.

9th May 1847 From B.W. Newton
    **To R.C Chapman**

Acceptance of invitation to visit him. Willing to come at once 'for the sake of manifested fellowship', but does not see his way clear to coming directly unless the Lord should enable it.
Original copy of letter - TC. Listed in CBA 6998 as in Folio 4, 1847. F.W. Wyatt's copy in MS Book 1 (TC), p.184.

15th May 1847 **From H.P.E. de St Dalmas**
    To B.W. Newton

Announcing B.W. Newton's excommunication. 'An astonishing letter' (F.W. Wyatt in the 'Rough Notes').

One of the five 'Brixham letters', others from Wolston, Kendrick and Morris.
Original (copy) - TC. Listed in CBA 6998 as in folio 5, 1847. F.W. Wyatt's copy in MS Book 1 (TC), pp.187 ff.

16th May 1847 **From R.W. Wolston**
To B.W. Newton
Expressing disapproval of de St Dalmas' action, and sympathy with B.W. Newton. One of the five 'Brixham letters'.
Original (copy) - TC. Listed in CBA 6998 as in Folio 5, 1847.
F.W. Wyatt's copy in MS Book 1 (TC), pp.187 ff.

16th May 1847 **From W. Morris**
To B.W. Newton
Expressing disapproval of de St Dalmas' action, and sympathy with B.W. Newton. One of the five 'Brixham letters'.
Original (copy) - TC. Listed in CBA 6998 as in Folio 5, 1847. F.W. Wyatt's copy in MS Book 1 (TC), pp.187 ff.

---

17th May 1847 **From R.C. Chapman** Barnstaple
**To H.W. Soltau** Plymouth
Withdrawing the invitation to visit him, for fear of offending others. It appears his intention had been for 'face to face' meetings with critics in Barnstaple.
Original copy (on a flimsy) –TC. Listed in CBA 6998 as a copy of a letter in folio 4, 1847. F.W. Wyatt's copy in MS Book 1 (TC), p.185 'from a flimsy'.

---

18th May 1847 **From H.W. Soltau** Plymouth
**To R.C. Chapman** Barnstaple
Rebuke of R.C. Chapman for his withdrawal of invitation.
Concerned at the apparent change in the purpose of the meeting. Concludes 'Little children, let us not love in word, or in tongue, but in deed and in truth' [1 John 3:18].
Original copy (flimsy) - TC. Listed in CBA 6998 as a copy in folio 4, 1847. F.W. Wyatt's copy in MS Book 1 (TC), p.186.

---

24th May 1847 From R.W. Wolston
To B.W. Newton
Describing the steps taken to oppose Dalmas, and the lifting of the excommunication of 15th May 1847 upon B.W. Newton. One of the five 'Brixham letters'.
Original (copy) - TC. Listed in CBA 6998 in folio 5, 1847. F.W. Wyatt's copy in MS Book 1 (TC), pp.187 ff.

25th May 1847 **From W. Morris**
[To B.W. Newton?]
Also describing the steps taken to oppose de St Dalmas, and the lifting of the excommunication of 15th May 1847 upon B.W. Newton. One of the five Brixham letters'.
Original (copy) - TC. Listed in CBA 6998 as in folio 5, 1847.
F.W. Wyatt's copy in MS Book 1 (TC), pp.187 ff.

Section 9 – B.W. Newton Correspondence

| 7th June 1847 | **From C. McAdam** | Countess Wear, Exeter |

**To Geo. Treffry**

Regarding Amy J.T. Toulmin's copy of notes of Kate Gidley of an address by B.W. Newton on Psalm 6. Declining to return the notes. 'The said notes to which you refer are in my wife's possession as she wishes to retain possession of them for the present. She has written to Miss Toulmin to say so and explain the reason for so doing'.
F.W. Wyatt's copy in MS Book 1 (TC), p.192.

| June 1847 | **From Mrs Anna Newton** | From 'Mrs Brown's' Victoria Villa, Weston Road, Bath |

**To Amy J.T. Toulmin**

Regarding McAdam calling people together to read extracts from the notes [of Mr Newton's address on Psalm 6] 'this evening'. Concern at the possible harm.
F.W. Wyatt's copy in MS Book 1 (TC), pp.187 ff.

| 10th June 1847 | **From George Treffry** | 169 Fore Street, Exeter |

**To Brethren and Sisters at Exeter**

Objection to 'notes' on B.W. Newton's lecture on Psalm 6 being read at the proposed meeting. States that Mr McAdam had obtained the notes, which were his (George Treffry's), without his consent.
Original letter – TC. Listed in CBA 6998 in folio 6, 1847. F.W. Wyatt's copy in MS Book 1 (TC), p.192.

| 11th June 1847 | **From G.T. [George Treffry]** Exeter |

**To Amy [J.T. Toulmin]**   10, Gasking Street, Plymouth

Reporting the meeting 'last evening' when C. McAdam read 'extracts' from Amy J.T. Toulmin's copy of the notes of B.W. Newton's lecture on Psalm 6 that had been taken by Kate Gidley. There was objection raised at the meeting that only extracts were read. He describes the subsequent criticism levelled by C. McAdam, and J.L. Harris. The letter also refers to family matters, J.L. Harris, and Thomas. It expresses the wish that B.W. Newton and H.W. Soltau hold a meeting. He orders her to 'restore the stolen notes to me'. 4 pages.

[Note on letter of 11th June 1847 continued]. The letter indicates that she was at '10 Gasking St' (sometimes spelled Gascoigne). It was the address of B.W. Newton's mother and Miss Toulmin). The original manuscript copy notes on Psalm 6 referred to were in the Fry Collection. CBA 6998 lists them as in 1847, Folio 3. See also Section 3, B.W. Newton's Published Works.
Original letter - TC. CBA 7180(36) Xerox copy of original. Listed in CBA 6998 in folio 6, 1847. F.W. Wyatt's copy in MS Book 1 (TC), pp.187 ff.

| June 1847 | **From Mrs Anna Newton** | 'staying at Exeter' (Wyatt) |

**To Amy J.T. Toulmin**

Two Original letters of the same date. Regarding her visit to Dawlish, the MS notes, and her distress at Harris and McAdam.
Original letters - TC. Listed in CBA 6998 as in folio 6, 1847. F.W. Wyatt's copy in MS Book 1 (TC), p.197.

## Section 9 – B.W. Newton Correspondence

> 23rd June 1847      **From G.T. [George Treffry]**    Exeter
>     **To Amy J.T. Toulmin**
> Simply confirming 'Mr McAdam returned your notes to me on Friday'.
> Original letter - TC. Listed in CBA 6998 in folio 6, 1847. F.W. Wyatt's copy in MS Book 1 (TC), p.193.

> ND [1847?]      **From Mrs Anna Newton**
>     To unknown
> An extract of a letter referring to a lecture B.W. Newton delivered in Exeter, probably in 1847, her brother Henry Treffry in the chair. Describes the atmosphere, etc. Considers her son 'the prophet of this generation'.
> This may not fit here in this sequence, but it does concern a meeting in Exeter.
> F.W. Wyatt's copy in MS Book 1 (TC), p.221.

25th June 1847      **From George Treffry**      Exeter
    To B.W. Newton
'The Darbyites are busy trying to undo what you did on Monday'.
Regarding a meeting that [C] McAdam ('the editor'), Woodman, Owen, Ord, Freeman and others had held last Friday, at which they confirmed by their signatures that their printed proof was a correct copy of Amy J.T. Toulmin's original. Regarding Owen's comments (of which he has taken a copy for Mr Newton) on B.W. Newton's paper Doctrines of the Church in Newman Street in *The Christian Witness*. The satisfaction of those who had gathered at 'the reading meeting' at the explanation B.W. Newton gave then. Treffry's refusal to take Owen's hand. Hoping that B.W. Newton will soon come up and lecture. Reference to Mrs Aldous, Rev. Cornish, and 'Aunt'. 3 pages.
Original letter - TC. CBA 7180(37) Xerox copy of original. F.W. Wyatt's copy in MS Book 1 (TC), p.194.

> 1st November 1847    **From H.W. Soltau**
>     **To J.G. Deck**[1]
> Replying to J.G. Deck's letter, which had sent quotations of B.W. Newton's supposed teaching at meetings. Defending teaching that Deck had recently confessed as holding in error. 'I intreat you to take only Newton's declared statements written and published by himself as the grounds of any conclusion you may arrive at'. Deck later printed a confession of error on 14th November 1847.
> Note copied by F.W. Wyatt from Amy J.T. Toulmin 'HWS herein defends and maintains the things taught by BWN, which things 3 weeks later he disavowed and determined to oppose!'
> Original (copy in Soltau's hand on a flimsy) - TC. Listed in CBA 6998 in folio 8, 1847. F.W. Wyatt's copy in MS Book 1 (TC), pp.202-206.

---

[1] For further information relating to J.G. Deck, see notes on other letters to him, and notes on B.W. Newton's *A Letter to a Friend Concerning a Tract recently published in Cork*, in Section 3, B.W. Newton's Published Works of this Guide.

Section 9 – B.W. Newton Correspondence

> **8th November [1847] - S.P. Tregelles's dated notes on B.W. Newton's tract 'Doctrines of the Church in Newman Street'**
> This was prepared by S.P. Tregelles before *A Statement and Acknowledgement Respecting Certain Doctrinal Errors* was published. It was appended to that item when it was published on 26th November 1847. It is a two page history of B.W. Newton's tract, *Doctrines of the Church in Newman Street*.
> Original of S.P. Tregelles's notes - TC. Listed by CBA 6998.

18 November 1847      **Samuel Lloyd [sen.]**      Farm, near Birmingham
     To B.W. Newton
     His [B.W. Newton's] cousin [Amy J.T. Toulmin] had been staying at Wood Green. He expressed sympathy with Newton in his trials. The letter indicates that he had seen J.N. Darby's *Observations...*[1], and *Plain Statement*.[2] 'I consider them both most disgraceful and outrageous'. 'Your continued forbearance in silence <u>without any reply</u> is the best way of meeting such abuse'.
     F.W. Wyatt's copy in MS Book 1 (TC), pp.207,208.

> **26th November 1847.**
> B.W. Newton published *A Statement and Acknowledgement Respecting Certain Doctrinal Errors*.

7th December 1847      From B.W. Newton      Plymouth
     **To Mr Treby**
     Speaks of Christ's sufferings as voluntary, and assumed by him. Assures Mr Treby of his belief in the 'perfect and entire holiness of Christ'. 4 pages.
     Original (copy by Miss Amy J.T. Toulmin) - TC. CBA 7180(38) Xerox copy of original. Listed in CBA 6998, 1847, Folio 9. F.W. Wyatt's copy in MS Book 1 (TC), p.211.

> **8th December 1847**
> B.W. Newton left Plymouth with his mother and cousin Amy J.T. Toulmin and did not reside there again.[3] The letters are from Liskeard, until February 24. When he speaks of having recently removed to St Austell.
> 'No letters are preserved by Miss Toulmin after April. They cease altogether for some reason. Only one appears in the year 1849. Miss Toulmin then ceased to be in his household. Those after that date (1850 and after) are simply copies she was allowed to make in her duodecimo books which

---

[1] J.N. Darby, *Observations on a Tract entitled 'Remarks on the Sufferings of the Lord Jesus: A Letter Addressed to Certain Brethren and Sisters in Christ' by B.W. Newton*, 1847.
[2] J.N. Darby, *A Plain Statement of the Doctrine on the Sufferings of Our Blessed Lord*, 1847.
[3] See the note of regret of this in the *Plymouth, Devonport and Stonehouse Herald and General Advertiser* of 11th December 1847, Quoted in *A Story of Conflict, the Controversial Relationship between Benjamin Wills Newton and John Nelson Darby*, Jonathan D. Burnham, p.200.

were subsequently numbered, approximate to their date' (Quote from F.W. Wyatt in the 'Rough Notes'). However, about eight years later Tregelles thought that Amy Toulmin was living in BWN's household. See his letter of 24 March 1856

---

9th December 1847 **From Amy J.T. Toulmin**
 To her 'cousin'
Referring to 'cousin Newton's letters'. Regarding going to Liskeard. Concerning various personal matters and her travels. Reference to H.W. Soltau, and R.C. Chapman. Note referring to events on 14th December. 4 pages.
Original letter - TC. CBA 7180(39) Xerox copy of original. Listed in CBA 6998 1847, folio 9. F.W. Wyatt's copy in MS Book 1 (TC), p.209.

---

Undated [12th December 1847]   From B.W. Newton
 **To 'My dearest brother' [S.P. Tregelles]**
An open letter to S.P. Tregelles. No date, but endorsed by Amy J.T. Toulmin as the above date, for the meeting on 13th December at Ebrington Street.
Denying the teachings falsely attributed to him (B.W. Newton) and making statements of what he (B.W. Newton) does hold. Asking that these be conveyed to others, and for S.P. Tregelles to be the means for doing this. 4 pages.
Original copy - TC. CBA 7180(40) Xerox copy of original. Listed in CBA 6998, 1847, folio 9. F.W. Wyatt's copy in MS Book 1 (TC), p.213.

15th December 1847   **From Henry Woodfall**
 To B.W. Newton
Regarding events at Ebrington Street. The letter refers to the meeting on 'Monday evening'. 'We did all we could to deter Soltau and Batten from acting in such a way as would require us to openly differ from them, but in vain. Soltau has withdrawn, and no doubt Batten will follow'. If they do not return, he urges Mr Newton to return and resume his post 'and that very speedily'. Duty requires him to return. He states that he is doing all he can to strengthen and encourage Tregelles. 'I have been almost surprized to witness the general feeling spontaneously manifested in your favour'.
Original letter - TC. CBA 7180(41) Xerox copy of original. Listed in CBA 6998, 1847 folio 9. F.W. Wyatt's copy in MS Book 1 (TC), p.210.

15 December 1847   **From unknown [not from Woodfall]**
 To 'beloved brother' [B.W. Newton]
Giving an account of the meeting at Ebrington Street. Transcribed by Amy J.T. Toulmin in her narrative for Mrs Tyndale, see note at 8th January 1848.
F.W. Wyatt's copy in MS Book 1 (TC), p.271.

18th December 1847   From B.W. Newton   Liskeard
 **To Mrs Haydon**
Defends 'the tracts'. 'In the ordinary sense of the word all his [Christ's] sufferings were vicarious'.

An extract in B.W. Newton's handwriting of this letter, and of letters to (Mrs) S.A. Tregelles (25th December 1847), and S.P. Tregelles (4th January 1848), were 'copied for Amy Toulmin at her request'.
Original - TC. Listed in CBA 6998 in folio 9 (and 10?), 1847 (as [Captain aka Admiral] W[illiam] Haydon). F.W. Wyatt's copy in MS Book 1 (TC), pp.214-217.

> 22 December 1847. H.W. Soltau printed his *Confession of Error*. Listed in CBA 6998 Tract No.40.

22nd December 1847      From B.W. Newton
**To 'My Dear Sister'**
Regarding the trial of the present circumstances.
Original copy - TC. Listed in CBA 6998 as in folio 9, 1847. F.W. Wyatt's copy in MS Book 1 (TC), pp.217-220.

> 23 December 1847. J.E. Batten printed his withdrawal from B.W. Newton in *A Letter to the Saints Meeting in Ebrington Street, Plymouth...* Listed in CBA 6998 Tract No.18.

25th December 1847      From B.W. Newton      Liskeard
**To Mrs S.A. Tregelles**[1]
Regarding the Lord's condition and his relations in his humanity.
An extract of this letter in B.W. Newton's handwriting, and of letters to Mrs Haydon (18th December 1847) and to S.P. Tregelles (4th January 1848), were 'copied for Amy Toulmin at her request'.
Original - TC. Listed in CBA 6998 as in folio 9, 1847. F.W. Wyatt's copy in MS Book 1 (TC), p.214.

27th December 1847      From B.W. Newton      Liskeard
**To Captain [Richard Courtenay] Johnson**
Regarding the 'great truths' concerning the Lord as a man, and as the Israelite. Rejects the proposed interpretation now being suggested that the revelation of the Lord in the Psalms is only typical.
F.W. Wyatt's copy in MS Book 1 (TC), p.220.

> 31 December 1847. W.B. Dyer printed his *Confession of Doctrinal and Practical Errors*. Listed in CBA 6998. Tract No.41.

4th January 1848      From B.W. Newton      Liskeard
**To S.P. Tregelles**
Regarding the Lord's relations in his humanity.
An extract in B.W. Newton's handwriting of this letter and of letters to (Mrs) S.A. Tregelles (25th December 1847), and to Mrs Haydon (18th December 1847), were together 'copied for Amy Toulmin at her request'.

---

[1] S.P. Tregelles's wife, née Sarah Anna Prideaux (1807 – 1882. Married 1839)

Original (copy) - TC. F.W. Wyatt's copy in MS Book 1 (TC), pp.222-224. Listed in CBA 6998 in folio 9, 1847. Listed in F.W. Wyatt's list of S.P. Tregelles's letters in the 'Rough Notes' (In the Christian Brethren Archive as FRY/1/2/1).

6th January 1848          From B.W. Newton          Liskeard
    **To Rowe**                   Torpoint

'The true doctrine of the Lord's Humanity has always been one of Satan's chief subjects of attack'. Responds to particular questions. Quotes various Psalms.

Copied extracts, probably in Amy J.T. Toulmin's hand (the item has 'A.J. Toulmin' on the back in her hand).

Original copy - TC. Listed in CBA 6998 as in folio 1 1848. F.W. Wyatt's copy in MS Book 1 (TC), p.224

> 7th January 1848. G.J. Walker printed his *A Confession and Retraction of Two Doctrinal Errors*. Listed in CBA 6998 Tract No.43.

> **8th January 1848. Sketch of the Controversy at Plymouth in 1847, drawn up for Mrs Tyndale**
>
> This is a manuscript by Amy J.T. Toulmin, dated 8th January 1848. It includes the letters of B.W. Newton to S.P. Tregelles (4th January 1848), (Mrs) S.A. Tregelles (25th December 1847) and to Mrs Haydon (18th December 1847).
>
> Original in Miss Toulmin's hand – TC. Copied in F.W. Wyatt's MS Book 1 (TC), p.269. It is listed in CBA 6998 1848, folio 1.

> **10th January 1848. Printed statement issued by the Ebrington Street Assembly**
>
> *Statement from Christians assembling in the name of the Lord in Ebrington Street, Plymouth*. F.W. Wyatt's copy in MS Book 1 (TC). Listed in the 'Rough Notes'. See Appendix 3, Select Publications List.

19th January 1848          From B.W. Newton          Liskeard
    **To Miss [Emily?] Weston**

Regarding 'the tracts'. 'I see nothing of importance that I would wish to retract in them'. 'If there are any expressions that need to be guarded or explained, I should be most willing to do so, but I could not forgo the general tenor of statement that is in them. Refers to an earlier controversy he had with the Arian tendencies of F. Newman[1], and makes comparisons with the current controversy.

F.W. Wyatt's copy in MS Book 1 (TC), p.228. Listed in the 'Rough Notes'.

---

[1] Francis William Newman (1805-1897). Brother of John Henry Newman; who tutored B.W. Newton in 1827; went to join Anthony Norris Groves in his missionary exploits in Baghdad; and later became a deist, and wrote *Phases of Faith; or Passages from the History of My Creed* (London 1850) as an account of his journey to that position.

21st January 1848                From B.W. Newton            Liskeard
    **To Mrs Haydon**

She had sent [G.J.] Walker's tract (he had also withdrawn from B.W. Newton). B.W. Newton comments on it. It is 'indeed a sorrowful paper'. Considers that the controversialists are now moving on to a denial of the Lord's real humanity.
F.W. Wyatt's copy in MS Book 1 (TC), p.230. Listed in the 'Rough Notes'.

[after 21st January 1848]      From B.W. Newton
    **To Mrs Haydon**

Original, but unfinished note. Mr Newton states all the sufferings of Christ were vicarious.
F.W. Wyatt places it after the 21st January 1848 letter.
F.W. Wyatt's copy in MS Book 1 (TC), p.233. Listed in CBA 6998 as in folio 10 1847.

28th January 1848                From B.W. Newton            Liskeard
    **To Mrs Brown**

Regarding the humanity of Christ. Hopes the current controversy will establish many in a clear apprehension of the truth of Christ's humanity.
F.W. Wyatt's copy in MS Book 1 (TC), p.234.

29th January 1848                From B.W. Newton            Liskeard
    **To 'My dear brother'**

Affirms Christ's voluntary entrance into suffering. Acknowledges that page 34 of his *Observations on a Tract* is open to misconception, but the latter part of the paragraph guards it.
F.W. Wyatt's copy in MS Book 1 (TC), p.236.

> February 1848       **From Miss Amy J.T. Toulmin**
>     **To Mrs Brown [or Browne]**
> Two letters or notes made by Miss Toulmin for Mrs Brown regarding 'the origin and nature of the present sad controversy'. Speaks of 'when we first met together' at Plymouth, and of Mr Darby and his friends' attempts 'to stop Mr Newton's mouth'.
> Original - TC. F.W. Wyatt's copy in MS Book 1 (TC), p.264. Listed in CBA 6998 1848, folio 6 as original 'Remarks'

2nd February 1848               From B.W. Newton
    **To 'My dear brother'**

Refers to the 'simple and Scriptural' statement that 'you' have recently issued from Ebrington Street [*Statement from Christians assembling in the name of the Lord in Ebrington Street, Plymouth* of 10th January 1848], which he approves. States his willingness 'to sign all the creeds and doctrinal articles adopted by the Scotch and English Churches on the disputed questions'. Speaks of Christ in relation to Israel. Suggests that those who oppose imagine something Divine was mingled with Christ's human nature. 10 pages.
Original copy - TC. Listed in CBA 6998 as in Folio 2, 1848. F.W. Wyatt's copy in MS Book 1 (TC), pp.238-241.

7th February 1848   From B.W. Newton
    **To Miss Bryan**
Regarding doctrinal matters, mainly respecting the humanity of the Lord. It asserts Christ is truly God and truly man, and defends his doctrine.
Listed in CBA 6998 as a copy of the letter in folio 2, 1848. F.W. Wyatt's copy in MS Book 1 (TC), pp.242-249.

10th [or 16th] February 1848  From B.W. Newton   Liskeard
    **To 'Dear sister'**
Regarding recent troubles. 'The events of the last few months seem to me almost like a dream'. 'The being so suddenly and unexpectedly bereft of those with whom I had so long laboured almost without a discordant thought or feeling, and their now violent repudiation of doctrines which they had before so deliberately and cordially sanctioned'. 'I almost feel as if I could never have confidence in anyone any more'. 18 pages.
Original copy in B.W. Newton's hand - TC. Listed in CBA 6998 in folio 4, 1848. F.W. Wyatt's copy in MS Book 1 (TC), pp.249-257.

15th February 1848   From B.W. Newton   Liskeard
    **To Mr G. Haydon**
Regarding Christ's humanity. Regarding recent troubles. Replies to accusations. 16 pages.
Original copy - TC. Listed in CBA 6998 as 1847 folio 10. F.W. Wyatt's copy in MS Book 1 (TC), pp.257-261.

19th February 1848   From B.W. Newton   Liskeard
    **To Mr [George J.] Walker [of Teignmouth]**
This was probably a first draft of the letter of 2nd March 1848.
F.W. Wyatt comments on the letter dated 2nd March in MS Book 1 'A duplicate only as far as line 10 of 133 [[i.e. from pp.128-133]] in red book No 1 is dated Feb. 19'.
Recorded in 'Rough Notes' as 'imperfect'.
F.W. Wyatt's copy in MS Book 1? (TC).

24th February 1848   From B.W. Newton   St Austle (*sic*)
    **To a 'sister'**   Barnstaple
Speaks of his removal from Liskeard to St Austell. Discusses the principles governing where, and how, we should fellowship.
F.W. Wyatt notes 'enclosed duplicate shows she was at Barnstaple'. Written on flimsy. 4 pages.
Original copy - TC. Listed in the 'Rough Notes' as in Folio 5, and as undated in CBA 6998. F.W. Wyatt's copy in MS Book 1 (TC), p.261.

26th February 1848          From B.W. Newton
### To Mr [George J] Walker [of Teignmouth]
On Mr G[eorge] J[ames] Walker's tract.[1]

This is probably a second draft of the letter recorded as 2nd March 1848 (see also the entry at 19th February 1848). 8 pages.

Original copy in Mr Newton's hand with revisions - TC. Listed in CBA 6998 as in folio 3, 1848.

---

26th February 1848     **From Amy J.T. Toulmin**          St Austle [sic]
### To Miss Kate Gidley
Responds to the suggestion that those who made public confessions might set them aside. Miss Gidley had reported that more than once Batten has said they are anxiously awaiting reunion with 'us', and also that Batten has said of Soltau that he has great love for Mr Newton and would like a re-union. Refers to Soltau having written a few lines to Mr Newton announcing the death of Clulow, and that he (B.W. Newton) had accordingly written to his widow. Miss Toulmin doubts whether any reconciliation will be possible after the solemn step that they had taken in repudiating the doctrines they had defended for so long.

Miss Gidley was the amanuensis of the original notes on Psalm 6, which Miss Toulmin copied. Wyatt refers to her as 'Miss Catherine Gidley'.

Original letter, listed in CBA 6998 folio 6, 1848. F.W. Wyatt's copy in MS Book 1 (TC), pp.265-268.

---

2nd March 1848          From B.W. Newton
### To [George J.] Walker [of Teignmouth]
Refers to Mr Walker's tract[2], and clings to the hope that he may reconsider and alter his present judgement. This is a lengthy doctrinal letter regarding the incarnation, and the imputation of Adam's sin. See the items noted at 19th February, 26th February, and 10th April 1848.

F.W. Wyatt's copy in MS Book 1 (TC), pp.128-135.

3rd April 1848          From B.W. Newton          St Austle [sic]
### To Mrs Browne [or Brown]
Refers to a 'consecutive statement of his doctrines on the subject of the recent controversy' that he had left with Ebrington Street to publish if they wish. His *Brief Statements in the form of Answers to Questions* is attached. The letter is mostly concerned with how to view and respond to the current events in Europe in relation to prophecy.

Original (copy or draft of letter in B.W. Newton's hand) TC. Listed in CBA 6998 in folio 9, 1848, and in the 'Rough Notes'. F.W. Wyatt's copy in MS Book 1 (TC), pp.276-281.

10th April 1848          From B.W. Newton
### To 'Dear Brother' [George J. Walker of Teignmouth]
Concerning issues relating to the Lord's humanity.

The appendix to this letter, copied in Amy J.T. Toulmin's hand, was what appears to be a quotation from Newton's tract, *Letter on Subjects connected with the Lord's Humanity* with certain changes noted by F.W. Wyatt. It could however represent a draft that preceded the publication

---

[1] CBA 6998 lists (under 'various other tracts' No.43) G.J. Walker's, *A Confession and Retraction of Two Doctrinal Errors*, dated 7th January 1848, which appears to be missing from the Fry Collection.

[2] Ibid

of 'the Letter'. See the note at the entry for the published item in Section 3, B.W. Newton's Published Works.

F.W. Wyatt heads this as the second letter to Mr Walker. Compare the letter of 2nd March 1848 and the other references there.

Original copy in Mr Newton's hand - TC. Listed in CBA 6998 in folio 7, 1848 (1849). F.W. Wyatt's copy in MS Book 1 (TC), pp.282-289.

12th May 1848          **From 'E'**          Plymouth
   To [B.W. Newton??]
   Giving an account of 'the Bath meeting'[1] in connection with a letter from [H.W.] Soltau.
   Transcript of letter CBA 7050, pp.248, 249

15th May 1848          **From 'M'**
   [to B.W. Newton??]
   Concerning the second day [of the Bath meeting]
   Transcript of letter CBA 7050, p.249.

---

10th December 1848   **From S.P. Tregelles**
   **To Miss Amy J.T. Toulmin**
Listed in CBA 6998 as an original letter. Listed in F.W. Wyatt's list of S.P. Tregelles's letters in the 'Rough Notes' (In the Christian Brethren Archive as FRY/1/2/1). Untraced. See note on letter 15th December, S.P. Tregelles to Amy J.T. Toulmin, which is not listed in CBA 6998.

---

15th December 1848   **From S.P. Tregelles**   6, Portland Square, Plymouth
   **To Miss Amy J.T. Toulmin, c/o Mrs Brown, 6 Buckingham Villas, Clifton, Bristol**
Comments 'I see that the devil wants to discredit all testimony to prophetic truth; this is the reason of the endeavour to crush it, and those who teach it; I believe that the Lord will uphold his servant, Mr Newton, and that some of the sheep of Christ will be freed from delusion: may this soon be wrought!'
[Note on letter of 15th December 1848 continued]. Original - TC. F.W. Wyatt's copy in his S.P. Tregelles Correspondence Book, acquired by the Christian Brethren Archive in 2011 (FRY/1/1/4).

---

25th December 1848   **From S.P. Tregelles**   Plymouth
   **To Miss Amy J.T. Toulmin, c/o Mrs Brown, 6 Buckingham Villas, Clifton, Bristol**
Advising her to 'act wisely and according to God in keeping as quiet as you can'.
Original - TC. Listed in CBA 6998. Also listed in F.W. Wyatt's list of letters by S.P. Tregelles. F.W. Wyatt's copy in his S.P. Tregelles Correspondence Book, acquired by the Christian Brethren Archive in 2011 (FRY/1/1/4).

---

[1] The meeting at Bath, 10th May 1848, was convened for the leaders of the Brethren movement, excluding those still associated with B.W. Newton. It included Lord Congleton, J.N. Darby, R.C. Chapman, and many others, as well as those (such as W.B. Dyer) who had recently seceded from the Ebrington Street meeting. W.B. Neatby, who calls it 'the closing act of the long tragedy', was very critical of the account of the meeting given by William Trotter in his *The Whole Case of Plymouth and Bethesda*. He provided an alternative account of the proceedings given to him by a participant. W.B. Neatby, *A History of the Plymouth Brethren*, pp.147-148.

> February 1849. **Statement of G. and H. Woodfall at Bethesda, Bristol.** Printed single leaf quarto listed in the 'Rough Notes', but apparently no longer extant in the Fry Collection. Listed in F.W. Wyatt's Index of correspondence, CBA 7002 as at p. 291 of MS Book 1 (TC), but not verified as having been seen by CG.

12th April 1849  **From Sir H. Rawlinson**  Bagdad
    To B.W. Newton

Refers to B.W. Newton's letter of January, which was about Babylon, and the conditions in its environs. He stated that Babylon proper cannot be regarded as a scene of desolation. He answered seven questions of B.W. Newton, including information regarding the town of Hillah on the site.

Reference is made to Sir Henry Rawlinson in the Fry Manuscript (CBA 7049), p.317, and in *Babylon and Egypt* (Third Edition), p.56n. He was introduced to Mr Newton by Dr J.P. Riach.[1]

F.W. Wyatt's copy of the original in MS Book 1 (TC), p.66.

---

**B.W. Newton married Maria Hawkins in Edinburgh, 24th April 1849.**[2]

---

1st July 1849  **From S.P. Tregelles**  Paris [postmarked Amiens]
    To B.W. Newton  11, Victoria Grove Terrace, Bayswater

Regarding his (S.P. Tregelles's) travels, etc). Regarding the Syriac version of the Gospels supplied by Mr [William] Cureton[3].

Original letter - TC. Listed in CBA 6998. F.W. Wyatt's copy in his S.P. Tregelles Correspondence Book, acquired by the Christian Brethren Archive in 2011 (FRY/1/1/4). Annotated transcription of the whole letter in T.C.F. Stunt, *Life and Times of Samuel Prideaux Tregelles* (2020) pp.227-230.

5th September 1849  From B.W. Newton
    **To Samuel Lloyd**

With this letter he sent tracts to him at the request of his (B.W. Newton's) mother, but expresses concern at his [Samuel Lloyd's] 'severe sufferings'.

Described in the 'Rough Notes' as 'last note to dear old S. Lloyd' with 'his lithographed of 1835' (not present).

Original (copy by Amy J.T. Toulmin) - TC. Listed in CBA 6998 in folio 8, 1848 (1849)

F.W. Wyatt's copy of the Miss Toulmin's in MS Book 1 (TC) p.291.

---

[1] The First Edition of *Thoughts on the Apocalypse* makes reference to another letter from a European traveller to Babylon. See Appendix 1, Comparison of Editions of *Thoughts on The Apocalypse* on the Thoughts on Revelation 18

[2] B.W. Newton's (second) Marriage Certificate was in the original Fry Collection and is currently held by Tom Chantry. See note in the section on Miscellaneous Biographical Items and Memorabilia. Maria Newton (née Hawkins) died 25th December 1906. She was born in Madras, 19th January 1815 (from her gravestone), the eldest daughter of William Hawkins of the Madras civil service (DNB). The Census records vary in their statements of her age (and of B.W. Newton's age).

[3] William Cureton (1808-1864), who, as Curator of the British Museum, had assisted S.P. Tregelles with access to the Syriac Nitrian Palimsest.

ND [pre 1850?]   From B.W. Newton
   **[to Dr J[oseph].C. Cookworthy[1]**
Letter referring to his [Dr Cookworthy's] alteration in relation to his former friends. Refers to the tract that B.W. Newton has just written, apparently on the believer's involvement in politics. B.W. Newton declares opposition to worldly methods to remedy the evils of the day.
[Pencil note (in Mrs L.S. Riach's handwriting) referring to 'this tract sent to Dr C'. If the tract B.W. Newton refers to is *On the Exercise of Worldly Authority*, this would date the letter pre-1850. See other letter to Dr Cookworthy [1844?] in the CBA Box 23(10), and the various letters in defence of B.W. Newton, of which he was a signatory. 2 pages.
Christian Brethren Archive, Box 23(10) (ex- The Stirling Collection, Spurgeon's College).

16th April 1850   **From G[rey] Hazlerigg [sic][2]**   Carlton Hall [Leicester]
   To B.W. Newton
Grey Hazelrigg wrote enquiring of Mr Newton's teaching on the humanity of Christ. He wrote of his [G. Hazlerigg's] desire to receive all who come to him in Christ's name. F.W. Wyatt's copy in MS Book 1 (TC), p.292. Listed in the 'Rough Notes'[3] where they are called by F.W. Wyatt (?) 'the Hazelrigg letters'.

22nd April 1850   From B.W. Newton   London
   **To G[rey] Hazlerigg [sic]**   Carlton Hall [Leicester]
   Reply to his letter
In the letter, Mr Newton wrote of the evenings when he saw him. 'I advised not to connect yourself with me until you had satisfied your mind'. 'I think you have heard me expound the Scriptures so often'. He refers to his published statements, and states his doctrinal position in answer to his questions.
F.W. Wyatt's copy in MS Book 1 (TC), pp.295-300. Listed in the 'Rough Notes' where they are called the by F.W. Wyatt (?) 'the Hazelrigg letters'. See note on letter of 16th April 1850.

2nd May 1850   **From G[rey] Hazlerigg [sic]**   Carlton Hall [Leicester]
   To B.W. Newton
   Answer to previous letter
'I think you did well in answering my letter, and though I do not quite think your reproof merited, it does not cause me any bitterness of feeling, because given in a kind, though perhaps somewhat stern spirit'. He [Hazlerigg] stated that he had united with the saints at Duke Street, and that he desired reassurance for others, not for himself.

---

[1] Joseph Cookworthy had been mayor of Plymouth (1839-41) a position of which BWN had not approved; see T.C.F. Stunt, *The Elusive Quest* p 37n.28. Joseph Cookworthy must not be confused with his younger brother John who died in 1835 but, with his family, had also worshipped with the Brethren in Plymouth. Originally they were part of a large Quaker family.

[2] Grey Hazelrigg (1818-1912). Later a leading Strict Baptist. Pastor of Trinity Chapel, and then Zion Baptist Chapel, Leicester from 1861. One time editor of the *Gospel Standard* magazine. It would be interesting to know whether there is a connection between Hazelrigg and the Leicester Lectures, which Mr Newton gave in 1853 and 1854. See Section 3, B.W. Newton's Published Works *Priesthood and Sacrifice Essential to Worship*, and *The True Unity of the Church of God in Time and Eternity*.

[3] 'The Rough Notes' – see Section 10, Duplicated and Manuscript Items, 'Manuscript Items added to the Fry Collection in 2011', item 7. The 'notes' are catalogued in the Christian Brethren Archive as FRY/1/2/1.

F.W. Wyatt's copy in MS Book 1 (TC), pp.300-302. Listed in the 'Rough Notes' where they are called the by F.W. Wyatt (?) 'the Hazelrigg letters'. See note on letter of 16th April 1850.

11 July 1850          From B.W. Newton
   **To person unknown**
Listed in the A.C. Fry Rough Notes as being 10 pages long. The comments 'if it could be of any real use', and 'in print also' are added to the sketchy note.
Missing from the Fry Collection.

---

**17th August 1850**
**Birth of B.W. Newton's only child, Maria Anna Constantia Hawkins Newton.**

---

23 November 1850          From B.W. Newton
   **To his mother**
In the letter B.W. Newton confirms that he intends to have two meetings on Lord's Day mornings in London. Firstly, a lecture, and, secondly, communion where any person of recognised gift (such as Mr Offord) can take part. There appears to be a little concern from Plymouth regarding the changed ministry arrangements. Mr Newton confirms he values the continuing link with the Plymouth meeting.
F.W. Wyatt's copy (from a copy by Miss Amy J.T. Toulmin) in MS Book 1 (TC), p.303. Listed in the 'Rough Notes'

25th November 1850          From B.W. Newton          London
   **To 'My dear friend' [Dr James Pringle Riach]**
This is concerned with 'Ministry' (or ministerial appointment). Mr Newton rejects the charge of clericalism that had been levelled against him, and explains his position.
This letter is linked with four others on Ministry which the 'Rough Notes' refer to as 'Five on Ministry'. The other four are also to 'Riach'[1] – see letters 7th December 1850 onwards.
When Church Principles was published in *Perilous Times*, July 1906 - September 1907, the statement was made that this was 'written by Mr B.W. Newton more than fifty years ago, but has not been previously published'. However, these letters are not that document.
F.W. Wyatt's copy in MS Book 1 (TC), p.18. Listed in the 'Rough Notes'.

27th November 1850          From B.W. Newton          London
   **To S.P. Tregelles**
Relating to the ministry in the Duke Street meeting, and the changes that were then taking place. 'Whilst at Plymouth I conversed with yourself, and with other brethren, respecting a proposed change in the form of our meeting in Duke Street'. The initial order was to meet just for

---

[1] James Pringle Riach, MD (c.1798-1865) – see A.C. Fry in CBA 7049, p.315 regarding him. He was one of Mr Newton's staunchest supporters at, and following, the division at Plymouth. The Riach family was continuously linked to his ministry. Mrs L.S. Riach (Louisa Sophia Riach) was involved with his circle to his death. See later correspondence. For further details of Riach's career see T.C.F. Stunt, *The Elusive Quest*. . .p.231n.60

exposition and prayer, followed by Communion. Mr Newton felt Communion at Duke Street should be after the exposition. He had nevertheless yielded to the feelings of others, and for the last eighteen months the meeting was on the same principles as at Plymouth. But circumstances were different in London. There was not plurality of ministers; therefore, a lengthy service with pauses was not appropriate. In the letter he rejects the 'sin of clericalism', 'which is appointment by human authority'.

F.W. Wyatt's copy in MS Book 1 (TC), p.32. Listed in the 'Rough Notes'

7th December 1850          From B.W. Newton          London
### To John Offord[1]

Also relating to the ministry in the Duke Street meeting.

Writes regarding Mr R. Offord and Mr Turner who assisted at Duke Street when he was away at Plymouth, but who, under the changed arrangements, are not playing any part in the ministry. 'Seeing that your brother, Mr R. Offord, and Mr Turner may be said to be the only [two] brethren who have acted in the meeting at Duke St…'. He states it was never intended that they should take such a position. It is implied they accepted the change. 'I do not class them among the number of those who believe in a necessity for pauses during worship for some supposed impulsive gift'.

F.W. Wyatt's copy in MS Book 1 (TC), p.36. Listed in the 'Rough Notes'

7th December 1850          From B.W. Newton          London
### To [Dr James Pringle] Riach

'In answer to your first question, whether any Christian brother should pray or give out a hymn in the congregation unless he has a proved and acknowledged gift for ministry in the Word and doctrine: I answer that I believe many may have a proved and acknowledged gift for ministry in prayer who never minister in other ways. I esteem prayer in the congregation to be one of the most important things'.

One of 'Five on Ministry' or 'ministerial appointment'. See note on the letter of 25th November 1850.

F.W. Wyatt's copy in MS Book 1 (TC), p.20. Listed in the 'Rough Notes'.

10th December 1850          From B.W. Newton          London
### To [Dr James Pringle] Riach

The principles of the Epistles to Timothy and Titus are ours to act on still, as much as any other part of the Word of God. 'Indeed they are the special directory during the latter days of those who are obliged to act in certain circumstances'. There is need for the right qualification of all those who act in a congregation.

One of 'Five on Ministry' or 'ministerial appointment'. See note on the letter of 25th November 1850.

F.W. Wyatt's copy in MS Book 1 (TC), p.23. Listed in the 'Rough Notes'.

---

[1] John Offord (c.1810-1870). He supplied ministry to the continuing congregation which Tregelles was still connected with at Plymouth. See T.C.F. Stunt, *The Life and Times of Samuel Prideaux Tregelles*, p178. B.W. Newton had 'worked closely with him in the West of England', but it appears that he came to London at the time of the closure of B.W. Newton's Bayswater work, and set up a separate chapel then and B.W. Newton dissociated with him. CBA 7064, p139, conversation 14th March 1898.

13th December 1850          From B.W. Newton          London
   **To [Dr James Pringle] Riach**
Regarding the place that faith and prayer ought to occupy in relation to the governmental agency of the Church. 'If Paul commanded some to be restrained whose gifts were real, how much more those who have no proved gifts'. There is a danger of governing the Church by self-devised principles rather than by the governmental principles of God.
One of 'Five on Ministry' or 'ministerial appointment'. See note on the letter of 25th November 1850.
F.W. Wyatt's copy in MS Book 1 (TC), p.26. Listed in the 'Rough Notes'.

18th December 1850          From B.W. Newton          London
   **To [Dr James Pringle] Riach**          [Plymouth]
Compares the ministry in London with that in Plymouth (where Riach is), in relation to open meetings, etc. 'In past life I have felt myself victimised to half-declared principles. Though constantly avowing them, I have been perpetually hindered in their practical unfolding. I trust it may never be so again'.
One of 'Five on Ministry' or 'ministerial appointment'. See note on the letter of 25th November 1850.
F.W. Wyatt's copy in MS Book 1 (TC), p.29. Listed in the 'Rough Notes'.

30th December 1850          From B.W. Newton
   **To 'A Friend'**
Published letter under the title *Reflections Suggested by the Present Movement in England against Romanism. A Letter to a Friend*.
See Bibliography of printed works for details

8th February 1851          From B.W. Newton
   **To his mother**
Regarding the opening that has developed for him to minister in London.[1] He writes of the destitution and sorrow of the last three and a half years. He is willing to return to Plymouth – 'nothing would give him greater pleasure' - but it would be impossible until his work in London is thoroughly consolidated. Refers to Dr [J.P.] Riach.
An extract by A.J.T. Toulmin. Quoted on pp.8,9 of *Teachers of the Faith and Future* by G.H. Fromow, Second Edition, 1969.
F.W. Wyatt's copy in MS Book 1 (TC), p.306.

29 March 1851          **From [John David] Macbride**[2]
   To B.W. Newton
   Addressed to 'Dear Newton'
   'I sincerely hope that you are now comfortably settled from a worldly point of view and far more that you enjoy peace in your creed and whatever outward form of Christianity

---
[1] There is reference to this in CBA 7064, p56. 'I got connected with a remnant of Mr Molyneux's congregation'.
[2] John David Macbride (28 June 1778 – 24 January 1868). Macbride was Principal of Magdalen Hall, Oxford [re-founded as Hertford College in 1874]. He was also a Fellow of Exeter College in 1800. See further notes on pages 1 and 119 of MS Book 1 (TC).

you prefer you are a genuine member of that invisible Church…'. Willing to help [S.P.] Tregelles in his work. Refers to [Dr William] Sewell[1].
F.W. Wyatt's copy in MS Book 2 (TC), p.117. Listed in the 'Rough Notes'.

---

**Census 30th March 1851**

Address: Paddington.
Benjamin Wills Newton 42 [sic]; Maria Newton 36, born Madras; Maria Anna 8 months; Mary Bolt, servant.

Address: 10 Gascoigne Street, Plymouth.
Mrs Anna Newton 68, born Beer Ferris, Devon; Amy Toulmin 38, born Birmingham; a servant.

---

8th July 1851      **From S.P. Tregelles**      Plymouth
    To [B.W. Newton] My beloved brother
Regarding the text of the Codex Vaticanus on Romans 1. He considers the text of the Codex here in a far better condition than in any other book of the New Testament.[2]
F.W. Wyatt's copy in his S.P. Tregelles Correspondence Book, acquired by the Christian Brethren Archive in 2011 (FRY/1/1/4). Original letter listed in CBA 6998, but now missing from the Fry Collection.

2nd April 1853      From B.W. Newton      London
    **To Mrs S**      A -- Rectory L---
Not able to decipher the recipient.
Spiritual counsel. The Serpent of Brass. The need to study the Scriptures as a whole
F.W. Wyatt's copy in MS Book 1 (TC), pp.307-309. Listed in the 'Rough Notes'.

December 1853      From B.W. Newton      London
    **To Mrs Haydon**
B.W. Newton thanks her for the information she has given regarding affairs at Plymouth.
F.W. Wyatt's copy in MS Book 1 (TC), p.309. Listed in the 'Rough Notes'.

2nd August 1855      From B.W. Newton      Maidenhead, Berkshire
    **To 'My Dear Sir'**
Largely regarding how to treat those who hold to infant baptism 'I fully admit that we should not allow in any congregation over which we may be watching infant baptism, or any doctrine that we know to be wrong, to be habitually taught. But to restrain certain teaching and to reject from the Lord's Table are two very different things'. Regarding excommunication etc.
F.W. Wyatt's copy in MS Book 1 (TC), p.310. Listed in the 'Rough Notes'

---

[1] One of B.W. Newton's two tutors at Oxford [F.W. Newman was the other). See CBA 1/1/1 p. 86
[2] NB Tregelles's letter of 26th December 1855.

## Section 9 – B.W. Newton Correspondence

14th August 1855        From B.W. Newton        Maidenhead
    **To 'My Dear Sir'**

Regarding *Pilgrim's Progress*, and its defects. The cross should be set in the City of Destruction, as the Serpent of Brass was set up in Israel. 'There is great danger in so presenting the gospel as to imply that certain experiences <u>must</u> first be gone through as pre-requisites to a right saving faith'. Suggests that Bunyan would probably have agreed.

F.W. Wyatt's copy in MS Book 1 (TC), p.315. Listed in the 'Rough Notes'

5th September 1855        From B.W. Newton        Maidenhead
    **To 'My Dear Sir'**

Regarding the humanity of Christ. He is in complete agreement with Bishop Pearson's statements on Christ's 'necessity of dying' [in his commentary on the Creed]. Concludes 'your controversy is clearly with Scripture, not with me'.

F.W. Wyatt's copy in MS Book 1 (TC), p.316. Listed in the 'Rough Notes'.

---

**September 1855. Death of B.W. Newton's only child, Maria Anna Constantia Hawkins Newton**

---

Friday morning [September] 1855      From B.W. Newton      Bayswater, London
    **To [Rev.] John Cox**

This gives his thanks for John Cox's sympathetic letter, and for his willingness to conduct his (B.W. Newton's) daughter's funeral. He writes in the letter of her faith and of his (B.W. Newton's) grief and affliction.

The register of burials gives B.W. Newton's address as 15, Victoria Grove Terrace, Bayswater, Paddington, although a note from Wyatt indicates that Mr and Mrs Newton did not return to their home after the funeral.

Maria Anna Constantia Hawkins Newton was born 17th August 1850. The exact date of her death is not known, but the burial record gives her age at death as 5 years 1 month. The date of the burial was 22nd September 1855. She is buried at Kensal Green, in the Parish of All Souls.

Copied (by Wyatt?) in MS Book 2 (TC), p.97. Further copy by F.W. Wyatt recovered by the Christian Brethren Archive (2011), uncatalogued at the time this guide was prepared. A.C. Fry's secondary copy CBA 7049, pp.440-442. Reprinted in *Teachers of the Faith and Future*, Second Edition, pp.13,14 – [NM 8.3] as: A Letter to Rev. John Cox Regarding the Funeral of His Only Child.

26th December 1855      **From S.P. Tregelles**      Plymouth
    To B.W. Newton

Regarding Mr Newton's tract 'Remarks on Romans 1 and 2'.[1] 'I hope your new pamphlet will be well circulated at Oxford'.

---

[1] *The First and Second Chapters of the Epistle to the Romans, Considered...* 1856

F.W. Wyatt's copy in MS Book 1 (TC), p.317. Listed in the 'Rough Notes', and in the short calendar of S.P. Tregelles related correspondence (with the 'Rough Notes'), simply as 'December 1855'.[1]

Undated [December 1855]      **From Cowan**
    To B.W. Newton

Gives thanks for Mr Newton's 'valuable book' on the 1st and 2nd chapters of Romans[2], which he had sent to him.

F.W. Wyatt's copy MS Book 1(TC), p.316. Listed in F.W. Wyatt's list of S.P. Tregelles's letters in the 'Rough Notes' (In the Christian Brethren Archive as FRY/1/2/1).

10th February 1856     **From S.P. Tregelles**     Plymouth
    To B.W. Newton     St Johns Wood, London

Reference to the Arabic New Testament [see regarding Eli Smith in the letter of 20th April 1856]. Regarding Tregelles's Greek Testament. 4 pages.

Original letter CBA 7181(1). F.W. Wyatt's copy in his S.P. Tregelles Correspondence Book, acquired by the Christian Brethren Archive in 2011 (FRY/1/1/4).

8th March 1856     **From S.P. Tregelles**     Plymouth
    To B.W. Newton

Regarding the Greek text of Philippians 2:15. Regarding S.P. Tregelles's Greek New Testament (the section on Mark's Gospel). 3 pages.

Original letter CBA 7181(2). F.W. Wyatt's copy in his S.P. Tregelles Correspondence Book, acquired by the Christian Brethren Archive in 2011 (FRY/1/1/4).

24th March 1856     **From S.P. Tregelles**     Plymouth
    To B.W. Newton

Regarding the Greek Text of Romans 1:29. Regarding Newton's wife, mother, and Amy J.T. Toulmin. Regarding S.P. Tregelles's Greek New Testament (Mark's Gospel). 3 pages.

Original/copy CBA 7181(3).[3] F.W. Wyatt's copy in his S.P. Tregelles Correspondence Book, acquired by the Christian Brethren Archive in 2011 (FRY/1/1/4).

11th April 1856     **From S.P. Tregelles**     Plymouth
    To B.W. Newton

Regarding Spanish matters[4]. Valera's Spanish Bible, the Trinitarian Bible Society, a Spanish teacher [for B.W. Newton] in London (Sarah Anna [his wife] has written to make enquiries). Regarding Seville and Madrid as bases for missionary work. Recommending

---

[1] 'The Rough Notes' –see Section 10, Duplicated and Manuscript Items, 'Manuscript Items added to the Fry Collection in 2011' in this Guide, item 7. The 'notes' are catalogued in the Christian Brethren Archive as FRY/1/2/1).
[2] *The First and Second Chapters of the Epistle to the Romans, Considered...*
[3] It is possible that there is another copy held by TC. Unable to verify
[4] For the context and the interest in Spain see T.C.F. Stunt, *The Life and Times of Samuel Prideaux Tregelles* 8.6.

that 'Brown' be sent to the North of Spain. References to M. Bosh[1], and to Haldane's notes. 7 pages

Original letter CBA 7181 (4). F.W. Wyatt's copy in his S.P. Tregelles Correspondence Book, acquired by the Christian Brethren Archive in 2011 (FRY/1/1/4). See reference to this and the following letter in T.C.F. Stunt, *The Life and Times of Samuel Prideaux Tregelles*, p99, 100.

20th April 1856       **From S.P. Tregelles**       Plymouth
    To B.W. Newton

Concerns regarding Spain: Valera's Spanish Bible, Trinitarian Bible Society. Reference to Dr Eli Smith[2] of Beirut. 4 pages.

Original CBA 7181(5). F.W. Wyatt's copy in his S.P. Tregelles Correspondence Book, acquired by the Christian Brethren Archive in 2011 (FRY/1/1/4).

16th January 1857       **From S.P. Tregelles**       Plymouth
    To B.W. Newton

Notes on 2 Peter 1. Reference to Mrs Lillington.

Original letter CBA 7181(6), 3 pages. F.W. Wyatt's copy in his S.P. Tregelles Correspondence Book, acquired by the Christian Brethren Archive in 2011 (FRY/1/1/4).

29th January 1857       **From S.P. Tregelles**       Plymouth
    To B.W. Newton

Reference to Mr [T.S.] Green's book[3], Dr Cumming, Littlewood, Duke of Manchester, Père Lambert's book on prophecy[4], President Agier's commentaries, J.N. Darby, the Paulicians, and Olshausen. Regarding S.P. Tregelles's Greek Testament.

The letter is quoted by T.C.F. Stunt in *Prisoners of Hope*, p.65, and *The Life and Times of Samuel Prideaux Tregelles*, as evidence of the influence of Lambert, and Agier on the development of J.N. Darby's prophetic views. It is quoted at length in T.C.F. Stunt in 'The Tribulation of Controversy: A Review Article' Brethren *Archivists and Historians Network Review*, No.2 (2003): pp.91-98,

Original letter CBA 7181(7). F.W. Wyatt's copy in his S.P. Tregelles Correspondence Book, acquired by the Christian Brethren Archive in 2011 (FRY/1/1/4). 4 pages.

---

[1] M. Bost in F.W. Wyatt's transcription
[2] Eli Smith 1801–1857. Translator of the Bible into Arabic
[3] A note by F.W. Wyatt on his transcription says, "The book referred to must be T.S. Green's *Course of Developed Criticism on Passages of the New Testament* (Bagsters London). A copy of it was given by Tregelles to BW Newton about a week before the date of this letter. It is in my possession. It is inscribed 'B.W. Newton from S.P.T. ... Jan. 23rd 1857'"
[4] Le Père Bernard Lambert, *Exposition des Prédictions et des Promesses Faites à l'Église pour Les Derniers Temps de la Gentilité*, Paris 1806. President Pierre Jean Agier *Les Prophètes nouvellement traduits sur l'Hebreu, avec des Explications et des Notes Critiques*. Paris 1820-1822, 10 vols. See S.P. Tregelles's comments on these works in *The Jansenists: Their Rise, Persecutions by the Jesuits and Existing Remnant* (1851), pp.96,97.

4th February 1857 **From S.P. Tregelles** Plymouth
    To B.W. Newton
    Referring to obtaining an abridgement of Goodwin's works, as B.W. Newton had requested. Reference to Père Lambert's book on prophecy, President Agier's commentaries, Green's book, and Wordsworth's Greek Testament. Regarding Tregelles's Greek Testament. 3 pages.
    Original letter CBA 7181(8). F.W. Wyatt's copy in his S.P. Tregelles Correspondence Book, acquired by the Christian Brethren Archive in 2011 (FRY/1/1/4).

9th February 1857 **From S.P. Tregelles** Plymouth
    To B.W. Newton
    Regarding the Greek text of Philippians 2:15. Reference to Eli Smith (Beirut). Regarding S.P. Tregelles's Greek New Testament (to Luke). 3 pages.
    Original letter CBA 7181(9). F.W. Wyatt's copy in his S.P. Tregelles Correspondence Book, acquired by the Christian Brethren Archive in 2011 (FRY/1/1/4).

14th March 1857 From B.W. Newton London
    **To [R.C.] Chapman**
'I trust I have never cherished feelings contrary to 'brotherly kindness' concerning yourself'. Declines the interview he proposes. 'I could never under any circumstances again connect myself with "The Brethren" as a body, nor with any of their assemblies'. 'Yours in Christian love'.[1]
F.W. Wyatt's copy MS Book 1(TC), p.363. Listed in the 'Rough Notes' as being in the 'parchment book'.

17th April 1857 **From S.P. Tregelles** Plymouth
    To B.W. Newton
    Regarding Tregelles's Greek Testament. Regarding Westcott and Hort's proposed edition of the Greek New Testament, and his wish to complete his edition first[2]. 3 pages.
    Original letter CBA 7181(10). F.W. Wyatt's copy in his S.P. Tregelles Correspondence Book, acquired by the Christian Brethren Archive in 2011 (FRY/1/1/4). Quoted in T.C.F. Stunt, *The Life and Times of Samuel Prideaux Tregelles*, p169.

> May 1857 **From S.P. Tregelles**
>     **To Chambers** Plymouth
> On the occasion of a violent appeal from H.W. Soltau to 'Chambers'. Refers to S.P. Tregelles's *Three Letters to the Author of 'A Retrospect of Events that Have Taken Place Amongst the Brethren'*, etc.
> F.W. Wyatt's copy MS Book 1 (TC), p.318. Listed in F.W. Wyatt's list of S.P. Tregelles's letters in the 'Rough Notes' (In the Christian Brethren Archive as FRY/1/2/1 – the list on accounts paper).

---

[1] B.W. Newton's gravestone bears a verse of R.C. Chapman's hymn 'O happy morn! The Lord will come'.
[2] See comment in T.C.F. Stunt, *The Life and Times of Samuel Prideaux Tregelles*, p169ff. on this letter and relations with B. F. Westcott and Fenton J.A. Hort

June 16th 1857          **From S.P. Tregelles**          Plymouth
     To B.W. Newton

     Original letter listed in CBA 6998, but now missing from the Fry Collection.
     T.C.F. Stunt has a copy that he transcribed from the original.

27th June 1857          **From S.P. Tregelles**          Plymouth
     To B.W. Newton

     Regarding money for S.P. Tregelles while abroad. Reference to Littlewood.
     2 pages.
     Original letter CBA 7181(11). F.W. Wyatt's copy in his S.P. Tregelles Correspondence Book, acquired by the Christian Brethren Archive in 2011 (FRY/1/1/4).

29th July 1857          **From S.P. Tregelles**          Geneva
     To B.W. Newton

     Expressing concern over B.W. Newton's illness. Reporting meeting with Dr Marriott. Referring to Basle Bible Society, tract distribution, the Misses Taylor of Florence, M. Guers, family matters. 4 pages.
     Original letter CBA 7181(12). F.W. Wyatt's copy in his S.P. Tregelles Correspondence Book, acquired by the Christian Brethren Archive in 2011 (FRY/1/1/4).

4th November 1857          **From S.P. Tregelles**          Plymouth
     To B.W. Newton

     Expressing concern over B.W. Newton's illness. Notes on the Greek word πας. Referring to 'present difficulties', and the need to shun identification with Brethrenism. Referring to financial matters. 10 pages.
     Original letter CBA 7181(13). F.W. Wyatt's copy in his S.P. Tregelles Correspondence Book, acquired by the Christian Brethren Archive in 2011 (FRY/1/1/4).

February 1858          From B.W. Newton
     **To Mrs [Miss?] Brown**          Knackers Knowle

Regarding ministry at Knackers Knowle [near Plymouth]. Noted in the 'Rough Notes' as being in Light Colour Quarto Letter Book, p.328 [= MS Book 1 (TC)? Not verified]. Listed in CBA 7002, F.W. Wyatt's index of Correspondence as being at p. 1 of 'Yellow Quarto'. Apparently no longer extant.

3rd February 1858          **From S.P. Tregelles**          Plymouth
     To B.W. Newton

     Regarding printing of Tregelles's Greek Testament. Referring to [F.H.A.] Scrivener. 3 pages.
     Original letter CBA 7181(14). F.W. Wyatt's copy in his S.P. Tregelles Correspondence Book, acquired by the Christian Brethren Archive in 2011 (FRY/1/1/4).

10th February 1858      **From S.P. Tregelles**      Plymouth
     To B.W. Newton
     Regarding Tregelles's Greek Testament. Referring to Tischendorf's transcript of the Nitrian palimpsest, Tregelles's poor eyesight[1]. 3 pages.
     Original letter CBA 7181(15). F.W. Wyatt's copy in his S.P. Tregelles Correspondence Book, acquired by the Christian Brethren Archive in 2011 (FRY/1/1/4).

13 February 1858      From B.W. Newton      70, New Finchley Road
     **To Mr [R.B.] Brooks**      Canada
Expresses thanks for R.B. Brooks's kind letter, and sends tracts, including *Ancient Truths*. States his doctrine on the sufferings of Christ in response to Brooks's query. Comments on the use of 'instead of', etc. in connection with Christ's vicarious work.
F.W. Wyatt's copy MS Book 1 (TC), pp.320-327. Transcript of letter by Wyatt CBA 7050, pp.33-40. Listed in the 'Rough Notes'.

20th April 1858      From B.W. Newton      70, New Finchley Road
     **To 'My Dear Sir'**
Regarding sanctification. The Greek verb ελλογεομαι not to be confused with λογιζομαι.
[See *Occasional Papers on Scriptural Subjects*: Note on the Words λογιζομαι, to impute, Rom. 4:6: ελλογεω, to enter in account, Rom. 5:13, λογιζομαι ΕΙΣ, to impute FOR, Rom. 4:5].
F.W. Wyatt's copy MS Book 1 (TC), p.328, which notes that this is taken from two copies - by Miss Amy J.T. Toulmin, and by B.W. Newton's mother. Listed in the 'Rough Notes'.

17th May 1858      **From S.P. Tregelles**      Plymouth
     To B.W. Newton
     Regarding Tregelles's Greek Testament. Commenting on Mai's edition of Codex Vaticanus. 3 pages.
     Original letter CBA 7181(16). F.W. Wyatt's copy in his S.P. Tregelles Correspondence Book, acquired by the Christian Brethren Archive in 2011 (FRY/1/1/4).

24th May 1858      **From S.P. Tregelles**      Plymouth
     To B.W. Newton
     Commenting on Codex Vaticanus. 3 pages.
     Original letter CBA 7181(17). F.W. Wyatt's copy in his S.P. Tregelles Correspondence Book, acquired by the Christian Brethren Archive in 2011 (FRY/1/1/4).

12th August 1858      **From S.P. Tregelles**      Kingsbridge
     To B.W. Newton      London
     Referring to accounts of B.W. Newton's poor health, and B.W. Newton's proposed going to Lake Geneva for his health.[2] Commenting on tract distribution on the Rhine steamboats. Commenting on George Müller's German tracts, and B.W. Newton's French

---
[1] See the quote from this letter and comment on Tregelles eyesight and health in T.C.F. Stunt, *Life and Times of Samuel Prideaux Tregelles*, p173ff.
[2] See B.W. Newton's passport in the Miscellaneous Biographical Items and Memorabilia section

tracts, which he found in Geneva. Advising about circulation of tracts in the Italian language. Referring to Mr [J.P.] Riach, Mr [Thomas] Adams, S.P. Tregelles's Greek New Testament, and Tregelles's rest in Kingsbridge. 4 pages.
Original letter CBA 7181(18). F.W. Wyatt's copy in his S.P. Tregelles Correspondence Book, acquired by the Christian Brethren Archive in 2011 (FRY/1/1/4).

2nd April 1859          From B.W. Newton
    **To Miss Hawkshaw**

Answers a question regarding access to the Lord's Table at Duke Street chapel. 'Very few strangers, I believe, come to the chapel who do not belong to this class [not linked to families etc]. Indeed almost all who are present in the morning are personally known to me. Sometimes it may happen that persons whom we cannot recognise as believers come, but they do not partake. From time to time I am accustomed to request publically that none would partake except they are introduced as Christians by some already in communion, or unless they apply personally to myself'. Miss Hawkshaw seems to have been pained at sitting with people at the Lord's Table whom she did not know to be Christians.
F.W. Wyatt's copy MS Book 1 (TC), p.331. Listed in the 'Rough Notes'.[1]

24th December 1859     **From Horatius Bonar**          Kelso
    To B.W. Newton

B.W. Newton that had commented favourably on an article on the Brethren that had appeared in the Journal of Prophecy. Horatius Bonar accepted responsibility for it, as he indicated that he had thoroughly revised it himself.
F.W. Wyatt's copy MS Book 1 (TC), p.333. Further transcript of letter by Wyatt CBA 7050, p.17.

22nd March 1860         From B.W. Newton
    **To Sir J. Crompton**      St Petersburg

To the British Ambassador in St Petersburg, concerning S.P. Tregelles.
Noted in the 'Rough Notes'. Now missing from the Fry Collection.

24th March 1860         From B.W. Newton
    **To Sir J. Crompton**      St Petersburg

To the British Ambassador in St Petersburg re- Tregelles.
Noted in the 'Rough Notes'. Now missing from the Fry Collection.

29th March 1860         From B.W. Newton
    **To Sir J. Crompton**      St Petersburg

To the British Ambassador in St Petersburg concerning Tregelles.
Noted in the 'Rough Notes'. Now missing from the Fry Collection.

---

[1]'The Rough Notes' –see Section 10, Duplicated and Manuscript Items, 'Manuscript Items added to the Fry Collection in 2011' in this Guide. The 'notes' are catalogued in the Christian Brethren Archive as FRY/1/2/1).

5th May 1860  **From S.P. Tregelles**  Plymouth
 To B.W. Newton

Regarding Tregelles's Greek Testament. Referring to [Dr J.P.] Riach, Codex Sinaiticus and [Constantine] Simonides.

Partially quoted (first three, and last paragraph) in T.C.F. Stunt, 'Some Unpublished Letters of S.P. Tregelles relating to Codex Sinaiticus' : *Evangelical Quarterly* Vol. 48 (January 1976), pp.18,23.

CBA 7181(20).

11th October 1860  **From S.P. Tregelles**  Plymouth
 To B.W. Newton

Thanking B.W. Newton for proofreading sheets of his (Tregelles) Greek Testament. Answering questions on the divisions of Alexander's empire. Referring to Lord Shaftesbury, the situation in Spain, and Tischendorf. 5 pages.

CBA 7181(21).

16th March 1861  From B.W. Newton  70, New Finchley Road
 **To Miss Haldane**

She had written to Mr Newton's wife. He thanked her for the invitation [to speak at a meeting?], but declines for the present. Mr Newton says he is pained at the current expectations of great blessing (as a result of changes affecting the Papacy etc). Says it runs counter to his expectations over thirty years.

F.W. Wyatt's copy, from a copy 'in Mrs N's hand', MS Book 1 (TC), p.334. Listed in the 'Rough Notes'.

---

**Census. 8th April 1861**

Address: 70, Finchley New Road, London.
 Benjamin Newton, 53 [*sic*], fundholder, born Devon, Stoke Damerel;
 Maria Newton, 46, born Maccrass [*sic* - for Madras], East Indies; Sophia C. Hawkins, 40, fundholder, born Hampton Court.

Address: 5, Belsize Terrace, London.
 Anna Newton, fundholder, 78; Amy Toulmin, 48; 2 servants, Sarah A. Barrett, aged 16 (cook), and Frances -?-, 19 (maid).

---

29th June 1861  **From [Dr] David Brown**
 To B.W. Newton

Refers to 'your kindness in coming to call on me and sending me so many of your writings. I shall value them and assuredly shall try to give them a prayerful and unprejudiced attention'. Indignant at attempted persecution of Mr Newton. [For B.W.

Newton's response to Dr Brown's popular book, see *Occasional Papers on Scriptural Subjects* Vol. 2 (1862); Vol. 3 and Vol. 4 - Examination of a Work.... by Rev. David Brown; reprinted in *The Second Coming of Christ: It Will Be Premillennial*].
Transcript of letter CBA 7050, p.18.

4th November 1861     From B.W. Newton     70, New Finchley Road
    **To Miss Smith**
Greatly pained by her step of joining with 'the Brethren' without speaking to him. She will have to burn *Thoughts on the Apocalypse, Aids* [*to Prophetic Enquiry*], etc. because they consider most of the New Testament Jewish, etc.
F.W. Wyatt's copy. MS Book 1 (TC), pp.336-338. Listed in the 'Rough Notes'.

3rd January 1862     **From S.P. Tregelles**     Plymouth
    To B.W. Newton
Regarding comments of Gesenius upon Psalm 1:2. [B.W. Newton adopted this proposed translation in his *Notes on Psalm 1*[1]]. Regarding the discovery by Professor [Franz] Delitzsch of a Greek MS used by Erasmus in translating the Book of Revelation. 'It takes away all possible ground for defending many false and troublesome readings' (see Tregelles's letter of 11th August 1862 to B.W. Newton). Stating he thinks his (S.P. Tregelles's) only vocation is textual criticism. Regarding getting Bibles into Portugal. 4 pages.
Original letter. CBA 7181(22). F.W. Wyatt's copy in his S.P. Tregelles Correspondence Book, acquired by the Christian Brethren Archive in 2011 (FRY/1/1/4). Quoted at length in T.C.F. Stunt, *Life and Times of Samuel Prideaux Tregelles*, p56.

23rd January 1862     **From William Cureton**[2]     Deans Yard
    To [B.W. Newton?]
Regarding Mr Cowper and a 'memorial' to be made to the Prime Minister [on behalf of S.P. Tregelles?]. 2 pages.
Original letter CBA 7182(13), Listed in CBA 6998. F.W. Wyatt's copy in MS Book 1 (TC), p.334.

4th February 1862     **From S.P. Tregelles?**
    To B.W. Newton
A lost letter noted by F.W. Wyatt simply as 'envelope only Simonides'. In F.W. Wyatt's list of S.P. Tregelles's letters in the 'Rough Notes' (In the Christian Brethren Archive as FRY/1/2/1). NB this could be an error as there is an extant letter regarding [Constantine] Simonides dated, 4th February 1863.

---

[1] *Notes on Psalm 1*, in *Occasional Papers on Scriptural Subjects*, No.2, 1862.
[2] William Cureton (1808-1864). See S.P. Tregelles's letter of July 1st 1849.

5th February 1862      **From S.P. Tregelles**      Plymouth
     To B.W. Newton

Regarding support for the Spanish prisoners, and sending money to Spain.[1] Returning letters from Mr and Mrs [R.B.] Brooks. 3 pages (see following item)
Original letter CBA 7181 (23). F.W. Wyatt's copy in his S.P. Tregelles Correspondence Book, acquired by the Christian Brethren Archive in 2011 (FRY/1/1/4).

5th February [1862]      **From Mrs S.A. Tregelles**
     To B.W. Newton

The year is not given in the letter, but it is 1862, as her letter is referred to in her husband, S.P. Tregelles's letter of the same date. Regarding support for the [Spanish] prisoners, and money collected on their behalf. Referring to Trigo, Gurney Prideaux, Mr Marsh, Manuel Matamoros, and Mr and Mrs [R.B.] Brooks. 4 pages.
CBA 7181(121), (see preceding item). F.W. Wyatt's copy in his S.P. Tregelles Correspondence Book, acquired by the Christian Brethren Archive in 2011 (FRY/1/1/4).

2nd June 1862      **From S.P. Tregelles**      Leipsic
     To B.W. Newton

Extract of a letter, which has this date, but a note on it identifies it as the letter from S.P. Tregelles dated 20th June 1862. See below on that date.

20th June 1862      **From S.P. Tregelles**      Leipsic
     To B.W. Newton

Extract of a letter. Does not doubt that Tischendorf's edition of the Greek NT will be out by the end of the year, and therefore he does not intend to collate the [Codex Sinaiticus] MS himself. Unhappy with Tischendorf, who gives little access, and interrupts continuously. He does not behave as a scholar and a gentleman ought. He (S.P. Tregelles) will leave for Berlin shortly.
The original letter may have been used to discredit Constantine Simonides's claims that he wrote the Codex Sinaiticus. See also a letter to *The Manchester Guardian*, 23rd January 1863, from Henry Bradshaw, who inspected the Codex Sinaiticus with S.P. Tregelles.
The letter is quoted at length and discussed in *Some Unpublished Letters of S.P. Tregelles*, by T.C.F. Stunt in *The Evangelical Quarterly* Vol. 48 (January 1976), pp.18,23.
This is a copy of S.P. Tregelles's letter, written in B.W. Newton's own hand, and entitled, 'Extract of a letter from Dr Tregelles'. It was originally in an envelope also endorsed by B.W. Newton, 'Copy of Dr Tregelles letter, Sinaitic MS'. The letter has the date of the 2nd of June 1862, but has a note on it correcting the date to 20th June 1862.
Original copy - TC. Original copy of the letter listed in CBA 6998. F.W. Wyatt's copy in his S.P. Tregelles Correspondence Book, acquired by the Christian Brethren Archive in 2011 (FRY/1/1/4).

---

[1] See the two page circular *Persecution of Protestants in Spain* (1862) In Section 4, Contributions to Other Publications, of this Guide.

Section 9 – B.W. Newton Correspondence

1st July 1862            From B.W. Newton
    **To Rev. Medhurst**          Coleraine

He thanks him for his desire to defend him against attacks, but declines that he should do this publicly, 'as I desire not even indirectly to be drawn back into any controversy with "the Brethren". 'They were at first, I think, Eutychian and are now becoming Valentinian, as Dr Carson says'.

F.W. Wyatt's copy. MS Book 1 (TC), pp.338-342. Listed in the 'Rough Notes'.[1]

July 1862               From B.W. Newton
    **To Dr Carson**[2]             Ireland

Offers to let him have a sight of the bound up pamphlets, if he visits London. 'It is not very easy to injure my reputation. A slain man is slain and cannot be killed a second time'. Refers to his other later tracts.

F.W. Wyatt's copy. MS Book 1 (TC), p.342. Listed in the 'Rough Notes'.

3rd July 1862          **From S.P. Tregelles**          Berlin
    To B.W. Newton

The letter discusses the value of Codex Sinaiticus (e.g. on Rev. 22:14), which Tischendorf had lately published in facsimile. Comments on Tischendorf's faulty judgement in some instances (e.g. relating to Arabic marginal notes). Russian exploitation of the discovery of the Codex (for diplomatic ends in the Red Sea area).

The letter is quoted at length in *Some Unpublished Letters of S.P. Tregelles*, by T.C.F. Stunt in *The Evangelical Quarterly* Vol. 48 (January 1976), pp.18,23.

Original (a copy by 'a lady' Wyatt) - TC. Listed in CBA 6998. F.W. Wyatt's copy in his S.P. Tregelles Correspondence Book, acquired by the Christian Brethren Archive in 2011 (FRY/1/1/4). There is an extract of this letter in F.W. Wyatt's hand bound into a volume with the cover title *Textual Criticism of the Greek N.T. S.P. Tregelles*, held by C.W.H. Griffiths. He titles it 'Copy of extract [in AJT.'s hand] from Dr Tregelles letter ...', i.e. the copy was by A.J. Toulmin.

17th July 1862         **From S.P. Tregelles**     Written in Vienna, but posted in
                                                            England, having been enclosed in a letter to Dr W. Cureton
    To B.W. Newton                    70, New Finchley Road, London

His travel to Vienna through Bohemia and Moravia. Tregelles's sister[3]. He writes of distributing B.W. Newton's tracts on *Justification*[4], and *The Blood that Saveth*. He desires to stay with Mr Newton and to converse. Hoping for his (S.P. Tregelles's) recovery to better health. The perverse conduct of [Nicolas] Alonzo.

---

[1] 'The Rough Notes' –see Section 10, Duplicated and Manuscript Items, 'Manuscript Items added to the Fry Collection in 2011' in this Guide. The 'notes' are catalogued in the Christian Brethren Archive as FRY/1/2/1).
[2] James Crawford Ledlie Carson (1815?-1886). An Anti-millennialist. Published *The Heresies of the Plymouth Brethren*, in 1862.
[3] Anna Rebecca Tregelles (1811-1885), who accompanied S.P. Tregelles and his wife on their continental trip. He took a month-long excursion with her to Brittany in the summer of 1865. See the further reference to this in his letter of 31st May 1865.
[4] *Ueber die Rechtfertigung*. 1860. See Section 3, Published Works.

Original letter listed in CBA 6998. F.W. Wyatt's copy in his S.P. Tregelles Correspondence Book, acquired by the Christian Brethren Archive in 2011 (FRY/1/1/4). Annotated transcription of the whole letter in T.C.F. Stunt, *Life and Times of Samuel Prideaux Tregelles* (2020) pp.235-237.

28th July 1862      **From S.P. Tregelles**      Nuremberg
     To B.W. Newton

Hoping Newton is in better health. Asking if he (S.P Tregelles) and his wife can stay with B.W. Newton in August. Referring to [J.P.] Riach, Mr Harry [independent minister of Bournemouth]; tract distribution in Vienna. Regarding Tregelles's Greek Testament. 3 pages.

Original letter CBA 7181(24). F.W. Wyatt's copy in his S.P. Tregelles Correspondence Book, acquired by the Christian Brethren Archive in 2011 (FRY/1/1/4).

31st July 1862      **From S.P. Tregelles**      Nuremberg
     To B.W. Newton      London

Regarding Tregelles's Greek Testament, Tregelles's travels, Tregelles's proposed book, *Pastoral Relations*. Referring to [Prof. F.] Delitzsch ('godly and orthodox'), B.W. Newton's visit to the continent for his health.[1] Eliza Pigeon. 4 pages.

Original letter CBA 7181(25). F.W. Wyatt's copy in his S.P. Tregelles Correspondence Book, acquired by the Christian Brethren Archive in 2011 (FRY/1/1/4).

11th August 1862      **From S.P. Tregelles**      Trèves
     To B.W. Newton      London

Regarding B.W. Newton's proposed continental journey, the situation in Spain, and family matters. The Greek version of Revelation held by Professor [Franz] Delitzsch (see letter of 3rd January 1862), and the blunder of Erasmus's 'false readings' which it elucidates. 4 pages.

Original letter CBA 7181(26). F.W. Wyatt's copy in his S.P. Tregelles Correspondence Book, acquired by the Christian Brethren Archive in 2011 (FRY/1/1/4).

27th August 1862      From B.W. Newton      Ireland
     **To Mr Edgton [Eggerton?]**

Affirms his belief that the Saviour continued to be the object of the Father's complacency, delight, and love, even whilst bearing wrath for our sins. He clarifies the sense in which Christ was 'made sin for us' on the cross

F.W. Wyatt's copy. MS Book 1 (TC), pp.345,346. Listed in the 'Rough Notes'.

29th August 1862      **From S.P. Tregelles**      Plymouth
     To B.W. Newton      London

Referring to money received for the Spanish prisoners, Darbyites in London. Commenting on Greek text of Luke 9:16. Regarding Tregelles's Greek Testament.

---

[1] See the note on B.W. Newton's passport in Section 12, Miscellaneous Biographical Items.

Referring to Miss E[gerton], Mr [J.C.L.] Carson, Tischendorf, and Elise Hupfeld. 4 pages.
One paragraph is quoted in *Some Unpublished Letters of S.P. Tregelles*, by T.C.F. Stunt in *The Evangelical Quarterly* Vol. 48 (January 1976), p.21.
Original letter CBA 7181(27). F.W. Wyatt's copy in his S.P. Tregelles Correspondence Book, acquired by the Christian Brethren Archive in 2011 (FRY/1/1/4).

31st August 1862          **From S.P. Tregelles**          Plymouth
     To B.W. Newton          London

Regarding the Vienna edition of B.W. Newton's 'two tracts in German' the publication in which he (B.W. Newton) had evidently assisted[1]. Regarding money for suffering Protestants in Spain. Regarding B.W. Newton's letter to Miss Dorothy Haydon on the possible retention of Compton Street Chapel, Plymouth, and problems there[2]. Regarding J.N. Darby deriving his teaching on the Church from Olshausen. Referring to C.H. Mackintosh, Darbyites in London, *The Record*, the translation of Jeremiah 33:16, Mr Rew, H. Fletcher, and Mr and Mrs Riach.
3 pages.
Quoted in relation to the Brethren rapture teaching in T.C.F. Stunt, 'The Tribulation of Controversy: A Review Article'. *Brethren Archivists and Historians Network Review*, 2, pp.91-98.
Original letter CBA 7181(28). F.W. Wyatt's copy in his S.P. Tregelles Correspondence Book, acquired by the Christian Brethren Archive in 2011 (FRY/1/1/4).

26th September 1862      **From S.P. Tregelles**          Plymouth
     To B.W. Newton

Concerning R.B. Brooks' enquiry about B.W. Newton, and Brooks's itinerary. Referring to Mr and Mrs. Riach, and Miss Dorothy Haydon. 1 page.
Original letter CBA 7181(29). F.W. Wyatt's copy in his S.P. Tregelles Correspondence Book, acquired by the Christian Brethren Archive in 2011 (FRY/1/1/4).

12th October 1862        **From S.P. Tregelles**          Plymouth
     To B.W. Newton

Regarding letters that B.W. Newton had shown him, which 'came as a blow' to him. Regarding Matamoros and the Spanish prisoners. Referring to Mr [William] Greene's publication, and its 'absurdly false' statements regarding the Spanish prisoners. Asking whether the Darbyites or the Soltau party have replied to recent notices. Regarding the 'false witness' of the Brethrenites. Referring to Señor de Sarravia, [Mrs] Alhama [Trigo].
3 pages.
Original letter CBA 7181(30). F.W. Wyatt's copy in his S.P. Tregelles Correspondence Book, acquired by the Christian Brethren Archive in 2011 (FRY/1/1/4).

---

[1] B.W. Newton produced five or six tracts in German at about this time, but we are unaware of any published in Vienna.
[2] For the Compton Street Chapel problems at Plymouth see T.C.F. Stunt, *The Life and Times of Samuel Prideaux Tregelles*, p178ff., and the following correspondence.

15th October 1862       **From S.P. Tregelles**       Plymouth
To B.W. Newton

> Listed in a calendar of S.P. Tregelles related correspondence prepared by F.W. Wyatt, but not noted elsewhere. It has the word 'not' against it in pencil on the list, perhaps indicating that it was lost at an earlier point. Missing from the Fry Collection. The calendar is in the Christian Brethren Archive as FRY/1/2/1.

17th October 1862       **From S.P. Tregelles**       Westbrook
To B.W. Newton

> Regarding Horsley's sermons and his discussion of the Greek word διά. Commenting on a tract by C. S[tanley].[1] Referring to a letter from Sarah Anna [Tregelles] to B.W. Newton regarding Trigo. Asking for his (Tregelles) name to be added to the appeal for the Spanish prisoners' children. Referring to Bishop Colenso[2], and to Mr Greaves. 3 pages
> Original letter CBA 7181(31). F.W. Wyatt's copy in his S.P. Tregelles Correspondence Book, acquired by the Christian Brethren Archive in 2011 (FRY/1/1/4).

31st October 1862       **From S.P. Tregelles**       Plymouth
To B.W. Newton

> Referring to an article by Bishop Horsley. Referring to Bishop Colenso, *The Record*. 4 pages
> Original letter CBA 7181(32). F.W. Wyatt's copy in his S.P. Tregelles Correspondence Book, acquired by the Christian Brethren Archive in 2011 (FRY/1/1/4).

1st November 1862       From B.W. Newton       70, New Finchley Road
    **To Sarah Anna [Tregelles]**

Regarding Spain, [William] Greene and Alonzo.
F.W. Wyatt's copy. MS Book 1 (TC), p.347. The following pages of MS Book 1 give further notes on Alonzo. Listed in the 'Rough Notes' (FRY/1/2/1).

15th December 1862       **From S.P. Tregelles**       Plymouth
To B.W. Newton

> Regarding Mr [Henry] Heywood and Mr [William] Haydon. 3 pages.
> Original letter CBA 7181(33).

17th December 1862       From B.W. Newton
    **To [William] Haydon**
    Regarding 'Compton Street'

---

[1] Regarding Charles Stanley, see B.W. Newton's publication, *Remarks on a Tract Entitled 'Justification in the Risen Christ'*, 1870 (by Stanley).

[2] John William Colenso (1814-1843), Bishop of Natal, whose heterodoxy was a catalyst for the first Lambeth Conference (1867). He was a former pupil of a friend of Tregelles; see T.C.F. Stunt, *Life and Times of Samuel Prideaux Tregelles*, p140. See also the comment on *The Spread of Neology in England*, Section 3, 1863 B.W. Newton's Published Works.

Listed in CBA 7002, F.W. Wyatt's index of Correspondence, as being at p. 19 of 'Yellow Quarto'. This letter is apparently no longer extant, but was written at the suggestion of Tregelles, in his letter of 15 December

21st December 1862          **From S.P. Tregelles**          Plymouth
To B.W. Newton

    Successful effect of BWN's letter to Haydon[1]. Regarding Manuel Matamoros and the situation in Spain. Referring to [William] Greene's publications; Miss Hupfeld, Count von Bernsdorff, Mr Bird, Washington Irving, William Cowper. 4 pages
    Appended: News about [Nicolas] Alonzo; Papers read by [H.B.] Bulteel about [J.L.] Harris.
    Original letter CBA 7181(34).

22nd December 1862          **From S.P. Tregelles**          Plymouth
To B.W. Newton

    Referring to Matamoros; Mr Haydon; [H.B.] Bulteel preaching at Compton Street Chapel, Plymouth. 2 pages.
    Original letter CBA 7181(35).

29th December 1862          **From S.P. Tregelles**          Plymouth
To B.W. Newton

    Referring to Mr [R.B.] Brooks. Commenting on Genesis. Referring to Tischendorf, Codex Sinaiticus, Delitzsch, Robert Young. 3 pages
    Two paragraphs are quoted in *Some Unpublished Letters of S.P. Tregelles*, by T.C.F. Stunt in *The Evangelical Quarterly* Vol. 48 (January 1976), p.22.
    Original letter CBA 7181(36).

7th January 1863          **From S.P. Tregelles**          Plymouth
To B.W. Newton

    Asking about papers by Rev. E.A. Litton on 'Plymouth Brethren'. Commenting on J.N. Darby's pamphlet that had dismissed the doctrine of imputed righteousness as 'Newtoninanism'[2]. Regarding Tregelles's Greek Testament. Referring to W. Kelly, Miss Egerton. 2 pages.
    An extract is quoted in *Some Unpublished Letters of S.P. Tregelles*, by T.C.F. Stunt in *The Evangelical Quarterly* Vol. 48 (January 1976), p.22.
    Original letter CBA 7181(37).

---

[1] See T.C.F. Stunt, *The Life and Times of Samuel Prideaux Tregelles*, p179 for the context. Haydon was a potential candidate for the pastorate of Compton Street whom Tregelles disfavoured.
[2] Eventually published in J.N. Darby *Collected Writings 7* (Doctrinal 2) as 'The Righteousness of God', and answered by S.P. Tregelles in his *Five Letters to the Editor of 'The Record' on Recent Denials of Our Lord's Vicarious Life*. See T.C.F. Stunt, *Life and Times of Samuel Prideaux Tregelles*, p184ff.

Section 9 – B.W. Newton Correspondence

10th January 1863     **From S.P. Tregelles**     Plymouth
To B.W. Newton

> Regarding Tregelles's Greek Testament. Reference to Codex Sinaiticus, Tischendorf, and [S.P. Tregelles's book] *Pastoral Relations*. 3 pages.
> Original letter CBA 7181(38).

13th January 1863     **From S.P. Tregelles**     Plymouth
To B.W. Newton

> Regarding a petition in Spanish and English[1], Mr McGregor and a Toronto publication. 2 pages.
> Original letter CBA 7181(39).

15th January 1863     **From S.P. Tregelles**     Plymouth
To B.W. Newton

> Regarding Codex Sinaiticus, W. Cureton, and [Constantine] Simonides. 3 pages.
> The whole letter is quoted in *Some Unpublished Letters of S.P. Tregelles*, by T.C.F. Stunt in *The Evangelical Quarterly* Vol. 48 (January 1976), p.24.
> Original letter CBA 7181(40).

21st January 1863     **From S.P. Tregelles**     Plymouth
To B.W. Newton

> Regarding Codex Sinaiticus, W. Cureton and [Constantine] Simonides, and a Toronto Tract. 3 pages
> Original letter CBA 7181(42).

2nd February 1863     **From S.P. Tregelles**     Plymouth
To B.W. Newton

> Hoping that Newton's health has improved. Hoping that William Elliott[2] will visit Newton. Regarding Codex Sinaiticus, [Constantine] Simonides, and W.A. Wright. 3 pages.
> Two paragraphs are quoted in *Some Unpublished Letters of S.P. Tregelles*, by T.C.F. Stunt in *The Evangelical Quarterly* Vol. 48 (January 1976), pp.24-25.
> Original letter CBA 7181(41).

4th February 1863     **From S.P. Tregelles**     Plymouth
To B.W. Newton

> Expressing concern regarding B.W. Newton's neuralgia. Regarding S.P Tregelles's actions in connection with W. Elliott and Compton Street Chapel. Expressing his thanks for B.W. Newton's support, he expresses his willingness to comment on texts in Romans.

---

[1] See the preceding correspondence, and Section 4, B.W. Newton's Contributions to Other Publications – the circular *Persecution of Protestants in Spain*, 1862.

[2] William Elliott (1829-1904). He was inducted as pastor of Compton Street 4th March 1863. See T.C.F. Stunt, *The Life and Times of Samuel Prideaux Tregelles*, p179ff for an account of Elliott's call to the pastorate, and the later exit of S.P. Tregelles from Compton Street.

Regarding [Constantine] Simonides and the Codex Sinaiticus. Referring to Sir C. Eardley. 3 pages.
Two paragraphs are quoted in *Some Unpublished Letters of S.P. Tregelles*, by T.C.F. Stunt in *The Evangelical Quarterly* Vol. 48 (January 1976), pp.24,25.
CBA 7181(43),

| | | |
|---|---|---|
| 8th February 1863 | **From S.P. Tregelles** | Plymouth |

To B.W. Newton

Expressing pleasure that [W.] Elliott has seen B.W. Newton. Referring to Haydon, and Mrs Brookes. 1 page.
Original letter CBA 7181(44).

| | | |
|---|---|---|
| 10th February 1863 | **From S.P. Tregelles** | Plymouth |

To B.W. Newton

Regarding translation and printing of B.W. Newton's account of Matamoros. Regarding B.W. Newton, Tregelles, and Elliott. Large numbers at Compton Street Chapel, Plymouth, and Tregelles's influence there. Referring to Elise Hupfeld, Dr Messner, Mr Haydon, and Codex Sinaiticus and [Constantine] Simonides. 3 pages.
Original letter CBA 7181(45).

| | | |
|---|---|---|
| 11th February 1863 | **From S.P. Tregelles** | Plymouth |

To B.W. Newton

Expressing concern at B.W. Newton's depression. Regarding Compton Street and Elliott. Criticism of Dr Carson's pamphlet attacking Tregelles, B.W. Newton, et al. Referring to Codex Sinaiticus, [Constantine] Simonides, and W. Cureton. Quote from Augustine. 3 pages.
Original letter CBA 7181(46).

14th February 1863           From B.W. Newton
   **To S.P. Tregelles**
Regarding [S.P. Tregelles book?] 'Pastoral Relations'
Listed in CBA 7002, F.W. Wyatt's index of Correspondence, as two letters with the same date and subject at pp. 22, 23 of 'Yellow Quarto'. These letters are apparently no longer extant.

| | | |
|---|---|---|
| 16th February 1863 | **From S.P. Tregelles** | Plymouth |

To B.W. Newton

Regarding Compton Street Chapel, and *Pastoral Relations*. Refers to [Frederick] Whitfield, Charnock, Dr Carson, and J.C. Cookworthy. 3 pages
Original letter CBA 7181(47).

| | | |
|---|---|---|
| 28th February 1863 | **From S.P. Tregelles** | Plymouth |

To B.W. Newton

Regarding Mr Rooker and a Bill introduced by Sir George Grey to give standing and salary to Romish priests. 2 pages.
Original letter CBA 7181(48).

8th April 1863          From B.W. Newton      Belsize Terrace [Hampstead]
    **To Miss Smith**

Re- 'us' in Rev. 5:9.[1] 'There can be no doubt it should be retained in the text', reference to Tregelles, Tischendorf, Codex Sinaiticus, and Kelly.

F.W. Wyatt's copy. MS Book 1 (TC), p.347. Listed in the 'Rough Notes'.

7th May 1863          **From S.P. Tregelles**      Plymouth
    To B.W. Newton

    Expressing concern regarding B.W. Newton's illness, and his (B.W. Newton's) worries regarding the Spanish prisoners. Thanking B.W. Newton for money. Regarding H.B. Bulteel's pronouncement of W. Elliott as 'the right man'. Regarding [Nicolas] Alonzo's preaching. Regarding Codex Sinaiticus and Tischendorf.
    3 pages.
    Original letter CBA 7181(49). Quoted by T.C.F. Stunt, *Life and Times of Samuel Prideaux Tregelles* in connection with Alonzo.

30th May 1863          From B.W. Newton
    **To Rev. John Cox**

Regarding 'Bunyan's tract, etc'

Listed in CBA 7002, F.W. Wyatt's index of Correspondence, as being at p. 24 of 'Yellow Quarto'. This letter is apparently no longer extant.

31st May 1863          **From S.P. Tregelles**      Plymouth
    To B.W. Newton

    Referring to Mr Cowper, W. Cureton, and Delores Garcia. 1 page
    Original letter CBA 7181(50).

16th July 1863          **From S.P. Tregelles**      Plymouth
    To B.W. Newton

    Agreeing with B.W. Newton, and Mr and Mrs Rew, regarding the exiled and imprisoned Spanish Protestants. Referring to Mr Wilbraham Taylor, the Barnet Conference, H.B. Bulteel, and the Haydons. 3 pages.
    Original letter CBA 7181(51).

12th August 1863          **From S.P. Tregelles**      North Malvern
    To B.W. Newton          London
        See 13th August 1863.

13th August 1863          **From S.P. Tregelles**      North Malvern
    To B.W. Newton          London

    Referring to his [Tregelles's] visit to North Malvern, Dr Macbride, Exeter College, Miss Boniface, and Miss Egerton.

---

[1] See *Thoughts on the Apocalypse*, 2nd and 3rd editions *in loco*, and Appendix B.

The date of the CBA catalogue (12th August 1863) is incorrect. Date is as recorded in CBA 6998. 4 pages.
Original letter CBA 7181(52).

21st August 1863      **From S.P. Tregelles**      North Malvern
To B.W. Newton
> Referring to his (Tregelles's) vacation. Regarding Mr and Mrs Riach, The Barnet Conference, H.B. Bulteel's health and his (Bulteel's) former church. Regarding B.W. Newton's cold, B.W. Newton's 'estimate of Oxford'. Referring to Mr Schwartz, Mr [D.K.] Shoebotham, and Mr [Robert] Nelson. 4 pages.
> Extracts of this letter were cited in Earle Hilgert, Two Unpublished Letters Regarding Tregelles' 'Canon Muratorianus', *Andrews University Seminary Studies 5* (No.2 1967), p.130 n18. Also, see letters at 28th October 1865, and 13th March 1868.
> Original letter CBA 7181(53).

24th September 1863      **From S.P. Tregelles**      Plymouth
To B.W. Newton
> Expressing concern at B.W. Newton's ill health. Stating that he has copied part of B.W. Newton's letter, and has sent it to Bulteel. Tregelles writing to *The Record* on doctrinal points. Referring to Tregelles's Greek Testament.
> 3 pages.
> Original letter CBA 7181(54).

21st October 1863      **From S.P. Tregelles**      Kingsbridge
To B.W. Newton
> Referring to Mr Brendon, Miss Hawkins, Lady Radstock, Tregelles declining an invitation to speak at a conference in East Barnet on the Lord's return, Mrs Bevan. 2 pages.
> Original letter CBA 7181(55)..

23rd October 1863      **From S.P. Tregelles**      Plymouth
To B.W. Newton
> Referring to Lady Radstock, to the ill-health of Bulteel, Ministerial support' by Brendon and W. Elliott, Spanish matters, *The Inquirer*, Mr Bird, death of M. le Comte de Tharon, Mr Adams, Tregelles's new tract. 3 pages.
> Original letter CBA 7181(56).

November 1863      From B.W. Newton
    **To a Clergyman**
Concerning B.W. Newton's position vis-à-vis the Brethren.
This extract, and a letter dated 15th April 1864, were enclosed with the letter from S.P. Tregelles on 15th April 1864. See letter of this date CBA 7181(66). There is a copy (placed after a letter dated 23rd April 1864) in F.W. Wyatt's book of S.P. Tregelles related correspondence, acquired by the Christian Brethren Archive in 2011 (FRY/1/1/4).

### Section 9 – B.W. Newton Correspondence

6th November 1863      **From S.P. Tregelles**      Plymouth
To B.W. Newton
> Thanking B.W. Newton for money. Referring to ill health of Bulteel, attacks on Tregelles's pamphlet [*An Appeal to the Law and to the Testimony, from Five Letters to the Editor of 'The Record'*, signed 'C.C.', but by S.P. Tregelles], 4 pages. CBA] by Rev. J.E. Carr, and a reply to it by Captain Catesby Paget.[1] Regarding Tregelles's Greek Testament. 3 pages
> Original letter CBA 7181(57).

17th November 1863      From B.W. Newton
**To Mrs Peddie**
On the subject of Spanish missions
Re-Matamoros and the Spaniards – 'the more they say the less I believe'. He states he can see little evidence of the hand of the Lord working in Spain.
F.W. Wyatt's copy ('from a copy, probably in Mrs N's hand') MS Book 1 (TC), p.355. Listed in the 'Rough Notes'.

24th November 1863      From B.W. Newton
**To Rev. Robt. McGhee**
Responding to the correspondent's enquiry. 'It is impossible, I believe, that anyone <u>could</u> feel a greater or more intense hatred of Popery than myself. I loathe it from the very bottom of my heart'. 'I was the first person who ever publicly opposed Mr John Newman'. The letter states that he (B.W. Newton) is on the committee of the Protestant Alliance. Clarifies his position vis a vis 'the Brethren'.
F.W. Wyatt's copy. MS Book 1 (TC), pp.357,358.

5th December 1863      **From S.P. Tregelles**      Plymouth
To B.W. Newton
> The letter asks B.W. Newton's opinion of the possibility of Tregelles writing a tract on the coming of the Lord. Captain Caldwell's reply to *Tregelles's Five Letters...* Asking whether B.W. Newton will attend the meeting of the Protestant Alliance. Referring to Robert Baxter, John Morley, Wilbraham Taylor, Mr Gardner, British and Foreign Bible Society, and Plutarch regarding 'leaven'. 3 pages.
> Original letter CBA 7181(58).

9th December 1863      **From S.P. Tregelles**      Plymouth
To B.W. Newton
> Commenting on the Greek text of Ephesians 1:6.[2] Regarding the Barnet Conference organised by William Pennefather, which Tregelles had attended. Referring to Mr H.H. Snell, George Müller, Mr Birk, Mr Pratt of Macclesfield, Mr Gilbert, and Capt. Caldwell. 4 pages.
> Original letter CBA 7181(59).

---

[1] For further comment on this, see T.C.F. Stunt, *Life and Times of Samuel Prideaux Tregelles*, p185, 186.
[2] See *Occasional Papers No.3* – 'Notes on the Greek of Ephesians 1'.

## Section 9 – B.W. Newton Correspondence

12th December 1863      **From S.P. Tregelles**
> To B.W. Newton

Concerning the Bible Society's uncritical publication of Romish versions made from the Vulgate [in French, Italian, and Spanish]. The errors of the Clementine Vulgate. Quoted in T.C.F. Stunt, *Life and Times of Samuel Prideaux Tregelles.*
Original letter listed in CBA 6998, but now missing from the Fry Collection. T.C.F. Stunt has a Xerox copy.

16th January 1864      **From S.P. Tregelles**      Plymouth
> To B.W. Newton

Referring to B.W. Newton's *Occasional Papers on Scriptural Subjects No.2* in reference to I Corinthians 1. Referring to Lady Radstock, Mr [William] Chalk[1], Louisa Freeman, Capt. Paget, Miss Massie, and Elizabeth Wakefield. Regarding progress on Tregelles's Greek Testament. 4 pages.
Original letter CBA 7181(60).

21st January 1864      **From S.P. Tregelles**      Plymouth
> To B.W. Newton

Referring to [Rev] Jacob Tomlin[2], *The Record*, Brethrenite influences, Miss Kinnaird, H.B. Bulteel in connection with Irvingism, Mr Goodhart, Tregelles's *Five Letters* [*An Appeal to the Law and to the Testimony, from Five Letters to the Editor of 'The Record'*, signed 'C.C.', but by S.P. Tregelles], Capt. Paget, Miss Massie. 3 pages.
Original letter CBA 7181(61). F.W. Wyatt's copy in his S.P. Tregelles Correspondence Book, acquired by the Christian Brethren Archive in 2011 (FRY/1/1/4).

29th January 1864      **From S.P. Tregelles**      Plymouth
> To B.W. Newton

Expressing the hope that B.W. Newton may be able to rest, having finished the latest *Occasional Papers on Scriptural Subjects Vol. 3*. Regarding sorrowful news from Spain, following his visit. Referring to [Rev. Jacob] Tomlin, Wetstein, Capt. Paget, Tregelles's health, Olshausen. 3 pages.
Original letter CBA 7181(62). F.W. Wyatt's copy in his S.P. Tregelles Correspondence Book, acquired by the Christian Brethren Archive in 2011 (FRY/1/1/4).

5th February 1864      **From S.P. Tregelles**      Plymouth
> To B.W. Newton

Thanking B.W. Newton for money. Referring to Mr [W.] Pennefather leaving Barnet. False dispensational teaching, [Rev] Jacob Tomlin writing to *The Record* regarding the Received Text. Refers favourably to Mr Bevan. 3 pages.

---

[1] William Chalk (1814-1878). See T.C.F. Stunt, *The Life and Times of Samuel Prideaux Tregelles*, 13.1 A Long-Standing Friendship.
[2] Rev. Jacob Tomlin (1793-1880). A defender of the Received Text of the New Testament to whose article in *The Annotator* S.P. Tregelles replied, and who later published a critical review of Tregelles work. See T.C.F. Stunt *The Life and Times of Samuel Prideaux Tregelles*, p137ff.

Original letter CBA 7181(63). F.W. Wyatt's copy in his S.P. Tregelles Correspondence Book, acquired by the Christian Brethren Archive in 2011 (FRY/1/1/4).

> 29th February 1864 **From S.P. Tregelles** Plymouth
> To B.W. Newton 70, New Finchley Road, London, NW
> Regarding S.P. Tregelles's Greek New Testament (Acts and Catholic Epistles). 2 pages. Original letter CBA 7181(64), (see CBA 7181(124)). F.W. Wyatt's copy in his S.P. Tregelles Correspondence Book, acquired by the Christian Brethren Archive in 2011 (FRY/1/1/4).

> 8th March 1864 **From J... (H... M...)** Cooksville, Canada
> To B.W. Newton
> Regarding an agent for the circulation of B.W. Newton's works in Canada. Referring to Mr Brookman, Mr Gregg, and Mr Brown of Toronto. Referring to the Plymouth Brethren and Brethren writings, Tregelles's writings, Mrs Pengelley, Miss Holditch.
> CBA 7182(14), 5 pages.

5th April 1864 From B.W. Newton 70, New Finchley Road
> To **Dr Desanctis**[1]

In the letter Mr Newton expresses great concern at the publication of a book by Dr Desanctis in England that associates his name with the Brethren. It referred to 'Newtonians'.

B.W. Newton clarifies his own, and S.P. Tregelles's, ecclesiastical position and their differences from the Brethren in Italy. This, and another letter dated 'November', were enclosed with the letter from S.P. Tregelles, 15th April 1864. See the letter of that date CBA 7181(66).

F.W. Wyatt's copy. MS Book 1 (TC), pp.359-361. A copy of this is given, as an example of F.W. Wyatt's transcription, in *A Pictorial Memoir of Benjamin Wills Newton* – the supplement to this Guide. See the Advertisement at the end of this volume..

> 10th April 1864 **From Dr L. Desanctis** No 9, Ponte di Carignano, Genoa
> To B.W. Newton
> In this letter, Dr Desanctis asks his pardon regarding the book (see letter 5th April 1864), as the English translation had been published without his consent, apparently from an unrevised text. Stated that he had never forgotten his conversation with Mr Newton, which was truly edifying to him. He stated that he values Mr Newton highly.
> MS Book 1 (TC), p.362.

> 11th April 1864 **From S.P. Tregelles** Plymouth
> To B.W. Newton
> Referring to Dr Desanctis, and Tregelles's book on the Second Coming[2]. 2 pages. Original letter CBA 7181(65). F.W. Wyatt's copy in his S.P. Tregelles Correspondence Book, acquired by the Christian Brethren Archive in 2011 (FRY/1/1/4).

---

[1] Dr Luigi de Sanctis (1808-1869). For further reference to Dr de Sanctis, see *Babylon and Egypt*, 3rd edition, p.542n. See also T.C.F. Stunt, *Life and Times of Samuel Prideaux Tregelles*, in connection with the Tuscan protestants (*Fratelli*).
[2] Samuel Prideaux Tregelles, *The Hope of Christ's Second Coming, How is it Taught in Scripture?*, 1864.

15th April 1864 **From S.P. Tregelles** Plymouth
    To B.W. Newton

Regarding the situation in Italy. Referring to Dr Desanctis, Maria Fox, *News of the Churches*[1], Count Guicciardini, the Foreign Aid Committee, Mr Burgess, a pamphlet to Darbyites in Switzerland, S.P. Tregelles's Greek New Testament, and Tregelles's health. Enclosed with this letter were two others, one dated November 1863, and another letter dated 5th April 1864. 2 pages. Quoted T.C.F. Stunt, *Life and Times of Samuel Prideaux Tregelles*, p. 95, which gives the context of these letters.
Original letter CBA 7181(66). F.W. Wyatt's copy in his S.P. Tregelles Correspondence Book, acquired by the Christian Brethren Archive in 2011 (FRY/1/1/4) (placed in error after a letter dated 23rd April 1864).

17th April 1864 **From S.P. Tregelles** Plymouth
    To B.W. Newton

Referring to Dr Desanctis, Brendon, Tregelles's tract [on the Second Coming], Mrs Dennison, secret rapture teaching, and the Church of England. 1 page
Original letter CBA 7181(67). There is a copy in F.W. Wyatt's book of S.P. Tregelles related correspondence, acquired by the Christian Brethren Archive in 2011 (FRY/1/1/4).

18th April 1864 **From S.P. Tregelles** Plymouth
    To B.W. Newton    London

Regarding Dr Desanctis apparent view that Tregelles is an upholder of Brethrenism. Count Guicciardini. 2 pages.
Original letter CBA 7181(68). F.W. Wyatt's copy in his S.P. Tregelles Correspondence Book, acquired by the Christian Brethren Archive in 2011 (FRY/1/1/4).

Undated [April 1864] **From S.P. Tregelles** Plymouth
    To B.W. Newton

Referring to Dr Desanctis correspondence with him (S.P. Tregelles), and the effect of 'Scotch Presbyterianism' forcing people into Brethrenism in Italy. The letter is undated but placed by F.W. Wyatt in his MS book of Tregelles's letters between January 21st and January 29th 1864 – relating it to the correspondence regarding Desanctis etc. at this time. 1 page.
Original letter CBA 7181(69), F.W. Wyatt's copy in his S.P. Tregelles Correspondence Book, acquired by the Christian Brethren Archive in 2011 (FRY/1/1/4) (copied after 21st January 1864). This is probably the undated letter listed in CBA 6998 as original letter at April 1864.

23rd April 1864 **From S.P. Tregelles** Plymouth
    To B.W. Newton

Regarding Tregelles's visit to London. Referring to Wilbraham Taylor, Tregelles's pamphlet, [Dr J.P.] Riach. 2 pages.

---

[1] *The News of the Churches and Journal Of Missions.* Journal published 1854-1863 and continued as *Christian Work*.

Original letter CBA 7181(70). F.W. Wyatt's copy in his S.P. Tregelles Correspondence Book, acquired by the Christian Brethren Archive in 2011 (FRY/1/1/4). Apparently listed in CBA 6998 as 25th April 1864.

25th May 1864        **From S.P. Tregelles**        Plymouth
    To B.W. Newton
Hoping that B.W. Newton's mother got safely to Worthing. Regarding the paper Newton has been preparing to send to Mr Bevan. Referring to Lightfoot's review of Stanley and Jowett in the *Journal of Philology*, and Admiral Haydon[1]. 2 pages.
Original letter CBA 7181(71). F.W. Wyatt's copy in his S.P. Tregelles Correspondence Book, acquired by the Christian Brethren Archive in 2011 (FRY/1/1/4).

30th May 1864        **From S.P. Tregelles**
    To B.W. Newton
Protestant Alliance matters (Mr Bird). Letter from a clergyman, and Bishop Ellicott's comments on the presentation of his [S.P. Tregelles's] Greek New Testament text. Publishing issues regarding his Greek New Testament. Concern at 'fraternisation' with Dean Stanley.
Original letter listed in CBA 6998. F.W. Wyatt's copy in his S.P. Tregelles Correspondence Book, acquired by the Christian Brethren Archive in 2011 (FRY/1/1/4).

4th June 1864        **From S.P. Tregelles**
    To B.W. Newton
Commenting on the draft of *Propositions for the Solemn Consideration of Christians*, which B.W. Newton had sent him. Suggests minor changes. Comment on error regarding the doctrine of justification. *Old Truths*. Reprinting his (B.W. Newton's) *Five Letters...*
Original - TC. Original listed in CBA 6998. F.W. Wyatt's copy in his S.P. Tregelles Correspondence Book, acquired by the Christian Brethren Archive in 2011 (FRY/1/1/4).

21st July 1864        **From S.P. Tregelles**        Plymouth
    To B.W. Newton
Referring to the death of Admiral Haydon. Regarding Mr Sharpe, and Mrs Pengelley. Regarding Tregelles's Greek Testament. 3 pages.
Original letter CBA 7181(72), F.W. Wyatt's copy in his S.P. Tregelles Correspondence Book, acquired by the Christian Brethren Archive in 2011 (FRY/1/1/4).

26th July 1864        **From S.P. Tregelles**        Plymouth
    To B.W. Newton
Suggesting that B.W. Newton, Mr Cox, Mr Goodhart, and others, come together to form a strong group to influence Christians. Referring to Mrs Pengelley in Canada, Haydon

---
[1] Captain William G. Haydon (1779-1864).

family, criticising Govett's paper in *The Rainbow*.[1] Advising B.W. Newton not to go on too long itineraries because of his health. 4 pages.
Original letter CBA 7181(73). F.W. Wyatt's copy in his S.P. Tregelles Correspondence Book, acquired by the Christian Brethren Archive in 2011 (FRY/1/1/4).

1st August 1864      **From S.P. Tregelles**      Plymouth
    To B.W. Newton
Referring to [Bishop] Ellicott, Frank and Emily Ball[2], Mrs Pengelley, and the death of H.W. Soltau. Regarding Tregelles's Greek Testament. 4 pages.
Original letter CBA 7181(74). F.W. Wyatt's copy in his S.P. Tregelles Correspondence Book, acquired by the Christian Brethren Archive in 2011 (FRY/1/1/4).

2nd August 1864      **From S.P. Tregelles**      Plymouth
    To B.W. Newton
Referring to Miss Pigeon, and Mrs Pengelley. Regarding Tregelles's Greek Testament. 1 page.
Original letter CBA 7181(75). F.W. Wyatt's copy in his S.P. Tregelles Correspondence Book, acquired by the Christian Brethren Archive in 2011 (FRY/1/1/4).

11th August 1864      **From S.P. Tregelles**      Hendre, by Caernarvon
    To B.W. Newton      70, New Finchley Road, London NW
Referring to B.W. Newton going abroad. Regarding the paper Tregelles is writing on the First Resurrection for Mr Cox[3]. Referring to Bishop Ellicott, and Eliza Pigeon. Regarding Tregelles's Greek Testament. 3 pages.
Original letter CBA 7181(76). F.W. Wyatt's copy in his S.P. Tregelles Correspondence Book, acquired by the Christian Brethren Archive in 2011 (FRY/1/1/4).

13th September 1864      **From S.P. Tregelles**      Plymouth
    To B.W. Newton      Post Office, Felixstowe by Ipswich
Refers to the likely terminal outcome of Mr Riach's illness. Reports on the ill health of Mrs Tregelles's mother. Expresses his hopes that B.W. Newton will take care not to overwork when he returns to London. Of his (S.P. Tregelles's) generally better health and sight.
Original letter CBA 7181(124). F.W. Wyatt's copy in his S.P. Tregelles Correspondence Book, acquired by the Christian Brethren Archive in 2011 (FRY/1/1/4).

---

[1] Further criticism of Govett vis–à–vis 'partial rapture theory' is in *Old Truths*, Vol. 1 1867, pp.170, 171, which also gives comments by S.P. Tregelles. F. Roy Coad wrongly associates B.W. Newton with partial rapture teaching. See comment on *A Letter to a Friend on the Study of Prophecy* in Section 7 on *The Christian Witness* article, and in Section 3, B.W. Newton's Published Works.
[2] Emily Ball was the sister of S.P. Tregelles's wife Sarah Anna.
[3] Samuel Prideaux Tregelles, *The First Resurrection* Published posthumously in 1876, edited by John Cox, jun.

5th October 1864 **From S.P. Tregelles** Plymouth
    To B.W. Newton                 70 New Finchley Road, London, NW

Regarding Mr Chapman's influence on [Nicolas] Alonzo in Spain. Referring to Mrs Riach, Dr Pusey's lecture on the authenticity of Daniel, and Bishop Ellicott. Suggesting B.W. Newton writes to Bishop Ellicott. 4 pages.

Original letter CBA 7181(77). F.W. Wyatt's copy in his S.P. Tregelles Correspondence Book, acquired by the Christian Brethren Archive in 2011 (FRY/1/1/4).

6th November 1864     **From S.P. Tregelles**         Plymouth
    To B.W. Newton                c/o Thomas [Graham] Graham[1], Esq.,
                                                               Park Crescent, Worthing

Referring to Newton's visit to Mr and Mrs Graham of Worthing. Referring to money sent by Newton to Tregelles. Concerning Pusey on Daniel, Bishop Ellicott, Mr Lyne, Newman's autobiography[2], Mrs Steane (née Pigeon). Appears to be wrongly dated in CBA catalogue (see note on 16th November 1864 below). 4 pages.

Original letter CBA 7181(78). F.W. Wyatt's copy in his S.P. Tregelles Correspondence Book, acquired by the Christian Brethren Archive in 2011 (FRY/1/1/4).

November 1864           From B.W. Newton
    **To S.P. Tregelles**

Regarding 'Dr Pusey'

Listed in CBA 7002, F.W. Wyatt's index of Correspondence, as being at p. 24 of 'Yellow Quarto'. This letter is apparently no longer extant.

    [16th November 1864     **From S.P. Tregelles**         Plymouth
        To B.W. Newton

This date is as described in Susan Noble's description of CBA 7181(78). It appears to be the letter of 6th November 1864, which bears that date in the listing of CBA 6998 and F.W. Wyatt's transcription – see above for 6th November 1864].

26th November 1864     **From S.P. Tregelles**         Plymouth
    To B.W. Newton                 70 New Finchley Road, London, NW.

Expressing concern at hearing of B.W. Newton's ill health. Referring to the illness of Tregelles's mother-in-law, Mrs Pengelley and Canada, Mrs Nottage, Mrs Alfred Hingston, Mr [J.P.] Riach. Regarding Tregelles's Greek Testament. 3 pages.

Original letter CBA 7181(79). F.W. Wyatt's copy in his S.P. Tregelles Correspondence Book, acquired by the Christian Brethren Archive in 2011 (FRY/1/1/4).

19th December 1864     **From S.P. Tregelles**         Plymouth
    To B.W. Newton                 70 New Finchley Road, London, NW

Regarding H. Bonar's recent work. Referring to a letter written to Miss Whately regarding his [S.P. Tregelles's] loss of all confidence in Matamoros. 2 pages.

---

[1] Obituary of T.G. Graham, *Perilous Times*, January, February. March, April, and May 1906.
[2] John Henry Newman, *Apologia Pro Vita Sua*. First published in 1864

Original letter CBA 7181(80). F.W. Wyatt's copy in his S.P. Tregelles Correspondence Book, acquired by the Christian Brethren Archive in 2011 (FRY/1/1/4).

18th February 1865      **From Mrs S. Riach**      Plymouth
    To B.W. Newton

The letter announces her husband's death. This letter was subsequently sent by B.W. Newton to S.P. Tregelles, who returned it to him with the following letter [21st February 1865].

F.W. Wyatt's copy in his S.P. Tregelles Correspondence Book, acquired by the Christian Brethren Archive in 2011 (FRY/1/1/4).

21st February 1865      **From S.P. Tregelles**      Plymouth
    To B.W. Newton      70, New Finchley Road [London]

Informing of the death of Mr [James Pringle] Riach. S.P Tregelles encloses, and returns to B.W. Newton, Mrs S. Riach's letter [of 18th February 1865, announcing her husband's death], which B.W. Newton had earlier sent to S.P. Tregelles. S.P. Tregelles writes 'for more than twenty years Mr Riach has been so valued and so intimate a friend. May the Lord abundantly bless Mrs Riach and Hugh'.[1]

Listed in CBA 6998, but missing from the Fry Collection. F.W. Wyatt's copy in his S.P. Tregelles Correspondence Book, acquired by the Christian Brethren Archive in 2011 (FRY/1/1/4).

17th March 1865      **From S.P. Tregelles**      Plymouth
    To B.W. Newton

Regarding Tregelles's Greek Testament. 2 pages

Original letter CBA 7181(81). F.W. Wyatt's copy in his S.P. Tregelles Correspondence Book, acquired by the Christian Brethren Archive in 2011 (FRY/1/1/4).

30th March 1865      **From S.P. Tregelles**      Plymouth
    To B.W. Newton

Referring to M. Jayer [so transcribed by F.W. Wyatt. Susan Noble in her catalogue of the Fry Collection reads 'Jayet'] of Lausanne, Mr Rew, Rev. W. Linwood. Tregelles seeing [H.B.] Bulteel. 3 pages.

Original letter CBA 7181(82). F.W. Wyatt's copy in his S.P. Tregelles Correspondence Book, acquired by the Christian Brethren Archive in 2011 (FRY/1/1/4).

31st May 1865      **From S.P. Tregelles**      Plymouth
    To B.W. Newton      70, New Finchley Road, London, NW

Regarding Tregelles's Greek Testament. Referring to a proposed visit to Brittany and Normandy[2], Marcus Spittler, Mrs Riach, Miss Egerton, General [Anthony] Marshall. 3 pages

---

[1] Their son, born 1846

[2] See the letter of S.P. Tregelles dated 17th July 1862. An account of the visit to Brittany was published by S.P. Tregelles, *Notes of a Tour of Brittany* (1865).

Original letter CBA 7181(83). F.W. Wyatt's copy in his S.P. Tregelles Correspondence Book, acquired by the Christian Brethren Archive in 2011 (FRY/1/1/4).

27th July 1865     **From S.P. Tregelles**     Plymouth
    To B.W. Newton         70, New Finchley Road, London NW
Referring to Polybius on 2 Thessalonians 2:2. Regarding a book on the text of Revelation by Rev. Jacob Tomlin purporting to show the common text is better than that of Tregelles.[1] 1 page.
Original letter CBA 7181(84). F.W. Wyatt's copy in his S.P. Tregelles Correspondence Book, acquired by the Christian Brethren Archive in 2011 (FRY/1/1/4).

31st July 1865     **From S.P. Tregelles**     Victoria Place, Kingsbridge
    To B.W. Newton         70, New Finchley Road, London NW
Recommending that no time be wasted on writers in *The Rainbow* such as Rev. Richard Chester, who have devoted themselves to the Brethrenite system of teaching. 2 pages.
Original letter CBA 7181(85). F.W. Wyatt's copy in his S.P. Tregelles Correspondence Book, acquired by the Christian Brethren Archive in 2011 (FRY/1/1/4).

28th August 1865     **From S.P. Tregelles**     Plymouth
    To B.W. Newton         Walshaw's Crystal Gardens, Scarborough
Expressing concern regarding B.W. Newton's ill health. Referring to Tregelles's wife in Frankfurt Street [Plymouth; her mother's home]. Regarding Tregelles's Greek Testament. 3 pages.
Original letter CBA 7181(86). F.W. Wyatt's copy in his S.P. Tregelles Correspondence Book, acquired by the Christian Brethren Archive in 2011 (FRY/1/1/4).

29th September 1865     **From S.P. Tregelles**     Plymouth
    To B.W. Newton
Regarding B.W. Newton's visits to Scarborough, Ilkley and elsewhere. Referring to B.W. Newton's mother's fall. Referring to Tregelles's pension and Miss Ker. Regarding Tregelles's Greek Testament. 3 pages
Original letter CBA 7181(87). F.W. Wyatt's copy in his S.P. Tregelles Correspondence Book, acquired by the Christian Brethren Archive in 2011 (FRY/1/1/4).

28th October 1865     **From S.P. Tregelles**     Roebuck Hotel, Oxford
    To B.W. Newton         London
Regarding Oxford University matters[2]. Conveying a message to the Vice Chancellor on B.W. Newton's behalf. Planning to visit him [B.W. Newton]. Referring to Mrs Charles

---

[1] Rev. Jacob Tomlin, *Improved Renderings and Explanations of Many Passages in the Authorized Translation of the Scriptures: From the Hebrew and Greek* [?] (1865)

[2] T.C.F. Stunt comments 'For some reason ... Newton had always avoided returning to his *alma mater* and whenever Tregelles visited Oxford, he always made a point of passing on to Newton the latest 'news ...'. *Life and Times of Samuel Prideaux Tregelles,* p191n.

Gillett [formerly Gertrude Tregelles], the Bishop of Peterborough, Dr Symons, and Dr Payne Smith. 3 pages.
Copies of this letter were provided by T.C.F. Stunt for citation in Earle Hilgert, *Two unpublished letters regarding Tregelles, 'Canon Muratorianus'; Andrews University Seminary Studies 5* (No.2, 1967) p.130 n18. See 21st August 1863, and 13th March 1868.
Original letter CBA 7181(88). F.W. Wyatt's copy in his S.P. Tregelles Correspondence Book, acquired by the Christian Brethren Archive in 2011 (FRY/1/1/4). Quoted in *The Life and Times of Samuel Prideaux Tregelles* by T.C.F. Stunt, p. 192.

20th November 1865     **From S.P. Tregelles**     Oxford
    To B.W. Newton     70, New Finchley Road, London, NW
Referring to B.W. Newton's excitement at the quotations from [H.] Bullinger's *Decades*. Stating he had spoken to the Vice Chancellor about Mr Harrington. Tregelles's advice at the Under-graduates' Prayer Meeting to study [H.] Bullinger's views on baptism. Quoting a story told by Professor Payne Smith that raises the question whether the Brethrenites got their doctrine from the Irvingites. Referring to Mr Ziegler. 2 pages.
Quoted in relation to the Brethren rapture teaching in T.C.F. Stunt, 'The Tribulation of Controversy: A Review Article'. Brethren Archivists and Historians Network Review, 2: pp.91-98
Original letter CBA 7181(89). F.W. Wyatt's copy in his S.P. Tregelles Correspondence Book, acquired by the Christian Brethren Archive in 2011 (FRY/1/1/4).

20th November 1865     From B.W. Newton
    **To Mr Ware**
'Theological'
Listed in CBA 7002, F.W. Wyatt's index of Correspondence, as being at p. 26 of 'Yellow Quarto'. This letter is apparently no longer extant.

22nd November 1865   From B.W. Newton
    **To Unknown**
'Theological'
Listed in CBA 7002, F.W. Wyatt's index of Correspondence, as being at p. 17 of 'Yellow Quarto'. This letter is apparently no longer extant.

29th November 1865     **From S.P. Tregelles**     Plymouth
    To B.W. Newton     70, New Finchley Road, London, NW.
Regarding the attack on Mr Rew regarding M[anuel] M[atamoros] in *Christian Work*. Referring to alterations to Exeter College, Oxford, and 'the Prideaux Connection'. 3 pages.
Original letter CBA 7181(90). F.W. Wyatt's copy in his S.P. Tregelles Correspondence Book, acquired by the Christian Brethren Archive in 2011 (FRY/1/1/4).

2nd December 1865      **From S.P. Tregelles**      Plymouth
    To B.W. Newton

Regarding M[anuel] M[atamoros]. Approving B.W. Newton's letter to *Christian Work*. [Mrs] Alhama [Trigo]'s difficulties with M[anuel] M[atamoros]. Suggesting B.W. Newton write to Mr Dallas to arrange a meeting in London. Referring to Mrs Rew, Miss Whately, Baptist Noel, C.J. Stewart, Miss Ziegler, and Miss Hawkins. Postscript dated 3rd December 1865. 3 pages.

Original letter CBA 7181(91). F.W. Wyatt's copy in his S.P. Tregelles Correspondence Book, acquired by the Christian Brethren Archive in 2011 (FRY/1/1/4).

December 8th 1865      From B.W. Newton
    **To Dr Ziegler**

Regarding 'isolation'

Listed in CBA 7002, F.W. Wyatt's index of Correspondence, as being at p. 27 of 'Yellow Quarto'. This letter is apparently no longer extant.

December 8th 1865      From B.W. Newton
    **To Mr Baker**

Regarding 'isolation'

Listed in CBA 7002, F.W. Wyatt's index of Correspondence, as being at p. 28 of 'Yellow Quarto'. This letter is apparently no longer extant.

13th January 1866      From B.W. Newton
    **To 'Governor [Ker Baillie] Hamilton**

Listed in CBA 7002, F.W. Wyatt's index of Correspondence, as being at p. 28 of 'Yellow Quarto'. This letter is apparently no longer extant.

7th February 1866      From B.W. Newton
    **To Mrs Riach**

On [the first anniversary of] the death her husband [Dr James Pringle Riach], 'one whose faithful friendship and affection were to me thro' a long series of sorrowful years a peculiar source of comfort and encouragement'.

See letter of 18th February 1865. 2 pages.

Christian Brethren Archive, Box 23(10) (ex-The Stirling Collection, Spurgeon's College). A copy of this letter is given, as an example of B.W. Newton's letter writing, in *A Pictorial Memoir of Benjamin Wills Newton* – the supplement to this Guide. See the Advertisement at the end of this volume.

27th February 1866      **From S.P. Tregelles**      Plymouth
    To B.W. Newton

Commenting favourably on B.W. Newton's *Propositions*… Suggesting its advertisement in *The Record*. Commenting on the tone of letter from [Mrs] Alhama [Trigo], and on one from M[anuel] M[atamoros]. Referring to Mr Haldane, Papal censors, Tregelles's ill health, Miss Haydon and Mrs Knight, Lord Shaftesbury, the Lausanne Report. 2 pages.

Original letter CBA 7181(93). F.W. Wyatt's copy in his S.P. Tregelles Correspondence Book, acquired by the Christian Brethren Archive in 2011 (FRY/1/1/4).

5th March 1866      **From S.P. Tregelles**      Plymouth
To B.W. Newton
Regarding charges against M[anuel] M[atamoros]. Regarding Joseph Chambers, who once opposed B.W. Newton's views, now becoming a clergyman. Referring to M. Nogaret, the Lausanne Report, Mr Southall, Mr Bird, Mrs Rew, Miss Whately, Mr Haldane, the omission of Brethrenites from almanacs, Gavazzi. 4 pages.
Original letter CBA 7181(94). F.W. Wyatt's copy in his S.P. Tregelles Correspondence Book, acquired by the Christian Brethren Archive in 2011 (FRY/1/1/4).

8th March 1866      From B.W. Newton
**To Mrs Meredith**
Regarding 'convicts'
Listed in CBA 7002, F.W. Wyatt's index of Correspondence, as being at p. 2 of 'Yellow Quarto'. Apparently no longer extant.

15th March 1866      From B.W. Newton
**To Mrs Meredith**
Second letter regarding 'convicts'
Listed in CBA 7002, F.W. Wyatt's index of Correspondence, as being at p. 3 of 'Yellow Quarto'. Apparently no longer extant.

15th March 1866      From B.W. Newton
**To G[eorge] W. Mylne**
Letter regarding 'the Law'
Listed in CBA 7002, F.W. Wyatt's index of Correspondence, as being at p. 4 of 'Yellow Quarto'. See further lost letters to him at May 1866. This letter is apparently no longer extant.

16th March 1866      **From S.P. Tregelles**      Plymouth
To B.W. Newton
Regarding an attack by Brethrenites, orchestrated by [W.] Kelly on Rev. Nassau Cathcart of Guernsey because of his statements on 'Our Lord's Divinity', and on the 'heavenly humanity' of the Lord that was being propounded by C.H. M[ackintosh]. 1 page.
Original letter CBA 7181(95). F.W. Wyatt's copy in his S.P. Tregelles Correspondence Book, acquired by the Christian Brethren Archive in 2011 (FRY/1/1/4).

4th April 1866      **From S.P. Tregelles**      Plymouth
To B.W. Newton
Relating problems with Mr Elliott's ministry at Compton Street Chapel, Plymouth, and with the deacons there. Referring to Miss M. Freeman, Mrs Edlin, and the looseness of the trust deed of Compton Street Chapel. 5 pages.

Original letter CBA 7181(96). F.W. Wyatt's copy in his S.P. Tregelles Correspondence Book, acquired by the Christian Brethren Archive in 2011 (FRY/1/1/4).

6th April 1866        **From S.P. Tregelles**        Plymouth
     To B.W. Newton

Regarding the trust deed of Compton Street Chapel, and resignation to the unhappy course of events. 1 page.
Original letter CBA 7181(97)

11th April 1866        **From S.P. Tregelles**        Plymouth
     To B.W. Newton

Regarding the Compton Street trust deed, and the dispersal of former members of the congregation. Referring to Mr [Henry] Heywood and the possibility of his commencing 'breaking bread' with others. 3 pages.
Original letter CBA 7181(98). F.W. Wyatt's copy in his S.P. Tregelles Correspondence Book, acquired by the Christian Brethren Archive in 2011 (FRY/1/1/4).

14th April 1866        **From S.P. Tregelles**
     To B.W. Newton

Reference to Dr McCaul's reply to articles in *The Morning Watch* c.1830. His (S.P. Tregelles's) mother's loss of sight, Thomas Adams. More confusion over the mortgage of Compton Street Chapel.
Listed in CBA 6998, but missing from the Fry Collection. F.W. Wyatt's copy in his S.P. Tregelles Correspondence Book, acquired by the Christian Brethren Archive in 2011 (FRY/1/1/4).

25th April 1866        **From S.P. Tregelles**        Plymouth
     To B.W. Newton

Regarding the discontinuance of the Compton Street Chapel School, and the possibility of a new meeting for communion. Regarding Tertullian, Montanism, and millennial teaching in the second and nineteenth centuries. Reference to the Bible Society, family matters, and Tregelles's Greek New Testament. 4 pages.
Original letter CBA 7181(99). F.W. Wyatt's copy in his S.P. Tregelles Correspondence Book, acquired by the Christian Brethren Archive in 2011 (FRY/1/1/4).

29th April 1866        **From S.P. Tregelles**        Plymouth
     To B.W. Newton

Regarding attacks [on B.W. Newton] by Mr T[homas]. Ryan. Referring to Mr Guinness, Mr [Henry] Bewley, Dorothy Haydon's Scripture Catechism, Georgina Haydon, Major [Richard Courtenay] Johnson, and Compton Street Chapel. 5 pages.
Original letter CBA 7181(100). F.W. Wyatt's copy in his S.P. Tregelles Correspondence Book, acquired by the Christian Brethren Archive in 2011 (FRY/1/1/4).

## Section 9 – B.W. Newton Correspondence

15th March 1866          From B.W. Newton
    **To G[eorge] W. Mylne**
'Theological" letter.
Listed in CBA 7002, F.W. Wyatt's index of Correspondence, as being at p. 4 of 'Yellow Quarto'. See further lost letters to him at 15th March 1866 and May 1866. This letter is apparently no longer extant.

15th March 1866          From B.W. Newton
    **To G[eorge] W. Mylne**
'Theological Doctrinal' letter.
Listed in CBA 7002, F.W. Wyatt's index of Correspondence, as being at p. 5 of 'Yellow Quarto'. See further lost letters to him at 15th March 1866 and May 1866. This letter is apparently no longer extant.

16th April 1866          From B.W. Newton
    **To T. Ryan**
Regarding the tract 'Amicus'.[1]
Listed in CBA 7002, F.W. Wyatt's index of Correspondence, as being at p. 6 of 'Yellow Quarto'. This letter is apparently no longer extant.

16th April 1866          From B.W. Newton
    **To H. Bewley**
Regarding 'Guinness publishing extracts'.
Listed in CBA 7002, F.W. Wyatt's index of Correspondence, as being at p. 6 of 'Yellow Quarto'. This letter is apparently no longer extant.

3rd May 1866          From B.W. Newton
    **To W.J. Turpin**
Listed in CBA 7002, F.W. Wyatt's index of Correspondence, as being at p. 6 of 'Yellow Quarto'. This letter is apparently no longer extant.

10th May 1866          From B.W. Newton
    **To A. Haldane**
'Regarding Lord Shaftesbury's speech, etc at the Pastoral Aid Society'.[2]
Listed in CBA 7002, F.W. Wyatt's index of Correspondence, as being at p. 7 of 'Yellow Quarto'. This letter is apparently no longer extant.

    5th January 1867          **From S.P. Tregelles**          Plymouth
        To B.W. Newton
        Regarding a quotation of Cyril of Jerusalem, or Cyril of Alexandria, which B.W. Newton was trying to locate. Expressing concern at B.W. Newton being so 'overwearied and

---

[1] *A Word of Warning to the Recent Converts in Ireland on the Peculiar doctrines of Mr. Darby and Mr. Newton*, by Amicus. [Extracted from] The Revival, no. 366. CBA 2249.
[2] See Section 3, Bibliography, *Occasional Papers on Scriptural Subjects 4*, item 12.

overworked'. Referring to Professor Payne Smith, Tregelles's wife's health, Georgina Haydon, Mrs H.B. Bulteel after her husband's demise. 3 pages.
Original letter CBA 7181(101).

> 24th January 1867    **From John Cox (jun.)**    Kensington
> **To C.H. Spurgeon** [as Editor]    London
> Responding to an article in *The Sword and Trowel* that gave C.H. Spurgeon's reply to the accusations of 'the Darbyites' that he [C.H. Spurgeon] was a blasphemer (Vol. 1, p.325). John Cox stated that Mr Newton had been 'entirely disconnected' from the Brethren for nearly twenty years and 'he is altogether opposed to their views and practices'. He states that the charges of heresy the Darbyites make against him are false and malicious. See also the article 'There Be Some That Trouble You' in the same issue of *The Sword and the Trowel* (page 343).
> Published in Vol. 1 *The Sword and the Trowel*, p.351.

28th January 1867    From B.W. Newton
**To Mr Foster**
'Theological. Luke 21:34'
Listed in CBA 7002, F.W. Wyatt's index of Correspondence, as being at p. 7 of 'Yellow Quarto'. This letter is apparently no longer extant.

6th February 1867    From B.W. Newton
**To Miss (T?)ucker**
'Exhibition'
Listed in CBA 7002, F.W. Wyatt's index of Correspondence, as being at p. 8 of 'Yellow Quarto'. This letter is apparently no longer extant.

> 4th March 1867    **From Miss Amy J.T. Toulmin**
> **To Henry Groves**
> Regarding his late pamphlet on Darbyism.[1] He referred to her (Miss Toulmin) in his pamphlet, and gives an account of the actions of [George] Müller and [Henry] Craik when she wished to have communion at Bethesda. She refers to misrepresentations, which she accepts may have been unintentional.
> Wyatt notes he did not reply – but note the missing letters at June 1867.
> F.W. Wyatt's copy. MS Book 1 (TC), pp.80,81. Listed in the 'Rough Notes' where strangely 'in print too' is added.

> 5th April 1867    **From Ker Baillie Hamilton**
> **To Miss Olway**    Cambridge
> Re- Mr Newton's writings. 'From a copy in Miss Toulmin's handwriting'
> Copied into CBA 7050, p.42

---

[1] *Darbyism, Its Rise, Progress and Development*, by Henry Groves (1818?-1891), eldest son of Anthony Norris Groves (1795-1853). First edition published 27th December 1866.

## Section 9 – B.W. Newton Correspondence

> June 1867
> Note of 'Toulmin and Groves Four Letters' in A.C. Fry's list from the "Smooth Red Leather MS book". Missing from the Fry Collection.
> Duodecimo Letter Book (Vol. 3), p.80. Information from 'The Rough Notes'.

26th July 1867        **From S.P. Tregelles**        Neath
     To B.W. Newton

Responding to B.W. Newton's comments on Hebrew words. Referring to Miss Wright, Mr Adams, matters concerning Compton Street Chapel, Henry Heywood and Dr Hingston. 3 pages.
Original letter CBA 7181(102).

13th March 1868        **From S.P. Tregelles**        Plymouth
     To B.W. Newton

Regarding Tregelles's edition of the Canon Muratorianus[1], which he had arranged to send to B.W. Newton. Referring to Tregelles's health, John Tyndale, Mary Boniface. Refers to the better health of Newton's mother.
Extracts of this letter were cited in Earle Hilgert, Two Unpublished Letters Regarding Tregelles' 'Canon Muratorianus'; *Andrews University Seminary Studies* 5 (No.2 1967), p.130 n18. See letters of 21st August 1863, and 28th October 1865. 3 pages.
Original letter CBA 7181(103).

> March 1867        **From Miss Amy J.T. Toulmin**
>      **To [R.C.?] Chapman**
> Listed in the 'Rough Notes' as being included in her letter of August 1889 to Mr Newton. Neither appear to be extant, although F.W. Wyatt' note says 'in print too' of this letter.

12th August 1868        **From S.P. Tregelles**        Plymouth
     To B.W. Newton

Concerning reports Tregelles had received of B.W. Newton's ill health. Referring to Mary Pigeon, Georgina Haydon, and Governor [Ker Baillie] Hamilton. Regarding S.P. Tregelles's Greek New Testament (Colossians, and 1 and 2 Thessalonians). 3 pages.
Original letter CBA 7181(104).

19th October 1868        **From S.P. Tregelles**        Plymouth
     To B.W. Newton

Regarding his [Tregelles's] Greek Testament, regretting it has occupied so much of his life[2]. Referring to death of Miss M. Boniface; Mr [William] Chalk, Aunt Mary Prideaux. 4 pages.
Original letter CBA 7181(105).

---

[1] S.P. Tregelles, *Canon Muratorianus, The Earliest Catalogue of the Books of the New Testament* ... (1867).
[2] See the quotation regarding this in T.C.F. Stunt, *Life and Times of Samuel Prideaux Tregelles*, p176.

29th January 1869  From B.W. Newton
**To Mrs Corsbee**
'External evidences of Christianity'
Listed in CBA 7002, F.W. Wyatt's index of Correspondence, as being at p. 8 of 'Yellow Quarto'. This letter is apparently no longer extant.

18th February 1869  **From S.P. Tregelles**  Plymouth
To B.W. Newton
Regarding the Protestant Alliance and Protestant Societies, Mr Bird [secretary Protestant Alliance].  2 pages.
Original letter CBA 7181(106).

17th March 1869  **From S.P. Tregelles**
To B.W. Newton
Re- C.S. Malan
Original letter Listed in CBA 6998, but now missing from the Fry Collection, nor is it in the Tregelles's Correspondence copied by F.W. Wyatt, although it is in F.W. Wyatt's list of S.P. Tregelles's letters in the 'Rough Notes' (In the Christian Brethren Archive as FRY/1/2/1). T.C.F. Stunt has a Xerox copy of the original letter.

27th April 1869  **From S.P. Tregelles**  Plymouth
To B.W. Newton  Tunbridge Wells
Regarding Protestant Alliance matters.  Commenting on B.W. Newton's reference to Dr H. Biesenthal on Hebrews.  Referring to Mr Bird (secretary, Protestant Alliance), Sir Robert Peel, Robert Nicholas Fowler, MP, Mr Bellson, and family matters.  Regarding Tregelles's Greek Testament.  3 pages.
Original letter CBA 7181(107).

19th May 1869  From B.W. Newton
**To Mr [John] Cox [jun.]**  [Worthing]
Regarding his correspondence with James Grant (author of *The Religious Tendencies of the Times*, and later of *The Plymouth Brethren, their History and Heresies*). Regarding his [Mr Newton's] tract, *The Doctrines of the Church in Newman Street*. He asks to point out that he withdrew the criticised statement in 1847 as soon as attention was drawn to it. Mentions a tract he published in 1845 whilst in the controversy in which he strongly maintained the heavenliness of the person of Christ as 'a new thing in the earth'.[1]
MS Book 1 (TC), pp.403-406. The handwriting may be A.C. Fry's. A note is added that Mr Cox kindly allowed him to make a copy of the letter.

---

[1] There is a reference to the verse (Jere. 31:22) in *A Second Letter...Ebrington Street*, p.23 (1845). B.W. Newton had referred to the verse in *Doctrines of the Church in Newman Street* (1835), p.121, and quotes it later in *A Letter on Subjects connected with the Lord's Humanity* (1848), p.9. Compare Bishop Pearson's use of the verse in his commentary on the Apostles' Creed, Art. 3, (born of the Virgin Mary), p.250. B.W. Newton adhered closely to Bishop Pearson's theological position, and published a corroborating quotation from him at the time of the controversy.

26 May 1869                  From B.W. Newton
     **To Mr [John] Cox [jun.]**          [Worthing]
A second letter regarding the correspondence with [J.] Grant. Quotes and opposes statements of [C.H.] Mackintosh and [J.N.] Darby on the Atonement. Quotes Hodge and Clarkson as exemplars of the doctrine of the Reformed church, and of the Scriptures, which he holds.
MS Book 1 (TC), pp.406-413. The handwriting may be A.C. Fry's. A note is added that Mr Cox kindly allowed him to make a copy of the letter.

Undated [May/June 1869]     From B.W. Newton
     **To Mr [John] Cox [jun.]**          [Worthing]
Refers to 'my preceding letter' (evidently 26th May 1869). Expounds several Scriptures regarding the Atonement, including Isa. 53 and Romans 5.
MS Book 1 (TC), pp.413-417. The handwriting may be A.C. Fry's. A note is added that Mr Cox kindly allowed him to make a copy of the letter.

Undated [May/June 1869]     From B.W. Newton
     **To Mr [John] Cox [jun.]**          [Worthing]
Continues writing regarding justification. Criticises a tract by Mackintosh
MS Book 1 (TC), pp.417-422. The handwriting may be A.C. Fry's. A note is added that Mr Cox kindly allowed him to make a copy of the letter.

Undated [May/June 1869]     From B.W. Newton
     **To Mr [John] Cox [jun.]**          [Worthing]
Following on from earlier letters. Further criticism of the teaching of Darby and Macintosh.
MS Book 1 (TC), pp.422-425. The handwriting may be A.C. Fry's. A note is added that Mr Cox kindly allowed him to make a copy of the letter.

26th July 1869            **From S.P. Tregelles**         Plymouth
     To B.W. Newton
Regarding Tregelles's health, Mr [William] Chalk and S.P. Tregelles's Greek New Testament (Revelation). Referring to death of Uncle Charles Prideaux, B.W. Newton's mother's poor health, Dr H. Biesenthal. 4 pages.
Original letter CBA 7181(108). Quoted in *The Life and Times of Samuel Prideaux Tregelles* by T.C.F. Stunt, p. 197.

23rd November 1869       From B.W. Newton
     **To Mrs Cox**
Recorded in the 'Rough Notes'[1] as being in the 'Quarto book'. Missing from the Fry Collection

---

[1] 'The Rough Notes' – see 'Manuscript Items added to the Fry Collection in 2011' in this Guide. The 'notes' are catalogued in the Christian Brethren Archive as FRY/1/2/1).

## Section 9 – B.W. Newton Correspondence

17th December [1869]     **From S.P. Tregelles**
　　To B.W. Newton

Letter quoted in the 'Advertisement' to the Second Edition of *Thoughts on Scriptural Subjects*. 'It was written to me a few weeks before the illness which terminated his *public* labours'. It expresses S.P. Tregelles's concern at various teachings that had the effect of setting aside the finished work of Christ.

The letter has not otherwise been preserved.

ND [February 1870?]     From B.W. Newton 11 Broadwater Down, Tunbridge Wells
　　**To Mr Stewart,**     11, King William street, West Strand, WC

F.W. Wyatt identifies the recipient as 'Stewart the publisher'. In the letter B.W. Newton relates that S.P. Tregelles did not inherit the ample fortune he should have received at the death of his grandfather. During the greater part of the last thirty years the private resources of Dr Tregelles have scarcely reached £40 annually. A life pension was granted, [in 1862] thanks to Lord Palmerston, of £100 as encouragement to persevere with his work etc.

Suggests establishing a fund – and of seeking to interest Gladstone to approve support for S.P. Tregelles.

[The position in Wyatt's notebook suggests May 1870, but it seems to fit better before the following letters. However, see letter referred to at 6th August 1870].

F.W. Wyatt's copy in MS Book 1 (TC).

5th February [1870]     **4th Earl of Ashburnham**     Battle
　　To B.W. Newton

Regarding S.P. Tregelles, Tregelles's Greek Testament, Tregelles's ill-health[1], and public acknowledgement of Tregelles's work. Referring to Sir Thomas Gladstone. 4 pages.
CBA 7182(1).

[1870]     From B.W. Newton
　　**To Lord Ashburnham**

Draft or copy letter regarding the poor health of S.P. Tregelles. Reference to Miss Prideaux. 1 page.
CBA 7182(12)

21st March [1870]     **4th Earl of Ashburnham**     [Battle]
　　To B.W. Newton

Regarding S.P. Tregelles, Tregelles's health, and financial support for Tregelles from the Government. 4 pages.
CBA 7182(2).

---

[1] S.P. Tregelles had his second stroke in this year. His first was in 1861. See CBA 7049, p.32, quoting the *Dictionary of National Biography*.

## Section 9 – B.W. Newton Correspondence

[1870]                  From B.W. Newton
     **To Lord Ashburnham**

Draft of a letter on applying for financial support from the Government on behalf of S.P. Tregelles.

(There is a draft of a circular to raise funds to support S.P. Tregelles by way of a subscription as a 'testimonial' in MS Book 1 (TC). 'The greater part of the work having now been completed and the publication of all the books of the New Testament with the exception of the Revelation being about to take place, there is a need to meet the expenses of the printing'. S.P. Tregelles's pension commencing from July 1870, but will not be received by him until July 1871).

CBA 7182(11) 1 page.

29th March [1870]      **4th Earl of Ashburnham**      [London]
     To B.W. Newton

Declining [B.W. Newton's] suggestion that he (Lord Ashburnham) acts on Tregelles's behalf to get support from the Government. Referring to Mr Gladstone. 4 pages.
CBA 7182(3).

May 1870            From B.W. Newton     Broadwater Down, Tunbridge Wells
     **To 'My Dear Sir'**

Refers to a pamphlet sent to him (written by the addressee) on substitution, and Christ's propitiatory offering for sin. B.W. Newton identifies disagreements on Atonement, which he regards as completed on the cross. Comments on various Greek words. Notes on Leviticus 16. B.W. Newton objects to the notion that Christ entered into sinful flesh.

Transcript of letter CBA 7050, pp.42-47 ['in a lady's hand', and 'altered in places by B.W. Newton's'].

4th May 1870      **4th Earl of Ashburnham [London]**
     To B.W. Newton

Regarding S.P. Tregelles, Tregelles's health, and suggesting Tregelles's friends bring his case for financial support before Mr Gladstone. 3 pages.
CBA 7182(4).

10th May 1870        From B.W. Newton          Tunbridge Wells
     **To Lord Ashburnham**

Promises to speak to those who have helped S.P. Tregelles in his work. Regarding Lord Ashburnham's letter. He has decided not to appeal for assistance from the Government. On S.P. Tregelles's continuing ill health. 4 pages
CBA 7182(5,6), [Draft or copy letter]

18th May 1870      **From Mrs S.A. Tregelles** [1]      Plymouth
     To B.W. Newton
     [Writing for S.P. Tregelles?]

---

[1] S.P. Tregelles wife, née Sarah Anna Prideaux (1807 – 1882. Married 1839)

In the list of S.P. Tregelles's letters made by F.W. Wyatt in the 'Rough Notes' (In the Christian Brethren Archive as FRY/1/2/1). Not in the Fry Collection.

22nd May 1870      **From Mrs S.A. Tregelles**      Plymouth
     To B.W. Newton
Writing for S.P. Tregelles. Regarding B.W. Newton seeing Mr Chalk and/or Mr Stewart about the Book of Revelation in Tregelles's Greek Testament. 4 pages.
Wrongly dated in CBA 6998 as 22nd May 1871.
Original letter CBA 7181(109).

1st June 1870      **From Mrs S.A. Tregelles**      Plymouth
     To B.W. Newton
Writing for S.P. Tregelles. Regarding Tregelles's Greek New Testament. Referring to Bishops Wilberforce and Ellicott, Mr Cox, Emily Wright, Dean Jeremie. 3 pages
Original letter CBA 7181(110).

2nd June 1870      **From Helen MacLachlan** Bournemouth
     To B.W. Newton
Renewing her acquaintance with B.W. Newton.
The 'Rough Notes' suggest a reply to this from B.W. Newton in June 1870 but it is not extant.
Transcript of letter CBA 7050, p.72.

4th June 1870      **From Mrs S.A. Tregelles**      Plymouth
     To B.W. Newton
Writing for S.P. Tregelles. Regarding Tregelles's Greek Testament. Tregelles unwilling to make the collation of Codex Vaticanus and Codex Sinaiticus. 4 pages.
Original letter CBA 7181(111).

15th June 1870      **From Mrs S.A. Tregelles**      Plymouth
     To B.W. Newton
The date is wrong in CBA 6998. It should be 18th June 1870. See below.

18th June 1870      **From Mrs S.A. Tregelles**      Plymouth
     To B.W. Newton
Writing for S.P. Tregelles. Regarding Tregelles's Greek Testament. Referring to Rev. A. Townsend, Dr Lightfoot, and Mr Gladstone. Wrongly listed in CBA 6998 as 15th June 1870. 5 pages.
Original letter CBA 7181(112).

---

6th August 1870      **From Charles James Stewart** (bookseller)
     **To Lord Ashburnham**
Listed in a calendar of correspondence relating to S.P. Tregelles prepared by F.W. Wyatt in the 'Rough Notes' (In the Christian Brethren Archive as FRY/1/2/1). Missing from the Fry Collection. [See letter placed at February 1870].

## Section 9 – B.W. Newton Correspondence

10th August 1870          **From Mrs S.A. Tregelles** Plymouth
    To B.W. Newton
[Writing for S.P. Tregelles?]
Listed in a calendar of correspondence relating to S.P. Tregelles prepared by F.W. Wyatt in the 'Rough Notes' (In the Christian Brethren Archive as FRY/1/2/1). Missing from the Fry Collection. Possibly 10th August 1871, or this is the true date for that item – see note there.

11th August 1870          **From Charles James Stewart** (bookseller)
    To B.W. Newton
Regarding S.P. Tregelles's Greek New Testament and Tregelles's financial affairs. Referring to Lord Ashburnham, Mr Braithwaite. 4+4 pages.
CBA 7182(7).

5th November 1870          **From Mrs S.A. Tregelles**      Plymouth
    To B.W. Newton
Writing for S.P. Tregelles. Regarding Tregelles's Greek Testament. Referring to money sent by B.W. Newton, S.P. Tregelles's continuing ill health, A.L. Vansittart. 4 pages.
Original letter CBA 7181(113).

15th December 1870          **From Mrs S.A. Tregelles**      Plymouth
    To B.W. Newton
Writing for S.P. Tregelles. Regarding Tregelles's wish that B.W. Newton should be at liberty to act for him [in relation to Tregelles's Greek Testament]. Referring to Miss Boniface, Miss Egerton, Mr Chalk, shares, Tregelles's suffering, and death of Alice Treffry (wife of Joseph Treffry). 5 pages
Original letter CBA 7181(114).

17th December [1870]          **From 4th Earl of Ashburnham**      London
    To [B.W. Newton]
Offering to help Tregelles financially. 4 pages.
CBA 7182(8).

23rd December [1870]          **From 4th Earl of Ashburnham**      Battle
    To B.W. Newton
Regarding his donation to Tregelles. Referring to the 'packet of game' he is sending B.W. Newton. 4 pages.
CBA 7181(9).

25th December 1870          **From Mrs S.A. Tregelles**      Plymouth
    To B.W. Newton
Writing for S.P. Tregelles. Regarding the illness of B.W. Newton's mother. Regarding Tregelles's Greek Testament. Referring to Joseph Treffry. 5 pages
Original letter CBA 7181(115).

26th December [1870?]   **From 4th Earl of Ashburnham**   Battle
    To B.W. Newton
Regarding financial support for Tregelles. 2 pages.
CBA 7182(10).

> 14 January 1871   **From Mrs S.A. Tregelles**   Plymouth
>   **To F.J.A. Hort**   Cambridge
> Listed in a calendar of correspondence relating to S.P. Tregelles prepared by F.W. Wyatt in the 'Rough Notes' (In the Christian Brethren Archive as FRY/1/2/1). CBA 6998 lists a letter from A Vansittart from [Mrs] S.A. Tregelles of this date, and of 18th January 1871. Missing from the Fry Collection.

> 18th January 1871   **From Mrs S.A. Tregelles**   Plymouth
>   **To F.J.A. Hort**   Cambridge
> Listed in a calendar of correspondence relating to S.P. Tregelles prepared by F.W. Wyatt in the 'Rough Notes' (In the Christian Brethren Archive as FRY/1/2/1). CBA 6998 lists a letter from A Vansittart to [Mrs] S.A. Tregelles of this date, and of 14th January 1871.

17th January 1871   **From H. Bewley**   Dublin
    To B.W. Newton
Refers to [Plymouth] controversy, withdrawn pamphlets, etc.
Transcript of letter CBA 7050 pages 73, 74.

27th January [1871]   **From Mrs S.A. Tregelles**   Plymouth
    To B.W. Newton
Writing for S.P. Tregelles. Regarding Tregelles's Greek Testament. Approving B.W. Newton's plan for different individuals to deal with the Gospels, and thereby to make best use of the Codices Vaticanus and Sinaiticus. Referring to Dean Alford, A.L. Vansittart [see CBA 7182(15), (16)], S.P. Tregelles's poor health. 5 pages
Original letter CBA 7181(120). Listed in CBA 6998 as 27th January 1872 with a question mark against the year, but more probably 1871.

12th February 1871   **From Mrs S.A. Tregelles**
    To B.W. Newton
Listed in CBA 6998, and also listed in a calendar of correspondence relating to S.P. Tregelles prepared by F.W. Wyatt in the 'Rough Notes' (In the Christian Brethren Archive as FRY/1/2/1), but now missing from the Fry Collection.

1st March 1871   **From Horatio Darby**   Parsonstown, Ireland
    To B.W. Newton
In the letter Horatio Darby asks Newton to tell him what he believes, and why he keeps himself aloof from the brethren ('or the brethren aloof from you'). He writes that he has heard a lot about errors, and wants an answer straight from Mr Newton himself. 'I might

in justice add – 1st I have no connection with my brother J.N. Darby. 2nd that no one knows that I have written to you. 3rdly that no one shall know your answer except by your permission'. See letters at 9th March 1871, and 14th March 1871.

F.W. Wyatt's copy MS Book 2 (TC), p.115. Listed in the 'Rough Notes'

2nd March 1871         From B.W. Newton
   **To F[rank] White**

Listed in the 'Rough Notes' as being in the quarto exercise book, but apparently no longer extant.

2nd March 1871         From B.W. Newton
   **To [Miss] van Monen**

Listed in the 'Rough Notes' as being in the quarto exercise book, but apparently no longer extant.

9th March 1871         From B.W. Newton         Tunbridge Wells
   **To Horatio Darby**

Apologises for delay, as he is overpressed with engagements. 'I remember with pleasure the intercourse I had with you at Parsonstown nearly forty years ago'. Enclosed his *Propositions for the Solemn Consideration of Christians*, in confirmation of his orthodoxy. States he cannot co-operate with anyone who systematically opposed those Propositions. Hopes to send another tract that he is about to publish on justification. See letters of 1st March 1871, and 14th March 1871.

F.W. Wyatt's copy MS Book 2 (TC), p.116. Listed in the 'Rough Notes'.

   13th March 1871         **From F.J.A. Hort**         Hitchin
      To B.W. Newton

   Regarding Tregelles's Greek Testament. Promising to send the Corrigenda for Matthew's Gospel. 4 pages.
   Original letter CBA 7182(17).

   14th March 1871         **From Horatio Darby**         Parsonstown, Ireland
      To B.W. Newton

Thanks B.W. Newton for his kind note. He had forgotten they had met 'in old and happier days'. He states that he is burdened by the divisions of those who professedly love the Lord. He could not subscribe to all of Mr Newton's *Propositions…*, and does not feel such should be proposed as a test for fellowship (breaking of bread) [B.W. Newton did not suggest that they should be such 'test of fellowship']. See letters of 1st March 1871, and 9th March 1871.

F.W. Wyatt's copy MS Book 2 (TC), p.116. Listed in the 'Rough Notes'.[1]

---

[1] 'The Rough Notes' –see Section 10, Duplicated and Manuscript Items, 'Manuscript Items added to the Fry Collection in 2011' in this Guide. The 'notes' are catalogued in the Christian Brethren Archive as FRY/1/2/1).

5th April 1871        **From S.P. Tregelles**        Plymouth
     To B.W. Newton
     Regarding Tregelles's Greek Testament. Referring to Mr [S.] Bloxsidge[1] (see letter B.W. Newton to S. Bloxsidge below). 2 pages
     Original letter CBA 7181(116).

[5th April 1871]        From B.W. Newton
     **To [S.] Bloxsidge**
Note appended to letter of S.P. Tregelles to B.W. Newton (5th April 1871), expressing distress regarding Tregelles's note, and ignorance of to what S.P. Tregelles refers.
CBA 7181(116) (see above)

5th April 1871        **From Mrs S.A. Tregelles**        Plymouth
     To B.W. Newton
     Writing for S.P. Tregelles. Relating that B.W. Newton's replies to [S.] Bloxsidge were incorrect (see CBA 7181(116)). 4 pages.
     Original letter CBA 7181(117).

---

**Census 2nd April 1871**

<u>Address:</u> 129, Queens Road, Paddington.
     B.W. Newton – fundholder - 64; Maria Newton, 56, born Madras; Sophia Hawkins, 50, born Hampton Court; David Briggs, 22, 'letter sorter'; Charlotte Briggs, 23.

<u>Address:</u> Tunbridge Wells:
     Anna Newton – income, interest of monies, 88; Amy Toulmin, cousin, 58.

---

3rd May 1871        From B.W. Newton
     **To Bunbury**
Listed in the 'Rough Notes' as being in the quarto exercise book, but apparently no longer extant.

18th May [1871??]        **From Mrs S.A. Tregelles**        Plymouth
     To B.W. Newton
     Thanking B.W. Newton for his letter and money. Authorising B.W. Newton to act for S.P. Tregelles in relation to Tregelles's Greek Testament. Further comment regarding S.P. Tregelles's Greek Testament. Referring to Mr Chalk. Tregelles's health. 4 pages.
     CBA 7181(122),

---

[1] S.J.B. Bloxsidge, Died June 15th 1928 aged 86 years. Graduate of Exeter College. Author of *Inspired Words Realized (published by Hunt, Barnard)*, in which he acknowledges his 'vast debt, directly and indirectly to the late Mr B.W. Newton: in public ministry and personal intercourse, from 1868 to 1872; since then mainly through his writings'. Brief obituary *Watching and Waiting*, August 1928. Longer reminiscences of him *Watching and Waiting* July-August 1959, pp.157-159. Bloxsidge is mentioned several times in this Section.

## Section 9 – B.W. Newton Correspondence

[22nd May 1871 **From Mrs S.A. Tregelles**
    To B.W. Newton
Listed in CBA 6998, but date wrongly transcribed, as it is dated 22nd May 1870].

26th May 1871 From B.W. Newton
   **To Olway [Lady Otway[1]?]**
Listed in the 'Rough Notes' as being in the quarto exercise book, but apparently no longer extant. See the further letter to her (? – Miss Olway) dated 5th April 1867

25th July 1871 From B.W. Newton     Tunbridge Wells
   **To J.H. Parker**
Copy (?) of a letter requesting that he send him (B.W. Newton) a list of errors he (J.H. Parker) has found in the proof text of Tregelles's Greek New Testament. 3 pages.
CBA 7182(18) copy or draft in B.W. Newton's hand.

10th August [1871] **From Mrs S.A. Tregelles**    Plymouth
    To B.W. Newton
Writing for S.P. Tregelles. Expressing concern regarding B.W. Newton's health. Referring to Dr Rieu and the American readings, Mr Hernfetter and Mr Partner.
3 pages. Possibly 1870. See note for that date as recorded in the 'Rough Notes'.
Original letter CBA 7181(118).

22nd August 1871 From B.W. Newton
   **To [Miss] van Manen**
Listed in the 'Rough Notes' as being in the quarto exercise book, but apparently no longer extant.

23 August 1871 From B.W. Newton
   **To Parker**
Listed in the 'Rough Notes', but apparently no longer extant.

November 1871 From B.W. Newton.
   **To [Ker Baillie] Hamilton**
Listed in the 'Rough Notes', but apparently no longer extant.

4th November 1871 **From Ker Baillie Hamilton[2]**
    To B.W. Newton
Comments on B.W. Newton's statements on France, European politics, etc.
Transcript of letter CBA 7050, p.50.

---

[1] See note on *The Blood that Saveth - Il Sangue che Salva*.
[2] Ker Baillie Hamilton, 1804-1889. Former colonial governor of Newfoundland, and Antigua and the Leeward Islands. Buried in Tunbridge Wells. See *Dictionary of Canadian Biography*, Vol. 11. A picture of him is included in *A Pictorial Memoir of Benjamin Wills Newton* – the supplement to this Guide. See the Advertisement at the end of this volume.

## Section 9 – B.W. Newton Correspondence

December 1871          From B.W. Newton
    **To [Ker Baillie] Hamilton**
Listed in the 'Rough Notes', but apparently no longer extant.

4th December 1871      **From Mrs S.A. Tregelles**      Plymouth
    To B.W. Newton
Writing for S.P. Tregelles. Thanking B.W. Newton for his help, and expressing concern about B.W. Newton's ill health. Regarding financial and administrative matters relating to S.P. Tregelles. Regarding Tregelles's Greek New Testament.
Further item in Mrs Tregelles's handwriting, and signed by S.P. Tregelles, expressing concern at B.W. Newton's illness, and thanking him for his kindness. Regarding Tregelles's Greek Testament. Referring to B.W. Newton's wife, Miss Hawkins, B.W. Newton's mother, and A.J.T. Toulmin. 5+4+1 pages.
Original letter CBA 7181(119).

18th December 1871      **From Ker Baillie Hamilton**
    To B.W. Newton
Refers to the return of papers sent to him.
Transcript of letter CBA 7050, p.51.

26th December 1871      **From [Hebrew letters]**[1]      Spring Gardens, London, SW
    To B.W. Newton
Expresses appreciation for light received through B.W. Newton. The 'Rough Notes' give the probable reason for the coded name. A letter from 'Francis A King, of the Admiralty' to B.W. Newton is listed with this date.
Transcript of letter CBA 7050 between p.50 and p.51.

3rd January 1872      From B.W. Newton
    **To Rev. John Cox**
Regarding the Bayswater work?
Listed in the 'Rough Notes', but apparently no longer extant.

3rd January 1872      From B.W. Newton
    **To his Mother**
'Re- ill-judged letter respecting BWN's health [sent to his congregation]'
Noted in F.W. Wyatt's index of letters, CBA 7002, where it is indicated as at MSS 2 p. 53. The note is followed by a further one 'reprinted circular respecting the Chapel and BWN'. Apparently no longer extant.

4th January 1872      From B.W. Newton
    **To his Mother**
Noted in F.W. Wyatt's index of letters CBA 7002 without comment. It is indicated as at MSS 2, p. 54. Apparently no longer extant.

---

[1] Compare the use of Hebrew for the initials of the recipient of the letter of 14th May 1877. The Hebrew letters here are indistinct.

6th January 1872          **From Ker Baillie Hamilton**
     To B.W. Newton

This gives the writer's thoughts on Mr B.W. Newton's withdrawal from the work in Bayswater. 'A few mornings ago the following thought occurred to me about the Church in London, "If he who proclaimed these truths was one out of 100, or even 50, who also taught them the congregation would have to be considered, but those truths are proclaimed by <u>one</u> person only in this country; and therefore can any one congregation or place exclusively claim him, now that the Providence of God appears to indicate that he should be unlocalised?'

A note appended refers to the instruction in Bayswater being withdrawn due to B.W. Newton's 'temporal suffering"'.

Transcript of letter CBA 7050, pp.51,52.

18th January 1872         **From F.J.A. Hort**
     To B.W. Newton

Listed in a calendar of correspondence relating to S.P. Tregelles prepared by F.W. Wyatt in the 'Rough Notes' (In the Christian Brethren Archive as FRY/1/2/1). Compare the letters listed at 18th January 1871, and 18th June 1872.

[27th January 1872       **From Mrs S.A. Tregelles**
     To B.W. Newton

Listed in CBA 6998 with a question mark against the year, but wrongly dated. See letter at 27th January [1871].

18th February 1872       From B.W. Newton
     **To Mrs Hurst**

The letter is headed 'On giving up Bayswater work'. 'from A.J.T[oulmin]'s copy' 'apparently unfinished'

In the letter he writes of the decision as his, but desires 'that our minds might be mercifully guided to the same conclusions'. Says he feels 'exhausted'. 'I do not think my friends in London have understood this'. See also the letter to Mrs Hurst recorded in this *Guide* at the start of 1875. Quoted in *A Story of Conflict, the Controversial Relationship between Benjamin Wills Newton and John Nelson Darby* by Jonathan D. Burnham, pp.216,217.

Transcript of letter CBA 7050, p.53

2nd March 1872          From B.W. Newton Broadwater Down [Tunbridge Wells]
     **To 'My Dear Friend'**

This is a reply to a critical letter, evidently regarding the closure of the Bayswater work. He speaks of the severity of censure, accusations of erring in judgement, etc. Says 'the circular' most deeply pained him. He writes that he intends to resume the management of his tracts and printing.

F.W. Wyatt's copy MS Book 2 (TC), p.53. ['A.J.T[oulmin]'s copy']. Also in CBA 7050, pp.54,55.

2nd March 1872          From B.W. Newton
    **To Rev. John Cox**
Regarding the Bayswater work?  See also the letter of 1st July 1872.
Listed in the 'Rough Notes', but apparently no longer extant.[1]

9th March 1872          From B.W. Newton                    Blackheath
    **To Miss Langford**
Regarding the ending of his ministry in Bayswater.  Sympathy expressed
Transcript of letter CBA 7050, pp.55,56.

    11th March 1872     **From Miss Langford**
        To B.W. Newton                              Blackheath
    Regarding the ending of his Bayswater ministry.  Concerned chiefly with his disposal of the chapel.  She asks for a 6 month delay in this.
    Transcript of letter CBA 7050, pp.56,57.

26th April 1872          From B.W. Newton                   Tunbridge Wells
    **To Mrs [Louisa Sophia] Riach**[2]
Comforting her at the death of her mother.  He gives his address for correspondence as 129, Queens Road, Bayswater.  Refers to Mrs Harris, Miss Fletcher, Mr Fletcher (Mrs Riach's brother), Miss Langford, Mrs Newton, and Miss Hawkins.  Black edged paper.  3 pages.
Christian Brethren Archive, Box 23(10) (ex- The Stirling Collection, Spurgeon's College).

30th May 1872           From B.W. Newton                    Folkestone
    **To person unknown**                     at 'Clonak'
Regarding allegations still made about his doctrines.  He repudiates the doctrines attributed to him.  Reminds the writer that such slander is against the Civil Law, although he does not intend to take legal action.
Quoted in *A Story of Conflict, the Controversial Relationship between Benjamin Wills Newton and John Nelson Darby*, by Jonathan D. Burnham, p.227.
Transcript of letter CBA 7050, pp.57,58.

    18th June 1872          **From F.J.A. Hort**
        To B.W. Newton
    Original letter, listed in CBA 6998.  Not traced.  NB similarly untraced letter listed at 18th December 1872 (Hort to Newton) in a calendar of correspondence relating to S.P. Tregelles prepared by F.W. Wyatt in the 'Rough Notes' (In the Christian Brethren Archive as FRY/1/2/1).

---

[1] John Cox wanted the Bayswater work to continue, and this caused a great deal of difficulty to Mr Newton.  See CBA 7064, note dated 13th September 1897, p56 and 57; and note dated 14th March 1898, p139.
[2] Louisa Sophia Riach died in Worthing, 16th December 1904, aged 85.  Obituary *Perilous Times*, January 1905, p.4.

1st July 1872                 From B.W. Newton
    **To John Cox [jun.]**
Regarding Finchley Road. There may be reference to a letter from John Cox with this (the note is ambiguous). See the letter of 2nd March 1872.
Listed in the 'Rough Notes', but apparently no longer extant.

September 1872            From B.W. Newton
    **To Revd J. Bennett**        Ashbourne, Derbyshire
Regarding two of his books, which he has arranged to send from Tunbridge Wells. Regarding the views of Pearsall Smith. Regarding the formation of the Free Church of England – 'I believe the individual position, humbly taken, with the Bible in our hand, is the only safe one now'. Instances the Brethren as the failure of good motives on wrong principles. Notes that he (B.W. Newton) is still unwell.
Copy in B.W. Newton's own hand in the Autobiographical Notebook that is mainly concerned with the closure of the work at Bayswater, recovered by the CBA in 2011. A photocopy is held by the SGAT. CBA FRY/1/1/3.

23rd September 1872        From B.W. Newton
    **To Ker B[aillie] Hamilton, Esq., CB**
Extract of a letter. Comments 'we must not be surprised if our efforts should fail in quarters where we would most desire them to succeed'. Refers to the overtures of the Church of England to the Old Catholic Church. Refers to his letter to Rev. J Bennett of Ashbourne, Derbyshire regarding the Free Church of England (see previous entry). Concludes 'There is only one right place now – the individual place with the Bible in our hands. That is the only right position at present for the little remnant, poor and afflicted, whom grace will deliver in these evil hours of the exaltation of worldliness and falsehood, but we may well be content with Baruch's position. An honoured and blessed position it was (see Jeremiah 45). Too honourable perhaps for us, yet we may desire it, for we must seek the thoughts and position of Jeremiah, though we may hold it in weakness'.
Copy in B.W. Newton's own hand in the Autobiographical Notebook that is mainly concerned with the closure of the work at Bayswater, recovered by the CBA in 2011 – FRY/1/1/3. A photocopy is held by the SGAT.

    11th October 1872 (postmark) **From Miss Freeman**      Winchester
        To B.W. Newton                         129, Queens Road, Bayswater
        Suggests the possibility of another person providing ministry at Bayswater, possibly on a temporary basis.
        Transcript of letter CBA 7050, pp.58,59

11th October 1872 (postmark)     From B.W. Newton     129, Queens Road, Bayswater
>
> **To Mrs Steane**[1]

Mr Newton returns a cheque from Dr Steane in view of his association with the Dean of Westminster [Dr Stanley, a neologian]. He denounces his action as 'a public man' (one of the chief office bearers of the Evangelical Alliance) accepting an invitation from Dr Stanley. The principle B.W. Newton follows is that we should not be partakers in the evil deeds of another.
Transcript of letter CBA 7050, pp.59-61.

30th October 1872     From B.W. Newton     129, Queens Road, Bayswater
> **To Mr [S.] Bloxsidge**[2]

Regarding the birth of his (S. Bloxsidge's) child. Adds 'it is most probable that those now born will have to encounter that dread coming hour when the system of wickedness now rising around us will reign, and be drunk with the blood of the servants of Jesus. All such reflections ought to be ever present with our souls now, and though no doubt there is a sorrow in them, yet it is holy and blessed sorrow, conducive to trustfulness and to true joy'.
In B.W. Newton's own hand. Possibly a draft - one page has been crossed out, and it ends with an unfinished sentence. Otherwise an incomplete extract.
This is included in the autobiographical notebook that is mainly concerned with the closure of the work at Bayswater, recovered by the CBA in 2011 – FRY/1/1/3. A copy is held by the SGAT.

18th December 1872     **From F.J.A. Hort**
> To B.W. Newton

Untraced letter listed in a calendar of correspondence relating to S.P. Tregelles prepared by F.W. Wyatt in the 'Rough Notes' (In the Christian Brethren Archive as FRY/1/2/1). NB another untraced letter dated 18th June 1872 (Hort to Newton) listed in CBA 6998.

8th March 1873     From B.W. Newton
> **To Mrs Steane**

Listed in the 'Rough Notes' as in the Morocco octavo notebook, but apparently no longer extant.

2nd August 1873     From B.W. Newton     Clatterford, Carisbrooke, I.W.
> **To Mrs Steane**

Speaks of his poor health. Expresses sorrow at the interruption of his friendship with Dr [Edward] Steane. He has cancelled the cheque she sent.
Listed in the 'Rough Notes' as Morocco octavo. Transcript of letter CBA 7050, p.62

---

[1] Née Pigeon: see CBA 7181(78). B.W. Newton favourably quotes Dr Steane in Appendix 1 of *Salvation by Substitution* (1866). See the note by B.W. Newton regarding this incident copied in CBA 7049, p. 382, 383.

[2] S.J.B. Bloxsidge, Died June 15th 1928 aged 86 years. Graduate of Exeter College. Author of *Inspired Words Realized* (published by Hunt, Barnard), in which he acknowledges his 'vast debt, directly and indirectly to the late Mr B.W. Newton: in public ministry and personal intercourse, from 1868 to 1872; since then mainly through his writings'. Brief obituary *Watching and Waiting*, August 1928. Longer reminiscences of him *Watching and Waiting* July-August 1959, pp.157-159. See letter 5 April 1871, etc

## Section 9 – B.W. Newton Correspondence

22nd November 1873        From B.W. Newton    Clatterford House, Carisbrooke, I.W
  **To his mother**
Regarding the Scriptures, 'deaconesses' and 'Dorcas Societies'.
Transcript of letter CBA 7050, pp.63,64 ('extract from a letter').

6th March 1874        From B.W. Newton    Clatterford House, Carisbrooke, I.W
  **To Admiral H[aydon?]**
Regarding a book that B.W Newton is sending. Political observations, Christians in the legislature, Ireland, political Protestantism, ultramontanism, and cleaving to Scripture.
Transcript of letter CBA 7050, pp.65-71.

4th June 1874 **From Messrs Tompson, Pickering, Styans, and Neilson** [his solicitors]
  To B.W. Newton
  Re- the sale of [the chapel] premises in Queens Road [Bayswater] to a coachbuilder. [Reply is 7050, p.74].
  Transcript of letter CBA 7050.

[June 1874] ND        From B.W. Newton    Clatterford House, Carisbrooke, I.W
  **To Messrs Tompson, Pickering, Styans and Neilson** [his solicitors]
[Reply to letter of 4th June 1874]. Agrees to sale, but he will arrange for the removal of the chapel in -?- so that it should not fall into the hands of papists or ritualists.
Transcript of letter CBA 7050, p.74.

5th June 1874        From B.W. Newton    Clatterford House, Carisbrooke, I.W
  **To Miss Skinner**
To a woman isolated from fellowship, giving counsel regarding holding meetings.
Transcript of letter CBA 7050 pp.75,76.

2nd July 1874        From B.W. Newton
  **To unknown**
Regarding Pearsall Smith
Listed in the 'Rough Notes', but apparently no longer extant.

15th July 1874        From B.W. Newton    Clatterford House, Isle of Wight
  **To my Dear Mary [Boniface?]**[1]
Writes to her as someone who evidently holds him in high regard. 'You must not invite me to return to the past'. 'I have retired to a private place. It is vain to speculate on the future. It may be that I shall never be strong enough to quit my present privacy'. Feels under necessity to refrain from correspondence, and to remain in complete seclusion.
F.W. Wyatt's copy MS Book 1 (TC), p.119.

---

[1] See letter of 14 May 1877, placed next to it in F.W. Wyatt's MS Book 1.

## Section 9 – B.W. Newton Correspondence

26th September 1874        From B.W. Newton    Clatterford House, Carisbrooke, I.W
**To his mother**
Extract. Refers to the hymn [by William Cowper] 'Oh for a Closer Walk with God' as 'most revolting'. Objects to the hymn lines 'I'm Waiting for the Fire...'[1], etc.
Transcript of letter CBA 7050, p.76.

11th October 1874        From B.W. Newton    Clatterford House, Carisbrooke, I.W
**To his mother**
Extract. He comments on [Edward] Hoare's book *Sanctification: Expository Sermons*. Refers to an anonymous letter by 'Evangelical Churchman' in *The Record*.
Transcript of letter CBA 7050, pp.77,78.

24th October 1874        From B.W. Newton
**To Mr Haldane**
Listed in the 'Rough Notes' as in the black quarto [book], but no longer extant.

27th October 1874        From B.W. Newton
**To Fox**
Listed in the 'Rough Notes' as in the black quarto [book], but no longer extant.

11th November 1874        From B.W. Newton
**To Haldane**
Listed in the 'Rough Notes' as in the black quarto [book], but no longer extant.

12th November 1874        From B.W. Newton
**To Brooke**
Listed in the 'Rough Notes' as in the black quarto [book], but no longer extant.

24th November 1874        From B.W. Newton
**To Fox**
Listed in the 'Rough Notes' as in the black quarto [book], but no longer extant.

27th October 1874        From B.W. Newton
**To Carron [Canon?] Bell[?]**
Listed in the 'Rough Notes' as in the black quarto [book], but no longer extant.

1875        From B.W. Newton
**To a person unknown**
Extracts. Commenting on Pearsall Smith's teaching.
Transcript of letter CBA 7050, p.90? (between p.90 and p.242).

---

[1] From hymn by Mary D. James? *My Body, Soul and Spirit, Jesus I Give to Thee*.

## Section 9 – B.W. Newton Correspondence

1875?  From B.W. Newton
    **To Mrs Hurst**

In reply to Mrs Hurst, regarding the closure of the work at Bayswater. Speaks of a hostile circle that formed, and of his conclusion that 'Intercourse, whether epistolatory or personal, could only (as things now are) awaken bitter remembrances of the past, without bringing any healing power into the present'. Refers to his retirement, and of the friends at Blackheath. 10 pages. See also the letter to Mrs Hurst of 18th February 1872.

The letter is included in the autobiographical notebook in B.W. Newton's own hand, which is mainly concerned with the closure of the work at Bayswater, recovered by the CBA in 2011 – FRY/1/1/3. A copy is held by the SGAT.

1st January 1875  From B.W. Newton
    **To Dr Angé**

Listed in the 'Rough Notes' as in the black quarto [book], but apparently no longer extant.

March 1875  From B.W. Newton
    **To T[homas] G[raham] Graham**

Regarding Pearsall Smith. On perfectionism, etc.
Transcript of letter CBA 7050, pp.89,90.

28th March 1875  From B.W. Newton  Clatterford House, Carisbrooke, I.W
    **To Mrs Hurst**

Regarding her husband's death.
Transcript of letter CBA 7050, p.78.

17th April 1875  From B.W. Newton  Clatterford House, Carisbrooke, I.W
    **To Ker Bailie Hamilton**

This gives B.W. Newton's comments on the preaching of Mr Moody. Likes his preaching better than his hymns. He does not doubt that the work as a whole is of God. However, he fears the latitudinarian effects of the campaign, sweeping aside differences, and allowing men to agree to differ. He accepts the events as a time of visitation for the world, but desires a time of visitation for the Church. Refers to the struggle against Popery in Germany. Refers to Mr Pearsall Smith's meeting.
Transcript of letter CBA 7050 pp.79-81.

---

**24th April 1875. Death of S.P. Tregelles**

---

25th April 1875  **From Mrs S.A. Tregelles**
    To B.W. Newton

Letter to B.W. Newton regarding S.P. Tregelles's death. Listed in a calendar of correspondence relating to S.P. Tregelles prepared by F.W. Wyatt in the 'Rough Notes' (In the Christian Brethren Archive as FRY/1/2/1). Apparently no longer extant.

> 27th April 1875     **From K.B. Hamilton**     Tunbridge Wells
>     **To Lord Shaftesbury**
> Re- *Prospects of the Ten Kingdoms*. Commends B.W. Newton's writings on prophecy.
> Transcript of letter CBA 7050, pp.82-84.

28th April 1875     From B.W. Newton     Clatterford House, Carisbrooke, I.W
    **[To Ker Baillie Hamilton?]**
Extract. Regarding Mr Pearsall Smith. Regarding hyper-Calvinists condemning Moody.
Transcript of letter CBA 7050, p.81.

29th June 1875     From B.W. Newton     Christchurch Road, Winchester
    **To Ker Baillie Hamilton**
Regarding a tract against Mr Moody's preaching. Refers to 'brazen serpent preaching'.[1]
Commends Spurgeon. Moody is not a teacher. H. Bonar knows Moody well, and vouches for his orthodoxy. There is reference to a postscript on different paper in the 'Rough Notes'.
Transcript of letter CBA 7050, pp.85-89.

24th August 1875     From B.W. Newton
    **To Rev. W.H. Papendale**
Listed in the 'Rough Notes', but apparently no longer extant.

3rd September 1875     From B.W. Newton
    **To Alex Haldane**
An extract of a letter to Alex[ander] Haldane is listed in the 'Rough Notes', but apparently no longer extant.

9th October 1875     From B.W. Newton
    **To Mr H**
'Theological'
Listed in CBA 7002, F.W. Wyatt's index of Correspondence, as being at p. 9 of 'Yellow Quarto'.
This letter is apparently no longer extant.

13th October 1875     From B.W. Newton
    **To Mr H**
Regarding '*Grace for Grace* by R.W. James'
Listed in CBA 7002, F.W. Wyatt's index of Correspondence, as being at p. 10 of 'Yellow Quarto'.
This letter is apparently no longer extant.

23rd October 1875     From B.W. Newton
    **To Mr B**
Regarding 'Dr Bonar's book and Mr D's criticism'
Listed in CBA 7002, F.W. Wyatt's index of Correspondence, as being at p. 11 of 'Yellow Quarto'.
This letter is apparently no longer extant.

---

[1] The Bible reference is to John 3:14, and Numbers 21.

3rd November 1875        From B.W. Newton
   **To Mr Adams**
Listed in the 'Rough Notes', but apparently no longer extant.

6th November 1875        From B.W. Newton
   **To Mr Haldane**
Listed in the 'Rough Notes', but apparently no longer extant.

9th November 1875        From B.W. Newton
   **To Mr Haldane**
Listed in the 'Rough Notes', but apparently no longer extant.

11th November 1875       From B.W. Newton
   **To Lord Shaftesbury**
Listed in the 'Rough Notes', but apparently no longer extant.

> 19th November 1875  **From K.B. Hamilton**        Tunbridge Wells
>    **To Earl of Shaftesbury**
> Listed in the 'Rough Notes', but apparently no longer extant.

December 1875        From B.W. Newton
   **To 'My Dear Georgina' [Haydon?]**
Listed in the 'Rough Notes', but apparently no longer extant.

11th December 1875      From B.W. Newton      Christchurch Road, Winchester
   **To Mr Bath**[1]
Commenting on Hebrews 4, etc.
Transcript of letter CBA 7080.

1876        From B.W. Newton        Winchester
   **To 'My Dear Sir' ('see Smith')**
On Rev. 5:9, and the Greek word ημας used there.
The Rough Notes record this as 'also in choc. penny book', but it is apparently no longer extant

January 1876        From B.W. Newton
   **To Mr [Alexander] Haldane**
Listed in the 'Rough Notes'[2], but apparently no longer extant.

18th January 1876        From B.W. Newton
   **To person unknown**
Listed in the 'Rough Notes', but apparently no longer extant.

---

[1] The notes of B.W. Newton's addresses by Mr Bath form the basis of several typescript volumes held by the SGAT. See Section 10, Duplicated and Manuscript Items.

[2] 'The Rough Notes' –see 'Manuscript Items added to the Fry Collection in 2011' in this Guide. The 'notes' are catalogued in the Christian Brethren Archive as FRY/1/2/1).

> 24th January 1876  **From F.J.A. Hort**
>    **To Mrs S.A. Tregelles**  Plymouth
> Concerning the publication of the 'Prolegomena' to S.P. Tregelles's Greek New Testament. 9 pages. [Correspondence regarding the Prolegomena runs between 24th January 1876, and 2nd March 1879. It consists of 9 letters].
> Original letter CBA 2251.

28 January 1876  From B.W. Newton
   **To 'My Dear Sir'**
Re Carron [Canon?] C. Listed in the 'Rough Notes', but apparently no longer extant

February 1876  From B.W. Newton
   **To Nancy Pols**
Listed in the 'Rough Notes', but apparently no longer extant.

2nd February 1876  From B.W. Newton
   **To Miss Van Monen**
Listed in the 'Rough Notes', but apparently no longer extant.

17th February 1876  From B.W. Newton
   **To Mr [Alexander] Haldane**
Listed in the 'Rough Notes', but apparently no longer extant.

14th March 1876  From B.W. Newton  Dunwear
   **To Mr W.**
Listed in the 'Rough Notes', but apparently no longer extant.

3rd April 1876  From B.W. Newton
   **To 'My Dear Sir'**
Listed in the 'Rough Notes, but apparently no longer extant.

April 1876  From B.W. Newton
   **To 'My Dear Friend'**
Listed in the 'Rough Notes' ('blue marble quarto'), but apparently no longer extant.

1st April 1876  From B.W. Newton  Christchurch Road, Winchester
   **To Mr Haldane**
This is in his own hand, and evidently a draft letter, with some deletions. It demonstrates uncertainty as to whether to sever his link with Mr Haldane. The issue is on one of clear separation from evil. Amongst others, the doctrine of Patrick Fairbairn (a fellow Free Church minister) is cited as in error.[1] Although it has a line through it, the closing paragraph reads, 'I do not forget that I have in past days received many kindnesses from you which have been a

---

[1] Patrick Fairbairn (1805-1874), Principal and Professor of Church History and Exegesis at the Free Church College, Glasgow from 1856 to 1874. See B.W. Newton's comment on his theology in *Erroneous Statements concerning the Atonement and Its Results*.

comfort to me in seasons of sorrow and trial. Consequently, I regret the more the divergency of our future paths. But as I feel the duty imperative, I have no alternative'.

The letter was recovered by CBA in July 2011 (CBA FRY/1/6/5). A transcript by C.W.H. Griffiths is held by the CBA, and by the SGAT.

15th April 1876   From B.W. Newton
 **To Mr P[?]ennell**

Listed in the 'Rough Notes', but apparently no longer extant.

15th April 1876   From B.W. Newton
 **To Mrs D--**

'and attached 'My dear friend' 16pp + printed'.
Listed in the 'Rough Notes', but apparently no longer extant.

27th April 1876   From B.W. Newton
 **To Mrs Rew**

Regarding 'Mildmay, etc'[1]
Listed in CBA 7002, F.W. Wyatt's index of Correspondence, as being at p. 13 of 'Yellow Quarto'.
This letter is apparently no longer extant.

9th May 1876   From B.W. Newton
 **To Mr Haldane**

Regarding 'remarks in *The Record*'
Listed in CBA 7002, F.W. Wyatt's index of Correspondence, as being at p. 14 of 'Yellow Quarto'.
This letter is apparently no longer extant.

July 1876   From B.W. Newton
 **To Nancy Pols**

Listed in the 'Rough Notes', but apparently no longer extant.

5th July 1876   From B.W. Newton
 **To Miss Pennell**

Regarding 'Atheism'
Listed in CBA 7002, F.W. Wyatt's index of Correspondence, as being at p. 15 of 'Yellow Quarto'.
This letter is apparently no longer extant.

13th July 1876   From B.W. Newton
 **To Miss Brazier**

Regarding 'Secession from the Church of England'
Listed in CBA 7002, F.W. Wyatt's index of Correspondence, as being at p. 16 of 'Yellow Quarto'.
This letter is apparently no longer extant.

---

[1] See CBA 7064, p. 69. Mrs Rew was one of those who pressed B.W. Newton to return from his 'seclusion' at Winchester, and have a room at Mildmay in which to lecture.

17th October 1876  **From a person unknown**
> To B.W. Newton
Letter on spiritualism
Listed in the 'Rough Notes', but apparently no longer extant.

January 1877  From B.W. Newton
> **To Nancy Pols**
Listed in the 'Rough Notes', but apparently no longer extant.

19th February 1877  From B.W. Newton  Winchester
> **To F.J.A. Hort**
Extract of a letter (Copied or drafted by Mrs S.A. Tregelles?). Thanking him for undertaking to publish the Prolegomena to S.P. Tregelles's Greek New Testament. Requesting that he (F.J.A. Hort) omits any textual authorities not sanctioned by S.P. Tregelles. 10 pages.
[Correspondence regarding the Prolegomena runs between 24th January 1876, and 2nd March 1879. It consists of 9 letters].
Original letter CBA 2256.

21st February 1877  From B.W. Newton  Winchester
> **To Mrs S.A. Tregelles**  Plymouth
Referring to an enclosed copy of a letter [not present, but see letter of 28th February 1877] from B.W. Newton to F.J.A. Hort; Commenting on the inaccuracy of the transcriber of the Codex Sinaiticus. 3 pages.
Original letter CBA 2253.

28th February 1877  From B.W. Newton  Winchester[1]
> **To F.J.A. Hort**
Extract (copied to Mrs S.A. Tregelles?) regarding the inaccuracy of the transcriber of the Codex Sinaiticus. Comments regarding [A.W.] Streane's preparation of S.P. Tregelles's Greek New Testament for printing. 4 pages.
Original letter CBA 2254.

> March 1877  **From Dr [Cecil Yates?] Biss**
> > **To A.A. Rees**  Sunderland
> A letter on ministry. See further letter dated 15 November 1882.
> Listed in the 'Rough Notes' as on p.114 of the Smooth Red Leather Duodecimo Letter Book (Vol. III). Missing from the Fry collection.
> There must be some doubt on this entry, as Dr Biss, in his letter of 15th November 1882, introduces himself as 'a stranger writing to you'.

---

[1] Regarding B.W. Newton's 'seclusion' at Winchester, where he first met F.W. Wyatt see CBA 7064 p. 29. He was driven to seclusion by 'my long experience of the uselessness of uniting on mere evangelical grounds apart from doctrinal agreement'.

## Section 9 – B.W. Newton Correspondence

2nd March 1877  From B.W. Newton
   **To Mrs S.A. Tregelles**
Referring to enclosed copies of letters from B.W. Newton and F.J.A. Hort [not present but see correspondence 19th and 21st February 1877]. Commenting on [F.J.A.] Hort and [B.F.] Westcott's views regarding John 13 in Tregelles's Greek New Testament. 3 pages.
Original letter CBA 2255.

---

**March 1877**

   Statement on 'the London Ministry'. Listed in the 'Rough Notes' as being at page 120 of the Smooth Red Leather Duodecimo Letter Book (Vol. III) with a further note of Miss Amy J.T. Toulmin reading the statement 'to one concerned in it, May 1877'.
[Note on the London Ministry statement continued]. This is in MS Book 1, now held by Tom Chantry. See the section of this *Guide* regarding Duplicated and Manuscript Items.[1]

---

9th March 1877  **From F.J.A. Hort**  Cambridge
   **To Mrs S.A. Tregelles**
Regarding the publication of the Prolegomena of S.P. Tregelles's Greek New Testament. 3 pages.
[Correspondence regarding the Prolegomena runs between 24th January 1876, and 2nd March 1879. It consists of 9 letters].
Original letter, CBA 2257.

---

12th March 1877  **From F.J.A. Hort**  Cambridge
   **To Mrs S.A. Tregelles**
Regarding the publication of the Prolegomena of S.P. Tregelles's Greek New Testament. 4 pages.
[Correspondence regarding the Prolegomena runs between 24th January 1876, and 2nd March 1879. It consists of 9 letters].
Original letter CBA 2258.

---

26th April 1877  **From F.J.A. Hort**  Cambridge
   **To Mrs S.A. Tregelles**
Regarding the publication of the Prolegomena of S.P. Tregelles's Greek New Testament. See copy letter 19th February 1877, and 2nd March 1877, etc. 5 pages.
[Correspondence regarding the Prolegomena runs between 24th January 1876, and 2nd March 1879. It consists of 9 letters].
Original letter CBA 2259,

---

[1] See also the autobiographical notebook that is mainly concerned with the closure of the work at Bayswater, recovered by the CBA in 2011 – FRY/1/1/3. A copy is held by the SGAT. See Section 10, Duplicated and Manuscript Items in this Guide.

14th May 1877  From B.W. Newton
**To 'Amy' transliterated into Hebrew (אמי) [Miss Amy J.T. Toulmin]**
Regarding false rumours concerning him, following the end of the Bayswater ministry. Agreeing the letter can be read to Mary Boniface[1] (her surname also written in Hebrew transliteration). Refers to the memorandum of his position [pages 120-127 in MS Book 1 (TC)]. The memorandum states that it was not his object to form a Church at Duke Street or at Bayswater, as 'the foundations of all things are out of course'. None should attach themselves to his ministry exclusively unless they felt led to do so. He could not afford to do some of the things they desired. Extended efforts, not localised efforts, were needed, as new truths were being taught. It was necessary for him to write as much as possible and, as he was under constant attack, he had to defend himself and his doctrines. Refers to his exertion at Weston-Super-Mare and his subsequent breakdown. His returning to London in 1871. He had been forced to act under different principles at Plymouth, but, when he commenced the work at Duke Street, he resumed the original principles that he had held when he left the Establishment
Both the letter, and the memorandum, were originally in Miss Amy J.T. Toulmin's hand, and found by F.W. Wyatt when he was sorting out Miss Toulmin's effects, subsequent to her death. The letter of 15th July 1874 was placed next to it in MS Book 1.
F.W. Wyatt's copy MS Book 1 (TC), pp.127 ff.

23rd May 1877  **From Dr George Smeaton**[2]  Edinburgh
  To B.W. Newton
Thanking him for his contribution to sound theology [*Salvation by Substitution* ?], 'which rescues salvation and imputation from a caricature'. Thankful that his (B.W. Newton's) health is yet strong.
Transcript of letter CBA 7050, p.15.

**8 June 1877 Death of B.W. Newton's mother** [3]

20th December 1877  **From F.J.A. Hort**  Cambridge
  **To Mrs S.A. Tregelles**
Regarding the publication of the Prolegomena of S.P. Tregelles's Greek New Testament. See copy letter 19th February 1877, and 2nd March 1877, etc. 5 pages.
[Correspondence regarding the Prolegomena runs between 24th January 1876, and 2nd March 1879. It consists of 9 letters].
Original letter CBA 2261 [incomplete – last page defective].

---

[1] See letter of 15th July 1874
[2] See further reference to his friendship with George Smeaton in *Babylon and Egypt*, 3rd edition, p.542n.
[3] Mrs Anna Newton (née Treffry), 12 August 1782 - 8 June 1877. Buried in Frant Cemetery, Tunbridge Wells. A photograph of her gravestone (giving her dates) is given in *A Pictorial Memoir of Benjamin Wills Newton* – the supplement to this Guide. See the Advertisement at the end of this volume.

31st December 1877      **From Dr Smeaton**      Edinburgh
     To B.W. Newton
     Further appreciative letter. Refers to Mr Cox, and 'the Darbyites'.
     Transcript of letter CBA 7050, pp.15,16.

January 1878      From B.W. Newton
     **To A.M. Gay [Alice Mary Guy?]**[1]
Listed in the 'Rough Notes', but apparently no longer extant.

17th January 1878      From B.W. Newton
     **To Miss Amy J.T. Toulmin**
Advising against a person being baptised in Dublin or engaging in wrong associations there.
F.W. Wyatt's copy MS Book 1 (TC), p.364. Listed in A.C. Fry's rough notes.

21st February 1878      From B.W. Newton
     **To Miss D**
Listed in the 'Rough Notes' as being in the 'blue marble quarto' book, but apparently no longer extant.

20th April 1878      From B.W. Newton      38, Broadwater Down, [Tunbridge Wells]
     **To 'My Dear Sir'**
Regarding the Church's persecution in the Tribulation.
Listed in the 'Rough Notes'[2] as being in the 'blue marble quarto' book. Transcript of letter CBA 7154 (unnumbered pages).

21st April 1878      From B.W. Newton
     **To Mr Campbell**
Listed in the 'Rough Notes' as being in the 'blue marble quarto' book, but apparently no longer extant.

     4th May 1878. An advertisement in *The Morning Post*, London, indicates that he was lecturing 'every Thursday' on 'Prophetic Scripture' at this time.

11th May 1878      From B.W. Newton
     **To Unknown**
'Theological'
Listed in CBA 7002, F.W. Wyatt's index of Correspondence, as being at p. 17 of 'Yellow Quarto'. This letter is apparently no longer extant.

---

[1] Alice Mary Guy. Died 2nd June 1919. In Memoriam notice, *Watching and Waiting*, July 1919, p.42.
[2] 'The Rough Notes' – see 'Manuscript Items added to the Fry Collection in 2011' in this Guide. The 'notes' are catalogued in the Christian Brethren Archive as FRY/1/2/1).

June 1878                           From B.W. Newton
   **To Unknown**
'Presbyterianism'
Listed in CBA 7002, F.W. Wyatt's index of Correspondence, as being at p. 18 of 'Yellow Quarto'. This letter is apparently no longer extant.

4th June 1878                       From B.W. Newton
   **To Miss [Amy J.T.] Toulmin**
Listed in the 'Rough Notes', but apparently no longer extant.

31st July 1878                      From B.W. Newton
   **To The Committee of the R[eligious] T[ract] Society**
Listed in the 'Rough Notes' as in the 'blue marble quarto' book, but apparently no longer extant.

22nd August 1878                    From B.W. Newton
   **To Macauley, The Committee of the R[eligious] T[ract] Society**
Listed in the 'Rough Notes' as in the 'blue marble quarto' book, but apparently no longer extant.

19th October 1878                   From B.W. Newton
   **To Mr Hamilton**
Listed in the 'Rough Notes' as being in 'a brown penny book', but apparently no longer extant.

> 21st December 1878   From **F.J.A. Hort**,          Cambridge
>    **To Mrs S.A. Tregelles**         Plymouth
> Explaining why he would not include the preface proposed by B.W. Newton to the Prolegomena of Tregelles's Greek Testament. He did not feel it appropriate to have Dr Tregelles's 'theological opinions' recorded. B.W. Newton had asked to include an extract from the preface of Tregelles's work on the Book of Revelation.[1] He comments on B.W. Newton's subsequent desire to have his (B.W. Newton's) name removed from S.P. Tregelles's Greek New Testament - 'Mr Newton has been so much connected with the work throughout that injustice would be done not only to him, but to fact by ignoring his name'. He considered that it was 'an exaggerated feeling of isolation' that led B.W. Newton to make his request. 8 pages.
> [Correspondence regarding the Prolegomena runs between 24th January 1876, and 2nd March 1879. It consists of 9 letters].
> Original letter CBA 2262.

> 25th February 1879    **From F.J.A. Hort**                Cambridge
>    **To Mrs S.A. Tregelles**
> Regarding the honorarium to be paid to [A.W.] Streane for his proof-reading for publication of S.P. Tregelles's Prolegomena of his edition of the Greek New Testament.
> [Correspondence regarding the Prolegomena runs between 24th January 1876, and 2nd March 1879. It consists of 9 letters]. 3 pages.
> Original letter CBA 2263.

---

[1] S.P. Tregelles, *The Book of Revelation in Greek, Edited from the Ancient Authorities; with a New English Version and Various Readings*, Bagster and sons 1844.

2nd March 1879          From B.W. Newton          Tunbridge Wells
     **To Mrs S.A. Tregelles**          Plymouth

Incomplete. Regarding the honorarium to be paid to [A.W.] Streane for his proof-reading for publication of S.P. Tregelles's Prolegomena of his edition of Greek New Testament. [Further letters between A.W. Streane and Mrs Tregelles regarding this, and other letters regarding the publication of S.P. Tregelles's Greek New Testament, are held in the Christian Brethren Archive, but are not recorded in this B.W. Newton resource as not relevant to this *Guide* to the works of B.W. Newton]. 1 page

[Correspondence regarding the Prolegomena runs between 24th January 1876, and 2nd March 1879. It consists of 9 letters].

Original letter CBA 2264.

20th November 1879        From B.W. Newton          Tunbridge Wells
     **To Mr Sears**[1]

Referring to the recipient's tract *Church Life*. Felt it unwise as tending to encourage an attempt to take a public position with very high pretensions. B.W. Newton sees 'neither government, nor pastorship, nor teaching' at present. Individual rectification must precede Church rectification, and in individual rectification is included rectification of doctrines and principles, as well as practices. This, and the supplying of the power of government, teaching, and a 'Timothy and Titus' ministry, are necessary prerequisites. 2 pages (unnumbered)

Transcript of letter CBA 7071.

    August 1880            **From Miss Amy J.T. Toulmin**
        To B.W. Newton

Letter relating to her letter to [Henry] Groves of [4th] March 1867, and to a tract *High Church Claims* [*of the Exclusive Brethren*, W.H. Dorman 1868].

Refers to her conversion in 1829.

F.W. Wyatt's copy MS Book 1 (TC), pp.81,82. Listed in the 'Rough Notes'.

September 1880           From B.W. Newton
     **To Mackenzie**                Redlands, Bristol

   Listed in the 'Rough Notes'. Missing from the Fry collection.

October 1880             From B.W. Newton
     **To Mackenzie**                Redlands, Bristol

   Listed in the 'Rough Notes'. Missing from the Fry collection.

26 March 1881           From B.W. Newton
     **To Mr ? Tufnel**

'Theological'

Listed in CBA 7002, F.W. Wyatt's index of Correspondence, as being at p. 19 of 'Yellow Quarto'. This letter is apparently no longer extant.

---

[1] Not Septimus Sears

> **Census 3rd April 1881**
>
> <u>Address:</u>  38 B[roadwater] Down, Frant.[1]
>   Benjamin Wills Newton (Head), 73 [sic], born Stoke Darenwell [sic] – stocks and house property, Fellow of Oxford;  Maria Newton (Wife), 66, born Madras (British subject); Sophia C. Hawkins (sister-in-law), 60, born Hampton Court Palace, house property; Elizabeth Miller (servant) 17, born Winchester – Cook Dom.; Eliza Curd (servant) 14, born Burgess Hill, Sussex, Household Dom.

4 August 1881        **From Mr Haldane**        Godden Green, Sevenoaks
    To B.W. Newton
He had sent Mr Newton's review to the editor, and given it his full approval. Regarding Dean Stanley and Lord Shaftesbury.
F.W. Wyatt's copy MS Book 1 (TC), p.112.  Listed in the 'Rough Notes'.[2]

18th May 1882        **From Mrs S.A. Tregelles** [3]        Plymouth
    To B.W. Newton
Acknowledging letter and money.  Concerning S.P. Tregelles's sufferings.  Authorising B.W. Newton to act in the matter of his Testament.  2 pages.
CBA 7181(122).

9th June 1882        **From Mrs S.A. Tregelles**
    To B.W. Newton
Asking if S.P. Tregelles accepted Mr Liebstein's correction to [S.P. Tregelles's] *Remarks on Daniel* (with reference to 5th Edition).  2 pages.
Original letter.  CBA 7181(123).

> **15th September 1882.  Death of Mrs S.A. Tregelles (1807 – 1882.  Married 1839).**

[15th November 1882]        From B.W. Newton
    **To Rev. A.A. Rees**[4]        Sunderland
Covering note by B.W. Newton to a letter on his behalf to Rev. A.A. Rees (see the following entry), explaining why he (Dr Biss) was replying on his (Mr Newton's) behalf.  The note is included as an undated letter [dated 15th November 1882 by Wyatt] in MS Book 1 (TC), p.114.

---

[1] Frant is about 8 km South of Tunbridge Wells, East Sussex.
[2] 'The Rough Notes' –see 'Manuscript Items added to the Fry Collection in 2011' in this Guide.  The 'notes' are catalogued in the Christian Brethren Archive as FRY/1/2/1).
[3] S.P. Tregelles wife, née Sarah Anna Prideaux.
[4] Rev. Arthur Augustus Rees was a prominent premillennialist who wrote *The Question Answered: Will the Millennial Reign of Christ be Spiritual Alone, or Both Spiritual and Personal?* 1856.  For further information on A. A. Rees, and his views on worship and ministry, see 'The Early Development of Arthur Augustus Rees and his relations with the Brethren;' by Timothy C.F. Stunt, *Brethren Archivists and Historians Network Review* (BAHNR) 4:22-35.

## Section 9 – B.W. Newton Correspondence

> 15th November 1882 **From Dr [C.Y.] Biss** 'Claremont', [Sydenham Park, SE] **To Rev. A.A. Rees** Sunderland
> Written on B.W. Newton's behalf. The letter confirms Mr Newton's substantial agreement with his letter of 14th May 1846[1] on worship and ministry, and notes his present reservations on certain points. F.W. Wyatt's copy in MS Book 1 (TC), pp.114-119 indicates from Dr [C.Y.] Biss to Rev. A.A. Rees.
> See also the 'Rough Notes' record of a letter from Dr Biss to A.A. Rees, dated March 1877.
> F.W. Wyatt's copy MS Book 1 (TC), pp.114-119, and also in CBA 7065, p.126. A further copy, in F.W. Wyatt's hand, is held by C.W.H. Griffiths.

23rd November 1882    **From A. Prideaux**
    To B.W. Newton
Regarding S.P. Tregelles's works
Reported that he had seen his sister, S.P. Tregelles's wife. They were very glad that Mr Newton was willing to take on all that concerns Dr Tregelles's works. He expressed the hope that it would be possible to bring out a manual version of Tregelles's Greek New Testament.[2]
F.W. Wyatt's copy MS Book 1 (TC), pp.112,113. Listed in the 'Rough Notes'.

21st December 1882   **From Frederick W. Wyatt**   Whitecliffe Mill Street, Blandford
    To B.W. Newton
Relating the circumstances of his separation from the Open Brethren Assembly at Blandford, following his being summoned to a meeting on 19th December 1882. F.W. Wyatt's teaching had become unacceptable to the leaders of the Assembly. They challenged him regarding the lectures he was giving in Blandford. They sought to label him with the same heresy of which Mr Newton had been accused - that Christ was under a curse, as a child of Adam and as an Israelite. Whilst accepting that Christ was truly one of Adam's race, and that he was an Israelite (both under curse), Wyatt qualified his answer by saying that Christ was himself personally free from all and every infliction, and could have gone up to Heaven again at any moment if his personal deservings were the only consideration. He wrote of possibly leaving Blandford. He sent greetings to Mrs Newton and Miss Hawkins, and requested that the letter be shown to Dr Biss. 8 pages.
Copy in F.W. Wyatt's hand. One of the F.W. Wyatt letters held by C.W.H. Griffiths.

March 1883    From B.W. Newton
    **To Marshall**
Listed in the 'Rough Notes'. Missing from the Fry collection

---

[1] See Section 3, B.W. Newton's Published Works entry on *Letter on Worship and Ministry*.
[2] C.W.H. Griffiths has a copy of the manual version with the initials 'B.W.N.' embossed on the spine. See also the note on the manual edition in Section 4, B.W. Newton's Contributions to Other Publications.

24th June 1883           From B.W. Newton
    **To person unknown** (a young convert)
Replying to the addressee's letter. Advises on the condition of the believer, and makes practical suggestions for the person's new Christian life. Warns against Farrar's books. Recommends the writings of John Newton, and Wylie's *History of the Reformation*. Recommends several of his own writings.
Reprinted in *Perilous Times* July 1905, pp.1,2, and subsequently published as a tract, *Counsels to Converts* (NM 5.1).

23rd November 1884      From B.W. Newton           Avonstowe, Orpington
    **To Mrs [George] Müller**
Related his separation from Mrs Pinstone because of her association with C.H. Spurgeon. Regretted that Spurgeon countenanced Bradlaugh [a prominent atheist] taking up his Parliamentary seat.
Transcript of letter CBA 7050, p.90? [between p.90 and p.242].

1st June 1885           From B.W. Newton           Orpington, Kent
    **To Mr I. Arnold Lake**      Camden Town, London
Expressing appreciation for the 'kind letter', and for enclosing the letter to him (B.W. Newton) from E.K. Groves. Cannot approve Groves' synopsis. 'It is beyond the power of any living individual to write an accurate or truthful account of the complications of Brethrenism during the last forty years'. Speaks of the doctrinal differences separating him from J.N. Darby since 1834. Of Tregelles's pamphlets on the Plymouth controversy. Attaches a list of tracts and books [not present]. Has been labouring since 1827 against the very doctrines that they have tried to fix on him. States his position on the issues of the controversy. Requests that the proposed book be focused on the present points of difference, and not on the past. Hopes that [R.C.] Chapman and [George] Müller will exert their influence to prevent the publication of the book [published as *Conversations on Bethesda Family Matters*]. See note too in Section 8, Publications Produced from Notes of Addresses, and Posthumously Published Letters and Manuscripts (N.M. 8.8).
Quoted on, pp.162-164 of the Second Edition of *Teachers of the Faith and Future* by G.H. Fromow, Second Edition, 1969.
F.W. Wyatt's copy. MS Book 1 (TC), pp.269-270.

> 5th June 1885         **From Miss Amy J.T. Toulmin**
>     **To Edward K. Groves**[1]
> Comments on his [E.K. Groves] proposed work *Conversations on Bethesda Family Matters*.[2] She relates events at Bethesda, and meetings with Müller and Craik when she visited a friend at Clifton.
> F.W. Wyatt's copy MS Book 1 (TC), p.83. Listed in the 'Rough Notes'.

---

[1] Edward Kennaway Groves (1836-1917. Son of Anthony Norris Groves and half-brother of Henry Groves.
[2] Published in 1885. See B.W. Newton's reported comments in CBA 7049, and the following correspondence in this section.

> 6th June 1885 ,          **From Edward K. Groves**    11 Greenway road, Redland, Bristol.
>     **To Miss Amy J.T. Toulmin**
> Reply to her letter. Concludes Mr Newton was more sinned against than sinning. Had submitted the part of the manuscript, giving his judgement, to Mr Newton for comment, but so far had had no reply.
> F.W. Wyatt's copy MS Book 1 (TC), pp.83, 84.

> 29th July [1885]        **From [Dr] C.Y. Biss**    Claremont, Sydenham Park, S.E.
>     **To F.W. Wyatt**
> F.W. Wyatt evidently appealed to Mr Wright [ruling elder?] at Bethesda. Dr Biss concludes, 'It is evident that there is no disposition to be fair at Bristol, and in all probability the result of your appeal will be to lead them to say that Mr Newton and his friends are terribly afraid of being exposed'. The elders could have stopped the book if they had so desired. 4 pages.
> One of the F.W. Wyatt letters held by C.W.H. Griffiths.

10th February 1886        From B.W. Newton
    **To unnamed [Thomas Graham Graham]**[1]

His [B.W. Newton's] relation to him has been seriously affected by his having presided over a meeting in January in which Mr Gregory of Brighton gave the address and others took part. Speaks of the principles of Haggai, Zechariah 3, and Nehemiah, 'I cannot acknowledge as co-labourers any who refuse to distinguish between rubbish and stones'. Asks them to take time to consider their positions. Does not take up an antagonistic position, nor will refuse aid to 'your ----- pastoral fund'.

F.W. Wyatt's copy MS Book 1 (TC), p.71. Listed in the 'Rough Notes', which identifies the recipient as Mr Graham.

11th June 1886        From B.W. Newton
    **To Lord Lichfield**[2]

Regarding Gladstone and his policy decisions, particularly in relation to Irish Home Rule. 'When Catholic emancipation was granted, Great Britain was ruined. Cromwell knew it would be so'. Romans 1 teaches that God punishes idolatry. This is not a question of liberty of conscience.

F.W. Wyatt's copy MS Book 1 (TC) pages 72-75. Listed in the 'Rough Notes'.

13th June 1887        From B.W. Newton        Avonstowe, Orpington
    **To Dr C.[Cecil] Y[ates] Biss**[3]

On mesmerism[4]. He wrote because a suggestion had been made that Dr Biss had an interest in mesmerism.

---

[1] Thomas Graham Graham . For further information on T.G. Graham and the Worthing venture see *Mr Newton at Worthing* by C.W.H. Griffiths.
[2] See note in *Watching and Waiting* July-August 1950, p.64, regarding the Second Earl's association with Mr Newton.
[3] Cecil Yates Biss. Obituary *Perilous Times*, February 1912. Died 20th January 1912, aged 66. Reminiscences of him *Watching and Waiting*, December 1920, p.240-241. CBA 7064 p139 refers to the 'violent quarrel' he had with the Brethren and the ministry he established at Wells Hall.
[4] See the letter from B.W. Newton placed after January 1840 regarding Mesmerism.

Transcript of letter CBA 7052, pp.1-8.

30th June 1887      **From Dr C[Cecil] Y[ates] Biss**      Harley Street, London
     To B.W. Newton
Regarding mesmerism. Regretted the false impression that he had a professional interest in mesmerism.
Transcript of letter CBA 7052, pp.9-17.

5th July 1887      From B.W. Newton      Avonstowe, Orpington
     **To Dr C[ecil] Y[ates] Biss**
On Mesmerism. Still anxious about Dr Biss's connection with mesmerism. Mr B.W. Newton considered it a delusion comparable to spiritualism. Quotes sources on the nature of mesmerism.
Transcript of letter CBA 7052, pp.36-38

30th July 1887      **From Dr C[ecil] Y[ates] Biss**      Harley Street, London
     To B.W. Newton
Regarding mesmerism. Regarded mesmerism to be a bad system, and therefore indirectly Satanic.
Transcript of letter CBA 7051, pp.1-16.

30th July 1887      From B.W. Newton      Avonstowe, Orpington
     **To Dr C[ecil] Y[ates] Biss**
On mesmerism. Mr Newton was determined to take decided ground on the question. Enclosed press cuttings.
Transcript of letter CBA 7052, pp.36-38.

4th August 1887      From B.W. Newton      Avonstowe, Orpington
     **To Mr [Ker Baillie?] Hamilton**[1]
Regarding his [Hamilton's] previous letter. Regarding prophetic truth. The need for separation from evil more needed now than 40 years ago. The spread of error now is far greater. '*Pari passu* the state has been divesting itself of all responsibility for acknowledging the Bible in Government, and has during the last year crossed 'the narrow ledge of theism''.[2] Regarding Darwin.
F.W. Wyatt's copy MS Book 1 (TC), p.75. Listed in the 'Rough Notes'.

---

[1] Ker Baillie Hamilton, 1804-1889. Former colonial governor of Grenada, Newfoundland, and Antigua and the Leeward Islands. Buried in Tunbridge Wells. See notes on Section 9, B.W. Newton's Correspondence, November 1871 onwards and on Prospects of the Ten Kingdoms in Section 3. See *Dictionary of Canadian Biography*, Vol. 11. A picture of him is included *A Pictorial Memoir of Benjamin Wills Newton* – the supplement to this Guide.

[2] W.E. Gladstone's phrase. See *The Acknowledgement of God by Earthly Governments* in Section 3, B.W. Newton's Published Works of this Guide.

29th August 1887          From B.W. Newton          Avonstowe, Orpington
### To Dr C[ecil] Y[ates] Biss
Regarding Dr Biss's letter of 30th July. B.W. Newton opposed mesmerism because it arrogates the power of the will to the person applying it.
Transcript of letter CBA 7051, pp.17-39.

1888          From B.W. Newton
### To an unknown person
To a friend troubled by hyper-Calvinism. Refers to perplexity about hyper-Calvinism as the first trial of his Christian life.
Reprinted in *Perilous Times*, June 1906 and July 1906, under the title: Divine Sovereignty and Human Responsibility. See note in Section 8 of this *Guide*, Derived Publications, NM 5.2 Letter on Hyper Calvinism, and the comment on Mr Newton's letter of 30th December 1847 linking this with Dr Robert Hawker of Charles Church, Plymouth, although it could also relate to H.B. Bulteel's high Calvinism.
CBA 7031a (incl.) Copied by G.M. Bartlett.

     February 1889          **From [Arthur?] Andrews**
         To B.W. Newton
         Listed in the 'Rough Notes', but missing from the Fry Collection.

14th July 1889          From B.W. Newton          Avonstowe, Orpington
### To Arthur Andrews
Regarding discipline and oversight at meetings of believers, the Lord's Table, etc.
Reprinted (edited) in the anthology, *B.W. Newton on Ministry and Order in the Church of Christ*.
Transcript of letter CBA 7061, pp.16a-18; and 7187(49).

2nd October 1890          From B.W. Newton          Isle of Wight
### To 'Dear Mr –'
Transcribed by G.L. Silverwood-Browne 25th December 1948. Source not known, but identified as 'a letter from B.W.N., not before published'.
Sets out the principles on which we should act, in relation to the doctrines and principles of the apostolic period. 1 page of small MS book.
MS copy, G.L Silverwood-Browne's MS book: B.W. Newton Lectures held by C.W.H. Griffiths. It was published in *Watching and Waiting* January/February 1942 (pp.15,16).

November 1890          From B.W. Newton
### To A.M. Gay [Alice Mary Guy?]
Listed in the 'Rough Notes'.[1] Missing from the Fry collection.

---

[1] 'The Rough Notes' – see 'Manuscript Items added to the Fry Collection in 2011' in this Guide. The 'notes' are catalogued in the Christian Brethren Archive as FRY/1/2/1).

## Section 9 – B.W. Newton Correspondence

> **Census 5th April 1891**
>
> <u>Address:</u> Wicliffe Villa, St John's Road, Carisbrook, IW.
>   B.W. Newton, 83 of private means. Birthplace: Stoke Demerel, Devon.
>   Maria Newton, 76 of private means. Birthplace: Madras, East Indies
>   Sophia Hawkins, 70 of private means. Birthplace: Hampton Court Palace.
>   Anna Marshall, 24, servant cook. Birthplace: Rochester, Kent.

> 7th November 1891  **From John Cox [jun.]**  Bedwardine, Upper Norwood, S.E.
>   **To F.W. Wyatt**
> The letter concludes, 'Is Mr Newton still at Newport. If so, do you know when he returns to Orpington? … I hear that he has bought a house in Shanklin and will probably reside there altogether'. 2 pages.
> One of the F.W. Wyatt letters held by C.W.H. Griffiths.

10th July [189?]  From B.W. Newton  Ermstowe, Shanklin, I.W.
  **To Dr [A.J.W.] Dalzell**
Regarding Latitudinarianism, etc.
CBA (7066?), pp.116a-117.

> 7th June 1893  **From John Cox [jun.]**  Bedwardine, Upper Norwood, S.E. [London]
>   **To F.W. Wyatt**
> Extract from a letter, in A.C. Fry's hand.

26th September 1893  From B.W. Newton
  **To Mrs Stirling**
Regarding types and ritualism
Transcript of letter CBA 7066 pages 73-78

2nd January 1894  From B.W. Newton  Ermstowe, Shanklin, I.W.
  **To Mrs N**
On prophecy and Brethrenism. Advises against Newbury's and Rotherham's Bibles. S.P. Tregelles on his deathbed was greatly pained by the manner Rotherham[1] used his Greek New Testament. Newbury 'has drunk too much of Brethrenism'.
Transcript of letter. CBA 7066, pp.143-145.

> **1st April 1895 Death of Amy J.T. Toulmin.**[2]

---

[1] Joseph Bryant Rotherham (1828–1910), editor of the magazine, *The Rainbow*, had used S.P. Tregelles's Greek New Testament text as the basis of his revision of his *New Testament Critically Emphasised*.

[2] Amy Jane Treffry Toulmin, B.W. Newton's cousin. Born 28th March 1814. See Timothy Stunt's index note regarding her in *From Awakening to Secession* (p.398). F.W. Wyatt notes he knew her from 1883, and attended her burial (MS Book 2, p.122 and CBA 7049, p.50). A brief account of B.W. Newton's address at her burial is recorded in CBA 7049, pp.437, 438. She is buried in Shanklin Cemetery.

## Section 9 – B.W. Newton Correspondence

18th July 1895     From B.W. Newton     Ermstone, Shanklin, I.W.
**To Miss [Jessie] Leake**[1]

In the letter he refers to the time that he resided at Maidenhead. Miss Leake had contact with Christians in Norway. She proposed translations[2], including S.P. Tregelles on Daniel. B.W. Newton criticised Tregelles's comments on Daniel 11, and indicated that he did not believe that Tregelles himself would have wished his thoughts on that part of Daniel republished[3]. B.W. Newton indicated that he intended to do further writing if he was spared.
Transcript of letter CBA 7050, pp.242-244.

12th August 1895     From B.W. Newton     Ermstone, Shanklin, I.W.
**To Miss [Jessie] Leake**

Mr B.W. Newton's sight had failed, and an amanuensis wrote this letter. Acceded to the printing of Tregelles on Daniel to the end of chapter 9, and of his own works (*The Blood that Saveth*; *How does the Blood Save?*; and *Acceptance with God*) into Norwegian. Sent *Gospel Truths*, and *Atonement and Its Results*. Requested information on the cost of translating and printing, and indicated that he will meet the cost if he can.

He again expressed difficulty with Tregelles's interpretation of Daniel 11. He confirmed his [B.W. Newton's] position that there is no detailed Gentile history in prophetic Scripture, except in connection with Jerusalem nationally existing.
F.W. Wyatt's copy MS Book 1 (TC), p.84. Transcript of letter CBA 7050, p.245.

[1895] ND     From B.W. Newton     Hampton Villa, Argyll Street, Ryde, I.W.
**To Miss [Jessie] Leake**

Written by A. Andrews as amanuensis to B.W. Newton, due to Mr Newton's loss of sight. Sent £5 for the expense of producing *Gospel Truths* [in Norwegian]. Suggested the translation of *The Day of the Lord*; *The First Resurrection*; and *The World to Come*'
Transcript of letter CBA 7050, pp.245-247.

1896     From B.W. Newton
**To W.L. Holland**

This is Mr Newton's response to a letter that W.L. Holland had received from 'one of the "Brethren" at Glasgow'. He had forwarded it to B.W. Newton for comment 'some two years ago'. It replies to the Brethren attacks on his doctrine made in *The Believer's Almanac, or Christian Remembrancer*. The substance of the attacks relate to the Suretyship of Christ. Mr Newton distinguishes Christ's circumstantial and personal position before God. The extracts run to three pages. It is probably Mr Newton's last recorded statement on the subject.
Extracts are printed in *The 'Archbishop' of Canterbury and 'Modern' Christianity* (1898), in a section on the Person of the Lord, between pages 195 and 202.

5th January 1896     From B.W. Newton     Ermstowe, Shanklin

---

[1] Miss Jessie Leake. Died at Tunbridge Wells 4th February 1928, aged 75 years. Obituary *Watching and Waiting*, March 1928, p.128
[2] See the 'authorised translation' of a selection of B.W. Newton's works in Retfærdiggjörelsen og Helligjörelsen, noted in Section 3, B.W. Newton's Published Works
[3] S.P. Tregelles, *Remarks on the Prophetic Visions in the Book of Daniel*, first published Plymouth, Tract Depot, 1847, Xerox copy CBA. The Fifth Edition, 1864 [1862] was the last published in his lifetime.

**To Mrs [Mary E.] Stirling**

The letter was dictated because of Mr Newton's failing eyesight. 'My eyes prevent me from consulting any books now in any language'. He had written with the assistance of 'Mr Wyatt of Ryde'.

He wrote on Genesis 3:15, in reply to a letter (not extant) from her (or her husband) regarding the Vulgate translation '*she* [i.e. interpreted as Mary] shall bruise thy head' [*ipsa* conteret caput tuum], and the alleged rules of Hebrew grammar of argued by a priest for that translation. B.W. Newton affirms that the text is unassailable, and confirmed by the rules of Hebrew grammar. Any change is without critical authority.

The letter is signed 'B.W. Newton and Fred W. Wyatt'.

A copy of the letter in F.W. Wyatt's hand was recovered by the CBA in July 2011, (CBA FRY/1/6/3). There is a transcript of letter in the manuscript book CBA 7063 pages 77, 77a without an identified date.

5th February 1896   **From [Mrs] Mary E. Stirling** 31 Chepstow Place, Bayswater, W
   To B.W. Newton

Regarding Mr Newton's reply of 5th January 1896. She reported that the priest had denied that there was a grammatical rule regarding masculine verbs and feminine substantives.

A copy of the letter in F.W. Wyatt's hand recovered by the CBA in July 2011 (CBA FRY/1/6/3). There is a transcript of letter in the manuscript book CBA 7063 pp.77,77a without an identified date.

8th February 1896              From B.W. Newton              Ermstowe, Shanklin, I.W.
   **To Mrs [Mary E.] Stirling**

Dictated letter because of Mr Newton's failing eyesight. Regarding Mrs Stirling's letter of February 5th 1896. Affirms that in Gen. 3:15 there is no grammatical peculiarity, or grammatical difficulty, whatever. The issue is not a grammatical one, but of the primacy given to the Vulgate by the Catholic Church, its claim to exalt tradition, and the decision of the Church over Scripture - as declared by the Council of Trent. Nevertheless grammatical authorities are appended – Müller, Ewald, Gesenius, Green, Davidson, and Tregelles.

A copy of the letter in F.W. Wyatt's hand recovered by the CBA in July 2011, (CBA FRY/1/6/3). There is a transcript of letter in the manuscript book CBA 7063, p.77a without identified date.

February 11th 1896   **From [Mrs] Mary E. Stirling** 31 Chepstow Place, Bayswater, W
   To B.W. Newton

Regarding Mr Newton's reply of February 8th 1896. The priest had acknowledged Jerome's admission regarding the verse, but prevaricated on the importance of the translation. Stated 'Mr Stirling is now conducting Protestant classes to teach young people how to answer the cunning activities of Roman Catholics'. 'Bayswater is called the Pope's Parish so there is need to warn the young'. Concluded by saying that Mr Stirling is tired, but that he hopes to write soon himself.

A copy of the letter in F.W. Wyatt's hand recovered by the CBA in July 2011, (CBA FRY/1/6/3).

## Section 9 – B.W. Newton Correspondence

    1896                        **From F.W. Wyatt**
        To B.W. Newton
        CBA 7117. Transcript of a letter.

27th July 1896           From B.W. Newton          Ermstone, Shanklin, I.W.
        **To Edward Crossley**[1]
Relating Mr B.W. Newton's withdrawal from the Ryde meeting led by Crossley. Refers to his 'little meeting' with Dr [A.J.W.] Dalzell, F.W. Wyatt, and Arthur Andrews.[2]
2 pages (unnumbered).
Transcript of the letter in CBA 7048.

1st August 1896          From B.W. Newton          Ermstone, Shanklin, I.W.
        **To Edward Crossley**
Expressing friendship to Crossley, and proposing fellowship on a private level. Refers to his (B.W. Newton's) poor health.
Transcript of the letter in CBA 7048, 3 pages (unnumbered).

    2nd August 1896        **From Edward Crossley**       Southfield, Ryde
           To B.W. Newton
        Declining to meet B.W. Newton because of his withdrawal from the meeting.
        Transcript of the letter CBA 7048, 1 page (unnumbered).

2nd August 1896         From B.W. Newton          Ermstone, Shanklin, I.W.
        **To Edward Crossley**
Distinguishing two kinds of withdrawal from fellowship. Expressing great regret if separation is total.
Transcript of the letter CBA 7048, 2 pages (unnumbered).

    4th August 1896        From Edward Crossley        Southfield, Ryde
        **To B.W. Newton**
        Curt letter confirming his earlier decision not to meet Mr B.W. Newton.
        Transcript of the letter CBA 7048, 1 page (unnumbered).

---

[1] Regarding Edward Crossley and Arthur Andrews, see Section 4, Contributions to Other Publications, 11. A Statement of Doctrines Held by a Body of Christians Meeting in the Evangelical Protestant Chapel, Newport Street, Ryde, Isle of Wight. Compiled By Arthur Andrews.

[2] For further background, see Section 4, Contributions to Other Publications section of this Guide, on *A Statement of Doctrines Held by a Body of Christians Meeting in The Evangelical Protestant Chapel, Newport Street, Ryde, Isle of Wight* - compiled by Arthur Andrews. It is possible there was a later reconciliation, as suggested there.

## Section 9 – B.W. Newton Correspondence

---

27th February 1899    **From [Miss] A.S. Butcher**
   **To F.W. Wyatt**
Regarding the withdrawal of W.L. Holland from B.W. Newton to join Frank White.[1]
4 pages.
CBA 7187(7)

---

March 1899    **From F.W. Wyatt**
   **To 'Miss ---'**
Regarding Mr B.W. Newton's opinion on W.L. Holland's withdrawal to Frank White.
3 letters attached (1) W.L. Holland to Mrs W. regarding his withdrawal: (2) W.L. Holland to Miss C. regarding his withdrawal and desire to be sure of Frank White's doctrinal position: (3) Mrs W. to W.L. Holland in reply to W.L. Holland's letter. 2 pages.
CBA 7187(10).

---

**21st May 1899. Mr Newton's final charge to his friends**
Recorded in a printed 'in Memoriam' card.
'Give my love to all, in the Circle of Christian Friends. Give them all fulness of love and to all of them; and tell them I commend them to God, and to those paths wherein they will find the Shepherd care of God. There are many obstacles in their way I know, which God, however, will in His good time remove; and say to them, that if I had my time over again, I WOULD MAINTAIN THE SAME TESTIMONIES THAT I HAVE DONE, ONLY MORE STRONGLY' [capitals in the printed item].
Copy in the CBA and reprinted on page 164 of *Teachers of the Faith and Future*, Second Edition. A copy of the card is given in *A Pictorial Memoir of Benjamin Wills Newton* – the supplement to this Guide. See the Advertisement at the end of this volume.

---

[1] Frank Henry White, born 15th April 1836. Died 20th March 1915. For a note on B.W. Newton's separation from Frank White's ministry at Talbot Tabernacle whilst he had his meeting at Bayswater, see E.J. Poole-Connor *Evangelical Unity*, p.31. See too MS book CBA Fry 1/1/1, p.45 regarding B.W. Newton's concern regarding Frank White's compromise. Biographical note on Frank H. White (without mention of the separation of Mr Newton from him) *Watching and Waiting*, August 1921, pp.51-53.

> 5th June 1899       **From Dr Arthur [J.W.] Dalzell**[1]    'Sunnyside', Rusthall[2]
> **To Col. [Rowland] Walkey**[3]
> Regarding Mr B.W. Newton's state, and his statements in his last illness. B.W. Newton's comments on the awfulness of a soul facing eternity unforgiven. His wanderings, but his unwavering faith.
> Transcript of letter CBA 7061, pp.1,1a; and 7049, pp.443,444.

## 26th June 1899. Death of B.W. Newton

### Undated, and of unknown date

ND       [From B.W. Newton]
   **To person unknown**
On the suretyship of Christ.
Transcript of letter CBA 7061, pp.21a-22

ND       From B.W. Newton
   **To person unknown**
Replying to enquiries regarding his doctrines, particularly regarding Christ's sufferings, and sending some of his publications to the recipient. 6 pages.
Transcript of letter CBA 7182(19).

ND       **From J.N. Darby**
   To Mrs B.W. Newton
Copy of a letter that is in J.N. Darby's hand
'My name I am sure cannot but be now painful to you, though I am not unmindful of kindnesses received, but I write having heard that Mr Newton is very ill…'. He asked her to communicate to him his desire for B.W. Newton's blessing 'and the Lord's mercy to be fully towards him', despite being unchanged in his public position, which he regarded as his duty. He wishes to be remembered to Misses Treffry and Amy Jane Toulmin. The letter is unfortunately undated, but refers to it as 'my duty after long delay' – possibly indicating that it was sent during one of B.W. Newton's bouts of illness in the 1860s or 1870s. 2 pages.

---

[1] Arthur John Wilson Dalzell (1864-1911). For more information regarding Dr Dalzell and his subsequent settlement in Australia, see the shortly to be published *Arthur J.W. Dalzell: B.W. Newton's Physician and the Kyneton Settlement* by C.W.H. Griffiths. A deeply flawed account both of Dr Dalzell and the Australian settlement is given in *Holy City': The Brethren Community at Kyneton, 1900-1911*, by Guy Featherstone: Brethren Historians and Archivists Network, BHR (2008) 5:2-24.

[2] Rusthall is two miles from Tunbridge Wells, where Mr Newton died and is buried. It is not known when he moved there from the Isle of Wight, but CBA 7064, p228 gives an account of a meeting with him in November 1898 where 'we here at Tunbridge Wells' is used.

[3] Rowland Walkey (1840-1928). Lieutenant Colonel, Royal Artillery (*Hart's Annual Army List, Militia List, and Imperial Yeomanry List*, 1891). Buried Heene Cemetery, Worthing where he resided in the latter part of his life. His gravestone gives his birth, death, and born-again dates.

CBA. Printed in Max C. Weremchuk, *John Nelson Darby*, 1992, p.224.

Also, see undated letter from S.P. Tregelles to B.W. Newton placed at 19th April 1864 in this *Guide*, and the undated letter from Mrs Anna Newton (his mother) placed at June 1847.

---

The 1901 Census indicates that Maria Newton (née Hawkins), his widow; Sophia Constantia Hawkins, his sister-in-law; a cook; and a 55 year old female companion were living at 2, Clanricarde Gardens, Tunbridge Wells.

Sophia Hawkins died at 2 Clanricarde Gardens, on 6th September 1904 aged 83. She was born at Hampton Court Palace, 1821.

Maria Newton died at 2, Clanricarde Gardens, on December 25th 1906 aged 91. She was born in Madras January 19th, 1815.

# SECTION 10

## DUPLICATED AND MANUSCRIPT ITEMS

Section 10 – Duplicated and Manuscript items

# DUPLICATED AND MANUSCRIPT ITEMS

This section records unpublished written materials in handwritten or duplicated form.

Letters, and manuscript copies of letters, are recorded separately in date order in Section 9, B.W. Newton Correspondence, with reference to where the letters are held.

Manuscript copies of published works (e.g.) are recorded in Section 3, B.W. Newton's Published Works.

The items from the Fry Collection donated to the Christian Brethren Archive in 1982 are available to the public and were catalogued by Susan Noble of the Royal Commission on Historical Manuscripts shortly after their accession. We have not attempted to duplicate or augment the Library's own catalogue of these items. The only exception we have made concerns The Fry Manuscript (CBA 7049). Because of its importance we have given an index of its contents.

We have given as full a record as possible of the contents of all the remaining items, including those items from the Fry Collection that were acquired by the Christian Brethren Archive in 2010.

## Contents of the Section

      A. Explanatory Note on The Fry Collection

      B. Items from The Fry Collection Donated to the Christian Brethren Archive In 1982

      C. Fry Collection Manuscript Items Recovered by the CBA in 2011

      D. Stirling Collection (now in the Christian Brethren Archive)

      E. The S.G.A.T. Collection

      F. Items held by C.W.H. Griffiths

      G. Items held by Tom Chantry

      H. Manuscript Items, the whereabouts of which are Unknown

Section 10 - Duplicated and Manuscript items

## A. EXPLANATORY NOTE ON THE FRY COLLECTION

The Fry Collection includes material from several sources. It consists of approximately 12,000 pages of manuscript notes in the Collection at the John Ryland University Library (CBA 7004-7082). Additional manuscript notes from the Collection are in the possession of Tom Chantry.

The Collection in its manuscript form derives mainly from F.W. Wyatt. There is no doubt that F.W. Wyatt, with his meticulous recording and copying, played a key part in its preservation. However, it is very likely that its earlier origins and organisation (and perhaps its collation after B.W. Newton's death) were strongly influenced by John Cox, jun. In the 1860s, and till his retirement in 1894, John Cox was Registrar to the Ecclesiastical Commission (the forerunner of the Church Commissioners). In that role, he was responsible for preparing and administering a vast filing system recording assets. The text from the catalogue entry for the Ecclesiastical Commissioners files reads, 'The series is numbered from 1 to 96,000 totally irrespective of subject and formed part of a highly centralised filing system which operated down to the creation of the Church Commissioners' in 1948. This numbering system was developed in the 1860's by John Cox and developed in conjunction with a series of letter books of outgoing letters arranged in a sequence of individually numbered letters which have not survived.' It is hard to imagine that, as a close associate his advice and help was not sought by B.W. Newton, or posthumously by F.W. Wyatt.

A.C. Fry preserved the collection and made some additions to it. His son C. Everit Fry later donated most of the Collection to the Christian Brethren Archive of the John Ryland Library of the University of Manchester. An account of the provenance of the Collection is given in T.C.F. Stunt, *From Awakening to Secession*, Appendix A, 2000.

Frederick William Wyatt[1] (3rd March 1842-1933), was born, christened, and spent his childhood in Romsey, Hampshire, with his brother Alfred and his younger sister. He was a watchmaker by trade, as was possibly his father. He first met B.W. Newton in 1875-1877 during B.W. Newton's 'seclusion' in Winchester.[2] He wrote to B.W. Newton on 21st December 1882, recounting his separation from the Brethren with whom he was then associated at Blandford (see Section 9, B.W. Newton's Correspondence). In the letter he considers the possibility of leaving Blandford. He subsequently moved to the Isle of Wight to be near, and later to assist, B.W. Newton. He acted as his private secretary, and as an amanuensis when Mr Newton lost his sight. He resided at Ryde. On the Isle of Wight he formed a close friendship with Alfred C. Fry. After B.W. Newton's death he conducted a ministry in the London suburb of Blackheath. He later resided at Blandford again, and possibly Tunbridge Wells. According to his obituary in *Watching and Waiting*, he became 'feeble minded' in old age.

While living on the Isle of Wight he took notes of addresses given by Mr Newton, and of conversations of a select group of friends with him. In the years that followed Mr Newton's death, F.W. Wyatt continued the work of preserving B.W. Newton's legacy, collecting, and transcribing notes of B.W. Newton's addresses. He also transcribed many original letters relating to B.W. Newton's early years at Oxford, and relating to J.N. Darby's controversy with him. A letter to A.C.

---

[1] A photograph of F.W. Wyatt is included in *A Pictorial Memoir of Benjamin Wills Newton* – the supplement to this Guide.
[2] CBA 7064 p. 29.

Fry, dated May 1912[1], refers to him having completed nine MS book volumes of transcribed notes, the first of which had lately been lent to A.C. Fry. Twelve numbered miscellany books were eventually completed, and several other unnumbered volumes. Much of the material of the Fry Collection consists of these carefully indexed notebooks, prepared by F.W. Wyatt. Examples of his notes and transcription are given in *A Pictorial Memoir of Benjamin Wills Newton* – the supplement to this Guide. See the Advertisement at the end of this volume. Notes of addresses and Scripture annotations by F.W. Wyatt and A.C. Fry are also in the collection. A photograph of him as an old man is also reproduced in the *A Pictorial Memoir of Benjamin Wills Newton*.

F.W. Wyatt was very meticulous in recording detail, and completely committed to the work, ministry, and message, of B.W. Newton. He compiled a Scripture index of 48 of his (B.W. Newton's) principal published works for his own personal use. This listed some 10,000 references. He also produced a subject index of B.W. Newton's works of a similar size (see Section 11, Indexes of B.W. Newton's Works). A letter A.C. Fry to FW. Wyatt (4th April 1918 – Letter 23) held by C.W.H. Griffiths confirms that F.W. Wyatt was also responsible for preparing for publication the 534 page *Lectures on the Epistle to the Romans*, based on notes of B.W. Newton's addresses over a 33 year period.

At F.W. Wyatt's death (or perhaps earlier, as F.W. Wyatt had mental weakness/dementia towards the end of his life), A.C. Fry became the custodian of his notebooks and other items.

B.W. Newton's widow had, in 1906, bequeathed to her executors and trustees 'all books, papers, manuscripts and documents (other than deeds, legal instruments and securities for money) and also all pictures, miniatures and photographs ...'.[2] It would appear that the trustees decided that the items were safest together in one collection on the Isle of Wight with A.C. Fry. In any event, C.T. Walrond, the principal executor, remained a close friend of A.C. Fry, and stayed with him from time to time.[3]

Alfred Charles Fry[4] (1869-1943) had assisted in the Sunday School at Mr Newton's meeting on the Isle of Wight, and acted as a colporteur for him on the island[5]. He later led a meeting at the Clifford Street Hall, Newport, Isle of Wight. In her will, Mrs Newton provided a regular annuity of £50 whilst he maintained the school and mission at Newport. As well as providing for their

---

[1] Letter held by C.W.H. Griffiths.

[2] See Section 12 of this Guide Miscellaneous Biographical Items E,5 for further details of Mrs Newton's will.

[3] See notes on Mrs Newton's will in Section 12, Miscellaneous Biographical Items. Information on C.T. Walrond and A.C. Fry's friendship from F.W. Wyatt letters held by C.W.H. Griffiths. A photograph of C.T. Walrond is included in *A Pictorial Memoir of Benjamin Wills Newton* – the supplement to this Guide.

[4] Alfred Charles Fry – Evangelist (Rosemary Stewart's memories of her grandfather) *Isle of Wight Family History Society Journal* February 2007. Obituary, *Watching and Waiting*, November/December 1943, and *Isle of Wight County Press*, 28th August 1943. For a remembrance of the Sunday School run by A.C. Fry at Clifford Street, Newport, I of W, see *Journal of the Isle of Wight Family History Society*, November 2006: The Fry Family in Newport, by Colin Jeffries. The Census record of 1891, is incorrect as it, states he was 24 then, giving a birth date of 1867. His granddaughter (Mrs Rosemary Stewart), and the SGAT obituary, give a birth date of 1869. His son, C.E. Fry confirmed his birthdate as 6th May 1869. According to a letter from C.E. Fry to Susan Noble, dated 30th June 1984, he attended Miss Hawkins's Sunday School and was converted at the age of 17. Income from his wife, and a legacy from Mrs Newton, supported him in his Christian work, but in 1918 he became a Rural Postman to support himself and his family. C.W.H. Griffiths placed a picture of A.C. Fry in the Christian Brethren Archive in 2002, courtesy of Rosemary Stewart. A portrait of A.C. Fry is included in *A Pictorial Memoir of Benjamin Wills Newton* – the supplement to this Guide.

[5] See Section 12, C.8 – Colportage records.

safekeeping, A.C. Fry copied extracts from Wyatt's notebooks into a large quarto MS volume, now at the Christian Brethren Archive, and catalogued as CBA 7049. This is often referred to as 'The Fry Manuscript'. At A.C. Fry's death the magazine *Watching and Waiting* commented, 'He has left a goodly volume of MSS. of B.W.N.'s life story, letters, and works, which we feel should be edited, and published. If anyone feels moved to pay the costs, it will be a worthy service to the memory of both the teacher and the pupil'. It appears that no-one offered to meet the cost of such a venture during World War 2. Extracts from it appeared in *The Evangelical* Quarterly in 1950 and 1954, and George Fromow quoted it in his *Teachers of the Faith and Future* (First Edition 1959). Use was made of the Collection, and, in particular, of the Fry Manuscript, by Harold H. Rowdon[1], F. Roy Coad[2], and Timothy C.F. Stunt[3]. Timothy Stunt compiled a list of the manuscripts in the Collection in 1962 (CBA 6998).

According to C.E. Fry[4] 'An important link in the transmission of some of the material was Charles T. Walrond, a civil engineer of Holland Park, London, who was Mr Newton's executor and publisher of his books. When he died, I think in the '30s, certainly after 1935, a lot of material came to my father'. As C.T. Walrond died in 1942, a year before A.C. Fry, the transfer of material must have taken place earlier, as A.C. Fry would have done little work on this newly acquired material. G.L. Silverwood-Browne apparently borrowed some of the material from A.C. Fry from April 1929 onwards[5], so perhaps the approximate date, although not the circumstance of Mr Walrond's death, was correct. The Collection was then stored in the loft of C.E. Fry's chemist shop in Newport after his father's death.

Dr Ulrich Bister (1948-2008) also visited Mr C. Everit Fry and offered to help him sort out the collection. He borrowed a number of items and took them to his home in Germany. Some of the items were not returned, and remained in Dr Bister's personal possession until his death. Some are still missing, including five irreplaceable volumes of S.P. Tregelles's Greek Testament with his own manuscript correcting notes.

Perhaps concerned at the apparent loss of important items (although always trusting Dr Bister's integrity) C. Everit Fry presented the collection to the Christian Brethren Archive (CBA) of the John Rylands University Library in Manchester, in September 1982. J.A. Green, who had encouraged the transfer, conveyed it to the Library.

A.C. Fry maintained a Gospel Mission, adhering to B.W. Newton's principle of decided separation from Brethrenism. However, his son took a different course. His first wife's family was from the Kelly branch of the Brethren, and he joined the Lowe-Kelly meeting on the Isle of Wight in 1950. Later, after the meeting broke up (c.1956), he joined the Open Brethren in Newport, Isle of Wight (later Bethany Evangelical Church)[6]. The interest shown in the Collection after the death of his

---

[1] Harold H. Rowdon, *The Origins of the Brethren*, 1967
[2] F. Roy Coad, *A History of the Brethren Movement* 1968
[3] Timothy C.F. Stunt, e.g. *Early Brethren and the Society of Friends* (Christian Brethren Research Fellowship 1970). This research item has been republished with some amendments as Chapters 1 and 2 of *The Elusive Quest of the Spiritual Malcontent: Some Early Nineteenth-Century Ecclesiastical Mavericks*, by T.C.F. Stunt., 2015.
[4] C. Everit Fry. Born 1908. Died 30 Dec. 1991. Letter from C.E. Fry to Susan Noble, 30th June 1984, in the possession of C.W.H. Griffiths.
[5] See Part F of this Section – Items held by C.W.H. Griffiths.
[6] Information from a letter to C.W.H. Griffiths 2nd June 1987.

father was largely from Brethren historians. The choice of the Christian Brethren Archive as a safe repository for the B.W. Newton material (despite Mr Newton being the subject to such opprobrium from the Brethren throughout his life) was therefore an inevitable, although strangely perverse, decision.

After Ulrich Bister's death, Ian Deighan purchased his huge personal library and archive. Most of the missing items were recovered, although some are now in private collections. Tom Chantry of Blackheath holds the important volumes of F.W. Wyatt's notes. A few of the items were purchased from Ian Deighan for the Christian Brethren Archive, and were thus re-united with the original Fry Collection.

C.W.H. Griffiths, during a visit to Mr C. Everit Fry in 1987, ascertained that miniature portraits of B.W. Newton, his father, and the two Hawkins sisters (one of whom was B.W. Newton's second wife) were in the care of Mr C.E. Fry's sister-in-law (née Lilian Irene Newcombe), wife of his younger brother Kenneth (born 1911 and died of meningitis in 1940). He visited her, and obtained photographs of these. The miniatures (apart from that of Mr Newton's father) were donated to the Christian Brethren Archive by her daughter (Mrs Rosemary Stewart) when her mother died in 2002. The miniatures were thus reunited with the original 'Fry Collection'. The miniature of B.W. Newton senior was sold at auction to an unknown buyer. See the note on these items in Section 12, Miscellaneous Biographical Items, and photographs of them in *A Pictorial Memoir of Benjamin Wills Newton* – the supplement to this Guide.

## B. ITEMS FROM THE FRY COLLECTION DONATED TO THE CHRISTIAN BRETHREN ARCHIVE IN 1982

It is beyond the remit of this *Guide* to compile a detailed account of the content of the Christian Brethren Archive Collection relating to B.W. Newton, or even of The Fry Collection. The definitive catalogue of the Fry Collection was made by Susan M. Noble of the Royal Commission on Historical Manuscripts in her *Report on Correspondence and Papers of Benjamin Wills Newton (1807-1899)*, reproduced for the John Rylands University Library of Manchester, 1984, 97 pages. This forms the basis of the indexing of the Fry Collection.

Susan Noble corresponded with C. Everit Fry regarding the authorship of the MSS, asking him to identify sample handwriting of different items[1]. The identification given then by C. Everit Fry may be of help to researchers. CBA 7092 Habakkuk = A.C. Fry. CBA 7073 Zechariah XI = A.C. Fry, 'He often semi-printed in his younger days, probably in the '90s'. CBA 7185 miscellaneous MSS include writing in several hands – Micah 7 is again F.W. Wyatt. The other sample of CBA 7185 she gave him, dated Dec 22nd /95, and CBA 7080 Psa. 62, 'could be my mother's, or possibly her mother-in-law's. They both attended Mr Newton's Bible lectures and took notes, I believe'. Samples of F.W. Wyatt's transcriptions and notes are given in *A Pictorial Memoir of Benjamin Wills Newton* – the supplement to this Guide. See the Advertisement at the end of this volume.

As well as the cataloguing of the collection itself by the Royal Commission, CBA 6998 should be noted, as an independent record made by T.C.F. Stunt in 1962, long before the collection was donated to the Christian Brethren Archive.

Many of the notes of B.W. Newton's ministry are in manuscript books that have been carefully indexed by the note takers, or by F.W. Wyatt. It would be a lengthy, but comparatively easy task to produce an overall index. It would be a great help to researchers if the Christian Brethren Archive were able to produce such an overall index at some point.

The following is a summary of the materials in the Fry Collection held at the Christian Brethren Archive of the John Ryland Library of the University of Manchester prior to 2010[2].

### Fry collection catalogue references of items directly related to B.W. Newton

    CBA 6999 - 7003    Indexes of Newton letters etc.
    CBA 7004 Letters [by B.W.N?] regarding R. Pearsall Smith.
    CBA 7005-7010a    Notes [by B.W. Newton?].

### Notes of lectures of B.W. Newton

    CBA 7006 - 7027
    7037,7038,7039,7041,7043,7045,7050(incl.),7055,7058,7059(incl.),7061(incl.), 7063(incl.), 7065(incl.),7066(incl.),7067(incl.),7069,7070,7072,7073,7074, 7080(incl.).

---

[1] Letter Susan Noble to C.E. Fry, dated 21st June 1984, and his reply dated 30th June 1984, both in the possession of C.W.H. Griffiths.
[2] Several of these MS books are referred to by these catalogue references, and quoted extensively, in T.C.F. Stunt, *From Awakening to Secession;* and in *The Life and Times of Samuel Prideaux Tregelles.*

## Copies of notes of B.W. Newton on the Bible, and on various issues

7028-7036, 7040, 7042, 7047, 7053, 7054(incl.) ,7056(incl.) ,7068(incl.), 7071(incl.), 7076, 7077, 7078, 7079, 7081, 7082(incl.).

## Various items

| | |
|---|---|
| 7046 | Thoughts on the Death of Captain Bird Allen (MS). |
| 7050 | Various letters + Draft of a tract (incl.) ['How B.W. Newton Learned Prophetic Truth']. |
| 7049 | Notes and collection by A.C. Fry for a biography of B.W. Newton. Letters and recollections, mainly, but not exclusively drawn from other items in The Fry Collection. Known as 'The Fry Manuscript'. See separate note in this section. |
| 7057(incl.) | The beginning of a proposed New Testament Greek lexicon. |
| 7057,7059(incl.)7060,7065(incl.), 7061(incl.) | Conversations F.W. Wyatt and B.W. Newton |
| 7062(incl.) | Conversations F.W. Wyatt, Dr [A.J.W.] Dalzell, and B.W. Newton |
| 7063(incl.) | Notes of meetings (of F.W. Wyatt?) with B.W. Newton |
| 7064(incl.) | Notes of meetings with B.W. Newton, F.W. Wyatt, Dr [A.J.W.] Dalzell, W.L. Holland between 2nd February 1895 and 18th November 1898 (mostly 1898). It has a 15p index of topics and Bible references. 311p. |

## Recollections of B.W. Newton

7065(incl.), 7066(incl.), 7067(incl.), 7068(incl.), 7082(incl.), 7185, 7187(9); 7187(10); 7187(47).

## CBA 7049

This 444 page document is sometimes called 'The Fry Manuscript'. It was produced by Alfred C. Fry, who was a colporteur for B.W. Newton. The following quotations describe the manuscript book in A.C. Fry's own words, 'This MS Book contains a collection of interesting things during the lifetime of the late Benjamin Wills Newton.... Apart from various letters from his mother and others, some of which relate to his early experiences with the Plymouth Brethren, most of the things recorded fell from his own lips and pen, and were taken down by his friend, the late Frederick W. Wyatt (of Blandford, Dorset) in a system of shorthand of his own, and copied out more fully by him in his old age. I have taken most of the things mentioned from F.W. Wyatt's MS books and put them up together as near as I could according to their dates... There is no thought in this book of preparing for publishing, but only collecting of material that it might not be lost. If someone more skilful than myself ever wished to publish that noble gentleman's life story they will find here much useful matter'. If it was originally A.C. Fry's intention to recount the whole of Mr Newton's life, the book does not really go beyond the end of Mr Newton's association with Plymouth and 'the Brethren'. A biographical account of the remainder of his life is lacking.

The Fry Manuscript (CBA 7049) is a collection of disconnected quotations derived from F.W. Wyatt's researches, notebooks of conversations with Mr Newton, and copies of letters. All of the material quoted was originally in the Fry Collection. All of the letters mentioned in CBA 7049 have been noted in the Section 9 of this *Guide* - B.W. Newton Correspondence. CBA 7049 provided a major source for H.H. Rowdon's *The Origins of the Brethren 1825-1850*, and the earlier sections of F.R. Coad's *History of the Brethren Movement*. The index to the book gives a sketchy outline of content, with some matters left unmentioned. A.C. Fry's headings are as follows. The index does not go beyond item 76, page 384. We have added the remaining headings.

1. Pedigrees of B.W. Newton, Miss Toulmin, and the Hawkinses.   pages 15 [sic]-25
2. Relatedness between B.W. Newton and S.P. Tregelles (& his works). pages 26-34
3. The Hawkinses.   pages 35-39
4. B.W. Newton – Marriages, birth, and infancy.   pages 42-45
5. – Going to school and Schoolmaster. Byrth.   pages 45-46
6. – Goes to Oxford, etc.   pages 56-60
7. – Tutors [William Sewell and Frank Newman].   pages 60-65
8. – Matriculates (Dec. 10 1824 Aged 16).   page 66
9. – Takes his Fellowship – wearing gowns.   pages 67-68
10. – Letter to his mother (16th October 1825).   pages 69-73
11. – Conduct etc. William Dalby. Sewell.   pages 73-74
12. – Elected Fellow of Exeter College (30th June 1826).   page 75
13. – In the University.   pages 76-83
14. – A valuable tract.   pages 84-94
    [Reprinted as *How B.W. Newton Learned Prophetic Truth*].
15. – and his friend Henry Bellenden Bulteel.   pages 95-124
16. – His conversion.   pages 125-128
17. More about Bulteel.   pages 129-137
18. Conversion of Bulteel.   pages 137-140
19. Mr Darby's first appearance.   page 139
20. Irving's error. Mr Douglas [T. Dowglass] (an Irvingite 'Angel' that B.W.N. knew).
    Page 141
21. B.W.N in Scotland.   pages 145-153
22. The Two Flocks by B.W. Newton [a parable].   pages 153
23. Casting Pearls before Swine – The New Covenant.   pages 159-160
24. 'Professorship' offered B.W. Newton [in Calcutta].   pages 166-176
25. B.W. Newton in Berlin – and Sibthorpe – Moody Stuart.   pages 176-183
26. Oxford 1829 – Nicholls – Pusey – Tractarians.   pages 184-187
27. B.W. Newton and India [offered Tutorship in Calcutta College].   page 187
    [Letters to his mother, etc.].   pages 188-192
28. Death of B.W. Newton's grandmother.   page 193
29. B.W. Newton – J. Newman – Gladstone – Pusey.   pages 194-233

## Section 10 – Duplicated and Manuscript items

30. B.W. Newton and Prophetic Truth [its first revival in 19th century].   pages 233-234
31. B.W. Newton and J.N. Darby.   pages 235-253
32. Beginnings at Plymouth – Captain Percy F. Hall.   pages 254-258
33. Mr [George V.] Wigram.   pages 259-266
34. [J.L.] Harris – [H.] Borlase – Douglas [T. Dowglass] [including various conversations]   pages 267-279
35. Early days at Plymouth.   page 280
36. Lady Powerscourt.   pages 281-287
37. Lord Roden.   page 287
38. Henry Borlase and *The Christian Witness*.   pages 288-293
39. About Plymouth beginnings.   pages 300-304
40. B.W. Newton's illness.   pages 304-306
41. Tregelles's (Tract) Christian Union.[1]   pages 307-308
    [+ Notes of conversations on various things].   pages 308-310
42. The Ministry of the Holy Spirit.   pages 310-315
43. Unworldliness in Plymouth.   page 315
44. Dr Riach. Sir Henry Rawlinson.   page 316
45. Triggs [member of Dr Hawker's congregation in Plymouth].   page 317
46. B.W.N.'s work in Exeter.   page 318
47. The storm in 1845.   page 319
    [The beginning of Darby's controversy with B.W.N.].
48. Darby's letters to Newton.   pages 320-324
49. Newton's reply.   pages 324-328
50. Letter from B.W.N. to Harris, Soltau, and Batten.   pages 328-331
51. A memorandum by B.W.N. on the beginning of Darby's attack   page 331
    on the brethren at Plymouth in 1845.
53. [*sic*] Another letter to Darby and Darby's reply.   pages 332-333
54. Newton's answer.   page 334
55. Darby's reply.   pages 335-336
56. Newton's answer and Darby's reply.   page 337
57. Newton's answer and letter to Mr McAdam.   pages 338-340
58. Newton's letter to Mr Harris.   pages 341-343
59. Harris to Newton announcing his breach.   pages 343-346
60. Newton's answer.   page 346
61. Two letters from Congleton and others to Darby.   page 347
62. Darby's reply.   pages 348-351
63. Their answer to Darby.   page 351
64. Darby's reply.   page 352
65. Clulow.   page 353
66. A Fragment – by B.W.N.   page 354
    [Regarding the efforts to subvert Plymouth].

---

[1] *The Blood of the Lamb and the Union of Saints* – withdrawn by Tregelles

## Section 10 – Duplicated and Manuscript items

67. A long letter by B.W.N. (on early Plymouth affairs). pages 356-362
68. Miss Jeremie's explanation [regarding Darby's *Letter to the Saints meeting in Ebrington Street*]. pages 363-365
69. 3 Letters from – Congleton – Robt. H. Rickards and W. Morris pages 365-367
70. Letter from Mr Rhind to Mr Soltau. page 368
71. Soltau's letter to Robert Howard. page 369-373
72. B.W.N. - to unknown [regarding *Doctrines of…Newman Street*]. page 373
73. Letter from Lord Congleton. page 374
74. E.K. Groves's book *A History of Bethesda* + Remarks by B.W.N. pages 375-379
75. Craik and important remarks on 'Relation' + 'Relationship'. pages 379-382
76. Dr Steane – Sidmouth and the Brethren. pages 382-384
[77. Douglas [T. Dowglass] - article wrongly copied a second time. See p.141] pages 384-386]
[78. Encouragements in the Sunday School work.[1] pages 386-388]
[79. B.W. Newton's address at Miss Toulmin's burial (1895)]. pages 437-439 [*sic*]]
[80. B.W. Newton's letter to John Cox (sen.) re-the death of B.W. Newton's daughter]. pages 440-444]

---

[1] C.W.H. Griffiths has the original of this. It is headed 'Duke Street Chapel, St James' Park, 1856' and 'Encouragement in the Sunday School Work'. See Part F of this section.

## C. FRY COLLECTION MANUSCRIPT ITEMS RECOVERED BY THE CBA IN 2011

1. **Notebook of B.W. Newton's Addresses and Conversations copied by A.C. Fry**

   Catalogued as FRY/1/1/1. Photocopy held by the SGAT. 132 pages.

   Probably from F.W. Wyatt's notebooks. It probably preceded his writing of 'The Fry Manuscript' (CBA 7049). It includes a list of dates to 1847.

   Contents
   1. The last words of B.W. Newton to his circle of Christian friends.
   2. Lessons on the Tabernacle. [July 6, 1901. By A.C. Fry].
   3. Psalm 73:10. 'Therefore his people'.
   4. The Greek prepositions προς, μετα, συν.
   5. Burial Places of the Patriarchs.
   6. Fasting.
   7. The Authority of Scripture.
   8. King Saul.
   9. David, and the Lame and the Blind - 2 Sam. 5:8.
   10. Leaven. 1 Cor. 5 and Hebrew. Newton's examination at Oxford.
   11. Our legal oneness with Adam – Augustine, Owen, Calvin, Cunningham.
   12. Lecture on Philippians 1. [Sept. 30 1889].
   13. Lecture on Romans 5 and 6. [Evening Sept. 30 1889].
   14. Christ made sin, and legal oneness ['before 1884'].
   15. The blood of the Lamb cannot be the basis of unity (referring to Tregelles's tract[1]).
   16. Psalm 47. One of our midnight songs.
   17. [Conversations at Newport. Messrs [T.G.] Graham, [John] Adams, [B.W.] Newton, and F.W. [Wyatt]].
   18. 1 Cor. 9:21. The Law, the Church and Israel, now and in the Millennium.
   19. The limits of the Roman Empire, [General C.G.] Gordon, Ishmael.
   20. A Reformation needed. A Gentilised message, Bishop [M.S.] Alexander[2].
   21. Isaiah 45:8 and the Millennium.
   22. Joel 2:21-23. The Pearl Testimony[3] and our Testimony.
   23. Conversations [John] Adams, F.W. Wyatt, B.W. Newton.
   24. Psalm 110.
   25. Jeremiah cursing the day of his birth.
   26. Jews in Jerusalem and the Pearl Testimony [see 22. Above].
   27. Titus 3:5. The Washing of Regeneration.
   28. The Old Testament Saints part of the Church.
   29. True Circumcision. Darby's arrival at Plymouth.

---

[1] *The Blood of the Lamb and the Union of Saints.* S.P. Tregelles's regret at having published the tract is recorded in CBA 7049, pp.302,303,307.

[2] See the 1904 Supplementary Note added to the Note on Rev. 11:8 in the Third Edition of *Thoughts on the Apocalypse,* commented on in Appendix 1 of this Guide, A Comparison of the Editions of *Thoughts on the Apocalypse.*

[3] Regarding the 'Pearl Testimony', see NM 10 in Section 8, Publications Produced from Notes of Addresses, and Posthumously Published Letters and Manuscripts.

30. Our 'impossible principles'. Breaking the link of co-operation. Frank White.[1]
31. Man does not have natural power to turn to God. Rom. 3.
32. God's Justice in Election.
33. Jonathan Edwards.
34. Note on General Gordon.
35. Luke 22:37. Healing and miracles. [Newport, February 21st 1884].
36. Ezek. 36:26. The Stony Heart.
37. 1 Cor. 2. The Character of ministry, 2 Cor. 5 and 6, Henry Drummond [22 February 1894].
38. Legal oneness. Being made sin. An exchange of imputation 2 Cor. 5:21.
39. Hyper Calvinists: Col. 1:27: 2 Pet. 3:9: 2 Tim. 3:16: Rom. 5:12.
40. Principles of Hezekiah.
41. Texts of Scripture that teach man's responsibility.
42. A Conversation with Mr Newton on the Doctrinal Controversy at Plymouth: Bethesda.
43. E.K. Groves's book. Christ in the Psalms. [1885].
44. A Conversation on Holiness. [between G[raham], N[Newton], and S[tirling?].
45. Mr Newton's reminiscences of his days at Oxford, visit to Scotland, etc.
46. Stealing Israel's blessings and claiming them for the Church. Newman, Darby etc.
47. Reminiscences of 1836, Powerscourt, and ministry at Plymouth. [June 1885].
48. A parallel account of 1836.
49. Rome, Irving, and Darby seeking a Body on earth with an authoritative voice.
50. The Christian Witness. Early stages of controversy with Darby. Capt. Wellesley.
51. Beginnings at Plymouth. [April 1885].
52. Another account, Hall, Wigram, the error of taking a false position, etc.
53. Trigg of [Robert] Hawker's congregation in Plymouth.
54. [Joseph] Wolff the Jewish missionary.[2]
55. The Oxford Tractarians, Newman, Sewell as his tutor.
56. Gifts of the Spirit, Irving, Hall, Bulteel.
57. Conversation with Craik – [Horatius] Bonar, [George] Smeaton.
58. Christ never endured damnatory wrath in his life time.
59. A conversation on involvement with civil government, application of prophetic truth,
60. Darby's attack on *Thoughts on the Apocalypse*. Habakkuk. [2nd June 1885].
61. The Sufferings of Christ in the Psalms. The view of [J.G.] Bellett and the Brethren.
62. Dr Riach, Sir Henry Rawlinson, Mr Newton and the invitation to India. [June 1885].
63. Clulow, the Tract Depot, the gift of 'governments' (1 Cor. 12:28).
64. Lord Roden [Second Earl], and principles of civil magistracy.
65. Dr [E.B.] Pusey.
66. Admiral Sir James Hawkins Whitehead – Mrs Newton's uncle.
67. William Pitt the Younger and Catholic Emancipation.

---

[1] Frank Henry White, born 15th April 1836. Died 20th March 1915. For a note on B.W. Newton's separation from Frank White's ministry at Talbot Tabernacle whilst he had his meeting at Bayswater, see E.J. Poole-Connor *Evangelical Unity*, p.31. Biographical note on Frank H. White (without mention of the separation of Mr Newton from him), *Watching and Waiting*, August 1921, pp.51-53. CBA 7064 p8 highlights a point of difference as Frank White not accepting the Pearl Testimony teaching (perhaps a comment by F.W. Wyatt).

[2] CBA 7064, p45. 'The best convert I knew from Judaism was Wolff'.

68. God's object in granting greater prophetic light – ruined for the present.
69. Dr Malan of Broadwinsor[1] – in relation to Pusey and Tregelles.
70. Seraphim.
71. Demonic agency - Newman, hymns, the Crusades, Bulteel, testing the supernatural.
72. Demonic activity in the Magicians of Egypt (Exod. 7:11, 12), and in the Pythoness of Acts 16.
73. [C.T.] Walrond's family.
74. A threefold curse on Spain: Spaniards [Nicolas] Alonzo and Mora; [William] Green[e].
75. Corporate Church-standing, 1 Tim. 3:15. Early unity at Plymouth. [Vol. 3 p.81].
76. When did Christ become the Second Adam? Mic. 5:2, Brethren views, F.[W.] Newman.
77. Bonaparte, Mr Newton's childhood games, etc. [Vol. 9 p.161].
78. Mr Newton's work at Exeter.
79. Second copy of 'Corporate Church-standing'. [Vol. 3, p.181].
80. Key early dates to 1847.
81. A.C. Fry's index of the book.
82. Another listing of key early dates.

2. **F.W. Wyatt's notebook, which copies original letters relating to S.P. Tregelles, listed in CBA 7181 (lost from the original Fry Collection).**

This 142 page notebook contains copies of 106 letters from 18th January 1846 and 29th April 1866. The majority, but not all of these, relate to B.W. Newton, and are listed in the correspondence section of this *Guide*. See too the notes regarding CBA 7181 at the beginning of the section on Correspondence. Recovered by the Christian Brethren Archive in July 2011, and catalogued as FRY/1/1/4.

3. **Autobiographical MS book in B.W. Newton's own hand, mainly describing the nature of the work at Bayswater, and the events around the closure of the Bayswater meeting.**

Dated (by F.W. Wyatt?) c.1877. 'I explained publicly and in private what my position was. I said that I stood in Bayswater Chapel as in a place that was as completely under my own control and management as was my own house; that all that I professed to do was to endeavour to unfold the Scripture from time to time to Christ's people, and to afford an opportunity to all who desired it of gathering without distinction of sect or party, around the Lord's Table – that I did not profess to gather into what is commonly called Church organisation – that I would have no officers (such as elders, deacons or the like,) nor attempt to appoint any to any official position – that I made no demand upon the constant adherence to me of those who came either to the Chapel or to the Lord's Table – that I wished to receive all Christians'.[2]

---

[1] Solomon Caesar Malan (1812 –1894). Son of Dr Henri Abraham César Malan of Geneva. Broadwinsor (or Broadwindsor) is in Dorset.

[2] It appears that John Cox (jun.) attempted to continue the Bayswater work, and this caused a great deal of difficulty to Mr Newton. See CBA 7064, note dated 13th September 1897, p56 and 57.

It includes copies of letters to Mrs Hurst, and to Rev. Bennett of Ashbourne, Derbyshire[1], an extract of a letter to Ker Baillie Hamilton, and a draft(?) of a letter to [S] Bloxsidge regarding the birth of his [S. Bloxsidge's] child.

45 pages. Recovered by CBA in 2011 (FRY/1/1/3), having been lost from the original Fry Collection. A photocopy is held by the SGAT.

4. **'The Famous Appendix' to B.W. Newton's 'Five Letters…'**

Manuscript copy of most of the letter to J.N. Darby (1840-41) in Mr Newton's hand, but without the specific reply to each of J.N. Darby's points.

It concerned 'the Tares' of Matthew 13, and was a reply to J.N. Darby's objections to *The Five Letters…*. This formed what J.N. Darby referred to as 'the famous appendix' to *The Five Letters…*, circulated by Miss Jeremie, and later published with them in the 1847 edition to which S.P. Tregelles wrote a preface.[2]

Now in the CBA, catalogued as FRY/1/6/6. A transcript and photocopy is held by the SGAT.

5. **Note on Mr Newton's relation to the Quakers**

One page manuscript note and family tree by A.C. Fry (or F.W. Wyatt?) regarding the Society of Friends, and B.W Newton's family relation to Samuel Lloyd (son of the founder of Lloyd's Bank). Obtained by CBA July 2011 (CBA FRY/1/2/17). A copy of this is given as an example of F.W. Wyatt's notes in *A Pictorial Memoir of Benjamin Wills Newton* – the supplement to this Guide. See the Advertisement at the end of this volume.

6. **Note on the Sufferings of Christ**

This is an undated six page document in Mr Newton's own hand. There is a note in F.W. Wyatt's hand on it 'Valuable. A fragment (untraced)'.

It addresses the central issue of the final controversy with J.N. Darby - whether all Christ's life sufferings were vicarious, or only those experienced on the Cross. He distinguishes four classes of sufferings that Christ endured. Added to the CBA in July 2011. A transcript by C.W.H. Griffiths (although the manuscript writing is difficult, and subject to a little uncertainty in places) is held by the CBA (FRY/1/2/16). A copy of the transcript is also held by the SGAT.

7. **Rough Notes and Calendars prepared by F.W. Wyatt and A.C. Fry**

A synthesis of the contents of these lists has been made by C.W.H. Griffiths, and is held by the CBA (FRY/1/2).

These were evidently made in the process of recording and organising the correspondence, and other items, in the Fry Collection. The 18 pieces of paper and larger sheets are the residue of materials recovered by the CBA in July 2011 from items that were in the original Fry Collection.

---

[1] Of September 1872? See Section 9, B.W. Newton's Correspondence.
[2] See J.N. Darby *Collected Writings* Vol. 20, p.19 – *Narrative of Facts*.

They are random, mainly rough, notes of the manuscript materials (chiefly correspondence). Most use date sequence, but some are in subject order.

Having been able subsequently to check MS Book 1 and MS Book 2, together with the original materials purchased by Tom Chantry, it became clear that a substantial part of the notes relate to MS Book 1. This was variously referred to in the 'Rough Notes' as, 'Red Leather Duodecimo Letter Book', 'Stamped Brown Leather Duodecimo Letter Book', 'Smooth Red Leather Duodecimo Letter Book', and 'Dark Red Leather Duodecimo Letter Book'. A possible explanation for the diversity may be that F.W. Wyatt bound several of these together to make MS Book 1.

We have therefore not made reference to these notes in this *Guide* where the items indicated have been located, unless the 'Rough Notes' suggest further information – for example on date or authorship.

These notes have been separately catalogued at the Christian Brethren Archive as items FRY/1/2/2 – FRY/1/2/15.

There are two further sets of Rough Notes, mainly relating to S.P. Tregelles's correspondence, headed 'Mr Cox's volume' (FRY/1/2/1). A list of the letters referred to in these, prepared by C.W.H. Griffiths, has been added to contents pages for the S.P. Tregelles's Correspondence book copied by F.W. Wyatt (FRY/1/1/4).

## D. STIRLING COLLECTION (now in the Christian Brethren Archive)

Mrs Mary E.J. Stirling and her husband were associated with B.W. Newton's Bayswater chapel and subsequently corresponded with him. They were members of the close circle of friends of B.W. Newton[1]. Mrs Stirling was a correspondent of A.C. Fry, and Louisa S. Riach. There is some evidence from the letters in the collection that she was involved in acquiring and distributing items by B.W. Newton.

As it was located there by C.W.H. Griffiths in 1988 …, this Collection is assumed to have been donated to Spurgeon's College by one of Mrs Stirling's sons. It consisted of two sets of B.W. Newton's works. The first, a five volume set, has the inscription 'Charles Goodbarne Stirling, with his mother's best love. Jan. 23: 1906'. The second set (perhaps his mother's, Mary E. Stirling, as her inscription is in Volume 7, *Thoughts of Parts of the Prophecy of Isaiah*) consisted of seventeen volumes. Volume 16 includes some rare items – e.g. several in German. When, during the course of this research, it was checked, a set of loose letters was found in the pages of its bound volumes. The Collection, books and MSS, were transferred to the Christian Brethren Archive in Manchester in 1995, after protracted negotiations. The books of the Collection are integrated into the Christian Brethren Archive's library. The MSS and letters of the Collection are in CBA Box 23(10).

The Collection included a bound set of B.W. Newton's principal works. The volumes were either for Mrs Stirling's personal use, or prepared by her for her son. An inscription in one of the volumes gives a comment on the manner of B.W. Newton's death. (see Section 12, Miscellaneous Biographical Items, E. Items Relating to his Death, etc, 1. Note by Mrs Stirling). Her collection of B.W. Newton's works shows an attempt to be as comprehensive as possible - it included a hand-written copy of two of Mr Newton's early tracts, tracts in German by him and the only copy of a children's tract *The White Robe*, ascribed by her to B.W. Newton. We have noted these items in Section 3 of this *Guide* - B.W. Newton's Published Works.

The Collection included personal correspondence relating to Mr Newton and his circle. Four letters directly relevant to this *Guide* are noted in Section 9, B.W. Newton's Correspondence.

The following manuscript item is unique to the Collection.

### Luke 18:15,16

This is written in Mrs Stirling's handwriting, and it ends 'B.W.N. Dec. 15. 1857'. It may be that Mrs Stirling has made a copy of notes of a meeting where Mr Newton preached at the presentation of children by parents. This appears to be the case, as the item is unpolished, and there are some loose ends in its statements. It very specifically refers to the circumstances, 'This is the reason why I have asked you to assemble today…' (p.12).

---

[1] A letter in the Stirling Collection from Louisa Riach refers to Mrs Stirling's parents meeting B.W. Newton in the West Highlands, and then commencing a long friendship with him, possibly much earlier in the nineteenth century. Mrs Stirling was the wife of Rev. C.E. Stirling, formerly vicar of New Maldon and Coombe, Surrey, and mother of W.H. Stirling, who emigrated to Australia in 1900 with Arthur J.W. Dalzell. W.H. Stirling's obituary, *Watching and Waiting* July/August 1961, p.353, and November/December 1961, p.385). W. H. Stirling met B.W. Newton in 1897 at Shanklin, Isle of Wight, when he was 27. Note also *A Companion to the Authorised Version of the New Testament*, 1900, compiled by A.J.W. Dalzell and W.H. Stirling and published by Lucas Collins, and the Kyneton Letter noted in Section 12 Miscellaneous Biographical Items, Reminiscences.

In the case of *Thoughts on the Death of Captain Bird Allen*, also copied in hand by Mrs Stirling, the publication details are given, which is not done here. The writer/ speaker maintained the salvation of unconscious infants on the basis of Rev. 20:12 and Romans 5:13 (see p.3 of the manuscript). The same argument for it, based on the same texts, is found in Mr Newton's *The Doctrine of Scripture respecting Baptism*, p.57.

The item is not an exposition of Luke 18, but is an address on a range of subjects relating to children. It touches upon infant baptism, the salvation of unconscious infants, the fallen state of the Church, the position of the child before God, and the responsibilities of parents. We can find nothing inconsistent with B.W. Newton's teaching elsewhere, although this would be the only evidence that B.W. Newton practised any such presentation of children to the assembly of believers.

We conclude that it is an account of an address by B.W. Newton. Probably a copy of notes of the address. There is no evidence that it was printed or published.

26 hand-written pages. CBA Box 23(10) with a transcript by C.W.H. Griffiths.

## E. S.G.A.T COLLECTION

See Section 2, Libraries and Collections, Sovereign Grace Advent Testimony, for further background information regarding the SGAT Collection. The most significant publications by B.W. Newton in the SGAT library (but not all the books in the SGAT store if there are copies available elsewhere with public access) are recorded in the list of publications - Section 3, B.W. Newton's Published Works.

Commenting on manuscript materials held by the SGAT, the Introduction of *Teachers of the Faith and Future*, by George H. Fromow stated, 'The Editor has volumes of MSS. and typescript, by B.W. Newton which he would gladly see published; such as Lectures on Matthew's Gospel; Lectures on the Acts of the Apostles; and Lectures on the Hebrews; beside many miscellaneous papers'. He also stated on page 41, 'We hold many letters from Mr Newton's numerous correspondents, among them, Lord Shaftesbury, whom he held in very high esteem; Alexander Haldane, Esq.[1]; Ker Baillie Hamilton, Esq., C.B...[2] his cousin, Miss Toulmin, and Pastor Frank White'. Mr Fromow bequeathed his large house in Chiswick, West London, to the SGAT. His wish was that, upon his death, the new SGAT secretary would live in the property, and continue to operate the Testimony from there. This did not happen. The problem of accommodating 50 years accumulation of papers and letters resulted in substantial bonfires, and only a small collection of key manuscript items were retained by the SGAT (along with copies of published books and tracts)[3]. Most of the documents and manuscripts to which Mr Fromow referred in his book must have perished. We are aware of no letters dating from the lifetime of B.W. Newton that have survived in the collection.

The following are the typescript and MS items held by the SGAT

1. **Lectures on the Epistle to the Hebrews**

    Volumes 1,2, and 3. Duplicated typescript.

    'Notes taken by Mr [Thomas Graham] Graham of Worthing'.[4]

    Continuous numbering. 915 pages. 26cm.

2. **Notes on Hebrews**

    A book of duplicated typescript notes which belonged to, and was evidently bound by, C.T. Walrond. It is undated. 164 pages. It has the description 'early Plymouth notes by Miss Jessie Johnson'.

---

[1] Alexander Haldane (1800-1882). Proprietor of *The Record*.
[2] Ker Baillie Hamilton, 1804-1889. Former colonial governor of Grenada, Newfoundland, and Antigua and the Leeward Islands. Buried in Tunbridge Wells. See *Dictionary of Canadian Biography*, Vol. 11. A portrait of him is included in *A Pictorial Memoir of Benjamin Wills Newton* – the supplement to this Guide.
[3] Keith Sheppard, who bought the house, was a lecturer colleague of C.WH Griffiths at the time and related the bonfires made by Mr Harvey, the then chairman. Stephen Toms, the SGAT secretary confirmed the account but said he was helpless to stop the wanton destruction of the records. At least the Fry Collection was safe elsewhere!
[4] Obituary of T.G. Graham, *Perilous Times*, January, February. March, April, and May 1906. Died 25th December 1905 aged 81 years. For further information regarding T.G. Graham and his work at Worthing see the soon to be published *Mr Newton at Worthing* by C.W.H. Griffiths.

It also contains other unconnected notes of a Lecture by Mr Newton on Hebrews 6:9. From MS notes by Mrs Rew. 5 pages separately numbered.

A further set of lecture notes on Isa. 6:1-5. From MS notes by Mrs Rew. Dated March 1878. 8 pages separately numbered. 26 cm.

According to an advertisement in *The Times* (28th March 1878) Mr Newton was giving lectures on prophetic Scripture every Thursday at the Christian Young Men's Association [sic] rooms, 48 Great Marlborough Street, Regent Street [London] at that time.

3. **Notes of Lectures**

A book of duplicated typescript notes that belonged to and was evidently bound by C.T. Walrond. The inscription inside is 'Notes of Lectures by the late B.W. Newton copied from a MS volume in the late Mr Bath's handwriting, which volume is in possession of Mr M. Barkey' – 'C.T. Walrond, 126, Holland Road, Kensington, London'. There is also a note indicating it was typed and bound in Witham in 1914.

- Ezek. 7 – Stafford Rooms, 14 June 1887, pp.1-10.
- Heb. 13 (pp.11-12), and Gen. 15, Stafford Rooms, 23 June 1887, pp.12-19.
- Encouragement to the study of prophetic truth, based on Zech. 12. Newport. 22nd September 1887. This lecture was also reproduced in *The Time of the End Series No.8*. However, although virtually word for word, there are differences - e.g. Time of the End No.8 omits comments on Zech. 12:7, and this book omits comment on Hos. 2 and Zech. 13, and is therefore considerably shorter. Either Mr Bath's handwriting must have been very difficult, there has been significant editing (but by whom?) or these are two accounts of the same lecture; if so, they are so close that they must have both been in shorthand. pp.20-30.
- Zechariah 12:6-14. This is a continuation of 'last week', but not reflected in *The Time of the End No.8*. 29th September 1887 – Newport, pp.32-41.
- Teaching on Hebrews 1, and the Quotations from the Old Testament – April 1887 – Newport, pp.42-51.
- Hebrews 2:1-8. Sunday morning, 25th September 1887, (Newport), pp.52-58.
- Jeremiah 1 (pp.59,60), and Heb. 2:8-17– Sunday evening, September 1887 (Newport), pp.60-63.
- Genesis 1:1,2,14, and 2:5 – Wednesday 28th September 1887 (at Miss Wright's), pp.64-66.
- Jeremiah 18:15 - end. Sunday morning, 2nd October 1887, pp.67-77.
- Rev. 10. Sunday evening 2nd October 1887 (Newport), pp.78-81.
- Rev. 10-12. Thursday 6th October 1887 (Newport), pp.82-90.
- Psalm 119. Sunday morning 9th October 1887 (Newport), pp.91-100.
- Psalm 73:22, pp.101-102, and Acts 16:6-8, Sunday evening 9th October 1887. Place not given pp.102-106.
- Zech. 12, 13, and Rom. 11 – Thursday 13th October 1887 (Newport), pp.107-112.

- Rom. 15:16 linked to Lev. 23. The New Meat offering. Sunday morning 16th October 1887 (Newport), pp.113-120. Compare Patmos Series 29. The New Meat Offering.
- Rom. 1:1-7. Sunday evening 16th October 1887 [no place], pp.121-129.
- Isa. 22. Thursday evening 20th October 1887 [no place], pp.130-135.
- 1 Cor. 1:4-18. Sunday morning 23rd October 1887 [no place], pp.136-141.
- Heb. 9:24 -10 end. Sunday evening 23rd October 1887 [no place], pp.142-152.
- Psalm 10 and Imputed Righteousness. 8th November 1887. Stafford Rooms, pp.153-162.
- Jer. 45 and Baruch. (pp.163,164), and Gen. 12 – note on Irvingism and Brethrenism (pp.164-173). 15th November 1887 - Stafford Rooms.
- 3 days (John 1 35,36,43, and 2:1). Includes reminiscences and comments on Irving, Darby, [(Irvingite Apostle) Nicholas] Armstrong[1], [Henry Bellenden] Bulteel, [George Hawkins] Pember. 24th January 1888 – Stafford Rooms, pp.174-184.
- Zech. 5 - the Flying Roll (pp.185-187), 1 Peter 3:18-20 (pp.187-188), and Laying on of hands (pp.189,190) [no date or place]. [MS Book 1 (TC) includes F.W. Wyatt's copy of the item on the Laying on of Hands].

4. **Lectures on Matthew**

   Typescript. Volumes 1 and 2. 'Copied from notes by MCF'.
   Continuous numbering. 768 pages. 26cm.
   This appears to be substantially the same twin volume set as that held by C.W.H. Griffiths. See Part F. 1 below in this Section.

5. **Retranslations of various portions of Holy Scripture extracted from the works of the late B.W. Newton**

   Typescript.
   Note that *Perilous Times* (June 1915 pp.126,127) gives a translation of Isaiah 53 compiled from *Isaiah 53, Considered: Being an Extract From a Work Entitled 'Thoughts on Scriptural Subjects'*.
   Lucas Collins? 52 pages. 26cm.

6. **'Rough notebook. Conversations and notes re - B.W. Newton'**

   Handwriting not identified. The notes are variously dated in 1897.
   A photocopy has been provided to the Christian Brethren Archive.
   Approx. 80 pages. 18cm

7. **Genealogy of B.W Newton's family**

   This book consists mainly of *The Herald and Genealogist*, August 1867, bound in with which, and interleaved, are a number of hand drawn family trees, and other handwritten material. The issue of *The Herald and Genealogist* has significant material concerning the name 'Newton'. The

---

[1] See T.C.F. Stunt *From Awakening to Secession*, p.259 n.71 and index for more information regarding Nicholas Armstrong (1801-1879), and B.W. Newton's securing Magdalen Hall for him to preach in Oxford in 1831.

book bears the title on the spine 'Newton, Wills and Calmady Pedigrees'. Its handwritten inscription is 'Maria Newton with the affectionate love of her cousin Amy J.T. Toulmin'.

Note: the Fry Manuscript (CBA 7049) also has an account of B.W. Newton's genealogy.

In addition to these items, photocopies of materials have been provided to the SGAT by C.W.H. Griffiths from the 'missing items' of the Fry Collection, following his purchase of these, and prior to their transfer to the Christian Brethren Archive in 2011. See Part C, Fry Collection Manuscript Items Recovered by the CBA in 2011, in this Section.

## F. ITEMS HELD BY C.W.H. GRIFFITHS

1. **Lectures on St Matthew by B.W. Newton**

   Volumes 1 and 2. Continuous numbering. 744 pages. 26cm. Typescript.
   There is no indication of ownership or provenance, apart from a typescript note at the end of volume 2 'copied from notes of MCF'. This may, however just refer to the final item. This is not a continuous exposition, and there are parallel expositions of some chapters. The core studies in the book appear to be a weekly series that ran weekly at least from January to May 1852. Not all of the items are dated. The earliest is dated 1st June 1847 (on Matt. 15 and 16), and the latest November 1862 (on Matt. 6). The last section (10 pages), after the exposition of Matthew, is on 'The Kingdom of Heaven'. This is headed 'A few thoughts expressed at a reading meeting in Plymouth on "The Kingdom of Heaven"'. Page 301 (ending notes on Matthew 10), has 'Miss Freeman's notes'. A letter from S.P. Tregelles at Plymouth dated 4th April 1866 (see Section 9) refers to a Miss M. Freeman (=MCF?).

2. **Clifford Street Sunday School Log Book**

   Manuscript book received via C.E. Fry. Notes attendances. Commences, '<u>1888</u>. Sunday April 29th. Clifford Street Sunday School was opened at 2 p.m. Miss Brooks [the Superintendent], and Miss Hawkins were present. Eleven children attended'. Brief weekly records continue until Sept. 6th 1896.[1]

3. **Encouragement in the Sunday School Work**

   A message delivered at 'Duke Street Chapel, St James' Park 1856'. This manuscript item was received via C.E. Fry. Two pages of the eight and a half pages of notes are transcribed in CBA 7049, the Fry Manuscript, pp.386-388. The notes state, 'At the first place at which I ministered in London a few years ago, there was a small Sunday School established in connection with that congregation'.

4. **Manuscript books transcribed by G.L. Silverwood Browne**

   These are believed to have been copied from items in the Fry Collection through Mr Silverwood-Browne's acquaintance with Alfred C. Fry. All are in the handwriting of Mr Silverwood-Browne. There are other notebooks, not listed here, believed to be notes of addresses by A.C. Fry or F.W. Wyatt, 1903-1910, which are transcribed in A.C. Fry's hand (?). The manuscript books were given to C.W.H. Griffiths by Mr Silverwood-Browne in 1992.

---

[1] For a remembrance of the Sunday School as later run by A.C. Fry, see *Journal of the Isle of Wight Family History Society*, November 2006: The Fry Family in Newport, by Colin Jeffries. Note also the obituaries in *Watching and Waiting*, November/December 1943, and *Isle of Wight County Press*, 28th August 1943. Mrs Newton's will indicates that Miss Hawkins, her sister, started the Sunday School. In a letter from C.E. Fry to Susan Noble dated 30th June 1984 in the possession of C.W.H. Griffiths, he stated that his father (A.C. Fry) attended the school run by Miss Hawkins, whilst Mr Newton was at Clatterford House, Carisbrooke. The surviving correspondence of B.W. Newton indicates he was there between 1873 and 1875. If so, the Sunday School must have re-started in 1888.

### 4.1. Book titled 'Lecture Notes and Works Now Out of Print'

Small MS book. Copied from 30th March 1930 - 18th March 1934. Approx. 180 pages. Transcribed between 12th Feb. 1932, and 8th March 1934

- Church Principles.
- Counsels to Converts.
- A Letter to R.W. Sibthorpe.
- Thoughts on the Death of Capt. Bird Allen.
- Notes of a Lecture on 1 Tim. 2. BWN – 'from notes of N.J. Heywood'
- Notes of a Lecture on Luke 22 and Phil. 2. BWN.
- Notes on the Ministry of the Spirit. When the word Presidency is used in relation to the Holy Spirit in what sense it is used [page headed 'Patmos Series 37'].
- Notes of a Lecture on Psalm 3. BWN – 'Notes from Mr Newton taken by C.G'.
- Notes of a Lecture on Ruth 1. BWN. Dated in the MSS '27th November 1870'.
- Notes of a Lecture on Micah 4 and Dan. 2. BWN – 'Westbourne Hall. 1st Lecture. March 26th 1861'.

### 4.2. Book labelled on spine 'B.W. Newton Lectures' (SB 6) and inside 'not published'.

Small MSS book. Transcribed between 19/3/34 and 27/3/68. 183 pages.

- Hebrews 11:1-7 - 'August 10th 1851'
- Exodus 30:12 to end – 'Feb. 3rd 1856'
- A Lecture on Ministry Eph. 4:11-16. 'Nov. 20th 1845 rep. by Kate Gidley, Regent Street, Plymouth' includes an observation by Mr Soltau.
- A Lecture on Phil. 1. 'Dec. 31st 1845 rep. by Kate Gidley, Regent Street, Plymouth'
- Notes. Lecture on Ministry. Mr Soltau. 'Rep by A.J. Toulmin Nov. 24th 1845'
- Notes. Lecture on Psalms 24-25. 'taken down from Mr Newton's lecture early (no date)'
- A Letter from BWN not before published. 'Isle of Wight. October 2nd 1890'
- The Blood that Saveth.
- How does the Blood Save?
- Acceptance with God.
- Notes on Psalm 110 'same as Time of the End Series No.7' dated 'BWN 20th Feb. 1886'.
- Notes on Psalm 91. 'BWN. 22nd October 1871'.
- Leviticus 16.
- Ezek. 36:26.
- Matthew 11:12.
- Matthew 19:28.
- Matthew 16:14-19.
- Gen. 12:6 and 13:14-15 'BWN March 1854'.
- How BWN learned prophetic truth.
- Thoughts on Psalm 138. 'Notes of an exposition given by B.W. Newton July 1870'.

### 4.3. 'B.W. Newton Matthew' on the spine (SB 7)

Small MS book. Inside notes read 'BWN's private lectures not published' 'Probably 1847' (Note on Matthew 5 is 'March '47' and on Matt. 5, April '47'). Note after Matt. 6 reads 'Mr Fry regrets that there are no notes on Matt. 7 to hand', otherwise the notes run consecutively from Matthew 1-13. 198 pages.

### 4.4. Larger Green Manuscript Book (SB 5)

Headed inside, 'Notes of Lectures by Benjamin Wills Newton, M.A.' and dated '7/29'. Approx. 210 pages.

- Heb. 11:23-40; Jere. 20; and Zech. 6.
- Isaiah 53:3.
- Isaiah 54:55.
- Eph. 1:13-23 etc. Part 1 and Part 2.
- Psalm 4 (with pencil note 'already? pub. WW'). Dated 'Dec. 8th 1872'.
- Psalm 73 (with pencil note 'already? pub WW'). 'Notes of a Lecture del. in the I of W on March 31st 1872'.
- Psalm 138 (with pencil note 'already? pub WW'). 'imperfect. July 1870. E.W.'.
- Ezekiel 1 & 2.
- 2 Chronicles 35.
- Hos. 2.
- Amos 3
- Amos 5:4-13.
- Haggai 2:11, 13.
- Ruth 1 (Pearl Testimony[1]). Dated Nov. 27 / 1870.
- Exodus 40:17- end. Dated 1885.
- Address. Revelation 1. 'Address August 1892 – Notes taken by F.W. Wyatt'.
- Address. Rev. 10 is like Isa. 1 'Saturday May 13th 1893'.
- Address. Isa. 30:8 'Address. Sunday Morning May 14th 1893 Shanklin'.
- 2 Cor. 2:18 'A fragment, the beginning of an address. May 1893'.
- Conversation on 2 Cor. 2:18 with F.W. W[yatt] 'after the above'.
- Acts 16. 'Sunday morning. 28th May 1893'.
- Psalm 7:1-6 (note). 'Recollections written afterwards 28th May 1893 on Sunday in Shanklin'.
- Lam. 3:22 (an address). 'Sunday June 4. 1893. Shanklin'.
- Notes on the Priesthood of Believers. 1 Pet. 2:5. by James Lovell.
- Prophecy its importance and general scope – John Cox [jun.] (cutting).
- The Sacred Calendar of the History of Redemption (hand drawn table on the Jewish Year with notes).

### 4.5. Notes on Psalm 91 by Benjamin Wills Newton

- Stitched manuscript sheets. 9 pages. at the end 'B.W.N. 22nd October 1871'.

---

[1] Regarding the 'Pearl Testimony', see NM 10 in Section 8, Publications Produced from Notes of Addresses, and Posthumously Published Letters and Manuscripts.

**4.6. Thoughts on Psalm 138. Notes of an Exposition given by B.W. Newton July 1870**

- Stapled sheets, 9 pages.

**4.7. Thoughts on Psalm 4. Notes of an exposition given by B.W. Newton, December 8th 1872**

- Stapled sheets. 8 pages.

## G. ITEMS FROM THE ORIGINAL 'FRY COLLECTION' HELD BY TOM CHANTRY

Tom Chantry of Blackheath, London[1] was able to purchase a substantial part of the correspondence relating to B.W. Newton, two important manuscript books[2], and several other items relevant to this *Guide*, when Ian Deighan sold part of Ulrich Bister's Collection in 2011. These are held in his private collection.

He kindly allowed access to these to enable this *Guide* to be complete.

The original letters held by him are noted in the Correspondence section.

The two manuscript books contain copies by F.W. Wyatt of letters and other items. We have not prepared a separate list of the letters copied into the two Manuscript books, but have recorded the copies in Section 9, B.W. Newton's Correspondence. Timothy Stunt noted most of the letters copied in F.W. Wyatt's MS Book 2 in 1962 (CBA 6998).

Some of the material in these books was further copied by A.C. Fry (CBA 7049 - the Fry Manuscript), and noted as 'MS Book 1' and 'MS Book 2' by him.

Subsequent to the visit to Tom Chantry's home in 2012 to access the materials he has, several of the Fry Collection manuscripts that he acquired have now been scanned and posted on his website, https://www.brethrenarchive.org/. He can be contacted at tomchantry@gmail.com.

1. **Manuscript Book 1**

    The following items are copied in MS Book 1:
    - An item on *Original Sin: Original Guilt: Original Condemnation: Original Corruption*. Dated 1887. F.W. Wyatt notes this is itself copied from a manuscript book, and may be incomplete, pages 79, 80.
    - *Notes of a lecture in Stafford Rooms, Titchbourne Street, April 19th 1881. Regarding the Earl of Beaconsfield's death*. Benjamin Disraeli (Lord Beaconsfield) died on 19th April 1881. B.W. Newton's lectures at Stafford Rooms were given on Tuesdays. The date of death, and the date of this weekly lecture, fell on the same day, p.89.
    - Statement by B.W. Newton dated March 1877 – regarding his ministry at Duke Street and Bayswater. He states his object in ministering at Duke Street and Bayswater. It was not was not to form a church; 'all things are out of course'. This is attached to a letter to Amy J.T. Toulmin dated 14th May 1877, pp.120-126.

2. **Manuscript Book 2**

    Apart from copies of correspondence, F.W. Wyatt's MS Book 2 contains the following biographical material [the numbering is somewhat irregular with blank pages, etc]:
    - Bulteel (p.1).
    - University men – Nicholls, Pusey, Buckland, Macbride, Duke of Wellington (p.7).

---

[1] Tom Chantry can be contacted by email - tomchantry@gmail.com
[2] On their covers they are named MSS 2 and MSS 5, which are their numbers in the larger series of twelve MS books. See T.C.F. Stunt's note on 'The Fry Collection', Appendix A of *From Awakening to Secession*.

- Hahn, Sibthorpe and B.W.N., Jowett, Jacobson, Delane, B.W.N.'s Fellowship 1826, the Newmans, Watts, Andrew Bonar [states that Andrew Bonar was interested in prophecy before endorsing the 'lunacy' of the 1859 revival], Jonathan Edwards [and revival] (page 8).
- Rev. R. Treffry [Wesleyan minister] and B.W.N., Earl of Kintore, Death of T.H. Treffry, Miss Amy J.T. Toulmin, B.W.N. saw Great Storm 1824, Dr Fox and B.W.N. (p.9).
- Certificate of B.W.N.'s birth (p.10).
- Memo of B.W.N.'s mother when he was a child (p.14).
- 'Pedigree Chart' (p.19).
- Portraits painted by Miss Amy J.T. Toulmin (description), some quaint books, and B.W.N.'s early schooldays (page 32).
- B.W.N.'s grandfather and relations. Roger Treffry b. 1746 (p.91).[1]
- List of occurrences by Miss Toulmin [valuable summary of key dates], Soltau, Batten (pp.93-95).
- On Certificate of birth [see p.10], Conversation with the late Miss Emily Wright [See letter from S.P. Tregelles 26 July 1867, etc], conversation with B.W.N. (p.96).
- Napoleon on the [H.M.S.] *Bellerophon* (p.97).
- B.W.N. and S.P.T[regelles] – relatedness (p.99).
- Lady Powerscourt's meetings 1833 [from Craik's published diary. See A.C. Fry's secondary copy CBA 7049 p.281] (p.118).
- Dates in B.W.N.'s own handwriting, 1820, and some Fellows of Exeter College – B.W. Newton, William Dalby, Henry Bellenden Bulteel, James Lampen Harris, Macbride (p.119).
- Some verses by B.W.N. [poetry – not religious poetry!] (p.157).

3. **Notebooks containing notes of addresses**

Notebooks of Amy J.T. Toulmin of addresses [by B.W. Newton]. The notebooks are small, and in the small compact handwriting of Miss Toulmin.
- Matthew 4. 'Notes of an exposition of Matthew 4'. (25 pages).
- Mathew 5:3, dated April 1847. (32 pages).
- Matthew 5. 2nd part Tuesday evening lecture March 28 1847. (32 pages).
- Matthew 8. (31 pages).
- Matthew 13 'Notes of an exposition of Matthew 13'. (29 pages).
- The Psalms. 'Notes of a Lecture by B.W.N taken by C.G.' on Psalms 1 and 2. (41 pages).
- Hebrews 4:11 - 6:12. (23 pages) [Notebook in a different handwriting, and of a different size, although also of an address, presumed to be by B.W. Newton].

4. **A Manuscript stitched booklet.**

Titled, 'The Substance of a Lecture delivered at Duke Street Chapel, Westminster on Tuesday July 8th 1856 by Mr B.W. Newton'.
Concerning Leviticus 23:1-3. 5. 10. 15. 16. 24. 27. 34.
This chapter refers to 'the future history of Israel when the veil shall be taken away from their hearts…'

---

[1] See further note regarding him in CBA 7064, p67 and 68.

The cover is laid out as the frontispiece of a book. It is unclear whether this was a draft for publication (the writing, in an unknown hand, is in places very widely spaced), or a personal item, perhaps circulated. The content does not reflect any known publication.

Original. 96 pages.

5. **'A Brief Account of Mr Newton's Paper on the Doctrines of the Church in Newman Street' by S.P. Tregelles.**

    This manuscript is written in S.P. Tregelles's own hand. It is dated 8th November 1847 and 'was written in reply to a private inquiry, and not for publication'. It was, however, attached to the Second Edition of Newton's *A Statement and Acknowledgement Respecting Certain Doctrinal Errors* as an appendix when it was republished.[1]

    Original. This is listed in CBA 6998 1847 Folio 8.

6. **'Statements I Desire to Oppose'.**

    MS in Mr Newton's own hand.

    Original. Listed in CBA 6998 (1847 Folio 10).

---

[1] See further comment on this in Section 3, B.W. Newton's Published Works on *A Statement and Acknowledgement...*

## H. MANUSCRIPT ITEMS, THE WHEREABOUTS OF WHICH ARE UNKNOWN

1. **Miss Amy J.T. Toulmin's notes on Psalm 6.**

    CBA 6998 1847, folio 3, lists this as 'Copy by Miss Toulmin of notes taken by Miss Kate Gidley at N's address on Psalm 6'. These were therefore the notes used by J.L. Harris and C. McAdam to make their attack upon B.W. Newton. This item disappeared from the Fry Collection before Susan Noble catalogued the collection at the Christian Brethren Archive.

2. **'Original fragment from N's mother re-Lecture on Psalm 6'.**

    An item listed in CBA 6998 as '1847, folio 10', but now missing from the Fry Collection.

3. **Miniature notebook.**

    Manuscript notes in Amy Toulmin's hand of an address by Mr Newton on Matthew 5, dated March 1847. 46 pages.

    Not examined in detail. Possibly the basis of *The Sermon on the Mount: An Outline*, published by Hunt, Barnard.

    Current position unknown. Ian Deighan offered it for sale in 2011.

4. **Manuscript address on Hebrews 11:1-7.**

    Handwriting unknown. The address is dated 1851, and it is probably by B.W. Newton

    Current position unknown. Ian Deighan offered it for sale in 2011.

5. **Memorandum on Arianism.**

    August 1878. Presumed to be by B.W. Newton. Listed in the 'Rough Notes', but apparently no longer extant.

# SECTION 11

## INDEXES OF B.W. NEWTON'S WORKS

# INDEXES OF B.W. NEWTON'S WORKS

1. **Index of texts explained or referred to in the works of Benjamin Wills Newton**

    'Compiled by F.W. Wyatt for his personal use'.
    'Typed, duplicated and bound in July 1939' – as per *Watching and Waiting* of that date.
    This indexed 48 of B.W. Newton's principal post-1850 publications.

    1939   E.J. Burnett, Worthing.   25cm.              86 pages           SG

2. **Index of Scripture references in the works of B.W. Newton**

    This is virtually identical to the 'index of texts' compiled by F.W. Wyatt, and almost certainly was the basis for it.  Copy at SG

3. **Classified List and General Index of the Works of the late Benjamin Wills Newton**

    This printed book is independent of the indexes of texts produced by F.W. Wyatt.  It has less Scripture indexing.  It includes an index of subjects, names, and Scripture references, drawn from 55 post-1850 publications (some of which overlap in content).

    ?      Hunt, Barnard, Aylesbury         18cm              61 pages    CBA, SG

4. **Subject index to the works of B.W. Newton**

    Duplicated pages, but bound as a book.  The subject index is different from the index of subjects and names in Hunt, Barnard's 'Classified List'.  54 publications post 1850 are indexed.

    1910           Lucas Collins, London.   26cm              159 pages.         SG

5. **Supplementary subject index and index of texts**

    C.W.H. Griffiths has a MS subject index and Scripture index of works not included in items 1-4 of this section, compiled for his own use.

6. **Index of works derived from notes of addresses, letters, etc.**

    We have included in this *Guide* a short index of publications derived from notes of addresses, and posthumously published letters and manuscripts at the end of Section 8.

See also CBA 7001 for F.W. Wyatt's manuscript Scripture and Subject Index, which was the basis for some of these indexes.

A number of the Fry Collection MS books transcribed by F.W. Wyatt have Scripture and Subject Indexes of their contents, for example CBA 7064 has an index of 15 pages.

CBA 6999, 7000, 7001, 7002, 7003 are separate indexes prepared by F.W. Wyatt, totalling 245 pages.

# SECTION 12

# MISCELLANEOUS BIOGRAPHICAL ITEMS AND MEMORABILIA

# MISCELLANEOUS BIOGRAPHICAL ITEMS AND MEMORABILIA

There are six parts to this section:

- A. Biographical Records and Personal Effects
- B. Pictures
- C. Conduct of Meetings etc
- D. B.W. Newton as a writer
- E. Items relating to his Death etc
- F. Reminiscences

## A. BIOGRAPHICAL RECORDS AND PERSONAL EFFECTS

1. The Blackwell Dictionary of Evangelical Biography (1730-1860)
2. Genealogy of B.W Newton's family in the SGAT Collection
3. Census records
4. Birth certificate
5. First book
6. College rooms at Exeter College, Oxford
7. Association with missionary work at Oxford
8. Distribution by B.W. Newton of J.N. Darby's tract at Oxford
9. Guardianship of H.W. Soltau's younger brother
10. Personal Greek Testament
11. Frederick Prideaux's remembrance of B.W. Newton as his Greek tutor
12. Marriage certificate (second marriage)
13. Passport

## B. PICTURES

1. Sketch of B.W. Newton in his seventies
2. Pictures at the Christian Brethren Archive
3. Sketch owned by G.L. Silverwood-Browne

## C. CONDUCT OF MEETINGS etc.

1. The account of Rev. John Jackson of Taunton in 1844
2. Mr Newton at Bayswater in 1870
3. Mr Newton at Ryde, Isle of Wight 1893
4. Reminiscence from C.E. Fry (from his father A.C. Fry) to C.W.H. Griffiths
5. Advertisement of Meetings
6. Hymnbook used by B.W. Newton's meetings on the Isle of Wight
7. Isle of Wight Sunday School records
8. Isle of Wight Colportage records

## D. THE PUBLISHING OF B.W. NEWTON'S BOOKS

1. His publishers
   1.1 Early publishing
   1.2 Houlston:
   1.3 Lucas Collins
   1.4 Publishing by B.W. Newton's trustees
   1.5 SGAT and other publishing
2. Mr Newton's amendments to *Occasional Papers on Scriptural Subjects*
3. Mrs Newton's copy of *Thoughts on the Apocalypse* amended for the Second Edition
4. Advertisement of books

## E. ITEMS RELATING TO HIS DEATH

1. Note by Mrs Stirling
2. Obituaries
3. 'In Memoriam' card
4. Gravestones
5. B.W. Newton's will, and that of his wife
6. Answer to the suggestion that, before his death Mr Newton 'changed his views'

## F. REMINISCENCES

1. Published in *Perilous Times* and *Watching and Waiting* (17 items)
2. Kyneton letter, September 19th 1938
3. Reminiscence from C. Everit Fry to C.W.H. Griffiths

# Section 12 – Miscellaneous Biographical Items and Memorabilia

## A. BIOGRAPHICAL RECORDS AND PERSONAL EFFECTS

This section records information of interest that has generally not been noted elsewhere in this *Guide*. It is not the object of this section to enable the production of a biography or even to give a representative selection.

There is much biographical material in the Fry Collection transferred to the Christian Brethren Archive in 1982. We have not included that material in this section. A summary of the MS material that was transferred is given in Section 10, Duplicated and Manuscript Items, and copies of correspondence are noted in Section 9 of this *Guide*.

1. *The Blackwell Dictionary of Evangelical Biography (1730-1860)*

    This gives a concise, informative, curriculum vitae of B.W. Newton by T.C.F. Stunt.

2. **Census records**

    Relevant Census records exist for 1841, 1851, 1861, 1871, 1881, and 1891. We have noted some details from the Census in the historical sequence of the record of Correspondence in Section 9.

3. **Birth Certificate**

    B.W. Newton was born on 12th December 1807 at Dock in the parish of Stoke Damerel, Devon. Plymouth Dock was the former name of Devonport. His father (also Benjamin Wills), whom Anna Treffry had married on 23rd March 1807, had died on 1st December 1807, eleven days before the birth.
    This Certificate was recovered by CBA in July 2011 (CBA FRY/1/3/2). It is believed to have been in the original Fry Collection.

4. **First book**

    Edwin Cross had a book in his private collection in 1992 with the inscriptions – 'B.W. Newton' (in a child's handwriting), and (in a different handwriting) 'The first book that he bought with his own money. 10th March 1813'. The book was *Grammatical Institutes or, an Easy Introduction to Dr Lowth's English Grammar designed for use in Schools and to lead young gentlemen and ladies into the knowledge of the first principles of the English language. 1807.* By John Ash LLD [1724?-1779]. Its current whereabouts are unknown.

5. **College rooms at Exeter College, Oxford**

    Written by B.W. Newton whilst he was at Exeter College, Oxford. It describes the appalling accommodation provided. CBA 7059 (Wyatt small MS Book #4), pp.43,44. For more information regarding his accommodation at Oxford, see his letter from Exeter College to his mother, dated 16th October 1825.

6. **Association with missionary work at Oxford**

    B. W. Newton was closely involved in the work of the Church Missionary Society at Oxford University, and played a leading role in ousting John Henry Newman from the secretaryship of the C.M.S. there. See CBA 7049, pp.136,194,195, and H.H. Rowdon, The Origins of the Brethren, p.64,65.

He was also Co-Secretary of the London Society for Promoting Christianity amongst the Jews (the Jews Society) at Oxford, with John Hill, Vice President of St Edmund Hall. See the quotation of a letter from John Hill's diary in T.C.F. Stunt, *From Awakening to Secession*, p.279n. Note also his acquaintance with Michael Solomon Alexander, the first Anglican bishop at Jerusalem.[1]

### 7. Distribution by B.W. Newton of J.N. Darby's tract at Oxford

Regents Park College Library (Angus catalogue), Oxford University, holds a copy of J.N. Darby's anonymous (ΟΥΔΕΙΣ) tract, *The Doctrine of the Church of England ... Briefly Compared with the Remarks of the Regius Professor of Divinity*, 1831, with the inscription 'The Rev. T.G. Tyndale with B.W. Newton's kind regards' in his handwriting. The tract has 'Revd. Benj$^n$ Newton of Exeter College' written on the title page in an unknown hand. Rev. T.G. Tyndale was the evangelical rector of Holton, Oxfordshire.[2]

In a bound volume of tracts 1801-1860 entitled on the spine, 'Dissent and the Established Church'.

### 8. Guardianship of H.W. Soltau's younger brother[3]

In her will of 1831, H.W. Soltau's mother nominated three people as guardians to be responsible for her young undergraduate son William Francis, who was still under age, having matriculated at Balliol College, Oxford a few months earlier. These were her brother William Symons, her son Henry, and another (we may presume) family friend, Benjamin W. Newton. She specifically required her trustees, in the event of her death, to raise from her estate the sum of £300, and to pay 'Benjamin W. Newton of Exeter College, Oxford, Esq.', to be applied or expended by him during the long vacations at Oxford, or in such manner as Mr. Newton may think fit, in addition to her son William's allowance for the furtherance of his studies. [A copy of the will and probate in the Public Record Office (Prob. 11/1877, indexed under 'Soltan') .... There is a copy of the will in the Plymouth and West Devon Record Office (81/Y/10/11)].

### 9. Personal Greek New Testament

B.W. Newton's Greek Testament. Dated May 1842, with his name in his handwriting in the inside cover. The printed preface is dated 20th December 1827. 'E. Hawkins' may have been the original owner. It is the Received Text.

The Gospels, the early chapters of Revelation, and some other parts, have extensive written amendments to the text (in Greek) in B.W. Newton's hand. The textual amendments of the Book

---

[1] See the 1904 Supplementary Note added to the Note on Rev. 11:8 in the Third Edition of *Thoughts on the Apocalypse* (pp. 213, 214), commented on in Appendix 1 of this Guide, A Comparison of the Editions of *Thoughts on the Apocalypse* for further information and other references to him in B.W. Newton's works.

[2] Regarding Thomas George Tyndale and other evangelical clergy in Oxfordshire at this time, see T.C.F. Stunt, *From Awakening to Secession*, pp.189-192 and index.

[3] For further information on B.W. Newton's connection with the Soltau family see T.C.F. Stunt, *The Elusive Quest of the Spiritual Malcontent: Some Early Nineteenth Century Ecclesiastical Mavericks*, 2015. H.W. Soltau was one of the leaders of the Plymouth meeting with B.W. Newton. See Section 9 of this Guide, B.W. Newton's Correspondence.

of Revelation generally agree with Tregelles's Greek text.[1]  However, there are significant differences, even where it is possible to make a close comparison (e.g. chapter 1). He consulted S.P Tregelles on particular points during the course of writing *Thoughts on the Apocalypse*[2].

There would have been no need for B.W. Newton to amend his Greek testament after S.P. Tregelles's book was printed in 1844. It is therefore likely that he made the amendments to the personal Greek Testament in 1842-1844. It is tempting to speculate that B.W. Newton's growing concerns at this time regarding the state of the text of the Book of Revelation led him to encourage S.P. Tregelles to start on his great work.[3]

B.W. Newton's position on the New Testament text was, 'The multiplicity of the variations shows the danger which has threatened the Scripture through the carelessness of men; the character of the variations proves the vigilance with which the faithful Providence of God has watched over and protected the substantial integrity of His Word'.[4]

There are no exegetical notes. C.W.H. Griffiths has this item, obtained from T.C.F. Stunt. Two pages of the amendments are illustrated in *A Pictorial Memoir of Benjamin Wills Newton* – the Supplement to this *Guide*. See the Advertisement at the end of this volume.

## 10. Frederick Prideaux's remembrance of B.W. Newton as a Greek tutor

*In Memoriam F[rederick] P[rideaux]: A Letter to his nephews and nieces from F[Frederick] A[sh] P[rideaux]* was privately published as a manuscript book, and dated 1891. The Library of the Society of Friends, London, holds a copy. It gives a happy reminiscence of Mr Newton as Frederick Prideaux's Greek tutor (pp.29,30). Frederick Prideaux (1817-1853) was the brother of S.P. Tregelles's wife (née Sarah Anna Prideaux)[5].

## 11. Marriage Certificate (second marriage)

The wedding took place in Edinburgh, on 24th April 1849. The witnesses were Maria Hawkins' mother, Sophia Constantia Maria's sister[6], and S.P. Tregelles. Original - TC.

## 12. Passport

This gives information on summer journeys, with visits to France, Austria, Switzerland[7], Belgium, and the Netherlands between 1855 and 1863. A summary of the contents was produced by C.W.H. Griffiths and is held in the Christian Brethren Archive.

This was recovered by CBA in July 2011. It is believed to have been in the original Fry Collection. CBA FRY/1/3/1.

---

[1] Perhaps more likely that of Griesbach. From the comparison that we made, the changes did line up fairly well with S.P. Tregelles's *The Book of Revelation in Greek, Edited from Ancient Authorities; with a New English Version and Various Readings*, 1844. See the Comparison of Editions of *Thoughts on the Apocalypse*, Appendix 1 of this Guide for further relevant information.

[2] See, for example, p.68 of the First Edition.

[3] For further comment of B.W. Newton's use of S.P. Tregelles's Greek text in *Thoughts on the Apocalypse*, see its entry in Section 3, B.W. Newton's Published Works, and Appendix 1, Comparison of Editions of *Thoughts on the Apocalypse*, on the Advertisement to the Second Edition.

[4] *Remarks on the Revised English Version of the Greek New Testament*, p. 355

[5] See also the references to Frederick Prideaux in Section 9, the listing of correspondence c.1846. See further information regarding him in T.C.F. Stunt, *Life and Times of Samuel Prideaux Tregelles*.

[6] Sophia was by the 1861 Census a member of the Newton household, and remained so until her death in 1904.

[7] See Correspondence 12th August 1858, regarding a visit to Lake Geneva for the sake of B.W. Newton's health, a letter dated 31st July 1862, etc.

Section 12 - Miscellaneous Biographical Items and Memorabilia

**B. PICTURES** (See *A Pictorial Memoir of Benjamin Wills Newton* published by Pearl Publications).

1. **Sketch of B.W. Newton in his seventies**

    The following note appeared in *Perilous Times*, April 1902, p.5.

    'Mr [Edward] Penstone[1], of 31 Stayton Street, Chelsea, has recently published an engraved portrait of Mr Newton. India proofs are 5s. each, and are suitable for framing. The portrait was sketched by the artist twenty years ago, and does not, therefore, represent Mr Newton as his friends knew him at the close of his life. He had, as is well known, a strong objection to being photographed, and this may explain the difficulty experienced in getting any really satisfactory likeness'.

    Reproduced in *Teachers of the Faith and Future* by George H. Fromow. A copy of this is given in *A Pictorial Memoir of Benjamin Wills Newton* – the supplement to this *Guide*. See the Advertisement at the end of this volume.

2. **Pictures at the Christian Brethren Archive**

    Photographs of the following items were provided to the Christian Brethren Archive by C.W.H. Griffiths, who located them after a visit to C.E Fry in 1988. Subsequently, Mrs Rosemary Stewart, daughter of Kenneth Fry (younger son of A.C. Fry), upon the death of her mother, donated items 2.1-3 to the Archive in 2002. She first offered them for sale at an Isle of Wight Auction Room and they were purchased by C.W.H. Griffiths with a view to transfer to the Archive. Mrs Stewart then refunded the auction price to C.W.H. Griffiths and they were transferred to the CBA. 2.4 was sold at a much higher price to an unknown bidder. We intend to include photographs of these in *A Pictorial Memoir of Benjamin Wills Newton* – the supplement to this *Guide*. See the Advertisement at the end of this volume. See the further note regarding their provenance in Section 10, Duplicated and Manuscript Items, The Fry Collection, and E5 of this part of the *Guide* – Mrs Newton's will.

    2.1. 100 mm oval Miniature of B.W. Newton as a young man. The miniature has a note on the reverse in an unknown hand 'believed to be Benjamin Wills Newton the Expositor'. There is no reason to doubt that it is of B.W. Newton. The miniatures were left in Mrs Newton's will to her trustees, and had together been passed to A.C. Fry and then Kenneth Fry. Mrs Newton would have had no need to identify the subject, and Newton's associates, who would not have known him as a young man, would have been bound to exercise caution, hence the note. An aquiline nose is common to both Penstone's sketch and the miniature. A copy of the miniature is included in *A Pictorial Memoir of Benjamin Wills Newton* – the supplement to this *Guide*. See the Advertisement at the end of this volume.

    2.2. Two miniatures. One of each of the Hawkins sisters. Unfortunately the identity of each is not known, however, Mrs Maria Newton was 6 years older than her sister, and readers can make their own guess! An investigation could be made by the Archive to see if there is identification within the framing or on the back of the paintings themselves. A copy of these

---

[1] Edward Penstone was also the owner of the copyright for the widely used portrait of J.N. Darby included in W.B. Neatby, *History of the Plymouth Brethren* (1902)

is included in *A Pictorial Memoir of Benjamin Wills Newton* – the supplement to this Guide. See the Advertisement at the end of this volume.

2.3. A sketch, and four paintings, by Amy J.T. Toulmin of persons unknown.

2.4. A photograph of a miniature of 'Benjamin Wills Newton of Plymouth Dock' (B.W. Newton's father), who died in 1807, eleven days before his only son's birth. The miniature was sold at auction on the Isle of Wight to an unknown buyer in 2002. It was subsequently resold by Bonhams of London in a sale of Portrait Miniatures and Silhouettes on 27 February 2007 for a hammer price of £400 (£480 including buyer's premium). It was bought by a private customer based in the UK. The auctioneer's description was "Benjamin Wills Newton (d.1807), wearing black coat with velvet collar and white buttons, frilled white chemise and cravat. Attributed to Soloman Polack (Flemish, 1757-1839) Gold frame, reverse engraved at the top Benjamin Wills Newton/ of Plymouth Dock, died 1807/ and at the bottom Father of Benjamin Wills Newton/ the Expositor, central aperture glazed to reveal plaited hair. Oval, 67mm (2 5/8in) high". A copy of this is included in *A Pictorial Memoir of Benjamin Wills Newton* – the supplement to this *Guide*. See the Advertisement at the end of this volume.

3. **Sketch owned by G.L. Silverwood-Browne**

    Mr Silverwood-Browne stated when C.W.H. Griffiths visited him in 1992 that he had a sketch, made by his uncle, of B.W. Newton wearing a top hat. This, however, could not be located by his daughter when he died. It is assumed to be lost.

## C. CONDUCT OF MEETINGS etc.

1. **The account of Rev. John Jackson of Taunton in 1844**

    B.W. Newton gave three lectures in Taunton on prophetic matters. The local General Baptist minister, Rev. John Jackson, attended. He published a response, titled *The Pre-millennial Advent and Earthly Reign of Jesus Christ, Irreconcilable with the Character of the Christian Dispensation and Common Sense*. In it he gives independent indications of B.W. Newton's conduct of meetings at this period. See the bibliographical note for *A Letter to the Minister of Silver Street Chapel, Taunton in Reply to his Recent Lecture against the Pre-Millennial Advent of the Lord* in Section 3 – Bibliography of B.W. Newton's Published Works.

    For the nature of his meetings in this period, see also T.C.F. Stunt, *The Elusive Quest of the Spiritual Malcontent: Some Early Nineteenth Century Ecclesiastical Mavericks*, 2015, which has a paper focussing on B.W. Newton's and S.P. Tregelles's accounts of the early Plymouth Assembly. Note also the correspondence in Section 9 from 23 November 1850 onwards, where B.W. Newton discussed the changes that he made at Duke Street Chapel, after he had left Plymouth.

2. **Mr Newton at Bayswater in 1870**

    This was first published in the 24th May 1870 edition of *The Daily Telegraph*. It was a first-hand account by C. Maurice Davies of a lecture by B.W. Newton. It was later published in a book in 1873, with his accounts of a series of visits to the Seventh Day Baptists, the Plymouth Brethren and others, as *Unorthodox London, or Phases of Religious Life in the Metropolis*, Tinsley bros, London, BL. It was a nineteenth century version of the mystery shopper (or mystery worshipper) approach. The visit to the meeting was prior to its closure in 1872.

    *Mr Newton at Bayswater, from 'The Daily Telegraph'* was republished by
        S.R. Cottey, London [c.1930] CBA
        The Irish Christian Mission (ICM) [1996].

    See also the MS giving autobiographical comment by B.W. Newton on the nature of the work at Bayswater in Section 12 – Duplicated and Manuscript Items, Fry Collection MS Items Recovered by the CBA in 2011, Item 3.

3. **Mr Newton at Ryde, Isle of Wight 1893**

    An article appeared in *The Freeman*[1] on September 29th 1893, giving a somewhat critical account of a meeting in Ryde, Isle of Wight, at which Mr Newton spoke, towards the end of his life. C.W.H. Griffiths has a copy.

4. **Reminiscence from C.E. Fry (from his father A.C. Fry) to C.W.H. Griffiths**

---

[1] *The Freeman* was a Baptist publication which became *The Baptist Times and Freeman* in 1899, and simply *The Baptist Times* in 1925

'When he first moved to the Isle of Wight Mr Newton hired a room to speak, in John Street, Ryde. He was seeking peace from the persecution he suffered'.

'The Ryde Chapel was in Newport Road. E. Crossley founded it. It was eventually closed by Arthur Andrews'.

See the account of Item 11. *A Statement of Doctrines Held by a Body of Christians Meeting in the Evangelical Protestant Chapel, Newport Street, Ryde, Isle of Wight. Compiled by Arthur Andrews*, in Section 4, B.W. Newton's Contributions to Other Publications, for further information regarding the chapel

## 5. Advertisement of meetings

Advertisements appeared in *The Times* on at least two occasions.

1st June 1857 for 'Lectures at Duke Street Chapel, St James Park (entrance Storey's Gate) – The following lectures will be given (D.V.):- Tomorrow Evening, June 2, at 7 o'clock – General Scope of the Book of Revelation. Sunday Evening, June 7th at half-past 6 – The Scripture Doctrine of Baptism'. A copy of this is included in *A Pictorial Memoir of Benjamin Wills Newton* – the supplement to this *Guide*. See the Advertisement at the end of this volume.

28th March 1878 'Benjamin Wills Newton will Lecture on Prophetic Scripture every consecutive Thursday, at 11:30, until further notice, at the Rooms of the Christian Young Men's Association [sic], 48 Great Marlborough Street, Regent Street'. A copy of this is included in *A Pictorial Memoir of Benjamin Wills Newton* – the supplement to this *Guide*.

Jonathan Burnham[1] notes further advertisements in *The Bayswater Chronicle and Local Journal*, 24th October – 28th November 1860; 27th March 1861 – 12th June 1861; 19th October – 23rd November 1861.

The Christian Brethren Archive has a printed notice of 'a few lectures' to be given by B.W. Newton at the Stafford Rooms, Titchbourne Street, Edgware Road on 'Prophetic and Other Parts of Scripture', commencing 10th May 1887, at 11:15 on Tuesday mornings. (CBA 7188(1)), 14cm. A copy of this notice is included in *A Pictorial Memoir of Benjamin Wills Newton* – the supplement to this *Guide*.

## 6. Hymnbook used at B.W. Newton's meetings on the Isle of Wight

C. E. Fry identified the hymnbook that was used at Mr Newton's meetings on the Isle of Wight as the same as that used by George Müller in his meetings[2]. C.W.H. Griffiths has a hymnbook given to him by Mr G.L. Silverwood-Browne, which he stated was used at B.W. Newton's meetings – *Hymns and Spiritual Songs. Compiled in Bristol,* Third Edition. Bristol: The Bible and Tract Warehouse of the Scriptural Knowledge Institution for Home and Abroad, 78 Park Street.

---

[1] Jonathan D. Burnham, *A Story of Conflict, the Controversial Relationship between Benjamin Wills Newton and John Nelson Darby*, p.215n.
[2] *How the Leaven has Wrought*, by T. Weston, 1894, an Exclusive Brethren tract against B.W. Newton and addressed to Open Brethren, quotes (disparagingly) letters by Mrs Müller (1882) and George Müller (1893) which commend B.W. Newton's works. It also quotes a letter from George Müller which states that he (George Müller) and his wife had travelled from Folkestone to attend a Bible Reading of Mr Newton in Tunbridge Wells.

1896. 544 pages. 618 hymns. However it is surprising that it does not have the hymn 'O happy morn! The Lord will come' by R.C. Chapman, the middle verse of which is on his gravestone.

7. **Isle of Wight Sunday School records**

    The **Clifford Street Sunday School** was commenced in 1888 by Sophia Constantia Hawkins (Mr Newton's sister in law).[1] See 'log book' of the Sunday School in Section 10, Duplicated and Manuscript Items – C.W.H. Griffiths.[2] C.E. Fry said that the Sunday School was started because Mr Newton found the noise of the children difficult whilst he was preaching, but there is more positive evidence of his commitment to children's work, e.g. 'Encouragements in the Sunday School work' (at Duke Street Chapel) CBA 7049.

8. **Isle of Wight colportage records**

    Manuscript diary of colportage work carried out for B.W. Newton, between 20th April 1891 and 10th March 1892 in Mr Fry's own hand. 114 pages.

    Whilst this does not provide theological or controversial material, it provides a human day to day picture of his life on the Isle of Wight, working with B.W. Newton, and the strong emphasis on evangelism that this entailed. He travelled around the island villages on a bicycle.

    In the CBA Collection from July 2011 (CBA FRY/1/1/2) and a photocopy held by SGAT.

---

[1] So stated in Mrs Newton's will. Sophia was the younger of the two sisters. She was born in 1821

[2] For a remembrance of the Sunday School, later run by A.C. Fry, see *Journal of the Isle of Wight Family History Society*, November 2006: The Fry Family in Newport, by Colin Jeffries. Note also his obituary in *Watching and Waiting* November/December 1943, and *Isle of Wight County Press*, 28th August 1943.

## D. THE PUBLISHING OF B.W. NEWTON'S BOOKS

### 1. His publishers

The distinction between the various branches of the book trade were not closely observed in the nineteenth century and firms held different roles – booksellers, publishers, stationers, printers, and so on, during their history. This accounts for some of the confusion of publishers' details relating to Mr Newton's works during the period 1849-53. The use of over stickers in the twentieth century has also caused confusion in some library cataloguing.

The following summary of his publishers outlines those involved with his works. We have not included here an account of Hunt, Barnard and Co, as its contribution was almost wholly concerned with secondary materials, concerning which comment is given in Section 8, Publications Produced from Notes of Addresses, and Posthumously Published Letters and Manuscripts.

#### 1.1 Early publishing

In the period before 1850, publication and printer's dates of B.W. Newton's works are confused. Useful work could be done in establishing publication dates of undated works (by Mr Newton and others) by confirming the years of operation of various printers. Clulow and Soltau (C&S) or the Plymouth Tract Depot[1] published many items, and, '1, Warwick Square' [I.K. Campbell (1835?-1847) then John Keylock Campbell 1847-)]. Wertheimer features as a printer of early articles by Mr Newton, as does Geo. Hunt. Publication data 1841-1853 is also confused, with the involvement of Hamilton-Adams, Partridge and Oakey, and J. Nisbet.

#### 1.2 Houlston:

During most of his lifetime B.W. Newton used Houlston as his printer and publisher. These are the dates of Houlston as publishers, derived from the dates of his works.

Houlston and Wright [1838]-1856
Houlston and Stoneman 1853-1869
Houlston and Sons 1870-1904

'Correspondence, Memoranda etc. regarding Houlston and Wright 1827-1861', is held as an archive of documents of the publisher in the British Library (British Library Manuscript 45413). This has been carefully checked. Unfortunately, here is little or nothing of real interest regarding Mr Newton. According to the Manuscript, Houlston and Stoneman started on 15th September 1845. John Stoneman's interest was bought out by Thomas Houlston 5th April 1860. He had died 5th April 1856. The first reference to Houlston and Wright is 9th November 1861. It is difficult to reconcile this with the publishers' details of B.W. Newton's works.

#### 1.3 Lucas Collins

Lucas Collins took over the publication of Mr Newton's works after his death. Lucas Collins is given as the publisher of B.W. Newton's books (firstly with Houlston and Sons, and then

---

[1] Soltau returned from India in 1834. Clulow dated his conversion from 1837. The start of their tract work must have been after that date. However, note B.W. Newton's letter of 22nd April 1830, in which he expresses pleasure at hearing of plans for regular tract distribution in Plymouth.

independently) between 1900-1913. C. Everit Fry had memories of being taken to see 'Luke Collins' by his father Alfred C. Fry. Lucas Collins died in 1917. His obituary in *Perilous Times*, May 1917, p.221 stated, 'Mr Collins had a long association with Mr Newton, extending, we believe, over a period of more than 50 years, beginning at the chapel in Bayswater. At a time when many failed Mr Newton, Mr Collins, with others, stood by him, and the friendship between the two continued to the end of Mr Newton's life'.

### 1.4 Publishing by B.W. Newton's trustees

*Teachers of the Faith and Future* (2nd Edn. pp.12-14) gives an account of the arrangements for circulating his books after the death of his wife [née Maria Hawkins] in 1906. Her will (see item 4.2 below) established a trust fund gifted with existing copies of his published works, and with a sum of £1,500. This operated separately from the publishing work of Hunt, Barnard and Co, which G.T. Hunt heavily subsidised.

The trustees of the publication fund were:
- C. T. Walrond[1],
- E.J. Burnett[2]
- G.L. Silverwood-Browne[3]

The trust fund was expended by the late 1950s).

The trustees republished Mr Newton's works under the publishers' names of:

- Lucas Collins, whose name appears as a publisher until 1913
- Tucker's Publishing Office (Miss C.M. Tucker) – undated publications
- E.J. Burnett, whose name appears as a publisher between 1924 and 1954
- G.L. Silverwood-Browne, who published between 1955 and 1957.

### 1.5 SGAT and other publishing

From its formation in 1919 the SGAT valued B.W. Newton's works. After the Second World War it obtained 'loose sheets' of several of B.W. Newton's books, which it re-bound and circulated. After the publications trust fund was expended, it took over the re-issuing of B.W. Newton's publications, often in edited form. In 2015 it embarked on an ambitious programme of reprinting several of B.W. Newton's major works[4].

Hunt, Barnard and Co did not re-publish B.W. Newton's works, but it did circulate them along with derivative publications, from notes of addresses. It issued a catalogue of his works produced by E.J. Burnett.[5]

---

[1] Charles Troubridge Walrond. Died 2nd January 1942, aged 84. Obituary of C.T. Walrond, Watching and Waiting, March/April 1942, p.26. He wrote *Scriptural Watching, A Reply to those who Expect the Lord's Return 'at Any Moment'*, and a booklet on British Israelism. His obituary also makes reference to Mrs B.W. Newton and her school. See letters to and from him in CBA 7187(51), etc. A photograph of him is included in *A Pictorial Memoir of Benjamin Wills Newton* – the supplement to this Guide.

[2] Ernest John Burnett. Born Ryde, Isle of Wight, 1876. Died 1959. Obituary *Watching and Waiting*, July/August 1959, with some useful notes of the starting of the meeting at Ryde, Isle of Wight, in 1894 Younger brother of W.E. Burnett, missionary to China.

[3] Gerald Leighton Silverwood-Browne. Born 1904. Died 1994, Worthing, Sussex.

[4] For further comment on the SGAT see Section 2, Libraries and Collections, The Sovereign Grace Advent Testimony.

[5] See Section 8, Publications Produced from Notes of Addresses, and Posthumously Published Letters and Manuscripts, for information regarding the publications of Hunt, Barnard and Co.

S.R. Cottey's name appears on some publications between 1918-1933[1]. He lived in Chiswick near to the Secretary of the SGAT, and operated a lending library of B.W. Newton's books.

2. **B.W. Newton's amendments to *Occasional Papers on Scriptural Subjects***

   Until his health failed, Mr Newton continued writing, and editing earlier publications. In particular, he anticipated a revised edition of *Thoughts on the Apocalypse*.[2] He was also preparing *Occasional Papers on Scriptural Subjects* (or parts of the volumes) for republication. In producing *Expository Teaching on the Millennium and Israel's Future* in 1913, Lucas Collins added a prefatory note that the papers extracted from *Occasional Papers on Scriptural Subjects* had been 'revised by the author for the press'. C.W.H. Griffiths has this item with Mr Newton's amendments. There are few handwritten amendments to *Occasional Papers* beyond those printed in *Expository Teaching on the Millennium and Israel's Future*. An example of this editing is included in *A Pictorial Memoir of Benjamin Wills Newton* – the supplement to this *Guide*. See the Advertisement at the end of this volume.

3. **Mrs Newton's copy of *Thoughts on the Apocalypse* amended for the Second Edition**

   The book has the inscription 'Maria Hawkins, S. James Place, Hyde Park Square' [i.e. it belonged to his second wife before their marriage]. Parts of it have been edited in B.W. Newton's hand, which aligns with the changes appearing in the Second Edition. It was evidently used for that purpose. Meticulous changes are made – e.g. a comma changed to a colon. C.W.H. Griffiths has this item. A sample page of this is included in *A Pictorial Memoir of Benjamin Wills Newton* – the supplement to this *Guide*. See the Advertisement at the end of this volume.

4. **Advertisement of books**

   Mr Newton's books were advertised by his publisher's lists, and also in newspapers.

   - In his letter to B. W. Newton of 27th February 1866, S.P. Tregelles suggested the advertisement of his *Propositions for the Solemn Consideration of Christians* in *The Record*.
   - Three of his works published by Houlston and Sons were advertised for sale in *The Times*, 30th December 1875.

---

[1] Stephen Robert Cottey. His obituary is in *Watching and Waiting*, October –December 1946, p. 51.
[2] See F.W. Wyatt's comments in a letter to Miss Martin dated 1913 copied in Appendix 1, Comparison of editions of *Thoughts on the Apocalypse*.

# Section 12 - Miscellaneous Biographical Items and Memorabilia

## E. ITEMS RELATING TO HIS DEATH

Note the circumstances of his last days as recorded in Section 9, B.W. Newton Correspondence.

1. **Note by Mrs Stirling**

    The following note appears in the front of 'Thoughts on Parts of the Prophecy of Isaiah' from the Stirling Collection[1], in Mrs Stirling's handwriting

    'Mary E. Stirling

    From Benjamin Wills Newton, the Author, May 19th 1899.

    Our beloved and revered Friend died June 26th 1899 1 a.m. aged 91.

    at 2, Clanricarde Gardens, Tunbridge Wells, as he wished – alone'.

    The volume is now in the CBA.

2. **Obituaries**

    <u>The Christian</u>, Obituary by Henry Varley in Thursday July 20th 1899 edition, with some personal reminiscence, as he had attended the meeting at Bayswater 'week after week'. It has certain inaccuracies, as noted in Section 3, B.W. Newton's Published Works item for *Plain Papers on Gospel Themes*.

    <u>The Record</u>, 7th July 1899.[2] F.W. Wyatt adds a correcting note in MS Book 2 (TC) p.1 that B.W. Newton did not gain a 'double first class' degree.

    <u>The Times</u>, 28th June 1899

    <u>Isle of Wight County Journal</u> September 2nd 1899. Photocopy at the CBA.

3. **In Memoriam card**

    A copy of the text of this was printed in *Teachers of the Faith and Future* by G.H. Fromow. A copy of the card is included in *A Pictorial Memoir of Benjamin Wills Newton* – the supplement to this *Guide*.

4. **Gravestones**

    4.1. A photograph of his gravestone with that of his mother (adjoining). The gravestone of his mother is now illegible. His mother's gravestone has the first verse of 'My hope is built on nothing less than Jesus' blood and righteousness. Interestingly, the gravestone of Mr and Mrs Newton has the second verse of R.C. Chapman's hymn 'O happy morn! The Lord will come'. Although he rejected Brethrenism, he retained brotherly affection for R.C. Chapman. See his letter of 14th March 1857. C.W.H. Griffiths has this picture. It is included in *A Pictorial Memoir*

---

[1] The Stirling Collection. See Section 10, Duplicated and Manuscript Items.
[2] F.W. Wyatt records '7th July 1900' in MS Book 2 (TC), but this is surely a mistake

*of Benjamin Wills Newton* – the supplement to this *Guide*. See the Advertisement at the end of this volume.

4.2. Black and White photograph of the grave of B.W. Newton and his wife. Copy printed in *Teachers of the Faith and Future* by B.W. Newton. The grave's reference in the graveyard is No A.298.Gen.Tunbridge Wells.

## 5. B.W. Newton's Will, and that of his wife

5.1 B.W. Newton's will is held at the National Record Office, London. At his death on 26th June 1899, B.W. Newton was listed as residing at 2, Clanricarde Gardens, Tunbridge Wells. Probate was given to Maria Newton and Sophia Constantia Hawkins, spinster. His effects totalled £21,390. He bequeathed a sum to the family of his first wife.

5.2 Mrs Maria Newton died 25th December 1906. There is a brief obituary in *Perilous Times*, February 1907. 'Her last remembered words were, "Jesus, Lover of my soul, let me to Thy bosom fly"'. Probate was given to Charles Troubridge Walrond[1] and Henry Tufnell Campbell. Her effects totalled £34,339. She provided an annuity to support the work being carried out by A.C. Fry. She gave a legacy of £1,500 'in providing for and promoting the sale of books written by my late husband'. She left all books, papers, manuscripts, documents, pictures, photographs, miniatures and the 'silver loving cup' to C.T. Walrond and H.F. Tufnell 'for their own use absolutely'. Provision was made for a number of other single gifts and annuities. The residue of the estate was bequeathed to the Aged Pilgrims' Friend Society.[2]

## 6. Answer to the suggestion that, before his death Mr Newton 'changed his views'

The answer is given to the suggestion 'being circulated' was evidently given by Mr Newton's friends. The claim is met by a quotation of Mr Newton's last message on Sunday 21st May 1899. '…If I had my time over again, I would maintain the same testimonies that I have done, only more strongly'. Printed card (11.5 x 9 cm) dated 'London: May, 1912'. Copy held by C.W.H. Griffiths.

---

[1] C.T. Walrond: See the note regarding him and the portrait in *A Pictorial Memoir of Benjamin Wills Newton* – the supplement to this Guide.

[2] On the connection with the A.P.F.S., see also *Watching and Waiting*, August 1938, p.268. The A.P.F.S. is now known as 'Pilgrim Homes'.

## F. REMINISCENCES

Note that the Hunt, Barnard publications with the title *Reminiscences...* (NS 1, NS 2, NS 3, NS 22, and NS 23 – see Section 8, Publications Produced from Notes of Addresses, and Posthumously Published Letters and Manuscripts) are not personal or circumstantial reminiscences relating to B.W. Newton, but a series of short comments he made on Scripture texts and subjects.

1. **Reminiscences in the Fry Collection**

   The Fry Collection contains a great deal of personal recollection of B.W. Newton and information on his family connections. It includes, for example, what are evidently the results F.W. Wyatt's interviewing of Mrs Newton, presumably after B.W. Newton's death, regarding the Hawkins family – copied by A.C. Fry from F.W. Wyatt's 'vol. 6, p.47 (CBA 7049, pp. 36-39).

   A.C. Fry recorded a number of F.W. Wyatt's biographical notes in the Fry MS (CBA 7049). An example is a memo in his mother's handwriting '<u>17 Dec. 1811, 4 years old</u>. My child reads very well and spells as well as he reads. He also points out the principle [*sic*] divisions of Europe, etc. He takes great delight in reading "Original Poems", and will repeat many of them'.
   F.W. Wyatt's copy in Vol. 2. p.121. Copied in A.C. Fry's MS (CBA 7049), p. 44.

2. **Published in *Perilous Times* and *Watching and Waiting***

   | | | |
   |---|---|---|
   | 1. | A poem that gave solace to Mr Newton in his closing years. | August 1902 (PT), p.7. |
   | 2. | Regarding England being humbled | Dec. 1907 (PT) p.119. |
   | 3. | In the obituary of John Cox, jun. | April 1915 (PT) p.113. |
   | 4. | Biographical note on Mr Newton | Oct. 1920 (*W&W*) p.190. |
   | 5. | Linked to a biographical note on S.P. Tregelles | Oct. 1920 (*W&W*) p.214. |
   | 6. | Biographical outline of Mr Newton, in connection with Aged Pilgrims' Friend Society, Matamoros etc. | Dec. 1921 (*W&W*) p.103. |
   | 7. | Biographical sketch of B.W. Newton | Feb. 1923 (*W&W*) p.229. |
   | 8. | Reference to Mrs Newton and her school. | March-April 1942 (*W&W*) p.26. |
   | 9. | Reference in A.C. Fry's obituary | Nov.-Dec. 1943 (*W&W*). |
   | 10. | Reminiscences of W.H. Stirling | Oct.-Dec. 1944 (*W&W*) pp.138,139. |
   | 11. | W.H. Stirling's account of a conversation | Oct.-Dec. 1947 (*W&W*) pp.128,129. |
   | 12. | W.E. Burnett's contacts with Mr Newton | July-Sept. 1948 (*W&W*) pp.199, 200. |
   | 13. | B.W. Newton and the 2nd Earl of Litchfield 'friend and follower'[1] | July-Aug. 1950 (*W&W*) p.64. |
   | 14. | In W.E. Burnett's obituary. Account of meeting with Mr Newton | Sept.-Oct. 1950 (*W&W*) p.69. |

---

[1] i.e. Thomas George Anson, MP for Litchfield 1847-54. 18/08/25-7/1/1892. There is nothing relevant in the National Register of Archives

| | | |
|---|---|---|
| 15. | Note of a meeting with Mr Newton, by Mr Licence. | July-Aug. 1953 (*W&W*) pp.334-336 |
| 16. | In obituary of Thomas Houghton. Correspondence with Mr Newton | March-April 1951 (*W&W*) p.113. |
| 17. | Biographical note on B.W. Newton [full of errors. G.H. Fromow unwell!] | July-Aug. 1956 (*W&W*) p.255. |
| 18. | Note on the starting of the Meeting at Ryde, Isle of Wight and Mr Newton's ministry there. | July-Aug 1959 (*W&W*) p.159 |

### 3. Kyneton letter, September 19th 1938

This is a letter with remembrances of Mr Newton from Miss Martin, who had, with a party of likeminded Christians, emigrated to Kyneton, Victoria, Australia. The letter is dated Sept. 19th 1938. It is apparently a copy (was the original on airmail paper?). It is recorded 'for Alfred Fry'. There are significant inaccuracies in the account – 'BWN was one of 7, I think', 'His thirst for learning was shewn by his spending his first half-crown given by his uncle on a Hebrew grammar at a very early age' – as we have noted elsewhere in this Section of the *Guide* (Sub-section A.4, Biographical Records and Personal Effects), his first book was an English grammar. There are nevertheless strong memories of his physical appearance 'He was tall and erect in youth and middle age and beyond, until his sickness brought him low with weakness and failing eyesight and drooping eyelids'. The letter is held by C.W.H. Griffiths.[1]

### 4. Reminiscence from C. Everit Fry to C.W.H. Griffiths

The following statements were made by Mr C.E. Fry in 1987. Mr C.E. Fry was not a contemporary of B.W. Newton, but a close associate of many who had been.

'B.W.N. was a tall plain man who always wore a frock coat and a silk hat'. He turned down the collar of the coat. He had grey hair swept back. 'He was on the tall side, slim'. He addressed the people in very cultured English.

B.W. Newton's fondness of a top hat was also confirmed by G.L. Silverwood-Browne, who likewise knew many of Mr Newton's acquaintances.

---

[1] For more information regarding the group that moved to Kyneton, Australia under the leadership of A.J.W. Dalzell, W.H. Stirling and Arthur Knapp see the shortly to be published *Arthur J.W. Dalzell: B.W. Newton's Physician and the Kyneton Settlement*, by C.W.H. Griffiths.

Section 12 – Miscellaneous Biographical Items and Memorabilia

# APPENDIX 1

## COMPARISON OF THE EDITIONS
### OF
## 'THOUGHTS ON THE APOCALYPSE'

# Appendix 1. A Comparison of the Editions of *Thoughts on the Apocalypse*

# COMPARISON OF THE EDITIONS OF 'THOUGHTS ON THE APOCALYPSE'

This appendix supplements and extends the information given on *Thoughts on the Apocalypse* in Section 3 of this *Guide*.

    A. Background

    B. General Comment on the Editions

    C. Overview of B.W. Newton's Exposition

    D. Contents

    F. The French Edition (1847)

    G. B.W. Newton's interpretation of Revelation 7 - F.W. Wyatt's letter

## A. Background

The general structure of the commentary is binary. There is a dissertation on a chapter (in some cases, chapters) - 'Thoughts on' – which is followed by 'Notes'. For the most part the notes comment on the text and individual verses.

The First Edition was written in parts during an itinerant ministry[1] alongside pastoral responsibilities at Plymouth. It was written during the period when B.W. Newton's first wife was dying, and in the context of J.N. Darby's ongoing controversy with him, particularly at that time on prophetic matters. The Second Edition was issued at a time of settled ministry in London, and following his remarriage. Significant changes would be expected in such changed circumstances. The Second Edition is significantly rearranged, with the addition of new material. However, it reveals no discernible theological changes.

In particular, no changes are apparent in response to J.N. Darby's lengthy and violent polemic[2], although he attacked the First Edition almost line by line. Neither of the first two editions refers to Mr Darby or controversy. With one exception, included in an appendix, no use seems to have been made of B.W. Newton's replies to J.N. Darby.

Apart from the opening chapters, the greatest changes to the text are made in connection with chapter 12.

## B. General Comment on the Editions

There are, effectively, only two editions, as the Third Edition claimed to be a word for word reprint of the Second Edition. The French Edition derives from the First English Edition has few variations from it.

The First Edition was published in twelve sections, which were issued successively as a series or part work.

---

[1] CBA 7049 and George H. Fromow, *Teachers of the Faith and Future* Second edition, p.4.
[2] The addition of an appendix on Psalm 110:1 is the only obvious example.

# Appendix 1. A Comparison of the Editions of *Thoughts on the Apocalypse*

The Second Edition was a revision of the First. Allowing for changes in typefaces and page sizes, the Second Edition has approximately 145 additional pages, an increase of nearly one third. C.W.H. Griffiths has the copy of the First Edition used by B.W. Newton for his revision. A sample page of this is included in *A Pictorial Memoir of Benjamin Wills Newton* – the supplement to this *Guide*. See the Advertisement at the end of this volume.

The Third [posthumous] Edition makes only slight additions to the text of the Second Edition. It updates some of the spellings (e.g. Affghanistan), adds a prefatory note, some additional footnotes (in square brackets), and retrospective comments on the events to which the Second Edition refers. It also adds alphabetical and Scripture indexes.

F.W. Wyatt indicated that it was B.W. Newton's intention, had he lived, to re-issue *Thoughts on The Apocalypse* with some changes, notably to Revelation 7. See the notes that follow in this section with F.W. Wyatt's letter to Miss Martin.

## C. Overview of B.W. Newton's Exposition[1]

Chapter 1 is an introduction to the Apocalypse. It draws attention to the condition of those to whom the instruction is addressed. It prepares them (and us) for the revelation that follows.

Chapters 2 and 3 of Revelation give letters to seven then-existing Churches as representative of Gentile Christianity ("things that are" Rev. 1:19).[2] It describes more fully the condition of those who should receive the message of the Book of Revelation, and Christ's relationship with his Church.

Chapters 4 and 5, read as one, describe the circumstances in which the Revelation was given to John.

Chapters 6-18 relate to the present dispensation, specifically to the period immediately before Christ rises to 'rule in the midst of his adversaries'. They (1) describe the forms human evil will take before the Day of the Lord; (2) indicate the manner in which the Lord will send judgement upon this evil; (3) give indications of the glory that shall follow. This part (as the Book of Daniel) consists of several complete and self-contained visions, each referring to the same short time period.

Chapters 19:1-10 Introduces the period which is the subject of the last part of the book.

Chapter 19:11- 21:8 gives consecutive events at and following the return of the Lord onward to the eternal state.

---

[1] Compare the outline of *Thoughts on the Apocalypse* given here with NS 12. *Elementary Studies on the Facts of Prophetic Scripture in the Book of Daniel and the Book of Revelation*. Part Two, Revised, noted in Section 8 – Publications Derived from Notes of Addresses.

[2] The only surviving exposition of B.W. Newton on these chapters is given in the notes of lectures on the Seven Churches published by Hunt, Barnard, and Co. in the *Patmos Series* – see Section 9, Publications Derived from Notes of Addresses (NP 8-13, 15, 17, 19). W. Lancelot Holland's book, *The Seven Candlesticks of Gold, or A Brief Exposition of the First Three Chapters of the Book of Revelation*, published in 1902, shortly after B.W. Newton's death, no doubt also closely reflects his teaching. His exposition was first published in the magazine *Perilous Times* in a series of 'Short Readings on the Book of Revelation' between March 1900 and December 1903 in 35 parts, and extended to Revelation 11.

# Appendix 1. A Comparison of the Editions of *Thoughts on the Apocalypse*

Chapter 21:9 – 22:5 reverts back to the Millennial period, and describes the New Jerusalem, the home of the risen saints.

Chapter 22:6-21 gives closing exhortations.

B.W. Newton's book does not claim to be a commentary on the whole of the Apocalypse, but merely selected "Thoughts". Apart from two sections (1) Christ in Relation to the Churches / On Revelation, and (2) The Seven Candlesticks of Gold, it deals exclusively with the prophetic parts of the book. It gives virtually no comment on chapters 2 and 3 and almost none on chapter 22:6-10.

## D. Contents

After the opening sections, the format of the book is uniform in all editions, with selected 'notes' on each chapter (or chapters) following more general 'thoughts' on the chapter (or chapters). The notes are not simply textual notes, and it is sometimes difficult to see why they have been separated from the 'thoughts' (compare, for example, the 'thoughts' and 'notes' on the closing chapters of the book).

The headings of the chapters in the First and Third Editions are given in the table below. The arrangement and headings of the first edition is somewhat ragged, no doubt due to it having been a part work. This was not fully corrected in the later English editions. In the First Edition the 'notes' were helpfully distinguished by the use of a smaller typeface:

|     | First Edition | Third Edition |
|-----|---------------|---------------|
| 1.  | Map & Explanation of the Map (17 pages) | - |
| 2.  | - | Prefatory Note (2 pages) + errata |
| 3.  | - | Advertisement to the Second Edition (3 pages) |
| 4.  | Introductory Observations (7 pages) | Introductory Observations (12 pages) |
| 5.  | The Revelation Treats Mainly of the Present Dispensation (3 pages) | - |
| 6.  | Christ in Relation to the Churches (7 pages) | On Revelation 1 (17 pages) |
| 7.  | 'The Seven Candlesticks of Gold' (12 pages) | 'The Seven Candlesticks of Gold' (14 pages) |
| 8.  | Notes on the First Chapter (6 pages) | Notes on Revelation 1 (19 pages) |
| 9.  | Thoughts on the Fourth and Fifth Chapters of the Apocalypse (18 pages) | On Revelation 4 and 5 (25 pages) |
|     | Thoughts on the Fifth Chapter (6 pages) | On Revelation 5 (8 pages) |
| 10. | Notes on the Fourth and Fifth Chapters (6 pages) | Notes on Revelation 4 and 5 (13 pages) |
| 11. | Thoughts on the Sixth Chapter of the Apocalypse (16 pages) | On Revelation 6 (21 pages) |
| 12. | Notes (5 pages) | Notes on Revelation 6 (19 pages) |
| 13. | Thoughts on the Seventh and Two Following Chapters of the Apocalypse (10 pages) | On Revelation 7 (13 pages) |
| 14. | Chapters 8 and 9 (10 pages) | On Revelation 8 and 9 (10 pages) |
| 15. | Notes (6 pages) | Notes on Revelation 7,8 and 9 (12 pages) |
| 16. | Thoughts on the Tenth & Eleventh Chapters of the Apocalypse (5 pages) | On Revelation 10 (6 pages) |
| 17. | Chapter 11 (8 pages) | On Chapter 11 (9 pages) |
| 18. | Notes (7 pages) | Notes on Revelation 10 and 11 (14 pages) |

Appendix 1. A Comparison of the Editions of *Thoughts on the Apocalypse*

| | | |
|---|---|---|
| 19. | - | Supplementary Note Added in 1904 (2 pages) |
| 20. | Thoughts on the Twelfth Chapter of the Apocalypse (13 pages) | On Chapter 12 (16 pages) |
| 21. | Notes (5 pages) | Notes on Revelation 12 (pp. 231-251) |
| 22. | Thoughts on the Thirteenth Chapter of the Apocalypse (19 pages) | On Chapter 13 (20 pages) |
| 23. | Notes (8 pages) | Notes on Revelation 13 (21 pages) |
| 24. | Observations on 2 Thessalonians 3 (5 pages) | - |
| 25. | Thoughts on the Fourteenth Chapter of the Apocalypse (22 pages) | On Revelation 14 (23 pages) |
| 26. | Notes to Chapter 14 (6 pages) | Notes on Revelation 14 (13 pages) |
| 27. | Thoughts on the Fifteenth and Sixteenth Chapter of the Apocalypse (14 pages) | On Revelation 15 and 16 (15 pages) |
| 28. | Notes (6 pages) | Notes on Revelation 15 and 16 (13 pages) |
| 29. | Thoughts on the Seventeenth and Eighteenth Chapters of the Apocalypse (17 pages) | On Revelation 17 and 18 (34 pages) |
| 30. | Eighteenth Chapter (19 pages) | On Revelation 18 (22 pages) |
| 31. | Appendix [letter re-Babylon] (3 pages) | - |
| 32. | Notes on Chapter 17 [and Chapter 18 as French Edn.] (10 pages) | Notes on Revelation 17 [and Chapter 18 as French Edn.] (36 pages] |
| 33. | Thoughts on the Nineteenth, Twentieth, and Part of Twenty-First Chapters of the Apocalypse (18 pages) | On Revelation 19, 20, and 21 to Eighth Verse Inclusive (19 pages) |
| 34. | Notes (6 pages) | Notes on Revelation 19, 20, and 21 (13 pages) |
| 35. | Thoughts on the Twenty-Second Chapter of the Apocalypse, Beginning at the Ninth Verse [...of Chapter 21', as French Edn.] (16 pages) | On Revelation 21 Beginning at Verse 9 [...of Chapter 21', as French Edn.] (17 pages) |
| 36. | Notes (3 pages) | Notes on Revelation 21 Verse 9 [... to chapter 22 end. French Edn. – 'notes on the same chapter'] (11 pages) |
| 37. | - | Appendix A: Note on Psalm 110:1 (3 pages) |
| 38. | - | Appendix B: On Revelation 5:9 (2 pages) |
| 39. | - | Note Appendix B (2 pages – posthumous note) |
| 40. | - | Index |
| 41. | - | Index of Texts |

Unless otherwise stated the Third Edition is the same as the Second Edition in the summary below. We have given fuller comment and analysis where the editions diverge.

## 1. Map and 'Explanation of the Map'

A map, and an 'Explanation of the Map', page numbered with roman numerals, are bound in at the beginning of Maria Hawkins' (his second wife's) copy of the First Edition.[1] The French Edition (1847) also includes this section, but with continuous numbering to the rest of the book (the first nineteen pages in roman numerals, and the 'Thoughts' commencing at p.20). We may assume that

---

[1] The map disappeared when C.W.H. Griffiths's copy was rebound.

the map and its explanation were produced after *Thoughts on the Apocalypse* was completed, and were therefore fully incorporated into the later French Edition.

The explanation of the map (page x) places strong emphasis on Rev. 17 and 13 as defining the extent of the territory given to the Beast, hence the map's relevance to the commentary.

A similar account (without the map) is found in *Aids to Prophetic Enquiry* (Third Edition, pp.162 ff.), which perhaps removed the need for it to appear in the Second Edition of *Thoughts on the Apocalypse*.

## 2. Third Edition - Prefatory Note

This is a two page note, dated December 1904. It confirms that the edition was a "word for word" reprint of the Second Edition. It draws attention to a footnote relating to B.W. Newton's 'Note' on Revelation 6:11. Although the exposition was left unaltered, it was suggested that S.P. Tregelles's revised reading would have probably been adopted by B.W. Newton. It also says that some explanatory notes have been added in relation to dates and incidents which would have been more familiar when the Second Edition was issued, and that square brackets had been used to distinguish these comments. We are unaware of this causing a problem, but on occasion square brackets used by B.W. Newton have been carried forward to this edition.

## 3. Advertisement to the Second Edition (2½ pages)

This states:

1. Re-examination had confirmed the radical principles adopted. Minor changes confirmed Mr Newton's increasing certainty. Changes in the text replace 'probably' with 'doubtless', 'must' for 'should', and strike through 'I think', 'I believe', 'I suppose', 'it appears to me that' many times.

2. The 'slight' amendments are explained as mainly to give the reasons for the conclusions reached.[1] Mr Newton also referred readers to the three Series of *Aids to Prophetic Enquiry*, S.P. Tregelles on Daniel, and Andrew Bonar's *The Development of Antichrist*, as providing background and explanation.

3. B.W. Newton stated that S.P. Tregelles's Greek text of the Book of Revelation had been used for the Second Edition (in his 'Advertisement' to the book

    In the First Edition, B.W. Newton was able to make use of some of S.P. Tregelles work on the text of the Book of Revelation[2] - p.68 wrote on a particular point, 'I have sought information … from a friend … who is now engaged in examining the text of the Revelation, and in preparing a corrected version of the Greek text, accompanied by a literal translation'. S.P. Tregelles in his *An Account of the Printed Text of the Greek New Testament*, 1854 (p.270 note) went further than this

---

[1] One of the initial criticisms by J.N. Darby in *An Examination of the Statements made in the 'Thoughts on the Apocalypse'...* (p.1) is 'the mass of statements, and that of the most extraordinary kind, with which the "Thoughts" abound, without any scripture to warrant them'.

[2] In S.P. Tregelles, *The Book Of Revelation in Greek, Edited from Ancient Authorities; with a New English Version and Various Readings*. 1844.

and stated that Mr Newton followed the revised Greek text that he published in 1844, although perhaps he is just referring to the reading και παρεσται at Rev.17:8.[1]

Whereas the First Edition of *Thoughts on the Apocalypse* has Greek readings on the authority of 'Scholtz and Griesbach' (Rev. 14:15) in the Second Edition the comment on these verses changes to – 'on the authority of Tregelles'! B. W. Newton's translations of the text do not follow S.P. Tregelles's translation.

The publishers of the Third Edition ensure that the readings adopted in Dr Tregelles's final New Testament Greek text are taken into account. For example, at p.138 they give a note of Dr Tregelles's final reading of Rev. 6:11, and its benign impact on the exposition. At page 514 of the Third Edition there is a page and a half note, which comments on the growing evidence in favour of the reading adopted by Mr Newton.

4. That the foundation doctrines of Protestantism are dearer than life to him, including Christ's '<u>true</u>, though sinless, humanity'.

The Advertisement to the Second Edition gives place and date – 'London, October 18th 1853'.

### Errata – Second Edition

The Second Edition has a minutely detailed 'errata', which even corrects the accents of Greek words that appear in the text. The corrections are made in the Third Edition.

## 4. Introductory Observations

The First and Second Editions each have Introductory Observations (7 pages First Edition; 9 pages Second Edition), but they are quite different.

### First Edition – Introductory Observations (numbers indicate paragraphs)

1. Doubt cast upon the Apocalypse, and our unfaithfulness, has caused darkness, but 'recently' giving heed to the prophetic word, as 'a light shining in a dark place', has brought definiteness, decision, and direction to those who have been recalled to it.

2. Overview of the Book of Revelation.

    a. It is especially addressed to Churches.

    b. It throws light on schemes of earthly greatness.

    c. It reveals the nature and manner of God's future judgement.

    d. It teaches the character of the glory reserved for those now 'in the tribulation, and kingdom, and patience of Jesus Christ'.

    e. It treats mainly earthly scenes, but is peculiarly heavenly. It is given from the throne in Heaven – it is addressed to those on earth with a heavenly calling – it refers almost exclusively to the heavenly glories of the redeemed, rather than the earthly promises recorded in the Old Testament.

---

[1] See also the note on B.W. Newton's personal Greek New Testament in Section 12 Miscellaneous Biographical Items,

# Appendix 1. A Comparison of the Editions of *Thoughts on the Apocalypse*

3. Preparedness of heart is necessary to receive its instruction (1 Cor. 3:2).

4. It is essential to be 'established in grace' to read it with profit. It speaks of holiness, terrors, ruin, and evil – so we need to be settled in the peace of the Gospel as a prerequisite to reading it with comfort (1:5,6).

5. It is necessary to have the spirit of a servant, as well as of a son [Rev. 1:1]. The Apocalypse has been neglected by the Church in times of comfort and self-interest, but used and valued at times when the Church was in a place of service or witness - the early Church against pagan Rome; the Waldenses and Reformers against Papal abominations. It will be so again in the closing testimony of the Church.

6. We must read looking beyond our personal or individual circumstances. We must recognise the character of mankind demonstrated through successive dispensations – the Lord's commission to Noah and the subsequent failure; the Lord's calling of Abraham and Israel's failure; the Church dispensation and its failure. We must recognise the present time in its true aspect.

7. John's eyes had been opened to the failure of successive dispensations. He understood Israel's glory and the depth of their fall. He had planted and watered the Church, but was a witness to its decline; therefore he was chosen to receive this revelation.

8. The Book of Revelation takes for granted those things that had been promised by the prophets since the world began, and John was instructed in these things – the times of refreshing and restitution - Christ's return to re-establish Jerusalem in the earth - the saints rising in the First Resurrection to reign with Christ. Without such understanding, a reader of the Book of Revelation will be stumbled at every step.

9. The Book of Revelation completes the picture of the closing hours of our dispensation by showing
    a. The exact character of the closing scene.
    b. The manner and place in which the combined apostasy of man, Israel, and the Church will be finally developed.
    c. The mode of God's interference in chastisement.
    d. The mission of the Son in judgement.

This is what John receives to declare to the Churches.

**Second/Third Edition - Introductory Observations**

These Observations are more discursive and descriptive of current circumstances than those of the First Edition.

1. It highlights dispensational failure, punctuated by God's interference to rekindle light.

2. Protestantism has compromised and deluded itself that all is tending to the millennial day of rest.

3. Neglect of Old Testament prophecy is one of the chief hindrances to understanding the Book of Revelation. New Testament prophecies supplement those of the Old Testament. They complete the earlier outlines.

4. The hour of judgement on the gathered nation of Israel has been the subject of particular neglect (Ezek. 22:18-22).

5. The rising importance of the Greek or Eastern division of the Roman Empire is inescapable. The two halves of that empire have remained distinct. That empire will reappear in a corporate, though divided, form. These two halves will be the mainspring of the world's energies during the last hours of its evil history, and the final apostasy will be met with vengeance.

6. The prophetic parts of Revelation belong to the closing hours of human history. It is not a history of the world. It does not record the successive steps that man takes to achieve his final worldly greatness.

7. The Book of Revelation records how and where man's apostasy will finally be developed, the mode of God's chastisement, and the mission of his Son in judgement. It describes in various visions the glory of those who have endured tribulation, and who will reign with Christ when truth is at last exalted.

8. The Book of Revelation assumes the path of human progress to be evil. It assumes the failure of the Church's testimony. It assumes that truth will never be established in the earth until judgement comes and Christ's servants are taken to mansions of glory. Those who will not admit these things cannot receive the instructions of the Book.

### 5. 'The Revelation treats mainly of the present dispensation' (3 pages) [First Edition]

This follows the Introductory Observations in the First Edition. It is omitted from the Second Edition. This chapter maintains that only the conclusion of the Apocalypse (chapter 19 onwards) is concerned with Christ's future glory, authority, and kingdom. The majority of the Book is concerned with the characteristics of our dispensation; 'Christ hidden – Israel blinded – the Gentiles supreme and glorious – the Church suffering'.

### 6. 'Christ in relation to the Churches' / 'Chapter 1: On Revelation 1'

Christ in relation to the Churches [of Rev. 1 and 2] (7 pages) is the second section of the First Edition, and directly relates to Revelation chapter one. It is substantially rewritten in the Second Edition as 'Chapter 1: On Revelation 1' (13 pages). Although the theme is the same, there is little verbal similarity.

#### First Edition – Christ in relation to the Churches (7 pages)

1. The relation of the throne of God to the nations, and the manner in which he will visit them in wrath, is the chief subject of the Book of Revelation, but it also reveals the present relation of Christ to the Churches.

2. God's rule over the nations is secret. The immediate government of the nations has been delegated to men. They are allowed to exercise their own principles and laws.

3. The Church, on the other hand, is under the immediate government of Christ. This kingdom is his, and his only, to govern. It is a kingdom in the midst of kingdoms.

4. It is natural, therefore, that Christ is seen in the opening chapter in his relation to the Churches - as the Son of Man glorified, walking in the midst of the candlesticks of gold. This is in contrast to:

    - His present relation to the nations – hidden in his throne.
    - His future relation to the nations – coming forth to break them with a rod of iron.

5. The reference to 'candlesticks of gold' is a tabernacle reference. The candlesticks belong to the Sanctuary and the presence of God in heaven, yet are, for a season, in the world where Satan's seat is - a place of darkness, corruption, and death.

6. John, as a labourer amongst the Churches, saw them here in a new relation. He did not visit them individually in his vision, but saw them together in a secret holy place.

7. Christ walked among the candlesticks (not the Churches) as an assessor and judge. In the first chapter he appears therefore not as king with a diadem, but as a judge - albeit with a priestly vestment.

8. He appeared as wholly Divine, and the Churches also had those Divine characteristics (they were of gold). If they were obedient (if they 'had ears to hear'), Christ could and would maintain them through his priestly ministrations.

**Second Edition – 'Chapter 1. On Chapter 1'**

1. Although the great object of The Book of Revelation is to communicate instruction respecting the future, especially concerning the nations and their evil, before the Lord enters into these things he directs attention to the condition of those to whom the instruction was addressed - the Churches. They were numbered among 'the things that are' (Rev. 1:19).

2. The Jerusalem Church had been destroyed when the Book of Revelation was written, but the Gentile Churches remained as a united and separate testimony, although with diminished power. They had a heavenly testimony, whilst Israel was blinded, and whilst the nations were fierce and devouring monsters.

3. Seven Churches were selected to give a complete representation of the practical condition of Gentile Christianity *at that time*. They are to be regarded as representing *all* Gentile Christianity *as it was then*. There was one focus of light in each locality, but they shone collectively in the world around them. Proper unity is gone if individual or collective testimony is wanting.

4. The symbolism of the candlestick relates to the candlestick in the inner court of the Temple. Zechariah's vision represented the millennial glory of Israel as a candlestick (Zech. 4:2). What Israel will be as to light, the Gentile Churches already were. Although *they* would fail, Israel's brightness will then never wane or be scattered. But, although the Gentile candlesticks and Israel's candlestick are circumstantially different, their light is essentially the same.

5. John had known the earthly Churches, but was taken to a heavenly Sanctuary in which they collectively shone.

6. The Churches were at that time collectively 'the pillar and ground of truth', and had a unity secured by him who walked among them and who held the seven stars in his right hand. Their unity was also secured by unlocalised ministry, firstly of the Apostles, and then of Timothy,

Titus, and others. Elders or bishops were always localised. The circulating ministry was not localised. It was by the circulating ministry that elders were appointed. This ministry ensured that the Churches were not independent of one another.

7. In this vision Christ walks among the Churches, demonstrating his awareness of their condition. He exercises his role of assessing, correcting, supplying grace, and, if required, of removing candlesticks. Few things are more important than remembering this relation of Christ to the Churches.

8. Christ walks as an assessor and judge.[1] In the first chapter he appears therefore not as king with a diadem, but as a judge, albeit with a priestly vestment.

9. Christ came to the Churches in grace, not in judgement. If they 'had ears to hear', and were obedient, he would rectify what was wrong.

10. We find it difficult to conceive, from our experience of the compromised state of the Church, what the apostolic Church was. It was not perfect, but error and failure was immediately met and corrected. It did not seek the authority of Caesar's courts, or of false corporate ecclesiastical authority. Truth was known and loved as something definite and fixed.

11. Gentile Christianity was, however, fast waning when the Book of Revelation was written. It is easy to forget the value that Truth has in itself, apart from the condition of its servants, and apart from its successes. John was bidden to give a final warning. It was not heeded, and the 'candlestick' condition of the Gentile Churches forever ceased.

12. The removal of the candlestick did not mean that Christianity would be removed, or that the external features of a Church would be removed. The hour when the Lord removed the candlestick would be discovered gradually, by its consequences. The leaven of wickedness would grow, once the candlestick was removed. 'Unless the corporate forms of Christianity, such as they have been seen in the East and in the West, during the last 1800 years are to be defended, we must admit these things'.

13. When the corporate testimony of the Church ceased, the corporate testimony of false Christianity became the ally of the world's worst energies. It has been a potent force in helping the nations to the present point of their progress, and the Book of Revelation speaks of how that shall develop. Yet a remnant shall be preserved. The testimony of this book, sometimes hidden, sometimes perverted, will be valued and, maintained in its integrity, in the closing day of evil.

## 7. Seven Candlesticks of Gold [First and Second Editions]

This is a separate section in both the First and Second Editions. The text of the two editions again differs, but it is sufficiently similar to consider both editions together.

---

[1] This was criticised by J.N. Darby in his *An Examination of Statements Made in the 'Thoughts on the Apocalypse' by B.W. Newton* ..., p.53. Mr Newton responded to this in his *Letter to the Brethren and Sisters...*, pp.53, 54 stating 'the candlesticks were only symbolically the Churches', but drops the statement completely in the Second Edition. See paragraph 7 of the summary of the parallel sections in the first edition.

# Appendix 1. A Comparison of the Editions of *Thoughts on the Apocalypse*

The Second Edition adds the note at the beginning of the chapter – 'Those who may not feel interested in this subject, and who desire to consider The Revelation in its prophetic parts only, may pass on to the next chapter'.

This chapter gives instruction on the order of the Gentile Churches. We are mistaken if we believe that the question of Church order is left open, to be decided by our own judgement, or on the varying rules of expediency. The question of Church order affects all who desire to honour God by an obedient recognition of his arrangements.

The Church was not ordered (to the form that the Lord Jesus intended it) whilst he was personally on earth. He was concerned with collecting, rather than arranging; with preparing, rather than building. Believers were not, until the day of Pentecost, 'builded together for an habitation of God through the Spirit' (Eph. 2:22).

The Church was constituted on the day of Pentecost as a visible body in the earth. It was constituted at Jerusalem, which was intended to be a centre of light and control to other Churches for a season. Its standing, hopes, and laws were all heavenly. [Second Edition adds as a footnote, '…of late an ingenious, but most false and dangerous system, has been invented by some, by which all these things, and others no less important, are denied, and the Pentecostal Church been supposed to be earthly and Jewish in its standing, and its hopes'].

This Church order was first 'metropolitan' – with the Jerusalem Church like a sun in the centre of a planetary system. One candlestick with many branches and many lamps would have been a more appropriate representation of it than the seven candlesticks of Rev. 1. This will again be the character of Jerusalem in her metropolitan position in the Millennial Earth (Zech. 4:2).

When Jerusalem had rejected the testimony of the Church, St Paul was raised up to carry the same Gospel to the Gentiles. But the order of the Gentile Churches was not metropolitan. The Churches were separate – all equal – all alike – independent of one another, but not independent of him who invisibly walked among the candlesticks, and who was their invisible bond of unity. Nevertheless, it was tangible unity – recognised by the believer and the world alike.

Christendom is divided into two classes -
1. those who insist that the Church is one - that its unity should be visible, and that its order is prescribed by God (Rome, and those who follow Rome).
2. those who scorn the notion of visible unity, and vindicate the present divisions of Christianity (Dissenters).

True servants of God have almost exclusively been found amongst low Churchmen and Dissenters. In their anxiety to recover the Gospel, and to testify against the doctrines and pretensions of Rome, they have rejected Rome's false claim to unity, but have failed to account for why unity is absent. The true way to account for its absence requires humbling confession of past sin, and of present weakness. Neglect of what Scripture says of unity has given a weapon to the enemies of truth [in relation to the Oxford Movement].

The Scripture pattern is for one Church in one city. This is the only pattern given for the Gentile Churches. 'Any spiritual Christian, who has been trained in the principles of low Churchism or dissent' has either been careless about this, or considers that Christians may be rightly gathered around their respective points of difference – they may worship separately, teach separately, act separately - and yet still be rightly acknowledged as Churches of God. However, to neglect God's pattern is a sin. To act, uncontrolled by the directions of God's Word, cannot but be evil.

[Second Edition adds, 'it is plain that not being "perfectly joined together in unity of mind and of judgement" incapacitates us for concurrent action; for we cannot act together, if our doctrines be different and our principles various. We must needs remain, in that case, more or less in separation from (it may be in opposition to) each other. Such separation may be necessary, for we must not compromise the Truth for the sake of apparent union; but is it a necessity to be gloried in, or to be deplored? Shall we quietly acquiesce to it? - or shall we do all that in us lies towards the rectification of such a condition, by seeking after Truth, and union in it'].

All pretensions of unity have assumed centralised power. The pattern for Gentile Churches given in the Book of Revelation has been trampled underfoot.

We must repudiate the pretensions of any body which claims the reverence and regard due to a Church of God, without any of its credentials.

True Church-standing depends upon a candlestick remaining, and hence Christ's action. We may refuse his sentence, say that we will raise up another candlestick, speak about ordination and successional order, but 'the Lord will laugh at it'.

The claim to Church-standing and authority is not confined to Romanists. It would seem as if Protestants imagined that Luther was another St Paul, commissioned to re-establish the Churches in all the perfectness of their original standing.

Luther and the Reformers were specially employed by God to establish the paramount authority of Scripture, but they did not even restore local, much less catholic, unity. The Reformation commenced a period in which division has multiplied upon division. The history of Protestantism has manifested features as deadly and dark as Popery itself.

It is sinful to pretend to a Church-standing, when unity has ceased to exist, for it is found neither generally nor locally. Individual saints, and companies of saints, will remain; 'But as to unity – the proper and once realised unity of the Gentile Churches – it is gone, and gone forever'. 'He that hath an ear to hear may still hear what the Spirit said unto the Churches: but we cannot hear it as Churches, for Churches have ceased to be'. [Deleted in Second Edition].

[Second Edition. 'We have nevertheless the consolation that some will testify faithfully, even to the end, and will preach the Gospel, and minister to the saints. By these means some union in truth will be preserved. If we have grace and wisdom so to unite…our union will not be without some results of blessing. There are few texts more needful at the present time than Eph. 4:11. The body of Christ will not be edified unless saints individually minister to each other, and unless pastors and teachers are given to enable this'].

'I do not mean that because the proper unity of our dispensation is gone, we are therefore driven into isolated individuality'. 'The New Testament knows nothing of isolation'. We must not neglect 'the assembling of ourselves together'. The continuance of pastors and teachers secures the union (the visible union) of all those who are obedient to Christ. But such union is very different from the unity of unfallen Churches. It is a remnant testimony of those who do not bow the knee to Baal, of those who stand with Haggai and Nehemiah. This is a key to understanding the Book of Revelation, 'for its testimony is in great part founded upon the lapse of Christianity'.

## 8. Notes on Chapter 1

The 'Notes' in the Second Edition are considerably fuller and generally on additional verses or phrases than the First Edition. Most of the 'Notes' were rewritten.

The notes are on the introduction to the book, verses 1-10.

1. The 'revelation' is either that communicated to him or possessed by him.

It is not the revelation of him in glory. All the inflictions of judgement before chapter 19 refer to the present, not the next dispensation. Christ has not yet assumed the authority of his peculiar kingdom (Psa. 110). He is not yet revealed in his glory.

It is the communication of God through Jesus to declare these things in the Churches. We receive its instruction as servants.

1:1 'Speedily'. The Church is always to regard the fulfilment as near at hand.

In the Spirit in the Lord's day indicates he was in a trance with supernatural visual and hearing powers. The Lord's day is the first day of the week, the first day of the week – not the millennium.

The First Edition makes comment on verse 19, which the Second Edition does not.

## 9. Thoughts on chapter 4 and 5

The Second Edition uses the First as a template, with additional material woven around it, with some omissions, some rewriting. The Second Edition follows the first more closely in its 'Thoughts' on chapter 5 than on chapter 4.

John is taken to heaven to receive instruction, away from mankind in its idolatry, Israel in its judicial blindness, the Jerusalem Church scattered, the Gentile Churches about to be chastened, and the united corporate testimony of Christianity about to cease. In heaven he saw the stability of God's power and superintendence. The rainbow reminded him of God's covenant faithfulness in the face of human wickedness. He is shown the church of the firstborn, symbolised by the 24 elders. The Sinai-like thunderings, lightnings, and voices indicate that the glory shown is future. The seven spirits symbolise God's providential governance. The 'sea of glass like unto crystal' adopts the symbol of the brazen sea of the Temple showing the nature of the purity given by Christ. The 'living creatures' are the cherubim, who symbolise the redeemed – they with the elders give the praise of redemption (5:8,9). The power of the Church is characterised by the forms of the four living creatures. The symbolism of the Lion of Judah and the Lamb are described. The joyful song there sung was to abide with and comfort the Church through all its present and future sorrows as spoken of in this book.

The Second Edition adds a footnote (p.60), drawn from an anonymous article published in *The Christian Witness* Vol. 5 April 1838 - Thoughts on the Tabernacle. Its authorship is universally assigned to Mr Newton by MS attributions on early copies[1].

---
[1] See further notes on this in Section 7, Articles in *The Christian Witness*.

## 10. Notes on chapter 4 and 5

It should be noted in these chapters, and throughout the Revelation that many of the symbols used are those of the Temple – but applied to government not to the Temple service.

The 24 elders seated upon thrones is a symbol for the whole enthroned priestly body.

'There are few more unfortunate translations than that of 'beasts' for Ζωα - 'living creatures'.

The cherubim sing the song of redemption and therefore are a symbol of the Church

The new song is new because it is millennial

There is one phrase commented on in the First Edition but not in the Second – 'as of a trumpet talking with me' (4:1). Otherwise, the first is a close template for the Second Edition, with some variation and additional comment.

## 11. Thoughts on chapter 6

Apart from added emphasis to these principles, the Second Edition closely follows the First Edition paragraph by paragraph, but does update comments on events affecting the lands of the East.

The sealed roll has been opened and we pass into the strictly prophetic part of the book. The general principles of interpreting chapters 6-18 are set out. Whilst again the First Edition acts as a template, the Second Edition emphasises more strongly the two principles of interpretation adopted (already present in the former edition).

> Firstly, the principle of recurrence in Biblical teaching is evident from the narrative of the creation onwards.

> Secondly, consummation of blessing is recorded first, prior to the events of evil that precede and introduce it.

The principles are then applied to chapter 6. Its leading principle is the infliction of Divine chastisements. This first section of prophetic teaching is wide and general. The final triumph is put first in the chapter. The seals were opened, not to accomplish the various events, but to instruct us concerning them. Psalm 45 is the best commentary on the first seal.

Some faithfulness remained. The saints were seen under the place of the priestly intercession of Christ – the golden altar. During the time of Israel's blindness the place of blessing is turned into a place of judgement. The sixth seal shows the signs which shall immediately precede the manifestation of the Lord in glory. They portend judgement on the Roman world and perhaps beyond.

## 12. Notes on chapter 6 (First Edition simply 'Notes']

The editions all commence these 'notes' by giving a one page outline of Revelation 6-18, before commenting on the text of chapter 6.

The Second Edition comments on additional phrases and verses that were not the subject of comment in the First Edition. Mr Newton expands his consideration of the order of resurrection in 1 Corinthians 15, and of the Greek words parousia (παρουσια), epiphaneia (επιφανεια) and apocalypsis (αποκαλυψις) to five pages - probably in response to the criticisms of the First Edition made by J.N. Darby.

On Rev. 6:11 Mr Newton argues, apparently from S.P. Tregelles's 1844 text of the Book of Revelation, that one robe was given to the company. The Third Edition adds a footnote correcting this in the light of S.P. Tregelles's 1872 edition of the Greek text, but commenting that the argument of the paragraph is unaffected, as (whether one robe was given to the company or one robe to each) it was merely a token or guarantee that each should minister in such a holy garment at the resurrection.[1]

In his comments on 6:12, B.W. Newton argues forcibly for the literality of the prophecy, rather than its supposed 'symbolic' fulfilment in the days of Constantine.

## 13. Thoughts on chapter 7

The Second Edition follows the first with little additional material or restructuring.

B.W. Newton considers the chapter, which speaks of some, even in Jerusalem who will bear testimony to the truth at the last time. He regarded the reference to the 144,000 as relating to the preserved and converted remnant of Israel.

See the notes, later in this Appendix of Mr F.W. Wyatt's letter to Miss Martin, in which he indicates that B.W. Newton had a change of view on the interpretation of this chapter. He later considered the 144,000 as representing those converted through the 'Pearl Testimony' during the Great Tribulation.

## 14. Thoughts on chapter 8 and 9

The changes made in the Second Edition are very minimal, and amount to little more than a word or two on each page.

After the reassurance to God's people in Chapter 7, trumpets are blown by angels of God to awaken the messengers of God's wrath against Israel and the earth. The consciences of men will bear witness that this is the work of God, and yet they will not repent.

The instruction given in these chapters is more definite than chapter 6, but still does not specify place or time.

## 15. Notes on Revelation 7, 8 and 9

The notes set out the progressive nature of the afflictions that will come. Very minimal changes are made, and the same verses are the subject of comment in both editions.

## 16. Thoughts on chapter 10

Amendments between the versions are again very minimal.

---

[1] On this verse, see the comments on the children's tract *The White Robe* in Section 3, B.W. Newton's Published Works, and in Section 5, Anonymous Publications Ascribed to B.W. Newton.

Chapter 10 is a preface to chapters 11, 12 and 13[1], which give more minute detail of persons, time and place.

In chapter 10 the mighty angel, as in chapter 7, is considered to be the Lord Jesus, who here lays claim to earth and sea. Although the prospect is bright, the message communicated for the present (the little book) is sorrowful.

## 17. Thoughts on chapter 11

There is slightly greater divergence, in word, but not in substance, from the First Edition to the Second.

The chapter gives the history of Jerusalem during the period that immediately precedes its final visitation. At this time the Temple is restored, its worship re-established, the city a centre for the nations, bewitched by the flatteries of Antichrist, who is about to unleash his destruction upon it. When those 1260 days begin, Christianity will withdraw from Judah and Jerusalem, but God will raise up a unique testimony. The message of the Two Witnesses will be of judgement, not of grace. Their death and the earth's rejoicing over it will immediately precede the Lord's return. He will be invested with the power long delegated to the hands of men, and, at the sounding of the seventh trumpet, he commences his long-awaited reign.

## 18. Notes on chapters 10 and 11

The 'Notes' of the Second Edition have been rewritten, but mainly follow the structure of the First Edition.

With the exception of comment on Rev. 10:7, all the 'Notes' relate to chapter 11.

The Second Edition makes additional comment on the following verses:

10:7 regarding:
1. The New Testament prophets.
2. The (Brethren) teaching that the Church is called 'a' or 'the' mystery, which he strongly repudiates.
3. The unity of all saints, including those of the Old Testament and those saved during the Millennium, which will constitute one redeemed body.

Note that, although the Third Edition uses square brackets to indicate material added posthumously, the square brackets of this verse were used in, and copied from, the Second Edition.

11:1 explaining his [Mr Newton's] statement that the inner courts of the Sanctuary, and those who enter into them, symbolise us, and our worship.

11:8 commenting on the circumstances of the appointment of the first Anglican Archbishop of Jerusalem. Jerusalem is called 'Sodom and Egypt' in the verse.

11:15 relates to the investiture of the Son of Man. There is no comment in the First Edition.

---

[1] There seems to be a mistake in B.W. Newton's numbering of the three following chapters in paragraph 2 of this section in the Second and Third Editions. The three chapter numbers were added in his own hand.

# Appendix 1. A Comparison of the Editions of *Thoughts on the Apocalypse*

The Second Edition omits comments on the following verses:

11:4 Removing the comparison of the two candlesticks with the two olive trees of the prophecy of Zechariah; Removing Hebrew and Greek grammatical comments on the abstract sense of 'standing' here.

11:10 Removing the statement expressing the difficulty of distinguishing 'the earth' and 'the land' here, and commenting that the difficulty is peculiarly felt in relation to Isaiah 24. On this, see *Babylon and Egypt,* Third Edition p.372, where the difficulty is expressed in relation to the passage in Isaiah.

11:18 Removing the note on the 'true rendering', given in the First Edition as 'the nations have been angered'.

## 19. Supplementary Note Added in 1904

This explains the circumstances of the appointment of Michael Solomon Alexander as the first Anglican bishop of Jerusalem, to which B.W. Newton refers in his comment on Rev. 11:8.[1]

## 20. Thoughts on Chapter 12

Apart from the opening chapters, this section is the most thoroughly rewritten. However, close examination shows that, with the exception of paragraph 7 of the First Edition, all the others are replicated to some degree in the Second Edition. The sequence of some of the paragraphs is changed, and additional comments are made.

The chapter describes God's system of truth before its future establishment in glory. Both its glory and the hideousness of Satan are seen initially 'in heaven'. That future position of glory is pictured with similar symbol in Isaiah 66. In Revelation 12 Satan is described in possession of all the power of the ten kingdoms of the Roman world (having seven heads, ten horns and seven diadems upon his heads) persecuting the woman and the remnant of her seed. Although applicable to all the family of faith in one sense, the interpretation of the woman in this chapter is constrained by the chronological markers given – the ten horns of the dragon, his expulsion from heaven following the birth of the man-child, the woman in the wilderness for the 1260 days of Antichrist's power. At that time Christianity will be found in the midst of unbelieving Israel in Jerusalem. Its travailing to bring forth a testimony of strength will provoke an attempt at its destruction, which will in turn be the occasion of Satan's expulsion from heaven. Exposed to Satan's aggravated wrath, Christianity will be banished from the domain of Antichrist's kingdoms. His instrument in this is the subject of Revelation 13.

---

[1] See the references to Bishop Michael Solomon Alexander (1799-1845) in *The Prospects of The World in Connection with the Approaching Return of the Lord Jesus Christ* p.15,16; *Europe and the East* 2nd Edition, p.46; and the *Time the End Series* booklet No.5 'Apostolic Succession', a Review of 'Protestant Christendom'. (NT 5). See also FRY/1/1/1 (Noted in Section 10, Duplicated and Manuscript Items, C. 1 - Notebook of B.W. Newton's Addresses and Conversations copied by A.C. Fry). He was a rabbi converted and baptised in Plymouth in 1825. B.W. Newton knew him and met him with warnings, just before his departure to Jerusalem. Note too B.W. Newton's association with The Jews' Society at Oxford recorded in Section 12 – Miscellaneous Biographical Items and Memorabilia, A.6 - Association with missionary work at Oxford.

## 21. Notes on Chapter 12

12:1  Regarding 'the woman', the Notes in the Second Edition are longer and fuller, with some parts of the First Edition incorporated.  Some of the deleted comments of the First Edition help to clarify the Second Edition Notes.

12:3  In relation to 'the Dragon', the Second Edition lays more emphasis on commerce as a controlling influence.

12:5  The note on 'the man child' in the First Edition (seven lines) is expanded to more than four pages in the Second Edition, identifying him with the unified body of the redeemed that will at the time of the end shake Israel and disturb the slumber of the civilized earth.

New notes are added on the future rule of the man child, the child being caught away, and the duration referred to - namely '1260 days'.

12:17  The Second Edition moves the comment on the translation of 16:7 in this verse to the 'Notes' on chapter 16.

## 22. Thoughts on Chapter 13

In contrast to the significant changes made to the 'Thoughts' on the previous chapter, this chapter is virtually identical between the editions, apart from some additional comments on 13:11.

A footnote regarding the use of universal terms in relation to each of the four great empires is moved to the comments on 13:7 in the 'Notes' section in the Second Edition.

The Antichrist, described here, will distil in one person all the diversities of outward greatness of the great world empires which were foretold by Daniel's prophecies.  Satan will exalt this mighty monarch.

The seventeenth chapter gives the earlier history of Antichrist.  He is there seen with uncrowned horns (the crowns are still upon the dragon in chapter 12), sustaining the harlot and virtually subordinate to her.  In chapter 13 he arises from the (Mediterranean) Sea crowned and in his full development.  The predominant feature of the complex beast is the leopard of Greece.  Miracles will be wrought by this delegate of Satan.  Antichrist is to be the new centre of religion, complete with image ('the abomination of desolation') and priest.  It will be a thoroughly harmonised combination of civil and religious power.

## 23. Notes on Chapter 13

The opening preface is largely rewritten in the Second Edition.  It forms a 5 page preface to this section.  This comment describes the usurpation of the Pope over secular power and gives ten reasons why the description of the beast in this chapter cannot apply to popery.

13:1  'Notes' on the 'ten kings' in the Second Edition replace the less developed 'Thoughts' in the First Edition.  Mr Newton delineates the Roman Empire at its widest extent.  The note on the 'seven heads' in this verse in the First Edition is transferred to the Notes on Rev. 17:9 in the Second Edition.

Additional 'Notes' are added regarding 'on his horns, ten diadems', 'and on his heads, names of blasphemy'.

13:2 A note in the First Edition on 'the beast that I saw', which makes comparisons with Napoleon, is absent from the Second Edition. Comment on 'a leopard' - the deduction that Antichrist will arise from Greece - is omitted in the Second Edition.

13:5  The Second Edition expands the note on Antichrist, and the duration of his authority.  It identifies the Beast of Revelation 13 with the 'little horn' of Daniel.

13:6 The Second Edition omits comment on 'them that dwell in heaven'.

13:8 The Second Edition adds comment on this verse.

13:10 The Second Edition adds comment on this verse, but omits the First Edition comment on 'he that leadeth into captivity', in which B.W. Newton suggests that this is a reference to Isaiah 33 [verse 1].

13:11 The Second Edition adds further comment on this verse.

13:18 The Second Edition omits the following comment (on '666') 'But this and all other points of similar detail are probably not intended to be understood till the time comes, because no moral principles flow therefrom, to direct conduct now'.

## 24. Observations on 2 Thessalonians 2

These notes apparently first circulated with B.W. Newton's *Five Letters*.

After the Notes on chapter 14, the First Edition has this short section: Observations on 2 Thessalonians 2. At the end of this, the First Edition adds a one page note – 'Since the above was written, it has been suggested to me by a friend that the translation of the seventh verse of 2 Thess. 2 as it now stands…' and proposes the translation 'there is at present one that witholdeth'. The note is identified by reference to 'this present year (1846)'. The French Edition omits the reference to the 'friend' etc., but retains the date. We may speculate that the friend was S.P. Tregelles (see comments on the French Edition].

This section was omitted from the Second Edition, but was included, in an expanded form, with a different translation of the text, in *Prospects of the Ten Kingdoms*. A two page excursus on 'the mystery of lawlessness' (2 Thess. 2:7) is added by the Second Edition at its Note on Rev. 17:5.

## 25. Thoughts on chapter 14

The Second Edition follows the First very closely in this section.

No interference on the part of God to stem the onslaught of evil is mentioned in chapter 13. Chapter 14 gives the antidote to those events.  The Lamb is contrasted to the dragon.  Christ's return manifests the full results of redemption in this world and on Mount Zion. That will be the place of Divine glory and omnipotent power.  It will be the foot of Jacob's ladder.

From verse 6 onwards the chapter develops its principal theme.  It describes the manner in which God acts amongst the antichristian nations, both in testimony and judgement.  The character and sequence of events is given, but not the time at which they will occur.  The harvest field is Christendom, not the world in general.  The ripened clusters of 'the vine of the earth' will be fit only for the winepress of the wrath of God. It is, as Joel 3 shows set up at the Valley of Jehoshaphat. The vision closes without its fulfilment and a new vision commences in the next chapter.

Mr Newton wavered in his translation of Rev. 14:13. The First Edition has 'their works do follow with them'. The French Edition likewise did not add 'with'. Mr Newton crossed out 'with' in his proof for the Second Edition, but then wrote 'stet "with"' in the margin. 'With' appeared in the Second Edition, but the errata stated that it should be deleted. It is accordingly missing from the Third Edition. 'Follow with' (Greek μετα – meta) is the literal translation adopted by the Revised Version.

### 26. Notes on chapter 14

The 'Notes' of the First Edition are crossed through, and 'Here turn to manuscript', written by Mr Newton in his revising copy. Curiously, however, the changes between the two editions are comparatively minor.

On 14:14 one minor change is significant. The First Edition stated, 'It is not likely that any more nations will profess Christianity before the Lord comes'. The Second Edition changes 'any' to 'many', perhaps showing a change in his expectancy of the Lord's return, even in the short period that elapsed between the editions.

### 27. Thoughts on chapters 15 and 16

Very few changes are made in the Second Edition with regard to the 'Thoughts' on these chapters, which are considered as one vision. It reveals the last inflictions of the wrath of God, which precede the still more terrible wrath of the Lamb. The commission of Christ to act is given as soon as the ministration of vials ends (Psa. 110. cf. Rev. 16:15, which portends his entrance on the scene).

As in all former visions, the revelation of final blessing (v. 1-4) precedes the description of the following judgements. The imagery of the vision parallels that of God's judgement upon Egypt, and so it is preceded by the 'song of Moses and of the Lamb'. The song is the song of the risen Church of the firstborn. Mercy will be yet available to those who survive God's judgements (Psa. 68:31, Isa. 19:24).

The vision of the vials of God's wrath follows. The vessels of the Temple, because of the Israel's rejection of the Gospel are turned into instruments of wrath. The expectation is that the plagues described in chapter 16 will be literally fulfilled.

Chapter 16 again proceeds until the end of the day of man. As with preceding visions, it goes no further. The next chapter commences a new vision.

### 28. Notes on Chapters 15 and 16

15:1 A paragraph is added in the Second Edition, proving that none of the vials are poured out before Antichrist has established himself - because the first vial is directed toward those who had the mark of the beast and worshipped his image.

15:3 A comment is added on the Song of Moses and of the Lamb.

15:4 The section on this verse is rewritten in the Second Edition, with biblical passages quoted to explain the meaning of the Greek word οσιος (hosios).

15:6 The Second Edition expands the exposition of the two different Greek words translated 'linen' and 'fine linen' in the A.V.  Rev. 15:6 [λινον]; and Rev. 18:16, 19:8 (x2) and 14 [βυσσινος].

16:10 The Second Edition deletes the following note 'on the throne [AV 'seat'] of the Beast': 'I do not know whether this is to be understood of Babylon, or Jerusalem; but probably of the latter, for we find in Isaiah that the king of Babylon says, "I will exalt my throne above the stars of God, I will sit also on the mount of congregation, on the side of the north"' [Isa. 14:13].  Mr Newton does not clarify his view on this elsewhere in his writings, or bring the verse in association with Isaiah 14:13 when he commented on that elsewhere. *Answers to the Questions considered…at Plymouth* (1836, p.65) commented, 'We do not now inquire where the great power of the earth will be again concentrated. The seat of the beast's empire is expressly mentioned (Rev. 16:10) and must have a definite existence somewhere'.

16:7 The Note on 12:17 of the First Edition has been moved here.

## 29. Thoughts on Revelation 17

The comments of the two editions are almost identical, with a sentence added here or there.

The chapter is considered to relate to a preceding period. "It ends where the thirteenth begins". Here Antichrist holds his glory from and with another.  This is as has often been the case, where leaders have risen to greatness under the favours of some system they have served, until they cast off its patronage.  Many such godless systems have arisen, and been thought in past ages to be the fulfilment of this chapter, 'but the exactness of prophetic statement must not be destroyed by applications'.  The fulfilment is altogether future.  The ten horns indicate the final ten kingdoms. The seven mountains indicate the assumption of all authority in this area.  He saw the growth of capitalism and commercial interdependence as factors leading to the greatness of Babylon.  The sword is not mentioned in the chapter, but the wares of Babylon are enumerated at length.  The organs of Government are subject to this ephah system and will reach full development when finally associated with Babylon (Zech. 5).  B.W. Newton traces seven forms of monarchy which will precede the type of rule of the Beast (Rev. 17:11).  The system of Babylon will be destroyed.  The city with its wealth will continue, as will Antichrist's reign over it until his doom, and that of Babylon itself, comes.

The Second Edition added a footnote to the comments of the First Edition on the democratic uprising in France in 1848. (First Edition p.244; Second Edition p.270; Third Edition, p.368).

A three page section is inserted in the Second Edition, concerning 'the ephah going forth' (Zech. 5:6) (First Edition, p.253; Second Edition, pp.277-280; Third Edition pp.377-381).

The Second Edition adds a footnote in the last paragraph regarding 'the two women' who lifted up the ephah in Zech. 5:9 – 'we cannot say with certainty what the two women represent'.

## 30. Thoughts on Revelation 18

Very little change is made to the First Edition of this chapter.

## Appendix 1. A Comparison of the Editions of *Thoughts on the Apocalypse*

B.W. Newton anticipated the revival of the Euphratean Babylon and defended this position by noting the features of the prophecies of Isaiah 13 and 14, and Jeremiah 50 and the history of Babylon to the present time. He proceeds to demonstrate this from the book of Revelation – the reference to Babylon and the Euphrates in chapter 16. 'Every purpose of the Lord shall be performed against Babylon, to make the land of Babylon a desolation without inhabitant'.

A paragraph is added to the First Edition, affirming that, in Scripture, the final destruction of Babylon is universally identified with the final forgiveness and restoration of Israel - Jeremiah 50:4, 18, etc. (First Edition, p.268; Second Edition, pp.292, 293; Third Edition pp.398, 399).

Where the circumstances of Babylon are referred to (First Edition, p.270; Second Edition, p.295; Third Edition p.401), the Second Edition refers to further information in *Aids to Prophetic Enquiry, Second Series* [*Babylon and Egypt*].

The Appendix to this chapter in the First Edition (a letter received from someone who had visited Babylon 'eight or nine years ago') is deleted from the Second Edition. It was included in *Babylon and Egypt* at the end of the chapter on 'The Present Condition of Babylon.[1]

In commenting on the merchandise of Babylon (Rev. 18:13, Second Edition, p.299, Third Edition, p.407), Mr Newton refers to trafficking in the bodies and souls of men, which he relates to 'the state of our manufactures' and the sale of advowsons. The Third Edition updates with reference to the sale of benefices, and refers to Lord Shaftesbury's campaign, which resulted in the Factory Acts.

The allusion in the First Edition to a circumstance where 'a great mercantile army' was destroyed (First Edition, p.276) is clarified in the Second Edition (p.299). An additional note identifies the location as 'in Affghanistan' [*sic*]. The Third Edition (p.408) adds a fuller note describing the debacles suffered by a British Army in Afghanistan in 1837 and 1841-2, 'after an assault by the natives'.

**31. Notes on Revelation 17** [The chapter heading of the English Editions is incorrect, as the 'Notes' relate to both chapter 17 *and* 18. The French Edition has the correct heading]

The Notes on these chapters are re-written, slightly changing the interpretation.

17:1 'The Great Harlot' – The Second Edition omits, 'it should be observed that the symbol is a harlot, not an adulteress. This alone would be sufficient to show that an ecclesiastical body is not meant. Babylon is never represented as being married to the Lord – Israel and the Church are'. The Second Edition adds an argument for the futurity of this chapter.

17:5 The comment on this verse in the First Edition gives a circumstantial date reference for the Notes – 'There have been during the last month, multiplied religious meetings held in London'. The note of the First Edition is absent from the Second Edition.

The Second Edition draws the conclusion from verse 7 that the mystery pertains to the woman, not merely her name.

---

[1] See also the letter from Sir Henry Rawlinson to B.W. Newton, dated 12th April 1849, and the Section 3, Published Works of this Guide regarding *Babylon and Egypt*. Reference is made to Sir Henry Rawlinson in the Fry Manuscript (CBA 7049), p.317.

# Appendix 1. A Comparison of the Editions of *Thoughts on the Apocalypse*

A two page section follows on 2 Thess. 2:7 – 'the mystery of lawlessness', in the Second Edition. See our comment above on 'Observations on 2 Thessalonians 2' which follows the Notes on chapter 13 in the First Edition.

17:8 The Second Edition has a lengthy new note giving three possible interpretations of the Beast 'who was, and is, and is to come'. He regarded the correct interpretation to be that Antichrist was about to become 'a second Nebuchadnezzar'. The comment of the First Edition is much more tentative. It simply says 'about this, I would express no opinion', and concluded, 'But this, and the number of the name of the beast, in the thirteenth chapter, may be safely left for time to unfold. We shall understand it in due season'.

17:9 The First Edition has a brief thirteen line paragraph. The Second Edition expands this to two pages of Notes that apply the symbolic meaning of 'seven' and 'mountains' to Babylon morally (or 'Babylonianism'). Notes of the First Edition on 13:1 are moved here.

17:10,11 There is a considerable expansion of the Notes of the First Edition in the Second Edition, from three paragraphs to more than two pages. There is an exegetical argument in the Second Edition, refuting the identification that some have attempted of the 'kings' with the 'heads' and 'mountains' of the previous verse.

17:12. The First Edition draws a parallel between
>   17:12 and 19:19-21 and
>   13:12-14 and 19:20

>   proving that chapters 13 and 17 refer to the same person. This note is absent from the Second Edition.

17:16 The Second Edition gives a translation from Tregelles's Greek New Testament, and defends it against possible objections.

17:18 The Second Edition adds 'Notes' here regarding 'that great city which is sovereign [η εχουσα βασιλειαν]'[1], arguing against the assumption that this referred to the city then reigning – i.e. Rome. A corroborating comment on 'which reigneth' is inserted from *Aids to Prophetic Enquiry, Second Series* [Babylon and Egypt, 1859], thus enlarging the note to four pages.

18:3 'Come out of her'. In the note of the Second Edition on this exhortation, Mr Newton concedes that 'In a former edition, I regarded these words as addressed to a remnant of Israel who are to be delivered when Babylon falls: but, on further consideration, they appear to me to have a wider and more important application, as being addressed to those who have wisdom and grace, to discern the signs of times and to quit the sphere of moral danger and temptation, before (like Lot in Sodom) they are driven out by the actual intervention of judgement'

'The kings of the earth'. Different 'Notes' occur in the two editions, commenting on the state of international affairs when each was written, and making analogies and observations from them. In both cases these illustrate 'the characteristic principles of the day'. Notes included in all editions

---

[1] A.V. 'That great city which reigneth over the kings of the earth'

refer to civil war in Italy 'at this present moment' and to the first Italian trading vessel in India 'lately', both of which, according to a note in the Third Edition, occurred in 1844.[1]

A footnote in the First Edition, commenting on this verse gives a precise indication of when the section, was written. It quotes the Courier Francais [*Le Courrier français*] of the present week' (p.291).

18:13 'slaves and the souls of men'. In the Second Edition, Mr Newton comments on slavery in the light of the avarice of 'commerce', with reference to the then situation in America. The Third Edition adds a note regarding the circumstances in the early to mid-nineteenth century, and concerning the abolition of slavery.[2]

18:15 'The merchants of these things, which were made rich by her'. The First Edition laments urbanisation and the manufacture of 'luxuries', when God has commanded us to 'fill the earth'. The note is absent from the Second Edition.

Re 18:24 'And in her was found the blood of prophets, and of saints, and of all that were slain upon the earth'. The Second Edition adds a note showing lawlessness and 'latitudinarianism' are culpable, by sustaining and encouraging evil.

## 32. Thoughts on the nineteenth, twentieth and part of the twenty first chapters of the Apocalypse [to 21:8]

In the First Edition this is headed, Thoughts on the Nineteenth, Twentieth, and Part of Twenty-First Chapters of the Apocalypse (pp.297-312). In the Second Edition it is headed, On Revelation 19, 20, and 21, to Eighth Verse Inclusive.

The Second Edition is virtually identical with the first. The only changes are extremely minor.

Each of the preceding visions from chapter six onwards lead to 'the end of the age', when the Lord Jesus will return. Chapter 19 gives the results of the Lord's coming and the resurrection of the saints in relation to the ten kingdom area of Antichrist's reign. The moment the Lord terminates the history of Christendom and takes his saints to meet him in the air is the same moment when he gives the final blow to Babylon. The chapter thus begins with the saints with the Lord in glory giving thanks for that final destruction. The Lord then goes forth against Antichrist. The saints 'fall into the train of his glory'. The character of his conquering power is shown, which he afterwards exercises. Human greatness is destroyed at 'the supper of the great God'. The long reign and deceit of Satan is ended (but for a little season) forever. It is the Old Testament that describes the millennial period. The book of Revelation describes the heavenly instrumentality (the exaltation of Christ and his risen saints) by which that period is reached. The Millennium is passed over briefly in Revelation, almost as though it was simply to show again the repeated hopelessness of man's evil heart, the sinfulness of the flesh, even apart from Satan's agency.

At last the final judgement will come and all things will be made new. The heavenly city, apart from the earth during the millennium will descend into it.

---

[1] There were uprisings in Italy in 1830-1, 1833-34 and 1848-9. The only violence in 1844 was the Calabrian Expedition organized by the Bandiera brothers (note from T.C.F. Stunt).

[2] See his letter to his mother dated, 22nd April 1830, in which he refers to a petition he had written to both Houses of Parliament regarding West Indian slavery.

The first eight verses of Revelation 21 take us further into the future than any other part of Revelation, or of Scripture. 'They alone treat of the new heavens and the new earth'

**33. Notes on Revelation 19, 20 and 21** [to verse 8]

The notes in the Second Edition are headed, 'Notes on Revelation 19, 20, and 21', In both the First and Second Edition Notes, the last comment is on Rev. 21:1.

The section starts with an introduction on the chapter divisions of the last part of the book of Revelation. 'There is, perhaps, no part of the Scripture which needs more a new division of chapters'. It proposes:
1. Rev. 19:1-10 forms chapter 19. It gives references that are later developed, in the same relation as chapter 14 to chapters 15-18.
2. Rev. 19:11 – 21:8 forms chapter 20. This gives consecutive events that will be happen in the order given, and should therefore be one chapter.
3. Rev. 21:9 – 22:5 forms chapter 21. This gives the condition of the heavenly city during the Millennium.
4. Rev. 22:6-21 forms the conclusion of the book.

There are very few changes in these Notes, apart from the following:

19:8 A note on the 'righteousness' referred to in this verse is deleted in the Second Edition. Mr Newton wrote, 'The righteousness (δικαιωματα) represented by the fine linen refers, I think, not to the righteousness of Christ, in which they have been accepted, but to the practical righteousnesses, in the power of which they will live and act'. See the comment on the Rev. 15:6 'Note'.

19:11 The Second Edition adds a note affirming that the verse teaches the character of the power with which the Lord Jesus will be invested.

21:1 The reference to 'no more sea' distinguishes the millennial from the new earth – 'for in the millennial earth the sea is frequently mentioned'.

**34. Thoughts on Revelation 21:9 to 22:21** [This is wrongly titled in the First Edition, and the French Edition, as 'Thoughts on the Twenty-Second Chapter of the Apocalypse, Beginning at the Ninth Verse. The Second and Third Editions also wrongly title it as 'On Revelation 21 [only] beginning at verse 9'].

This section in the First and Second Editions appears to be identical.

Revelation does not give a description of the millennium, but it does represent the manifold heavenly glory of the saints and the agency of the earth's blessing. The connection between the millennial earth and the heavenly city is most fully described in this section. The heavenly city is looked upon as seen from below, externally and afar off, rather than as known within itself.

Its characteristics will be (1) heavenly glory (Rev. 21:10-22): (2) Light given in love (Rev. 21:23, 24; conf. Luke. 1:78, 79, and 2 Sam. 23:4): (3) A ministry of grace (refs. to the Lamb, healing, open gates). (4) The earthly Jerusalem 'will form, as it were, the exterior court of the temple of God' and earth will bring its gifts mediately to it (Rev. 21:25-27; conf. Isa. 60:11). (5) The preciousness of the

Church's testimony will be recognised (Rev. 21:14 – foundation of the Apostles). (6) The city will be Divinely excellent (Rev. 21:15, 16 – golden rod, perfect cube). 'Such are some of our prospects'.

Sweet words of comfort are given to the Church in the last chapter.

**35. Notes on Chapter 21:9 to Chapter 22 end** [The heading of the First Edition is simply 'Notes', as in each of these sections. The chapter heading of the Second and Third Editions is again faulty, 'Notes on Revelation 21 verse 9'].

21:10 The 1½ page note of the First Edition is expanded to a six page note in the Second Edition. It gives fuller comment on the distinctions between the Millennial Earth and the New Earth. It affirms the unity of the redeemed, which must include the Old Testament saints.

A paragraph of the First Edition is deleted. This suggests a possible difference as to honour and privilege between those who inhabit the New Jerusalem, and the rest of those who inhabit the New Earth, drawing an analogy with the citizens of Jerusalem and those of the rest of the cities of Israel in former times. He had qualified this by stating that such a distinction would be merely 'official', and not destroying the union of all who have been made alive in Christ.

22:16 The last note in the First Edition (out of sequence with the previous note on 22:17) is omitted from the Second Edition. It reads:

'I Jesus have sent my angel to testify unto you' (Rev. 22:16). – The sealed book which Jesus took from the throne [Rev. 5:1 ff.] – God's gift unto Him, appears to have been intended for Him alone. No one else opened its seals, or looked upon it, or read it; and no one ever will. That Book pertains to Jesus alone. It seems to have been a book of direction to Him, as to the subjects which He was commissioned to reveal to his servants, and that he guided Himself thereby, choosing His own means of making the communication; and using chiefly the instrumentality of an angel, by whom visions, accordant with the directions of the sealed book, were shown to John. This, I think, shows the relation of the sealed Book to the Revelation as a whole'.

**36. Appendix A: On Psalm 110:1**

The Second Edition adds two short appendixes; One on Psalm 110:1 (2 pages), referring to the present session of the Lord Jesus. The paragraphs concerning the eighth psalm are drawn from his *Letter to…Ebrington Street* (p.18). The other appendix (a single page) concerns the critical reading of the Greek of Revelation 5:9. This is expanded in the Third Edition by a further one and a half pages, giving evidence of increased textual weight for Mr Newton's reading. The posthumous *Time of the End* tract No.4 (produced two years before the Third Edition) gives these comments in a fuller form, as an account of an address by Mr Newton. The appendix seems to have been in relation to comments in J.N. Darby's *An Examination of the Statements made in the 'Thoughts on the Apocalypse'* (*Collected Writings*. Vol. 8 p.70).

**37. Appendix B: On Revelation 5:9**

This enlarges the case for the preferred reading, following comment on the verse in the 'thoughts' on chapter 5. B.W. Newton sets out the textual evidence in favour of 'thou hast redeemed us to God'. The word 'us' was deleted 'by some critics'. Its inclusion confirms that the cherubim are not angelic creatures, but 'the redeemed in certain aspects of their future glory'. He states, however, that the interpretation does not wholly depend upon this reading.

### 38. Note on Appendix B

This is a posthumous note in the Third Edition. It is a detailed note on the textual evidence and other circumstances since the issuing of the Second Edition. The inclusion of 'us' in the verse in the Received Text, is supported by its inclusion in Codex ℵ (Sinaiticus - discovered in 1859 by Tischendorf). Erroneous statements by William Kelly, purporting to quote Tischendorf, led to 'us' being absent from Alford's Greek New Testament. Alford would have amended his text and commentary following correspondence with S.P. Tregelles, but died before this could be done.[1]

## F. The French Edition (1847)

The First (English) Edition gives prominence to France in its description of European developments, for example, in its description of commercial enterprise (pp.244-245).

It is also significant that Mr Newton quotes the Courier Francais [*Le Courrier français*], of the present week' in the First Edition (p.291). Either he, or someone close to him, had good knowledge of French, and was following French interests very closely when he was preparing the book.

There are no explicit indications of who initiated the publication or translated the French Edition. However, there is significant internal evidence of the involvement of S.P. Tregelles.

**This evidence may be summarised as follows**:

1. Mr Newton is unlikely to have been directly involved in producing a French Edition at the height of the controversy with J.N. Darby, or of preparing it for publication in the period following the death of his first wife (18th May 1846).

2. Reference is made to an editor.

    At page 98 an editor's note (*Editeur*) adds comments on the thought of the author.

    It is difficult to imagine anyone other than S.P. Tregelles whom Mr Newton would have allowed to edit his commentary, or who would have presumed to have done so during the controversy at Plymouth.

3. There are corroborating quotations attributed to S.P. Tregelles as footnotes on pages 29 and 30.

4. The short section at the end of 'Notes' on chapter 13 and the 'Observations on 2 Thessalonians 2' is introduced, in the English version, by 'Since the above was written, it has been suggested to me by a friend that the translation of the seventh verse of 2 Thessalonians 2 as it now stands…'. This 'friend' was in all probability S.P. Tregelles. Mr Newton sought the authority of Dr Tregelles's knowledge of the Hebrew and Greek in his *Letter to … Ebrington Street* (in

---

[1] Υμας [you] was left out of Westcott and Hort's text, and from the text of the Revised Version. It is not in the current Nestle-Aland Greek text, nor the United Bible Societies Greek text. Bruce Metzger's *A Textual Commentary on the Greek New Testament* accounts for its absence by a text-critical argument, and an interpretation of the meaning of the text. Τω θεω (to God) is accepted into the text (although the evidence for it is 'slight') because 'this reading best accounts for the origin of the others'. The critical texts then prefer βασιλευσουσιν in v. 10, 'as more suited to the meaning of the context'.

which he defended *Thoughts on the Apocalypse* against the attacks of J.N. Darby). The French Edition omits the reference to 'the friend'. At the end of the (English) Thoughts on chapter 18, there is another postscript 'Appendix' that refers to a friend in India. Here the French Edition retains the reference to *'un ami chrétien'*.

5. Dr Tregelles had produced his Greek text of Revelation in 1844, and this had been used by B.W. Newton in his *Thoughts on the Apocalypse*. We find the Greek repeatedly introduced into the text of the French Edition, for example on pages 67, 84, 108, 185, 255, 311, 318, and 334.

6. Where Mr Newton refers to 'the Florentine Latin Version' the French adds *'ayant pour titre* Codex Amiatinus'. Dr Tregelles relied heavily on this manuscript of the Vulgate. It appeared (Codex Amiatinus) as a parallel column of his final Greek New Testament.

7. There is further evidence that the translator or editor was very concerned with exactness. Where Mr Newton relates the request of 'the mother of James and John' (p.132), the French Edition more precisely refers to 'La *mere des fils de Zébédée'* (compare Matthew 20:20 and Mark 10:35). Likewise, page 243 of the French Edition gives a more precise explanation to the note of page 220 in the English – *'que l'Eglise des premiers-nés héritera son partage céleste'*.

8. In 1851 Dr Tregelles published his book on *The Jansenists*, in which he thanks 'my friend, the Count de Tharon of Paris', and refers to his travels[1]. The French Edition was published in Paris. It is at least possible that his connection with France was developing in the preceding years.

**Against the involvement of S.P. Tregelles it could be argued.**

1. J.N. Darby had questioned the correctness of Mr Newton's reference to Griesbach on Rev. 5:9,10, and commented on Dr Tregelles's reading.[2] This seems to be behind Mr Newton's Appendix B in the Second Edition. The French Edition, however, does not enter into the debate, and simply translates Mr Newton's comments.

2. Likewise, the reference to 'a friend… who is now engaged in examining the text of the Revelation' (page 68) is simply translated without comment.

**Other features of the French Edition are as follows:**

1. It is not an edited version in any real sense of the word. There are no deliberate reductions or significant changes that can be discerned.

2. The Forward is simply concerned with the character of the translation, and issues concerning the printing of the book.

3. There are minor additional notes and changes, for example a footnote is added on the first page of the 'Preliminary Observations', where a comment is made regarding the title of the Book of Revelation. There is a further explanatory footnote on page 41. Mr Newton's footnote at page 48 (First Edition) is placed in the text, and a translator's (*'Trad.'*) footnote is added, p.67 (French).

---

[1] After his time of exile, when he served in the British army, Le Comte de Tharon [1786-1863] had known both B.W. Newton and S.P. Tregelles in Plymouth; see T.C.F. Stunt, *The Life and Times of Samuel Prideaux Tregelles* (2020) p.228 n.56.
[2] J.N. Darby, *An Examination of the Statements made in 'The Thoughts on the Apocalypse'* (Collected Writings Vol. 8, p.70).

# Appendix 1. A Comparison of the Editions of *Thoughts on the Apocalypse*

4. It adds the Scripture references of quotations, and indicates quotations with quotation marks where this was not done in the English First Edition.

5. There is some changing of paragraphing, with some joined paragraphs, and some split.

6. Reference to uncultivated areas of Canada (First Edition, p.293) is omitted in the French Edition (at p.317).[1]

## G. B.W. Newton's interpretation of Revelation 7 - F.W. Wyatt's letter

There are two copies/drafts of this letter by F.W. Wyatt in the Fry Collection, catalogued as 7187(24), and dated 25th July 1915. They are in Mr Wyatt's handwriting, and addressed from Tunbridge Wells to Miss Martin. Because of the letter's importance to the exposition, we copy the drafts/copies in full.

### First draft/copy

Dear Miss Martin,[2]

Mr Newton said repeatedly to persons now living – of whom I may mention Miss Butcher[3], Mr Alfred Fry, and myself – that he would expound the 7 of Revelation somewhat differently from the way he has done in his book. And if God would give strength and health, he would re-issue that work with those alterations. As that was not given him, and as no one was deputed by him to alter anything, it was not altered in the Third Edition, but remained as he left it, except a few historical notes to explain what he alluded to. You will see that that is very different from altering anything which he had written.

The alterations he proposed, do not concern the main Exposition. If we may compare it to a tree, the trunk will remain as it was, and the main limbs or branches are unaffected, and the greater part of the little twigs everywhere. But just a few little twigs on one small portion of the foliage are meant to be different.

Mr Newton spoke of this change both in public lectures and in private conversation, and in my notebooks I wrote down his words at the time, with the questions and remarks that Mr Fry or Dr Dalzell, or myself, or whoever was present at the time, made as well as Mr Newton's reply.[4] Dr Dalzell would quote Mr Newton's book, and he would reply, 'Yes, I did think that then, but I believe I was then mistaken'.

The change is of the paragraph beginning 'The vision, therefore, of those here mentioned, etc.' It is on page 98 of the First Edition 1844, on p.116 of the Second Edition 1853, and on p.158 of the Third

---

[1] Perhaps because of sensitivities in regard to recent unrest in French Canada.

[2] This was probably the Miss Martin who emigrated to Australia. See Section 12 Miscellaneous Biographical Items and Memorabilia, Reminiscences, Kyneton letter.

[3] Probably Miss Annie S. Butcher. Died 8th June 1919 at Tunbridge Wells. Obituary *Watching and Waiting* August 1919, p.55. Two of the F.W. Wyatt letters held by C.W.H. Griffiths refer to Miss Butcher - 7th July 1910 refers to her suffering and 'mortal illness'; and 'May 1912', which refers to a 'loose case of Notes in Miss Butcher's handwriting' received from A.C. Fry that F. W. Wyatt will undertake to copy. There is also a reference to the obituary in *The Times* of a Miss Butcher in a letter to him, 'I suppose it was the sister of your friend'. F.W. Wyatt also corresponded with Francis E. Butcher of Southborough regarding Hebrew. A letter from A.C. Fry to F.W. Wyatt, dated 4th April 1918 refers to Miss A. Butcher.

[4] We regret that we have not had the opportunity to check the notebooks in the Fry Collection at Manchester to locate the record to which F.W. Wyatt refers.

## Appendix 1. A Comparison of the Editions of *Thoughts on the Apocalypse*

Edition 1904. By the words 'the preserved remnant of Israel' Mr Newton meant those Jews who would be preserved through the terrors of the day of the Lord, and will form the new nation upon earth during the Millennium. In the First Edition (p.99) he translated 7:14 'came out of the Great Tribulation' which in the second he altered so as to mean all tribulation from Abel downwards. He wished that the article [the] had been kept. He believed that the innumerable multitude were Gentile converts born to God during the 3½ years of the Great Tribulation through the preaching by the 144,000 Israelites sealed in chapter 7, who are the Manchild that is born (chapter 12) before those 3½ years begin. You can see that that Manchild is born before the crowns are transferred from the seven heads to the ten kings and that is, before the arising of Antichrist to supremacy 17:12, for 'they receive power at one hour (one and the same hour) with the beast'. That fixes the date of the arising of this much desired group, a corporate body therefore 'Manchild', a symbol taken from their nation's conversion Isa. 66, standing exactly where the nation will stand when they are converted, born in a day. These are the much desired 'Pearl of great price', Matt. 13. For the first time in eternal history a body of power, purity and rare value. Unlike national Israel, however, they are crushed as a body by Satan and his servant the Roman Empire. The symbol is taken away to heaven, kept there for the nation 3½ years later. The men remain. Just as when the symbol candlestick was taken from Ephesus (2:5). The men remained, and Church work went on as usual, heedless of the change in their aspect as seen by God. So the company in Zion and neighbourhood is broke up. The devil raised up his instrument, 'Antichrist', who has his statue put in the Temple. The Manchild disciples flee and carry their Evangelic power (Rev. 14:6,7) with them, North, East, South and West, and this multitude is shown to John as the result of their labours.

Consequently, these 144,000 are the Israelitish branch of the Olive tree in this dispensation, and the multitude is part of 'the fullness of the Gentiles' of this dispensation (Romans 11) - during its last 3½ years. Consequently, too, they are not the entire 'Church of the first born ones', as Mr N. said in his book, but only a part of it.

The 144,000 of chapter 7 also are a prominent part (not the whole, but the most prominent) of the 'worshippers' in 11:1 in the inner Sanctuary. God accepts them and recognises them all through the 42 months (verse 2), even though Jerusalem and Palestine is smitten and given over. They are driven out, like Daniel, Shadrach and Meshak, etc., but they are inner-Sanctuary worshippers at Zion, being Israelites indeed, as Daniel while outwardly in Babylon (Dan. 6:10). So what a bright and glorious prospect! This cheered Mr Newton immensely. When Jews go back, there will be three sorts, worldly Jews, pious Old Testament Jews and Christian Jews. But a fourth will be brought out by God that will cast all Christianity to shame by their pearl-like purity and value to heaven. Earth will hate and despise their characteristics but Christ will at last see on earth and within Israel what he has for centuries been looking for. The treasure is not said to be disconnected from the field – that is, the Reformation never took or led the Church out of the world. The world appoints the clergy and the clergy of all sorts and forms of Christianity support the world. But these are a strong healthy Manchild able to rule all nations, if only the time was come.

I hope this is clear to you. If not, please let me know.

Yours sincerely,

Fred. W. Wyatt.

# Appendix 1. A Comparison of the Editions of *Thoughts on the Apocalypse*

**Second Draft/Copy**

Dear Miss Martin,

Mr Newton said to several persons in his later years, that he would expound the 7 chapter of Revelation differently from what he had printed in his book, if God would allow him health and strength to re-issue the book. He on one occasion spoke clearly and solemnly to that effect to the late Dr Dalzell and myself and I made memoranda at the time of what he said. We both of us cross-questioned him as to details, because of the great importance of the matter, and afterwards Dr Dalzell and I conversed about it with a clear apprehension of what Mr Newton said. One, or both, of us had said to Mr Newton when he first explained some item – 'But Mr Newton, this is different from what is in your book; you said there so and so'. And he replied 'Yes, I know it is: but that was my understanding of it at that time, and later consideration has shewn me I was mistaken; and if my life is spared and my strength, I will alter it in a new edition'. God did not renew his strength, and he died; and when the Third Edition was to be published the decision was that as he had left no writing we had better not make reference to the proposed alteration. The change makes no difference in the main and fundamental exposition as against the current wrong teaching in Christendom, but only affects one detail. No one should pretend or suppose that Mr Newton was infallible, or his judgement on every detail was unchangeable. We should be thankful for the remarkable steadfastness and accuracy that in his long life was really manifested.

Besides Dr Dalzell and myself, there are Miss Butcher[1] and Mr Alfred Fry to whom Mr Newton said pretty much the same.

Now as regards what the change is. In *Thoughts on the Apocalypse* p.158 the paragraph beginning 'The vision, therefore, of those here mentioned as sealed from among the tribes of Israel, I regard as having reference to the preserved remnant of Israel'. That, Mr Newton would alter. Those 144,000 he finally believed to be the Manchild that chapter 12 speaks of, and they belong to this dispensation, and the vision that follows in chapter 7 is a view of their converts, the result of their Gospel preaching after they have fled from Jerusalem and Palestine as our Saviour has commanded in Matt. 24. It (I mean Rev. 7:9-14) is therefore a view not of the whole Church of the firstborn ones, but only of a part of it – namely those converted during 3½ years which is the period of 'the Great Tribulation' Rev. 7:14. Thus what Mr Newton said in the next page (159) is quite true – that all in the Church of the firstborn have come out of great tribulation – 'all from Abel down to the very last convert will have known tribulation'. But the 14th verse should be translated, 'these are they which came out of The Great Tribulation' – for the Greek has the article.

In 12:3 the expected birth of this man-child, which is the conversion of the 144,000 who will be sealed as the Servants of our God (the angel's God) as destined to do an extraordinary work for God – the birth of this child is before the advent of Antichrist to supreme power. For the horns are not crowned but the heads only. Therefore the time is when the woman rules and not the ten kings Rev. 17:12. It is before 17:16 when he and his ten kings destroy the ruling system and rule despotically. And of course the Manchild birth is before the Antichrist breaks his covenant with the Jews in the midst of the week of seven years. For then begins the 3½ years of tribulation. and the image causing desolation is placed, and all disciples flee, and the Woman, Christianity, of whom

---

[1] See the note regarding Miss Butcher to which we refer in the other version of this letter given above.

the Manchild is born, is fed 1260 days in the wilderness. The symbol of the 'Manchild' is taken from the earth, taken from the 144,000, who therefore are no longer one body, but a lot of scattered units, dispersed among 'all nations and kindreds and peoples and tongues' 7:9, to whom they preach the everlasting gospel with power given from above, as symbolised in 14:6, 7. The angel had said they were 'the servants of our God' and sealed for a distinct work. If they had been allowed to stand and serve upon Zion, or in Jerusalem, their testimony would shake Satanic power greatly, and Antichrist knows that; therefore the devil stands ready to devour as soon as that body of men is formed and in working order. It says 12:5 that that body has everything necessary to enable them to rule all nations – millennial purity, millennial endowment, angelic help, and Christ's warm approval as the Pearl of great price for which, as a Merchantman, He has long been seeking, a goodly pearl. Therefore Satan destroys that body. One way of viewing their flight and dispersion is (Matt. 24:16) that they will obey the Saviour. Another way of describing it is that Satan is allowed to work his utmost and persecute them with all the power of the Roman nations, even breaking up the system of Babylonian harmonious liberality and latitudinarianism, and placing his statue or image in the Temple for Israel to worship. 'Her child was caught away to God and his throne' means like 2:5, 'I will remove thy candlestick'. In both cases it is only the symbol that is taken away from the men; the men remaining on earth as before. That symbol will come back to earth again when the nation is born to God. Isa. 66:8,9.

# APPENDIX 2

# A THEMATIC ARRANGEMENT OF B.W. NEWTON'S PRINCIPAL WORKS

# A THEMATIC ARRANGEMENT OF B.W. NEWTON'S PRINCIPAL WORKS

This arrangement was prepared at an early stage of this work, when some expressed interest in the publication of a Complete Works of B.W. Newton. Whilst it does not serve that purpose, it may be helpful to give a strategic view of his published works, and to give some idea of their scope and topics. The development of Print on Demand technology has brought down the cost of reprinting historic publications and (unexpectedly when this Guide was commenced decades ago) the main publications of B.W. Newton are now back in print.

What now appears to be needed is a digital, searchable, edition of his complete works.

This arrangement does not include all his published works. We have not included items published by others on the basis of notes of his lectures, although in the case of *Lectures on the Epistle to the Romans* this could be considered. An estimate is given of the approximate number of pages in each virtual volume.

Unless otherwise noted, the references are to the latest editions approved by B.W. Newton.

## EXPOSITION

### 1. On the Old Testament Saints..........367 pp.

| | |
|---|---|
| The O.T saints not excluded... (from *Narratives from the Old Testament*). | 36 pp. |
| Genesis 12,13,28,29 etc. (from *Narratives from the Old Testament*). | 77 pp. |
| *Moses, the Child of Faith.* | 66 pp. |
| *David, King of Israel.* | 164 pp. |
| The Rechabites (from *Narratives from the Old Testament*). | 24 pp. |

### 2. On Leviticus..........473 pp.

| | |
|---|---|
| *Thoughts on Parts of Leviticus.* | 404 pp. |
| On Leviticus 10 (from *Narratives from the Old Testament*). | 25 pp. |
| The Feasts of Israel (Lev. 23) (from *Thoughts on Scriptural Subjects*). | 37 pp. |
| Thoughts on the Tabernacle (from *Christian Witness*). | 7 pp. |

### 3. On the Psalms and Song of Solomon..........234 pp.

| | |
|---|---|
| *Prophetic Psalms in their Relation to Israel.* | 42 pp. |
| On Psalms 1, 2, 68, 84 (from *Expository Teaching on the Millennium and Israel's Future*). | 92 pp. |
| *Thoughts on Parts of the Song of Solomon.* | 100 pp. |

### 4. On Isaiah..........365 pp.

| | |
|---|---|
| *Thoughts on Parts of the Prophecy of Isaiah* (not including Note on Marcionism or Note on the Unity of the Redeemed. The Note on | 257 pp. |

Spiritualism is included in *Reflections on the Character and Spread of Spiritualism*).

On Isaiah 18 (from *Expository Teaching on the Millennium and Israel's Future*). — 18 pp.

Isaiah 53 (Two chapters from *Thoughts on Scriptural Subjects*). — 90 pp.

---

### 5. On the Prophecies of Daniel and Zechariah..............386 pp.

| | |
|---|---|
| On the Book of Daniel (from *The Investigator*, 1834). | 6 pp. |
| Chapters 1-3,5 and 7-11 of *Prospects of the Ten Kingdoms* | 232 pp. |
| *Israel in the Days of Haggai and Zechariah; with A Note upon the Prophecy of Haggai, Both Reprinted from 'Occasional Papers On Scriptural Subjects', also A Lecture Upon Zechariah 3... .* | 62 pp. |
| Zechariah 5 (from *Thoughts on Scriptural Subjects*). | 7 pp. |
| Zechariah 12,13 and 14 (*Aids to Prophetic Enquiry* chapters 4,5). | 30 pp. |
| *The Day of the Lord, a Lecture on Zechariah 14.* | 23 pp. |
| Notes on Zechariah 14 (from *Expository Teaching on the Millennium and Israel's Future*). | 26 pp. |

---

### 6. On Passages in the Gospels..............240 pp.

(Some editing needed because of overlaps. In total 252 pp.)

| | |
|---|---|
| *Thoughts on the History of Professing Christianity as Given in the Parables of Matthew 13.* | 36 pp. |
| *The Prophecy of the Lord Jesus as Contained in Matthew 24 and 25, Considered.* | 108 pp. |
| Thoughts on Matthew 24 (from *Aids to Prophetic Enquiry*). | 22 pp. |
| Luke 21 (from *Aids to Prophetic Enquiry*). | 21 pp. |
| *On Luke 21... the Substance of a Lecture... .* | 11 pp. |
| Regeneration ... (Jn. 3:1-15) (from *Gospel Truths*). | 34 pp. |
| Jesus Washing His Disciples' Feet (from *Atonement and Its Results*). | 20 pp. |

---

### 7. On Romans and passages in the Epistles..............350 pp.

| | |
|---|---|
| *The First and Second Chapters of the Epistle to the Romans, Considered... .* | 129 pp. |
| Justification (Romans 5: 1-11) (from *Gospel Truths*). | 22 pp. |
| Eternal Reconciliation (Romans 5) (from *Gospel Truths*). | 22 pp. |
| *The Seventh Chapter of the Epistle to the Romans, Considered.* | 84 pp. |
| No Condemnation (Romans 8) (from *Gospel Truths*). | 21 pp. |
| Notes on 1 Corinthians 1 (from *Occasional Papers on Scriptural Subjects*). | 27 pp. |

| | |
|---|---|
| On 2 Thessalonians 2 (chapter 12, *Prospects of the Ten Kingdoms*). | 22 pp. |
| On David Brown on 2 Thess. 2:8 (from *Occasional Papers on Scriptural Subjects*). | 6 pp. |
| Notes on 2 Peter 1 (from *Occasional Papers on Scriptural Subjects*). | 17 pp. |

## 8. On the Book of Revelation .................................................................. 544 pp.

| | |
|---|---|
| *Thoughts on the Apocalypse*, Third Edition | 532 pp. |
| Additional items left out of the Second Edition (see Appendix 1 of this Guide. A Comparison of the Editions of *Thoughts on the Apocalypse*). | 10 pp. |
| Frederick W. Wyatt's letter to Miss Martin regarding the interpretation of Revelation 7 and B.W. Newton's changed view of the chapter. | 2 pp. |

## 9. On the Hebrew Old Testament and Greek New Testament .................. 274 pp.

| | |
|---|---|
| *Notes Expository of the Greek of the First Chapter of Romans with Remarks on The Force Of Certain Synonyms, etc.* | 168 pp. |
| Notes on the Greek of Ephesians 1 (from *Occasional Papers on Scriptural Subjects*). | 55 pp. |
| Use of the Hebrew Future (Appendix 1 from *The Altered Translation of Genesis 2:5, as Given in the Revised Version, Considered*). | 12 pp. |
| Use of Hebrew word ראשית (*roshith* – beginning) (Appendix 2 from *The Altered Translation of Genesis 2:5, as Given in the Revised Version, Considered*). | 4 pp. |
| The [Greek] word κοσμος (*kosmos*) in 2 Peter 3:6 (Appendix 3 from *The Altered Translation of Genesis 2:5, as Given in the Revised Version, Considered*). | 6 pp. |
| Meaning of [Hebrew] היה (*hayah*) [and Greek] γινομαι (*ginomai*) (Appendix 4 from *The Altered Translation of Genesis 2:5, as Given in the Revised Version, Considered*). | 6 pp. |
| Note on the Greek ειναι (*einai*) and υπαρχειν (*huparchein*) (Appendix note from *The Altered Translation of Genesis 2:5, as Given in the Revised Version, Considered*). | 1 p.p |
| Notes on the words λογιζομαι (*logizomai*) etc. (from *Occasional Papers on Scriptural Subjects*). | 5 pp. |
| Use of ευλογεω (*eulogeo*) in the NT (from *Occasional Papers on Scriptural Subjects*). | 7 pp. |
| The use of the [Greek] preposition αντι (*anti*) in the New Testament (from *Thoughts on Scriptural Subjects*). | 10 pp. |

## 10. On Bible Translation and Versions............................................365 pp.

| | |
|---|---|
| *Remarks on the Revised English Version of the Greek New Testament.* | 355 pp. |
| *Dr Tregelles's Greek Testament; Remarks on Some Observations of the Bishop of Gloucester and Bristol* [C.J. Ellicott] *on Dr Tregelles's Revised Text of the Greek New Testament.* | 8 pp. |
| On the Septuagint Version of Daniel (Appendix D *Prospects of the Ten Kingdoms*, First Edition) | 2 pp. |

## DOCTRINE

## 11. On the Gospel...............................................................256 pp.

| | |
|---|---|
| *Acceptance with God.* | 4 pp. |
| *The Blood that Saveth.* | 4 pp. |
| *How does the Blood Save?* | 5 pp. |
| *Appointments of God in Judgment and Mercy.* | 55 pp. |
| *Atonement and Its Results* (omit Jesus washing His Disciples Feet). | 100 pp. |
| *Is Salvation by the Obedience of a Substitute a Fiction?* | 16 pp. |
| Imputation and Representation (from *Thoughts on Scriptural Subjects*). | 55 pp. |
| Truths concerning Christ as the Redeemer - (from *Old Truths* Vol. 2, 1867). | 2 pp. |
| *Salvation by Substitution* (without Appendix 4). | 15 pp. |

## 12. On Doctrinal Subjects...................................................369 pp.

| | |
|---|---|
| *Ancient Truths respecting the Deity and True Humanity* - (as published with *Christ, our Suffering Surety...*, and *Note on 1 Peter 2:4*). | 118 pp. |
| *Priesthood and Sacrifice essential to Worship.* | 10 pp. |
| *Doctrine of Scripture respecting Baptism.* | 154 pp. |
| Doctrine of the English Reformers on Baptism (Appendix B of *Judgement of the Court of Arches*) | 6 pp. |
| Note on the Lord's Supper; Note on Hebrews 13:10; Note on Certain Statements of Dean Goode on the Eucharist (from *Thoughts on Scriptural Subjects*). | 41 pp. |
| The Lord's Day our Sabbatic Day (from *Thoughts on Scriptural Subjects*) | 30 pp. |
| *The True Unity of the Church of God in Time and Eternity* | 10 pp. |

# PROPHECY

### 13. General and Introductory ..................................................................... **295 pp.**

| | |
|---|---|
| *How B.W. Newton Learned Prophetic Truth.* | 16 pp. |
| *A Letter to a Friend on the Study of Prophecy.* | 20 pp. |
| *A Second Letter to a Friend...Prophecy.* | 23 pp. |
| *Answers to...Questions...Considered at a Meeting...in Plymouth... 1834.* | 84 pp. |
| Introductory Observations (from *Aids to Prophetic Enquiry*). | 21 pp. |
| No Poetic Exaggeration in Scripture (from *Aids to Prophetic Enquiry*). | 19 pp. |
| *Thoughts on Unfulfilled Prophecy.* | 20 pp. |
| Preface to *Babylon and Egypt*. | 10 pp. |
| *The Prospects of the World in Connection with the Approaching Return of the Lord Jesus Christ.* | 24 pp. |
| *A Prophetic Map of the World; Intended to Exhibit its General Condition at the End of the Age* [with commentary]. | 20 pp. |
| Quotations from the Fathers (Appendix A, *Prospects of the Ten Kingdoms*). | 31 pp. |
| Extracts from Hippolytus (from *Babylon and Egypt*). | 6 pp. |
| *Map of the Ten Kingdoms of the Roman Empire.* | 1 p. |

### 14. Babylon, Egypt, Palestine, Syria, etc. ..................................................... **454 pp.**

| | |
|---|---|
| *Babylon and Egypt*, pp. 1-378 + Appendices B, C, D, E). | 410 pp. |
| Antichrist King in Babylon...present prospects... (from *Aids to Prophetic Enquiry*). | 16 pp. |
| *Remarks on the Ten Kingdoms of the Roman World.* | 12 pp. |

### 15. Europe in Prophecy ................................................................................ **326 pp.**

| | |
|---|---|
| *Europe and the East.* | 182 pp. |
| *European Prospects* (AD 1863). | 54 pp. |
| Sundry Remarks (Appendices B and C, Conclusion from *Prospects of the Ten Kingdoms*). | 90 pp. |

### 16. This Present Age .................................................................................... **350 pp.**

| | |
|---|---|
| *The Acknowledgement of God by Earthly Governments.* | 41 pp. |
| On the Natural Relations of Men and Governments to God (from *Prospects of the Ten Kingdoms*). | 20 pp. |
| *On the Exercise of Worldly Authority.* | 16 pp. |

| | |
|---|---:|
| *What is the Ephah of Zechariah 5? or, The Exhibition of 1851 Considered in Relation to the Principles of Modern Legislation.* | 40 pp. |
| Present Tendencies (from *Aids to Prophetic Enquiry*). | 32 pp. |
| *Thoughts on the Death of Captain Bird Allen and Other Christians Engaged in the Niger Expedition.* | 12 pp. |
| Christendom: A Retrospective and Prospective Outline (from *Babylon and Egypt*). | 174 pp. |
| *Babylon and Egypt.* Postscript 1. | 12 pp. |
| Preface, *Prospects of the Ten Kingdoms.* | 3 pp. |

## 17. Events to Precede the Lord's Return ...................... 247 pp.

| | |
|---|---:|
| *Order of Events Connected with the Appearing of Christ and His Millennial Reign* (from *Prospects of the Ten Kingdoms*). | 53 pp. |
| *Five Letters on Events Predicted in Scripture as Antecedent to the Coming of the Lord* (adjustments to be made in view of the later modification of *The Duty of Giving Heed...* and of *Thoughts on the Christian and Jewish Remnants at the Time of the End*. | 109 pp. |
| On the Duty of Giving Heed to the Predictions of Scripture Respecting Events That Intervene Between the Departure and Return of the Lord (an enlargement of one of the *Five Letters* from *Occasional Thoughts on Scriptural Subjects*).(from the above). | 6 pp. |
| *On the Prophecies Respecting the Jews and Jerusalem in the Form of a Catechism.* | 31 pp. |
| *Jerusalem, Its Future history.* | 48 pp. |

## 18. The Time of the End and The Millennium .......................... 318 pp.

| | |
|---|---:|
| *Thoughts on the End of the Age, Being in Part Compiled from Some Notes of Lectures Delivered at Sidmouth, and Elsewhere.* [Matthew 24, 25]. | 37 pp. |
| *Thoughts on the Christian and Jewish Remnants at the Time of the End.* | 24 pp. |
| The Future Siege of Jerusalem (*Investigator* 1833). | 4 pp. |
| Futurity of the Manifestation of Antichrist (from *Aids to Prophetic Enquiry*). | 26 pp. |
| Scriptures respecting Antichrist Compared (from *Aids to Prophetic Enquiry*). | 11 pp. |
| *The Antichrist Future, Also the 1260 Days of Antichrist's Reign Future.* | 83 pp. |
| *The Personal Return of the Lord Jesus necessary to the Introduction of Millennial Blessing.* | 18 pp. |
| Scriptural Proof of the Doctrine of the First Resurrection. (from *Aids to Prophetic Enquiry*). | 35 pp. |

| | |
|---|---:|
| Objections to the Millennial Reign considered (from *Aids to Prophetic Enquiry*). | 15 pp. |
| *The World to Come.* | 16 pp. |
| *Expository Teaching on the Millennium and Israel's Future* (first five sections). | 47 pp. |
| The Times of Restitution[1] (*Investigator* 1832). | 2 pp. |

## 19. Replies to Prophetic Views............................................................292 pp.

| | |
|---|---:|
| *A Letter to the Minister of Silver Street Chapel, Taunton in Reply to his Recent Lecture against the Pre-Millennial Advent of the Lord.* | 36 pp. |
| Examination of a Work Entitled 'Christ's Second Coming, Will It Be Premillennial?' by Rev. David Brown, DD (from *Occasional Papers on Scriptural Subjects*). | 47 pp. |
| Remarks on the Prophetic Statements of Mr Fleming (from *Aids to Prophetic Enquiry*). | 29 pp. |
| The Prophetic System of Mr Elliott and Dr Cumming Considered (from *Aids to Prophetic Enquiry*). | 73 pp. |
| Remarks on Bishop Wordsworth's Lectures on the Apocalypse (from *Aids to Prophetic Enquiry*). | 76 pp. |
| Extracts from the Works of Dr Lightfoot (in connection with Bishop Wordsworth, from *Aids to Prophetic Enquiry*). | 5 pp. |
| Augustine, Jerome, Lightfoot (from *Babylon and Egypt*). | 7 pp. |
| Prophecy and Ritualism (from *Old Truths*, Vol. 2, 1867). | 1 p. |
| The Future of Israel Denied by Modern Maintainers of Catholicity (Appendix D, *Judgement of the Court of Arches*). | 4 pp. |
| The Second Advent of Our Lord Not Secret But in Manifested Glory (from *Occasional Papers on Scriptural Subjects*). | 14 pp. |

## APOLOGETICS

## 20. Replies to Mr Darby and his Friends (1)..................................................297 pp.

### Before separating from 'The Brethren'

| | |
|---|---:|
| *A Letter to the Brethren and Sisters in Christ, Who Meet For Communion in Ebrington Street, Plymouth; Containing Remarks on a Recent Tract, Circulated Amongst Them* [this relates to J.N. Darby's pamphlet on *Thoughts on the Apocalypse*], 1845. | 63 pp. |
| *A Second Letter to the Brethren and Sisters in Christ, Meeting For Communion in Ebrington Street* [relating to J.N. Darby's further reply], 1845. | 68 pp. |

---

[1] NB This gives B.W. Newton's earlier view regarding the identity of Babylon

| | |
|---|---|
| *Letter to Clulow*. 1845. | 10 pp. |
| *Defence*. 1846. | 8 pp. |
| *Remarks on the Sufferings of the Lord Jesus: A Letter Addressed to Certain Brethren and Sisters in Christ*. 1847. | 49 pp. |
| *Observations on a Tract Entitled 'The Sufferings of Christ as Set Forth in a Lecture on Psalm 6, Considered'*. 1847. | 89 pp. |
| *A Statement and Acknowledgement Respecting Certain Doctrinal Errors*. 1847. | 10 pp. |

## 21. Replies to J.N. Darby and his Friends (2) ...................232 pp.
### After separating from 'The Brethren'

| | |
|---|---|
| *A Letter on Subjects Connected With the Lord's Humanity* 1848. | 55 pp. |
| *Brief Statements in the Form of Answers to Questions*. | 4 pp. |
| *Reply to a Tract of Mr Trotter Entitled 'What Are Mr Newton's Present Doctrines as to the Human Nature and Relationships of the Lord Jesus Christ?'*, 1850. | 12 pp. |
| *A Letter to a Friend Concerning a Tract Recently Published in Cork* (in reply to J.M. Code's tract), 1850. | 34 pp. |
| *Propositions for the Solemn Consideration of Christians* 1864. | 36 pp. |
| Note on Marcionism and the Unity of the Redeemed (from *Thoughts on Parts of the Prophecy Of Isaiah*) 1868. | 44 pp. |
| *Remarks on a Tract Entitled 'Justification in the Risen Christ'* (by C. Stanley) (from *Thoughts on Scriptural Subjects*. incl. Rom. 4:25) 1871. | 47 pp. |

## 22. On Quakerism, Irvingism, Spiritism and the Salvation Army ...................340 pp.

| | |
|---|---|
| *A Remonstrance to the Society of Friends*. | 110 pp. |
| *A Vindication of 'A Remonstrance to the Society of Friends'*. | 72 pp. |
| Letter on the Beacon Controversy (*Christian Observer*, April 1836). | 4 pp. |
| *Doctrines of the Church in Newman Street*. | 24 pp. |
| Letter on Irvingism (1835). Published in *Extracts from Baxter's 'Narrative of Facts'*. | 11 pp. |
| Note on the Doctrines of Mr Irving (from *Salvation by Substitution*, Appendix 4). | 8 pp. |
| *Reflections on the Character and Spread of Spiritualism*. | 88 pp. |
| *Address respecting the Methods of the Salvation Army*. | 23 pp. |

## 23. On Romanism ...................260 pp.

| | |
|---|---|
| *Doctrines of Popery as Established by the Council of Trent. No.1 On Holy Scripture and Tradition.* | 28 pp. |
| Doctrines of Popery as Established by the Council of Trent. No 2 On Original Sin. | 89 pp. |
| *'Falsification of the Meaning of the Word 'Justify' at the Council of Trent'* (from *Occasional Papers on Scriptural Subjects*). | 9 pp. |
| Remarks on Indefectibility (from *Aids to Prophetic Enquiry*). | 26 pp. |
| *Catholicity in a Dispensation of Failure, a Sure Token of Apostasy* | 46 pp. |
| *Reflections suggested by the Present Movement in England against Romanism.* | 21 pp. |
| *A Letter to Richard Waldo Sibthorpe [sic], B.D., Late Fellow of Magdalen College, Oxford on the Subject of his Recent Pamphlet.* | 34 pp. |
| John Wesley on the Toleration of Romanism (Postscript *Babylon and Egypt*). | 6 pp. |
| *Persecution of Protestants in Spain.* (pamphlet) | 1 p. |

### 24. On Anglicanism, Anglo-Catholicism, and Modernism..................…...…..248 pp.

| | |
|---|---|
| *Answers to Questions on the Propriety of Leaving the Church of England.* | 18 pp. |
| *Remarks on R. Pearsall Smith's Edition of Faber's Hymns.* | 194 pp. |
| *Judgements of the Court of Arches* (from *Occasional Papers on Scriptural Subjects*, without Appendices B and D listed elsewhere in this arrangement). | 84 pp. |
| Note on Dr Pusey's Statements (from *Babylon and Egypt*, Postscript 3). | 18 pp. |
| Comment on 'Ecce Homo' (from *Occasional Papers on Scriptural Subjects*). | 10 pp. |
| On the Spread of Neology in England (from *Occasional Papers on Scriptural Subjects*). | 24 pp. |

### 25. On Evolutionism…................................................................……..348 pp.

| | |
|---|---|
| *Remarks on 'Mosaic Cosmogony', Being the Fifth of the 'Essays and Reviews'.* | 103 pp. |
| *The Altered Translation of Gen. 2:5.* | 53 pp. |
| *Remarks on a Book Entitled 'Natural Law In The Spiritual World' By Henry Drummond, FRSI, FGS, Being the Substance of Four Lectures Given in London.* | 192 pp. |

### 26. The Evangelical Downgrade…..............................................…..........402 pp.

| | |
|---|---|
| Advertisement from the First Edition of *Aids to Prophetic Enquiry.* | 3 pp. |
| *The Excellency of the Person of Christ Unalterable. Remarks On The Doctrine of Olshausen* (from *Thoughts on Scriptural Subjects*). | 18 pp. |
| Modern Doctrines respecting Sinlessness considered [R. Pearsall Smith] (from *Thoughts on Scriptural Subjects* + Appendix) – 87 pp.. | 87 pp. |

| | |
|---|---:|
| Letter regarding R. Pearsall Smith's teaching (The Record). | 1 p. |
| *Tracts on Doctrinal Subjects* [1-6] (Patrick Fairbairn, etc). | 156 pp. |
| *Theological Opinions of Rev. Joseph Cook Of Boston, Briefly Considered.* | 137 pp. |

# APPENDIX 3

## A SELECT PUBLICATIONS LIST

relevant to the controversy of J.N. Darby with B.W. Newton and B.W. Newton's separation from the Brethren

# A SELECT PUBLICATIONS LIST
## relevant to the controversy of J.N. Darby with B.W. Newton, and B.W. Newton's separation from the Brethren

### INTRODUCTION

J.N. Darby and his friends branded B.W. Newton a heresiarch.[1] They excommunicated him from their circle of influence. Their attacks continued throughout his life, impugning his personal integrity and motives, and evoking Christological errors from anything he wrote. However, it was J.N. Darby and his friends who proved the truth of the Scripture 'with what judgment ye judge, ye shall be judged: and with what measure ye mete, it shall be measured to you again' (Matthew 7:2). The precious unity of the early Brethren Movement was shattered, and the Exclusive wing was riven by endless schisms, divisions, allegations, and counter-allegations, of heresy. 'Darby proved totally unable to keep clear of errors that, in the judgement of several of the foremost of his own adherents, were essentially the errors charged on Newton'.[2] In the end, it was Newton who Spurgeon, and many other esteemed leaders of the day, considered 'an honoured brother'.[3] Professor George Smeaton, himself a paragon of orthodoxy, later thanked him for his contribution to sound theology.[4]

It is no desire of this book to revive old hostilities that are still harboured by some of J.N. Darby's followers. But neither would it be right to give allegations a fresh airing by listing the torrent of vituperant publications that purported to be 'the whole case', 'a narrative of facts', 'plain statements' and so on. Such documents have been kept in print, and are still circulated by the followers of J.N. Darby. We therefore give a select list of other documents relevant to the controversy, rather than trying to be inclusive of all that was written. In the words of George Reynolds pamphlet, there is a need for *Audi Alteram Partem* – to hear the other side.

The first part of this Appendix, 'Contemporary Items', largely lists nineteenth century responses from B.W. Newton's circle to the attacks. Most of these items relate directly to B.W. Newton, but we have also included less directly related items by John Cox (sen. and jun.), and by S.P. Tregelles. B.W. Newton himself refrained from direct engagement after he had left the Brethren[5]. Many such items are long out of print, and we do not seek their republication. However, it does need to be recorded that there is a body of material that represents another side to the controversy. We believe this material breathes a very different spirit to that of the protagonists on J.N. Darby's side, as Horatius Bonar noted at the time.[6]

---

[1] See H.H. Rowdon, 'A Nineteenth Century Nestorius' in *Vox Evangelica*, June 1962, pp.60-75, in which he acquits B.W. Newton from the error with which he was charged; homologous to Nestorius being guiltless of Nestorianism.

[2] W. Blair Neatby. *A History of the Plymouth Brethren'*.

[3] See *The Sword and the Trowel* June 1889, etc.

[4] See letter 23rd May 1877. George Smeaton was professor at the Free Church of Scotland College. See the appreciation of him (George Smeaton) by W.J. Grier in the reprint of Smeaton's *The Doctrine of the Holy Spirit*, Banner of Truth Trust, 1958.

[5] See, for example the letter of 1st July 1862 to Rev. Medhurst of Coleraine, in which B.W. Newton declined to be drawn into any direct controversy with the Brethren, or to allow him to do so on his behalf. Section 6, B.W. Newton's Letters and Articles Published in Periodicals.

[6] See below under *The Quarterly Journal of Prophecy*.

# Appendix 3 A Select Publications List

The second part of this select list provides later items that take a broader perspective on the controversy at Plymouth and the development of Brethrenism. We feel that, taken together, they give a balanced view. There is a need however, to remember that B.W. Newton left Brethrenism in 1848 and ministered apart from the Brethren for fifty years after that. The circle in which he moved stayed very clear of either the 'exclusive' or 'open' wings of the movement. A balanced biography of his whole life has yet to be written.

This *Guide* shows that there never was any rapprochement, either at the beginning of the division, when J.L. Batten wished a 'reconciliation' in 1849[1]; or in correspondence with J.N. Darby's brother[2]. Time and again, he repudiated any association with the Brethren. When James Grant wrote his first book, and assumed B.W. Newton's connection with the movement, Mr Newton wrote to him, and had little difficulty in convincing him otherwise.[3] When a book by L. Desanctis implied B.W. Newton's continued connection with the Brethren, he was at pains to correct him, and Dr Desanctis gave a sincere apology.[4] One of his close adherents at the end of his life[5] wrote *Vitiated Brethrenism or Revived Marcionism*, clearly indicating that there was 'a great gulf fixed' between B.W. Newton and Open or Exclusive Brethren to the very end. It is therefore a supreme irony that 'The Fry Collection' forms a part of the Christian Brethren Archive, and that booksellers worldwide categorise his books as 'Brethren'.

## CONTEMPORARY ITEMS

### 1. *Plymouth Brethrenism Examined*
by Rev. John Cox[6]

In 1840, Rev. John Cox produced a short item regarding the Brethren.[7] He then published an enlarged booklet, *Plymouth Brethrenism Examined*, in 1845, prior to Newton's separation from the Brethren. It critiques articles in *The Inquirer*, and in *The Christian Witness*.

Before the Brethren division, he wrote almost prophetically, 'The Brethren would do well not to boast too soon of their superiority to other sects. They are only "putting on the harness"; their *system has yet to be tried.* In many respects it has been cradled on a bed of down, and what can do has been done for it. *It remains to be tried.* All new movements in religion present a show of superior sanctity at first'.

---

[1] See the letter of 26th February 1848 from Amy J.T. Toulmin in response to Miss Kate Gidley. Noted in Section 9 of this *Guide* - B.W. Newton's Correspondence

[2] See the letter of Horatio Darby to B.W. Newton dated 1st March 1871 and his reply. Noted in Section 9 of this *Guide* - B.W. Newton's Correspondence

[3] See James Grant, *The Religious Tendencies of the Times: or How to Deal with the Deadly Errors of the Day*, 1869.

[4] See letters, B.W Newton to Dr De Sanctis 5th April 1864, and Dr De Sanctis to B.W. Newton 10th April 1864 (in which he stated that he valued Mr Newton highly and that the book has been published without his consent from an old, unrevised, manuscript).

[5] Walter Lancelot Holland

[6] Rev. John Cox (1802-1878), Baptist minister. The integrated catalogue of British Libraries attributes 123 books and pamphlets to him. In connection with Brethrenism he also wrote *Test before you Trust; or The New Doctrine and the Old Divinity Compared*. He is to be distinguished from his son (also John Cox, 1829-1915), who was a keen supporter of Mr Newton and published *Old Truths* between 1865 and 1868.

[7] *Plymouth Brethrenism Exhibited: in Extracts from the Writings of the Brethren, with Remarks*, 1840, printed by James Black, 8 pages. (Listed in CBA 6998, Tract No.28. Copy held in the CBA)

It would be interesting to know what role, if any, this booklet had on Mr Newton's decision to leave the Brethren, and his subsequent friendship with Rev. John Cox. This friendship grew rapidly after B.W. Newton's withdrawal from the Brethren. John Cox conducted the funeral of Mr Newton's only child in 1855. Rev. John Cox's eschatology, and certainly that of his son (John Cox, jun.), moved closer to that of Mr Newton over time.

    1845[1]      Nisbet, and Ward & Co, London         40p.     BL

## 2. Correspondence etc. Relating to Mr Newton's Refusal to Appear before the Saints at Rawstorne Street, London, According to The Two Citations which issued from them, November 20th, to December 6th 1846

This was a collection of the letters and other items concerning the attempt of the leaders of the London Brethren Assembly at Rawstorne Street to arraign Mr Newton before them, together with the response of the leaders of the Plymouth Assembly with Mr Newton. It was published without comment by Lord Congleton, apparently to give objectivity, showing how each side had acted.[2]

For fuller description of this item see Section 4, B.W. Newton's Contributions to Other Publications, in this *Guide*.

    1846       Tract Depot, Plymouth              50p.     CBA 14162

## 3. Remonstrance and Protest addressed to the saints at Rawstorne Street, London, respecting their late Act of excluding Mr Newton from the Lord's Table

See the note regarding this published letter in Section 9 of this *Guide*, B.W. Newton's Correspondence at the date of the letter, 25th December 1846. Quoted in *History of the Brethren Movement* by H.H. Rowdon.

    1846       Tract Depot, 5 Cornwall Street, Plymouth, and sold by I.K. Campbell, 1, Warwick Square, London         12p.     CBA 8438

## 4. A Letter [from] Mr Tregelles to Mr [Henry] Gough Relative to the Exclusion of Mr Newton from the Lord's Table in Rawstorne Street, London

Three of those present at the London Brethren meeting held to judge B.W. Newton (William Blake, John Scoble, and Frederick Prideaux) published S.P. Tregelles's letter 'by permission', as it expressed the reasons they could not concur with the Rawstorne Street's 'act of excommunication'. For further detail on their letter (dated 22nd January 1847), and S.P. Tregelles's letter (dated 16th December 1846) see Section 9 of this *Guide*, B.W. Newton Correspondence. The letter has three appendices that were not a part of the original letter. They detail events, and circumstances relating to the events of November and December 1846.[3]

    1847       I.K. Campbell, London & Plymouth Tract Depot  24p.  CBA 13813

---

[1] After April 1845 – see p.36.
[2] John Vesey Parnell (1805-1883)
[3] The publication is quoted in T.C.F. Stunt, *Life and Times of Samuel Prideaux Tregelles*, p44,45.

### 5. 'Shibboleth' or the New Test of Communion amongst certain Brethren.

'A counter appeal to the Christians at Bethesda, Bristol, in Answer to G.V. Wigram's attack on Henry Craik. With Reflections'. Written under the pseudonym 'Vindex'.

Printed in Bristol. Anonymous. Quoted by W.B. Neatby and others.

[1848]     Houlston & Stoneman, London.            40p.      CBA

### 6. A Statement from Christians assembling in the Name of the Lord in Ebrington Street, Plymouth

This was the printed reply of those who remained at the Ebrington Street Chapel to the 'Confessions' of H.W. Soltau, J.E. Batten, and W.B. Dyer. Mr Newton wrote to a correspondent approving the statement (see the letter listed dated 2nd February 1848). Quoted by Blair Neatby, *A History of the Plymouth Brethren*, p. 71

Dated 10th January 1848. Original Printed Copy – TC. Listed in CBA 6998, 1848, Folio 1.

### 7. Three Letters to the author of 'A Retrospect of Events that have taken place among the Brethren'

by Samuel Prideaux Tregelles

The *Retrospect...* was anonymous.[1] It was to some extent a critique of J.N. Darby's *Narrative of Facts...* S.P. Tregelles's book has three sections, (1) Ministry, (2) Facts connected with the divisions at Plymouth, and (3) The Sufferings of our Lord, the application of the Psalms to Christ, and liberty of teaching on prophetic subjects. It also includes the doctrinal statements that were appended to B.W. Newton's *Letter to Clulow* [18 April 1845] (pp.64-66).

First Edition
1849     Plymouth                              34p.      CBA 14586 (Xerox)

Second Edition
1894     Houlston & Sons, London               76p.      CBA 1797, SG

### 8. The Quarterly Journal of Prophecy

For a view from outside Brethren circles on how the controversy with Mr Newton, and J.N. Darby's various pamphlets were received, the (Quarterly) *Journal of Prophecy* is a good source, with many items and reviews. Examples are Vol. 1 (1849), p.209 on *Remarks on 'A Letter on Subjects connected with the Lord's Humanity'* by J.N. Darby; Vol. 1 (1849), p.71 on *An Examination of the Statements made in the 'Thoughts on the Apocalypse' by B.W. Newton...* by J.N. Darby. A series was later run in 1862 on 'Darbyism and Socinianism', which was defended on, pp.176-177 of Vol. 14 for that year, with the added charge of Valentinianism, because of the teaching of the 'heavenly humanity' of Christ.

The Evangelical Library London has a full set of the Journal.

---

[1] A note by F.W. Wyatt in MS Book 1 (TC) states that Amy Toulmin indicated the author to be [Robert Mackenzie] Beverley. It was published by Benjamin Green, London, in 1849.

## Appendix 3 A Select Publications List

**9. *Test before you Trust; or The New Doctrine and the Old Divinity compared***
by Rev. John Cox [sen.]

Described by *The Quarterly Journal of Prophecy* (Vol. 14, 1862, pp.176-182) as 'calm, clear, forcible and satisfactory'.

First? Edition *Test Before you Trust; or the Innovations of the Brethren.*

ND [1862]　　　Nisbet & Co, London　　　1+28+4p.　CBA 13700

**10. *Christ the End of the Law for Righteousness: Five Letters to the Editor of* The Record *on Recent Denials of our Lord's vicarious Life***
by S.P. Tregelles

The five letters were published as a booklet. They relate particularly to the teaching of J.N. Darby and C.H. Macintosh. The booklet gives an account of the dispute with B.W. Newton at Plymouth, and describes the Church order there as 'modified Presbyterianism'.

First Edition
1863　　　Plymouth and London　　　31p.　BL

Second Edition 'with notes in square brackets'.
1863　　Plymouth, and Houlston & Wright, London　　31p.　BL

'Second Edition, reprinted'
1910　　Hunt, Barnard & Co, London and Aylesbury　40+2p.　CBA 1944

**11. *The Testimony of Mr B.W. Newton concerning the Divinity and Humanity of the Lord Jesus. Extracted from 'Old Truths'***

1867　　London　　　8p.　CBA 6377,(28)

**12. *Judge Righteous Judgement. Letters Respecting Certain Charges Made by The Brethren***
by John Cox [jun.]

John Cox wrote these letters to publications and individuals to refute the assumption that Mr Newton held the views attributed to him by the Darbyites. They appeal against the ongoing calumny directed at him.

Second Edition
1867　　Houlston & Wright, London　　　8p.　CBA 9043

**13. *A Refutation of Certain Charges made by the Brethren***
by John Cox, [jun.]

Reviewed in *The Quarterly Journal of Prophecy* (ed. Horatius Bonar], 1867, pp.401 ff. 'We thank Mr Cox, jun. for this excellent and satisfactory pamphlet. It shows the Darbyite zeal for sound doctrine, in the case of Mr Newton, has been a mere pretext for attacking an obnoxious rival. These sectarians have become the champions of worse heresies than anything charged against Mr Newton'.

First Edition
1867        Houlston and Wright, London            44p.        BL

Second Edition
1867        Houlston and Wright, London            44p.        CBA 6205

**14.** *An Earnest Expostulation. A Letter addressed to the Author of* **High Church Claims of the Exclusive Brethren**[1]

by John Cox, [jun.]

The letter is dated May 1869. W.H. Dorman had written of his changed perception of J.N. Darby and his teaching, after many years of association with him. John Cox sought to demonstrate J.N. Darby's misrepresentation of Mr Newton, and appealed to W.H. Dorman to reconsider his past, and currently expressed, allegations against him (Mr Newton). 'I still fearlessly maintain, and am prepared to prove, that Mr Newton does not and <u>never did teach or hold</u> the heretical doctrines so persistently attributed to him by Mr Darby'. The pamphlet gives a helpful account of the stages of the controversy, and particularly an account of the tract, *The Doctrines of the Church in Newman Street* by Mr Newton.

1869        Houlston & Wright, London            28+4p.     CBA 9028, BL

**15.** *A Letter to the Saints Meeting at Moscow Hall, Bayswater*

by A[nna] M[atilda] Hull

The perspective of one who had been connected with the Brethren for a long period and who was associated with W.H. Dorman, but left and joined Mr Newton's meeting. She wrote of her experience of Mr Newton's grace and forbearance at those who had so sorely wounded him, and his entire lack of asperity towards them.

1869        Geo. Hunt                                39p.        CBA

**16.** *Destroying and Building: or A Few Remarks on a Pamphlet*[2] *Entitled,* **The Step I have Taken: Being Letters to a Friend on Taking his Place with 'Brethren'**

by John Cox [sen. and jun. – see preface]

This does not relate directly to B.W. Newton, but is a further indication of the robust **response of both father and son to Darbyism. Edward Dennett (1831-1914) was a Baptist minister in Greenwich who resigned and joined the Brethren in 1873. He had published** *The Plymouth Brethren, their Rise, Divisions, Practice and Doctrine* in 1870. He was at one time a ministerial colleague of Rev. John Cox. This tract chiefly responds to Dennett's defence of 'The Presidency of the Holy Spirit'.[3]

C.H. Spurgeon was equally dismissive of Edward Dennett's pamphlet, and his claim to his 'friend' that 'besides yourself, I never met with a dissenting minister who held the verbal

---

[1] William Henry Dorman (1802-1878)
[2] By Edward Dennett
[3] On this subject, see Appendix of NP 37. *The 'Holy Spirit'; His Office and Work*, in Section 8, Publications Produced from Notes of Addresses, and Posthumously Published Letters and Manuscripts.

inspiration of the Scriptures', which presumably included Spurgeon himself, Rev. John Cox and a number of others![1]

| 1873 | Houlston and Sons, London | 16p. | BL,Bo,SG |

## LATER SOURCES RELEVANT TO B.W. NEWTON'S RELATIONS WITH THE BRETHREN, AND EARLY BRETHREN HISTORY

### 17. The Plymouth Brethren, Their History and Heresies
by James Grant.

James Grant qualified the title by explaining that he wrote regarding of 'that section of which Mr Darby is the recognised leader'. There are some useful sidelights on B.W. Newton, e.g. in relation to his later ministry 'to a congregation hardly surpassed for Christian excellence of social position – due regard being had for the relative numbers – by any Church and congregation which could be named', p.33.

| 1875 | William Macintosh, London | ii+98p. | BL,CU |

### 18. A History of the Plymouth Brethren
by William Blair Neatby.

A very readable and balanced account. Considers the division between B.W. Newton and J.N. Darby in a fair and even-handed way. He had access to first hand witnesses of many of the events described.

First Edition
| 1901 | Hodder & Stoughton | 357p. | BL, CU |

Second Edition
| 1902 | Hodder & Stoughton | 357p. | BL,CBA,CU,T |

'Second Edition'
| 2001 | Tentmaker, Stoke-on-Trent | 319p. | BL |

### 19. Mr B.W. Newton and his Traducers: A Letter to a Friend
by G[eorge] Reynolds

The tract is headed '*Audi Alteram Partem*' – i.e. 'Hear the other side'.

This is not a scholarly work, but an answer to the Darbyite calumnies at the time of B.W. Newton's death. George Reynolds the was pastor at an independent Church in Loddiges Road, Hackney.[2]

---
[1] See C.H. Spurgeon in *The Sword and the Trowel*, 1873, p.234.
[2] *Watching and Waiting*, September – October 1971, p.161.

1900  Houlston and Sons, London           20p.    CBA, EL

## 20. *Audi Alteram Partem* (Hear the other side)
by Dr R. Cameron

This was a 4 page tract using the same Latin phrase as George Reynolds. It was produced about 1917 'for private circulation', extracted from *Watchword and Truth* (ed. Dr R. Cameron of Seattle). It contains favourable quotations regarding B.W. Newton by George Müller, Jas. H. Brooks and J.N. Darby. This is the source of George Fromow's quotation of J.N. Darby of 'his esteem for him' in *Teachers of the Faith and Future*, p.27. This reported quotation of J.N. Darby was reprinted in *Perilous Times*, April 1917, and *Watching and Waiting* July 1950.

[1917]  Rectory Road, London SW              4p.     SG

## 21. The Pilgrim Church
by E.H. Broadbent

'Being some account of the continuance through the succeeding centuries of Churches practising the principles taught and exemplified in the New Testament'.

This is Church history from an Open Brethren perspective, which gives a brief account of early Brethren history and the division at Plymouth.

1931 and subsequent reprints.  Pickering & Inglis    421p.

## 22. B.W. Newton and S.P. Tregelles: Teachers of the Faith and Future
by G.H. Fromow.

This gives biographical notes on both B.W. Newton and S.P. Tregelles with an outline of their teaching in summaries and extracts. As might be expected, it is an appreciative eulogy by the long-time secretary of the SGAT. G.H. Fromow evidently made some use of the Fry Collection and other materials held by the SGAT in its preparation. With illustrations, including portraits.

First Edition
1959   SGAT, London                         174p.   BL,SG

Second Edition
1969   SGAT, London                         198p.

## 23. The Origins and Early Development of the Plymouth Brethren
by Peter L. Embley

University dissertation written in 1966, and made available by Bruederbewegung in 2003. Overall, an even-handed account of the period of B.W. Newton's association with the early Brethren and the manner in which J.N. Darby acted towards him.

1967   PhD Thesis                          278+16p.CBA (Xerox)

Available as a pdf download from the Bruederbewegung.com [German Brethren] website
   149 pages

## 24. The Origins of the Brethren 1825-1850
by Harold Hamlyn Rowdon.

Gives a well-documented account of the early development of the Brethren Movement, and B.W. Newton's separation from it.

| | | |
|---|---|---|
| 1967 | Pickering and Inglis, London, | xii+323p. |

## 25. History of the Brethren Movement: Its Origins, Its Worldwide Development, and Its Significance for the Present Day
by Frederick Roy Coad.

For many years the most widely accepted account of the development of Brethrenism, including the division at Plymouth.

First Edition
| | | |
|---|---|---|
| 1968 | Paternoster, Exeter | 327p. |

Second Edition
| | | |
|---|---|---|
| 1976 | Paternoster, Exeter | 336p. |

## 26. Gathering to His Name: The story of Open Brethren in Britain and Ireland
by Tim Grass.

This claims to be 'The first complete history of the Brethren Movement in Britain and Ireland'. Very well referenced, but uncritical of the allegations of J.N. Darby and his relentless attacks (he [Darby] was 'a winsome and passionate evangelistic preacher'), and accepting of the stereotype of B.W. Newton as autocratic, heretical and sectarian.

| | | |
|---|---|---|
| 2006 | Paternoster, Milton Keynes | 589+20p. |

## 27. A Nineteenth Century Nestorius.
by Harold H Rowdon.

A paper read at the Tyndale Fellowship for Biblical Research, Cambridge, December 1957. Published in *Vox Evangelica* – the journal of London Bible College. Dr Rowdon's thesis is that, like Nestorius, B.W. Newton was innocent of the heresy with which he was charged.

Vox Evangelica, June 1962, pp.60-75.

## 28. Prophetic Developments
by F. Roy Coad.

This endeavours to trace the background of prophetic views in the early nineteenth century, particularly as they relate to the development of dispensational views and the division between Mr Newton and J.N. Darby.

*Christian Brethren Research Fellowship Occasional Paper 2*, 1966, 31p.

## 29. Early Brethren and the Society of Friends
by Timothy C.F. Stunt.

Gives interesting sidelights to the Quaker roots of the early Brethren, and the context of the Beacon Controversy. It makes frequent reference to B.W. Newton.

*Christian Brethren Research Fellowship Occasional Paper 3*, 1970, 27p. This research item has been republished with some amendments as Chapters 1 and 2 of *The Elusive Quest of the Spiritual Malcontent: Some Early Nineteenth-Century Ecclesiastical Mavericks*, T.C.F. Stunt, 2015.

### 30. John Henry Newman and the Evangelicals
by Timothy C.F. Stunt.

Describes J.H. Newman's relation to the evangelicals at Oxford, particularly to the radical evangelicals, including B.W. Newton, H.B. Bulteel, G.V. Wigram, and J.C. Philpot.

*Journal of Ecclesiastical History* Vol. 21 – No 1 1st January 1970, pages 65-74.

### 31. The Humanity of Jesus Christ
by F.F. Bruce.

This highlights docetic tendencies of J.N. Darby and his followers in their reaction to the use of 'mortal' by B.W. Newton in relation to the Lord's humanity.

*Christian Brethren Research Fellowship Occasional Paper No.24*, 1973. pp. 5-13. CBA

### 32. J.N. Darby in Switzerland at the Crossroads of Brethren History and European Evangelism
by Christopher Smith.

This gives invaluable background to J.N. Darby's activities in the period immediately prior to his confrontation with Mr Newton in Plymouth in 1845.

*Christian Brethren Review No.34*, Nov. 1983.   42p.   CBA

### 33. Primitivist Piety. The Ecclesiology of the Early Plymouth Brethren
by James Patrick Callahan.

Part of a doctoral study. It makes a detached assessment of the views of Church order among the early Brethren and the relation of this to their views on prophecy. It gives a useful account of J.N. Darby's actions in relation to Plymouth and B.W. Newton.

1996            The Scarecrow Press,            287p.   CBA

### 34. From Awakening to Secession: Radical Evangelicals in Switzerland and Britain 1815-35
by Timothy C.F. Stunt

This takes a wide international perspective, which enables the development of Brethrenism to be seen in the context of the Swiss *Réveil*, and movements in Ireland and Scotland, as well as England. It provides a synthesis and re-interpretation of the origins of both the Brethren and Irvingism. It gives many helpful sidelights on both B.W. Newton and the early days at Plymouth.

2000            T&T Clark, Edinburgh            402p.   CBA

## Appendix 3 A Select Publications List

**35. A Story of Conflict: The Controversial Relationship between Benjamin Wills Newton and John Nelson Darby**

by Jonathan D Burnham.

The doctoral thesis of an American Free Church pastor. It gives a detailed account of the formative years of both J.N. Darby and B.W. Newton, and their growing tensions and eventual parting in the period 1830-1847. It gives some account of B.W. Newton's later ministry.

2004          Paternoster Press          267p.     CBA.

**36. The Elusive Quest of the Spiritual Malcontent: Some Early Nineteenth-Century Ecclesiastical Mavericks**

by T.C.F. Stunt

A series of well-researched, readable and fair essays that give much personal information and background regarding the early life of B.W. Newton. There is a wealth of information and insight in this book that is not found elsewhere.

2015          Wipf and Stock          556p.     CBA

**37. Benjamin Wills Newton (1807-1899), A Theological Biography**

by Nigel Pibworth

This is a study of Newton's thought within the cultural and historical context of the nineteenth century. It is arranged in ten self-contained chapters that consider; the Scriptures; 'the Fall of the Church'; Prophetic Interpretation; Orthodoxy and the Charge of Heresy; Brethrenism; Soteriology; and Society in General.

Unpublished. Draft completed 2003. Contact: Nigel Pibworth of Biggleswade, England. Email: nigelpibworth@yahoo.co.uk.

**38. The Life and Times of Samuel Prideaux Tregelles. A Forgotten Scholar**

by T.C.F. Stunt

As the definitive biography of S.P. Tregelles, this inevitably advances our knowledge of B.W. Newton, with whom his life was so intimately connected. The book was sixty years in the writing, during which time varied aspects of Tregelles life, including his correspondence in Welsh, and his connection with the Italian *Fratelli*, were thoroughly researched. Timothy Stunt's discipline as a historian frequently enables him to 'join up the dots', and so cast new light on his subject(s). The book concludes with six substantial, previously unpublished, letters; three of which were written to B.W. Newton. The book is thoroughly referenced, and has an extensive bibliography.

2020          Palgrave Macmillan          282p.     CBA

# ADVERTISEMENT

# A Pictorial Memoir of Benjamin Wills Newton

The Supplement is published simultaneously with this book. The intention of including it as an appendix was abandoned due to the impact this would have had on the cost of the *Guide*. It is important, as it takes the work beyond being a mere written account and catalogue. It enables the reader to relate to the subject material and the individuals involved with different insights. It adds human interest.

The content of the Supplement is as follows:

1. **Pictures of B.W. Newton and his immediate family**
    a. B.W. Newton's father.
    b. B.W. Newton as a young man
    c. The Hawkins sisters.
    d. Samuel Prideaux Tregelles.
    e. Sketch of B.W. Newton, aged about 75.

2. **Manuscript material by B.W. Newton**
    a. B.W. Newton's first book
    b. B.W. Newton's Greek Testament.
    c. Example of B.W. Newton's editing for a new edition (1)
    d. Example of B.W. Newton's editing for a new edition (2)
    e. Example of B.W. Newton's Letter writing

3. **Meetings**
    a. Illustration of an Iron Church
    b. Notice of Duke Street Meetings, 1st June 1857.
    c. Notice of Meetings at Great Marlborough Street, 28th March 1878.
    d. Notice of meetings at Stafford Rooms YMCA, 10th May 1887.

4. **His death**
    a. Note by Mrs Stirling
    b. In Memoriam Card.
    c. Gravestone of Mr Newton and his wife, with the gravestone of his mother.

5. **Examples of F.W. Wyatt's copies and notes**
    a. A Letter of B.W. Newton to Dr Luigi de Sanctis copied by F.W. Wyatt.
    b. The Quakers and Samuel Lloyd. Personal note of F.W. Wyatt.

6. **Pictures of B.W. Newton's associates**
    a. Alfred C. Fry
    b. Frederick W. Wyatt
    c. Charles T. Walrond
    d. W. Lancelot Holland
    e. Thomas Graham Graham and Jane Graham
    f. John Adams
    g. Ker Baillie Hamilton
    h. William Edward Burnett
    i. George T. Hunt

*A Pictorial Memoir of Benjamin Wills Newton*

Supplement to
*'A Guide to the Works and Remains of Benjamin Wills Newton'*

Paperback 978-1-901397-15-4
Hardback 978-1-901397-16-1

Pearl Publications intends to publish further items relating to B.W. Newton and his associates. It is also hoped to publish an enlarged second edition of *B.W. Newton on Ministry and Order in the Church of Christ*.

www.ingramcontent.com/pod-product-compliance
Lightning Source LLC
Chambersburg PA
CBHW081612100526
44590CB00021B/3417